ESSAYS IN MEDIEVAL HISTORY

University of Toronto Press

essays in medieval history

PRESENTED TO

bertie wilkinson

edited by

T. A. SANDQUIST AND
M. R. POWICKE

Copyright Canada 1969
by University of Toronto Press
printed in Canada

SBN 8020 5203 7

PROFESSOR BERTIE WILKINSON

This volume of studies is presented to Professor Bertie Wilkinson in the hope that the authors and subscribers may thereby acknowledge in some small part the many debts we owe to him as scholars and as friends. The essays are confined to the medieval period, largely to aspects of the later middle ages in England. In a sense this is especially fitting for it is here that Professor Wilkinson finds himself most at home exploring the greatest theme of history: "The unending story of men's efforts to reconcile order and liberty, the two essential ingredients of a truly great civilization." Professor Wilkinson's skill in the use and interpretation of contemporary sources is writ large over the course of English medieval history, his influence as a scholarly teacher is more extensive still, and his friendships on two continents transcend all bounds of discipline, class, and age. Those of us, young and old, who have known and worked with Professor Wilkinson will not soon forget that cherished privilege.

T.A.S.   M.R.P.   Toronto, June 1968

This work
has been published
with the help of a grant from the
SOCIAL SCIENCE RESEARCH COUNCIL
OF CANADA
using funds provided by the
CANADA COUNCIL

Table of Contents

ESSAYS IN MEDIEVAL HISTORY

Hadrian IV, the Byzantine Empire, and the Latin Orient J. G. ROWE

he pontificate of Hadrian IV (1154–59) was a period of great crisis for the Roman church, a time which saw several far-reaching changes in papal policy. The intention of this article is to present a group of facts (well-known in themselves to students of the period) in such a way that attention will be drawn to one particular development which has perhaps been insufficiently delineated by historians.

Since the pontificate of Gregory VII, the Byzantine Empire had been one of the chief protagonists in the drama of the Jerusalem crusade.[1] In Hadrian's day its significance for the Latin Orient was increasing. Certain events suggested that the empire was about to reach a long-cherished goal, the control of Antioch. The claim to Antioch was well founded. The leaders of the First Crusade had promised to return Antioch to the empire, but circumstances and the ambitions of the Norman adventurer, Bohemund, had conspired to place the city in Latin hands. The Byzantines never accepted the loss of Antioch. At the Treaty of Devol in September 1108, Alexius I Comnenus (1081–1118) had forced Bohemund to recognize his claim.[2] Even though for years afterwards the city continued to elude

1 For this article I have used some well-known abbreviations: *JL   Regesta pontificum romanorum*, ed. P. Jaffé, S. Loewenfeld, and others; *MGH Monumenta Germaniae Historica*, ed. G. H. Pertz and others; *PL   Patrologiae cursus completus, Series latina*, ed. J. P. Migne; *RHF   Recueil des historiens des Gaules et de la France*, ed. M. Bouquet and others; *RISS* (2) the new edition of L. A. Muratori, *Rerum italicarum scriptores*, ed. G. Carducci and others. In addition to these are the following: *DR   F.* Dölger, *Regesta der Kaiserurkunden des oströmischen Reiches* (Munich/Berlin, 1924–32); *RHC   Recueil des historiens des croisades*, ed. under the direction of the Académie des inscriptions et belles lettres; *RR   R.* Röhricht, *Regesta regni Hierosolymitani* (Innsbruck, 1893–1904).

2 *DR*, II, no. 1243, preserved in Anna Comnena, *Alexiade*, ed. and trans. B. Leib (Paris, 1937–45), XIII, 12, iii, pp. 125–39.

their grasp, the Byzantines never ceased to regard Antioch as right-fully theirs. In 1137–38 and 1142–43, the gifted Emperor John II Comnenus (1118–43) led his army before the walls of the city. Although John forced Prince Raymond of Antioch to acknowledge his suzerainty, actual possession of the city was denied him. On the eve of a new campaign which might have resulted in the occupation of the city, the Emperor died suddenly of a wound received in a tragic hunting accident in the forests of Cilicia.[3]

John's partial failure did not deter his famous successor, Manuel I Comnenus (1143–80).[4] Early in his reign, Manuel also obtained Raymond's oath of allegiance and fidelity, but the emperor was at first unable to compel Raymond to a more meaningful subjection.[5] The Second Crusade demanded all his attention. Yet once that un-happy expedition had passed away, Manuel decided to act. Unlike his father, Manuel chose not to proceed by force. Instead he tried another tack by exploiting the weakness of Antioch and assuming the role of a benevolent protector.

Certainly, Antioch was weak. The county of Edessa was lost to the infidel. The death in battle of Prince Raymond and many of his barons at the Fountain of Murad (29 June 1149) had reduced sub-stantially the strength of the principality,[6] and all appeals for help from the west had produced little significant assistance.[7]

3 William of Tyre (WT), Historia rerum in partibus transmarinis gestarum, XIV, 30; RHC, Historiens occidentaux, I, p. 653: "... fidelitatem suam domino Imperatori manualiter exhibuit." The best account of John at Antioch re-mains C. Cahen, La Syrie du nord à l'époque des croisades (Paris, 1940), pp. 347–67.

4 For a brilliant sketch of Manuel Comnenus, consult C. Diehl, La Société byzantine à l'époque des Comnènes (Paris, 1929), pp. 13–8. The standard work remains F. Chalandon, Les Comnène: I, Essai sur la règne d'Alexis Ier Comnène (1081–1118); II, Jean II Comnène (1118–1143) et Manuel I Com-nène (1143–1180), (Paris, 1900–12).

5 Cinnamus, Epitome historiarum, II, 3, ed. J. Meineke (Bonn, 1836), p. 35, 11: 19–23; Odo of Deuil, De profectione Ludovici VII in orientem, ed. and trans. V. G. Berry (New York, 1948), p. 70: "... et iam principi extorsit homi-nium. ..."; Michael the Syrian, Chronicle, ed. and French trans. J. B. Chabot (Paris, 1899–1910), III, p. 267.

6 WT, XVII, 9, pp. 771–3; Cinnamus, III, 14, pp. 122–3; Michael the Syrian, III, pp. 288–9; H. A. R. Gibb, The Damascus Chronicle of the Crusades extracted and translated from the Chronicle of Ibn Al-Qalanisi (London, 1932), pp. 291–2.

7 For a typical appeal for help at this time, see RR, no. 261; RHF, XV, pp. 450–1. There was some response in France to the news of the disaster, coming as it did close upon the unfortunate outcome of the Second Crusade. This new crusade enthusiasm produced no positive result. For a recent treatment in the context of European politics, see P. Rassow, Honor imperii (Munich/Berlin, 1940), pp. 26–40.

Seeking to demonstrate the quality of his intentions, Manuel advanced circumspectly. Beatrice of Edessa provided his opportunity. All that remained to the widowed countess in 1150 were a few forts which she lacked adequate resources to maintain. Manuel offered to occupy the forts and grant Beatrice a handsome pension. The countess hesitated and eventually consulted King Baldwin III of Jerusalem. Baldwin also showed indecision. The king was well aware of the growing weakness and confusion of the Latin Orient, particularly in the principality of Antioch. He realized that he himself could not defend the forts for long and that hopes for large-scale assistance from the west were vain. Finally he concluded with some cynicism that the Greeks might just as well take the forts. Baldwin had little confidence in their ability to defend them successfully, and it was better that they, not he, bear the responsibility for their loss. In the end, therefore, Baldwin agreed to Manuel's proposal. The immediate results were not altogether happy for the Byzantine Empire. As Baldwin suspected, the Greeks proved incapable within a year of holding the forts. Yet, no matter how much the Latin Orient might shake its head over Greek "effeminacy," a precedent of co-operation between the Greeks and the Latin Orient had been set which would not be forgotten.[8]

A second opportunity for Byzantine intervention appeared almost simultaneously with the first. The ruler of Antioch was Raymond's widow, the Princess Constance. Her widowed state alarmed both King Baldwin and her barons who urged her to marry again and provide the principality with a capable leader. On the other hand, the Patriarch Aimery urged delay. With only a woman to govern the principality, the patriarch was enjoying unusual power and influence.[9] Caught between barons and patriarch, Constance appealed to Manuel Comnenus to provide her with a husband. Manuel responded eagerly since a Greek prince would strengthen his influence in Antioch. Yet his efforts to provide her with a husband failed, for it was soon clear to Constance that the barons would accept only a Frank as prince of Antioch.[10] In the spring of 1153, she suddenly married a Frankish adventurer, the notorious Renaud de Chatillon.[11]

Manuel was not discouraged. He accepted Renaud gracefully, all the more so after he had persuaded the new prince to undertake a

8 *WT*, XVII, 16–7, pp. 784–9.
9 *WT*, XVII, 18, pp. 789–91.
10 Cinnamus, III, 14, pp. 122–3; IV, 17, p. 178, 11: 9–17.
11 *WT*, XVII, 26, p. 802; Cinnamus, IV, 17, p. 178.

6   J. G. Rowe

campaign against Thoros of Armenia who was attacking the Empire in Cilicia.[12] Unfortunately, at this point Manuel made a serious mistake. He failed to reward Renaud adequately for his help against Thoros. With that destructive megalomania which distinguished so much of his career in the Latin Orient, Renaud in revenge allied himself with Thoros, and together they launched a vicious raid on the island of Cyprus in the spring of 1156.[13] Curiously, the raid proved a blessing in disguise for Manuel for it won much sympathy for the Greeks. William of Tyre's account mirrors the sense of shame and dismay felt by responsible Latins when the news of Renaud's atrocities arrived in the kingdom of Jerusalem.[14] The attack on Cyprus came at a dark moment for the Latins, confronted as they were with the steadily mounting strength of the great emir, Nur ed-Din. The desperate military position of the Latin Orient made Renaud's savagery seem all the more senseless and irresponsible. The Greeks might be poor soldiers, but they did have money. Did not the Latin Orient need a patron willing to be generous with men, and, above all, with money?[15]

How could amends be made? The answer was found in Baldwin's need for a wife. Why should not one be found in Constantinople? Therefore, in the fall of 1157 an embassy led by Attard, bishop of Nazareth, was sent to the great city to seek a bride for the king of Jerusalem.[16] No one objected, not even the clergy. In times past, they had been accustomed to regard the slightest Byzantine intrusion into the Latin Orient as evidence of a desire to re-introduce Greek Christianity into the churches of Syria-Palestine. In 1143, Bishop Hugh of Jabala had ordered the Emperor John Comnenus out of the principality of Antioch in the name of Blessed Peter.[17] Now, a little

---

12 WT, xviii, 10, p. 834; Cinnamus, iii, 14–18, pp. 121–30. Manuel also solicited the aid of the Sultan of Iconium in the war on Thoros, DR, ii, no. 1393.
13 WT, xviii, 10, pp. 834–5; Cinnamus, iv, 17, pp. 178–9; Michael the Syrian, iii, pp. 314–5; Gregory the Priest, Chronicle, RHC, Documents arméniens, i, p. 187.
14 WT, xviii, 10, pp. 834–5.
15 WT, xviii, 16, pp. 845–6. Of Manuel, the Latins agreed (p. 846): "... tum quia princeps potentissimi et inter mortales locupletior, de suis copiis nostram, qua regnum maxime laborat, poterat relevare inopiam, et tenuitatem, mutata conditione, reddere superabundantem."
16 WT, xviii, 16, p. 846. Cf. M. W. Baldwin, "The Latin States under Baldwin iii and Amalric i, 1143–1174," in A History of the Crusades, ed. K. M. Setton (Philadelphia, 1955–   ), i, pp. 528–61, here 542.
17 WT, xv, 20, pp. 690–1; Otto of Freising, Chronicon, vii, 27, ed. A. Hofmeister, Scriptores rerum germanicarum in usum scholarum (Hanover/Leip-

more than a decade later, his hostility found no echo. William of Tyre makes no comment on this change in the Latin Orient's attitude towards the Byzantine Empire, and he, of all men, must have been aware of the change. In his great history Alexius I Comnenus fares rather badly,[18] whereas his portrayal of the emperors John and Manuel Comnenus is favourable, if somewhat marked by condescension.[19] Dire necessity had worked a transformation in the thinking of the Latin Orient. The crusaders in the east could no longer remain suspicious and hostile towards the Greeks.

Yet this growing rapprochement between Greeks and Latins would require papal blessing if it was to bear fruit. Would such be forthcoming? In the middle of the twelfth century the answer was in doubt. It is true that Gregory VII had long before thought in terms of both assisting the Greeks in their struggle against the Turks and bringing the eastern churches into harmony with Rome.[20] Urban II had also hoped that the First Crusade would draw the Greek church closer to the papacy.[21] However, these hopes had been thwarted by the animosities engendered in the confrontation of east and west during the crusade.[22] Relations between the churches became more hostile. In 1138 Pope Innocent II, hearing of the Emperor John's advance on Antioch, wrote a letter to the east denouncing John as excommunicate and prohibiting all service by Latins in the imperial

zig, 1912), p. 354. The fears of the Latin clergy were justified. Evidence in Odo of Deuil, pp. 68–71, indicates that wherever the Greeks established their power they unfailingly introduced the Greek hierarchy and that both John and Manuel were fully prepared to introduce a Greek patriarch into Antioch. Indeed, Alexius Comnenus had forced Bohemund to agree to this in the Treaty of Devol, *Alexiade*, XIII, 12, III, p. 134. *Infra* nn.57, 60.

18 Of Alexius's treatment of the First Crusade, William wrote, II, 20, p. 103: "Sicque quotidie magis et magis Graecorum dolus et fraus Imperatoris detegebatur: ita ut jam nemo esset de principibus cui non esset manifestum et luce meridiana clarius, quanto odio populum prosequebatur nostrum et omne Latinorum genus haberet invisum." Similar comments may be found in II, 7, p. 83; 13, p. 91; X, 13, p. 417; XI, 6, p. 460; XII, 5, pp. 517–8; XIV, 24, p. 642.

19 *WT*, XV, 23, p. 695; XXII, 5, p. 1069.

20 G. Hofmann, "Papst Gregor VII und der Christliche Osten," *Studi Gregoriani*, I (1947), 169–81.

21 For recent treatments of this subject, see S. Runciman, *The Eastern Schism* (Oxford, 1955), pp. 61f, 76–8; A. C. Krey, "Urban's Crusade: Success or Failure," *AHR*, LIII (1947–8), 235–50, and J. H. Hill, "Raymond of Saint-Gilles in Urban's Plan for Greek and Latin Friendship," *Speculum*, XXVI (1951), 265–76.

22 J. G. Rowe, "Paschal II, Bohemund of Antioch and the Byzantine Empire," *Bull. John Rylands Lib.*, XXXIX (1966), 165–202, here 167–76.

army.[23] Would Hugh of Jabala have defied John to his face if he had not been certain of papal support? Probably not.

Moreover, in recent years, despite Eugene III's attempt to use the Second Crusade as an occasion for healing the schism between Rome and Constantinople,[24] relations between the papacy and the Byzantine Empire had been exacerbated by the ambitions of Manuel Comnenus in the west.[25] The Greeks had never accepted the Norman conquest of southern Italy, and for their part the Normans had given evidence from time to time of their desire to conquer the Byzantine Empire. Inspired by the past glories of Byzantine power and mindful of present dangers, Manuel had set his heart on the destruction of the kingdom of Roger II of Sicily, and to this purpose he had, during the Second Crusade, concluded with Conrad III of Germany the Treaty of Thessalonica. The two monarchs agreed to invade Italy and attack the Norman Sicilian kingdom together. As his reward, Manuel would be allowed to re-establish Byzantine power in southern Italy.[26]

Much as Eugene III hated Roger of Sicily, the prospect of a Byzantine re-entry into southern Italy terrified him still more, and the pope bent all his efforts to the exclusion of the Greeks from Italy. Success was attained when the pope signed the Treaty of Constance with Conrad's successor, Frederick Barbarossa, in March 1153. Each party agreed that "Grecorum quoque regi nullam terram in ista parte maris concedet."[27]

The papacy was fully aware of the needs of the Latin Orient. Further, after surveying the damage wrought by the collapse of the Second Crusade, the papacy seems to have concluded that the possibility of massive western assistance to the Latin Orient was unlikely and even undesirable.[28] Even so, it is suggested that Greek

23 *JL*, 7883; *PL*, 179, cc. 354–5.
24 J. G. Rowe, "The Papacy and the Greeks (1122–1153)," *Church History*, 28 (1959), 115–30, 310–27, here 122–6.
25 *Ibid., passim.*
26 Rassow, *Honor imperii*, pp. 27–8, based on evidence in Cinnamus, II, 19; IV, 1, pp. 87, 135.
27 *MGH, Constitutiones*, I, p. 201, 11: 30–2, p. 202, 11: 6–7, p. 203, 11: 15–7. The treaty has been subjected to many analyses, of which the most perceptive is W. Ohnsorge, "Zu den aussenpolitischen Anfängen Friedrich Barbarossas," in *Abendland und Byzanz* (Darmstadt, 1958), pp. 411–33.
28 William of Tyre knew well that the Second Crusade had worked to the grave disadvantage of the Latin Orient and the Jerusalem crusade. See his comments, XVII, 6, pp. 767–8, and the terse observation, 9, p. 771: "Ab ea die coepit orientalium latinorum manifeste deterior fieri conditio." The memory

ambitions in Italy would cause the papacy to look with suspicion on any co-operation between Greeks and Latins in the east and that until the problems posed by those ambitions were resolved to the satisfaction of the papacy, it would be difficult, if not impossible, for the Roman church to grant its blessing to Manuel Comnenus as the self-appointed protector of the Latin Orient.

It was in the opening year of Hadrian's pontificate that Byzantine policy in southern Italy reached its crisis. Even though he could no longer expect from Frederick Barbarossa any military assistance in his plans to re-assert Byzantine power in southern Italy, the Greek emperor still decided to proceed independently.[29] Late in 1154 a Greek mission was sent to Ancona to fish in the troubled waters of Italian politics.[30] Manuel's courage and insight were soon rewarded. In the spring of 1155 the barons of Apulia, encouraged by Frederick Barbarossa's entry into Italy to receive the imperial crown at Rome from Pope Hadrian, began a rebellion against their new sovereign, William I of Sicily, a man of uncertain talent and untried capacity.[31] The rebels were slowly gaining ground when Frederick arrived at Rome in June 1155, only to hesitate in consternation when shortly

of the disaster also rankled in the minds of many in the west. Louis VII asked Hadrian in the final year of his pontificate to authorize a new crusade into Spain. The papal reply, *JL*, 10546, 18 February 1159; *PL*, 188, cc. 1615–17, reveals the cautious attitude of the Roman church which, according to Hadrian, had been severely criticized for the failure of the Second Crusade, c.1616C-D.

29 The early diplomatic negotiations between Frederick and Manuel Comnenus are exceedingly difficult to unravel. The most detailed examination remains H. von Kap-Herr, *Die abendländische Politik Kaiser Manuels* (Strassburg, 1881), pp. 148f. The surviving correspondence reveals that Frederick intended to invade Italy quite independently of Manuel. In other words, while Frederick wished to preserve the alliance with Manuel in some form, perhaps by his own marriage to a Byzantine princess, he regarded the essentials of the Treaty of Thessalonica as null and void. See Wibald of Corbie, *Epistolae*, ed. P. Jaffé, in I, *Bibliotheca rerum germanicarum* (Berlin, 1864), nos. 410, 411, 424, 432, pp. 548–50, 561, 568.

30 *DR*, II, no. 1396; Cinnamus, IV, 1, p. 135.

31 The standard account of the Norman rebellion is G. B. Siragusa, *Il regno di Guglielmo I in Sicilia* (2nd ed., Palermo, 1929), pp. 57–96. C. A. Garufi offers a brilliant character sketch of William in the introduction to his edition of the *Chronicon* of Romuald of Salerno, *RISS* (2), VII, 1, p. xi. Chalandon's analysis, *Histoire de la domination normande en Italie et en Sicile* (Paris, 1907), II, pp. 167–176, is more ample and derived from the *Liber de regno Sicilie* (ed. G. B. Siragusa for the *Fonti per la Storia d'Italia*, XXII, Rome, 1897), once attributed to Ugo Falcandus and now ascribed to the Admiral Eugenius of Palermo by E. Jamison, *Admiral Eugenius of Sicily* (Oxford, 1957), p. 200f.

after his coronation (18 June) he suddenly decided to return to Germany.[32] The rebellion was left without its expected leader. The rebels made a final appeal to Frederick in August at Ancona, but the German monarch refused their requests for assistance.[33] At this precise moment the Greeks intervened, offering to the rebels their fleet, a small but efficient corps of mercenaries, and seemingly limitless quantities of gold. Their offer was accepted, and a kind of alliance came into being.[34] Under Greek leadership the rebellion assumed greater force and direction in Apulia and along the Adriatic coast as city after city took up the cry "Liberty and Riches" and defected to the Byzantines and their Norman allies.[35] It is significant for our purposes to note that from the start the rebellion against William of Sicily had two foci, one in the region of Capua and the Terra di Lavoro, directed by Richard of Capua and Andrew of Rupecanina, and the other in Apulia under the leadership of the Greeks and Robert of Loritello, William's ambitious kinsman.[36] In September 1155, the papacy threw its lot in with Richard of Capua and his fellow insurgents. It seemed then that the hour had struck for the dissolution of the Norman Sicilian monarchy.[37]

But did the papacy ally itself with the Greeks against William of Sicily? William of Tyre clearly represents the pope as the soul of the rebellion, organizing both Greeks and rebels into one mighty struggle against the monarchy.[38] His views have been adopted by some

32 Otto of Freising, *Ottonis et Rahewini Gesta Friderici I. Imperatoris*, II, 34, ed. G. Waitz and B. de Simson, in *Scriptores rerum germanicarum in usum scholarum* (Hanover/Leipzig, 1912), pp. 142–3; Cardinal Boso's *Vita* of Hadrian in *Liber Pontificalis*, ed. L. Duchesne (Paris, 1886–92), II, p. 393.

33 Otto of Freising, *Gesta*, II, 35, pp. 144–5, and in Frederick's letter to Otto, summarizing his first Italian expedition, printed in the same edition, p. 4, 11: 22–30.

34 Cinnamus, IV, 2, pp. 136f.

35 See the account of the siege and surrender of Bari in Cinnamus, IV, 3, pp. 138–40.

36 This seems to emerge clearly from the accounts of the origin of the rebellion in Cinnamus, Romuald, the *Liber de regno Sicilie*, and Boso's *Vita*.

37 Romuald, *Chronicon*, p. 239, is surely wrong in placing the papal entry into the rebellion in June 1155. The papal itinerary, *JL*, II, pp. 112–3, and Boso's account in the *Liber Pontificalis*, II, 393, state otherwise.

38 *WT*, XVIII, 2, 7–8, pp. 818–9, 828–31. William believed that Hadrian urged all rebels, as well as both Frederick and Manuel, to attack William (2, p. 819): "... Romanam ecclesiam in perpetuum eis non defutaram, in verbo pontificali spondens eis firmissime. Utrumque nihilominus, imperatorem Romanorum videlicet et Constantinopolitanum, alterum ore ad os, et manifeste, qui adhuc erat in Italia; alterum vero per litteras, sed occulte, ad occupandum Siculi regnum sollicitat."

modern historians;[39] however, such an interpretation cannot be sustained. William wrote at some distance from these events, and besides, his account is flavoured with animosity towards the Roman church.[40] Other sources fail to confirm his account. Romuald of Salerno and the *Liber de regno Sicilie* say nothing concerning an alliance between Greeks and papacy. Cardinal Boso records that the Greeks offered the pope unlimited supplies of men, war machines, and money, if the pope would but grant them possession of three cities in Apulia. Boso does not tell us if the pope accepted this offer, but shifts at once to relate a counter-proposal made by the king of Sicily.[41] Cinnamus, in contrast, tells us that Hadrian approached the Byzantine leaders, offering full co-operation. The Byzantine response was something less than enthusiastic. Instead of accepting the papal offer, they sent Basilakios, the imperial secretary, to recruit mercenaries in the area around Rome.[42] The report of Cinnamus is consistent with his general picture of Byzantine strategy throughout the rebellion. The Greeks had come to conquer southern Italy for the Emperor Manuel. They were determined to do as much as they could on their own with a minimum of commitments to anyone, rebels and papacy alike.[43]

It is difficult to evaluate this evidence, and care must be taken to avoid a too easy synthesis. None the less, even if the reports in Cinnamus and Boso are completely accurate, they will not support the idea that the papacy and the Greeks concluded an alliance against Sicily. According to both accounts, an approach was made but no alliance occurred. These reports reflect, I believe, the situation in

39 P. F. Kehr, *Die Belehnungen der Süditalienischen Normannenfürsten durch die Päpste (1059-1192)* (Abhandlungen der preussischen Akademie der Wissenschaften, Philos-historische Kl., Berlin, 1934, no. 1), pp. 45-6; Chalandon, *Domination normande*, II, pp. 204-5, 210-2.

40 William's account is placed within the context of the appeal of the Patriarch Fulcher against the Hospitallers. The papal curia rejected his appeal out of hand to the great bitterness of the patriarch and his fellow clergy of the Latin Orient, a bitterness which colours William's account of the papacy's role in the Norman rebellion.

41 *Liber pontificalis*, II, pp. 393-4.

42 Cinnamus, IV, 5, pp. 146-7.

43 This is made clear by Cinnamus' report of the relations between the Greeks and their rebel supporters led by Robert of Loritello. When the campaign was going well, the Greeks treated the rebels in niggardly and humiliating fashion. Yet when military reverses revealed the essential weakness of their position, the Greeks were obliged to show both generosity and respect towards their Norman supporters. See IV, 6, 7-8, pp. 147-8, 151-2. Cf. Chalandon, *Domination normande*, II, pp. 215-6.

which the papacy found itself vis-à-vis the Greeks. To have entered
upon an alliance with them would have been to reverse dramatically
the papal policy which for years had been concerned to exclude the
Byzantine Empire from southern Italy. On the other hand, given
the rebellion and the uncertainty of the future, the Greeks could
hardly be ordered out of Italy. Perhaps both the papacy and the
Greeks made gestures of alliance towards each other. Even so, there
was no significant result, nor could there be since the objectives of
the papacy and the Greeks in southern Italy were not the same.[44]

The failure of Hadrian and the Greeks to come to agreement is but
part of a larger truth. The accounts of the rebellion in the *Liber de
regno Sicilie*, Romuald, Boso, and Cinnamus suggest that there was
no real unity among those opposed to William of Sicily. There were,
in effect, two rebellions, one in Apulia directed by the Greeks and
the other in Capua, to some degree directed by the papacy. William
of Tyre's picture of Hadrian as the generalissimo of all the enemies
of the Norman Sicilian monarchy must be rejected. The two rebellions proceeded, more or less independently of each other, towards
their appointed ends.[45]

The end for both was disaster. With dramatic suddenness, William
of Sicily roused himself to action, summoned his vassals, crossed
the straits, and by forced marches quickly arrived at Brindisi where
he annihilated both Greeks and rebels on land and sea.[46] His triumph
at Brindisi broke the rebellion. Within a few weeks resistance was at
an end.[47] On 18 June 1156 William concluded with Hadrian the Concordat of Benevento wherein the papacy recognized the unity and
integrity of the Norman Sicilian kingdom and was granted in return
far-reaching concessions touching the powers of the Roman church
over the churches of southern Italy and Sicily.[48] To that concordat,

44 The Greeks wished to restore Byzantine power in Apulia. The papacy wished
to break the rigid control exercised over the churches of southern Italy by
the Norman Sicilian monarchy and generally to weaken the ties between the
southern Italian baronage and the monarchy in favour of greater political
power for the papacy in southern Italy.

45 Otto of Freising, *Gesta*, II, 49, pp. 156–8, represents the revolt as a well-
organized movement under unified leadership. Unlike William, however,
Otto presents the Greeks as the leaders of the rebellion. He ignores the papal
role completely. Otto also wrote at some distance from these events and saw
them in the light of Frederick Barbarossa's relations with the Greeks.

46 Cinnamus, IV, 13, pp. 166–8.

47 *Liber pontificalis*, II, pp. 394–5; Romuald, p. 240; *Liber de regno Sicilie*,
pp. 21–2.

48 The best edition of the Concordat is found in Siragusa, *Il regno di Guglielmo*

Hadrian remained faithful. When the Greeks tried in 1157 to intervene once again in southern Italy, they found the papacy standing firmly on William's side.[49] Eventually disheartened by reverses in Italy and a savage Norman attack on the cities of the empire, the Emperor Manuel concluded in 1157 a treaty with William of Sicily which was at once the recognition by the Greeks of the Norman conquest in Italy and the relinquishment by the Normans of their longstanding dream of conquering the Byzantine Empire. Manuel Comnenus could now safely substitute dreams of expansion in the east for hopes of conquest in the west.[50]

While we cannot know precisely what role the papacy played in the conclusion of this treaty, it is clear that the pope had good reason to favour this renunciation by the Greeks of their ambitions in Italy.[51] In 1157 the growing tensions between the papacy and Frederick Barbarossa presaged a storm whose outcome no man could foretell. Peace between Greeks and Normans gave the papacy a more secure political position in Italy. Yet, beyond this, Hadrian and his cardinals now saw that the treaty had even greater possibilities. It was now possible for the papacy to make a new evaluation of the Byzantine Empire and its activities in the Latin Orient. Manuel Comnenus, who had once been the enemy of the Roman church in Italy, might now become the friend of the Roman church in the Latin Orient. The rapprochement of Greek and Latin in the east might prove a happy augury for the crusade and even for the resolution of that ancient problem, the relation between the Greek and Latin churches.

It is in this light that we should approach Hadrian's famous letter to the Metropolitan Basil of Ochrida and the equally famous reply which this letter received.[52] The purpose of the papal letter was to

I, pp. 381–8. A summary of its provisions may be conveniently consulted in R. Foreville and J. Rousset de Pina, *Du premier concile du Latran à l'avènement d'Innocent III* (being IX, 2, of *Histoire de l'Eglise*, ed. A. Fliche and others, Paris, 1953), pp. 24–6. An essential article for understanding these negotiations is V. Epifanio, "Sul preteso assedio di Benevento e sul concordato fra la chiesa e lo stato normanno del 1156," *Archivio storico per le provincie Napoletane*, n.s. XXVIII (1945), 49–74.

49 Cinnamus, IV, 14, pp. 170–1.
50 Chalandon, *Les Comnène*, II, pp. 376–81. See the penetrating remarks of G. Ostrogorsky, *History of the Byzantine State*, trans. J. Hussey (Oxford, 1956), p. 342.
51 Nicetas Choniates, *Historia: De Manuele Comneno*, II, 8, ed. I. Bekker (Bonn, 1835), pp. 127–8, depicts the pope in the role of mediator.
52 *JL*, 10437, *PL*, 188, cc. 1580–1. Basil's reply is in J. D. Mansi, *Sacrorum Con-*

open conversations with the Greeks on the subject of church union. It
is difficult for the historian in this century not to feel that Hadrian's
method of reopening the question was peculiar: the letter to Basil
contained a long recitation of papal claims, introduced by the pious
statement that Hadrian considered it his duty to seek out the lost
sheep, that is, the Byzantine Christians, and lead them safely back
into the fold.[53] On the other hand, while Basil's reply is marked by
deep irony as well as by a determination to exalt the patriarchate of
Constantinople to a position of equality with the see of Rome,[54] it is,
on the whole, a careful and respectful defence of the traditions of
orthodoxy. The metropolitan, for all his condescension, displays an
encouraging attitude towards church union. He emphasizes the Emperor Manuel's positive interest in the matter and suggests that the
conversations between Rome and Constantinople continue.[55]

Manuel Comnenus had every reason to view this reopening of
conversations on church union with the greatest satisfaction. During
the winter of 1157–58 he acted as host to the emissaries of the king
of Jerusalem who had come to the royal city to seek a wife for their
master. The emperor could, with some justification, choose to see in
this renewed concern for church union a kind of papal blessing on
closer relations between his empire and the Latin Orient. The marriage negotiations were soon concluded to the satisfaction of all concerned. In the spring of 1158, surrounded by every possible sign of
Byzantine opulence, the Princess Theodora was sent to the Latin
Orient where she became the wife of Baldwin III and received the
royal diadem at the hand of the Patriarch Aimery of Antioch. The
city of Acre was given to her as a dower for life.[56]

In the fall of the same year, Manuel decided that the time had come
at last for a great military demonstration against both Thoros of
Armenia and Renaud of Antioch. The emperor and his great army
marched quickly through Asia Minor and suddenly appeared in Cili-

---

ciliorum Amplissima Collectio (Florence/Venice, 1759–98), XXI, cc. 799–802.
Both Chalandon, Domination normande, II, pp. 211–2, and Runciman,
Eastern Schism, p. 119, place this correspondence in 1155 as part of an
attempt to effect a political alliance between the papacy and the Greeks
against William of Sicily during the war of 1155–56. There is nothing in
these letters to confirm or deny such an opinion. I believe they belong here,
1157–8, when the abandonment of Greek ambitions in Italy had made a
rapprochement between the churches possible.

53 PL, 188, c. 1581B.   54 Mansi, XXI, c. 802C.
55 Ibid., c. 802D–E.   56 WT, XVIII, 22, pp. 857–8.

cia. Thoros fled before the imperial advance; Renaud bowed to the inevitable. In the great square at Mamistra, he submitted to one of those elaborate humiliations which the Byzantines loved to inflict upon a repentant enemy. It demonstrated imperial power, wrath, clemency, and pardon in one dramatic ritual action. Grovelling before the imperial presence, Renaud acknowledged that his life was forfeit for his criminal raid on Cyprus. He professed himself the humble client of the empire. As its vassal, he would render military aid on demand. He would surrender the citadel of Antioch if required, and he would even introduce a Greek patriarch into the city. His abasement was complete. The emperor had obtained substantially what he wanted, and Renaud was accordingly restored to imperial favour.[57]

Shortly thereafter Baldwin III arrived in Mamistra, seeking to enhance his relations with the emperor. He showed himself eager to please and displayed the greatest deference towards his uncle-in-law and august patron. The king made the most favourable impression, all the more so when he and the Templars (enjoying a rare moment of unanimity and co-operation) persuaded Thoros of Armenia also to make peace with Manuel.[58]

The emperor remained in Mamistra until after Easter 1159. To demonstrate the totality of his triumph over Renaud he then moved towards Antioch. The reception of the Byzantine monarch in that city left little to be desired, and, in return, the feasts and tourneys were all calculated to display Byzantine magnanimity and generosity. We may question the sincerity of the protestations of fidelity and friendship which were offered on this occasion. We cannot, however, deny the brilliance of this encounter between Latin and Greek.[59] Perhaps during the festivities Baldwin intimated to Manuel that the introduction of a Greek patriarch into the city might be profitably delayed. Certainly a Greek patriarch did not appear in Antioch until several years later.[60] A compromise of this nature was acceptable to

---

57 WT, XVIII, 23, pp. 859–61; Cinnamus, IV, 17–8, pp. 178–83; Gregory the Priest, RHC, Documents arméniens, I, p. 188; Bar Hebraeus, Chronography, ed. and English trans. E. A. Wallis Budge (Oxford, 1932), I, pp. 285–6; DR, II, no. 1430.
58 WT, XVIII, 24, pp. 861–3; Cinnamus, IV, 19–21, pp. 183–6.
59 WT, XVIII, 25, pp. 863–4; Cinnamus, IV, 21, pp. 186–7. Cf. S. Runciman, A History of the Crusades (Cambridge, 1951–54), II, pp. 353f.
60 Cinnamus, IV, 20, pp. 185–6, suggests that the Antiochenes made their opposition to the introduction of a Greek patriarch plain to Manuel. A Greek patriarch eventually did appear c. 1165: Michael the Syrian, III, pp. 326, 332, 339.

Manuel. The Comneni had savoured their revenge and found it satis-fying. They were now disposed to be generous.

Unfortunately, we cannot know exactly what the papal reaction was when the news of these Byzantine triumphs arrived in the west. The lack of direct evidence may well be the result of the fact that during the closing months of his pontificate Hadrian was too occu-pied with the problems which Frederick Barbarossa and his ambitions posed for the Roman church to give any attention to developments in the Latin Orient. Nevertheless it is not too much to say that, when Hadrian died on 1 September 1159, a new era seemed to be opening for co-operation between the papacy, the Byzantine Empire and the Latin Orient. Developments in both east and west had led the Roman church to see that the new spirit of co-operation between Constan-tinople and the Latin Orient might prove favourable to the continu-ing strength of the crusader states and even work towards the ultimate reunion of the Greek and Latin churches. It matters little that these hopes in the end proved illusory. What does matter is the new constructive attitude which, I suggest, the papacy was now will-ing to entertain towards the Byzantine Empire and its relations with the Latin Orient.[61]

61 Herein lies the chief limitation of the oft-cited article by J. L. La Monte, "To what extent was the Byzantine Empire the suzerain of the Latin crusading states?," *Byzantion*, VII (1932), 253–64. The distinguished crusade historian fails to place Byzantine policy towards the Latin Orient in the context of the Empire's relations with western Europe in general and the papacy in particular.

An Unpublished Letter by Abbot Hugh II of Reading concerning Archbishop Hubert Walter G. CONSTABLE

The relations between Hubert Walter and the monastic orders would make the subject of an interesting study when the catalogue of his *acta* is complete.[1] There is no evidence that Hubert himself had any monastic leanings or deep spiritual interests,[2] but his concern for monastic affairs, both as a patron and as a visitor, went well beyond what would have been "the thing to do" for a highly placed and wealthy prelate. Aside from his great dispute with the monks of Canterbury, which was largely an inheritance from his predecessor Archbishop Baldwin, Hubert seems to have been on good terms with the English monastic leaders of his day and, more important, to have secured their support in several of the conflicts and crises in which he was involved.

Hubert's alliances with the new orders of Cistercians and Premonstratensians have long been known to scholars. Cheney described Hubert's relations with the Cistercians as "close, at least from 1195, when he sought the confraternity of the General Chapter."[3] He was

1 A book on Hubert Walter is in preparation by Professor C. R. Cheney and his *acta* are being collected by Dr. Eric John. I am indebted to both these scholars for advice on this article. On Hubert's monastic policy, see Kate Norgate, in *Dictionary of National Biography* (Oxford, 1921–22) (*DNB*), x, p. 140, and esp. C. R. Cheney, *From Becket to Langton: English Church Government, 1170–1213* (Ford Lectures, 1955; Manchester, 1956), pp. 37–40. On Hubert as justiciar, see Francis West, *The Justiciarship in England, 1066–1232* (Cambridge Studies in Medieval Life and Thought, N.S. 12; Cambridge, 1966), pp. 78–96.
2 Hubert Walter has commonly been considered a thoroughly secular figure, but Cheney, *Becket to Langton*, pp. 40–41, argues that he was a conscientious and competent churchman.
3 *Ibid.*, p. 38, citing J.-M. Canivez, *Statuta Capitulorum Generalium Ordinis Cisterciensis*, I (Bibliothèque de la Revue d'histoire ecclésiastique, 9; Louvain, 1933), p. 187.

especially friendly with the abbot of Meaux, who had been his
notary and helped to secure his intervention with King John on
behalf of the Cistercians in 1200.[4] According to Ralph of Coggeshall,
he intended before his death to replace the secular canons at Wolver-
hampton with Cistercian monks.[5] The special patronage of Hubert
and his family, however, was reserved for the Premonstratensians.
Hubert founded the Premonstratensian priory of West Dereham in
1188, while he was still dean of York, and "in his lifetime," according to Colvin, "he probably had a closer connexion with the white
canons than any other medieval English prelate who was not himself
a Premonstratensian."[6] This was partly owing to family tradition:
"A large proportion of the Premonstratensian houses in England,"
Stubbs concluded, "was thus founded by Hubert's kinsfolk."[7]

There is a suggestion of a more purely spiritual concern in Hubert's high regard for the Carthusians, which apparently dated from
his visit to Witham and meeting there with the famous Adam of
Dryburgh. "Thereafter he maintained a connection with Adam,"
said Bulloch, "and regarded the Carthusian order with special
honour."[8]

The Cistercians and Premonstratensians repaid Hubert's support
with loyalty and service. In the controversy with the monks of
Canterbury, which lasted from 1185 until 1201, "the whole Cistercian order, at home and abroad, espoused the party of Baldwin [and
Hubert] from principle and inclination."[9] This was especially so in
1198 when the new pope, Innocent III, showed himself ill-disposed
towards Hubert, causing seven English Cistercian abbots "and the
entire congregation of Cistercian abbots of England" to send a
strongly worded letter to the pope praising Hubert and his policy

4 Ralph of Coggeshall, *Chronicon anglicanum*, ed. Joseph Stevenson (Rolls
Series, 66; London, 1875), pp. 102–10; Annals of Margam, s.a. 1200, in
Annales monastici, ed. H. R. Luard (Rolls Series, 36; London, 1864–69), I,
p. 25.
5 Ralph of Coggeshall, *Chron.*, p. 160; cf. Norgate, *DNB*, x, p. 140; David
Knowles, *The Monastic Order in England* (2nd ed., Cambridge, 1963), p. 360;
Cheney, *Becket to Langton*, p. 38.
6 H. M. Colvin, *The White Canons in England* (Oxford, 1951), p. 135; cf. also
Knowles, *Mon. Order*, p. 360; Cheney, *Becket to Langton*, pp. 38–9.
7 William Stubbs in Roger of Hoveden, *Chronica* (Rolls Series, 51; London,
1868–71), IV, p. lxiii, n.l.
8 James Bulloch, *Adam of Dryburgh* (London, 1958), p. 28; cf. Knowles, *Mon.
Order*, p. 384, and Cheney, *Becket to Langton*, pp. 39–40, all citing the
sources.
9 *Chronicles and Memorials of the Reign of Richard I*, ed. William Stubbs
(Rolls Series, 38; London, 1864–65), II: *Epistolae Cantuarienses*, p. xliii.

with regard to the monks of Canterbury.[10] The Cistercians also co-operated closely with Hubert Walter in his long dispute with Gerald of Wales over the bishopric of St. David's (1198–1203).[11] Earlier, in 1194, eleven Premonstratensian abbots helped secure from Pope Celestine III a sentence against Hubert's enemy Archbishop Geoffrey of York.[12] Stubbs considered this sentence an outrage and "feared that the measure was pressed by the whole force of the royal agents acting under Hubert Walter's direction. The fact that the eleven complaining abbots were Premonstratensians, members of an order particularly affected by Hubert, looks like a strong confirmation of this conjecture."[13] There is thus evidence for co-operation between Hubert and the new orders in at least three major controversies.

Hubert's relations with the black monks are less clear. Naturally, in the voluminous correspondence of the monks of Canterbury, he is depicted as hostile to their interests. His policy as a strict monastic visitor and his disciplinary action at Thorney, Worcester, St Mary's at York, and other monasteries seems to point in the same direction.[14] Hubert was without question an efficient, and at times ruthless, financial administrator;[15] but there is no evidence that he was harsher on the black than on the white monks. Gervase of Canterbury admits that Hubert's actions as a monastic visitor were often necessary in the interests of reform.[16] And in the controversy with the monks of Canterbury, according to Knowles, Hubert "seems

10 *Ibid.*, pp. 423–5, no. 462; Gervase of Canterbury, *Historical Works*, ed. William Stubbs (Rolls Series, 73; London, 1879–80), I, pp. 569–71.
11 Knowles, *Mon. Order.*, pp. 666–7.
12 Hoveden, *Chron.*, III, p. 279; cf. D. L. Douie, *Archbishop Geoffrey Plantagenet and the Chapter of York* (St. Anthony's Hall Publications, 18; York, 1960), p. 8.
13 Hoveden, *Chron.*, IV, p. lxiii.
14 Gervase, *Works*, I, pp. 529–30; cf. Knowles, *Mon. Order*, pp. 651–2, who described Hubert as a "particularly active" monastic visitor, and Cheney, *Becket to Langton*, p. 141, who cites the charge (see *infra* n.20) that Hubert was "an oppressive and extortionate visitor." Pope Celestine III in 1195 forbade the archbishop and his officials to exact fines from the men of the Augustinian abbey of Waltham: Walter Holtzmann, *Papsturkunden in England* (Abhandlungen der Gesellschaft der Wissenschaften zu Göttingen, N.F. 25 and 3rd S. 14 and 33; Berlin/Göttingen, 1930–52) (*PU in England*), I, pp. 625–6, no. 326.
15 Cheney, *Becket to Langton*, p. 41; West, *Justiciarship*, p. 82.
16 Gervase, *Works*, I, p. 530: "Videns autem quod res ecclesiae et ordo monasticus in parte plurima deperissent, et inter monachos frequenter essent litigia, quosdam ex ipsis misit Cantuariam et alias per Angliam; duosque ex Cantuariensibus misit Wigorniam, qui ordinem et res dissipatas in bonum statum reformarent."

from first to last to have acted with honesty and considerable moderation, while the monks permitted themselves some very questionable actions."[17]

Hubert's generally good relations with the old monastic orders are shown by the support given him by black Benedictine abbots, especially in the crisis of 1198, when Innocent III ordered the destruction of Hubert's new church at Lambeth. "The king wrote to the lord pope on behalf of the archbishop," wrote Gervase, "the bishops wrote and … the abbots of the Cistercian order and other abbots were not entirely silent."[18] The Cistercians at the end of their letter urged the pope, if he was in doubt about the reliability of their testimony, to consult "those … who are of the black order."[19] On another occasion, when he was accused before the pope of oppressive practices, Jocelin of Brakelond said: "The legate [Hubert] therefore sent his clerks to the abbot [Samson of Bury St. Edmunds], asking him with other abbots to write to the lord pope and exonerate him. This the abbot said he would do and, speaking according to his conscience, he testified that the lord archbishop of Canterbury did not come to our church nor oppress it or any other."[20]

17 Knowles, Mon. Order, p. 326. The judgment of Cheney, Becket to Langton, p. 68, was less favourable to Hubert: "The monks of Canterbury, battling first against Archbishop Baldwin and later against Hubert Walter, show an excess of jealousy, obstinacy, and insubordination which is only matched by the violence and illegal obstruction which the archbishops employed."

18 Gervase, Works, II, p. 408; cf. Knowles, Mon. Order, p. 325.

19 Epp. Cant., pp. 424–5, no. 462; Gervase, Works, I, p. 571.

20 The Chronicle of Jocelin of Brakelond, ed. and trans. H. E. Butler (Medieval Classics; Edinburgh, 1949), p. 85. Butler dated this event in 1199 and said that the pope in question was Innocent III, but 1197 and Celestine III seem more likely to me. Jocelin repeatedly refers to Hubert as both legate and justiciar in this passage, but there is no evidence that Innocent III (who was elected pope on 8 January 1198) renewed Hubert's legation (see Raymonde Foreville, L'Eglise et la royauté en Angleterre sous Henri II Plantagenet, Paris, 1943, p. 556, n.4) and Richard I accepted Hubert's resignation as justiciar in July 1198 (West, Justiciarship, p. 96). Butler associates Archbishop Geoffrey of York's complaint against Hubert with his visit to Rome soon after Innocent's election (Chron. Jocelin, p. 85, n.2); but Geoffrey was also in Rome in 1196 and 1197: see Hoveden, Chron., IV, pp. 7–8, and W. H. Dixon, Fasti Eboracenses: Lives of the Archbishops of York, I, ed. James Raine (London, 1863), p. 272. Most important, Jocelin says that Hubert made his visitation through Norfolk and Suffolk in fine anni (i.e. in the spring, presuming that Jocelin began the year on Lady Day) and travelled through Colchester, Norwich, Castle Acre, and West Dereham and that Abbot Samson met him infra mensem on the king's highway between Waltham and London. Samson excused himself (somewhat disingenuously) for not having come to Hubert earlier, while he was in the diocese of Norwich, on account of the approach of Easter (Chron. Jocelin, pp. 83–4). This fits with the facts

The only known surviving testimonial written by a black Benedictine to the pope on behalf of Hubert Walter is the letter from Hugh II of Reading to Celestine III, which is published here for the first time from ms. Douai 887.[21] This is a composite manuscript in a variety of thirteenth-century hands, which came from the nunnery of Nuneaton in Warwickshire[22] and was given to the English College at Douai by Francis Barber in the first half of the seventeenth century.[23] The letter was copied between two works by Gerald of Wales and was incorrectly identified in the catalogue of the manuscripts at Douai as a well-known letter by Abbot Hugh I of Reading (later archbishop of Rouen),[24] which may account for its having hitherto escaped the notice of scholars.

The abbey of Reading was founded by Henry I in 1121 and was favoured by the royal family in the twelfth and thirteenth centuries. It was the burial place of Henry I, of his daughter the Empress Mathilda, of Henry II's eldest son William, and of other members of the royal family.[25] The rights of confraternity were granted to Eleanor of Aquitaine in 1158/65, and Henry II and John both appear

that Hubert is known to have been at St. Benet of Hulme, north-east of Norwich, on 1 April 1197 (West, *Justiciarship*, p. 94) and that Easter in 1197 fell on 6 April. Hubert would thus have been passing near Bury St. Edmunds during Lent, and Samson probably met him late in April ("within the month"). Hubert's request for the letter to the pope came soon after. The following year, in 1198, Hubert gave the abbey a valuable silk cloth which was used for wrapping the coffin of St. Edmund (*Chron. Jocelin*, p. 115).

21 MS Douai, Bibliothèque municipale, 887, f. 106ʳ⁻ᵛ. See the description by C. Dehaisnes in *Catalogue général des manuscrits des bibliothèques publiques des départements* (4to Series), VI: *Douai* (Paris, 1878), pp. 648–9.

22 N. R. Ker, *Medieval Libraries of Great Britain: A List of Surviving Books* (2nd ed., Royal Historical Society Guides and Handbooks, 3; London, 1964), p. 140.

23 The career of Francis Barber at the English College in Douai, where he served as general prefect and procurator, can be traced from 1609 until his death, apparently in 1632, in the diaries of the College: see Thomas Knox, ed., *The First and Second Diaries of the English College, Douay* (Records of the English Catholics under the Penal Laws, 1; London, 1878), pp. 21 and 287, and Edwin Burton and Thomas Williams, eds., *The Douay-College Diaries: Third, Fourth and Fifth, 1598–1654* (Catholic Record Society, 10–11; London, 1911), s.n., in index (II, p. 579).

24 Dehaisnes cites "Thes. anec., I.2, 297–300," referring to B. Pez, *Thesaurus anecdotorum novissimus* (Augsburg/Graz, 1721–29), I.2, pp. 297–300, = *PL*, CXCIV, coll. 1172–5, and *MGH, Libelli de lite*, III, pp. 285–6. The letter, which is embedded in the *Contra duos haereses* by Gerhoh of Reichersberg, is addressed "clarissimo suo domino W. abbati" and concerns the validity of the sacraments of excommunicated and deposed priests: cf. Peter Classen, *Gerhoch von Reichersberg* (Wiesbaden, 1960), p. 126.

25 Hoveden, *Chron.*, I, p. 190 and II, p. 86; Gervase, *Works*, I, pp. 92, 94–5, 258 and II, pp. 71–2; Stephen of Rouen, *Le Dragon normand*, ed. Henri Omont

in a thirteenth-century calendar from Reading.[26] Henry II visited the abbey on many occasions, including the dedication of the church by Archbishop Thomas Becket in 1164.[27] John gave the monks a golden cup in 1191 and a rent of a golden mark in perpetuity in 1192.[28] The abbey was jurisdictionally independent, but it followed the Cluniac observance and had close ties with Cluny.[29] In particular, it tended in the twelfth century to recruit its abbots from the Cluniac priory of Lewes. Hugh II, who became abbot in 1186, had (like Hugh I) been prior of Lewes; and he left Reading in 1199 to become abbot of Cluny.[30]

Very little is known about Hugh's background and personality. He was described in the annals of Waverley as "vir magnae religionis et honestatis vitae," and in the annals of Worcester and Winchester-Waverley he was said to have ruled Reading "strenue" for fourteen years.[31] These expressions might be merely conventional, except that as abbot of Cluny Hugh issued an important series of reforming statutes, including a provision (apparently modelled on the Cistercian constitution) for the visitation of Cluny itself.[32] He was also a

(Société de l'histoire de Normandie; Rouen, 1884), p. 18; Annals of Tewkesbury, s.a. 1232 and 1234, in *Ann. mon.*, I, pp. 89 and 93.

26 C. R. Cheney, "A Monastic Letter of Fraternity to Eleanor of Aquitaine," *EHR*, LI (1936), pp. 488–93.

27 R. W. Eyton, *Court, Household, and Itinerary of King Henry II* (London, 1878), p. 71 (and index, s.n. Reading, for other visits to the town and abbey). He attended a council concerning the see of Canterbury at Reading in 1184 and the following year met the patriarch Heraclius of Jerusalem there: Ralph of Diceto, *Opera historica*, ed. William Stubbs (Rolls Series, 68; London, 1876), II, p. 32, and Gerald of Wales, *Expugnatio hibernica*, II, 26, in his *Opera*, ed. J. S. Brewer, J. F. Dimock, and G. F. Warner (Rolls Series, 21; London, 1861–91), V, pp. 360–1.

28 C. W. Previté-Orton, "Annales Radingenses Posteriores, 1135–1264," *EHR*, XXXVII (1922), p. 401.

29 Knowles, *Mon. Order*, pp. 281–2. On the early history of the abbey of Reading, and its relations with Cluny, see the article (which appeared after the present article was written) of Hans Mayer, "Staufische Weltherrschaft? Zum Brief Heinrichs II. von England an Friedrich Barbarossa von 1157," *Festschrift Karl Pivec*, eds. Anton Haidacher and Hans Mayer (Innsbrucker Beiträge zur Kulturwissenschaft, 12; Innsbruck, 1966), pp. 272–6.

30 Previté-Orton, "Annales Radingenses Posteriores," p. 401; Annals of Winchester, s.a. 1199, Annals of Waverley, s.a. 1186 and 1199, Annals of Worcester, s.a. 1199 in *Ann. mon.*, II, pp. 73, 244, 251–2, and IV, p. 390; Annals of Winchester-Waverley, s.a. 1199 in F. Liebermann, *Ungedruckte anglo-normannische Geschichtsquellen* (Strassburg, 1879), p. 183.

31 *Ibid.*

32 *Bibliotheca Cluniacensis*, ed. Martin Marrier and André Duchesne (Paris, 1614), coll. 1457–72; cf. Rose Graham, *English Ecclesiastical Studies* (London, 1929), pp. 23–4.

generous benefactor of Cluny. "This Hugh while he was still abbot of Reading," according to the chronicle of Cluny, "equipped the entire refectory with precious cloths from England, and towels, and he also gave towels for the *mandatum*; and he had the close of St. Lazarus planted and maintained at his own expense until the community received the full produce. And he conferred upon us many other benefits," including paying the abbey's debts and the gift of "all his excellent books."[33] That he had an interest in learning is confirmed by an anecdote in the *Vita magna* of St. Hugh of Lincoln, which records that Hugh of Reading received a renegade Carthusian monk named Alexander, "owing to the privilege of letters and semblance of a great reputation," and made him his companion and attendant.[34] Taken together this evidence suggests that Hugh was a capable administrator and firm disciplinarian, and not without worldly ambitions and intellectual interests.

As abbot of Reading from 1186 until 1199, Hugh was a prominent figure in the English church and in close touch with the king, pope, and archbishop. He was a supporter of Richard, in spite of John's gifts to the abbey in 1191–92 and Richard's seizure in 1196 of the property of Cluny, La Charité-sur-Loire, St. Denis, and Marmoutier as surety for the good behaviour of the king of France.[35] Hugh appears with the royal clerk William of Ste.-Mère-Eglise (later bishop of London) in the pipe roll for 1190 as having crossed the sea with the royal treasure and chancery, presumably before Richard's departure on the Third Crusade.[36] In 1194 the monks of Reading helped Hubert Walter in his military operations against Marlborough castle, which was held by John's men.[37] Hugh of Reading appears again with the king and Hubert Walter at La Roche d'Andely in 1198.[38]

33 *Bibl. Clun.*, coll. 1663–4.
34 *The Life of St Hugh of Lincoln*, II, 12, ed. Decima Douie and Hugh Farmer (Medieval Texts; Edinburgh, 1961–62), I, pp. 82–3. After Hugh's departure for Cluny, Alexander tired of life at Reading and sought to re-enter a Carthusian house.
35 Hoveden, *Chron.*, IV, p. 4. Reading itself, as an independent abbey, was not affected by this move, but Hugh was doubtless concerned for the welfare of Cluny.
36 *The Great Roll of the Pipe for the Second Year of the Reign of King Richard the First*, ed. Doris Stenton (Pipe Roll Society, 39, N.S. 1, London, 1925), p. 131.
37 West, *Justiciarship*, p. 80; cf. Hoveden, *Chron.*, III, p. 237, and Gervase, *Works*, I, p. 523.
38 Lionel Landon, *The Itinerary of King Richard I* (Pipe Roll Society, 51, N.S. 13, London, 1935), p. 137.

Meanwhile, he was used as a papal judge by Clement III in 1186 and by Celestine III in 1191 and 1195.[39] He apparently visited Rome on behalf of Archbishop Baldwin in 1188 and later served as arbitrator and papal commissioner in the dispute between the archbishops and the monks of Canterbury.[40] Hugh requested and received a grant of the *pontificalia* from Clement III in 1191.[41] He also secured the support of the papacy for his plan to build a hospice for pilgrims and the poor outside the gates of the abbey. He granted various revenues to this hospice in 1189/90, "with the assent and consent of the diocesan bishop H. Walter,"[42] and a total of at least six papal bulls were issued by Clement III and Celestine III concerning the hospice and its revenues.[43]

Throughout these transactions Hugh seems to have been on good terms with Hubert Walter, and they help to explain his role in the controversy over the establishment by the archbishops of a collegiate church that threatened the rights of the monks of Canterbury.[44] Already in June 1188, when Baldwin was still archbishop, the monks wrote to the community of Reading that they had heard that Hugh was going to Rome "against us" and that this "will greatly displease both the lord [cardinal] of Ostia and the entire Cluniac order."[45] In November 1189 Hugh was present with the king and Hubert Walter at the council of Canterbury, when the issue was discussed;[46] and he was chosen, together with various other bishops and abbots, as one of a group of arbitrators who decided in favour of the archbishop.[47] In 1191–92, however, Hugh acted as a papal commissioner on behalf of the monks. On 28 May 1191 the pope wrote to the bishop of Bath and the abbots of Reading and Waltham instructing them to support

39 *PU in England*, II, pp. 429–31, nos. 236–7, and III, pp. 526–7, 562–7, nos. 435 and 471.
40 See *infra* n.45.
41 *PU in England*, III, p. 525, no. 433.
42 William Dugdale, *Monasticon Anglicanum*, ed. John Caley, William Ellis, and Bulkeley Bandinel (London, 1846), IV, pp. 42–3. Hubert Walter became bishop of Salisbury late in 1189 and was called to Normandy by the king in February 1190; he returned to England after the crusade only just before his election as archbishop of Canterbury (Norgate, *DNB*, X, p. 138).
43 *PU in England*, III, pp. 524–5, 575–7, 581–2, and 584–5, nos. 432, 481–2, 489–90, and 493.
44 The best account of this long and complex affair is by Stubbs in his introduction to the *Epp. Cant.*
45 *Epp. Cant.*, pp. 218–9, no. 237.
46 Landon, *Itinerary*, p. 18.
47 Gervase, *Works*, I, pp. 469 and 479.

the monks and see to the destruction of Baldwin's church at Hacking-ton.[48] Soon after this letter was received, in June or July 1191, the monks wrote separately to the two abbots asking them to execute the papal mandate.[49] This the three commissioners did with exemplary energy, ordering the suspension of divine services, the destruction of the church, and the suppression of the chapter.[50] They were apparently prevented only by the death of Archbishop Baldwin, and by specific orders from the chancellor, Bishop William of Ely, from proceeding against Henry of Northampton, William of Ste.-Mère-Eglise, and other clerks of the late archbishop.[51] The case dragged on because of the vacancy in the see. The monks rewarded the bishop of Bath for his support by electing him archbishop;[52] but he died in December 1191, before being consecrated. His place on the papal commission was taken by the bishop of Chichester. Celestine III wrote to him and the abbots of Reading and Waltham on 16 May 1192 telling them to close the new church at Lambeth (which the monks feared would take the place of the destroyed chapel at Hackington) and to absolve the canons from their oaths to Archbishop Baldwin.[53] This ended the first phase of the controversy, and the papal commission was presumably dissolved.

When, in 1197, Archbishop Hubert revived the project to establish a collegiate church at Lambeth,[54] Hugh of Reading again figured in the dispute, but in a new role. He was sent by the archbishop of Canterbury in November 1197, together with the abbots of Chertsey and Waltham, in order to convince the monks that the new foundation would not infringe their rights.[55] The monks refused to be convinced, however, and gained the support of the new pope Innocent

48 *Epp. Cant.*, p. 337, no. 358; Gervase, *Works*, I, pp. 498–9 and (with a different date) pp. 534–5; JL, 16711. The choice of commissioners is not without interest. Reginald of Bath was a known supporter of the monks (*Epp. Cant.*, pp. lxxxvi–lxxxvii). The attitude of the abbot of the Augustinian house of Waltham is uncertain, but Hubert Walter had to be enjoined by the pope in 1195 from molesting the abbey's men (see *supra* n.14). Hugh of Reading may therefore have been included on the commission on account of his support of the archbishop.
49 *Epp. Cant.*, pp. 338–9, no. 360.
50 *Ibid.*, pp. 339–42, nos. 361–6. Two of these are excuses from the bishop and from Hugh of Reading for their inability to attend some stage of the proceedings; but there is no hint of any lack of zeal.
51 *Ibid.*, pp. 342–3, nos. 367–9.
52 *Ibid.*, pp. 352–5, nos. 383–9.
53 *Ibid.*, p. 361, no. 397; Gervase, *Works*, I, p. 536; JL, 16878.
54 See Stubbs, in *Epp. Cant.*, pp. xciv–xcv.
55 Gervase, *Works*, I, p. 545.

III.[56] The king, on the other hand, and the group of Cistercians mentioned above, strongly supported the archbishop, who appealed against the papal mandate from Lambeth on 1 June 1198, in the presence of Hugh of Reading, the bishop of Rochester, and the abbots of Bury St. Edmunds, Waltham, and Chertsey.[57] Hugh appeared in the controversy for the last time on 22 June 1198, when he and the abbots of Chertsey, Faversham, and Waltham, and the prior of Coventry visited the convent – "not as envoys from the archbishop," according to Gervase, "but as special friends of the church of Canterbury" – and again tried to mediate between the two sides.[58] This effort failed, and the dispute was not finally settled until 1201. But in the meantime, in 1199, Hugh of Reading left England to become abbot of Cluny.

Hugh's letter to Celestine III can be dated between 18 March 1195, when Hubert was made legate,[59] and 8 January 1198, when Celestine died. The most probable date is early in 1197, when Hubert was mustering his resources, after a number of troubles in 1196,[60] for a renewal of the Canterbury controversy. At the time Hugh was writing this had not yet taken place, since he specifically praised Hubert for bringing "the perturbation of the church of Canterbury" to a peaceful conclusion, "which hitherto seemed impossible to many people." Hubert seems to have sent a mission to the pope late in the spring of 1197, and between 9 June and 5 July Celestine issued at least five bulls in Hubert's favour, confirming and augmenting his powers and permitting the foundation of a chapter at Lambeth.[61] I am inclined to believe that Hubert obtained the testimonial from Hugh of Reading to send to Rome at this time.[62]

It is a general letter of support and recommendation. Unlike the letters of the abbot of Bury St. Edmunds and the Cistercian abbots,

56 See *supra* n.20 for Innocent's attitude towards Hubert Walter.
57 *Epp. Cant.*, p. 407, no. 450.
58 Gervase, *Works*, I, p. 556. In the official account of this mission written by the monks of Canterbury (*Epp. Cant.*, p. 410, no. 450), the arbitrators appear more definitely as envoys of the archbishop, warning the monks of grave consequences unless they give up the papal mandate.
59 Hoveden, *Chron.*, III, pp. 290–3; Diceto, *Opera*, II, pp. 125–6; JL, 17202; cf. Z. N. Brooke, *The English Church and the Papacy from the Conquest to the Reign of King John* (Cambridge, 1931), pp. 12 and 218.
60 Stubbs, in Hoveden, *Chron.*, IV, pp. lxxxix–xc; Norgate, *DNB*, X, p. 139.
61 *Epp. Cant.*, pp. 371–2, no. 413 (JL, 17564); *PU in England*, II, pp. 479–82, nos. 286–9.
62 This would agree exactly with the dating proposed above (n.20) for Hubert's request for a testimonial from Abbot Samson of Bury St. Edmunds.

it does not appear to have been connected with any particular crisis or controversy, although at the end Hugh suggests that the Devil is trying to stir up trouble in the *Anglicana ecclesia*.[63] He urges the pope not to listen to Hubert's detractors and assures him of the archbishop's merit and devotion to the holy see. Aside from the preliminaries, most of the letter is an account of Hubert's career from his youth up through his appointment as legate in 1195. Some of this is obvious flattery, such as the comparison of Hubert to the sun and stars and the praise of his simplicity, gentleness, and humility. Even the factual parts add nothing to what is known about Hubert's life from other sources. But the letter is more circumstantial than most testimonials, and it confirms in various ways the impression of Hubert's position and personality given by other writers, including his enemies. Hugh praises in particular Hubert's honesty and charity as a judge, his contributions to the crusade,[64] and above all his pacification of England "disturbed by the perfidy of certain men." Hubert has wielded both swords, "that is, of the king and of the church,"[65] so justly that he has both brought peace to the church and restored the royal power to its former dignity. "And with all men joined to one another in peace, the *regnum* and the *sacerdotium* now agree perfectly in our country." Hugh does not suggest that Hubert was popular – indeed, he commends him for scorning popular praise – but he clearly felt sincere admiration for Hubert's achievement in bringing peace and unity to the troubled realm.[66]

63 On the phrase *anglicana ecclesia*, see Brooke, *Eng. Church*, pp. 1–21, who stresses its use in the Canterbury controversy (pp. 11–2) and by Hubert Walter (pp. 12–3).

64 See the *Itinerarium peregrinorum* in *Chron. and Mem.*, I, pp. 116, 134–7, 372, and 437–8.

65 On the use of the image of the two swords with reference to Hubert Walter, see the letter of Richard I to the bishop of London in 1195, in Diceto, *Opera*, II, p. 128, and *The Life of St Hugh of Lincoln*, IV, 6 (II, pp. 28–9): "This powerful man [Hubert], as he himself used to say with perfect truth, had both swords committed to his custody, for he was metropolitan in his own right, and by papal authority legate throughout England, and also the king's representative above the other secular justices." These sources and Hugh's letter leave no doubt that the royal or material sword here refers to civil power: see Hartmut Hoffmann, "Die beiden Schwerter im hohen Mittelalter," *Deutsches Archiv*, XX (1964), 78–114, with references to previous literature on this disputed point.

66 Hubert's enemy Gerald of Wales, who had attacked the archbishop in his *De invectionibus*, I, 5, and *De jure et statu Menevensis ecclesiae*, IV (*Opera*, III, pp. 29–30, 254, and *passim*), admitted in his *Retractationes* that Hubert was "animosus et strenuus" (cf. Hugh of Reading's "non minus prudenter quam strenue") and that he had promoted peace and curbed the tyranny of

At the very least, the letter shows that Hugh was willing to use his influence with the pope on behalf of Hubert Walter. It therefore confirms that in the controversy between the archbishops and monks of Canterbury (in which Hugh was involved for exactly a decade, from June 1188 until June 1198), his sympathies lay with the archbishops. Only when he was carrying out specific papal instructions, in 1191–92, did he act on behalf of the monks, though his behaviour at this time shows his fairness and efficiency and doubtless accounts for Gervase's later calling him a "special friend of the church of Canterbury." Even when he later re-entered the controversy, acting for the archbishop in 1197–98, there is no sign of any hostility to the monks. This view of Hugh's attitude is confirmed not only by the known friendly relations between himself and Hubert Walter in the period 1189–98[67] but also by the archbishop's strong support of Hugh after he became abbot of Cluny, in 1200–1, in a dispute with the earl of Warenne over the right to appoint the prior of Lewes.[68]

If it is true, as the recipient of this *Festschrift* maintains, that the value of documents is not "merely illustrative" but to "provide original material on which judgements must be made and by which theories are to be tested,"[69] this letter is not without value for the historian. By helping to establish the political position of Hugh of Reading in the Canterbury controversy, it goes a long way towards refuting the claim of Stubbs that "the whole order of Cluny, at home and abroad, undertook the defence of the convent, to which they were attached by their earliest traditions."[70] It is true that the monks of Canterbury seem to have had close relations with the Cluniacs, especially at the beginning of the dispute, and to have looked to them

the king (*ibid.*, I, pp. 426–7); cf. Hoveden, *Chron.*, III, pp. 299–300, on Hubert's peace edict of 1195; Cheney, *Becket to Langton*, pp. 33 and 41; West, *Justiciarship*, p. 94.

67 See *supra* nn. 37–8, 42, and 46, in addition to their contacts in connection with the Canterbury dispute.

68 Diceto, *Opera*, II, p. 173; G. F. Duckett, *Charters and Records among the Archives of the Ancient Abbey of Cluni, 1077–1534* (Lewes, 1888), I, pp. 87–101, nos. 284–9, with a brief account of the affair on pp. 86–7; and Auguste Bernard and Alexandre Bruel, *Recueil des chartes de l'abbaye de Cluny* (Collection de documents inédits sur l'histoire de France; Paris, 1876–1903), V, pp. 736–41, no. 4381 (Duckett, no. 284); pp. 750–2, no. 4390; pp. 752–3, no. 4392; pp. 758–9, no. 4397 (Duckett, no. 285); pp. 760–2, no. 4398 (Duckett, no. 289); pp. 780–4, no. 4408 (Duckett, no. 288).

69 Bertie Wilkinson, *Constitutional History of Medieval England* (London, 1948–64), I, p. xii.

70 Stubbs, in *Epp. Cant.*, p. xliii.

for support.[71] Also, as abbot of Reading Hugh was not a Cluniac in the strictest sense. But his election as abbot of Cluny in 1199 shows that the order did not disapprove of his policy. It proves, on the contrary, what can also be shown in the conflict between Mathilda and Stephen earlier in the century,[72] that the Cluniacs did not take sides as an order, but had adherents in both camps, and were thus certain of having friends on the winning side. With regard to the policy of Hubert Walter, this letter[73] is further evidence of his good relations with the old monastic orders and of his ability to muster their support in times of trouble.[74]

Appendix

Sanctissimo domino ac patri reuerendo, Celestino dei gratia summo pontifici, Hugo diuina miseratione humilis minister Radingensis ecclesie, salutem, et deuotam in Christo obedientiam.

Sanctam et apostolicam Romanam ecclesiam eggregie dignitatis sue priuilegio domino disponente ceteris per orbem ecclesiis preminere, nullus fidelium permittitur ignorare. Hec est quam sibi dominus beatorum Petri et Pauli magisterio specialem elegit, et quo preesset aliis et prodesset diffusius, eorum glorioso sanguine rubricauit. Hanc uestro sanctissime pater apostolatui uoluit committi, ut et uestro merito et exemplo proficiat, et amplius in ipso dilatetur et crescat. Hinc est quod cum eidem sancte matri nostre fidelium deuotio cedat ad gloriam, uobis non minus eorundem profectus in domino duplicabitur ad coronam. Et quidem uobis plenius honoris et glorie cumulant incrementum, hii quos in sanctarum uirtutum exercitiis illustrat

71 *Ibid.*, pp. 64, 186–7, 258, and 275, nos. 77, 202, 275, 292, and esp. pp. 218–9, no. 237.

72 See the appendix on "Peter the Venerable, the Lateran Council of 1139, and the Case between King Stephen and the Empress Mathilda" in my edition of *The Letters of Peter the Venerable* (Cambridge, Mass., 1967), II, pp. 252–6.

73 The letter is printed here exactly as it appears in ms Douai, Bibliothèque municipale, 887, f. 106$^{r–v}$, except for the expansion of abbreviations, the capitalization of proper names, and the substitution of commas for the . and : found in the manuscript.

74 Since the manuscript of this paper was submitted to the publisher, the biography of Hubert Walter referred to in note 1 has appeared: C. R. Cheney, *Hubert Walter* (London/Edinburgh, 1967). Another recent biography is: Charles R. Young, *Hubert Walter, Lord of Canterbury and Lord of England* (Durham, N.C., 1968).

illustrior titulus meritorum. E quibus uenerabilis dominus et pater
noster eximius Hubertus Cantuariensis archiepiscopus specialis filius
uester et deuotus, prerogatiua quadam sanctimonie, alter sol in nostro
emicat occidente. Domino teste quod mendosa non fingimus, sed
meram sicut est loquimur ueritatem, prout oculata fide comperimus,
et relatu multorum magni testimonii qui uirum a puero nouerunt, de
eo plene sumus edocti. Hic quidem a cunabulis cum adhuc secularibus
insisteret disciplinis, et uitiorum deuitauit uoraginem, et morum
honestate tenellam in puero exornauit etatem. Iuuenis uero mire
sagacitatis raptus ad tribunalia, deo et hominibus se talem exhibuit,
quod omnium sibi etiam emulorum gratiam uendicauit. Ecclesiarum
specialis tutor effectus, oppressorum adiutor, pius protector pau-
perum, pupillorum pater, defensor uiduarum. Hinc accidit quod ecclesia Saresberiensis pastorali destituta regimine, ipsum sibi concinno
assensu cleri et populi uolentem reniti sed minime ualentem in pas-
torem elegit. Promotus in episcopum, non talentum abscondere, sed
fructum centesimum domino de commissis studuit reportare. Cum
uero sanctam orientalem ecclesiam tirannica rabies deuastaret, et loca
sancta multis barbaries fedaret spurcitiis, non ferens diutius crucis
obprobrium, baiulans sibi crucem secutus est Christum. Studens se
casibus mortis obicere, ut loco sancto quem suo altissimus conse-
crauit martyrio, uel sic posset prodesse. Quantum ibi profecerit, qua
strenuitate qua animi uigilantia et ope et consilio Christi studuerit
promouere negotia, sanctitatem uestram latere non credimus, quod
omnis Romane uox urbis et orbis predicat uniuersus. Ut dicatur stella
de climate nostri progrediens occidentis, fulgoris sui lumine, ipsos
orientis radios illustrasse. Demum post multa pericula post labores,
Anglia iam quorumdam perfidia perturbata, et misere declinata tota
in precipicium, ipsius suspirare dicebatur regressum. Reuersus igitur
et non minus prudenter quam strenue aduersantium rabiem emol-
liuit, compescuit furorem, et ut est adhuc cernere, uniuersos continuo
reuocauit ad pacem. Cum autem metropolis sancta Cantuarie suo iam
esset uiduata pastore, et multarum pensitans merita personarum de
substituendo pertractaret pontifice, tandem uoto unanimi domini
nostri regis et regni, deo inspirante, clero uocante, populis acclaman-
tibus, auctoritate etiam uestra mediante, a Saresberiensi in Cantuariensem antistitem est promotus. Tantis igitur uirtutibus decoratus, et
moribus decorus, pontificali meruit a uestra clementia pallio decorari,
et tam excellenti sullimatus fastigio, ne humana possit potestate con-
cuti, legationis etiam offitio insigniri. De quo nunc illud cunctis pre-

dicatur mirabile, quod utrumque gladium in Anglia, uidelicet regis et ecclesie, tanta tam decenti moderatur temperie, ut ad honorem dei ecclesia plena tranquillitate uigeat, et regia potestas multis pridem ut diximus iniuriis lacessita, in pristinum decorem iam plenius conuales-cat. Et omnibus sibi counitis in pace, regnum a sacerdotio iam penes nos in nullo dinoscitur dissentire. Sed nec pretereundum arbitramur silentio, quod Cantuariensis ecclesie perturbatio ipsius ut liquet meritis et industria feliciter sedata, quod uidebatur hactenus pluribus impossible, conquieuit in pace. Qui cum tanta discretione polleat, tantaque ceteris premineat potestate, nec primam innocentiam nec innatam sibi simplicitatem exuit columbinam, non incedit tumide, non sapit superbe, sed popularis aure declinans extollentiam, consuete mansuetudinis et humilitatis Christi se zelantem exhibet amatorem. Perpendens in pontifice nichil humilitate splendidius elucere, et quo maior, eo factus humilior. Nunc igitur uestrum est pater serenissime paterne prospicere, ne antiquus ille qui suo in altissimis creatori inuidit, et tunicam inconsutilem Christi in terris laniare contendit, in ipsum preualeat malignitatis sue uirus euomere, et tantam unitatem Anglicane ecclesie uel per se uel per suos in aliquo perturbare. Quod si qui inuidie ueneno suffusi ausu dyabolico coram uobis compareant, ut tante quod absit detrahant ueritati, non illos admittat sancta uestra paternitas, ne falsitatem ueri palliantes ymagine, et discretionem uestram eludere, et gloriam in aliquo ualeant obfuscare. Sed merita patris nostri et deuotionem quam habet erga uos oculis dementie uestre contuentes, et eos sicut decet et eorum uelitis figmenta res-puere. Ut sic iusticia iusti super eum, et in caput proprium, propria retrudatur iniquitas malignantium. Ualerat dilecta nobis in Christo semper uestra discretio, sanctissime pater.

William de Montibus, a Medieval Teacher H. MACKINNON

illiam de Montibus was born in Wigford, a suburb of Lincoln, about the year 1140. A number of medieval scribes call him William de Monte and according to Gerald of Wales they did so "because he had lectured at Mont Ste.-Geneviève in Paris."[1] The name William de Montibus is preferable, however, not only because the majority of medieval scribes use it, but because beyond reasonable doubt William was a member of a de Montibus family, the name originating quite independently of its most famous bearer.[2] Modern writers have confused him with William of Sherwood and William of Durham, and he has been called by some William of Leicester.[3]

William de Montibus studied at Paris *circa* 1160–70 and afterward stayed to lecture at Mont Ste.-Geneviève. Gerald of Wales knew him in Paris about 1177.[4] St. Hugh, shortly after he became bishop of Lincoln in 1186, brought William back to Lincoln. William soon became chancellor and remained at Lincoln for the rest of his life. As

---

1 Gerald of Wales, *De Rebus a se Gestis*, ed. J. S. Brewer (Rolls Series, 1861), I, p. 93.
2 See Hugh MacKinnon, "The Life and Works of William de Montibus," unpublished D.Phil. thesis, Oxford, 1959, pp. 2 ff. The evidence comes largely from three sources: Brit. Mus. ms. Cotton Faustina B I, f.5ᵛ; *Final Concords of the County of Lincoln* (The Lincoln Record Society), XVII, 64, p. 148; and from the late Canon Foster's transcription of the *Thurgarton Priory Cartulary*, which Miss Kathleen Major of St. Hilda's College, Oxford, was kind enough to let me see.
3 See *Histoire littéraire de la France*, XVIII, pp. 391–2; W. E. Rhodes in *DNB*, "William of Leicester"; P. Glorieux, *Répertoire des maîtres en théologie de Paris au XIIIᵉ siècle* (Paris, 1933), I, p. 289.
4 Gerald of Wales, *De Rebus*, "... in Monte S. Genovefae legerat quem etiam ibi archideaconus tunc noverat." Gerald studied humanities under Peter Comestor about 1172 and theology and canon law from 1177–80. It is likely that he came to know William de Montibus during this second period.

chancellor he was in charge of the theological school, a school which enjoyed a considerable reputation for learning under him. Gerald of Wales studied there because he considered it to be the most promising school of theology in England at the time.[5] William de Montibus died in Scotland in 1213 and the following year, when Innocent III's interdict was lifted from England, his body was translated to Lincoln.

It is clear that the influence of Paris remained dominant throughout William's life. While at Paris he witnessed and became part of a theological movement which had far-reaching consequences for the medieval church. The movement is typified by the work of men like Peter Comestor, Robert Courçon, Stephen Langton and, in a particular way, by Peter the Chanter, an influential and perhaps the leading member of the movement. The influence of Peter the Chanter is especially apparent in the works of William de Montibus; it cannot be doubted that they knew one another, and it is probably that Peter was William's master in Paris.[6]

The movement itself evolved from certain developments in sacramental theology taking place in Paris in the second half of the twelfth century. One important and distinctive element in this movement was the attempt to transmit the new speculative sacramental theology of the schools to the parish priests. These churchmen, whose daily lives were occupied with the administration of the sacraments, needed the new theology in a practical and popular form. One of the more interesting facets of William de Montibus' career at Lincoln is the part he played in making this knowledge accessible and intelligible to the lower ranks of the clergy. A study of his works shows how much he was devoted to the movement and also demonstrates how the movement itself had an impact in the areas of the church not usually associated with the Paris schools.[7]

William de Montibus' major theological work is the *Numerale*.

5 Gerald of Wales, *De Rebus*, "Ubi sanius atque salubrius in Angliam theologicam scientiam vigere cognovit ... studii causa Lincolniam adivit." He chose to study in England because of the war between Philip II of France and Richard of England.

6 See MacKinnon, "Life and Works," pp. 20–1 and 158 ff. for the argument that they knew each other and that Peter the Chanter was William de Montibus' master. William de Montibus seems to have modelled his *Tropi* on a work of the same name by Peter the Chanter.

7 See V. L. Kennedy, "Robert Courçon on Penance," in *Medieval Studies*, VII (1945), 291–336; M. Gibbs and J. Lang, *Bishops and Reform 1215–1272* (Oxford, 1934), pp. 106 ff.; Hugh MacKinnon, "Life and Works"; P. Michaud-Quantin, *Sommes de casuistique et manuels de confession au moyen-âge* (xii–xvi siècle), *Analecta Namuracensia*, 12 (Louvain, 1962).

William himself referred to it as a *summa* but it is very different from the theological treatises produced by the schools. The *Numerale* is a practical book which presents the findings of the theologians rather than the speculation which led up to them. It is a practical book, too, in the manner of its presentation. It makes extensive use of various didactic devices meant to assist the reader in remembering the lessons taught. Another of his works, the *Versarius*, is partly theological in content. It is written in verse, obviously for didactic and not aesthetic reasons.

In addition to these theological works, William de Montibus was the author of a number of penitential works which one might expect, for the movement referred to above was particularly concerned with the sacrament of penance. One of these works, the *Speculum Penitentis*, is a practical guide for parish priests. In it he discussed various kinds of sins, placed them in several categories, and gave instruction on how the priest should hear confessions. In answer to a request from a friend, he also wrote a brief but doubtless useful manual of instruction on how to hear the confessions of religious. It is known as *Quomodo Religiosi Monendi Sunt ad Confitendum*.

Another manifestation of this theological movement is to be seen in William's efforts to assist the parish priest in his preaching. His *Tropi*, a text book of exegesis, was designed to give the priest a better understanding of sacred scripture which formed the basis of medieval preaching. The *Distinctiones* presented biblical and theological learning under various headings in schematic form and was intended to provide ready material for sermons. Two other works were meant to give the priest material to make his sermons attractive: the *Similitudinarius* is a collection of analogies drawn mainly from contemporary sermons, while the *Proverbia* is a collection of citations from sacred scripture, ecclesiastical writers, and above all from classical poets. In the *Proverbia* everything is arranged under appropriate headings and placed conveniently in alphabetical order. All of these works must have been of great service to a busy parish priest in the preparation of his sermons.

Another of William's works is *De Eliminatione Errorum*, a small and in many respects a curious liturgical book. In it he gave instruction on church services, the form of absolution, and some liturgical prayers. Finally, three sets of collected sermons, nearly two hundred in all, complete the corpus of his extant and identifiable works.[8]

8 There are a considerable number of extant mss. of his works. Most of them are located in England at Oxford, Cambridge, and in London. Two are in the

The most characteristic feature of William de Montibus' works is that they were all of a practical – one is tempted to say severely practical – nature. This can be seen not only in the matter he expounded but even more in the style and form he employed. An outstanding example of the latter is to be found in the *Numerale*, his major theological treatise. Even the choice of the title stems from the form into which he fashioned the work. The *Numerale* is divided into twelve chapters with each chapter subdivided into sections. Some of the chapters have many subdivisions while others have few. The division of the material itself is *secundum numerum*, the author grouping material in such a way that it can be somehow related to the corresponding number of the chapter. The result is an arrangement that is purely artificial. In chapter one we find: one God, one Faith, one Baptism, one Church. In chapter two: the Two Testaments, Faith and Works, Cleanness of Life and Knowledge. In chapter three: the Three Persons in the Trinity, the Three Substances in Christ, Faith, Hope, and Charity, and other groups of three. This artificial arrangement is carried out with remarkable fidelity throughout the twelve chapters and the treatise ends with a discussion of the Twelve Articles of the Faith, the Twelve Hours of the Day, and a short treatise on the Blessed Virgin, who is the woman in the Apocalypse with the crown of twelve stars upon her head. At first sight one might suppose some sort of symbolism was intended, some hidden meaning in the arrangement. There can be little doubt, however, that this form was meant to be nothing more than a pedagogical technique to assist the student to whom the work was directed. And it must have proved a useful book if we are to judge from the number of copies that were made and by the books in which it found a place.[9]

Bibliothèque Mazarin in Paris. Nearly all the mss. are of the thirteenth century, which suggests that his influence waned towards the end of the century. The provenance of the mss., where known, suggests that his influence was largely in the eastern part of England. It seems highly likely that he wrote all his works after his return from Paris. For numerous works attributed to William de Montibus see MacKinnon, "Life and Works," Appendix II. For manuscript references to the works of William de Montibus see *ibid.*, Appendix III, 1–77.

9 Merton College (Oxon.) ms. 257, which contains the *Numerale* and the *Similitudinarius*, was bought by Fitzjames in 1482 and put into Merton Library. Balliol College (Oxon.) ms. 222, which has the *Numerale*, the *Similitudinarius* and the *Tropi*, belonged to William Grey, Bishop of Ely (d. 1472) and came to Balliol after his death. This ms. is given over entirely to these three works. New College (Oxon.) ms. 98, which also contains only works by William de Montibus – the *Numerale*, the *Similitudinarius*, the *Tropi* and the *Proverbia* – was given to the college by its founder, William of Wykeham (d. 1404).

His concern for teaching techniques is seen, too, in the frequency with which he arranged his material in an alphabetical form. A good example of this can be found in his *Similitudinarius*, a sermon book. The scope of the work is practical rather than theoretical; it was not meant to be an *Ars Praedicandi*. It was not an original work but a collection of citations from a variety of sources as widely separated as St. Augustine's *City of God* and the sermons of his friend and contemporary, Alexander Nequam. As he wrote in the preface to the work, doctrine to be preached in sermons ought to be not merely stated but demonstrated by the use of authorities and reason and illuminated by examples and analogies. M. D. Chenu has shown how writers of this period were beginning to collect the sayings not only of the fathers but also of contemporary theologians and to present them as proofs of their doctrine.[10] William adopted this new technique for teaching theology but put it to use in a slightly different way, as a help to preachers in the composition of their sermons. He then added his own contribution by setting the collected sayings in alphabetical order. There are twelve extant copies of the work and an examination of them makes it clear that a variety of attempts have been made to group the material in alphabetical series and that this has been done in different ways and with varying degrees of success.[11] It seems very likely that William de Montibus spent considerable time on the work and that he added to it from time to time. It also would appear that the work was issued in, as it were, a number of "editions," that students took it away in varying forms, and that other copyists added material of their own. One thing is clear: it was a book ready to hand and easy to use and it was looked upon as very useful. Not only the considerable number of extant copies but the expenditure of time and effort in the various attempts at re-organiza-

10 M. D. Chenu, *La théologie au douzième siècle* (Paris, 1957), p. 358.
11 In some manuscripts the material is arranged in alphabetical form followed by other material in non-alphabetical form. Other manuscripts show that an attempt has been made to set this non-alphabetical material in an alphabetical form, and this is done in different ways. Some manuscripts have taken the non-alphabetical material and formed it into a second alphabetical series, others have taken the non-alphabetical and have integrated it with the alphabetical material to make one alphabetical series. In these attempts at re-arrangement there can be found imperfections and nearly all of them have included at the end of their different arrangements bits of added material still in non-alphabetical form. Finally, some manuscripts seem to show that a further revision was attempted, in which all the earlier attempts at re-organization have been used, and in one a new alphabetical series is put into order.

tion argues that the *Similitudinarius* was a manual worth working upon. In three other major works – *Distinctiones, Proverbis,* and *Versarius* – William used this alphabetical framework as a means of aiding the student to learn and to remember the lessons taught.

William de Montibus' keen interest in pedagogical techniques can be seen again in his use of what has been called the *"distinctio* method" of writing. The method had, as Miss Beryl Smalley tells us, "a long pedigree, going back on the one hand to alternative interpretations of the same word in patristic commentaries, on the other to lists of biblical words with their meanings, like the *Formulae Spiritualis Intelligentiae* of St. Eucher of Lyons, and the *Clavis Scripture* of the pseudo Melito."[12] But the form that was characteristic of William's writings was new and in that sense its origin lies somewhere in the later years of the twelfth century. It is reasonable to conjecture that the methods of studying the *sacra pagina* during the twelfth century had made the *distinctio* method natural until someone, in Miss Smalley's words, "had the brilliant idea of making a table of meanings for each word, according to three or four senses, and illustrating each meaning by a text."[13] When that happened the *distinctio* method was born. In its simplest form this method was a variety of exegesis.

The actual form in which the *distinctiones* were cast varied. Peter the Chanter and William de Montibus arranged their material alphabetically, sometimes as a commentary on the text of the psalter like the *Distinctiones super Psalterium* by Prepositinus and Peter of Poitiers.[14] The text of the work was sometimes written out, sometimes arranged schematically. A biblical text is usually attached to each meaning of the word but there are many exceptions to the rule. It is quite clear that the method was intended as an aid to preachers. Fr. Spicq is probably correct in describing various sets of *Distinctiones* as offshoots of the *Glossa Ordinaria,* and, as such, they were undoubtedly meant to assist the theologian in the classroom. Peter of Poitier's *Distinctiones super Psalterium* may have been written to supplement Peter Lombard's gloss on the psalter and, if so, it was meant primarily for teachers.[15]

However, William de Montibus used the *distinctio* method in a

12 B. Smalley, *The Study of the Bible in the Middle Ages* (Oxford, 1952), p. 246.
13 *Ibid.,* p. 247.
14 *Ibid.,* p. 248.
15 C. Spicq, *Esquisse d'une histoire de l'exégèse latin au moyen âge* (Paris, 1944), pp. 67–8.

special sense and applied it to meet a different but very pressing problem; to educate the clergy not for a career in the schools but for a career in the parish church.[16] This can be seen in the *Distinctiones*. A clear – even a classic – example is his treatment of the word "Jerusalem."

Historice: civitas scilicet illa terrena vel inhabitatores illius civitatis. Per metonomiam, unde "Jerusalem qui occidit prophetas" etc. Allegoria, ecclesia presens per totam orbem diffusa. Tropologica, queque anima sancta. Anagogica, patria celestis. Historia est ad litteram. Allegoria christi et ecclesie sacramenta figurat. Tropologia, more instruit. Annagoge, de futuris mistice disputat.[17]

He also made frequent use of the purely schematized form as in these examples:

From f.102ᵛ:

Christus est

per similitudinem	vitis
per nominis interpretationem	David, Salamon
per significationem	agnus paschalis
per rei veritatem	deus homo

From f.23:

Divitie

	Prohibetur circa eas	
avide queruntur		concupiscentia
solliciti servantur		tenacitas
cum tristitia perduntur		dilectio
cum labore adquiruntur		confidentia
cum timore possidentur		extollentia

In one place, after giving some *distinctiones* he adds some ideas which could be used when preaching to religious.[18] In another passage he suggests that the ideas presented would be useful for a sermon on the nativity.[19]

16 That the *distinctio* method was used in this special sense seems to be borne out by the scene Dr. R. W. Hunt describes as an early example of its use: Peter the prior of Holy Trinity Aldgate listened with delight and admiration to a sermon preached by Gilbert Foliot and wrote of it, "the whole sermon was varied by distinctiones, and adorned with flowers of words and sentences and supported by a copious array of authorities". See R. W. Hunt, "English Learning in the late Twelfth Century" in *TRHS.*, 4th series, xix (1936), 33–4.
17 Bodleian Library (Oxon) ms. 419 (SC 2318), f.40ᵛ.
18 *Ibid.*, f.63.
19 *Ibid.*, f.69.

From these examples the purpose of the *Distinctiones* is clear enough. Although it is easy to see how the *distinctio* method could have been and was used for exegesis in the classroom, William's purpose was definitely to aid in the preparation of sermons. Fr. Petit, therefore, certainly exaggerates and probably misleads when he sees in the *distinctio* method merely a turning away from older traditions with an almost superstitious reverence for patristic interpretations and the acceptance of new methods by which dialectic and logic were used to interpret sacred scripture.[20]

This distinguished medieval teacher must also be given credit for initiating a new form of teaching theology. His *Versarius* is a work of didactic verse written not later than the early years of the thirteenth century. Its importance lies not so much in the content of the work itself but in that it originated a method of teaching that became popular and influential in the later medieval period. There may have been earlier efforts in the use of didactic verse but they were limited to the teaching of grammar. The *Doctrinale* of Alexander of Villa Dei, composed at the end of the twelfth century, is perhaps the best known grammatical work of this kind. Early in the thirteenth century Eberhard of Bethune's *Graecismus*, a similar work, also gained great popularity. The use of didactic verse in the teaching of theology is a later development, which, it would seem, found its inspiration in the widespread use of versified grammatical works. William either wrote at the same time as Alexander and Eberhard or he immediately grasped the new technique and applied it to theology.

The teachers of theology used the verse form in a variety of ways. At times the verse was used to explain the text or to summarize it in a manner easy for the memory to retain; at times the text itself was put into verse to which was added a gloss to point the lesson or to explain the text. In the later years of the thirteenth century and in the fourteenth and fifteenth centuries this method of teaching theology in verse was used to present the great medieval theological works. Hugh of St. Victor, Peter Lombard, and St. Thomas Aquinas were all put into verse form. Two *Libri Sententiarum Versificati* are preserved at Cambridge.[21] Hugh of St. Victor's *De Sacramentis Christianae Fidei* was put into verse form[22] and Francis Penon, O.P.

20 P. Petit, *Ad Viros Religiosus: Quatorze sermons d'Adam Scott*, (Tongerloo, 1934), p. 30.
21 Gonville and Caius College (Cantab.) ms 258, fols. 1–27.
22 See S. de Ghellinck, "Medieval Theology in Verse," in *Irish Quart. R.*, ix, 35 (July 1914), 340.

did the same for the *Summa Theologica*.[23] These verse renditions of the great theological treatises, however, never gained the popularity of the works which, although less formidable theologically, were originally in verse form.

It is to this latter form of theological writing that William de Montibus' *Versarius* belongs. It is the earliest attempt at this method of teaching theology. Like the *Numerale*, the *Versarius* is a very artificially contrived work with its subject matter arranged alphabetically. The subject matter, therefore, is not logically ordered and the work possesses only extrinsic unity.[24] The whole work is generously glossed; at times it is the gloss that teaches the lesson, while the text itself is meant to be no more than a mnemonic device. In other instances both text and gloss are employed to teach the lesson. Sometimes a fairly lengthy verse passage with virtually no gloss is given and the entire lesson depends upon the text itself. In the latter case, the verse form is useful because it is more easily remembered as well as being more attractive in form. The *Versarius* is an unusual work of theology. The subject matter and the author's treatment of it are so varied that it is difficult to define its nature precisely. It can hardly claim to be entirely a work of theology; rather it appears to be a compilation of more or less random reflections – theological, moral, ascetical, liturgical – put together for instruction and edification. It may have been intended to be in part some kind of devotional work meant for occasional reading and meditation. At any rate it was the first attempt at a method of teaching theology which was to have considerable influence upon the instruction of students to the end of the medieval period.

Perhaps the most successful attempt to use this method of teaching theology was the penitential poem, *Peniteas cito*, which became one of the most widely used didactic poems of the middle ages. The first four lines of the poem are elegiac couplets, but from line five until the end the metre changes to the easier dactylic hexameter. It appears in a variety of forms, sometimes unglossed, more frequently with a gloss. In a work so widely copied and used it is not surprising to

---

23 *Ibid.*, 341.
24 Under the letter B, for example, some of the subjects discussed are: baptismus, brevitas vite, brevitas rerum, bellum, bone, benedicere, bonus homo, sanctus Benedictus, beneficia dei. A kind of internal unity seems to be aimed at with christus, corpus christi, victoria christi, testes christi, and vita et doctrina christi, but this is probably accidental, the unity being more apparent than real.

discover many variations in both text and gloss.[25] The general rule is that the texts compare very closely for the first fifty lines, which is roughly half the poem, and the variations are found in the latter part. These take the form of omissions of a line or lines, additions or merely variant arrangements of material. There is, naturally enough, wider divergence in the glosses. At the same time, the poem is always recognizable as the *Peniteas cito* and, while additions to both text and gloss were almost certainly made by various copyists, authorship in a real sense can be claimed by one man.

Copies of the *Peniteas cito* are almost innumerable in manuscripts of the thirteenth, fourteenth, and fifteenth centuries. Most of the copies are anonymous and some of the attributions are obviously erroneous. There are, however, good reasons for attributing this influential poem to William de Montibus. The contents and style of the *Peniteas cito* indicate that it was written late in the twelfth century or early in the thirteenth. It was certainly not written later than the first decade of the thirteenth century as extracts from it are found in William de Montibus' *Versarius*. It is probable, then, that the *Peniteas cito* was written during William's productive years and it is certain that it was the kind of work that interested him, the kind of work that he could do and had done. The matter and the manner of the work were within his compass and it resembles in a general way other known works of his on the same subject.

There are, moreover, two thirteenth-century manuscripts which attribute the *Peniteas cito* to William de Montibus. One attribution in the Cambridge University Library manuscript mentioned above is straightforward enough and calls for no comment. The attribution in the British Museum manuscript, on the other hand, presents a number of problems. The manuscript contains a number of works by different authors. The first work is a *Chronicon ab exordio mundi ad A.D. 1137* and runs from fols. 1–58. The second work is the *Speculum Penitentis* by William de Montibus, fols. 59–66, the third a

25 The text of Cambridge University Library ms. Ii i 26 has the same beginning and ending as the glossed version in Brit. Mus. ms. Cotton Vespasian D XIII, but it has twenty-five lines added internally. An unglossed version in the same ms. has an addition to the text and, therefore, its own ending. The Migne version of the poem, (vol. 207, col. 1153–4, *Series Secunda*, attributed to Peter of Blois), which represents ms. Codice Lamethano, n.36 and ms. Bruxellensi, n.1968, closely resembles all of them except for some additional lines. Vatican Library ms. Reg. Lat. 29, has fewer lines of text than any of those mentioned, and has lines not found in any of them and an ending different from them all.

Summa by Alan of Lille, fols. 66ᵛ–98, the fourth the *Liber de Miseria*
by Innocent III, fols. 98–112. On f.112 there is a title "Qualis debet
esse confessio hic versus notificatur" and what follows the title is the
Peniteas cito in an unglossed form, ending on f.113 with no attribution given. On f.113 there is the heading "Incipit tractatus magistri
Willelmi de Montibus de confessione" and what follows is a short
citation from a sermon by St. Bernard and once more the *Peniteas
cito*, this time in its more usual glossed form. It runs to f.116ᵛ and is
immediately followed by a title "Versus de confessione," a four-line
description in verse of what a good confession should be and then
brief notes on each of the qualities given in the short verse. The notes
come to an end on f.116ᵛ and are followed by the heading "Item
eiusdem unde supra" and part of the *Speculum Penitentis* by William
de Montibus, beginning with the words, "Hec sunt de quibus inquisi-
tio facienda est in confessione" and ending with the work's proper
ending on f.119. The rest of the manuscript contains seven other
works by various authors that have no bearing on our present
question.

The first problem is the duplication of the two penitential works in
the same volume, for we have the *Peniteas cito* given twice, once in
an unglossed form, once in a glossed form and the *Speculum Penitentis* given twice, once in its entirety and once in a substantial but
incomplete form. The latter duplication, perhaps, does not present a
great problem. Since the complete *Speculum Penitentis* begins on
f.69 and the incomplete one on f.116, it can be assumed that the
scribe did not recognize the incomplete *Speculum Penitentis* for what
it was and included it in a volume which was to contain a number of
penitential works. The other duplication is more difficult to understand since the copies of the *Peniteas cito* follow one another in the
manuscript. The one scribe, who wrote the whole section of this
volume, introduced the unglossed *Peniteas cito* without any attribution and immediately afterward and on the same page introduced the
glossed *Peniteas cito* as the work of William de Montibus. Two
things are worth noting; firstly, it is the glossed *Peniteas cito*, the
one attributed here to William de Montibus, which was popular and
influential and, secondly, there are too many variations in this copy
from the other ascribed *Peniteas cito* in the Cambridge University
Library copy mentioned above to allow that they immediately descend from a single source. In other words, these appear to be two
independent and early attributions of the *Peniteas cito* to William de
Montibus.

Attempts to establish the authorship of the *Peniteas cito* have been thus far unsuccessful because historians have assumed that the poem had from the beginning an independent existence. The assumption was based largely upon the fact that no one had demonstrated its relationship to or dependence upon similar contemporary literature. Recently, however, the interdependence of the *Peniteas cito* and William de Montibus' *Versarius* has been established.[26] A close examination of this interdependence demonstrates that the *Peniteas cito* consists essentially of excerpts from the *Versarius*. Its author extracted every item from the *Versarius* that had to do with the sacrament of penance and put them together to form a separate work, which came to be known as the *Peniteas cito*. For example, in the Migne version of the *Peniteas cito*, referred to above,[27] every line of the poem, except for a brief conclusion of three lines, can be found scattered through the *Versarius* as separate items in that work, each with its own title. Two early manuscripts,[28] both of which were written either during William de Montibus' lifetime or shortly after his death, help to demonstrate the genesis of the *Peniteas cito*. In these manuscripts the scribes have added interlinearly throughout the poem the titles which each item had been given in the *Versarius*.[29] It seems reasonably clear that the scribes have inserted the titles of each item throughout the poem because they recognized them as items from the *Versarius*. Later copyists dropped the titles as unnecessary when the less popular *Versarius* had been forgotten.

The inclusion of one item from the *Versarius* is particularly revealing. The item is ten lines long, has the title "Qualis debet esse prelatus" and in the *Versarius* begins thus: "Prelatus mitis, affabilis

26 See MacKinnon, "Life and Works," p. 121. It is here demonstrated that William de Montibus, if not the author of the *Peniteas cito*, is certainly the first author to have used it.

27 *Supra* n.25.

28 Bodleian Library (Oxon) ms. Musaeo 30 (SC 3580), and Cambridge University Library ms. Ii i 26. The scribe who copied the latter also attributed the work to William de Montibus. Thus we have the evidence of both an early ms. and a scribe who probably had possession of William de Montibus' *Versarius*.

29 The poem begins with an item – Que sunt necessaria penitenti (4 lines) – then continues with these items in sequence: De satisfactione (5 lines), Quod plenaria debet esse confessio (2 lines), De Fletu (3 lines), Qualis debet esse confessio (3 lines), Confessio (5 lines), De corporalibus et spiritualibus peccatis (8 lines), Que sunt vitia capitalia (2 lines), Confessio (2 lines), De quibus facienda est generalis confessio (6 lines), Que circumstantie aggravant peccata (3 lines), De penitentia infirmorum (5 lines), Cur instituta est confessio (4 lines), and so on to the end of the poem, always using the titles given in the *Versarius*.

atque benignus / Sit sapiens, justus, sit dulcis compatiensque." When this item appears in the *Peniteas cito*, however, the title is changed to "Qualis debet esse confessor," and the first line is changed to read, "Confessor mitis, affabilis atque benignus," while the rest of the item is left unchanged. Had the item as originally written described the qualities of a confessor, William de Montibus would have had no reason to transform it into an item describing the qualities of a prelate in order to include it in a work so general as the *Versarius*. However, it was necessary to transform *prelatus* into *confessor* to include it in a purely penitential work. It would seem then that this item and all the other items in the *Peniteas cito* were initially part of William de Montibus' *Versarius*.

In view of the above evidence, it can be asserted that William de Montibus was in the most fundamental sense the author of the *Peniteas cito*. Whether it was he or some other writer who originally extracted the items and put them together may be impossible to determine. However, in view of the nature of William de Montibus' other known works and his demonstrated interest in popularization, together with the variety of pedagogical techniques he employed, it seems highly likely that William de Montibus himself made the initial compilation of the *Peniteas cito*.

While commentators, medieval and modern, say very little about William de Montibus, there is pretty general agreement, explicitly stated or strongly implied, that he was a man of importance in his day and worth investigation today. Two chroniclers give brief but laudatory obituary notices of him. He is "pie memorie," "doctor sancte theologie," and one year after his death his body was translated to Lincoln "cum debita reverentia."[30] In the prologue of an anonymous life of Gilbert of Sempringham, he is praised as the first theological teacher in England,[31] while a thirteenth-century poem equates him with Gregory and Augustine.[32] In the *Scala Caelica*, a compilation of ascetical and theological sayings of the fathers and of St. Anselm, Hugh of Victor, and St. Bernard, he is given an honoured place. Among modern scholars there is again pretty general, if only implicit, agreement about his importance. Thomas Wright calls him "a friend of the most distinguished scholars of his day," and the

30 *Chronicon de Mailros*, ed. Joseph Stevenson (Edinburgh, 1835), p. 114.
31 Brit. Mus. ms. Cotton Cleo. B I, f.35.
32 See A. Wilmart, "Les mélanges de Mathieu préchantre de Rievaulx au début du XIIIᵉ siècle," in *Revue bénédictine*, LII (1940), 15–48.

founder of a school at Lincoln, "which became as famous as that which he had left at Paris."[33] Sir Maurice Powicke refers to him as "the learned chancellor" under whom "the theological school of Lincoln became famous."[34] Fr. de Ghellinck links his name with Langton's[35] and Fr. Paul Anciaux writes: "Parmi les sommes à l'usage des prédicateurs, la plus célèbre en Angleterre est celle de Guillaume des Monte."[36] J. C. Russell considers that "a critical study of his works is needed."[37] His name, a reference to his works, the implication of his importance keep cropping up in articles by scholars like Msg. Lacombe, Miss Smalley, and MM. Glorieux and Chenu. Dr. R. W. Hunt, however, notes the elementary character of his writings and judges that "his speculative bent can hardly have been great"[38] and Miss Eleanor Rathbone registers disappointment on reading his works.[39] They both are right, of course, but it is not in the matter of his writings that one should look for his achievement. William de Montibus was a man of ability but not a strikingly original man. It is not for what he wrote but for the method that he used that he is interesting. He was an early and forceful participant in a movement that was to transmit new ideas in a popular way to a particular audience. And there is perhaps no aspect of the movement to which he did not make a contribution – whether it be penitentials, distinctiones, biblical exegesis, sermon aids, or didactic verse. His writings were read and respected and one of them, the *Peniteas cito*, made a signal contribution to the penitential literature of the later middle ages. The total must be considered an achievement of consequence.

33 T. Wright, *Biographia Brittanica Litteraria* (London, 1842), p. 463.
34 F. M. Powicke, *Stephen Langton* (New York, 1965), p. 9.
35 J. de Ghellinck, S. J., *L'Essor de la littérature latine au XIIe siècle* (Louvain, 1946), I, p. 86.
36 P. Anciaux, *La Théologie du sacrement de pénitence au XIIe siècle* (Louvain, 1949), p. 88.
37 J. C. Russel, *Dictionary of Writers of Thirteenth Century England* (Bulletin of the Institute of Historical Research, Special Supplement no. 3; London, 1936), s.n. William de Montibus.
38 R. W. Hunt, "English learning," p. 21.
39 Eleanor Rathbone, "The Intellectual Influence of Bishops and Cathedral Chapters, 1066–1216," an unpublished Ph.D. thesis (University of London, 1935).

The Constitutional Problem in Thirteenth-Century England R. F. TREHARNE

𝕴n medieval times royal authority in England, as elsewhere in western Europe, was never absolute. Whether we consider its primitive tribal origins, its feudal form, or its Christian *ethos*, there was no basis for absolutism, nor room for its growth, in medieval England. Folk memory and ancient custom; the feudal habit of the upper ranks of society, with its emphasis on mutual obligation, devolution, and the almost exclusive duty of the aristocracy to provide the fighting forces of the kingdom; the Christian conception of kingship as a divinely instituted office whose holder was responsible to God and ultimately subject to ecclesiastical admonition and censure – all these things made genuine absolutism a contradiction in terms to medieval kingship. In fact, the medieval king lacked the essential means of absolutism. Since the disappearance of the *huscarles* after Hastings, he had no standing army of professional mercenaries; his financial resources were very limited and did not include the power to tax at will; and even the growth of a royal bureaucracy was sharply restricted by the lack both of money and of trained servants. "Angevin absolutism," then, is a very loose description of English royal authority about AD 1200!

Among those who were writing at this time on political theory and practice, as the late Dr. A. J. Carlyle showed us,[1] three great principles were universally accepted as beyond challenge: "the principle that the purpose or function of the political organisation of society is ethical or moral, that is, the maintenance of justice and righteousness; ... the principle of the supremacy of law as the concrete embodiment of justice; ... and the principle that the relation between the king

1 R. W. and A. J. Carlyle, *A History of Medieval Political Theory in the West* (Edinburgh and London, 1915), III, pp. 181–4.

and the people is founded and depends upon the mutual obligation and agreement to maintain justice and law." These writers "believed firmly in the divine nature of the state, they looked upon the ruler as God's representative and servant, but only so far as he really and in fact carried out the divine purpose of righteousness and justice. ... To them the conception of an arbitrary authority was simply unthinkable, and the distinction between the king who governs according to law and the tyrant who violates it was not a rhetorical phrase, but the natural and normal expression of their whole mode of thought." The "feudal" lawyers concurred fully in this conception of royal authority, expressing the same ideas in their own way. "There is no king where will rules and not law," "The King is under God and the law;" "La dame ne le sire n'en est seignor se non dou droit,"[2] are not empty platitudes falling meaninglessly from the pens of Bracton or of the authors of the Assizes of Jerusalem; they are expressions of a fundamental conviction on which these men based the entire legal and judicial system which they set themselves to describe and to justify, and in the operation of which they were proud to spend their lives. The revived study of Roman civil law, based upon Justinian's determined distortions in the interest of imperial absolutism, had already achieved great conquests and was to win many more. But, although even the most stoutly "feudal" lawyers were profoundly influenced by Roman civil law's massive and scientific jurisprudence, they resisted its hypnotic doctrine of efficiency under a centralized royal authority freed from all compulsion or restraint.

In England it was the royal authority itself which helped to preserve the nation from this dangerous allurement, for, as Professor McIlwain has shown us,[3] it was precisely the early establishment, by Henry II himself, with his reformed *curia regis*, his system of uniform writs, and his itinerant justices, of a specifically English common law sufficiently tough to resist the later onslaught of revived Roman law in Justinian's version, that saved England from a legal theory which taught that "the will of the prince has the force of law." "If Irnerius had taught, or Azo had written, a century before he did, or if a Henry III had followed Stephen on the throne of England, we might well be using the *Digest* of Justinian to-day in our American law-schools," Professor McIlwain tells us. While this may be an exaggeration, in

2 Cited *ibid.*, p. 184.
3 C. H. McIlwain, *Constitutionalism Ancient and Modern* (Ithaca, 1947), p. 59.

that other kingdoms in medieval Europe, without any Henry II to defend them, nevertheless escaped Justinian's deadly legacy, it is at least remarkable that Henry II, the founder of the miscalled "Angevin absolutism" and the strongest of all medieval English kings, should have done so much to make it impossible for a legal theory of absolutism to establish itself in England when so many states in Europe were falling under its spell.

The relation between the king and the law, though not formally stated, is clearly implied in the *Tractatus de Legibus et Consuetudinibus Anglie* which bears the name of Henry's great justiciar, Ranulf Glanvill. It matters little for our present purpose whether this treatise was written by Ranulf or by his still greater protégé and successor, Hubert Walter: in either case it states authoritatively the views current among the professional judges of the *curia regis* at the close of Henry's reign. In the text as we have it today, the most telling passage on this matter has been rejected by Dr. Fritz Schulz as a clumsy interpolation impossible to construe satisfactorily and interrupting the course of Glanvill's argument.[4] This rejection seems somewhat highhanded; if the passage could be allowed to stand, it would suggest that Glanvill so strongly disapproved of the famous maxim of Justinian's *Digest*, "quod principi placuit, legis habet vigorem," that, in a passage explaining why unwritten English customs are properly to be called laws, he went out of his way to drag the pernicious text irrelevantly into his exposition in order to render it harmless by means of a gloss which virtually reversed its obvious sense. What he says is that "this is the law, [that] that which pleases the prince has the force of law; that is to say, those things which have manifestly been promulgated upon doubtful matters which must be determined in the council with the advice of the magnates at least, and under the prince's authority." If this passage be genuine, its irrelevance to the argument in which it is embedded makes the reversal of meaning by interpretation all the more remarkable. But even if Dr. Schulz is right to reject the passage, there are still others in which Glanvill indicates his belief that the king is not *legibus solutus*, but is under the law. In his prologue he tells us that "in the king's court each decision is governed by the laws of the realm and by customs drawn from reason and long observed," and that "the King does not disdain to consult those of his subjects whom he knows to stand out by their virtue, by their skill in the law, and by the customs of the realm."

4 F. Schulz, "Bracton on Kingship," *EHR*, LX (1945), 171.

And Professor McIlwain, by recounting a judgment made by Glanvill himself in 1185 when the prior and convent of Abingdon, appealing against the arbitrary action of a royal *custos* during a vacancy, based their case on ancient custom, has shown that these were no empty words.[5] After hearing their statement, "Ranulf Glanvill, the chief of the justices, turning to the other judges, said that our customary rights had been established reasonably and wisely ... and that the lord king neither wishes nor dares to go against customs so ancient and so just, or to change anything respecting them"; and the justices "who were seated around" all concurred. How far removed constitutionally from the absolute emperor whose pleasure has the force of law is this great king who nevertheless "neither wishes nor dares" to contravene customary law in his courts!

Bracton, writing some seventy years later and treating his subject in a more detailed as well as a more philosophical way, tells us much more of his constitutional conception of the English monarchy which he was proud to serve.[6] At the outset we may spare ourselves the attempt to reconcile Bracton's very conservative constitutionalism with the startingly radical doctrines of the famous *addicio* (D3, 4) which claims "that the king has a superior, not only in God and in the law which makes him king, but also in his *curia*, that is, in his earls and barons, since the earls [*comites*] are, as it were, the associates [*socii*] of the king, and whoever has an associate has a master. And therefore, if the king is without a bridle, that is, without law, they should put a bridle upon him, unless they themselves are, like the king, without a bridle." In spite of Dr. Kantorowicz's defence of the authenticity of this passage and his assertion of its "genuinely Bractonian" flavour,[7] Professor McIlwain's demonstration that it is completely at variance with the rest of Bracton's teaching on this fundamental topic,[8] and Dr. Schulz's analysis of its derivation,[9] seem convincing. It must be regarded as a later addition, incongruously inserted into Bracton's text, probably by some legal enthusiast

5 McIlwain, *Constitutionalism*, pp. 63–6, where all of the passages from Glanvill cited in this paragraph are discussed.
6 The relevant passages from Bracton's *De Legibus et Consuetudinibus Angliae libri quinque* have been conveniently gathered together, punctuated, and distributed into numbered paragraphs to facilitate citing by Dr. Schulz, "Bracton on Kingship," 137–45; Dr. Schulz's numbering is employed in the references which follow, between brackets, in the text of the present article.
7 H. Kantorowicz, *Bractonian Problems* (Glasgow, 1941), pp. 49–52.
8 McIlwain, *Constitutionalism*, pp. 69, 157–8.
9 Schulz, "Bracton on Kingship," pp. 144–5, 173–5.

for the Montfortian cause. The proper place, therefore, to consider
the significance of its drastic doctrine is as a justification of the Montfortian reforms of 1258–65, and not as a regular part of the constitutional theory of a great conservative lawyer and judge writing a little
before that time.

But even if we discard the *addicio*, Bracton still has much to say
about the king's position in relation to the law and the constitution.
He is profoundly impressed by the might and majesty of the king's
dominion and power and by the dignity of the office which God has
conferred upon him. "He is God's minister and vicar upon earth
[A.16, 22], and has ordinary jurisdiction and power over all in his
realm." In his hand are all the rights which pertain to the crown and
to the lay power, and the secular sword of government in the realm;
he alone, therefore, can grant liberties (B.1). Justice and judgment
are his, so that in virtue of his jurisdiction as God's servant and
deputy, he may render to each whatever may be his (B.2); he alone,
and no other save by his commission, may exercise this jurisdiction.
To him belong all matters that concern the peace, so that the people
committed to his charge may live in tranquillity (B.3); his is the power
of coercion, to punish and restrain wrongdoers (B.4). It is in his
power to enforce the laws, statutes, and decrees provided and approved in his realm and to cause them to be observed by his subjects
(B.5). He must be above all of his subjects in power, and can have no
equal (A.10, 11, 14), for thus he would forfeit authority, since equals
have no power to command each other (C.1). Still less can he have
any superior, especially in doing justice, so that it may truly be said
of him "Great is our Lord, and great are his virtues [A.11, 12]." He
cannot be under any man, since thus he would be inferior to his own
subjects (C.1): no writ can run against him, but only a supplication of
grace that he should amend his action, and if he will not do so, then
God's vengeance is the sole penalty that can befall him (C.7).

But for all this elaboration of the king's supremacy, not for one
moment does Bracton consider him to be *legibus solutus*. These vast
powers are in effect a solemn responsibility, for they have been committed to him purely for specific and public ends. With a clear per-
ception of the essential realities of politics, Bracton begins his discussion of the royal powers with the coronation oath which, with but
slight alteration, every king of England since the founding of the
realm had taken – the triple pledge "in Christ's name to do his utmost
to preserve the peace of God's church and of the whole Christian

people committed to his charge, to forbid violence and all wrong-doing to men of all ranks in his kingdom, and to show equity and mercy in all judgments, so that by his justice all shall enjoy the blessing of secure peace [A.2]." He was chosen and created king, "that he might do justice to all men and that through his deeds God might show forth his judgments [A.3, 4]." As vicar of God upon earth, he must therefore decide between right and wrong, equity and injustice, so that all of his subjects may live decently, none harming another and each receiving his due (A.8, 9). If justice and judgment are his, it is so that he may give to each his rights (B.2), and whatever he has justly adjudged he must maintain and uphold; for if there were none to do justice, peace would swiftly perish, and it would be idle to establish laws and pronounce judgments if there were no one to enforce them (A.5, 6, 7). It is to this end too that he is the guardian of the peace, "that his people may live in tranquillity, and that none may beat, wound or ill-treat another, or seize the goods of another by force and robbery, or maim or kill his fellow-man [B.3]." This is why he has the power to compel his subjects to observe the law, and why he can coerce and punish evildoers (B.4, 5).

This weight of responsibility, in Bracton's eyes, constantly circumscribes the king's authority and imposes conditions on the exercise of his great power. His power is to do right, not injury, and since he is the champion of right, no cause of injury should spring from him who is the source of right (A.19, 20). He must exercise his power of right as the vicar and servant of God upon earth, since this power is of God alone, whereas the power of harm is of the devil and not of God (A.22). The king will be the minister of that power whose work he does – if he does justice, he is the servant of the Eternal King; if he falls into injustice he is the servant of the devil (A.23). As the earthly minister and vicar of God he can do nothing save what he can rightly do (A.16): he is styled "king" (*rex*) from "directing well" (*bene regendo*), not from "reigning" (*regnando*) for he is a king only while he rules well, and he becomes a tyrant when by violent domination he oppresses the people entrusted to him (A.24, 25). Let him, therefore, since the king's heart should be in God's hand, place upon himself the bridle of temperance and the reins of moderation, lest, unbridled, he fall into injustice (A.14, 15). Let him temper his power with law, which is the bridle of power, so that he may live by the laws (A.26), for there is nothing so proper to authority as to live by the laws (A.29), and to submit his own authority to the laws is still greater a thing than to command (A.30). He must not himself commit those very things which, by virtue of his office, he must forbid to others (A. 21): human law decrees that "the laws bind their maker" (A.27), and again it has been said "It is a worthy utterance of reigning majesty to profess that the prince himself is bound by the laws" (A.28): the famous *digna vox* principle stated originally by the emperors Valentinian and Theodosius, and enshrined in Roman law itself. "He is no king, if his will, not the law, rules [c.3]: let him therefore attribute to the law what the law confers on him – authority and power, for it is the law that makes him king [A.31]."

"And since the king should go armed, not only with weapons but with the laws, let him learn wisdom and cleave to justice [A.32, 33]. And God shall grant wisdom to him, and when he shall find it, blessed shall he be if he keep it [A.34], for there are honour and glory in the words of the wise, but the tongue of the foolish man is his overthrow [A.35]." "The rule of the wise king is stable, and the wise king shall judge his people; but if he be foolish, he shall bring them to destruction [A.36], for corruption of the members flows down from a corrupted head, and if wisdom and strength do not flourish in the head, it follows that the other members cannot fulfil their office [A.37]." "But not only must he be wise; he must be merciful, and mercifully just with wisdom [A.38], letting his eyes go before his feet so that his judgment shall not falter by imprudence, nor his mercy lack wisdom through incaution [A.40]."

With these manifold admonitions to the prince so clearly in his mind, Bracton, for all his profound knowledge of the civil law, was not to be seduced by Justinian's doctrine of imperial absolutism. He does, indeed, quote from the *Digest* and the *Institutes* the celebrated text, "Quod principi placuit, legis habet vigorem," but only to refute the justification of absolutism which had been founded on it (A.17, 18). The original text of Ulpian had been far too limited for the superstructure which Justinian's lawyers proposed to build upon it, and therefore they had flagrantly remodelled it to make it serve as a justification of their master's power.[10] Bracton, declaring that the king can do only that which he can do lawfully (A.16), takes up the challenge of this famous enunciation of absolute authority. "Nor can it be objected" he writes "that it is written 'That which pleases the prince has the force of law', for that same law continues '... since by the *lex regia* which is decreed concerning the imperial power ...';

10 Cf. *ibid.*, pp. 153–62.

wherefore it is not whatever the king's will may rashly presume, but that which, after discussion and deliberation on the matter, shall be lawfully decided by the counsel of his magnates, the king lending his authority to it [A.17, 18]." The abbreviated reference to the bearing of the *lex regia* on the famous maxim has puzzled commentators from Selden down to McIlwain, but Dr. Schulz, by a patient disentangling of the history of the passage,[11] has shown us that Bracton neither misunderstood the construction of the text nor deliberately misconstrued it in order to explain it away. Dr. Schulz argues convincingly that, on the contrary, Bracton perceived the falsity of the argument that the *lex de imperio* (*lex regia*) had made the prince absolute, and he says that Bracton's abbreviated reference to the *Digest* and the *Institutes*, when fully expanded, was meant to argue that, since the emperor derived his authority from the *lex de imperio*, by which the people conferred all their authority and power upon him, his authority was limited by the *lex de imperio* itself to the circumstances named in that act. According to Dr. Schulz, Bracton went behind the *Digest* to the presumed original meaning of Ulpian himself, arguing that only a limited and conditional power of lawmaking was conferred upon the emperor by the *lex de imperio*, and he then showed what these limits and conditions actually were by paraphrasing another passage from Justinian's *Codex* itself, whereby the emperor's legislative power was limited by formal rules of procedure requiring consultation and consent of the senate. Bracton equates this requirement to the need for formal consultation and consent of the king's great council; subject to this all-important requirement, the king can indeed make law, but he cannot do whatever he likes. Dr. Schulz may perhaps be right in dismissing as "only a rhetorical ornamental phrase" the designation of English law as "a common engagement of the republic" (*rei publicae communi sponsio*) which Bracton took from the *Digest*,[12] though Professor McIlwain treats it much more seriously.[13] But there is no mistaking the rest of Bracton's definition of law in England: "That has the force of law which has been justly declared and approved with the counsel and consent of the magnates ..., the authority of the king or prince preceding."[14] Moreover, he says, "these laws, since they have been approved by the consent of

---

11 *Ibid.*, pp. 153–69.
12 *Ibid.*, p. 171.
13 McIlwain, *Constitutionalism*, p. 69.
14 *Ibid.*, pp. 69–70, quoting from Bracton's prologue.

those using them, and confirmed by the oaths of kings, can neither
be changed nor destroyed without the common consent of all those
with whose counsel and consent they have been promulgated."[15]
There can be no question that, for Bracton, the rule of law was supreme and that the English constitution was a monarchy limited by
law: "the law makes him king and he must live by the law [A.29, 31,
B.2]: there is no king where it is not the law, but his will, that
governs [B.3]."

If Bracton's constitutional doctrine is so clear, why then have some
commentators held it to be self-contradictory? Probably much of the
difficulty in the past has sprung from treating the *addicio* (D.3, 4) as
part of Bracton's own text, instead of disregarding it as an incongru-
ous and propagandist interpolation by some unknown copyist. For
the rest, the apparent contradiction is the result of taking isolated
sentences and phrases and commenting upon them without due
regard for the sense of the whole: Professor McIlwain tells us that
in *Darnel's* case in 1627 both sides were able to quote Bracton in
contradiction of each other on the question whether the king can act
otherwise than in accordance with law.[16] On the one hand, we have
the unmistakable assertions that "neither justices nor private persons
ought to or can dispute concerning royal charters and royal acts"[17]
and that "no one can pass judgment on an act or charter of the king
so as to make void the king's act [D.1]"; and, in more general terms,
that no writ can run against him (C.7), that he alone has the powers
of justice, coercion, and punishment (B.2, 4), that he has no equal,
much less a superior, in the land (A.11, C.1), and that if he does wrong
and will not amend it, God's justice alone can bring him to book
(C.7). On the other hand are the no less emphatic assertions that he
is not *legibus solutus*, and that the rule of law limits his authority
wherever the two meet. Yet the contradiction disappears as soon as
we view his doctrine as a whole: it is a picture of the monarch free
from all human restrain but subject to the *vis directiva* of the law, as
Aquinas was soon to describe it. Bracton himself has stated the position with complete clarity in his famous phrase: "Rex non debet esse
sub homine, sed sub Deo et lege, quia lex facit regem": "the king
should not be under man, but under God and under the law, for the
law makes the king." (C.2)

Professor McIlwain, in discussing this supposed contradiction, has
given us a key to the better understanding of the constitutional prob-

15 *Ibid.*   16 *Ibid.*, p. 73.   17 *Ibid.*, p. 72.

lem of the thirteenth century, and a means of measuring the progress made by the men of that great age towards the solution of the central question of their political life. Professor McIlwain found the answer to the difficulties of the supposed contradictions by following the distinction which Bracton himself makes quite clearly between the two aspects of royal power: *jurisdictio* and *gubernaculum*.[18] By *jurisdictio* Bracton means the administration of justice, and the application of the law and custom of the land: by *gubernaculum*, the executive and political, the general administrative actions of government. According to Bracton, in administering justice or in performing any action to which the law and the custom of the realm can apply, the king may not set aside, break, or vary that custom or law, and if he does, the king's own judges should and will disallow his action or that of his officials.[19] But the *gubernaculum*, the executive and political government of England, is in his hand alone: not only is he the sole administrator, but he must have, of right, all powers needful for effective government. In this sphere no one, not even a judge, can question the legitimacy of his actions; he has no peer, much less a superior, and there exists neither man nor institution in the realm with the legal right to check him. Thus, in the framing of policy, in the executive action needed to carry out that policy, in the choice of counsellors and officials, in the day-to-day administration, the king is free from restraint or control, so long as he does not break the law or infringe the recognized custom of the realm. The only effective restraints on him are his own conscience and the practical fear of driving his subjects to revolt – the *vis directiva* of Aquinas – plus such common sense as the king may have. This view was a commonplace of thirteenth-century political thought, and though, as the *addicio* and as *Fleta*[20] prove, it had vehement opponents, it was the doctrine generally held in the church and in the schools, and it was uncompromisingly asserted by St. Louis in the Mise of Amiens[21] and by the papal legate and the royalist bishops and barons in the Dictum of Kenilworth.[22] It is adequately summed up in the maxim, "Rex debet esse sub Deo et lege, sed non sub homine." To avoid misunderstanding, it must be made clear that Professor Wilkinson's well-known

18 *Ibid.*, pp. 74–9.   19 *Ibid.*, pp. 85–6.   20 *Ibid.*, p. 78.
21 R. F. Treharne, "The Mise of Amiens, 23 January 1264" in *Studies in Medieval History presented to Frederick Maurice Powicke*, eds R. W. Hunt, W. A. Pantin, and R. W. Southern (Oxford, 1948), pp. 223–39; W. Stubbs, *Select Charters*, 9th edn., ed. H. W. C. Davis (Oxford, 1913), pp. 395–7.
22 Stubbs, *Select Charters*, pp. 407–8.

distinction between the *negotia regis et regni* and the *negotia regis*[23] is not at all the same as Bracton's. Bracton's is a lawyer's distinction between what the king may lawfully do and what it is unlawful for him to do: Professor Wilkinson's is an administrative and political distinction between what the king and his officers are accustomed to do without consultation and what they should do only after obtaining the advice of the great council.

The position described by Bracton was one of unstable equilibrium, depending for its balance on the personal character of the king and the nature of his rule, and the constitutional problem of the thirteenth century was to discover a more stable and permanent balancing factor than the personality of an individual owing his power to the accidents of hereditary succession. The Bractonian conception of monarchy placed a heavy burden of responsibility on the ruler, and only a great and strong king could bear it, for thirteenth-century England was not an easy society to rule. From the great days of Innocent III, papal influence over the clergy was at its height, and the church, claiming the ultimate power of directing all human life, making and deposing emperors, humbling kings and reducing their kingdoms to papal fiefs, must in duty challenge a ruler who abused his power, in England most of all. In this great age of universities, which could bring a Langton to the primacy of all England and later a Grosseteste to the moral leadership of the prelates, there were seldom wanting men of the highest intellectual quality in high places whence they could speak with authority on the shortcomings of mere temporal rule. The feudal barons, with their essentially contractual and mutual ideas of the bond between king and magnates, and their habits of counsel and consent, would not for ever stop short at mere criticism of any king who fell badly below their conception of good government. The county knights, already accustomed by the reforms of Henry II and Hubert Walter to play an ever-increasing part in local government, whether as officials or as jurymen and suitors in the shire and hundred courts, would not meekly endure royal despotism which infringed their rights or outraged their sense of justice. The men of the boroughs could be roused if their liberties were infringed or their trade damaged by the arbitrary action of royal officials, or if royal exactions taxed their wealth too severely. Even the peasantry,

23 B. Wilkinson, *The Constitutional History of England, 1216–1399*, (London, 1949), I, pp. 13, 71–4, *et passim*.

inarticulate and unorganized as they were, had learnt to look to the king's courts for justice, and if ever the time came, might show in action their resentment of official oppression or injustice. In such an England the king, already limited by the law in his *jurisdictio*, must show both strength and discretion in the exercise of his *gubernaculum*, even though no formal restraint was here imposed upon him. If he transgressed or failed badly, a mere legal theory would not be likely to stand for very long between him and the clamour of his subjects. And in saying this we must bear in mind the importance which Professor Wilkinson very rightly attaches to the ever-increasing part played by royal officials in the lives of ordinary men, making them more than ever aware of the royal power and very often arousing resentment by actions of their own for which the king was not immediately to blame: the very spread of royal power made it more than ever necessary that the king's officers should be firmly controlled lest they bring their master's rule into disrepute.[24]

The peaceful continuance of the legal position stated by Bracton thus depended in the first instance, and very largely, on the king himself and on the behaviour of his officials: if his will had the force of law, he must make the laws his will, or he risked rebellion. He must be firm and strong, wise, reasonable, and just: he must frame sound policy and execute it with discretion. He must consult his magnates frequently, winning at least their trust and respect, if not their affection: if he went to war, he must succeed, or at least he must not disgrace or humiliate them. He must appoint good judges and officials, who, though firm, would be just: he and they must keep the law, doing justice and right to all men as the law declares. Finally, his demands for extraordinary taxation must be moderate and clearly justifiable to those who would have to pay. These were the essential conditions of royal absolutism in thirteenth-century England; they were implicit, not explicit, in the Bractonian position, but they were none the less real for that. Even in his *gubernaculum*, the king's power was in fact not arbitrary but limited, though the limitations were implied, not openly declared.

This does not mean that, to avoid rebellion and deposition, the king must be a paragon of excellences, for he might fall short of the ideal and still provoke no serious challenge. But it does mean that he must be of the stature of an Edward I if he was to rule for long without arousing revolt – and even Edward endangered himself and the

24 *Ibid.*, pp. 8–13.

peace of his realm before his reign was over. Under so strong and acceptable a king the difficulties of the Bractonian position could be held at arm's length and passed on to future years, though that merely postponed and did not resolve the problem. Under such a king the feudal, and even the Christian, ideal of co-operation could be approximately realized, not indeed without all discord but at least in general harmony. I cannot too heavily underline Professor Wilkinson's timely comment on this fact, which is of fundamental importance, that "the basis of the medieval state was not a long-drawn-out struggle between the king and the magnates, based on opposed and irreconcilable interests and aims: it was exactly the opposite – a rough identity of interests between the ruler and the politically articulate and active section of the nation, which was based on a support of, and belief in, the political order which sustained both alike, and was fostered by the bonds of social intercourse, a common education, and a common membership in the knightly class." With respect to the late thirteenth century he wrote, "even Edward I, as he implied by his famous letter of 12 August 1297, was, in the final analysis, dependent on the active support of the nation for all his imposing royal power."[25] It is Sir Maurice Powicke's teaching of "the joint enterprise"[26] in medieval English society envisaged as a whole. All too often have we concentrated our attention on the dramatic episodes when king and magnates were in conflict. This was natural, for instance, in the days when Stubbs was working out the theme of his *Constitutional History*, for he had then to rely mainly on the chronicles, and in particular upon the great series of St. Albans' histories. Now, as Professor Galbraith has very pertinently remarked,[27] the aristocratic and constitutional tradition of the thirteenth-century St. Albans writings made them almost the official *apologia* of the opposition, and has coloured much of our teaching on constitutional history from the seventeenth century onwards. But now that the records of government have been printed so abundantly, the balance is redressed, and the king and his officers can be heard speaking for themselves, unaware that we are listening: there is no need any longer for us to dwell only on the sharp peaks of conflict for the quiet plains of concord are available for our scrutiny, and those plains, as we now well know, were very fertile in the growth of Eng-

25 *Ibid.*, p. 9. The date of the letter is there misprinted as August 10: but see *ibid.*, p. 219.
26 F. M. Powicke, *Medieval England, 1066–1485* (London, 1931), esp. pp. 216 ff.
27 V. H. Galbraith, *Roger Wendover and Matthew Paris* (Glasgow, 1944), esp. pp. 19–20.

lish government. It is not too much to assert that it is to the even stretches of co-operation that we owe most of the institutions which, in the long run, provided the solution of the problem we are discussing: while what we owe to the periods of conflict is rather the rules of their operation which ensured that no one part should become excessively dominant and that all should work together to a common end.

But although a successful king might postpone the problem, his success did not conjure the problem away. What was to happen when the successful king grew overweeningly strong and threatened the liberty of his subjects, or when he died and gave place to an incompetent or a tyrannical successor? The great defect of the Bractonian position was that it provided no lawful means of imposing restraints, of enforcing the implicit limitations, upon a recalcitrant king in the exercise of his *gubernaculum*: the only way left was the threat of force, with the immediate sanction of rebellion and civil war as the next step. This remedy, from whatever standpoint we view it, is a confession of political bankruptcy resembling, on a larger scale, the unhappy conclusion reached in the laws of Ethelred when the ealdorman either could not or would not do justice and a man must take the law into his own hands: "then let the ealdordom lie in unfrith."[28] The constitution would have broken down, and anarchy would prevail until force decided the issue. The thirteenth-century constitutional problem was thus how to make explicit the implied limitations on royal absolutism; to extend to the king's *gubernaculum* the restraints already explicitly acknowledged to lie upon his *jurisdictio*; to find, in a new constitution which the king would undertake to observe, the necessary legal sanction for control of his political, executive, and administrative power, hitherto unrestrained by any human agency other than his own discretion.

The achievement of this solution was bound to be a radical, or even a revolutionary process, for it was inconceivable that any king other than a minor or an imbecile would willingly agree, without a struggle, to surrender any significant part of his traditional powers. The opposition of the magnates was not the outcome of any abstract political theorizing on their part, and they would make no unprovoked demand or threat; but their opposition to the king was implicit in the constitutional position, and it would become explicit when, in their view, royal misgovernment eventually became intolerable. Failing the miracle of a succession of just, strong kings

28 Stubbs, *Select Charters*, p. 85.

voluntarily observing the implicit conditions of successful royal government, sooner or later the barons would be driven to make these limits explicit in the form of legal sanctions restraining the royal *gubernaculum* – that is to say, they would be forced to devise a new constitution. To achieve this end they would certainly have to threaten force, and unless they were, and remained, so completely united that the king would deem resistance useless, the barons would certainly have to use the force which they had threatened. The question was simply when and how this revolution would happen – for happen it must, sooner or later, and sooner or later the magnates would succeed, for the Bractonian position of unstable equilibrium could not endure for ever. Force and rebellion were obviously illegal, but to condemn them for that is irrelevant, for there was no other way of controlling the power of a king who misused it and who would not accept restraint voluntarily.

It was not in the nature of any Angevin king to abandon power of his own free will: he was the heir of a great tradition, for, from his West Saxon and Norman predecessors, it had been the kings of England who had built the state and shaped the nation. Monarchy was the political form which the young English nation-state had assumed, the *primum mobile* of its growth: why should the king voluntarily abdicate the functions by whose exercise his ancestors had built the state? Was not his authority of divine origin, and he the Lord's annointed? Who but he could or should wield the powers which were his sacred trust, or exercise the mysteries of kingship? Kings were not mere hereditary officials: something of the primitive superstitions of magic and priestcraft still invested their persons and their office with reverence and awe in the eyes of their subjects. In defending his prerogatives, the king was, on legal grounds, unassailable, and could reasonably hope to count upon the mistakes of his opponents, or even a mere revulsion of feeling, providing him with loyal supporters if only he would bow for a while before the blast of compulsion, and let instinctive conservatism and ingrained feelings of duty do their work. Indeed, it was in such deep irrational feelings, in human distrust of the rational and dislike of the radical, in men's love of what is proved and venerable, that the strength of the royal position lay. In this matter the law was most certainly on the king's side.[29] Yet in politics law is neither the first nor the last word: the constitution, which is the law of politics, must change with

29 Cf. Wilkinson, *Constitutional History*, I, pp. 134–5.

a changing society. If this process, as was virtually inevitable, involved rebellion and civil war, the blame rests on a king who provoked rebellion by his own misrule, and then resisted the restraints which he had impelled his subjects to place upon him. As for the rebels, we must judge them not simply by the inescapable illegality of their revolt, but by their programme, their actions, and the manner in which they rose to the occasion.

For to say that a grave breach of the implied limitations of royal authority would provoke the magnates to rebellion, and that a reasonably united baronage would almost certainly succeed in imposing its will on the king, is not to say that the problem would in this manner find an automatic solution. The barons had much to learn before their political education could be deemed adequate to the solution. Of course, they had wide and deep experience in administration, alike in the management of their own fiefs and honours and in playing their parts in local government under the king's commission: while in national politics they had, in the *magnum concilium*, in various high offices, and in many special missions, both the opportunity of acquiring experience and the chance of expressing their opinions on the conduct of national affairs. But, important and necessary though this was, it was still only a foundation for what was required. Some of the lessons, at least, could best be learnt in the periods of quiet co-operation, especially the change in the baronial views on national finance and the necessity of taxes: the thirteenth-century baronage was very far in temper from the mixture of pride and awe with which the modern Englishman contemplates the weight of taxation he can carry. The habit of co-operation with the ministers of the crown, and the development of a national, as distinct from a purely local or a class, outlook, could also be cultivated without a revolution in politics. But the practical measures for effective limitation of the king's *gubernaculum*, in the nature of the case, could be devised only in periods of opposition and conflict, while to test their validity in operation would require a political revolution. This, to begin with, would mean controlling the advice on which the king took his decisions – in other words, controlling the membership of his private counsel, converting it into a privy council, and binding the king to act upon the advice of this body and on no other counsel in matters of state. It would also mean controlling the king's great officers – choosing them or at least ratifying their choice, and developing a doctrine of ministerial responsibility.

In this process it would not be easy, once a start was made, to stop short of the complete conception of constitutional monarchy, with control of the entire machinery of government, both central and local, in the hands of whatever body might have been set up to exercise that control.

It is clear that, for limiting the king in his executive capacity, resolutions and standing orders would not suffice: the king must be controlled by persons, not by platitudes. The magnates, once the necessary conditions had been fulfilled, would have to take charge of the government and in some form or other run it themselves in the king's name. Were the magnates willing to do this? Would the extremity of the circumstances make them ready for the sacrifice of time and the diversion of their attention from their own affairs? Would they develop the necessary assiduity in attending regular and frequent councils and committees? Or would their efforts dwindle until the management of public affairs fell into the hands of a mere faction or a clique? Had they the ability requisite for the task? Would they be able to devise the technical means, the various committees and councils necessary when control by one man is replaced by control by many? Had they the public spirit required for the task, or would they seize power only to exploit it for their own ends? Could they command the obedience of the hundreds of officials who had worked for the king but who might feel very differently towards a mere council? Could they hold the loyalty of the king's subjects as kings had been wont to hold it, but without the magic of the royal name? These questions indicate the formidable nature of the problem which the men of the thirteenth century, sooner or later, were bound to face: to take over the king's power and put it into commission would be the beginning, not the end of their task. Two things are clear: if the attempt was to succeed at all, it must make use of the vast prestige of the royal authority: in form and appearance, at least, government must continue to be in the king's name and with the king's consent. And the magnates must be united: they would fail as soon as they broke up into cliques.

The men who framed the Great Charter of 1215[30] have often been described as "feudal reactionaries" devoid of any constitutional

30 The most useful narrative works for this section are: *The Oxford History of England* (Clarendon Press, Oxford): III, *Domesday Book to Magna Carta, 1087–1216*, by A. L. Poole (1951), and IV, *The Thirteenth Century, 1216–1307*,

ideas and concerned only to safeguard their own class privileges, to win more wealth, lands and power for themselves, and to humiliate and shackle King John.[31] This verdict cannot be maintained against any careful assessment of the meaning of the Charter's many clauses or of the circumstances in which it was drafted and sealed. Three clauses of the 1215 Charter, clauses 12, 14, and 61, are explicitly constitutional in substance and purpose. Clauses 12 and 14 defined the constituency which the king must consult whenever he required "extraordinary" taxation, and prescribed the manner of summoning this tax-granting body. Although this definition and prescription were conservative rather than novel, this was the first attempt to state formally and explicitly the constitution of the body which was held to be sufficiently representative of "the common counsel of the realm" to be able to grant or refuse the king a voluntary aid, and to have power, by a majority decision, to bind a dissident minority, and even those who were absent, to pay their proper contribution to any such tax granted. Here is an important constitutional advance along two lines – the baronial acceptance in principle of the necessity to vote "extraordinary taxes" and of the binding force of a majority decision, and the explicit requirement that the king should summon

by F. M. Powicke (1953); S. Painter, *The Reign of King John* (Baltimore, 1949); F. M. Powicke, *Stephen Langton* (Oxford, 1928), ch. iv and v.; J. C. Holt, *The Northerners; a Study in the Reign of King John* (Oxford, 1961), though several of the older books still retain much of their value. The most important commentaries on the Charter are: *Magna Carta Commemoration Essays*, ed. H. E. Malden (Royal Historical Society, London, 1917); W. S. McKechnie, *Magna Carta* (2nd ed., Glasgow, 1914) – a very full and learned legal commentary, but weak on the historical side; and J. C. Holt, *Magna Carta* (Cambridge, 1965), the best guide for the historian, with authoritative narrative chapters in addition to interpretative commentary, and an excellent bibliography. H. G. Richardson and G. O. Sayles, *The Governance of Mediaeval England* (Edinburgh, 1963), though of great value for the study of the machinery of English government before 1216, takes an eccentric and outdated line on the Charter, and has been disregarded in this essay. V. H. Galbraith, *Studies in the Public Records* (London, 1948) has a most valuable chapter (ch. v.) on the Charter.

31 McKechnie, *Magna Carta*, G. B. Adams, *The Origin of the English Constitution* (New Haven, 1920), ch. v., and Ch. Petit-Dutaillis, *Studies Supplementary to Stubbs' Constitutional History* (Manchester, 1929), III, especially pp. 315–8, are typical examples in varying degrees, though by no means all of the historians of this period followed the line of cynical interpretation – cf. A. B. White, *The Making of the English Constitution*, (2nd ed., New York, 1925), pp. 267–74. Among recent works, Poole, *Domesday Book* and Richardson and Sayles, *The Governance*, still reflect much of the cynical view of the Charter and its authors.

in set form a clearly defined body of his subjects to grant or refuse such a tax and to determine its form and amount if any such tax were granted. Here we have clearly an explicit limitation of the royal *gubernaculum*, debarring John from using the piecemeal methods of persuading special classes and local groups to make grants habitual under Henry II, and it takes the form of institutionalizing "the common counsel of the realm" into a defined and formally constituted "Great Council."

The "sanctions" clause (number 61) was even more obviously constitutional. It authorized the magnates to appoint a committee of twenty-five to ensure that John and his officials kept the terms of the Charter: it prescribed formal procedure for notifying John of any incident which the twenty-five considered to be a breach of the Charter: and it empowered the committee, if John, having thus been notified, failed to amend the breach, to "distrain" him by seizing his castles, lands, and goods, stopping short only of personal violence against John, his queen, and his children, to force him to comply with his sworn promises. It is this clause which has led modern commentators to condemn the framers of the Charter as feudal anarchists bankrupt of political ideas, or, worse still, as merely ensuring that they should have a legal justification for renewing their rebellion – "legalizing anarchy" is the phrase often used. Now, we cannot deny that clause 61 is an extremely crude attempt to solve the constitutional problem of the king's unlimited *gubernaculum*: the clause called the coercive action of the committee "distraint," and Professor Plucknett has insisted that this was all that clause 61 envisaged, since it forbade violence against the king's person.[32] But such "distraint" is scarcely distinguishable from civil war, and if John refused to amend breaches of the Charter after due warning, rebellion and civil war must inevitably result, for John was not the sort of man who would allow his barons to seize his castles and lands without resistance. Nevertheless, clause 61 was not intended to "legalize anarchy" – quite the contrary, for it is an attempt to prevent anarchy by organizing controlled and unified rebellion against a king who refused to be bound by law or by sworn promise. Few of the rebels of 1215 believed that John would keep his promises for a day longer than he was compelled to by superior force, while on the other hand

32 Taswell-Langmead's *Constitutional History of England* (10th ed., ed. T. F. T. Plucknett, London, 1946), pp. 97–8.

everyone knew that some of the baronial leaders were determined on personal vengeance against John or on exploiting John's weakness for their own material gain. The sanctions clause was therefore framed to prevent the anarchy which would result from individual action or rebellion by self-constituted groups, and to substitute for such isolated risings a national and organized rebellion of the whole baronage, lawfully proclaimed by the elected and representative committee of twenty-five after that committee had decided that a breach of the Charter had occurred and that John, after due warning, had refused to make redress. Only then could lawful rebellion be proclaimed, and only by the twenty-five, who were, moreover, empowered to call upon any of the king's subjects for an oath of support to the committee and, if need be, for armed action against the king. It need not surprise us that, when the inevitable civil war broke out, the committee of twenty-five attempted, with some regional success, to act as the lawful government of England, levying forces, raising taxes, and even issuing writs for a time in those areas where it had effective control.[33] The civil war of 1215-17 was indeed an ugly affair, but at least England was spared the anarchy of the "nineteen long winters" of Stephen's reign, and some of the credit for this must go to the much-abused sanctions clause. That clause did not, in fact, make rebellion and civil war more likely than they would have been had no such clause been included, but it did, to some extent, control and direct the rising and so prevent mere anarchy. Looked at in another way, the clause provided for a unified *diffidatio* made by a properly constituted body of tenants-in-chief on behalf of the entire baronage, and at the same time afforded a legal defence in the royal courts should John attempt, either during the rebellion or subsequently, to bring a court action against any individual rebel. We can admit that the sanctions clause, legalizing rebellion in certain circumstances and attempting to unify and control such a rebellion, could never be an effective and acceptable solution to the problem of limiting the arbitrary exercise of the royal *gubernaculum*, but at least the clause does not deserve the extreme censures which have been poured upon it. Constitutional documents must be interpreted, not *in vacuo*, but in the context of the political and personal circumstances which they are devised to meet: the failure to consider the

33 See the admirable article by H. G. Richardson, "The Morrow of the Great Charter," *Bull. John Rylands Lib.*, xxviii, 422–43.

great constitutional documents of our history in their proper political context has far too often been the source of grievous errors of interpretation, whether by the so-called "Whig" historians or by their cynical successors.

Fortunately for England, the unexpectedly early death of John in October 1216 altered the whole political situation so drastically that the sanctions clause of the Charter became completely irrelevant and the unpromising false start made in June 1215 could be abandoned, leaving the way open for a different and far better solution. John's successor was his nine-year-old son Henry III, who had offended no one and who for many years must, as a minor, reign without ruling; nor was there available any royal uncle or other close kinsman who might, as regent, have attempted to continue to govern England after John's fashion. In the circumstances, the royal power could be exercised only by a consortium of all the various interests supporting the young king: the pope as feudal overlord of the kingdom, working through his legate Gualo; the prelates, led by the greatest of all English archbishops, Stephen Langton, acting as the spiritual counsellors of the crown; the civil servants, under the justiciar, Hubert de Burgh, who would actually carry on the daily task of government; the foreign mercenaries, who had provided much of John's military power and who now tended to look to Peter des Roches, the Poitevin bishop of Winchester, for a lead; and finally, most important of all from our standpoint, those English barons who, led by the great William Marshal, earl of Pembroke, appointed regent of England by their own common choice, preferred to support the young and inoffensive Henry III rather than the alien Louis of France whom the rebels had called in to lead them against John. Even while John lived strong personal and feudal loyalties, outbalancing a recognition of the defects of John's rule, had kept many barons loyal to the king, and the replacement of John by Henry III brought many moderate men over to the king's side at once. But until the earl marshal died in 1219 it was his sagacity, moderation, and prestige, together with his professional military skill, that did most to win John's opponents over to Henry III's side, virtually to end the civil war in 1217, and speedily thereafter to restore peace and legality to England. Obviously, the earl marshal could not have done this single-handed: Hubert de Burgh's outstanding ability both as a warrior and as an administrator, the loyalty of John's mercenary captains and their men, the work of the civil servants, all played important parts. The prelates, too, intervened opportunely and influentially on critical occasions, though their help became more obviously important after rather than before the end of the civil war: and the legate Gualo, once Innocent III's death had removed papal rancour and prejudice as a factor in English politics, gave tactful and discreet support to the regent's policy of reconciliation backed by firmness.[34] The result was that within twelve months of John's death the entire English baronage, save for a mere handful who were irreconcilable, had been won back to loyal support of the regent's government in the name of John's son.

The history of the Charter during this decisive year after John's death shows both how the regent and his allies used it as an instrument of reconciliation and how the royal power was freed from some of the restraints placed upon it in 1215. The original Charter had not been the work of the embittered rebels, but of the more responsible, moderate, and public-spirited of the magnates, wisely supported and counselled by Stephen Langton, with the undoubted co-operation of the better baronial and bureaucratic leaders who had remained loyal to John. With the proviso that it had to include clauses which would satisfy the widespread fear and distrust felt against John personally, the 1215 version can reasonably be held to represent the convictions of the "maior et sanior pars" (to use a characteristic contemporary expression) of the magnates of England, lay and ecclesiastical, in the early summer of 1215. Obviously it was, after John's death, too valuable an instrument of reassurance and reconciliation to be ignored, and no less obviously John's death made some of its provisions unnecessary, now that the government of England must necessarily be conducted by the leading magnates themselves, with the support of as much of the rest of the baronage as they could win to their side. Predictably therefore, the first important act of the regent and his colleagues, explicitly supported by the papal legate in spite of Innocent III's annulment of the Charter in August 1215, was the reissue of the Charter on 11 November 1216. However, in this first reissue the Charter differed substantially from the version of 1215. Some twenty of the clauses of the original Charter were omitted as raising "grave and dubious" issues which must therefore be held over until further consideration could be given to them, with the promise that on all such deferred matters whatever might be best

---

34 The best guide to these years is F. M. Powicke, *Henry III and the Lord Edward*, I (Oxford, 1947).

for the common good would eventually be done. From the standpoint of this essay, the important omissions are the three constitutional clauses: the sanctions clause (61) and the clauses (12 and 14) defining the constitution and the mode of summons of a great council called to consider a voluntary grant to the crown.

The omission of clauses 12 and 14 from the revised Charter seemed a grave matter to historians who, like Stubbs,[35] regarded these clauses as being vitally important in the history of the origins and early development of parliament, and it is quite true that the 1216 version lists these two clauses among the matters to be deferred for fuller consideration, as being "grave and dubious." Most commentators today would regard this omission as far less important than it seemed to Stubbs. Undoubtedly it abandoned the attempt to define the constitution and mode of summons of the great council called to consider the granting of an extraordinary aid, and therefore it left the crown free to obtain such grants from whatever assemblies it might see fit to summon, and even to go back to the piecemeal methods of consultation employed by Henry II for this purpose. To that extent the omission of clauses 12 and 14 may be regarded as a retrogression: but was it really of great importance? As long as the crown contemplated extraordinary taxation on an exclusively feudal basis, these two clauses were both apt and necessary, and represented a genuine, if limited, constitutional advance. But by 1215 the fiscal needs of the crown and the state of the kingdom's economic development had both far surpassed the possibilities of additional taxation on a merely feudal basis, as the fiscal experiments of the later years of Henry II and of the reigns of Richard I and John had already shown, and this immensely important fact must have been obvious, not only to exchequer officials, but also to any prelate or baron intelligent enough to draw general conclusions from plain facts. The crown must henceforth inevitably and increasingly seek extraordinary taxes based far more widely than on mere feudal tenure, and every decade would make clauses 12 and 14 of the original Charter progressively less satisfactory as a definition of the body which must be consulted before any "special aid" could be levied. It is not likely that the retention of these two clauses in the later reissues of the Charter in Henry III's reign would in fact have limited the crown to this purely feudal great council when extra-

35 Cf. Stubbs, *Select Charters*, pp. 335–6.

ordinary taxation was needed: the tenants-in-chief would not have been able or willing to bear the whole burden themselves, and the crown, finding it increasingly necessary to tax non-feudal resources, would in any case have been driven by sheer necessity to exercise its right to afforce the feudal great council with non-feudal elements which must be consulted and persuaded if special aids were to be levied successfully on non-feudal wealth. The dropping of these two clauses certainly left the crown completely free to afforce the great council in whatever way might seem useful – if anyone nowadays really believes that clauses 12 and 14 of the original Charter would in fact have prevented or even delayed the summoning of non-feudal and representative elements to meetings of the great council at which their attendance was desired by the crown: after all, even in thirteenth-century England, no one was clamouring to be taxed! Probably by far the most important practical effect of the abandonment of clauses 12 and 14 in all of the reissues of the Charter was the prolongation of the right of individual tenants-in-chief, or of local groups, to refuse to share in paying a voluntary aid, on the grounds that they had never given individual assent to it – a practice which still caused occasional embarrassment to the government during the minority of Henry III, though it soon died out and was replaced by the more sensible idea that a majority decision bound all of the individuals concerned.[36]

The dropping of the "sanctions" clause was inevitable in the new circumstances. In the first place, the reissue of 1216 was genuinely a "free and spontaneous" grant of the new government, acting in the name of the young king, and not a treaty of peace extracted from an unwilling ruler by the threatened rebellion of his feudal baronage, and therefore no sanctions were needed to coerce the government which so freely reissued the Charter. Secondly, the "sanctions" clause of 1215 had been devised specifically to deal with John's faithlessness and tyranny; it was not in any sense a general attack on royal absolutism, or the outcome of political theory in the minds of those who had framed it, and now that John's government was replaced by that of the earl marshal and his baronial and episcopal allies, the sanctions of 1215 were no longer required. With the dropping of the "sanctions" clause, the reissue of Magna Carta in 1216

36 For fiscal developments in the thirteenth century, see especially S. K. Mitchell, *Studies in Taxation under John and Henry III* (New Haven, 1914).

marks the abandonment for the time being, and for many years to come, of any attempt to limit the royal *gubernaculum* by the institution of a supervisory body of magnates with power to proclaim lawful rebellion. In this respect, therefore, the royal executive authority was fully restored to its untrammelled condition of the time before the Charter – untrammelled, that is to say, by any human power or institution existing in the hands of the king's subjects. The second and the third reissues of the Charter, in 1217 and in 1225, confirmed this position by omitting all reference to any kind of sanctions, just as did the first reissue of 1216: the king is once more responsible to no man, or body of men, within his kingdom.

On one matter, which at first sight appears to be of merely judicial and administrative significance, important constitutional consequences followed from a reform which created no new office or institution. Clause 24 of the 1215 Charter forbade the sheriff henceforth to play any part, as sheriff, in judging pleas of the crown, and reserved the hearing of all such pleas to the king's justices and to other special commissioners appointed specifically to deal with crown pleas, as in the general eyre and in certain special commissions of enquiry. This clause, which was repeated and even strengthened in the subsequent reissues of the Charter, and was henceforth most strictly enforced, is usually regarded as a matter of legal and administrative history – as the last stage in the rapid decline of the sheriff from his mighty position in Norman times as chief judge and unchallenged ruler of the shire into the much humbler and more professional character of an essentially administrative, fiscal, and police officer, acting mainly under direction from the central authority, as he became in the thirteenth century.[37] This view of the change is quite correct, except that clause 24 was not the last step in the process, and no one, whether from the side of the crown or from among the baronial reformers in later years, ever proposed to reverse the change at any later time. The clause, which was already partly foreshadowed in the Articles of the Barons (clause 14), looks, as it appears in the Charter of 1215, very much like a suggestion which may initially have come from the baronial side, but which was taken up readily by the king's officials during the negotiations, and by them given both much clearer definition and far greater effect as a total prohibition. For the king's ordinary subjects, and particularly for

37 See especially W. A. Morris, *The Medieval English Sheriff to 1300* (Manchester, 1927).

those who were not strong enough to stand up to a powerful and unscrupulous sheriff, the prohibition was unquestionably a great boon, for now, in major matters of criminal law and of public obligation, they would be judged, not by a sheriff who was one of the greatest landowners in the shire, or one of the king's mercenary captains, but by the justices of the general eyre or by special commissioners holding the king's commission for this express purpose, and visiting the shire as representatives of the impartial and ultimate authority of the king himself, concerned primarily to do justice according to the law of the land. How much difference this made to local government, and especially to local justice, we can see by comparing the thirteenth-century sheriff in England with his much more powerful counterparts in France, the *bailli* and the *sénéschal*, who retained the high judicial powers which Magna Carta took away from the English sheriff. Constitutionally, the clause obviously meant a significant strengthening of the direct power of the crown and of its officials of the central government, in as much as the king now took back into his own hands a highly important sector of public jurisdiction which he had hitherto delegated to the sheriffs. In fact, however, this responsibility proved too heavy for the king's justices to discharge unaided, and throughout the thirteenth and early fourteenth centuries the crown had to turn increasingly to special *ad hoc* commissions to cope with those parts of the work which related to the preservation of public order and the king's peace. At length, in the middle of the fourteenth century, a new institution was evolved: the justice of the peace, a member of a commission of locally resident gentry, appointed directly by the crown and removable at the king's pleasure, but never paid for their heavy and responsible task of keeping the king's peace in the shire and hearing all pleas where a breach of that peace was alleged.[38] How important was this development, constitutionally no less than administratively, the later medieval and early modern history of England was to show: yet without clause 24 of Magna Carta the process would not have been started.

But over the centuries, and even from the beginning, the true constitutional significance of the Great Charter has lain, not in clauses

38 My pupil, Mr. Howard Ainsley, has worked out the details and the successive stages of this development in his Ph.D. thesis (Univ. of Wales), "The Problems relating to the maintenance of law and order in thirteenth-century England, with particular reference to the Custos Pacis," and I hope that before long he will publish this study.

12, 14, and 61, or even in any other specific clause or clauses, but in the Charter as a whole, and in the circumstances in which it was first granted and subsequently reissued and confirmed. The 1225 version of the Charter, confirmed and re-confirmed time and time again by Henry III and his successors, was not technically a statute, and yet it came in due course, and with significant speed, to be regarded as the first and most fundamental of the "Statutes of the Realm," and as the guarantee of the liberties and rights of the king's subjects, and of the strict observance of the law of the land. It is easy to pour ridicule on this traditional interpretation of the Charter, by pointing out on the one hand the triviality of a few of the clauses (especially clause 33, ordering the removal of fish-traps from inland waters), or by dwelling myopically on the strictly "feudal" clauses 2–8 and a few other clauses aimed at defining clearly the obligations and the rights of feudal tenants-in-chief: but this kind of comment, fashionable enough even among reputable historians in the first three decades of the present century, is now very much out-of-date and is to be found, with a very few egregious exceptions, only in the works of textbook writers and of others like them who have apparently never read the Charter – in any of its versions. The historical instinct of successive generations of Englishmen has not been mistaken on the significance of the Charter, even when we have allowed for the erroneous interpretations of the seventeenth-century lawyers and the nineteenth-century historians. Had the Charter been a trivial document, or a document of merely contemporary value, or "a document of feudal reaction," as it came to be styled by historians reacting from the nineteenth-century "Whig" interpretation, it could never have carried the enormously weighty superstructure which the succeeding centuries have laid upon it; not merely in English history, but also in the history of Canada, Australia, and New Zealand, and, not least of all, in the history of the United States of America.

    When all of its limitations have been freely admitted – and they are many – the Great Charter still deserves its place as the most important document in our constitutional history, partly on account of a handful of clauses providing fundamental rights and liberties, and still more when taken as a whole and in its contemporary context. We must not deduce the nature and quality of the Charter from the evil and unworthy motives of the most extreme of the leaders of the rebellion. The Charter was worked out by the moderate men among the baronial leaders, with the help and exhortation of Stephen Langton, and it represented the ideas of the most responsible and public-spirited of the magnates. The content of the Charter thus devised was reinforced by the circumtsances of its original issue, when a great majority of the English barons, firmly supported by most of the prelates, forced an unwilling and resentful king to acknowledge that the clauses of the Charter were the law of the land, which he must enforce and obey; while the later reissues, made by the governing party in the name of the young king as a free and unforced promise to his people, added further sanction to the authority of the Charter, which could no longer be denounced or repudiated as a promise extracted under duress. The final result of these successive proclamations of the Charter was to establish firmly in English minds that it was a guarantee of their laws and their liberties; the "myth of Magna Carta" had in effect been created as early as 1225.[39] That "myth," whatever misconceptions may later have gathered themselves to it, established the vitally important principle that the king is under the law as a practical basis for English politics, not merely as a pious platitude in theological treatises or as an abstract theory in writings on law, but as a hard historical fact which had cost one king his life after coming near to driving him from his throne, and was to remain as an effective warning and threat to any subsequent king who might prove either a tyrant or an incompetent. The first baronial attempt to limit the royal *gubernaculum* by human institutions had failed, but the limitations of his *jurisdictio* had been strikingly enforced in a most enduring fashion.

The substance of the Charter was not unworthy of the principle or even of the subsequent "myth": as the latest commentator on the Charter has said, "it set no mean standard."[40] Far from being a merely feudal document, the Charter, like several of the great statutes of the reigns of Henry III and Edward I, is a comprehensive and miscellaneous statement of the law on many different matters: feudal rights and obligations, legal principles quite unrelated to feudalism, reforms in judicial and administrative procedure, constitutional matters (in the 1215 version), clauses relating to trade,

39 The later history of Magna Carta has been studied in detail by Faith Thompson in *The First Century of Magna Carta* (Minneapolis, 1925) and in *Magna Carta: its Role in the Making of the English Constitution, 1300–1629* (Minneapolis, 1948). Holt, *Magna Carta*, ch. 1, has a brief but highly valuable discussion of this theme, centred especially on Coke and his later seventeenth-century critics.
40 Holt., *Magna Carta*, p. 292.

merchants, and boroughs, and even political and military clauses of immediate significance only. It was natural that many of the clauses should provide remedies for the feudal grievances of the magnates against John's tyranny and the high-handedness of his two Angevin predecessors: the barons provided the coercion which first extorted the Charter from John, and their grievances naturally stand near the head of the Charter. But even, for a moment, confining ourselves to a consideration of these feudal clauses, we must note that at no point did the barons demand unfair or unreasonable concessions for them-selves, and that they aimed at restating established custom or at defining rights and obligations hitherto left uncertain, without any-where affording justification for a charge of feudal reaction. Even the famous clause 34, restricting the use of the writ *Praecipe*, which was, fifty years ago, held to be evidence of the blackest feudal reaction, is now seen to have been of no great importance and of no reac-tionary significance, for it did not prevent the crown from using this writ, but merely ensured to the lord of any feudal court his right to try cases falling within his jurisdiction, provided he was both able and willing to do justice in such pleas, and even so the right of appeal to the king's courts remained unimpaired.[41] And finally, we must always bear it in mind that, in clause 60 of the original Charter, the magnates undertook to be bound, in their dealings with their vassals, by the same rules of law as those which they had won from the king, so that in so far as the Charter was a feudal document, it applied equally to all grades of feudal tenure, and was not devised merely for the benefit of the tenants-in-chief alone.

In fact, the feudal clauses, important though they were, form only a small part of the Charter. Its lasting merit, if we are considering individual clauses, lies elsewhere – in its non-feudal provisions. Of these, by far the most important is clause 39 (of the 1215 version): "no free man shall be arrested, imprisoned, dispossessed, outlawed or exiled, nor in any other way ruined, nor will we take or order action against him, save by the lawful judgment of his equals and according to the law of the land." Humanly speaking, this is the most precious single clause of the whole Charter,[42] not because it ensured that henceforth all men who fell foul of king or government would infallibly be given fair trial according to the law, for of course this

41 Holt, *Magna Carta*, p. 225; Naomi D. Hurnard, "Magna Carta, clause 34," *Studies in Medieval History*, pp. 157–79; M. T. Clanchy, "Magna Carta, clause 34", EHR, LXXIX, 542–8.
42 See especially Galbraith, *Studies on the Public Records*, pp. 130–3.

clause has been violated by later kings and governments on countless occasions; but it set the standard of justice and in due course rightly came to be regarded as the foundation of individual liberty. It is true that it did nothing to protect the property-rights of the villein or the serf, and that this was a serious defect in an age when so large a proportion of the king's subjects was still of servile status. But we must always remember that, in the most important matters of criminal law and of public obligations, as, for example, in pleas of the crown, the king's courts and the common law made no distinction between freeman and villein: as Sir Maurice Powicke has said, "in these matters even the villein had his free side" in the thirteenth century. And in time serfdom died out and all men were free, and therefore under the protection of this clause. If kings and governments often violated it, it still remained the standard to which appeal could be made, and the king's courts themselves have applied it and have so extended its meaning as to ensure that even rebels taken in arms against the king should be given fair trial.[43]

We may fairly add to this fundamental pledge clause 40, "To no one will we sell, deny or delay justice and right," clause 36, "Henceforth nothing shall be given or taken for a writ of inquisition where life or limbs are at stake, but such writs shall be granted freely and not denied," and clauses 20, 21, and 22, laying down the principle that amercements shall be inflicted only in proportion to the offences committed and after the verdict of a man's neighbours and equals, for these clauses go to the root of the matter of individual liberty, justice and the rule of law. All of them were preserved in substance in the reissues of 1216, 1217, and 1225, and so they passed into the body of English legal principle. Once again, the importance of these clauses is not that they were never broken, for successive kings and governments have frequently violated them from time to time. What matters is that these principles of the rule of law had been set up as a standard of government and justice in England for all time. And let us be quite clear that in these clauses *"liber homo"* means just what it says – "free man": only the perversity of too-ingenious lawyers could ever have sought to persuade us that these words meant "landholder by military tenure".

It is in these clauses chiefly, though not entirely, that the permanent value of the Great Charter lies, and it is mainly around these clauses that the "myth of Magna Carta" has gathered in the succeed-

43 See the case of the trial of Wolfe Tone in 1798, C. Grant Robertson, *Select Statutes, Cases and Documents 1660–1832* (4th ed., London, 1923), pp. 498–9.

ing centuries. No matter how often they were broken, appeal could still be made to them as binding all kings and governments, and their very generality made them capable of almost unlimited extension and interpretation. Strictly speaking, they are not constitutional clauses, but they are essential foundations for what we have come to call constitutional government and what the western world understands by "democracy." The men who first drafted the Charter in 1215, and those who reissued it in 1216, 1217, and 1225 had far transcended a merely feudal point of view, and were acting in a responsible and public-spirited way on behalf of the whole community of freemen, despite the limitations which are obvious enough to twentieth-century historians. We should not forget those other clauses of the Charter whereby the magnates provided remedies for the grievances of the Londoners and the citizens and burgesses of other cities and boroughs generally, or protection for merchants and their wares as they came into the country, travelled its roads and rivers, and finally left again, and even the brief glance at the right of the serf to protection of his livelihood. The administrative clauses, too, provided for reforms which would benefit all classes of men, and not merely the magnates, especially in the matter of doing justice in the shire and hundred courts. It is, in fact, hard to see how any open-minded historian, having read the Charter even once, could describe it as a document of feudal reaction: it is easy to understand why and how it has acquired its unique reputation, including the accretion of myth, over the seven centuries which separate its origin and our own age.

   To sum up, what had the Charter, and the two years of civil war which ensued, contributed to the solution of the constitutional problem of the thirteenth century, to making explicit the limitations upon the absolute royal *gubernaculum* which the conditions and circumstances of medieval English monarchy necessarily implied? In the end, nothing institutional had been achieved, for the sanctions clause offered no solution other than the intolerable prospect of legalized rebellion, while the attempt to define the constitution of the "counsel of the realm" for purposes of voluntary taxation was already out-of-date when it was devised; and both of these institutional remedies were abandoned in the reissues of the Charter. But although no institutional check on the king's executive power had resulted, the whole climate of opinion and of action in constitutional matters had been changed in such a way that the change could never be reversed. The proof of this is the contrast between the action of the magnates in the earlier years of Stephen's reign and the nature of the opposition to John in 1212–16: the magnates had begun to realize that royal absolutism was a problem, though as yet they saw it only in terms of the misrule of an individual king. They had attempted to solve the problem, as they saw it, by common action, though in fact unity among them was never achieved; and most of them had acted responsibly and with a good and even generous understanding of the common interest of all the king's subjects. If in the end they had achieved no institutional progress towards a solution of the constitutional problem, at least they had learnt a lesson which was not to be forgotten, and they had taught the kings of England something they, too, could never forget and which they could reject only at their extreme peril. They had given powerful and practical meaning to the theologians' and the lawyers' maxim that "Rex debet esse sub Deo et lege," and if, as yet, it was still true that the maxim continued "sed non sub homine," since no human institution had been devised to limit the king's executive power, the men of 1215 had set the stage for the effective solution of the problem, which was to be worked out, in its initial stages, in the reigns of John's son and grandson.

Not that the thirteenth century saw the solution of the problem – very far from it, for even at the end of Edward I's reign the fundamental nature of the problem had never yet been faced. The men of the middle ages – that is, the men capable of taking effective political action – never did face it, for they still accepted as their ideal the medieval conception of monarchy summarized in Bracton's phrase, "Rex debet esse sub Deo et sub lege, sed non sub homine." They believed that the true king, in the exercise of his absolute *gubernaculum*, would always be guided by the *vis directiva* of God's will towards the common good of the whole realm, and that any *vis coactiva* exerted by his subjects upon him would be an impious contradiction of the monarchical ideal. Yet time and again weak kings acting incompetently or strong kings acting so as plainly to threaten the rights, liberties, and even the lives of their subjects, forced the magnates and any other classes that were strong enough to defend themselves, to resist the king, to rise against him, and to coerce him by setting up institutions, councils, formally constituted and representative bodies of men who were the king's subjects and yet now made themselves his masters. This apparent contradiction is simply explained: medieval Englishmen, while continuing to revere the medieval ideal of kingship, were impelled to opposition and to revolt whenever the behaviour of a particular king fell sufficiently far below the unattainable ideal to make them feel that the misrule of this particular king could not be tolerated. They saw the problem, not in general and permanent terms, which would have required a quite different ideal of monarchy, a monarchy permanently limited by human institutions, but as a temporary and immediate aberration caused by the failure of a particular king, and not by any inherent flaw in their ideal. After the frightening disorders of the fifteenth century, the Tudor age was too bedazzled with the idea of divine right inherent in kingship, and, on the whole, was too well governed by exceptionally able rulers, to perceive the fundamental weakness of the whole ideal of Tudor – and medieval – monarchy. It was not until the less capable early Stuarts, by their combination of high pretensions and low ability, forced the men of the seventeenth century, who were now far more capable than their predecessors of generalizing about politics, to reconsider the fundamentals of the whole position, that at last, slowly and hesitantly at first, they began to see the problem as a permanent and inherent defect in English political thinking, requiring a revolutionary transformation of the former "absolute" kingship into something totally different – a permanently limited monarchy controlled by human institutions and constitutional laws. How this change of outlook came about, until men could see that "to admit reason of state in a particular case would open a gap through which *Magna Carta* and the rest of the statutes may issue out and vanish," has been most lucidly and cogently traced by Professor McIlwain:[44] there is no point in recapitulating his argument here. Yet, although in 1307 men were still more than three centuries away from the solution of their problem, they had at least made a start: they had grasped the need to limit incompetent kingship and royal tyranny by human institutions, even if they regarded the need for these remedies as temporary only. And, though in the main it had been created by the crown itself and for its own purposes, there had by 1307 come into existence, not as an occasional or temporary device, but as a lasting and a growing institution, the parliament which, in the seventeenth century, was to effect the revolutionary and permanent change from a theoretically absolute to a constitutionally limited monarchy.[45]

---

44 McIlwain, *Constitutionalism*, ch. v.
45 I am indebted to my friend and colleague, Dr. E. B. Fryde, for reading the typescript of this article and for making some helpful suggestions which I have incorporated in this study.

Notes on the Making of the Dunstable Annals, AD 33 to 1242 C. R. CHENEY

The Annals of Dunstable, first published by Thomas Hearne in 1733 and re-published by H. R. Luard in volume III of the *Annales Monastici* (Rolls Series) in 1866, hardly rank as a neglected source for thirteenth-century history, though they may have been underrated. They extend from AD 33 to 1297. While the material for the years before 1200 is wholly derivative, the annals of the next ninety-eight years, which fill 78 out of 85 folios in the single complete medieval manuscript, have never been associated with any other written work and have the air of an original production. Internal evidence makes it clear that the annals were compiled in the Austin priory of Dunstable in Bedfordshire. They are much concerned with the priory's domestic affairs, its relations with the townsfolk and neighbouring landlords, and its patronage of parish churches. Luard indicated the worth of the annals clearly enough.[1] Reinhold Pauli valued them for information on continental affairs, and edited extracts.[2] That the annals were compiled in Dunstable priory has been recognized since the time of Humphrey Wanley and Thomas Hearne. It has also been repeatedly stated that the annals to AD 1201 were derived in the main from the writings of Ralph de Diceto, dean of St. Paul's, and that Richard de Morins, prior of Dunstable, compiled the work down to the time of his death in 1242.[3] These findings would be the better for a little more precision and some modification. The present object is to examine the origin of the compilation and the way in which the annals were put together in the time of Prior Richard.

1 *Annales Monastici* (Rolls Series), III pp. xxxii–iv.
2 *Monumenta Germaniae Historica, Scriptores* (1885), XXVII, pp. 505–13.
3 Thus, most recently, F. M. Powicke, *The Thirteenth Century* (2nd ed., Oxford 1962), p. 733.

THE MANUSCRIPTS

To begin with, a few words about the state of the text. The whole is found in a thirteenth-century manuscript, Brit.Mus.ms. Cotton Tiberius A x, fols. 5ʳ–89ᵛ (*Tib.*). On the following folios to f.115ʳ are notes and documents, legal and historical, which record events of the fourteenth century and a proclamation of the year 1459.[4] This manuscript was damaged, but the text not seriously harmed, in the Cottonian fire of 1731. A close codicological study of it is precluded by the remounting of the leaves and by the contraction, distortion, and discoloration caused by fire and water; but at least one can see that the early portion was written by hands of the early part of the thirteenth century and that the later entries could have been written not very long after the events they record. Luard and Pauli saw a clear distinction of handwriting in the middle of the annal for 1210 on f.12ʳb.[5] They took this to be the first change of hand, and Luard remarked that the second hand broke off in the middle of a sentence at the foot of f.14ᵛa, s.a. 1215, after which (according to him) "the original hand goes on" (p. 45, n.3). But Luard's analysis of the hands was inadequate: he noted no other change of the main hand of the annals between 1215 and the ending in 1297. No full palaeographical analysis will be attempted here, for reasons to be explained; but some features of the manuscript must be noted which bear upon the compilation of the annals in the first half of the thirteenth century. In the first place, it is not certain that the variations which are seen in the folios preceding Luard's first distinction on f.12ʳb can all be explained by a mere change of pen or ink without change of scribe. On the very first leaf (f.5ʳa) a new start was made at AD 96 (and this corresponds to a new start at this point in the Harleian manuscript (*Harl.*) discussed below). Up to the year 96 the scribe of *Tib.* uses the tironian *et* with a stroke through it; for the rest of f.5ʳ and f.5ᵛ the stroke is missing (as it is in *Harl.*). From AD 96 punctuation is limited to a single point, and the *i* is never dotted. Instead of introducing the year by *Anno* the word is abridged to *a.* On fols. 6ᵛ–7ᵛ, by contrast, the year is expressed as *an.* (from AD 636 to 1095).[6]

Coming to AD 1210, the change in the style of writing on f.12ʳb

4 Luard printed some parts in his Appendix, *Ann. Mon.*, III, 409–20.
5 *Ann. Mon.*, III, 33, to which references are made hereafter by page-number only.
6 The remaining fragments of fols. 6 and 7 have been reversed in mounting, so that the text proceeds: 6ᵛ, 6ʳ, 7ᵛ, 7ʳ.

which Luard discerned is clearly visible. But it is at least possible that this hand was superseded by another on f.13^{r}b (s.a. 1213); and if, as Luard supposed, the scribe of fols. 13^{r}b–14^{v}a was in fact the scribe who took up his pen first at f.12^{r}b, the contrast between f.14^{v}a and f.14^{v}b (where Luard saw "the original hand" reappear) becomes less significant: this could be the work of the same scribe, whose adoption of a larger script produces a superficially different impression. Be that as it may, the hand of f.14^{v}b continues at least to f.17^{v}b (s.a. 1220), and thereafter several scribes take their turns recurrently at writing the annals.[7] The poor state of the manuscript does not permit collation by quires nor show how the ruling was carried out. The writing is disposed throughout on two columns to the page, varying from 37 to 49 lines in the column. A new and more careful ruling, apparently prepared leaf by leaf, allowing forty lines to the column, began on f.13^r (s.a. 1212).[8]

Before the Cottonian fire Humphrey Wanley had made, with his customary accuracy, a complete transcript of *Tib.* which is now in Brit.Mus.ms. Harl. 4886, and it was this that Hearne printed in his edition of 1733, quoting in his introduction Wanley's discerning remarks about the annals. Luard used both the Cottonian manuscript and Wanley's transcript in preparing his edition. He observed of his predecessor: "Hearne made little attempt at editing his author or investigating his authorities, confining himself to printing the text. His notes do not show much antiquarian or historical knowledge." (p. x) The criticism came ill from one who himself made egregious blunders and overlooked highly significant facts.

One other manuscript contains a small part of the annals. In 1714 Wanley acquired a thirteenth-century cartulary of Dunstable Priory, which is now Brit.Mus.ms. Harl. 1885.[9] In it he found the verso of

7 Another physical feature which deserves notice, though it probably has no bearing on the subject of this paper, is the rubrication of A in *Anno*, which occurs only for the years 1213 (f.13^{v}b), 1213 *bis* (f.14^{r}a), 1214 (f.14^{r}b), 1215 (f.14^{v}a), 1216 (f.16^{r}a). No space had been left for the rubric in the first two places.

8 The ruling continues to allow forty lines a page until f.31^r, except for fols. 22^v–24^r, which have forty-one lines; thereafter the number of lines constantly varies.

9 Extracts were printed by Hearne in *Chronicon sive Annales Prioratus de Dunstaple, una cum excerptis e Chartulario ejusdem Prioratus* (2 vols., Oxford, 1733), II, pp. 676–713, and a calendar of the whole by G. H. Fowler in *A Digest of the Charters preserved in the Cartulary of the Priory of Dunstable* (Bedfordshire Historical Record Society, Publications, X, 1926). Fowler

one leaf (f.41^v)[10] wholly filled by the annals for the years AD 33–
552, beginning with precisely the same preamble as occurs in *Tib.*
The recto of the leaf contained the usual material of a cartulary –
private deeds of Edlesborough, Chalton, and Hudnall – in an early
thirteenth-century charter hand. The annals, in a different small neat
hand of the same period, begin at the extreme top of the verso page,
above the original ruling, and are arranged in two columns. Changes
in colour of ink suggest new starts at AD 33, 96, ?277, 369, and 420;
but the only change of hand appears to be after the preamble, at
AD 33. The hand of the preamble may be that which makes some
references to the civil law and Gratian on f.77^r of the cartulary.
Wanley's study of the manuscripts led him to conclude that the
cartulary was started at the instance of Richard de Morins, prior of
Dunstable from 1202 to 1242: "This is the Man who ... began the
same partly with his own Hand, and partly by the Hands of Others
as Occasion Offered. After the Entries of many Matters ... he began
his Annals with his Own Hand; but then, perchance, considering
that they would, in time come to be the Foundation of the Annals of
the House, he kept on this Book for Chartulary, and began his
Annals again, in the same Words, and with the same (that is his
own Hand) in another Book, namely that Cottonian MS. above-
mentioned. ..."[11]

Leaving on one side for the moment the question whether author
and scribe can be treated as identical, we cannot doubt that the
bulk of the annals in ms.Harl. 1885, f.41^v was written by one hand,
and that the hand closely resembles one of the first hands of *Tib.*
Comparison of the two texts suggests not only a close connexion
between them, but (as Wanley supposed) the priority of *Harl.* The
close connexion appears s.a. 50, misplaced in both manuscripts before
the entry for AD 45, and s.a. 282, where both *Harl.* and *Tib.* mark
the words "Albanus beatus" for transposition. The priority of *Harl.*
is shown by mistakes in *Tib.* where *Harl.* is correct. Thus, s.a. 50:
Harl. secundo, *Tib.* secundus; s.a. 85: *Harl.* Limovicis, *Tib.* Limo-
nicis; s.a. 493: *Harl,* cxv, *Tib.* xcv. The last words of the entry
for AD 493: "concilio ... purgavit" are correctly inserted in *Harl.*
but have strayed to the entry for AD 467 in *Tib.* Therefore, either

failed to recognize the annals and describes them (p. 119) as "a Calendar of
Saints and Popes, from the Crucifixion a.d. 33 to a.d. 552."
10 At that time f.40^v, formerly p. 94 and not, as Wanley says, f.93^v.
11 Quoted Hearne, *Chronicon,* I, p. lxxix. Luard accepted the view that the hand
of the annals in *Harl.* was "not improbably the compiler's own" (p. ix).

Tib. was copied from *Harl.* or another text of the annals lies behind both these manuscripts. One curious feature strikes the reader. *Harl.* ends s.a. 552 at the bottom of the second column of a well-filled page. *Tib.* has smaller leaves. It reaches AD 552 at the bottom of the first column of its second page (f.5^{v}a); it then leaves the second column blank, resuming on the next leaf with an entry s.a. 584. Wanley may be right in his surmise that the author (or the scribe) decided after completing the first page of *Harl.* that it would be best for him to separate the annals from the cartulary; but we cannot determine whether or no the intention was to devote f.5^{v}b of *Tib.* to the events of the next thirty-two years (a generous allowance) and, if so, why the gap was not filled.[12] The explanation may be that *Tib.*, f.6 was intended originally as a continuation to the copy begun in *Harl.*, although written on a smaller leaf; and that the scribe, having decided to separate the annals from the cartulary, re-copied the contents of *Harl.* to make a new beginning.

THE ORIGIN OF THE ANNALS

I turn to the questions of origin and authorship, which are inevitably intertwined. Some of the internal evidence is so clear that it could hardly be overlooked by anyone who picked up the printed text. It is plain for all to see in the first sentence which reads: "Ab Adam usque ad Nativitatem Christi fluxerunt anni secundum Hebreos tria milia dccccxlviii, secundum Septuaginta Interpretes v milia cxcvi; et exinde usque ad octavum annum nostrum mccx." The author, that is, began his work AD 1210 and was then in the eighth year of the tenure of some office. This leads to the annal for the year 1202 for which year the only entry runs: "Ricardus canonicus Meretone, adhuc diaconus, fit prior de Dunstaple; et Sabbato quatuor temporum [21 September] ordinatus, die S.Michaelis [29 September] primam missam celebravit." The first sentence of the annals, therefore, was framed by that Master Richard de Morins who became prior of Dunstable in 1202 and whose death is recorded in the annals s.a. 1242.

This opening sentence (ultimately derived through Diceto from Eusebius) is followed by an annalistic sequence beginning: "Anno

12 An examination of text *C* of Diceto (see *infra*) shows only two annals marked for extraction in this period: 562 "Iustiniani temporibus Vigilius ..." and 565 "David qui et. ..." The latter is attached by a "sub quo" to the entry in the Dunstable annals (both *Harl.* and *Tib.*) for AD 552 "Pelagius papa."

xxxiii. Christus crucifixus est octavo kalendas Aprilis." The dependence of these annals on Ralph de Diceto's *Abbreviationes chroni-
corum* (to 1147) and *Ymagines historiarum* (from 1148 to 1201) was
asserted by T. Duffus Hardy, who declared that "the chronicles of
Florence of Worcester and Martinus Polonus can also be traced."[13]
This statement followed Luard, who had also referred to "some
source which I have not been able to trace" (pp. xiv–xv). It did not
occur to Luard and Hardy that Martinus Polonus flourished a generation after Richard de Morins, and they produced nothing from
Florence of Worcester that is not to be found in Diceto's *Abbreviationes*. Nor is it necessary to look further than a text of Diceto for
Luard's untraced source. To the end of the twelfth century the additions to Diceto are extremely few and unimportant. The Dunstable
annalist may be presumed to be responsible for a few reflexions of
his own and a few facts: for instance, s.a. 1135 "Hinc oritur werra";
under the same year he adds to a list of monasteries founded in
Henry I's reign "et prioratum de Dunstaple"; s.a. 1185 "terre motus"
is described as "apud Lincolniam" instead of "circa partes aquilo-
nares"; s.a. 1198 "Obiit Hugo Coventrensis episcopus"; s.a. 1199
"dictus de S.Marie Ecclesia." With the year 1200 the compiler abandoned Diceto, whose main texts stop before this year.[14]

The failure of previous editors and commentators to identify precisely the source for the years 33–1199 arose from their reliance on
the wrong text of Diceto's works. It should be remembered that
Stubbs did not produce his edition of Diceto until 1876. The text
used by Luard was Twysden's edition,[15] supplemented for the matter
before AD 589 by Brit.Mus.ms. Cotton Cleopatra E III (Stubbs's *B*).
This was Twysden's main text. It is, as Stubbs pointed out, a revised
recension of the original text of Lambeth ms. 8 (Stubbs's *A*), from
St. Paul's Cathedral. But *A* had been later corrected and its corrections had been mostly incorporated in Brit.Mus.ms. Royal 13 E VI
(Stubbs's *C*), where some peculiar passages were added in the text
and margins. Twysden made use of *C* (and of another text, *D*), but

13 *Catalogue of Materials of British History* (Rolls Series, 1871), III, p. 252.
14 *Radulfi de Diceto Decani Lundoniensis Opera Historica*, ed. W. Stubbs (2
   vols., Rolls Series, 1876), I, pp. lxxxviii–xcvi; cf. D. E. Greenway, "The succession to Ralph de Diceto, dean of St. Paul's," *Bull. Inst. Hist. Res.*, XXXIX
   (1966), 86–95.
15 *Historiae Anglicanae Scriptores X*, ed. Roger Twysden (1652), cols. 429–710.
   After giving a small part of the introductory matter of the *Abbreviationes*
   (ed. Stubbs, I, pp. 18–24, 34), Twysden omits everything before the annal for
   AD 589.

conflated in such a way as to obscure the differences between his texts. Comparison of them points unmistakably to the source used at Dunstable. The compiler used *C*; and he borrowed it, in the year 1209 or 1210, from the library of St. Albans Abbey, where it had probably been written.

C is a large and handsome manuscript, illuminated in gold and colour, written throughout on two columns in good bold bookhands, about 1200. A fine pen indicated in the margin where corrections were needed in the text, and the corrections were neatly executed. On f.i^r is the St. Albans library pressmark: "A 6 gradus 2 p." A comparison of this *C* text of Diceto's works with the extracts which are in the Dunstable annals shows some verbatim copying, a little condensation, and occasional misunderstanding of the original. Passages occur in the Dunstable annals which are not in *B* but are in *C*. One small but clear pointer occurs s.a. 1183, where the Dunstable annals read: "moritur Henricus rex iunior anno vicesimo octavo etatis sue." These words are taken over from a rubric in *C* (f.98^v), except that "iunior" replaces "regis Henrici filius"; they are not found in mss. *A* and *B* of Diceto. Again, the entry in the Dunstable annals s.a. 1195: "Obit Guarinus abbas sancti Albani" is derived from a passage added to Diceto by the St. Albans scribe in the bottom margin of *C* (f.125^{v}b, ed. Stubbs, II, 124 n.4). Text *C* of Diceto ends with the year 1199, and Dunstable transcribed with some abridgement the last three entries for that year.

That the original Dunstable annalist went to work with text *C* of Diceto before him is proved beyond doubt by inspection of ms. *C*. In its careful ruling, two parallel vertical lines on the left hand of each column mark the space commonly reserved for the rubricated initials. At intervals, from AD 386 in the *Abbreviationes* to the end of the *Ymagines* in 1199, certain entries have been marked lightly between the parallel lines by a diagonal stroke made with a reddish-brown pencil. When these marks are compared with the Dunstable annals a very close (though not perfect) correspondence appears between the strokes and the extracts of the annals. Very few of the passages marked in the Diceto ms. have been wholly omitted. In some cases the abridgement or conflation is particularly significant. Thus, Diceto has entries under the years 857, 859, 860, 862, 864, 868, 872. The only ones with pencil strokes against them are 857, 868, 872. In the Dunstable annals the items so marked are gathered up to make one entry under the year 857: "Nicholaus papa. Item

Adrianus papa [868] sub quo Adeldredus fit Cantuariensis archiepiscopus [872]." Occasionally a marginal "Nota," in the same reddish-
brown pencil, supplements or replaces the diagonal stroke in C; in
nearly all cases this points to an entry in the Dunstable annals.[16] It
looks very much as if Prior Richard, after announcing himself in the
preamble, extracted and edited the annals that interested him as far
as AD 369, and then marked later entries in Diceto with his pencil
so that somebody else could carry on the work on the pattern he had
set. The extracts were scanty, so that they occupy only eleven printed
pages (small type) compared with the 314 pages (large type) of
Diceto's book. Annals rather than a history were contemplated.

It was stated categorically above that Richard de Morins borrowed
C from St. Albans in 1209 or in 1210. Certainty is possible because
the St. Albans scribe of Diceto, terminating with King John's accession the copy of his exemplar from St. Paul's, had left half a column
blank on f.136^{r}b and was left with three blank pages in his last quire
of parchment.[17] They were ruled for writing like the preceding leaves
and invited new entries to keep the chronicle up to date. But there
was no attempt to produce a big and ambitious work on the lines of
Diceto's *Ymagines*. The original scribe of C left ten lines for additions for 1199. Thereafter the marginal dates allow fourteen lines for
1200, sixteen lines for 1201, twelve for 1202, sixteen for 1203, and
so on, irregularly spaced to 1215. The spaces are only partly filled,
and that by various hands which do not appear in orderly succession.
Some of these brief annals seem to have been written soon after the
events they record (e.g. an entry s.a. 1211), but at least one entry –
that for 1202 – has been so badly misplaced that it must have been
added several years later: it is in a hand which predominates in and
after 1211 and was probably written at the same time as the annals
of 1211–15.[18]

Liebermann printed these annals of St. Albans in 1879.[19] Elsewhere he observed that, "slender as they are and much concerned

16 The earliest "Nota" occurs s.a. 265 (f.12^r), concerning the Council of Antioch: this precedes the series of diagonal strokes.
17 The collation of the book is: [sig. 1^1] = f.i; sigg. I–XVI^8 = fols. 1–127; [sig.
XVII^{10}] = fols. 128–37. The signature marks are in roman numerals at the
foot of the last verso of each quire; there is no signature for the front flyleaf
or for the last quire. An unnumbered blank leaf follows f.52, in quire VII.
18 It sets the Easter crowning of King John in Canterbury in the year 1202,
giving the date of Easter (correctly for 1202) as 14 April. But the event
belongs to 1201 when Easter Day was 25 March.
19 *Ungedruckte anglo-normannische Geschichtsquellen*, ed. Felix Liebermann
(Strassburg, 1879), pp. 166–72.

with domestic matters, they are the first beginnings of real history by monks of St. Albans."[20] He also pointed out that Roger Wendover, naturally enough, had made use of these annals along with the preceding text of Diceto. (Wendover copied the erroneous annal of 1202 about the Easter crowning of King John.) Moreover, Matthew Paris made independent use of the annal for 1212: he took more of Diceto's *Ymagines* than Wendover had extracted, and he embellished the Diceto text with marginal additions in his own hand.[21] But neither Liebermann nor anyone else, to my knowledge, remarked that the Dunstable annalist, like the St. Albans historians, laid these annals under contribution. When text C of Diceto came to Dunstable it must already have contained some of the entries for the years 1200 to 1209.

Under the year 1200 the sole entry from St. Albans, recording the death of Bishop Hugh of Lincoln, appears in the Dunstable annals in the same form. Again, under the year 1201 the sole annal from St. Albans is copied, almost completely; and this is the more remarkable because it is a piece of domestic news of St. Albans: "Facta est [*om.* finalis] concordia in curia [*om.* domini] regis [*om.* Iohannis] inter ecclesiam Sancti [*for* Beati] Albani et Robertum filium Walteri [*om.* et heredes eius] super nemore de Northhawe [*for* la Norhawe]." The St. Albans annal of 1202 (already noted as a later addition) is not paralleled in the Dunstable annals; but after this twelve items in the St. Albans annals are matched, ending with the consecration of Otto as emperor at Rome on 4 October 1209. Within this period the only items omitted are three which were only of interest to St. Albans and the record of the election and consecration of Stephen Langton at Viterbo on 17 June 1207, which is noted in the Dunstable annals in different terms. There can, then, be no doubt that this ms. Royal 13 E vi came into the hands of the Dunstable annalist after the entry had been made concerning the coronation of Otto. This entry may have been made as early as November 1209, for already on 12 November, at Mountsorel in Leicestershire, King John had rewarded the messenger who bore him the news of his nephew's triumph.[22] On the

---

20 "Sane tenues sunt annales, plerumque in rebus domesticis versantes, sed vera historiae apud Albanenses prima initia," *MGH* (1888) xxviii, 7.

21 *Matt. Parisiensis Historia Anglorum*, ed. F. Madden (Rolls Series, 1866), I, p. x, note; *Catalogue of Royal MSS. in the British Museum*, ed. G. F. Warner and J. P. Gilson (1921), II p. 113; Richard Vaughan, "The handwriting of Matthew Paris", *Trans. Cambridge Bibliog. Soc.*, v (1953), 391.

22 *Rotuli de Liberate ac de Misis et Praestitis*, ed. T. D. Hardy (Record Com., 1844) p. 138.

other hand, whereas the St. Albans annals next record, with the date
20 December 1209, the consecration of Hugh de Wells as bishop of
Lincoln by Archbishop Stephen Langton at Melun, Hugh's promotion appears in a briefer form and a different context in the Dunstable annals. It may be guessed, then, that the news of the consecration of their diocesan had not reached the monks of St. Albans when
the manuscript was lent to Dunstable. The end of 1209 or the early
months of 1210 are indicated as the time of borrowing. This agrees
perfectly with the preamble to the Dunstable annals which an-
nounced 1210 to be "our eighth year" – the eighth year of Richard
de Morins's priorate.

It is one thing to determine the origin of the Dunstable annals in
the year 1210; it is quite another thing to discover how the work was
continued after the manuscript of Diceto had been returned to
St. Albans. It is one thing to feel justified in the inference that Prior
Richard was personally responsible for its inception; it is another
thing to be satisfied that he was the author of it from the point where
it ceased to depend on Diceto. Although it has been generally assumed that Richard de Morins composed it from the beginning to
his death in 1242, this assumption needs testing. Again, the relationship of author to scribe cries out for consideration. Does Tiberius A x
present us with the annals as they were first written down, so that
the changes of handwriting show stages of composition and changes
of authorship? Or is it the work of a series of copyists, told to make
a fair copy of a more disorderly original? If this is a fair copy, may it
not conceal under its uniformity additions made by others to the
author's original draft? One may not be able to settle all these matters with certainty, but the questions must be asked. I shall proceed
to some particular observations on the annals from 1200 to 1242 in
the hope that they will throw light on the problem and help to illustrate the way in which such works as this evolved.

THE ANNALS AD 33–1242: ORIGINAL OR COPY?

The mere external appearance of *Tib.* is enough to raise doubt
whether this can be the original manuscript of the compilation. It is
altogether too tidy. Several hands have been at work; but from beginning to end there is no sign of those second thoughts or retouch-
ings which an author could hardly resist. Spelling mistakes are very
rare; where they occur, they are uncorrected.[23] Very occasionally,

23 On f.9ʳb (p 20, s.a. 1171) "mandato ee" has been neatly corrected to read

two words are marked for transposition. In the entry for AD 493, already noted, an extract from Diceto is correctly placed in *Harl.* and wrongly placed in *Tib.* The change of script which Luard noted as a return to the original hand of f.14ᵛb of *Tib.* occurs in the middle of a sentence: it cannot indicate a change of authorship. At later points in the manuscript where new starts occur there appears to be an alternation of hands: if each were to represent a change of authorship the course of composition would seem most erratic. But if this is a fair copy it follows that changes of pen and ink and hand provide no proof of stages of production of the annals. Even if a palaeographer suggests approximate dates for the hands he will only be providing the dates before which certain parts of the annals were composed. To verify the view that *Tib.* is a fair copy we must look at the contents of the annals as well as at their physical appearance. If it is a fair copy it is only from the contents that we can form any idea of the process of composition.

AUTHORSHIP OF THE ANNALS

Comparison with the St. Albans annals has already established that the Dunstable extracts to the year 1209 were made in 1210 or very soon afterwards, for additions to the annals were made soon afterwards, when the book had been sent home. The Dunstable scribe of the lost exemplar which lay behind *Tib.* may have imitated the St. Albans scribe in leaving space for additions under each year from 1200 to 1209. He made numerous short additions, amounting to nearly five pages of Luard's printed text. Within each year they show no chronological order, and two entries (deliberately, it seems) overrun the ends of the years 1208 and 1209 in which they begin. If we reject the idea that *Tib.* is the autograph of the compiler we must reckon with the possibility that its exemplar was a composite work, compiled by several hands; unco-ordinated, unedited, marginal additions may have been grafted on to the original after it was first written down in 1210 or 1211. But the Dunstable annals of these years might well be material already assembled by Prior Richard with some such work in view when he borrowed the St. Albans Diceto. There is nothing in them which presupposes a knowledge of events later than 1210. Almost all the events, moreover, lie well within the

"mandato ecclesie," by the original hand, which adds "ecc^e" in the margin and expunges "ee" on the next line. This looks like the work of a copyist who had originally misread the abbreviation for "ecclesie" as that for "esse."

range of Prior Richard's experience and to some extent reflect his special interests.

Master Richard de Morins was a man of repute as a canonist. A graduate of Bologna, he was probably still a secular clerk, perhaps engaged in teaching and writing, until the year 1200.[24] Then he became an Austin canon at Merton Priory and in 1202 became prior of Dunstable. The annals of these years record his promotion, ordination as priest, and first celebration (above, p. 83). They contain many details connected with Dunstable Priory. The royal taxation of 1207 and 1210 is noted with special reference to what Dunstable paid. They tell of the prior's mission to Rome for the king in 1203, and of his activity as a delegate of the papal legate in 1206. They show an interest in ecclesiastical councils which Richard may have attended in 1200 and 1206. They record (as an event of January 1210) the hanging of two clerks at Oxford which caused the schools to disband. Under 1208 they note the otherwise unchronicled fact that Master Honorius, archdeacon of Richmond, was imprisoned at Gloucester. It is not fanciful to suppose that the prior was interested in the fate of this man, another distinguished canonist with whom he was certainly well acquainted.[25] It is unlikely that any ordinary canon of Dunstable would have thought the news noteworthy, even if it came his way.

But although the prior's mind may be behind the annals of these years, it would be unwise to attribute all to him. In the first place, it is difficult to believe that a man so well versed in public affairs would be guilty of two inaccuracies which occur. King John's second marriage (1200) is assigned to 1201. Under 1209 "Otto, son of the duke of Saxony" is said to have visited England before his coronation as emperor (pp. 31–32). Either there is confusion here with the visit of Otto's elder brother Henry in spring 1209, or the entry results from a faulty transcription of an annal for 1207, when Otto himself came to England. Neither mistake could very well be one made by the prior

---

24 J. C. Russell, *Dictionary of Writers of Thirteenth Century England* (1936), pp. 111–3; Stephan Kuttner, in *Dictionnaire de droit canonique*, ed. R. Naz (1960), VII, pp. 676–81. As Master Richard de Mores (the name given by Matthew Paris to the prior of Dunstable) he witnesses an act of Hubert Walter, archbishop of Canterbury, probably to be dated 1200 or 1201, without indication that he is a regular (*Acta S. Langton*, ed. Kathleen Major [Canterbury and York Soc., 1950], p. 50).

25 The Dunstable annalist is the only chronicler to report the death of Master John of Tynemouth (s.a. 1221), who belonged to the same circle of canonists.

of Dunstable in 1210.[26] In the second place, there are slight but un-mistakable signs that the compilation has received additions from written sources besides ms. Royal 13 E vi. Entries for 1200 and 1201 (pp. 27–28) resemble passages in the *D* text of Diceto (or his con-tinuator) under the year 1200,[27] and a list of episcopal promotions under the year 1209 (p. 31) offers a more correct version of a list which occurs in the annals of Tewkesbury.[28]

In the decade after 1210 the Dunstable annals show few if any features which could be construed as signs of the prior's authorship, although from time to time they record his personal activities. He investigates the churches' losses during the Interdict (p. 39), he attends the Fourth Lateran Council and spends a year in the theologi-cal schools of Paris on the way home (p. 44). Much later, in his old age, he acts as papal judge delegate in 1239, in an important lawsuit over metropolitan rights of visitation (p. 151). The fact that these records generally refer to "prior noster" hardly affects the question of authorship. Humphrey Wanley, who regarded him as the author, wrote: "I may believe that he might often dictate the Matter, even when he himself is mentioned in the Third Person, as we see that Moses often writeth of himself in that manner."[29] The personal element is exemplified in the record of the apparition (*visio*) to "our prior" on the night of St. Martin of two Jews who foretold to him the coming of Antichrist (p. 33). But even if the prior was instrumental in recording these facts, the main responsibility for the compilation

---

26 Other mistakes occur under the year 1208: the bishops of Salisbury and Rochester actually went to Scotland in November 1209, and Walter, arch-bishop of Rouen, died in November 1207. The abbot of Ramsey resigned, and the abbot of Chertsey died, in 1206.

27 Diceto, I, pp. xci–xcii and II, pp. 169–70.

28 *Ann. Mon.*, I, p. 59; cf. *ibid.*, IV, pp. 397–8 (Worcester annals) and Brit.Mus.ms. Cotton Faustina B I, f.24ʳ (Winchcomb annals) which omit the words "cancellarius regis in Coventrensem et magister Nicholaus de Aquila" and so erroneously make Walter de Gray bishop-elect of Chichester (Luard tried to correct by emending to Chester). The common source would seem to be that which Liebermann believed to lie behind so many south-country annals: see *Ungedruckte anglo-norm. Gesch.*, pp. 173–82; Moses Tyson, "The annals of Southwark and Merton," *Surrey Archaeological Collections*, XXXVI (1925), 24–57, and N. Denholm-Young, "The Winchester-Hyde Chronicle," *EHR*, XLIX (1934), 85–93, reprinted in his *Collected Papers on Medieval Subjects* (Oxford, 1946) pp. 86–95. Another trace of the common source is possibly the record in Dunstable, s.a. 1219: "Obiit Hugo Herfordensis episcopus, cui successit Hugo Foliot" (p. 55), also in Winton-Waverley annals (*Unge-druckte anglo-norm. Gesch.*, p. 188).

29 Hearne, *Chronicon*, I, p. lxxix.

might rest in other hands. The compiler, to be sure, displayed keen interest in legal matters concerning his priory, but such an interest does not necessarily denote the professional canonist, and it is equally a feature of the annals before and after Prior Richard's death. Any intelligent obedientiary of the house, acquainted with its temporal affairs, could chronicle these events, for which the priory's cartulary preserved complementary documents. Pauli, who thought that *Tib.* was the original authors' manuscript, saw no reason to think that Prior Richard composed the annals beyond the point where the hand of *Tib.* changes under the year 1210.

METHODS OF COMPOSITION

Granted that the annals before 1209 were for the most part written down by 1210 or 1211, what was the method of composition thereafter? Luard thought "that the greater portion of the chronicle was written from year to year as the events occurred or were reported" (pp. xxxi–ii). A thirteenth-century pattern for such a procedure is provided by the compiler of annals contained in ms. Cotton Vesp. E IV, f.153ʳ, called by Liebermann "Winton-Waverley."[30] The annalist begins by saying that he has assembled various chronicles and annals from neglected sources. He continues: "It will be your business to see that there is always a sheet attached to the book, on which may be noted in pencil deaths of illustrious men and anything in the state of the kingdom which is worth remembering, whenever the news comes to hand. But at the end of the year let a man appointed to the task – not just anyone who so wishes – write out briefly and succinctly, in the body of the book, what he thinks truest and best to be passed down to the notice of posterity. And then the old leaf can be removed and a new one put in." This sort of pattern may have been in the mind of Richard de Morins when he inaugurated an historical work in his priory; but, if so, it was not maintained in the decade after 1210.

At several points events have clearly been recorded at least three or four years after they occurred. Thus the prophecy of Peter of Pontefract, earlier than May 1213, is noted with a comment that could only have been written after King John's death in October

30 Liebermann, *Ungedruckte*, pp. 173–202. The preamble is not printed here, but is printed by Luard in his edition of the annals of Worcester, *Ann. Mon.*, IV, 355.

1216 (p. 34). With the imprisonment of Stephen Ridel in the summer of 1212 is also recorded his death several years later (p. 34). A lawsuit undertaken by the priory in July 1213 is said to have been interrupted by the outbreak of war: this must have been written later than May 1215, perhaps much later (p. 38). Delay is suggested when the fate of the pseudo-Emperor Baldwin is reported s.a. 1225 and the annalist observes: "Populares tamen *usque hodie* credunt ipsum verum comitem fuisse Baldewinum ... unde multa miracula in locis sue passionis postmodum acciderunt" (p. 95).[31] Now, it is theoretically possible that every one of these few examples of "hindsight" is the result of a later addition to a contemporary text, and that their origin as marginalia is obscured because in *Tib.*, instead of the original manuscript, we have only a fair copy which has smoothed out the anachronisms and irregularities. True though this is, we must take into account two other features of the annals which, when added up, make a systematic contemporary and unified composition unbelievable. These features are, first, inaccurate chronology in the decade 1210–20 and, secondly, duplication in the reporting of events both before and after 1220.

Pauli stated that "the author who first succeeded Prior Richard in the reign of King John made the mistake of ascribing everything not to its own year but to the preceding one."[32] Had this been the only error, we might have blamed it on the copyist of *Tib.* But in fact Pauli's own extracts show that the chronological confusion in this period was much more serious. Strangely enough, it was disregarded by Luard.[33] The author's disease was apparently infectious: not even the appearance of Magna Carta in 1214 moved Luard to dissent, and he was capable himself of speaking of the Fourth Lateran Council of 1214 (p. xi) and of the campaign between John and Lewis in 1215 (p. xvi).

If we look at the annal for 1210 an interesting fact emerges. The first entries (pp. 32–33) are all correctly assigned to this year – the year in which Prior Richard inaugurated the work. But as soon as a

31 Cf. s.a. 1235: "... ita quod *nondum habemus* in ea nisi veterem pensionem" (p. 141).
32 "Notandum vero ... auctorem, qui primus post Ricardum priorem Iohanne regnante annales continuavit, ita errasse, ut omnia non suo, sed precedenti singula anno ascriberet," *MGH*, XXVII, p. 504.
33 He refers to "errors and instances of confusion" only in relation to the doublets he cites (p. xxxi); see below, p. 94.

new hand appears in *Tib.* errors of dating appear. At first sight this might seem to support Pauli's view that this is the original manuscript and that the new hand is that of a less accurate annalist who took over the work from Prior Richard in 1210. But reasons have been given for supposing that *Tib.* is a copy, not the original. The fact that the quality of the annals changes with the change of hand in this copy can be understood on the supposition that the original annals first stopped at this point, hung fire for several years, and were only resumed by a less careful compiler (perhaps even in a different book) several years after our existing fair copy of the annals to 1210 had been made. It has already been noted that the annals for 1210–20 were written up at least three or four years after the events. The gap may have been longer, for the compiler seems to be chronologically all at sea. The prophecy of Peter of Pontefract (earlier than May 1213) is placed under the year 1210. Under this year, too, comes the peace with Scotland (1212), the death of Roger de Lacy (1211), and events of strictly local interest which would be well known at Dunstable: the death of Robert de Braybrook (1211) and a lawsuit over Pulloxhill church (1212). Almost all the events s.a. 1211 belong to 1213. But then many of the chief events of 1213 are recorded s.a. 1212. Here occur the details of King John's reconciliation with the church, the damages paid by John to the clergy, and the preaching of the crusade. A few of the entries under this year relate to the first months of 1214. The confusion continues in the following years. A complete analysis is unnecessary, but it is desirable to insist that the misplacement is not consistent. The first entry s.a. 1213 is the appointment of Master Alexander Nequam as abbot of Cirencester, and this did take place in July 1213; but the battle of Bouvines (July 1214) appears under the same year. S.a. 1214 events of that year are combined with the account of the baronial revolt and Magna Carta. S.a. 1215 the Fourth Lateran Council is correctly dated but the campaign of Prince Louis in England in 1216 and 1217 is also included. So it continues. Only in and after 1220 does the chronology at last become fairly reliable.[34]

    Another feature of the disorderly annals of 1210–19 is duplication. Luard noted entries which are (more or less) doublets, and commented thus: "There are not unfrequently traces of different authorities being employed, and thus many facts are repeated in different

34 Later examples of misdating occur s.a. 1238 (events of 1236 and 1239, p. 148) and s.a. 1241 (an event of 1240, p. 156).

language, and occasionally with different dates, – a rumour of an event having reached the priory before it really took place, and being at once inserted in the chronicle" (pp. xxx–xxxi). The examples which Luard proceeds to give (and some others) do not bear out his suggestion of anticipatory rumour and contemporary record. They do, none the less, show that the compiler (or compilers) of the annals in their present form had indeed access to several authorities, and had copied them slavishly, without regard to their redundancy or mutual incompatibility. The compiler shows his carelessness very early, for the first entry in *Tib.* written by the new hand s.a. 1210 reads: "Eodem anno rex Otto fit imperator per Innocentium papam" (p. 33). This event had already been correctly noted s.a. 1209, with its precise date (4 October), from the St. Albans annals. The election of a new abbot of Westminster appears both wrongly under 1213 (with a wrong initial) and rightly under 1214. These are the only doublets before the year 1220; whereas there are at least fifteen examples between 1220 and 1242. This again points to a different method of composition.

Doublets appear commonly in medieval annals, and must be taken as symptoms of the practice of conflation. For instance, the annals of Worcester, contained as a single series in the fifteenth-century manuscript from which Luard printed them, show reliance in part on "Winton-Waverley," in part on other sources. The compiler – or conflater – did not avoid the occasional doublet.[35] In the Winchcomb annals in Brit.Mus.ms. Cotton Faustina B I an intermediate stage can be visually observed. Here the scribe first abridged a series of Tewkesbury annals (which lay behind those printed by Luard). He set the entry for each year as an island in a little sea of blank parchment. Then he added new islets of text, spread all round the original entry: sometimes there are as many as six for one year. Their sources, Worcester annals and others, overlapped with the original source, so that (for instance) s.a. 1202 there are three accounts of the capture of Prince Arthur at Mirebeau.[36] Duplication of this sort was incidental to the normal habit of supplementing annals copied from one book by reference to another. It was most likely to arise when the annalist had access to several books of pre-digested annals; and this may well

35 *Ann. Mon.*, IV, pp. xxxix–xl. Cf. the doublet in the Waverley annals for the Third Lateran Council of 1179 (*Ann. Mon.*, II, 214) and the two eulogies of Abbot Walter in the Tewkesbury annals, s.a. 1202 and 1205 (*ibid.*, I, 56–8).
36 F.23ʳ. For an edition and critical study of the Winchcomb annals, 1182–1232, see the unpublished M.A. thesis (Manchester, 1949) of Mr. Eric John.

have been the position of the Dunstable compiler, filling out his local information with news of public characters and affairs, for the years 1220–42. But for the period 1210–19, when doublets are few and the chronology is confused, when the information is copious and excellent though the dating of it is wrong, a different method of composition is more likely. In the light of the observations made above one may envisage the following process.

Prior Richard de Morins had borrowed the St. Albans Diceto in 1210 to lay foundations for annals of his own time. He had begun the work of extraction himself but soon handed over the task to one of his canons. For the years 1200–10, when Diceto failed him, he could trust to his own experiences and memory for some information. That the scribe who wrote in 1210 was relying largely on personal reminiscences is implied by the comparative scarcity of precise dates in the earlier years, the greater precision as he approached 1210. The annals were brought up to date by the time Diceto's book had to be returned to St. Albans; though a few of the items for those years found in *Tib.* were probably added later. For the future the prior – if he took an interest in the sequel – may have proposed the method which the Winton-Waverley annalist wished to be observed. Pencilled notes of important events were to be jotted down as they were reported, and these were to be digested and edited annually. But his advice was a counsel of perfection: the Dunstable annals show what might actually happen. When we look at the annals for 1210–19 in *Tib.* – with their abundance of good material, evidence of later writing, and gross mistakes of dating – it is easy to imagine a background of rough jottings on odd scraps of parchment, allowed to accumulate in chaos and only edited when it was much too late. It may have been only about 1220 that something was done to bring order out of chaos, and then the work was not done intelligently. It is hardly credible that the existing muddle could have arisen if Prior Richard himself had supervised the compilation. But it is unlikely that the delay was longer. For from about 1220 onwards the standard of record-keeping was much higher and another and better compiler was at work. He made no attempt to revise the preceding annals; but for the future he introduced much better order. The range of information is now very wide, extending often to continental affairs; the entries are on an ampler scale than before; and documents concerning Dunstable Priory are sometimes quoted in full. Whereas the entries under the years 1200–9 occupy four and a half of Luard's printed pages and those under the years 1210–19 occupy twenty-four, the annals for 1220–29 fill sixty-eight pages, and those for 1230–41 nearly thirty-four. Perhaps Prior Richard, having observed the failure of the annalist to do his job properly between 1210 and 1219, lent a hand or kept an eye on the work during the rest of his priorate. He may have contributed items of his own. His academic interests had been revived by a year at Paris, and he may have had contacts there. This would explain the obituary on Philip Augustus, "pater populi et mater scolarium," and several entries about the university of Paris and the English scholars there (pp. 81, 97–98, 116, 125).[37] It is a plausible conjecture, but nothing more. The character and scale of the annals do not abruptly change when Richard de Morins dies in 1242. One detail, nevertheless, points to a change of direction in the year after his death. The annal for 1243 begins: "Anno incipiente a festo Annunciationis dominice" (p. 161, cf. p. 167). This marks an innovation, for although the practice of calculating the year of grace from 25 March was already very common in the English church, some chroniclers still preferred to reckon from Christmas to Christmas.[38] Diceto had used the Christmas dating;[39] and there are a few indications in the Dunstable annals, s.a. 1203, 1206, and 1221 which come near to proving – what is suggested by other entries – that the compilers used the same system.

Since much of this paper has been devoted to the shortcomings of the annals of Dunstable, it may be as well to conclude by endorsing Luard's high estimate of their historical value (p. xxxii). As they advance through the thirteenth century they give an incomparable view of the ordinary secular proceedings of an English monastery,[40] and at the same time preserve the texts of records and make interesting comments on public events, amplifying our information from other quarters. The prior of Dunstable, after all, was a man of some consequence, and the priory, about thirteen miles northwest of St.

37 No other English chronicler speaks of Philip Augustus in these terms (few do more than record his death) and none mentions the troubles of the University of Paris during the twenties.
38 Cf. Mr. Denholm-Young's comment on a change of practice in this matter in the Winchester-Hyde chronicle in 1261, *EHR*, xlix, 88–89.
39 Diceto, ii, 124.
40 The cartulary, calendared by G. H. Fowler, adds important documentation at many points.

The Ordines of the Third Recension of the Medieval English Coronation Order J. BRÜCKMANN

he broad outlines of the evolution of the medieval English coronation order are well known.[1] The extant liturgical *ordines* which determine the celebration of a coronation have been classified into four groupings, each containing texts that are generally similar to each other. These groupings fit readily into a chronological sequence; they are therefore referred to as the First, Second, Third, and Fourth

1 For major contributions towards the study of medieval English coronations, cf. the following works by B. Wilkinson: "The Coronation of Edward II," *Historical Essays in Honour of James Tait*, ed. J. G. Edwards, V. H. Galbraith and E. F. Jacob (Manchester, 1933), pp. 405–16; "The Coronation Oath of Edward II and the Statute of York," *Speculum*, XIX (1944), 445–69; *Constitutional History of Medieval England, 1216–1399*, (London, 1952), II, pp. 11ff, 85–111; *The Coronation in History* (Historical Association Pamphlet, G 23, general series; London, 1953); "Notes on the Coronation Records of the Fourteenth Century," *EHR*, LXX (1955), 581–600; *The Constitutional History of Medieval England* (London, 1958), III, pp. 72–111.

For a bibliography of primary sources for medieval English coronations, see P. E. Schramm, *A History of the English Coronation* (Oxford, 1937), Appendix, pp. 233–40, and especially P. E. Schramm, "Ordines-Studien II: die Krönung in England vom 10. Jahrhundert bis zur Neuzeit," *Archiv für Urkundenforschung in Verbindung mit dem Reichsinstitut für ältere deutsche Geschichtskunde*, xv (1938), Neue Folge, I (Heft 2), 305–91 (which also lists the earlier secondary sources, 306–9); as well as "Ordines-Studien III, Anhang" and "Nachträge zu den Ordines-Studien II–III," *ibid.*, XVI (1939), Neue Folge, II, 279–86. For a brief bibliography of some of the more important secondary sources, see R. S. Hoyt, "The Coronation Oath of 1308: The Background of 'Les leys et les custumes,'" *Traditio*, XI (1955), 235, n.1.

In addition to the works cited in these bibliographies, a list of the principal secondary sources contributing towards the study of the medieval English coronation order should also include the following: J. A. Robinson, "The Coronation in the Tenth Century," *J. Theological Studies*, XIX (1917), 56–72; Hope Emily Allen, "A Thirteenth Century Coronation Rubric," *Church Quarterly R.*, XCV (1922–23), 335–41; P. E. Schramm, "Die Krönung bei den Westfranken und Angelsachsen von 878 bis um 1000," *Zeitschrift der*

Recensions of the coronation order, respectively,[2] on the assumption
that a current form of the order was always used for all coronations
until a new recension was created to be used for all subsequent
coronations. On this basis it has thus far been generally accepted that
all medieval English coronations from 1308 onwards were celebrated
according to some form of the Fourth Recension, and that the coronations of the twelfth and thirteenth centuries were celebrated according to the Third Recension.[3] At present there seems little doubt
that the late medieval English coronations, starting with the coronation of Richard II in 1377, were performed according to the complete
and final form of the medieval order as it is preserved in the *Liber
Regalis* of Westminster Abbey and in the Missal of Abbot Litlington
of Westminster Abbey;[4] while the *ordo* used for the coronation of
Edward III has not yet been identified (if it was different from that
prepared for his predecessor's coronation), the order for the corona-

Savigny-Stiftung für Rechtsgeschichte, LIV (1934), Kanonistische Abteilung,
XXIII, 117–242; P. L. Ward, "The Coronation Ceremony in Mediaeval England," *Speculum*, XIV (1939), 160–78; E. Müller, *Die Anfänge der Königssal-
bung im Mittelalter* (Köln, 1939); P. L. Ward, "An Early Version of the
Anglo-Saxon Coronation Ceremony," *EHR*, LVII (1942), 345–61; Carl Erd-
mann, *Forschungen zur politischen Ideenwelt des Frühmittelalters* (Berlin,
1951), pp. 52–91; R. S. Hoyt, "The Coronation Oath of 1308," *EHR*, LXXI
(1956), 353–83; C. A. Bouman, *Sacring and Crowning* (Bijdragen van het
Instituut voor Middeleeuwse Geschiedenis der Rijksuniversiteit te Utrecht,
Groningen, 1957); C. A. Bouman, "De Oorsprong van de rituele zalving der
koningen," *Opstellen aangeboden aan Prof. Dr. D. Th. Enklaar* (Groningen,
1959), pp. 64–85; H. G. Richardson, "The Coronation in Medieval England:
The Evolution of the Office and the Oath," *Traditio*, XVI (1960), 111–202;
H. G. Richardson, and G. O. Sayles, *The Governance of Mediaeval England
from the Conquest to Magna Carta* (Edinburgh, 1963), pp. 136–52, 397–412.

2 Other nomenclatures have occasionally been used. Earlier English scholars
have at times referred to the Second Recension as the order for the coronation of Aethelred, and to the Third Recension as the order of Henry I, on the
basis of ms. attributions of highly dubious reliability (cf. the description of
ms. *B, infra*). P. E. Schramm, who first succeeded in establishing some order
in the interrelations of the numerous coronation *ordines*, calls the First
Recension the "Dunstan-Ordo," the Second the "Edgar-Ordo," the Third the
"Anselm-Ordo," and subdivides the Fourth into the order for Edward II and
the "Lytlington-Ordo." In spite of the fundamental importance of Schramm's
work, however, we follow here the numerical nomenclature which is now
more usual.

3 Richardson, "The Coronation in Medieval England," suggests that no English coronation was ever celebrated according to the Third Recension, but
that a "Roman order" was used instead. This suggestion is not convincing
and will be discussed below.

4 Schramm's "Lytlington-Ordo"; the text is published in L. G. W. Legg,
English Coronation Records (Westminster, 1901), pp. 81–112.

tion of Edward II is well known as the first form of the Fourth Recension to be used for a coronation.[5]

For the twelfth and thirteenth centuries, however, our knowledge of English coronations is much more conjectural. The so-called "official" documents (e.g. the entries in the patent rolls) are usually above suspicion as to the reliability of their information. Unhappily such documents are as a rule extremely brief; they merely note the occurrence of the event without any elaborate description. The most we can usually learn from these sources is merely the fact that the king was crowned, the place and date of the coronation, and sometimes the name of the celebrant. The reports of chroniclers, while usually much fuller than "official" documents, are never complete in their citations of the texts of prayers, blessings, or other formulae. And even though, unlike *ordines*, chronicles state explicitly which particular coronation they describe, the reliability of the description is hardly ever completely above suspicion. The chronicler himself may well not have been an eyewitness to the coronation, in which case he will probably have relied on some *ordo* for his description of it; this *ordo* may or may not have been a copy of the order actually used for the coronation. It is therefore not inconceivable that a chronicle may give a very detailed report of a coronation which never occurred as reported, for the simple reason that the *ordo* on the basis of which the chronicler thought he was describing the event had not been used to celebrate it. Such an error is particularly likely in view of the fact that a liturgical *ordo* is never intended for only one celebration of a ceremony, but is deemed authoritative for all celebrations of ceremonies of this kind, on the assumption that each would normally be celebrated exactly as it had been on previous occasions. This assumption would encourage a chronicler to treat the order as if it were fixed and invariable, and to treat each *ordo* as an equally reliable text of this invariable order. That *ordines* do, in fact, vary in

5 Slightly different forms of this order are extant in the following mss.: Brit. Mus.,ms. Harley 2901; Bodleian Library (Oxon), ms. Rawlinson C 425; Brit.Mus.ms. Harley 3763; Bodleian Library (Oxon), ms. Ashmolean 842; Brit.Mus.ms. Cotton Vitellius C XII; Brit.Mus.ms. Cotton Cleopatra D VII; Public Record Office, Coronation Roll 1 (C.57/1); Brit.Mus.ms. Royal 12 D III; Brit.Mus.ms. Hargrave 496; Exeter Cathedral, Exchequer Chamber, ms. Liber Pontificalis of Edmund Lacy. The text of the Public Record Office ms. is published in Thomas Rymer, *Foedera, conventiones, litterae* etc. (London, 1818), II, i, pp. 33–6; the edition of the *Liber Pontificalis of Edmund Lacy* by Ralph Barnes (Exeter, 1847), pp. 137–52 has a faulty and unreliable text.

their respective texts, and that changes are introduced from time to time into the order, does not alter this basic assumption. Anything a chronicler says must consequently be treated with a great deal of caution.

This leaves the *ordines* themselves as the remaining source of information. For such a purpose a liturgical *ordo* is far more useful than either an "official" document or a chronicler's report, for two reasons: it contains more precise information than other sources because, to be effective in its purpose, it must provide detailed information on all aspects of the ceremony which are deemed important, especially on the precise words of prayers, blessings, and other liturgical formulae; it is more reliable than other sources because it is liturgically authoritative, that is, while other sources describe an event, a liturgical *ordo* prescribes it. If, therefore, it can be ascertained that a specific *ordo* was in the hands of the archbishop at the celebration of a particular coronation, this *ordo* will be both the most complete and the most reliable source of information. If this cannot be ascertained, it is almost as useful to show what form of the order was used, and what relation this form has to other forms of the same recension, or what forms of the order were accepted as liturgically authoritative.

Since the Fourth Recension was created for the coronation of Edward II in 1308,[6] and since the Second Recension had apparently already been altered for the coronation of William the Conqueror[7] and was surely obsolete by the end of the eleventh century, the *ordines* which obviously come first into consideration for the coronations of the twelfth and thirteenth centuries are those of the Third Recension. It is therefore not surprising that until recently it has been generally assumed that the English coronations of the twelfth and thirteenth centuries were celebrated according to the Third Recension. Although a critical edition of the text of the *ordines* of the Third Recension has yet to be published,[8] an examination of the manuscripts containing *ordines* of the Third Recension, and a comparison of these texts with other coronation liturgies, can shed some light on

---

6 Cf. the articles by Wilkinson cited *supra* n.1, for the evidence that the text of the coronation oath of this recension was created immediately before the coronation of Edward II.

7 Corpus Christi College (Cantab), ms. 44; cf. P. E. Schramm, "Ordines-Studien III," No. 10, p. 317.

8 I propose to present such a text in my forthcoming edition of the medieval English coronation *ordines*.

the status of this Recension in the evolution of the English coronation liturgy and on some of the questions raised about the coronations of the twelfth and thirteenth centuries.

   Ordines of the Third Recension are extant in the following seven
pontificals.[9] (They will subsequently be referred to by the italicized
capital letter placed here immediately ahead of each manuscript
identification.)

A.   Cambridge, University Library, ms. Ee ii, 3, f.82ᵛ–91ʳ. The pontifical
is written in a liturgical hand of the early twelfth century. Maskell refers
to this ms. as the "Winchester Pontifical," doubtless because an early sixteenth-century note on the flyleaf indicates that it was then in the possession of St. Swithin's Priory in Winchester. While nothing definite is known
about the early history of the ms., it was probably not intended as a pontifical for a bishop of Winchester: in the order for the Holy Week liturgy
the rubrics for the office of Good Friday refer explicitly to cathedral
canons; this cannot be a reference to the monastic chapter of Winchester.
Since the *ordo* for the consecration of a bishop directs the bishop-elect to
make his profession specifically to the church of Canterbury, its place of
origin is somewhere in the province of Canterbury; it probably cannot be
determined any more closely.[10]

B.   Brit. Mus. ms. Cotton Claudius A iii, f.19ʳ–29ᵛ. The codex is a collection of texts, most of which are pertinent to a pontifical; but not all are
liturgical. It appears to consist of parts of three separate pontificals bound
into one volume. While part of the content of this compilation may well
have belonged to Bishop Osmund of Salisbury (1078–99), the general
nature of much of the material in the collection seems to indicate a provenance from the diocese of Winchester, and certainly from the province of
Canterbury. The beginning of the ms., written in a hand of the late tenth
or early eleventh century, contains an *ordo* of the Second Recension,
attributed in the ms. to the coronation of Aethelred. Immediately following
this earlier *ordo* comes the *ordo* of the Third Recension, written in a much
later and already slightly gothic hand of the twelfth century, perhaps of
the early twelfth century. A still later humanist hand has written at the
beginning of this *ordo*: "Coronatio Hen: primi Regis." An equally recent
illustration of a king between two mitred prelates, clearly much later than

9 P. E. Schramm has already briefly listed these in his "Ordines-Studien iii,"
    No. 12, p. 320.
10 For published notices of this ms., cf.: W. G. Henderson, *Liber Pontificalis
    Chr. Bainbridge* (Publications of the Surtees Society, lxi, Durham, 1875),
    p. xxxi; W. H. Frere, *Pontifical Services* (Alcuin Club Collections, iii, 1901),
    i, p. 98; H. A. Wilson, *The Pontifical of Magdalen College* (Henry Bradshaw
    Society, xxxix; London, 1910), pp. xxiv–xxv; W. Maskell, *Monumenta Ritua-
    lia Ecclesiae Anglicanae* (London, 1846), *passim*.

the text of the *ordo,* furnishes no further information about the provenance of the text.[11]

C.   Trinity College (Dublin), ms. B 3 6, fols. 149ʳ–154ᵛ. The pontifical is
written in a liturgical hand of the twelfth century and probably originated
in the province of Canterbury. It was acquired by Trinity College from
Archbishop Ussher. The contents of the ms., all pertinent to a pontifical,
are remarkably similar to those of mss. *D* and *E* described below. The
coronation *ordo* is incomplete; it is interrupted in the middle of a sentence
in the tradition of the sceptre at the bottom of f.154ᵛ. The remainder of
the *ordo,* as well as the presumably subsequent *ordo* for the coronation of
a queen, is missing. The nature of this interruption, and the fact that the
next folio starts out in a different hand, would indicate that several folios
were lost after the completion of the writing, rather than that the writing
of the coronation *ordo* was interrupted and never completed. (Nor would
these be the only missing leaves; at least two others, f.62 and f.74, have
disappeared, and a thorough examination of the whole ms. might well
reveal that still other folios were lost.) The English provenance of the
material in the ms., and its probable origin in the province of Canterbury,
are clear from the benedictional, in which special benedictions are cited for
the feasts of St. George, St. Alphege, St. Dunstan, St. Augustine, the translation of St. Alphege, and the ordination of St. Dunstan. In this ms.,
furthermore, the first of the litanies in the *ordo* for consecrating a church
adds St. Alphege to the standard list of saints invoked, and the second
litany adds St. Augustine and St. Dunstan.[12]

D.   Magdalen College (Oxon), ms. 226, fols. 99ʳ–110ʳ. The pontifical,
written in several liturgical hands of the twelfth century, with a few additions in thirteenth- and fourteenth-century hands, originated probably in
the archdiocese and certainly in the province of Canterbury. The ms. has
been called the "Hereford Pontifical," with the implication that it belonged

11 For published notices of this ms. cf.: J. O. Westward, *Facsimiles of the Minia-
tures and Ornaments of Anglo-Saxon and Irish Manuscripts* (1868),pp.126–7,
pl. 50; J. A. Robinson, "The Coronation Order," 56; Frere, *Pontifical
Services,* I, p. 95; E. G. Millar, *English Illuminated Manuscripts from the Xth
to the XIIth Century* (Paris and Brussels, 1926), p. 79, pl. 27b; D. Talbot
Rice, *English Art, 871–1100* (Oxford, 1952), p. 197; H. A. Wilson, *The Benedictional of Archbishop Robert* (Henry Bradshaw Society, xxiv; London,
1903), pp. xviii, xix, 168–98 *passim;* G. Ellard, *Ordination Anointings in the
Western Church Before 1000 A.D.* (Cambridge, 1933), pp. 80, 81; J. Planta,
A Catalogue of the Mss. in the Cottonian Library (1802), p. 188; Henderson,
Liber Pont., pp. xx, 268.
12 Despite a suggestion to the contrary by Henderson (*Liber Pont.,* p. xxxiii),
who states that St. Alphege is the only English saint mentioned in this
pontifical. For other published notices of this ms. cf.: Wilson, *The Pontifical
of Magdalen College,* p. xvi; T. K. Abbot, *Catalogue of the Mss. in the
Library of Trinity College, Dublin* (Dublin, 1900), p. 12.

to a bishop or to the cathedral of Hereford and contained the pontifical services according to the liturgy of the see of Hereford.[13] This conclusion is probably unwarranted. A note at the end of the table of contents, written in the fifteenth century, suggests perhaps that the ms. may at that time have been in Hereford. But an ambiguous fifteenth-century attribution is hardly authoritative for the provenance of a twelfth-century pontifical. The pontifical does, however, furnish real clues about its provenance in at least two places and both of these point to the see of Canterbury, not to the see of Hereford. The *ordo* for the *benedictio monachorum* formulates the monk's profession in the presence of an archbishop. While this makes sense in a Canterbury pontifical, a pontifical intended for Hereford would surely refer here to a bishop rather than to an archbishop. In the *ordo* for the installation of an abbot, the abbot-elect promises canonical obedience to the church and bishop of Canterbury rather than of Hereford; that is, it is taken for granted that the abbot to be installed is in the archdiocese of Canterbury.[14]

E.   Trinity College (Cantab), ms. B 11 10, fols. 104^r–110^r. The pontifical occupies fols. 7–124 of the ms. The first ninety-seven folios of the pontifical are written in a liturgical hand of the mid-twelfth century. H. A. Wilson dates the writing around 1150–75, and sees in it "some traces of the style of Christ Church, Canterbury."[15] The last twenty-one folios, beginning with the coronation *ordo*, are in a somewhat more recent liturgical hand, probably of the second half of the twelfth century. Wilson attempts to connect this latter part with the see of Ely,[16] but the evidence for such a specific provenance is very slender. A notation in a sixteenth-century hand mentions the name of Augustinus Styward among some heraldic sketches in the first six pages. M. R. James suggests that this must be a reference to the sixteenth-century mayor of Norwich, whose relative, Robert Styward, was the last prior of Ely.[17] This certainly does not prove that the pontifical was in the possession of the see of Ely, even in the sixteenth century, and it tells us absolutely nothing about the provenance, ownership, or place of use of the ms. four centuries earlier. The only other indication which

13 Henderson, *Liber Pont.*, p. xxxii, and W. H. Frere, *Bibliotheca Musico-Liturgica* (1894), I, p. 152.
14 The whole ms. has been published in Wilson, *The Pontifical of Magdalen College*; for a detailed examination of the ms. cf. Wilson's preface to this work, pp. vii–xxxii.
15 Wilson, *The Pontifical of Magdalen College*, p. xiv. The ms. also contains a letter, dated 26 January 1910, from H. A. Wilson to the Librarian, stating in part: "The main part of this book is, I think, of Canterbury origin and there are some features in the handwriting which seem to suggest that it was written at Christ Church, Canterbury."
16 *Ibid.*, p. xiv.
17 M. R. James, *The Western Manuscripts in Trinity College, Cambridge* (Cambridge, 1900), I, p. 348.

Wilson finds to suggest Ely as the place of origin is indeed contemporary, but does not point unambiguously to Ely. He says that "the names of saints invoked in the litanies for the sick seem clearly to point to Ely as the place for which this part of the book was written."[18] This is an overstatement. Nine saints whose cult is local to England are included in these two litanies; of these nine, three are associated with Ely, two with Minster in Thanet, two with Winchester, and two have the common veneration of England in general and the province of Canterbury in particular. The attribution of this part of the pontifical to Ely is therefore not convincing. Since the content of the manuscript is strikingly similar to that containing *ordo D* (as suggested in the description of *ordo C* above), and since at least the coronation *ordo* in this manuscript is a direct copy of *ordo D* (as will be indicated below), the relation of *D* to *E* would suggest that *E* is not a compilation of two fragments, and that Wilson's attribution of the greater part of the pontifical to Christ Church Canterbury might be equally valid for the last twenty-one folios containing the coronation order. This probability is strengthened by the provenance of ms. *D* from the archdiocese of Canterbury. *Ordo E* is therefore certainly from the province of Canterbury and probably from the archdiocese of Canterbury.[19]

F. Brit. Mus. ms. Cotton Tiberius B vIII, fols. 81ʳ–105ᵛ. Except for the coronation book of Charles v, which is a later addition to the manuscript and is now bound separately, the pontifical is written in a very clear early gothic liturgical hand of the late twelfth century. The order for the consecration of a bishop indicates that the pontifical was intended for use in the province of Canterbury. No clue, however, is provided towards the identification of the diocese. The order for the consecration of an abbot refers explicitly to the diocese of Glasgow, but this is much later, perhaps fourteenth century; if there was ever an earlier reference to a diocese in the province of Canterbury, it is now completely illegible.[20]

G. Bodleian Library (Oxon), ms. Rawlinson C 400, fols. 51ᵛ–87ᵛ. The pontifical was written in the early fourteenth century, when it was the property of the cathedral of Salisbury. The coronation *ordo* is incomplete; the text breaks off at the bottom of f.87ᵛ in the middle of the second ora-

18 Wilson, *The Pontifical of Magdalen College*, p. xiv.
19 For published notices of this ms. cf.: *ibid.*, p. xiv; M. R. James, *The Western Manuscripts*, I, pp. xx, 348–50.
20 The *ordo* is published in Legg, *English Coronation Records*, pp. 31–42. For other published notices of this ms. cf.: Planta, *Cat. Mss. Cotton*, p. 36; Henderson, *Liber Pont.*, p. xxxiv (also his *Manuale et Processionale ad Usum insignis Eboracensis ...*, Surtees Society, 63, 1875, p. 211). The *ordo* of Charles v is published in E. S. Dewick, *The Coronation Book of Charles V of France* (Henry Bradshaw Society, XVI, 1899), and the ms. is discussed by L. Delisle, "Notes sur quelques manuscrits du Musée Brittanique," in *Mémoires de la Société de l'histoire de Paris*, IV (1877), 226–9.

tion of the *ordo* for the coronation of a queen. Presumably several folios are missing at this point, even though the subsequently inscribed foliation continues without indicating a lacuna. The provenance of the pontifical is clearly indicated by a contemporary note at the bottom of the first folio: "Hunc librum legavit dominus Rogerus de Martival, Saresbiriensis episcopus, ecclesie cathedrali beate Marie Saresbiriensi. ..." Roger de Martival was Bishop of Salisbury from 1315 to 1329; nothing in the appearance of this manuscript, nor in what little is known of its subsequent history, puts the reliability of this note into question. The pontifical was probably in use at Salisbury in the fourteenth century. The only point which throws any doubt on its actual use is precisely the coronation *ordo* investigated here. It may at first appear strange that a pontifical of the fourteenth century should still reproduce the coronation order in the form of the Third Recension, when the Fourth Recension was already well established and had actually been used as early as 1308, seven years before the beginning of Roger de Martival's pontificate. There is, however, no reason why we must assume that a change introduced into the liturgy of the coronation, presumably in Westminster, must necessarily have come to the attention of the see of Salisbury within a few years, or that, even if such a change was known in Salisbury, a scribe copying a pontifical must have taken it into consideration, particularly since all the models at his disposal would no doubt still have presented the coronation order according to the Third Recension. Furthermore, the differences between the Third and the Fourth Recensions are not so overwhelming as to make it impossible for such a scribe to consider the coronation ceremony as being essentially the same, regardless of which recension furnishes his particular text.[21]

While the place of origin of three of these seven pontificals cannot be located in any particular diocese, two are known to come from Canterbury, one from Winchester, and one from Salisbury; all are English, and all are clearly the product of the province of Canterbury. With the exception of one late copy, all are of the twelfth century; at least one, and perhaps two, date from the early part of the century. The picture which emerges from this is one of a coronation order which appears early in the twelfth century in the province of Canterbury, gains very rapid acceptance throughout this province in the authoritative liturgical books, and appears to have become the sole form of the coronation order acceptable to English pontificals of the twelfth and thirteenth centuries. No other form of a coronation order

---

21 The text is published in Henderson, *Liber Pont.*, pp. 214–24, and in part in the *Liber Regalis* published by the Roxburghe Club (London, 1870), pp. 59–60. For notices of this ms. cf.: Henderson, *ibid.*, p. xxxvii, and W. D. Macray, *Catalogi codicum manuscriptorum Bibliothecae Bodleianae*, v, 185.

has been found in any of the extant English pontificals of this period, nor is there any evidence which would indicate that such another form ever existed in authoritative liturgical texts intended for use in England during these two centuries.[22]

P. E. Schramm has pointed out[23] (and both P. L. Ward and H. G. Richardson[24] have recently reiterated) that the compilation of the Third Recension was achieved by a conflation of texts taken from the Second Recension with texts taken from the coronation order in the "Roman" pontifical created in the tenth century (probably around 961) in the Abbey of St. Alban at Mainz, which Andrieu called "pontifical romano-germanique."[25] Schramm, however, did not specify which of the versions of this *Mainzer Ordo* served as a source for the compilation of the Third Recension. Richardson, who attempts a tabulation of the three orders in parallel columns, quotes indiscriminately from different forms of the *Romano-Germanicum*, as if they all contained the same texts, and thus constructs as one of the sources of the Third Recension an artificial conflation of texts which he selects as he needs them from different *ordines* of the *Romano-Germanicum*.[26] The recent publication of the edition of the *Pontificale Romano-Germanicum* by C. Vogel and R. Elze provides a text which furnishes the solution to the problem of the "Roman" source of the Third Recension.[27] The form of the *Romano-Germanicum* used as a model for the Third Recension is that still extant in two of the manuscripts used by Vogel and Elze in their edition: Wolfenbüttel, Herz.-August-Bibl., cod. 603 (*R*) and Vienna, Nationalbibliothek, cod. lat. 701 (*T*).[28] Of all the manuscripts Vogel and Elze use to estab-

---

22 An argument *ex silentio* is, of course, never completely convincing, but it strongly suggests that the Third Recension was authoritative for English practice in the twelfth and thirteenth centuries.
23 Schramm, "Ordines-Studien III," 321–3.
24 Ward, "The Coronation Ceremony," 174–6; Richardson, "The Coronation in Medieval England," 177–80.
25 M. Andrieu, *Le Pontifical romain au moyen-âge: I, Le Pontifical romain au XIIᵉ siècle* (Città del Vaticano, 1938), p. 4.
26 Richardson, "The Coronation in Medieval England," 178–80. The texts of the "Roman" order are selected from P. E. Schramm, "Die Krönung in Deutschland bis zum Beginn des Salischen Hauses," *Zeitschrift der Savigny-Stiftung für Rechtsgeschichte*, LV (1935), Kanonistische Abteilung, XXIV, pp. 309–24, and 325–32.
27 C. Vogel and R. Elze, *Le Pontifical romano-germanique du dixième siècle* (Città del Vaticano, 1963), I, pp. 246–61.
28 For a description of ms. *R*, cf. M. Andrieu, *Les Ordines romani* (Louvain, 1961), V, pp. 4–14; for a description of ms. *T*, cf. *ibid.*, I (1931), pp. 373–88.

lish their text, these two share a considerable number of significant mistakes and textual variants from the primitive form of the order of Mainz which are all reproduced in the *ordines* of the Third Recension. The general shape of the coronation order in these two manuscripts is an alteration of the order of Mainz and comes closest to a shape of the "Roman" order published by Melchior Hittorp as *Ordo romanus antiquus*.[29]

Thus far, the *ordines* of the Third Recension have usually been treated as if they were all identical, or at least as if the Third Recension consisted of only one form of the coronation order. This, unfortunately, is not so. While the differences between the various forms of this recension are not quite as obvious as the differences between the families of the Fourth Recension, the extant *ordines* of the Third Recension contain enough significant variations to indicate that this recension of the order underwent some deliberate alterations and re-workings. These variations occur in a pattern which is regular enough to allow the classification of these *ordines* into several families, as subdivisions of the Third Recension.

In almost every case an *ordo* of the Third Recension consists of two clearly differentiated parts: the order for the coronation of a king and the order for the coronation of a queen. Significant variations, on the basis of which the *ordines* can be grouped into families, occur in both these parts. If, for the moment, the order for the coronation of a king in all these *ordines* is examined separately from that for a queen, it becomes apparent that the Third Recension contains two distinct forms of the order. A comparison of each of these two forms with both the Second Recension[30] and the coronation order in the *Pontificale Romano-Germanicum*[31] (as the two sources for the Third Recension), as well as with the Fourth Recension,[32] indicates

29 M. Hittorp, *De divinis catholicae Ecclesiae officiis et mysteriis, etc.* (Paris, 1610), coll. 147–52.
30 The *ordines* of the Second Recension used to establish this correlation are those in the following mss.: Brit.Mus.ms. Cotton Claudius A III; Rouen, Bibliothèque municipale, mss. 368, 369; Corpus Christi College (Cantab), ms. 146; Bibl. Nat. ms. lat. 943.
31 The *ordines* of the *Romano-Germanicum* used to establish this correlation are those in Wolfenbüttel, Herz.-August-Bibl., cod. 603, and in Vienna, Nationalbibliothek, cod. lat. 701, as cited by Vogel and Elze in their edition of the pontifical (n.26 *supra*).
32 The text of the Fourth Recension used to establish this correlation is an unpublished edition of the first form of this recension (based on Brit.Mus. ms. Harley 2901) which I prepared as part of a doctoral dissertation under the direction of Professor Wilkinson.

clearly that one of these two forms is older than the other. Wherever the two forms differ, the same one is always in agreement either with the text of the Second Recension or with the text of the *Romano-Germanicum*, while the other agrees in these places with the text of the Fourth Recension. Evidently the later form of the order is the result of some alterations in the earlier form, and served in turn as a source for the Fourth Recension when the earlier form of the Third Recension had already been completely discarded. This relative dating of the two forms is supported by the general principle that as liturgical ceremonies develop they usually tend to become more rather than less complex, and the rubrics tend to become longer and more detailed. The relative dating is further confirmed by the fact that *ordo A*, which is contained in what is clearly the oldest of the manuscripts, has the earlier form. On the basis of the form of the order for a king only, the seven *ordines* of the Third Recension can thus be divided into two groups: one group consisting of those *ordines* containing the earlier form, and the other of those containing the later.[33]

If these seven *ordines* are now compared to each other on the basis of their order for the coronation of a queen (and on this basis only, excluding any attention to the order for a king investigated in the previous paragraph), such an examination will again reveal the existence of two clearly separate forms of the order. Again, a relative dating of the two forms can be established on the basis of a comparison of each of these two forms of the order for a queen with the sources and with the Fourth Recension. This relative dating is again supported by the general principle that liturgical ceremonies become longer and more complex and by the fact that the oldest *ordo* has the older version. Again, the *ordines* might be classified into two separate families on the basis of this examination of the order for the queen.[34]

33 The text of the earlier form of the order for a king is printed in Legg, *English Coronation Records*, pp. 30–6. The text of the later form is printed in Wilson, *The Pontifical of Magdalen College*, pp. 89–95.

34 The references to the printed texts of the two forms of the order for a queen are the reverse of those cited in n.28 for the two forms of the order for a king. The earlier form for a queen is in Wilson, *The Pontifical of Magdalen College*, pp. 95–7; the later form for a queen is in Legg, *English Coronation Records*, pp. 37–9. The difference between the opinion of Richardson, "The Coronation in Medieval England," p. 175, and the earlier opinion shared by Wilson and Ward (cf. *ibid.*, p. 175, n.6) about which of these two printed texts represents the earlier form can thus be settled by a compromise on the basis of a distinction between the evolution of the order for a king and the

Unhappily these two criteria do not result in a similar classification of the seven *ordines*. We have, rather, a triple classification into three families of *ordines*. The first family consists only of *ordo A*, which has the earlier form of the order for a king and the earlier form of the order for a queen. The second family consists of *ordines B, C, D,* and *E*, which have the later form for a king and the earlier form for a queen. The third family consists of *ordines F* and *G* which have the earlier form for a king and the later for a queen. No *ordo* has both the later form for a king and the later form for a queen.

Even though *ordo A* is both the oldest (judged on the basis of the dating of the hand) and the most archaic (since it has the earlier form for both the king and the queen) of the seven *ordines*, a simple comparison of the variants in the texts indicates that it cannot possibly be the original *ordo* from which other *ordines* of the Third Recension are descended; nor can any of the other *ordines* be this original since all the others contain either the later form for the king or the later form for the queen. The original *ordo* of the Third Recension is thus not available and probably no longer extant.

Evidently, from this lost original *ordo* three separate lines of filiation descended, each with its own development. *Ordo A* reproduces the original as closely as it is now possible to ascertain. The *ordines* of the second family, *B, C, D,* and *E*, are descendants of a lost *ordo* which we shall call *X*, in which the later form for the king had been substituted for the earlier form found in the original, without changing the order for the queen. The *ordines* of the third family, *F* and *G*, are descendants of a lost *ordo* which we shall call *Y*, in which the later form for the queen had been substituted for the earlier form found in the original without changing the order for the king. Within the second family, *D* is clearly a direct copy of *C*; it reproduces all the significant variants of *C* and has a few more of its own. The same kind of evidence indicates that *E* is a direct copy of *D*. *Ordo B*, however, does not fit into this straight line of filiation from *C* to *D* to *E* as ancestor, link, or descendant; nevertheless both *B* and *C* must have had *X* as their common ancestor. In the third family, neither *F* nor *G* was copied from the other, but both share *Y* as their common ancestor. The pattern of filiation for the *ordines* of the Third Recension can thus be indicated by the following stemma:

evolution of the order for a queen: Richardson was right for the order for a king; Wilson and Ward were right for the order for a queen.

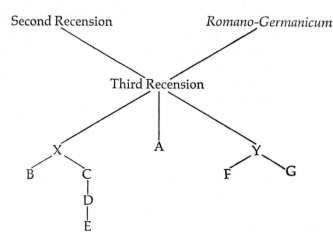

This stemma indicates that both the later form for the coronation
of the king and the later form for the coronation of the queen appeared very soon after the original compilation of the Third Recension, even if it does not indicate exactly how soon. Nor has it yet
been possible to specify which *ordo* or even which family of the
Third Recension was used for which of the coronations in the twelfth
and thirteenth centuries.[35] In any case, however, it is clear that the
second family had currency not only in the province, but also specifically in the see of Canterbury; this was exactly the period when the
archbishop of Canterbury succeeded (not without a struggle) in
having his right as sole ordinary celebrant of English coronations
prevail over the rival claims of the archbishop of York. Both the
second and the third families, however were deemed to represent the
authoritative English practice by the authors of the Fourth Recension, since both the later form for the king in the second family and
the later form for the queen in the third family were used as sources
for the compilation of the Fourth Recension.

H. G. Richardson raises a new and more basic question by his
recent suggestion that no English coronation was ever celebrated
according to an *ordo* of the Third Recension and in his attempt to
relegate these *ordines* to the status of a liturgical sport, a blind alley

35 The suggestion in Ralf de Diceto, *Historical Works* (Rolls Series, 68), ii, 69,
   that Richard i was anointed with chrism might perhaps indicate a use of an
   ordo of the second family (only the later form for a king prescribes an
   unction with chrism) in 1189, or perhaps from 1189 on; but such a suggestion must be treated very cautiously.

in the development of texts completely divorced from real liturgical practice.[36] The order which Richardson suggests was used instead of the Third Recension was some form of the *Romano-Germanicum*.[37] This is altogether unlikely, and therefore deserves a few brief final comments. Perhaps the strongest argument is simply that no *ordo* which fits Richardson's specifications exists, nor is there any direct evidence anywhere indicating that it ever did. That Richardson finds discrepancies between the text of the Third Recension and the reports of some chroniclers is not surprising; what is perhaps more noteworthy is rather that the generally very brief or liturgically sketchy reports by chroniclers do not contain more apparent inconsistencies with the text of the Third Recension.[38] In almost every case, the apparent incompatibility disappears if we keep in mind that an *ordo* (especially a medieval *ordo* with very rudimentary rubrics) does not specify every action that occurs, but rather provides a prescription for the spoken or sung words accompanying the actions; actions without accompanying liturgical formulae as well as "non-liturgical" actions can be inserted into the ceremony later, without being mentioned in the *ordo* and without violating its prescriptions. Nor can a chronicle be expected to report everything which occurs at a coronation; and the two need not coincide in what they select for mention. Roger of Howden's report of the coronation of Richard I, which constitutes Richardson's chief evidence against the use of the Third Recension, is a good example of this.[39] While it may well be based on a directory which is no longer extant, there is nothing in this report (and presumably, therefore, nothing in the directory), which is absolutely incompatible with an *ordo* of the Third Recension; but some details are incompatible with the *ordines* of the *Romano-Germanicum*. Richardson's attempt to explain these away,

36 Richardson, "The Coronation in Medieval England,"
37 *Ibid.*, p. 185.
38 The only real difficulty in reconciling chronicles with the liturgical text lies in the citation of the coronation oath in some of the chronicles. But even there, the oath cited is far more easily compatible with the oath in the Third Recension than with any oath found in an *ordo* of the *Romano-Germanicum*. This is particularly clear in the case of the oath cited by Roger of Howden in his report of the coronation of Richard I, which will be discussed immediately below. Howden reports the oath in indirect quotation: he paraphrases it rather than reproducing the king's *ipsissima verba*; the text which he paraphrases, however, is quite clearly not an oath of the Romano-Germanicum, but rather the oath of the Third Recension.
39 Roger of Howden, *Chronica Magistri Rogeri de Hovedene* (Rolls Series, 51), III, 9–11; cf. Richardson, "The Coronation in Medieval England," 181–9.

on the basis of Howden's alleged mistakes,[40] creates more difficulties than it solves. Nor is the absence of a proper coronation mass a convincing argument against the use of the Third Recension. Obviously the coronation was celebrated in conjunction with a mass; but many sacramentaries and most *missalia plena* (they had become numerous and readily available by the twelfth century)[41] contained a *missa pro rege*, and usually several of them for different occasions. (Or it could be simply the "mass of the day" that was celebrated.)[42] In the cases in which the reports of chroniclers appear to be difficult to reconcile with the Third Recension, they are even more difficult (or actually impossible) to reconcile with a "Roman" order.[43] Richardson, therefore, attempts to posit a "Roman" *ordo* (now lost) which deviates from all known *ordines* of the *Romano-Germanicum* in order to agree with the details on which he needs agreement. This attempt is unnecessary if we return to an at least tentative acceptance of the Third Recension as the form of the coronation order actually used during this period.[44] Such an acceptance is supported by the extant

40 The only evidence in Howden's account which relates unambiguously to a matter about which there is a clear difference between the prescription of the Third Recension and the prescription of the "Roman" order is his list of the sequence of the traditions of the regalia; there Howden agrees with the Third Recension and conflicts with the "Roman" order.

41 Cf. Adalbert Ebner, *Quellen und Forschungen zur Geschichte und Kunstgeschichte des Missale Romanum im Mittelalter – Iter Italicum* (Freiburg, 1896), p. 361.

42 If an *ordo* for a *missa pro rege* should not be available, or if for some other reason it should be decided not to celebrate such a mass, the mass in conjunction with which the coronation has to be performed must, of course, be the mass of the day. It is therefore interesting, and perhaps significant, that Howden (*Chron. Mag.*, III, p. 11) states: "Deinde inchoata est missa Dominicalis." (Richard I *was* crowned on a Sunday.) Since the *ordines* of the "Roman" order with which Richardson worked (cited according to P. E. Schramm, "Die Krönung in Deutschland bis zum Beginn des Salischen Hauses") have a special mass for the coronation while the *ordines* of the Third Recension do not, Howden's report that the mass of the day was celebrated is again compatible with a coronation performed according to the Third Recension, but not according to this "Roman" order.

43 Not to mention the difficulty involved in reconciling chroniclers with each other; the English *ordines* of the period, however, give a virtually unanimous testimony, aside from the relatively minor difference between the earlier and later forms of the Third Recension.

44 It also avoids the *circulus vitiosus* of attempting to establish the actual practice in England in the twelfth and thirteenth centuries without relying on the English liturgical sources because, allegedly, "we can discard the Third Recension as evidence of English practice" (Richardson, "The Coronation in Medieval England," 116) and concluding therefrom a "divergence of the Third Recension from practice" (*ibid.*, 118).

and authoritative liturgical texts: no known English pontificals of the twelfth or thirteenth centuries contain a "Roman" coronation order,[45] but the Third Recension is well documented in authoritative liturgical texts. The weight of the evidence available thus far suggests that at least for the present we must assume that English coronations of the twelfth and thirteenth centuries were celebrated according to some *ordo* of the Third Recension of the English coronation order.

45 A systematic survey of all Latin pontificals in British collections of mss. has produced only one pontifical containing a "Roman" coronation order which could have been copied in England: Corpus Christi College (Cantab.) ms. 163. Although it may perhaps have been written in Winchester (s. xi), it is not an English pontifical but rather a pontifical of Cologne. The saints included in the litany (p. 202) indicate quite clearly that it was intended for use on the Continent, in the province (and probably the diocese) of Cologne. The general nature of the contents of this pontifical agrees closely with the *Romano-Germanicum*. It provides thus for a consecration of a bishop "in romana ecclesia" followed by the preliminary examination "secundum gallos," as well as the "ordo qualiter ordinetur romanus pontifex"; in addition to the "Roman" order for crowning a king, it also makes provisions for the imperial coronation (R. Elze, *Die Ordines für die Weihe und Krönung des Kaisers und der Kaiserin*, M.G.H., Fontes iuris germanici antiqui, IX: Ordines coronationis imperialis (Hannover, 1960), Ordines I and II). Except for a very short Winchester addition – the formula for the dedication of an image of St. Swithin (p. 285) – everything in this pontifical points towards the Continent and nothing to England. Ms. C.C.C.C. 163 is not an English pontifical.

𝕸atthew 𝕻aris and the 𝕸ongols

J. J. SAUNDERS

𝕿he *Chronica Majora* of Matthew Paris is by common consent one of the most valuable historical memorials of the middle ages. The learned monk of St. Albans was an industrious seeker after information, not without skill in evaluating his sources, accurate and reliable according to the standards of his time, and wrote a Latin style characterized by a recent critic as "forceful, vigorous and direct ... blunt and straightforward, yet often lively and colourful."[1] Though he left the shores of England perhaps only once in his life, his outlook is far from insular and he never forgets that he is a member of the church universal. The events of the reign of Henry III are narrated in detail, but as often as he is drawn to refer to happenings outside the kingdom he enters into a full explanation of matters beyond the knowledge and experience of his countrymen. Thus in dealing with the crusading wars, he stops to summarize the religion of Islam, the teachings of the Prophet Muhammad, and the conquests of the caliphs, and when we recall the prejudices of the age, we are surprised more by the accuracy than by the distortions of his picture.[2]

1 R. Vaughan, *Matthew Paris* (Cambridge, 1958), p. 126. The same critic has calculated that Matthew, in the course of his history, cites some 350 documents. See also the eulogistic appraisal by A. L. Smith, *Church and State in the Middle Ages* (Oxford, 1913), pp. 167–79, and the more recent verdict of V. H. Galbraith: "There is nothing in any way comparable ... either for the contemporary history of England or of the Continent. In scope and in method, if not in critical ability, the great history of Matthew Paris marks the highwater mark of medieval historical writing in England. Above all, he is outstanding by his lavish use of archive and documentary material." *Roger Wendover and Matthew Paris* (David Murray Lecture, Glasgow, 1944), p. 24.

2 An instructive inquiry might be made into the sources of Matthew Paris's knowledge of Islam. His fullest account is given s.a.1236, and purports to be a report sent to Pope Gregory IX "from the countries of the East by preachers

When he reaches the years 1238–42, he feels it necessary to say a good deal and to cite not a few documents relating to the great Mongol invasion of Eastern Europe, notwithstanding that this dreadful barbarian assault on Christendom never got anywhere near England. It is a remarkable fact, and increases our respect for Matthew, that the English chronicler has given a fuller account of this episode than have most contemporary continental writers.

He introduces the subject under the year 1238 and describes two distinct occurrences, which indeed have one thing in common: they both arose out of fear of the approach of the Mongol invaders. This is what he says:

About this time, special ambassadors were sent by the Saracens, chiefly on behalf of the Old Man of the Mountain (*principaliter ex parte Veteris de Monte*), to the French king, telling him that a monstrous and inhuman race of men had burst forth from the northern mountains, and had taken possession of the extensive, rich lands of the East; that they had depopulated Hungary Major, and had sent threatening letters, with dreadful emissaries; the chief of which declared, that he was the messenger of God on high, sent to subdue the nations who rebelled against him. ... [There follows a vivid description of the "Tartars," their repulsive appearance and unpleasant habits]. The inhabitants of Gothland and Friesland, dreading their attacks, did not, as was their custom, come to Yarmouth, in England, at the time of the herring fisheries, at which place their ships usually loaded; and owing to this, herrings in that year were considered of no value, on account of their abundance, and about forty or fifty, although very good, were sold for one piece of silver, even in places at a great

who were frequently in those parts." The authorship of this document is unknown: a good deal of it seems to be taken from the *Risalah* ("Apology") of "al-Kindi," an oriental Christian who wrote in Arabic some time before the eleventh century and whose work was translated into Latin by Peter of Toledo around 1140. (See Sir William Muir, *The Apology of Al-Kindy* [London, 1882]). Though violently hostile to the Prophet, it contains a reasonably accurate summary of Muslim belief. Unfortunately, Matthew added from some other polemical source ("a celebrated preacher of great renown, who preached in rebuke of the law of the said Mahomet"), a nauseating fiction about Muhammad's end, which makes him die of a combination of drunkenness, epilepsy, and suffocation by a litter of pigs. Most of his material was doubtless drawn from the large corpus of works on Islam produced in the mid-twelfth century under the direction of Peter the Venerable, abbot of Cluny, which included a Latin translation of the Koran by Robert of Ketton and a short but well-informed tract called *Summula brevis contra haereses et sectam Saracenorum* (the latter printed in Migne, PL, 189, cols. 651–8). See the references in Norman Daniel, *Islam and the West* (Edinburgh, 1960).

distance from the sea. This powerful and noble Saracen messenger, who had come to the French king, was sent on behalf of the whole of the people of the East, to tell these things; and he asked assistance from the Western nations, the better to be able to repress the fury of the Tartars; and he also sent a Saracen messenger from his own company to the king of England, who had arrived in England, to tell these events, and to say that if they themselves could not withstand the attacks of such people, nothing remained to prevent their devastating the countries of the West. He therefore asked assistance in this urgent and general emergency, that the Saracens, with the assistance of the Christians, might resist the attacks of these people. The Bishop of Winchester, who happened to be present, interrupted his speech, and replied jocosely, "Let us leave these dogs to devour one another, that they may all be consumed, and perish; and we, when we proceed against the enemies of Christ who remain, will slay them, and cleanse the face of the earth, so the world will be subject to the one Catholic Church, and there will be one fold and one shepherd."[3]

A puzzling and intriguing passage, in which the famous Yarmouth herring-fishery story is embedded in a much longer account of the "Saracen" embassy to the west. The Yarmouth anecdote has attracted widespread notice and become one of the best-known tales connected with the Mongols. "It is whimsical enough [says Gibbon] that the orders of a Mongol khan, who reigned on the borders of China, should have lowered the price of herrings in the English market."[4] What lies behind it? "Gotland" is no doubt the Baltic island, and "Friesland" was in this age the common term for the Netherlands. Neither was directly menaced by the Mongols in 1238 or at any other time, but the story is clearly related to the Mongol conquest of Russia and particularly to the threatened capture of Novgorod in the winter of 1237–38. Batu, the grandson of Chingiz Khan, who led the first great Mongol invasion of Europe, crossed the frozen Volga in November 1237; Riazan fell amid frightful carnage just before Christmas; Vladimir was stormed in February 1238, and the Grand Duke Yuri of Suzdal, in whose territory Vladimir lay, was defeated and slain in March on the river Sita, a tributary of the Mologa. Yaroslav and Tver were sacked, and the invaders, "the accursed godless ones" as the Novgorod Chronicle calls them,[5]

3 *Chronica Majora*, ed. H. R. Luard (Rolls Series), III, 488–9. I use in this, and in subsequent passages quoted, the translation by J. A. Giles, *Matthew Paris's English History* (Bohn series, 3 vols.; London, 1852–54).
4 *Decline and Fall of the Roman Empire*, chap. 64.
5 *The Chronicle of Novgorod* (Eng. tr. Camden Society, 1914), pp. 81–4. Cf. G. Vernadsky, *The Mongols and Russia* (New Haven, 1953), pp. 49–52.

pushed westwards towards the Valdai Hills and Lake Ilmen. The road
to Novgorod, only sixty miles or so distant, lay open; the alarm, not
to say terror, in that rich commercial city, the Venice of the north,
must have been acute; every available citizen was doubtless mobi-
lized for its defence, and its shipping and trading activities during
that perilous winter must have been seriously curtailed. By a treaty
of 1195 Novgorod had trading agreements with Gotland (whose
principal town, Visby, was a great Baltic entrepot) and the Frisians,
but the Mongol danger this year precluded it from making the usual
herring deal and the fishing fleets stayed at home. Actually, Novgorod, the approaches to which were rendered difficult by extensive
swamps and marshes, escaped capture and destruction; with the
coming of spring the Mongols retired southwards to the lower Don,
probably fearing to be caught in the floods that followed the thaw.
Next season, presumably, the herring fleets sailed as usual.[6]

All this is reasonably clear, but the alleged embassy from the "Old
Man of the Mountain" is very much of a mystery, and Matthew's
narrative is here curiously vague and deficient in detail. No names are
cited; even the place where the envoys were received by Henry III is
unidentified. Two questions arise: where did these "Saracens" come
from, and why did they seek help in the distant and infidel west?

The Old Man of the Mountain was, of course, the chief of the
Nizari Isma'ilis, better known as the Assassins, the title being a
translation of the Arabic *shaikh al-jabal*, mountain lord.[7] Says
Matthew's predecessor Roger of Wendover:

There is a race of men who inhabit the mountains in the province of Tyre,
in Phoenicia; they hold ten castles, with large districts belonging to them,
and they amount to 60,000 men, or even more. These men, not by hereditary succession, but by the claim of personal merit, elect over them a
master or preceptor, whom they call by no other name or title than "Old

---

6 Matthew Paris, in all his sixty years or so, was out of England but once,
  when he crossed the North Sea to Norway at the request of King Haakon IV
  to inquire into and reform abuses in the Benedictine monastery of St. Benet
  Holm. He landed at Bergen in June 1248 and was back in St. Albans the
  following year. Did he on this trip pick up further details of the great
  Mongol scare of ten years before? Batu's advance on Novgorod must have
  aroused anxiety in Norway. As late as 1262 Pope Urban IV, in a letter to the
  Norwegian bishops, warned them to be on guard against fresh Mongol
  attacks in the north. Baronius-Raynaldus, *Annales Ecclesiastici*, ed. Theiner
  (1870), XXII, pp. 86–8.
7 On the whole subject of the Assassins, see M. G. S. Hodgson, *The Order of
  Assassins* (The Hague, 1955), now the standard authority.

Man of the Mountain," and they bind themselves to obey him readily and implicitly in everything, however difficult or dangerous; for besides other occasions, if any prince becomes an object of hatred or suspicion to these people, one or more of them receives a dagger from their chief, and without considering on the consequences or the punishment of such a deed, set out for the residence of the victim, whom they make the sole object of their attention until they murder him. These people are called Assassins, both by Saracens and Christians. ...[8]

There were two branches of the Assassin "order," the parent one in north Persia, with its headquarters at Alamut, in the Elburz Mountains, where the *imam* of the sect lived, and a subordinate one in Syria, centred on Masyad, a strongly fortified castle near Hama, whose most famous "grand master" (*mukaddam*), Rashid ad-Din Sinan, ruled his people for over thirty years (1162–93). Under Rashid, the original "Old Man," the Syrian branch achieved something like independence, but the Persians later re-established control, and subsequent grand masters were usually nominated by Alamut. Though the principal targets of the Assassins were the orthodox (Sunnite) Muslim leaders, their daggers were occasionally turned against the Crusaders; hence they acquired notoriety in the west, though little was known there of the Persian branch. It would appear at first more likely that the 1238 embassy came from the Syrian Assassins, who were well acquainted with the Franks and their European background, rather than from those of distant Alamut, where the Crusaders had never penetrated. But when we reflect on the political and military situation in western Asia in the 1230s, this becomes less certain.

Chingiz Khan's son and successor, Ogedei (1229–41), was directing a plan of world conquest. While Batu was overrunning Russia other Mongol armies under Chor-maghan were subjugating Persia and the Caucasus. Mongol detachments entered Azerbaydzhan in 1231, invaded Georgia in 1236, ravaged Armenia and sacked its capital Ani in 1239. Fighting was going on all around Alamut; an obscure reference in a Georgian chronicle has been taken to mean that a direct Mongol attack was launched on the great rock-fortress about this time.[9] Be this as it may, the Isma'ili chiefs must have been gravely

---

8 Roger of Wendover, *Flores Historiarum* s.a. 1150, à propos of the murder by the Assassins of Raymond II of Tripoli.
9 Sir Henry H. Howorth, *History of the Mongols* (London, 1888), III, p. 54, alleges a Mongol assault on Alamut at an unspecified date in the 1230s, on the authority of a Georgian chronicle translated by M. Brosset, *Histoire*

alarmed and cast about for allies; as hated heretics, they could expect
no help from their fellow Muslims, but in view of the fact that the
Mongol forces in the north were attacking a Christian country, perhaps an appeal to the Franks for joint action might be heeded.
Matthew Paris's narrative implies that it was the Assassin mission
that first brought the news of the invasion of Russia to France and
England; the "northern mountains" presumably refer to the Caucasus, and "Hungary Major" (*Hungaria Magna*) – probably the region
between the Volga and the Urals believed to have been the original
home of the Magyars – is specifically mentioned perhaps because it
had recently been reported on by Dominican missionaries from the
other Hungary.[10] The idea of a mission to the west probably originated in Alamut, but the details may have been worked out jointly by
the Persian and Syrian Assassins, and no doubt it was from a Syrian
port that the envoys set out for Europe.

But why did they make for France and England? One might have
expected them to apply first to the Emperor Frederick II, who had
been in Palestine on the Sixth Crusade from 1227 to 1229 and who
must therefore have been better known to Orientals than any other

ancienne de la Géorgie (St. Petersburg, 1849–51), "additions et éclaircisse-
ments," I, pp. 528–31. I do not have access to this work, but my friend
Professor C. F. Beckingham, of the London School of Oriental and African
Studies, who kindly checked the reference for me, is of the opinion that the
passage relates to the subsequent attack by Hulegu in 1256.

10 The exact location of Hungary Major is one of the controverted points of
medieval geography. It probably lay between the Volga and the Yaik or
Ural rivers, north of the Kirghis steppe and south of "Great Bulgaria"
along the middle Volga. This is roughly the area covered today by the
Autonomous Bashkir Republic of the Soviet Union. The Bashkirs, who have
always lived on the lower slopes of the Urals, were believed to be kinsmen
of the Magyars, part of whom stayed behind in their original home when
the rest of the nation moved westward to the middle Danube at the close
of the ninth century. The Hungarians were often called Bashkirs in the
Middle Ages, e.g. by the Persian historian Juwaini (*History of the World
Conqueror*, tr. Boyle (1958), I, p. 270). The relationship is obscure, the
modern Bashkirs being Turkish-speaking, whereas Magyar is a Finno-
Ugrian language. It is curious that Matthew Paris, in an otherwise geo-
graphically vague passage, should refer to Hungaria Magna as though it
were a region familiar to his readers. Possibly it had become tolerably well
known from the reports of Hungarian Dominican missionaries who visited
the land of their ancestors shortly before the Mongol invasion. See D. Sinor,
"Un voyageur de 13ᵉ siècle: le Dominicain Julien de Hongrie," *Bull. School
of Oriental and African Studies*, (1952), 589–602. The latest discussion of
this vexed problem is J. Németh, "Ungarische Stammesnamen bei den
Baschkiren," *Acta Linguistica Academiae Scientiarum Hungaricae*, XVI
(1966), 1–21, a reference I owe to the kindness of Professor Sinor.

Christian sovereign. Yet there was perhaps good reason why France and England should be the objectives of this mission. From their confreres in Syria, the Isma'ilis of Alamut must have learnt a good deal about the Crusaders, whom they might consider, not without justice, as a French colony in the east. The majority of the barons and knights of the kingdom of Jerusalem and the other Latin principalities and of the military orders were of French origin, and since 1204 a Latin empire, under a French-speaking dynasty, had been established in Constantinople. France must therefore have seemed to these Orientals the greatest nation of the west, the home of the crusading movement, and the most likely ally against the Mongols. As for England, that country's ruling class was French in speech and culture; the memory of its crusading king, Richard Lionheart, was still alive in the east, and the king of England, though he had lost Normandy, was still lord of Gascony, and as such, an important figure in European politics. The two western kingdoms had acted together during the Third Crusade of 1190–92 and had considerable interests in the Levant: it was not unreasonable to suppose that they might be persuaded to take action against the ferocious pagans from the steppes of Asia who, unless checked, might break through to the Mediterranean and from their bases in Russia overwhelm Christian Europe. Moreover, the situation in the Levant seemed favourable to such a design, because Frederick II's truce with Sultan Kamil of Egypt in 1229 had brought fighting between Christian and Muslim virtually to a standstill.

Matthew Paris tells us nothing about the French response to the Isma'ili overtures, but he implies that it was negative.[11] He leaves us in no doubt about the English reaction by quoting the remark of the bishop of Winchester which apparently decided the matter. The Assassins were unlucky in their request. The bishop of Winchester was the Poitevin Peter des Roches, the last man to favour a rapprochement between Christendom and any branch of Islam. He had gone on Frederick II's crusade in 1227 and had been present at the

11 The French, like the oriental, sources are silent on this embassy, but William of Nangis and other French chroniclers tell an odd story of two Isma'ili *fida'is* being sent to France in 1237 to kill Louis IX. The "Old Man" (they aver) then changed his mind, and sent two others to warn the king about the first! The latter were run to earth at Marseilles, and the second pair were sent home with gifts. William of Nangis, *Chronique latine de Guillaume de Nangis, de 1113 à 1300*, ed. H. Giraud (Paris, 1843), I, p. 188. Can it be that the sudden change in Assassin policy was due to an Alamut decision to seek help from the west against the Mongols?

signing of the truce of 1229, which suspended hostilities and gave the Christians possession of a demilitarized Jerusalem for ten years. That truce would expire in 1239, and Pope Gregory IX was already preparing to preach a new crusade in expectation of a renewed Muslim onslaught on the Holy City. If, in the bishop's view, the infidels were now being threatened by pagan Tartars from the heart of Asia, well and good; both were enemies of Christ, and could be safely left to tear each other to pieces! The Isma'ili envoys left Europe empty-handed.[12]

The French and English might scorn the Isma'ili warnings, but they soon had cause to recall them. Matthew Paris is again one of our chief authorities for the great Mongol drive into central Europe which put Christendom in graver peril than it had been since the days of Attila. After resting his forces on the lower Don for a year or two, Batu resumed his western offensive from the Ukraine late in 1240. Kiev fell in December of that year; simultaneous attacks were then mounted against Poland and Hungary. One army, sweeping across the Polish plains, pushed its way into Silesia, and annihilated the forces of Duke Henry at Liegnitz on 9 April 1241, the victors filling nine sacks with the ears of the slain. Two days later a second army, commanded by Batu in person, having crossed the Carpathians, crushed the resistance of King Bela IV at Mohi on the river Salo in northern Hungary. This double catastrophe frightened all Europe; no one knew where the next blow would fall; rumours and panic spread; German Jews were reported to be smuggling arms across the Polish frontier to the Mongols.[13] The two Mongol armies, joining up, overspread the Hungarian plain, killing and ravaging like locusts; King Bela fled from his shattered kingdom, vigorously pursued by the enemy; on Christmas Day 1241 Batu crossed the frozen Danube to take Buda and besiege Esztergom, and by the spring of

12 There is a curious footnote to the story of the Isma'ili mission to England. On the night of 9 September 1238, an attempt was made to murder Henry III at Woodstock, an intruder being caught with a knife in his hand trying to get into the king's bedroom. Under torture, he confessed he had been sent by William Marsh, an outlaw who made Lundy Island a base for piracy in the Irish Sea and the Bristol Channel, "to slay the king in the manner of the Assassins (more Assessinorum)." *Chron. Maj.*, III, pp. 497–8. Cf. Sir Maurice Powicke, *King Henry III and the Lord Edward* (Oxford, 1947), II, pp. 751–2. May the presence of Assassin envoys in England that year have inspired the deed?

13 *Chron. Maj.*, IV, pp. 131–3. The weapons were said to have been concealed in wine-casks. Anti-Jewish feeling was no doubt intensified by reports that the "Tartars" were descendants of the Ten Lost Tribes.

1242 the Mongol cavalry, overrunning Croatia and Dalmatia, were ranging up and down the Adriatic coast in search of the royal fugitive, who had found asylum in the island city of Trau or Trogir.[14] A Mongol patrol penetrated as far as Neustadt in Austria: both Italy and Germany were directly threatened. Suddenly Batu was stopped in his tracks by a message from Mongolia announcing the death in the previous December of the Great Khan Ogedei. He at once decided to suspend operations against Europe and retire to the Russian steppes, to be close enough to influence the election of Ogedei's successor. Moving back through the Balkans, he regained his encampments by the Volga at the end of 1242.

Matthew Paris collected a remarkable number of eyewitness accounts of these disasters. In the text of his chronicle, four documents are quoted:[15] 1. A letter from Henry Count of Lorraine to his father-in-law Henry I, duke of Brabant from 1235 to 1248; it is dated "Laetare" Sunday (10 March 1241), and reports that the Mongols are ravaging Hungary "with unheardof cruelty," and intend to attack Bohemia after Easter. The writer begs for arms and men immediately. The duke responded by forwarding the message to the bishop of Paris, who brought it to the notice of Louis IX. Queen Blanche asked her son what was to be done. He replied: "If these people, whom we call Tartars, should come upon us, either we will thrust them back into the region of Tartarus, whence they emanated, or else they will send us all to heaven."[16] 2. A circular letter of the Emperor Frederick II to the kings of Europe, dated from Faenza, near Ravenna, 3 July 1241; this refers to the fall of Kiev and the invasion of Hungary, claims that the enemy have been repulsed from Bohemia, but

14 For the Mongol campaign in Hungary, see D. Sinor, *History of Hungary* (London, 1959), chap. 8.
15 The first two, *Chron. Maj.*, IV, pp. 109–20.
16 The name "Tatar" is first met with in the Turkish Orkhon inscriptions in Mongolia under a date equivalent to AD 731. The original Tatars seem to have lived in the region of Buir-Nor. The Chinese came to call the northern nomads "ta-ta," and the name was probably carried westwards by traders and Nestorian missionaries. Since the Mongols, hitherto unknown, came from eastern Asia, they were universally dubbed "Tatars." Matthew Paris derived the word at first from a mythical river Tartar, but Louis IX's pun made popular its identification with Tartarus, the classical Hell. The Mongols themselves never used it: their name is from *mong*: brave, bold, daring. The word "Mongol" is not found in Matthew Paris, but his near-contemporary Vincent of Beauvais gave the title *Historia Mongolorum* to Plano Carpini's famous report which he published in his *Speculum Historiale*, 31:8. From this time onwards "Tartar" (or "Tatar") and "Mongol" are interchangeable terms in western literature.

are threatening Germany, according to information received from his son Conrad, ruling the German lands in his name, and the Hungarian ambassador to his court in Italy. The emperor urges his fellow monarchs to despatch "a complete force of brave knights and soldiers, and a good supply of arms." 3. A letter from Ivo of Narbonne to Archbishop Gerald de Mulemort of Bordeaux, undated but inserted by Matthew under the year 1243.[17] Ivo was at Neustadt when the Mongol armies approached the Austrian frontier from Hungary; he alleges that they retired in face of the advance of a large force under the command of King Ottakar of Bohemia and Duke Frederick of Austria. Yet the danger, he warns, is still acute: "six Christian kingdoms have already been destroyed, and the same fate hangs over the others." He tells the strange story of an unnamed Englishman who, being banished from his country for various crimes, went first to Acre, lost his money by gambling, wandered eastwards, was picked up by Mongol spies and induced to act as their interpreter; Batu employed him to carry his message to King Bela demanding the submission of Hungary. 4. A report or interview given in northern Italy by a fugitive Russian archbishop named Peter, in which he describes the devastation of his country and states that "thirty-four years have now elapsed since the time when they [the Mongols] first came forth from the desert."[18] Assuming that the "now" refers to the completion of the conquest of Russia in 1240, this would carry us back accurately enough to Chingiz's enthronement as Great Khan in 1206. This document, which Matthew cites under the year 1244 and which is said to have been laid before the Council of Lyons in 1245, lists a number of the Mongol commanders in Hungary; the names are mostly mangled beyond recognition, but "Bathatarcan" clearly stands for "Bahadur Khan," this being a title (*bahadur*: hero) borne by the great Subedei, the most outstanding of the Mongol generals.[19]

In his *Additamenta*, or appendix, Matthew reproduces seven further reports relating to the Mongol invasion.[20] 1. From an uniden-

---

17 *Chron. Maj.*, IV, pp. 270–7. Ivo refers to the invaders as "Tatars" and Matthew Paris calls attention to this correction.
18 *Chron. Maj.*, IV, pp. 386–9. The precise identity of this prelate has not been established.
19 Subedei led the van of the Mongol army in the invasion of Hungary, and his title is often mistaken by contemporaries for his personal name. See the article "Bahādur" in the *Encyclopedia of Islam*.
20 Six of these documents are printed by Luard as a continuous series and numbered 46 to 51, *Chron. Maj.*, VI, pp. 75–84; the seventh (no. 61), pp. 113–6.

tified Hungarian bishop to William of Auvergne, bishop of Paris, describing his interview with two captured Mongol spies; the enemy are near the frontiers of Hungary, and the date is apparently early 1241.[21] 2. From Henry Raspe, landgrave of Thuringia, to Henry I, duke of Brabant: the "Tartars" have destroyed all Russia and Poland as far as Bohemia and the middle part of Hungary; the date seems to be mid-1241. Both these letters refer to "Zingiton" (Chingiz Khan), "the King of the Tartars" as though he were still alive. 3. From the abbot of St. Mary's Abbey in Hungary dated Vienna, 4 January 1242, to any clergy who may see it; it reports the death of Duke Henry [at Liegnitz] with 40,000 men, the flight of King Bela after a battle in which 65,000 were slain, the Christmas crossing of the Danube by the Mongols, and begs for charity for the refugees. 4. From Friar Jordan, provincial vicar of the Franciscans of Poland, "to all the faithful in Christ," dated Pinsk,[22] 10 April 1242: Russia has perished with its seven dukes, the greater part of Hungary has been occupied, almost all Poland has been cruelly destroyed, and the invaders are on the borders of Germany and Bohemia; the king of Bohemia has gone out to meet them with a very numerous army. 5. From a Dominican and a Franciscan friar "to all their brethren," undated but probably late 1241, since they report that Russia has been in great part ravaged, Kiev[23] destroyed, Poland invaded "before Easter," most of Hungary occupied and King Bela expelled. All Germany is prepared for war, and if Germany were conquered no part of Christendom could resist. 6. From a Franciscan friar in Cologne to his brethren in the duchy of Brabant, enclosing a letter from Friar Jordan of Pinsk, written a little later than the previous one, since he reports that the Mongols entered Moravia "before Ascension Day." 7. A report submitted to the Council at Lyons from Friar Andrew and another (unnamed) Dominican, containing a general account of the Mongols, their religious beliefs, the extent of their empire, and the

---

21 Luard, *Chron. Maj.*, VI, p. 75, dates this letter 10 April 1242, but this must be an error, since it speaks of the Mongols as only on the frontiers and was clearly written before the actual invasion. Professor Sinor suggests, in "Un voyageur du 13ᵉ siècle," that the unnamed bishop might be the bishop of Vác (German Vatzen), who was soon afterwards sent by King Bela to beg assistance from the Emperor Frederick II.

22 *Datum Pyngensi.* But as in his second letter, Friar Jordan describes his fellow friar as *custos Prangensis*, it is uncertain whether Pinsk, in eastern Poland, or Prague is intended.

23 The text has *Rionam*, but this is almost certainly a scribal error for *Kionam*: Kiow or Kiev.

supposed connection of their "king" with Prester John.[24] This was no doubt the result of the famous mission despatched by Innocent IV in March 1248, consisting of three Franciscans, the best known of whom was John of Plano Carpini, and four Dominicans who were later joined by two others of their order, including Andrew of Longjumeau. This last document brings us to Matthew Paris's handling of the first diplomatic exchanges between the Mongols and the west, exchanges which were long to outlive him and continue well into the fourteenth century.[25]

Even before the formal opening of the Council of Lyons in April 1245, Innocent IV sent two missions, one to the Great Khan Guyuk in Mongolia and the other to Baiju or Baichu the Mongol governor of Persia. Their aim was to protest against the recent devastation of Christian kingdoms and to discover if these redoubtable pagans could be won over to the Christian faith. Since Batu's withdrawal in 1242 there had been no further threat to the west, but another invasion was likely if the new great khan (the throne had been vacant since Ogedei's death in 1241) was as aggressive-minded as his predecessors, and clearly something should be done to counter a fresh Mongol move against Europe. The papal embassy under John of Plano Carpini reached Mongolia in time to witness Guyuk's enthronement in July 1246, but Innocent's appeal received a brutal response: the pope was told that God had given the Mongols the rulership of the world and if he and his people wished to be spared he must come in person and make his submission to the khan![26] The second papal mission under Ascelin reached Baiju's camp west of the Caspian in May 1247 and got an even worse reception: its members were threatened with death for daring to claim that the pope, instead of the khan, was possessed of the world's highest dignity! Then Mongol policy suddenly reversed itself, and two Mongol envoys were ordered to accompany the Europeans back home and deliver a message to the pope. A new Mongol governor named Aljigidei had

24 According to this tale, the father of the "King of the Tartars" killed Prester John and married his daughter, their son being the present king. The historical basis for this is probably the overthrow by Chingiz Khan of Wang Khan, the chief of the Keraits, a Nestorian Christian people, in 1203.

25 The standard account of the negotiations between the Mongols and the West is P. Pelliot, "Les Mongols et la papauté," *Revue de l'orient chrétien*, XXIII, XXIV, XXVIII (1922–32).

26 Christopher Dawson, ed., *The Mongol Mission* (London, 1955), pp. 85–6 for the text of Guyuk's letter. Cf. E. Voegelin, "The Mongol Orders of Submission to the European Powers," *Byzantion* (1941).

taken over in Persia and a more conciliatory attitude to the west had been decided on.

Matthew Paris makes no mention of John of Plano Carpini or Ascelin, but he reports the arrival at the papal court in the summer of 1248 of the first Mongol embassy to Europe and the strange secrecy which surrounded it. "In the summer of this year," he says, "two Tartar messengers came from their prince to the Pope; but the particulars of their message were kept such a secret to all in that court, that they were not clearly known to clerks, notaries or others, however familiar they were with His Holiness. Their charter [sealed letter] which they brought to the Pope was translated from an unknown language to one more suited to the people, as they drew near the western countries." Rumours flew over Europe about the object of this mysterious embassy. "It was suspected from certain indications [Matthew goes on] that the letter contained an offer and design of the said Tartars to make immediate war upon Battacius [John Vatatzes, Greek emperor of Nicaea from 1222 to 1254], the Emperor Frederick's Greek son-in-law, a schismatic and one disobedient to the Roman Church. The offer, it was believed, did not displease the Pope. ..."[27] In his *Historia Anglorum*, Matthew says Innocent not only urged the khan to become a Christian, but suggested he should attack both Vatatzes and Frederick, to which the envoys replied that they were not free to put such proposals to their master. The two emperors were, indeed, sworn foes of the papacy, which was then trying to save the falling Latin empire of Constantinople, but the story may well be mere gossip.[28] A more likely explanation is that Aljigidei was contemplating an attack on the caliph of Baghdad, and a diversion by the Christians, in the form of a new crusade, would prevent the Muslims of Egypt from coming to the help of their spiritual chief.[29] Two pieces of evidence, both noted by Matthew, point in this direction: a second Mongol embassy to the west, this time to Louis IX of France, who was known to be planning a crusade against Egypt, and the rumour which spread from the east at this time, that the great khan had been baptized a Christian.

27 *Chron. Maj.*, v, 37–8. A. Atiya, *The Crusade in the Later Middle Ages* (London, 1938), p. 240, thinks the Mongol envoys were spies. One of them, Sargis or Sergius by name, was presumably a Nestorian Christian.
28 Matthew Paris, *Historia Anglorum*, ed. F. Madden, III, pp. 38–9. A. A. Vasiliev, *History of the Byzantine Empire* (Madison, 1952), pp. 531–2, dismisses the story and notes it is marked "dubium" in red in the margin of the ms.
29 This is Pelliot's suggestion, "Les Mongols et la papauté," XXIV (1923), 195.

In December 1248, the French king, then engaged in Cyprus in military preparations against Egypt, received two Nestorian Christians from Persia who brought him a letter from "Achatay" (Aljigidei), the French translation of which is given by Matthew in the *Additamenta*.[30] The envoys' names were David and Mark, and that of the first is cited in its full Arabic form, Saphadin Mephat Davi, or as we should transliterate it, Saif ad-Dīn Muzaffar Dā'ūd, "Sword of the Faith, Victorious David." Couched in unusually gracious terms, it hints at a Christian-Mongol alliance against "those who despise the Cross." In the body of his chronicle, under the year 1249, Matthew remarks: "About the same time, the most gratifying reports became frequent, namely, that the most potent king of the Tartars, influenced by the diligent preaching and persuasions of Peter, an Indian monk of the Black Order, was converted to Christianity and baptized ... the same king also sent consolatory messages to the French king, who was staying at Damietta, encouraging and persuading him vigorously to carry on the war against the Saracens, and to purify the whole land of the East from their impurities; and he also promised effectual and speedy assistance, as a faithful Catholic and baptized novice of Christ."[31]

It is characteristic of our St. Albans monk that he cautiously refrains from asserting as a fact Guyuk's conversion and treats it simply as a report, and a doubtful one at that, for he goes on to speak of "alii rumores umbratiles et ficti ad consolandum Christianos et forte ad animandum cruce signatos."[32] It is not mentioned in Aljigidei's letter to Louis IX, but the Nestorian envoys told the king verbally that Guyuk had been baptized on the feast of the Epiphany that year (6 January 1248) by a Nestorian bishop named Malachy. (Where Matthew got his Indian Benedictine from is impossible to say.) When John of Plano Carpini was at Karakorum in 1246 the

30 *Chron. Maj.*, VI, pp. 163–5. The Great Khan Guyuk is named in the letter: his death in east Turkestan in April 1248 was not known when it was written.

31 *Chron. Maj.*, V, p. 87.

32 *Chron. Maj.*, V, p. 87. William of Rubruck, who was in Karakorum a few years later, was scornful of these tales, which he treated as Nestorian inventions. Of the Nestorians he says "out of nothing they make a great rumour." Dawson, *The Mongol Mission*, p. 122. Guyuk's mother was certainly a Nestorian Christian and the khan may have occasionally attended Christian services, but the indications are that he lived and died a pagan. Yet it is fair to note that the Persian historian Juwaini, a contemporary writer, positively asserts that he was baptized. *History of the World Conqueror*, tr. Boyle, (Manchester, 1958), I, p. 259.

Nestorians there told him they firmly believed Guyuk was about to
become a Christian, but nothing the papal mission saw there justified
this optimism. It was, in fact, disquieted, not only by the khan's arro-
gant and uncompromising reply to the pope's message, but by signs
of a new Mongol offensive against Europe. As it happened, Christendom had another narrow escape, for Guyuk died in April 1248 after
a reign of less than two years, and the throne remained vacant until
the election of Mongke or Mangu in 1251, during which interval
major military operations were suspended.

Matthew Paris has not much more to tell us about the Mongols.
He says nothing of William of Rubruck's famous mission, sent by
Louis ix in 1253, but he mentions the destruction of the Assassins by
Hulegu in 1256, though he puts this event under the year 1257.[33] His
chronicle continues until 1259, but the fall of Baghdad in February
1258, which made so much noise in the world and excited such ex-
travagant hopes among many Christians, finds no place in it. However, what he has recorded of these extraordinary world conquerors
is of enormous importance.

From what sources did Matthew Paris derive this wealth of
material, of which he was, it seems, not unjustifiably proud? "If
anyone is desirous [he writes] of learning the impurities of the Tartars, and their mode of life and customs, or the superstitions and fury
of the Assassins, he may obtain information by making diligent
search at St. Albans,"[34] which gives the impression that the monastic
library was well stocked with transcripts of public and private documents relating to these subjects. St. Albans was, of course, a wealthy
Benedictine house, only twenty miles from London, in close touch
with the centre of government; important visitors were frequent, and
the king himself often made short stays there. Matthew knew personally Henry iii and many of his councillors and advisers; he had
access to the exchequer records, and may have been allowed to take
copies of diplomatic correspondence. Overseas travellers occasionally turned up at the abbey, and were no doubt closely questioned by
its historian; some of these were oriental Christians. In 1228 an unnamed Armenian archbishop stayed there, and told the monks the
story of the Wandering Jew; in 1245 the abbey was visited by the

33 Chron. Maj., v, 655.
34 Ibid. Ipsorum Tartarorum immunditias, vitam et mores si quis audire desi-
    derat, necnon et Assessinorum furorem et superstitionem, apud Sanctum
    Albanum diligens indagator poterit reperire.

bishop of Beirut, who was possibly a Maronite, and in 1252 we read of "some Armenians" being there. Contacts between Armenia (that is, the kingdom of "Little" Armenia in Cilicia) and the west had been multiplying since the closing decades of the twelfth century; its able chief Leo Rupen had a royal title conferred on him by the Emperor Henry VI in 1198; the Armenian church submitted to Rome; Armenian ecclesiastics were warmly welcomed in Latin Christendom, and as a curious instance of this intimacy, Thomas Becket, canonized by Alexander III in 1174, was within a few years commemorated as a martyr in Armenia. Under the long rule of the greatest of her kings, Haithum or Hayton (1226–69), Armenia attempted to act as mediator between the Mongols and Europe and to build up a Franco-Armenian-Mongol alliance against Islam. Some at least of Matthew Paris's information about the "Tartars" may well have come from this source.[35]

Much of his material came, no doubt, from Benedictine houses on the Continent. The great abbeys were in frequent touch with one another; the Mongol conquests scattered refugees from Russia, Poland, Hungary, and elsewhere over western Europe, and their tales of woe, repeated from monastery to monastery, would inevitably reach St. Albans before long. Moreover, the great general council summoned by Innocent IV to meet at Lyons in 1245, brought together, at the height of the Mongol scare, churchmen from east and west; indeed, ways and means of dealing with these dreadful pagans stood on the agenda next to the business of Frederick II. It was from Lyons in April 1245 that Innocent IV despatched the first great mission to "Tartary," that of John of Plano Carpini. If, as is almost certain, Matthew Paris had "correspondents" at Lyons, he would gather from them a mass of information some of which he never had time to incorporate into the body of his chronicle.[36]

But the fact remains that other monastic chroniclers of the time had equal, if not better, opportunity to set down a documented record of these tremendous events, and did not do so. It is to Matthew Paris's lasting credit that he had the curiosity and diligence to collect all the relevant evidence he could find and write it down for the

---

35 On Little Armenia, see the Pennsylvania *History of the Crusades* (Philadelphia, 1962), II, chap. 18, and the new (1966) Byzantine volume of the *Cambridge Medieval History*, chap. 14.

36 "Of many important events, like the Council of Lyons, his (Matthew Paris's) is the only contemporary description." A. L. Smith, *Church and State in the Middle Ages*, p. 169.

𝔄 𝔖tatue of 𝔥enry of 𝔄lmain   P. H. BRIEGER

𝕴n the *Codex Christianeum Altonensis* of Dante's Divine Comedy which was profusely illustrated, probably by a Pisan artist late in the fourteenth century, the illustration to Canto xii of the *Inferno* (f.21) contains a feature which can not be found in any other illustrated codex of Dante's poem. In separate panels inserted between the text columns, the illustrator shows a number of "violents against their neighbour" immersed in Phlegeton, the river of blood. The degree of their immersion is intended to indicate the measure of their sin. One of these tyrants is singled out sitting by himself, only his head emerging above the level of the river. His eyes seem to be focussed upon a seated figure in the opposite corner which is much larger than any other figure and is not nude like the sinners but is clothed in a long garment decorated at top and bottom by a broad hem and by a pattern above the chest. It is shown frontally, the eyes looking straight ahead, the feet supported by a slab. The head is crowned by a diadem. In the right hand is a chalice in which rests a heart pierced by an upright dagger; in the left hand is a blank scroll. Surely this represents, not a living figure, but a statue.

There is no reference to this figure in the text of the poem; Dante merely speaks of one of the tyrants in Phlegeton as:

> ... the man who dared to smite
> Even in the very bosom of God, the heart
> They venerate still on the Thames.   (*Inf.* xii., 119–21)[1]

Since he does not name either victim or slayer, he must have counted on his readers understanding that he speaks of Henry of Almain,

---

1 *The Comedy of Dante Alighieri*: i, *Hell*, trans. D. Sayers (Harmondsworth, 1960), p. 145.

son of Richard of Cornwall, and cousin of Edward I and of Guy de Montfort, son of Simon de Montfort.

The murder of Henry by Guy de Montfort made a deep impression upon contemporaries who reacted with horror and revulsion.[2] It was reported by English, French, and Italian chroniclers whose reports differ in some details. According to Sir Maurice Powicke only two facts are established beyond doubt: "the time was 13 March, 1271, during Mass and the scene was the church of San Silvestro. ..."[3] Furthermore, the crime was not premeditated, "an act of almost incredible folly ... I think that when the brothers learned that their cousin was in Viterbo, they were swept away by their memories of Evesham, by the thought of their disinheritance and humiliation, and by the knowledge that Henry was in their power."[4] To increase the elements of a detective story there was the question of complicity, not only of Guy's father-in-law, Count Rosso, but even of Charles of Anjou whose vicar he had become in Tuscany. And the crime was made so much more horrible in the eyes of the contemporaries, leading Dante to put Guy de Montfort in the river of blood, shot at by centaurs, by the fact that Henry had the reputation of a kind and pious man, that he was on return from a crusade, that King Edward, who was his cousin, had detached him from the crusading army with the purpose of creating peace between the king and the sons of Simon de Montfort, and most of all, that he was murdered in church while attending mass, "in the very bosom of God."

Dante and his commentators are partly responsible for the fact that the memory of the murder was kept alive much longer in Italy than in England and still aroused strong feelings many years later, even after the death of Guy in 1287, but it is also true that the dramatic tale of bloodfeud and unpunished murder in church made a stronger appeal to the Italian temperament than to the English. The English chroniclers limit themselves to a report of the murder, the transport of the body to the Abbey of Hailes where it was buried, and the preservation of the heart in a gold container near Edward the Confessor's shrine at Westminster Abbey.[5] Rishanger alone men-

2 See T. F. Tout, *Dictionary of National Biography*, s.n. Henry of Cornwall, XXVI, pp. 98–9.
3 F. M. Powicke, "Guy de Montfort (1265–71)," *Trans. Royal Historical Society*, 4th Series, XVIII, 15–16.
4 *Ibid.*, 17–18.
5 "Ex Annalibus Oseneiensibus et Thomae de Wykes Chronics," in *MGH, Scriptores*, XXVII, p. 500.

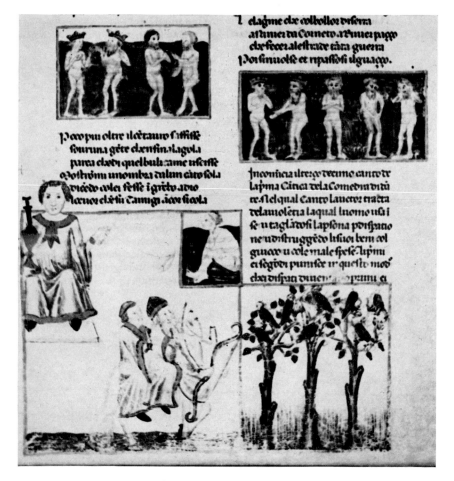

Dante's *Divine Comedy*, *Inferno* XII,
Codex Christianeum Altonensis, folio 21
Reproduced with the permission of the Christianeum, Altona

tions that the men of Viterbo caused a memorial to be painted upon the wall, presumably of the church where the murder had taken place, recording the manner in which the murder was committed.[6] No trace of such a mural has survived in any church at Viterbo. If it existed it must have helped to keep the memory of the horrible deed alive. The mural may have been similar to a miniature in a manuscript of Villani's chronicle (Vatican Cod. L vɪɪɪ 296 f.116ᵛ of the second half of the fourteenth century, attributed to Pacino di Bonaguida) which represents not the actual stabbing before the altar, but the even more brutal aftermath. One of the knights with Guy de Montfort reminded him that his father's corpse had been dragged from the battlefield of Evesham whereupon Guy turned back to the body of the murdered man and dragged him by the hair out of the church. In the miniature the protagonists are shown in the centre of the picture. Guy stands outside the church with his right hand on the dagger. His left hand clutches a strand of Henry's hair, whilst Henry himself lies prostrate inside, before the altar which carries the vessels for mass and behind which a priest is in the act of celebrating.

Villani continues his tale of the murder with his version of what happened to Henry's heart, and this brings us back to the Altona picture. He states at first that Edward, whom he calls Henry's brother, had the heart within a gold cup placed upon a bridge across the river Thames to remind the English of the outrage which had been inflicted upon them. Later (in an appendix) he mentions that a statue was placed upon this column, and that it held in its hand the gold cup.[7]

This location of a statue is much more difficult to explain than the story of the statue itself. As far as I can ascertain the custom of placing statues upon bridges was unknown at the time in western Europe, with one exception: the statue of "Mars," the ancient patron of the city of Florence. According to local tradition the heathen statue of Mars which stood in his temple, had been put away into a tower near the Arno when the temple was replaced by the Church of St. John the Baptist, the present Baptistery. Later, the mutilated statue was set up on the Ponte Vecchio.[8] It is alluded to by Dante in his *Inferno*

6 W. Rishanger, *Chronica et Annales*, ed. H. T. Riley (Rolls Series no. 28, 1865), p. 67.
7 *Cronica di Giovanni Villani*, Compilato da Franc Gherardi Dragomanni (1845), ɪ, p. 370; *Cronica di Giovanni Villani*, Appendix 112 (Firenze, 1823), p. 538.
8 R. Davidsohn, *Forschungen zur Geschichte von Florenz* (1908), ɪv.

(Canto xiii, 145–7). The only explanation of Villani's location of Henry's statue seems to be that he imagined it in analogy to the statue of Mars.

In attempting to explain the origin of the tale about a statue, one is on safer ground. It also seems to rest upon an analogy, but to an actual statue erected in Italy early in the fourteenth century. Guido da Pisa, one of the earliest of the commentators on the Divine Comedy,[9] gives the most detailed account of the statue which he locates in Westminster Abbey where, as he says, all English kings were buried. He states that Henry was buried in a chapel in which all tomb effigies of English kings were assembled, and above his tomb a guilded marble statue was erected. In the right hand it held a gold cup which contained a sculptured heart and a sword fixed into it. In the left hand it held a scroll with the inscription: "cor gladiis fessum do cui consanguineus sum." This description contains all the features which we find in the Altona picture, though there the inscription is omitted and the scroll left blank.

No such statue exists at Westminster Abbey today, nor was one ever mentioned by English writers of the time. Modern English historians either ignored or ridiculed the story as pure fiction. But even should it be untrue, as it seems to be, one cannot ignore the question of how such a story could originate in Italy, and the further question: did the Altona illustrator merely turn the verbal description of such a statue, which he found in the commentaries, into a fictitious visual image of a kind which never existed in reality? Or did commentators and possibly the illustrator know of effigies either in England or in Italy which made them believe in the existence of such a statue of Henry?

In regard to these questions, the most probable answer seems to be that of two main components of the statue as described by Guido da Pisa and depicted in the Altona *Codex* – the seated effigy and the heart held by it – one can be seen to stem from Italy, the other from England.

Early in the fourteenth century an exceptional elaborate tomb was erected in Pisa for the Emperor Henry vii which contained features rare in contemporary Italy and unknown outside of it. The tomb, designed by the sculptor Tino da Cammaino, exists today only in fragments. The most remarkable of these, now gathered in the

9 G. Biagi, *La Divina Commedia nella figurazione artistica e nel secolare commento* (1924), i, p. 348.

Campo Santo, is the seated effigy of Henry vii which towers over the standing figures on either side. Though much more slender than the figure of Henry of Almain in the Altona picture, the emperor sits in the same pose and his garment sags in v-shaped folds between his knees. Unfortunately both hands are broken off. The story and the image of the statue of Henry of Almain may well have been derived from this statue of another prince who came as a visitor to Italy, who died there suddenly and who was also called Henry.

There was another unusual feature connected with the burial of Henry vii: the tomb at Pisa housed the body only, while the heart was buried in the tomb of Margaret of Luxemburg, his wife, in San Francesco di Castellato at Genoa. This separate burial of heart and body was considered a northern custom in Italy. Referring to the burial of Henry of Almain's heart, L'Ottimo speaks of "L'usanza oltramontana."[10] Heart burials had found great favour in England by the middle of the thirteenth century, in knightly circles.[11] Furthermore a number of contemporary effigies have survived in which the figure of the dead holds his heart in his hand. The knightly effigies at Mappover (Dorset) and at Steeple Langford (Wiltshire) provide good examples, but the best representative of this type is the monument for Bishop Aylmer de Valance (died 1260), half-brother of Henry iii, in the choir of Winchester Cathedral. Here the half-length figure of the bishop is set in a trefoil niche within a mandorla which is decorated with stiff-leaf foliage and three coats of arms. The effigy holds his heart before his chest. We know that Henry's father wished to have his heart buried in the Minor's Church at London. There may have been a similar monument made at the time for Richard of Cornwall which does not now exist. In any case, knowledge that such statues with hearts in their hands existed in England may well have reached Italy and may have prompted writers and the illustrator to put the heart into the hand of the seated effigy of Henry of Almain.

There still remain the two other outstanding features of this statue: the dagger piercing the heart and the inscription. As far as the dagger is concerned, it was quite common in the thirteenth century for images of martyrs to have in their hands the tool by which martyrdom was inflicted upon them, as a means of identification. Dante's statement that the heart was still venerated in England and Henry's reputation as an inoffensive, sweet, and angelic youth may

10 G. Biagi, *La Divina Commedia*, p. 348.
11 See P. Brieger, *English Art 1216–1307* (Oxford, 1957), p. 103.

have given him the rank of a martyr in Italian eyes. In consequence, the weapon with which he was slain was added to the portrayal.

The inscription presents a more difficult problem. It could be either genuine or a later invention. If it was copied from an actual inscription connected with the burial of Henry's heart in the Confessors' chapel at Westminster Abbey, of which no trace is left, the *consanguineus* to whom the heart was given must be Edward the Confessor, near whose shrine the heart was buried and who acted as intercessor between Henry and God. The inscription would thus stress the blood relationship between the last Anglo-Saxon king and the reigning royal house in conformity with Henry iii's choice of St. Edward as a patron saint. The Italian writers of the following century, either quoting the inscription or inventing it, interpreted it quite differently. Henry's words are not directed towards the saint and through him towards God, but towards his blood relation Edward i to remind him of his duty to revenge the murder. They introduce the motif of blood revenge of which there is no trace to be found in England.

Some attempts were made by Edward i after the murder to obtain just punishment for the murderer, but they led to nothing. Guy was for a time excommunicated and banned, but was later reinstated. He was finally captured by a Sicilian admiral and died shortly afterwards in prison. Rishanger quotes a verse by an unknown versemaker which was inspired by the mural painting at Viterbo.[12] It was probably composed by an Englishman, to judge from the two last verses which say that God ordained the murder of Henry to prevent the recall of the sons of Simon de Montfort to England which might have caused the perdition of the whole English nation. There is no clamour for revenge in these verses whereas the feeling of resentment that the murderer escaped unpunished and the desire for punishment was strong in Italy and characteristic of the emotional temper in Italy of Dante's time. It was so strong that it was even infused into a tomb effigy, which usually at this time was intended to represent the resurrected body of the deceased, to whom all thoughts of vengance would be foreign. The root of the story about the statue grows from the same passionate desire to see sin punished which made Dante allot just punishment in hell to Guy de Montfort after his death since he had escaped human justice during his life.

12 W. Rishanger, *Chron. et Ann.*, p. 67.

The Commentary of Giles of Rome on the
Rhetoric of Aristotle J. R. O'DONNELL

he exact date of birth of Giles of Rome is unknown. The most plausible conjecture puts it somewhat before 1247, perhaps as early as 1243.[1] He was a student of St. Thomas Aquinas from 1269–72. After the condemnations of 1277, Giles refused submission on several points of anti-aristotelianism and, as a result, left Paris in 1278. In 1285 he returned to Paris, armed with a letter from Honorius IV; he made his submission and was declared a doctor. In 1292 he became general of his order, the Hermits of St. Augustine. In 1295 he was named archbishop of Bourges and died at Avignon on 22 December 1316. For a long period, Giles was thought to be a member of the famous Colonna family but this is highly improbable.[2]

Giles of Rome was a prolific writer and influential teacher. Two of his works on politics were of particular importance, the *De Regimine Principum*, dedicated to Philip, later Philip the Fair, and the *De Potestate Ecclesiastica*, dedicated to Boniface VIII.[3] It was from this

1 P. Mandonnet, "La carrière scolaire de Gilles de Rome," *Revue des sciences philosophiques et théologiques*, IV (1910), 481; E. Hocedez, "La condamnation de Gilles de Rome," *Recherches de théologie ancienne et médiévale*, IV (1932), 34ff; G. Boffito, *Saggio di bibliografia Aegediana* (Firenze, 1911); G. Bruni, "Catalogo dei manoscritti Egediani Romani," *Rivista di filosofia neoscolastica*, XXII–XXIII (1931).
    Le opere di Egidio Romano (Firenze, 1936); *Quadro cronologico della vita e delle opere di Egidio Romano: Saggio, una inedita "Quaestio de Natura Universalis" di Egidio Romano* (Napoli, 1935), pp. 26–43.
    A. Dyroff, "Aegidius von Colonna? Aegidius Conigiatus?" *Philosophisches Jahrbuch*, XXXVIII (1925), 18–25; K. Eubel, *Hierarchia Catholica Medii Aevi*, I (Padua, 1960), p. 138.
2 Dyroff, "Aegidius von Colonna?" 23.
3 "Domino philippo primogenito et heredi praeclarissimi viri domini philippi dei gratia illustrissimi regis francorum" (Venice, 1482), 1ʳa; "Sanctissimo

treatise that Boniface took a good deal of material for the famous
bull, *Unam Sanctam*. Giles defended the position of St. Thomas
Aquinas against the advocates of a plurality of forms.[4] Among his
philosophical treatises was a series of commentaries on the works of
Aristotle done between 1263 and 1278. Some of these commentaries
were dedicated to individuals, for example the commentary on the
Sophistici Elenchi was dedicated "filio praeclari comitis Flandrensis"
and on the *Posteriora Analytica* to an Englishman, Stephano de
Maulay. The commentary on the *Rhetoric* is dedicated to a person
left unnamed whom Giles in turn designates as "vestra discretio"
and "vestra tamen punctus dilectione." The coupling of the terms
discretio, used for bishops and nobility, and *dilectio*, used for ecclesiastics, would, perhaps, suggest a bishop as the dedicatee.[5]

The basic text of the *Rhetoric* which Giles used was the translation of William of Moerbeke made in 1260.[6] But he does make
references to other readings, which he calls "alia litera," "alia translatio," "textus arabicus," or "vetus translatio." These are references
either to the earlier translation, sometimes attributed to Bartholomew
of Messina, or to the version of Hermann Alemannus.[7] William of
Moerbeke borrowed heavily from the anonymous translation. For
example, compare "Ambae enim de talibus quibusdam sunt quae
communiter quodammodo omnium est cognoscere et nullius scientiae determinatae."[8] with "utraeque enim de quibusdam hujusmodi
sunt quae communia quodammodo omnium est cognoscere et nullius
scientiae determinatae."[9] Hermann describes his translation as "opus
praesentis translationis rhetoricae Aristotelis et ejus poetriae ex ara-

patri ac domino suo domino singulari domino Bonifacio" (ed. R. Scholz,
Weimar, 1929), p. 4.

4 E. Hocedez, "La condamnation," 37.

5 *discretio*, see DuCange, *Glossarium ad Scriptures mediae et infimae Latini-
tatis*, s.v.
dilectio, see Sr. M. B. O'Brien, *Titles of Address in Christian Latin Epistolo-
graphy to 543 A.D.* (Washington, 1930), index s.v.

6 G. Verbeke, in *Lexikon für Theologie und Kirche*, x (Freiburg, 1960), ed.
1140. On William of Moerbeke as a translator see G. Verbeke, "Guillaume
de Moerbeke et sa méthode de traduction," *Medioevo e Rinascimento: studi
in onore di Bruno Nardi* (Firenze, 1955), II, pp. 779ff.

7 L. Spengel, *Aristotelis Ars Rhetorica: Accedit Vetusta Translatio Latina*
(Leipzig, 1867), I, p. 177, n.2 cf. Bibliothèque Nationale, ms. latin 16673,
fols. 1–65, henceforth described as ms. *P*. On Hermannus Alemannus, see
G. Bonafede, in *Enciclopedia Filosofica* (Venezia/Roma, 1957), II, p. 22 and
ms. *P*. fols. 65ᵛ–172. Also Eubel, *Hierarchica*, I, p. 114.

8 Spengel, *Aristotelis*, p. 178.

9 Ms. *P*. f.1ʳa.

bico eloquio in latinam jam dudum intuitu venerabilis patris Joannis Burgensis episcopi et regis Castellae cancellarii inceperam."[10] The explicit of the *Poetics* reads as follows: "Explicit, deo gratias, anno domini millesimo ducentesimo quinquagesimo, sexto decimo die Martii apud Toletum, urbem nobilem."[11] Hermann also stated that he translated the glosses of Alpharabi on the *Rhetoric*. "Cujus glosae plusquam duos quinternos ego quoque transtuli in latinum."[12] Some examples of the cross references to the *aliae translationes* will demonstrate that they do not, for the most part, contribute much to the commentary. "Unde in alia translatione habetur quod rhetorica convertitur arti Topicae."[13] Hermann's translation reads "Rhetorica quidem convertitur arti Topicae."[14] "Habet alia translatio mactatio Victimarum," instead of "sacrificia."[15] "Ex alia littera, aptos ad quinque ludos" for "penthadeos."[16] "Superficialiter sive summatim ut habet alia littera."[17] "In aliis ambabus translationibus habetur pono"[18]; here Hermann reads "ponimus" and Giles reads "positio." "Adulatores, alia littera habet callidi et astuti."[19] Such detailed references seem to indicate that Giles had read the texts of both the anonymous translation and that of Hermann Alemannus. But the text used varies somewhat from that of ms.*P.*

Giles opens his commentary with an exordium; Aristotle had said this should be done.[20] Giles, however, seems to be more indebted to the *artes dictaminis* for the style of the exordium than to the *Rhetoric*.[21] He begins with a quotation from the *Nichomachean Ethics* to the effect that a man's purpose is dictated by his character.[22] The anonymous addressee of the commentary surely had such a lofty

10 Ms. *P.* f.65ʳa. On Joannis Burgensis, see Eubel, *Hierarchica*, ɪ, p. 151.
11 Ms. *P.* f.172ʳ.
12 Ms. *P.* f.65ᵛb; On ms. of Paris, see Biblio. Nat. ms. latin 16097 and I. Madkour, *L'organon d'Aristote dans le monde arabe* (Paris, 1934), p. 16.
13 All references are to the Venice edition of 1515. I am grateful to the British Museum for a photographic copy, henceforth referred to as *ed.* Where necessary the text of this edition has been corrected from ms. Vatican latin 766, henceforth referred to as ms. *V.*
14 Ms. *P.* 65ᵛb.
15 Ms. *P.* 8ᵛb; *ed.* 21ʳb.
16 Ms. *P.* 74ᵛb; *ed.* 21ᵛb.
17 Ms. *P.* 14ʳa; *ed.* 31ʳb.
18 *Ed.* 36ᵛb: ms. *P.* 17ᵛa and 85ᵛb; Spengel, *Aristotelis*, p. 218.
19 *Ed.* 93ᵛb; ms. *P.* 127ᵛb, on Aristotle 1405a22.
20 *Rhetorica*, ɪɪɪ, 14 (1414b19ff.).
21 L. Rockinger, *Briefsteller und Formelbücher des 11. bis 14. Jahrhunderts* (reprint, New York, 1961), ɪ, p. 18.
22 *Ed.* 1ʳa, Aristotle 1114a32.

purpose in asking for the commentary to facilitate a better knowledge of rhetoric. This is the *capatio benevolentiae*, traditional in the *artes dictaminis*. This should be followed by an expression of humility: Giles is really unequal to the task, because of the difficulty of the work in translation, the brevity of Aristotle's style, the multiplicity of texts (*ex multiplicitate exemplorum*) and the few helps (*et paucitate auxiliorum*) available and the stress of many and continuous tasks. But he will undertake the task and try to express what Aristotle had in mind "promulgabo sententiam qualem credam Aristotelem intendisse."[23] The difficulties which Giles alleged to be facing in his task are more or less a commonplace. Cicero had praised Aristotle for his brevity;[24] yet many commentators had complained of Aristotle's brevity, of the great number of the works of predecessors, and a busy life. For example Themistius alleges as difficulties the many commentators on Aristotle, the brevity of Aristotle's manner of speech, and the difficulty of the text.[25] Likewise Ammonius complains of the difficulty of the text and the many commentators.[26] Boethius, too, had said that the difficulties in understanding Aristotle had led him to write a double commentary on the *De interpretatione*.[27] All of these statements, and many others, were available to Giles of Rome.[28]

Giles' own exordium varies somewhat from Aristotle's stipulation that it contain enough information to introduce the audience to the material under discussion.[29] Nonetheless he takes Aristotle's definition of an exordium as an occasion to discuss in detail the place of rhetoric in the classification of the sciences. Also, Aristotle had not considered the exordium an essential part of rhetoric; Giles says that he would agree with this, were he going to talk about matters that are clear. "Si manifesta essent dicenda, non indigeremus praelocutione."

The problem of the classification of the sciences had long played an important role in philosophical speculation, from Plato (*Republic*, 509ff) in his attempt to correlate the noetic order with the objects of

23 *Ed.* 1ʳa.
24 *De inventione*, II, pp. 2, 6.
25 J. R. O'Donnell, "Themistius' Paraphrasis of the Posterior Analytics in Gerard of Cremona's Translation," *Mediaeval Studies*, XX (1959), 242.
26 G. Verbeke, *Ammonius, Commentaire sur le peri hermeneias d'Aristote* (Louvain, 1961), p. 1.
27 Boethius, *In librum de interpretatione*, P.L. 64, col. 293.
28 E. Quain, "The Medieval Accessus ad Auctores," *Traditio*, III (1945).
29 *Rhetorica*, 1414b19ff.

knowledge, through the twelfth and thirteenth centuries, to clarify and systematize by division and definition the nature of the science in question.[30] The opening statement of the *Rhetoric* is that "Rhetorica assecutiva dialecticae," or as it reads in the translation of Hermann: "Rhetorica convertitur arti Topicae," which Alpharabi, Giles tells us, explained as a kind of identification: "Alfarabius exponit hujusmodi conversionem esse quandam adaequationem et aequipollentiam."[31] Alpharabi was one of the few aids at Giles' disposal and whom he quotes considerably ("in quibusdam suis praeambulis quae edidit super rhetoricam").[32] This identification, Giles felt, entitled him to say that rhetoric is a part of dialectic or of logic. Alpharabi had enumerated eight parts of logic, namely, the *Categories, Perihermeneias, Prior and Posterior Analytics, Topics, Sophistics, Rhetoric,* and *Poetics;* the names of the books are substituted for the names of the sciences contained therein.[33] *Logica* is derived from *logos,* which is, in Latin, *sermo vel ratio;* therefore, logic is either a science of discourse or a rational science: "Est igitur logica sermocinativa vel rationalis scientia." This only partially locates rhetoric. Two more questions must be asked. How does logic differ from any other science or art which is based on reason? Again, why are logic and rhetoric labelled unqualifiedly as rational, when there are sciences which are much more cogently rational than either? To Giles the answers are clear. Each science, he says, has a different procedure. There is no ruling science which controls the methodology of any other science or art. Hence, even though rhetoric is part of dialectic or logic, the procedures are different. Dialectic proceeds by probable reasoning to produce opinion (*opinio*); opinion demands only a conditioned assent, an assent which does not exclude the possibility of another opinion about the same question being true. Rhetoric uses persuasive arguments to produce belief (*fides, credulitas*) which requires an act of the will or appetite of the believer. Finally, the demonstrative sciences, properly so-called, use syllogistic reasoning based on a knowledge of the causes. The difference between belief and science is apparent; if they do happen to coincide, it is by sheer accident. But the case is far different for belief and opinion.

30 J. Mariétan, *Problème de la classification des sciences d'Aristote à St. Thomas* (Paris, 1901); A. Maurer, *The Division and Methods of the Sciences* (Toronto, 1963); p. xxxiii ff.
31 *Ed.* 2ʳa.
32 *Ed.* 1ʳa.
33 A. G. Palencia, *Al-Farabi, Catálogo de las Ciencias* (Madrid, 1953), p. 95.

Superficially, it might be said that opinion gives greater certitude than belief. But we know that many believe more strongly than they opine. Alpharabi offers a possible way out of the difficulty by stating that opinion deals with universals, whereas belief has to do with particulars. To Giles this is not a satisfactory answer because one can believe more strongly about a particular fact than opine about a universal; for example we are of the opinion that the sun is larger than the earth, even though our senses tell us that the sun is only one foot in diameter.[34]

The distinction, therefore, between rhetoric, dialectic and logic cannot be based on the subjective norms of certitude. The basis of distinction is to be found in the fact that assent to belief comes from the intellect only when it is moved by the will or the appetite, whereas assent to opinion or scientific demonstration belongs to the intellect strictly as intellect: "Hoc autem si bene advertamus, habemus differentiam inter scibilia, probabilia et persuasibilia. Nam assensus credulitatis per rationes persuasivas competit intellectui secundum quod aptus natus moveri ab appetitu. Assensus vero scientificus et opinativus sive assentire per propositiones demonstrativas et probabiles competit intellectui ut est aptus natus moveri secundum motum proprium."[35] Again, the purpose of rhetoric is different from that of dialectic and logic. Its purpose is to show that something is good, not that it is true: "Magis est finis rhetoricae ostendere aliquid esse bonum vel malum quam esse verum vel non verum."[36]

Once it has been established that a distinction between dialectic and rhetoric could be made on the basis of the assent of the intellect, moved by the will or the appetite, and an assent of the intellect purely in terms of rational cogency, it becomes possible to attribute greater certitude to opinion than to belief. For as soon as appetites are involved, the objects of the appetites, as such, are also involved. But truth or falsity can exist only in a mental proposition or judgment and for this reason dialectic is a more rational science than rhetoric, because the objects of the appetites appear as good, and good exists only in things and not in the judgment. "Per rationes dialecticas magis probatur aliquid esse verum, per rhetoricas vero magis esse bonum. Nam cum verum et falsum sint in anima et objectum intellectus formaliter loquendo non sit bonum sed verum, quod

34 *Ed.* 1ᵣb; Palencia, *Al-Farabi,* p. 93.
35 *Ed.* 1ᵣb.   36 *Ed.* 16ᵣa.

terminat intellectum secundum se, oportet quod probet aliquid esse verum; unde bene dictum est quod verum sub ratione qua probabile intenditur a logico; nam hoc est habere opinionem alicujus, quia assentimus ei tanquam vero probabili; sed cum bonum et malum sint in rebus et bonum sit objectum appetitus, quod terminat intellectum ut habet ordinem ad voluntatem, debet ostendere aliquid quia bonum."[37]

The same principle, used to distinguish rhetoric and dialectic as sciences, can also be used to distinguish them from sciences of reality, that is the sciences whose objects are grounded in the physical world outside the mind (*scientiae reales*).[38] For example, geometry deals with magnitudes and consequently cannot strictly be called a rational science, but it is rational in the sense that its procedure is rational.

There are, to sum up, five ways in which rhetoric and dialectic differ: (1) The rhetorician tends to treat of moral questions or problems of the practical intellect; the dialectician deals primarily with speculative matters. (2) The rhetorician must take into consideration the passions, since appeals to the passions are means of persuasion, not as properly belonging to the subject matter of rhetoric, but as influences on the judge and audience. The dialectician, however, need not be concerned with the passions. (3) Those at whom the art of rhetoric is aimed are generally less learned and astute (*simplex et grossus*) than those engaged in dialectics who are more subtly minded (*subtilis et ingeniosus*). (4) The rhetorician uses enthymemes and examples to persuade, whereas the dialectician uses syllogisms and induction to demonstrate probability. Enthymemes are imperfect syllogisms (*syllogismus defectivus*, that is, *ateles*) and examples are imperfect forms of induction. Both rhetoric and dialectic use commonplaces, but differently. (5) The subject (*objectum vel subjectum*) of dialectic is universal, that of rhetoric is singular.[39]

Three of the above-mentioned differences Giles, following his bent of mind and competence, deals with in detail: the relation of rhetoric to moral philosophy,[40] the nature of enthymemes and examples,[41] and an analysis of the passions.[42]

---

37 *Ibid.*
38 *Ed.* 1ᵛa–b.
39 *Ed.* 1ᵛa, 15ᵛb.
40 *Ed.* 11ᵛb, see G. Bruni, "The 'De Differentia Rhetoricae, Ethicae, et Politicae' of Aegidius Romanus," *New Scholasticism*, vi (1932), 1ff.
41 *Ed.* 11ᵛb; 77ʳa; 89ʳa.
42 *Ed.* 49ʳa.

Can rhetoric be applied to politics? Enthymemes – the main means of rhetorical persuasion – are applicable to more than one science or art and especially to politics, since both rhetoric and politics deal with singulars. "Rhetorica vero non est de actibus rationis simpliciter et absolute sumptis, sed est de eis ut sunt applicabiles ad facta singularia; ideo ait philosophus [1094b3] quod accidit rhetoricam velut adnatam partem quandam dialecticae esse negotii, quod est circa mores."[43] In his treatise *De differentia rhetoricae, ethicae et politicae*,[44] Giles is more specific. Rhetoric is not properly part of politics because it does not directly give a knowledge of morals; rather it is a form of dialectics and gives directly a knowledge of certain things common to several sciences. It is also possible to compare rhetoric and dialectic much as optics and geometry can be compared. Geometry deals with lines as such, while optics is concerned with visible lines, that is lines which are subject to the senses; in much the same way rhetoric deals with common principles which are applicable to specifically concrete political facts; just as geometry and optics are separate sciences, so also are rhetoric and dialectics. However, Giles adds a note of caution; because optics is a science subalternated to geometry, it cannot be concluded that rhetoric is subalternated to dialectics. Subalternation is the relationship of one science to another in which the lower science derives its principles from the higher. In other words, optics would not be possible if geometry had not already established principles, which can be validly adapted to optics.[45] That is why Giles insists in this treatise that the statesman would be a sophist if he were to use the common principles of rhetoric without adapting them to politics.[46]

The statesman (*politicus*), it is true, studies enthymemes as does the rhetorician, but in a different way. The statesman considers enthymemes in their specific application to particular circumstances and facts; the rhetorician studies enthymemes only in so far as they are common means of persuasion. Giles returns to this principle again and again as a basis of distinction. To the question whether it is true that rhetorical reasoning is applicable to the natural sciences and to the speculative sciences, he says that the whole matter would be clear if we take into consideration a twofold and basic difference.

---

43 *Ed.* 14ᵛb–15ʳa.
44 Bruni, "De Differentia," 5.
45 *Ed.* 7ᵛb; see *Posterior Analytica*, I, p. 7ff.
46 Bruni, "De Differentia," 8.

"Duplex enim quasi radicalis differentia inter rhetoricam et dialecticam est. Prima est ex eo quod generatur ex eis; nam ex rhetorica aggeneratur fides quae terminat intellectum in ordine ad appetitum; ex dialectica vero opinio quae habet quietare intellectum secundum se."[47] In two of his later works, the *De regimine principum* and the *De potestate ecclesiastica*,[48] he states that reasonings in politics and on moral problems should not be profound and subtle, but plain and appealing to the senses, if we hope to persuade men to do good.

A second point with which Giles deals in detail is the nature of enthymemes. If enthymemes are the most important means of persuasion at the disposal of rhetoric, then this emphasis seems in order. The whole art of rhetoric is to persuade and this it does primarily by enthymemes and examples. "Rhetorica est principaliter de enthymemate ... simpliciter loquendo principalissimum genus persuasionum enthymemata erunt."[49] But Giles raises an objection: if enthymemes belong to rhetoric, then surely they have no place in dialectic. His answer to the objection is interesting. There are those who invent arts and there are those who teach how to use an art; for example, the inventor of the art of grammar need not have been a *grammaticus* as such, but rather a metaphysician who grasped the modes of understanding and of signification.[50]

Since enthymemes and examples are the chief instruments of rhetoric, and rhetoric is a part of dialectic, enthymemes and examples must be reducible to syllogisms and induction, the proper tools of dialectic. "Nihil enim est aliud enthymema quam rhetoricus syllogismus et exemplum quam rhetorica inductio."[51] To explain further Giles turns to the *Organon* for clarification. From the *Topica* we learn that induction is the progress from particulars to universals, that is from particulars which bear the same relationship to a universal.[52] Dialectical reasoning, however, progresses from generally accepted opinions. Demonstrative reasoning progresses from premises which are true, primary, and necessary. Again, a syllogism demonstrates through a middle term that the major term applies to a third term; induction, however, shows that the major term applies to the middle term through a third term. Giles suggests that the reason Aristotle

---

47 Ed. 15ᵛb.
48 *De regimine principum*, I, p. 1.
49 Ed. 4ᵛb., on 1355a3.
50 Ed. 4ᵛb–5ʳa.
51 Ed. 8ʳa ff.
52 Ed. 8ʳb; *Topica* I, p. 12 (105a10ff); also 68b30ff.

mentions only the *Topics* is because the definition from the *Prior Analytics* is too subtle. Giles confuses the treatise *Methodica* with the *Topics*, ("in Methodicis, id est in Topicis").[53]

In the *Posterior Analytics* (74b5) Aristotle required necessary premises for scientific demonstration. In rhetoric, however, it is rare that premises are necessary. If they happen to be necessary, it is merely accidental. Rather enthymemes are constructed from probable propositions and signs ("ex ycotibus et signis, ex eikoton kai semeion").[54] However, the general audience of rhetoric is more impressed by examples; "nam homines vulgares, qui sunt auditores rationum rhetoricarum volentes melius capere exempla, turbantur magis, si quis enim loquitur enthymemate."[55]

Signs are of three kinds, distinguished according to the three figures of the syllogism. First, those which belong to the first figure always and without fail call to mind the thing signified: milk indicates that a woman has given birth. Those that belong to the second figure generally, but not always, call to mind the thing signified: if anyone wanders about after dark, it is usually a sign that he is a burglar. In the third figure, the sign sometimes calls to mind the thing signified: we often associate diligence, wisdom, and goodness, because they are virtues sometimes found in one and the same person and we can build a rhetorical argument on such a sign.[56] The sign belonging to the first figure Giles calls a "prodigium, id est, signum magnum sive retinerium" or, according to another text, "detinar (tekmerion)"; it is so called because it sets a person's mind at rest ("quasi hominem retinens vel terminans"). Giles evidently either did not understand the text or misread it, because the text of William of Moerbeke reads *tecmerium* and the anonymous text of the translation has *tecmiridon, tecmirium*, and *tecmar* and ms. Vatican latin 776, f.112^{r}a reads "retinerium quasi hominem retinens"; *retinerium*, however, has been corrected in the manuscript.[57] In book II (1402b-13) Aristotle distinguishes *tekmerion* from sign and indicates that enthymemes can be constructed of four different components: "ychos, exemplum, tecmerium et signum"[58]; *exemplum* has been

---

53 P. Moraux, *Les listes anciennes des ouvrages d'Aristote* (Louvain, 1951), p. 24, nos. 52, 55, 55b; *Ed.* 8^{r}b on 1356b19.
54 *Ed.* 9^{r}b on 1357a29.
55 *Ed.* 8^{v}a on 1356b23.
56 *Ed.* 9^{v}a: see *Prior Analytica*, II, p. 27.
57 *Ed.* 9^{v}a; Spengel, *Aristotelis*, p. 186; ms. *P.* 4^{v}b.
58 *Ed.* 89^{r}b reads *dechamerium* ; text c has *thechamerium.*

added. A sign can be called an *ycos* (*eikos*), that is, "quasi imago vel similitudinarium," provided it is limited to the second and third figures of the syllogism, because these are probabilities (*versimile et probabile*), but in the case of the first figure, the sign is necessary and really cannot be identified with *ycos*.[59]

Because enthymemes are composed of examples and examples are a form of induction, some discussion of their differences is called for. An example differs from a syllogism in two ways and from induction in two ways. From a syllogism in that the major and minor terms are related through a middle term, and in that there is a descent from the whole to the part; all figures of the syllogism are reducible to the first figure, (*Barbara* and *Celarent*) whose premisses are either universal affirmatives or universal negatives. An example, on the other hand relates the terms, not through a middle term, but through a likeness to a third; nor does it descend from whole to part, but progresses from part to part. Giles seldom departs from the examples given by Aristotle and here borrowing from Aristotle, he shows us how an example works. Dionysius has asked for a bodyguard; therefore he probably intends to make himself a tyrant, for that is exactly what Pisistratus did when he asked for a bodyguard.[60]

An example differs from induction, for by induction the argument proceeds by way of enumeration of particulars, whereas an example concludes a term about the middle term through a likeness to a third. A third difference can be added to the above, namely, one term can conclude through a third term about still another term, other than the middle term.[61]

Both rhetoric and dialectics deal with all these points, but in a different way: the rhetorician in a broad and practical way, the dialectician in a more detailed and speculative manner. In short, the general principle that rhetoric tends to the particular, and is an applied art, especially to moral questions or politics, in order to persuade, by probabilities, examples etc., that good, real or apparent, should be done; the dialectician, however, attempts to prove that something is true. Rhetoric and dialectic are distinct, and this fact colours all Giles' discussions about commonplaces, signs, etc.

Although Aristotle claimed that the passions were, in essence, really outside the field of rhetoric (1354b25ff), nonetheless he admits (1378a18) that the passions or emotions cause men to change their minds, especially when moved by such passions as anger, pity, fear,

59 *Ed.* 9ᵛa.   60 *Ed.* 10ʳb on 1357b30.   61 *Ed.* 10ᵛa.

friendship, goodwill, etc.[62] Since rhetoric is aimed at persuasion and because the passions play a large role in persuasion, especially in forensic oratory, either to make it easy or difficult, we are not surprised that Giles goes out of his way to an amplified and codified analysis of the passions, specifically on their nature, number and interrelation. "Ad intelligentiam autem dicendorum quattuor sunt declaranda; nam, ut habeamus notitiam tractatus sequentis, ubi de passionibus agitur, primo videndum est quid sit passio; secundo ... numerus passiorum, tertio ... ordo ipsarum, quarto ... quomodo opponantur passiones ad invicem."[63]

In answer to the question: what is a passion, Giles does not begin with a definition which he will exploit; rather he attempts a description which will lead to a definition. The location of the passions is in the powers or faculties of soul as in a subject: for example, love exists in the will. Because the passions are accidents of the faculties or powers of the soul, they cannot be defined without reference to their subject. There is a threefold division of the powers according to the threefold partition of the soul into the vegetative, sensitive, and rational. The natural powers flow from the vegetative soul, the sensitive powers from the sensitive soul which are bound up with a sense organ, the rational powers are in the rational soul and not tied to organs. Although there might appear to be three souls, there is in reality only one; the vegetative soul exists in the sensitive soul and the sensitive in the rational. The rational or intellective soul contains within itself virtually both the vegetative and sensitive, that is, the intellective soul, of itself, exercises both vegetative and sensitive activities. "Sic omnes potentiae animae vegetativae reservantur in anima sensitiva et adhuc plures, et quicquid potest anima sensitiva potest intellectiva et adhuc amplius. Propter quod licet nos non habeamus tres animas, tamen, quia hujusmodi anima est intellectiva in qua virtualiter continentur vegetativum et sensitivum, omnia genera potentiarum nunc assignata est invenire in nobis."[64] To illustrate what he meant Giles uses the example of a triangle being contained by a figure of four angles which in turn is contained by a pentagon; in each case the contained is less than the container. This is a rather crude statement about the problem of the plurality of

62 Ed. 4ʳa–b.
63 Ed. 49ʳa on 1378a15; See O. Hieronimi, Die allgemeine Passionenlehre bei Aegidius von Rom (Würzburg, 1934).
64 Ed. 49ʳb.

forms, a problem which was to grow into a bitter dispute within the next few years and to which Giles will return in his *De gradibus formarum*. The problem was violently discussed as both a philosophical and theological question and ended with the Oxford condemnation by Robert Kilwardby on 18 March 1277, although this doctrine had not been numbered among the condemned theses at Paris on 7 March 1277.[65] In the commentary on the *Rhetoric* Giles does not seem to be seriously concerned with the problem; otherwise, surely, he would have used the occasion to deal more thoroughly with it. The statement in the *Rhetoric* is little improvement over that of Alcher of Clairvaux in his *Liber de Spiritu et Anima*, where he says that there is a threefold power of the soul, sensitive, rational, and intellectual, which the philosophers call virtual parts of the soul: "Hanc triplicem vim animae, id est sensualem, rationalem et intellectualem, philosophi partes vocaverunt, non integrales, sed virtuales, quia potentiae ejus sunt."[66] In the *De gradibus formarum*, Giles set out to prove that not only was the doctrine of the unity of form not contrary to faith; rather it is really the only doctrine that is consonant with the faith.

The passions are located in the powers of the soul. But in what powers? It cannot be in the natural powers, that is, in the vegetative powers of nutrition, generation, and growth, because these are active powers and in no way passive. "Potentiae naturales secundum quod hujusmodi videntur esse activae, non passivae."[67] The passions do not exist in the rational powers, if we understand by rational powers those not bound to a sense organ. It remains, therefore, that the subject of the passions is the sensitive powers. But some of the sensitive powers of the soul are cognitive and some appetitive. In knowledge things enter the soul; in appetition the soul goes out to the things desired and is modified by whatever things the powers of the soul undergo. In knowledge what is known is modified by the conditions of the knower. Giles quotes the axiom which he attributes to Boethius;[68] "quicquid cognoscitur cognoscitur secundum modum cognoscentis." In passion it is a contrary process: "passio secundum quod trahitur passum ad conditiones agentis." The passions, therefore, are in the sensitive powers of the soul and are moderated

65 D. A. Callus, *The Condemnation of St. Thomas at Oxford* (Oxford, 1955).
66 Alcher of Clairvaux, *Liber de Spiritu et Anima*, P.L. 40, col. 808.
67 Ed. 49ʳb.
68 *De Consolatione Philosophiae*, v, 4, 71; *ed.* 49ʳb.

according to the conditions of the objects desired. "Solum ergo erit passio in appetitu sensitivo, ut communiter ponitur, quia secundum appetitum trahitur ad conditiones objectorum." The appetite goes out to an object and is affected by the object; there is, in other words, a motion of the soul towards the thing which will affect or alter the powers of the soul. But action and passion are one and the same thing: "nam actio et passio sunt unus et idem motus, ut dicitur 3° Physicorum (201a19ff). Est enim eadem res motus et actio et passio." The way has now been opened for Giles' definition of a passion as a motion of the sensitive appetite; "declaratum est igitur quid sit passio quia est motus appetitus sensitivi; quod ostendere volebamus."

The number of the passions given by Giles is traditional.[69] The sensitive appetite is divided into the concupiscible and the irascible. The objects of these two appetites are particulars which are either simply or apparently good. The irascible appetite does not seek its object merely as a good, nor avoid an object merely as evil; for over and above the goodness or evil of the objects there is the additional note, that the object sought is a good difficult to attain or an evil difficult to avoid. The concupiscible appetite, however, seeks its object simply as a good or avoids an object simply as evil: "Omnes igitur passiones illae, quae sumantur respectu boni vel mali absolute sumpti, pertinent ad concupiscibilem. Illae vero, quae super talem rationem superaddunt rationem ardui vel difficilis, pertinent ad irascibilem."[70] To the concupiscible appetite belong love (amor) and its opposite, hate (odium); desire (desiderium) and its opposite, detestation (abominatio); pleasure (delectatio) and its opposite, pain or sadness (tristitia). To the irascible appetite belong hope (spes) and its opposite, despair (desperatio); fear (timor) and its opposite, boldness or courage (audacia); anger (ira) and its counterpart, meekness (mansuetudo, mititas).[71] A comparison can be made between the passions and physical objects. In physical objects (in rebus naturalibus) there is, first of all, a certain tendency (inclinatio), as in a heavy object there is the tendency to fall to earth; secondly, there is the exercise of this tendency, for example the rest (quies) the heavy object enjoys, when it comes to rest on the ground. In the passions love corresponds to the tendency of a heavy object to fall; desire cor-

69 Ed. 49ᵛa.
70 Ibid.
71 Contrast Aristotle 1125b26 with 1380a5 on ira and its opposite.

responds to the fall or descent of the heavy object; pleasure corresponds to the repose the heavy object enjoys when it comes to rest on the ground. The same pattern can be applied to the appetite in the face of evil. There is a tendency away from evil which is hate, the exercise of hate is detestation, and finally there is sadness or pain when we fall into inescapable evil.

Giles has defined a passion as a motion of the sensitive appetite and wants his division to fit the definition. That is why he introduces a statement of Aristotle (*Physics* 201a5) to the effect that motion belongs in the categories of quality, quantity, and place as well as in substance. Within substance there is no motion, because there is no contrary to substance; but emotional change is an accidental motion of the soul. The passions, therefore, achieve their roles either through motion or arrival at the term of motion. Arrival at the term of a motion can be instantaneous, in the sense that the power of the soul is affected immediately when it finds itself in the presence of its object. "Communiter ergo accipiendo motum omnis passio potest dici quidam motus animae; proprie tamen accipiendo motum, quaedam passiones habent rationem motus, quaedam vero habent rationem mutationis vel mutati esse."[72]

Two possible objections are introduced into the discussion.[73] Pleasure does not seem to correspond to the definition of a passion, since it is neither a motion nor a change; rather its whole essence seems to consist in a lack of change (*in immobilitate*). For example, in God and in the separate substances there is no change but rather a perfection and splendour of operation which suffers no impediments. The greatest pleasure is found in the activity of the intelligence; the fact that the passions are located, not in the intelligence, but in the sensitive appetite, diminishes the nature of the pleasure which can be found in them; there is, therefore, a *mutatio* or *mutatum esse* in the gap that exists between a perfect and a diminished pleasure. In this way the passion of pleasure can be made to comply with the general definition of passion. Although at this point Giles cites Aristotle by name, his terminology is more reminiscent of St. Thomas' commentary on the *Ethics*.[74]

There is also a difficulty in the case of meekness. If we face evil and rebel against it and through anger seek revenge, there can be no doubt that this is a motion. But if, on the contrary, we meekly submit to evil, there seems to be rest (*quies*) in that evil. Surely this does not

72 Ed. 49ᵛb.					73 Ed. 50ʳa.					74 cf. In vɪɪ Ethica, t.c. 14.

satisfy the definition of a passion. Nonetheless, Giles claims, meekness can, in a certain sense, be called a passion because every negation implies an affirmation. Meekness is a denial or negation of anger and desire for revenge; consequently it must be defined in terms of anger. For his authority, Giles invokes the second book of the *Sophistici Elenchi* ("semper in non facere intelligitur facere," (177b26).[75] The section closes thus: "sunt igitur duodecim passiones, sex in concupiscibili et sex in irascibili. Propter quod manifestatur numerus earum, quod volebamus declarare."[76]

The order of the passions (*ordo passionum*) can easily be codified on the basis of the distinctions already made. Yet at first glance the problem seems to be rather involved, for the passions of the concupiscible appetite are not entirely anterior to those of the irascible, nor are they entirely consequent to them. Some passions of the concupiscible appetite are essentially passions which require motion, while others imply that the terminus of a motion has been reached. In general, the passions of the irascible appetite presuppose that the term of motion has not been reached; on the contrary they specifically imply motion; of course, in the case of meekness there is a dubious exception. Also, since both hope and despair are concerned only with future goods as attainable or not, there can be no *mutatum esse*, because the term of motion has not been reached. Neither fear nor courage could possibly imply that the terms of their motion have been reached; for once a desired good has been attained or an evil avoided, there can no longer be hope or despair, nor can there be fear in venturing after it. No more can there be anger in the presence of evil, but rather either pain or meekness. The passions of the irascible appetite seem to find their proper location between the passions of the concupiscible appetite which imply motion and those which imply that a terminus has been reached: "Hujusmodi passiones (irascibilis) mediae sunt inter passiones concupiscibilis importantes motum et passiones concupiscibilis importantes mutatum esse."[77] In the first place, therefore, are the passions of love and hate, secondly those of desire and detestation. These are followed by hope and despair; next come fear and courage, and finally anger and meekness. In last place are pleasure and pain, since they imply a *mutatum esse*.

75 The *Sophistici Elenchi* was divided into two books: I, chaps. 1–15; II, chaps. 16–34.
76 Ed. 50ʳb.   77 *Ibid.*

So far, the passions have been compared two by two. Is there a priority between them considered individually? Giles thinks there is; he bases his argument on the priority of the good; for it is always some good which we seek; evil can be sought only under the guise of good. "Malum semper movet appetitum sub ratione boni."[78] Consequently love is prior to hate. Even hatred of another finds its origin in an inordinate self-love. For the same reason desire is prior to detestation. Hope is prior to despair, because hope seeks the good as such, despair turns from the good, not as good, but as a good too difficult to attain. Fear is prior to courage or boldness, because flight from evil through fear is prior to an assault on evil through courage. As a passion anger is prior to meekness; however, in a certain way meekness is prior to anger, inasmuch as meekness refrains from vengeance, whereas anger seeks vengeance. Finally, pleasure is prior to pain, because pleasure looks primarily to the good and pain is more immediately concerned with evil.

There is a relationship between the passions, but there is also a way in which they stand in opposition to each other. "Declarandum est quomodo hujusmodi passiones habent oppositionem ad invicem; in qua declaratione tangemus de effectibus et de speciebus passionum secundum quod spectat ad praesens negotium."[79] In the case of the passions of the concupiscible appetite, the opposition is clear; for love stands in opposition to hate, desire to detestation, and pleasure to pain or sadness. But the case of the passions of the irascible appetite is more complex; the concupiscible appetite is concerned with good and evil as such, whereas the irascible adds the note of "difficult." There is therefore, a twofold opposition between the good alone and the fact of it being "difficult to obtain." Consequently, hope is opposed both to fear and to despair, but in different ways: hope and fear have as their respective objectives a future good or a future evil, but hope is opposed to despair in the sense that despair is concerned with a future good which is difficult to obtain. The same principle can be applied in the same way to the rest of the passions.

One passion can cause more than one effect, and so the effects of the passions are much more numerous than the passions. For example, fear can cause coldness of the members or a flushed face. Fear of death causes a rush of the blood to the heart which results in coldness of the members; fear of a loss of honour causes the blood

78 *Ed.* 50ʳb.
79 *Ibid.*

to rush from the heart to the exterior which in turn causes the face to be flushed.

Giles' commentary on the *Rhetoric* follows one general pattern of thirteenth-century commentaries, namely the commentary accomplished, lemma by lemma, within the framework of books and *lectiones*. Neither the printed edition nor the manuscripts consulted are set up according to the division into *lectiones*. However, the task of making such a division would not be too difficult. At the end of each text of commentary on a lemma, the commentator adds "deinde cum dicit"; these words are omitted when a new *lectio* begins. There are several references to a *lectio* within the text of the commentary, such as "in fine tertiae lectionis declarabitur."[80] Giles does not stray very far from the text of Aristotle; rather he constantly documents his explanations by cross references to other works of Aristotle, supplemented by borrowings from Alpharabi and Averroes. There are no references to Cicero, Quintilian, or the important writers on the liberal arts, such as Cassiodorus or Martianus Capella. It is, in other words, a philosophical commentary of the kind that Giles was best equipped to do. There is a striking resemblance between Giles' discussions of the passions and those of St. Thomas Aquinas. Both the doctrine and terminology are so similar that I am led to believe that Giles had the text of St. Thomas before him.[81] The commentary constantly repeats explanations; it usually fails to refer to previous or later discussions of the same point. On technical points of rhetoric Giles makes no significant contribution to what Aristotle had to say. He uses normal terms, such as *cursus*, common in the *artes dictaminis*; he makes mention of *versus leonini*, a medieval technical term for rhymed hexameters, and objects to their use in speeches, because they would tend to distract the audience.[82] He treats Aristotle's *Rhetoric* as a complete unit and does not question either its structure or stages of composition, but is content to explain it as best he can with the means at his disposal, using, above all, Aristotle to explain Aristotle.[83] Finally, Giles seems to have done more than one redaction of the commentary: ms. Vatican latin 766 and ms. Vatican latin 833 are quite different.

80 *Ed.* 2ᵛb.
81 See *De Veritate* q. 26, art. 3; in III Sent; dist. 15; in II *Eth.*
82 See D. S. Raven, *Latin Metre* (London, 1965), p. 39; *ed.* 99ᵛb on 1408b23.
83 Moraux, *Les listes anciennes*, p. 97.

What Made a Medieval King Constitutional?

B. LYON

he bored but imaginative clerk responsible for the drawings of Edward I and Philip the Fair on the Memoranda Roll of the lord treasurer's remembrancer for the twenty-fifth and twenty-sixth years of Edward I certainly was under no illusion that he had sketched realistic portraits of the two kings whose historical trademarks have become French good looks and English honesty, celebrated in the words *Pactum Serva*. But his drawings do show two dour monarchs *tête-à-tête*, realistically appraising each other. Edward and Philip are depicted apparently talking at Tournai in January of 1298 during negotiations that led to peace and the return of Edward and his army to England.[1]

But what were they saying to each other? Obviously they engaged in diplomatic parlance, but what turn did their conversation take after the terms of peace had been arranged? Despite their antagonism they had much to talk about – common problems and objectives. It would be surprising if they had not discussed their power – those royal rights known as prerogatives – or if they had not compared notes to learn how each was managing the problems of his realm. They may even have considered their relations with the estates of the realm and discussed how successful they were in keeping on top of clergy, nobility, and the other estate emerging so rapidly as a third force. Philip probably evaluated his position more optimistically than Edward his. Was it not true, Philip could say, that

---

1 P.R.O., L.T.R. memoranda roll, no. 69, memb. 54. For a discussion of this drawing, see Elisabeth Kimball and Hilary Jenkinson, "Sketches of Edward I and Philip the Fair," *EHR*, LI (1936), 493–6. For kindly calling my attention to this record, I am indebted to Professor T. A. Sandquist of the University of Toronto and to Professor E. B. Fryde of the University of Wales at Aberystwyth.

as far back as he could look and remember, the French crown had known no serious challenge to its power, no serious protests of the nobles, no civil war? Edward could not boast of this. Had not the Mise of Amiens awarded by Philip's saintly grandfather been a brotherly gesture designed to uphold the royal prerogative and to bolster the shaky position of Henry iii and the Lord Edward in 1264? In France there had been no Provisions of Oxford, no Simon de Montfort. To be sure, Edward had tasted success in Wales and Scotland but so, too, had Philip in extending his control over France and pushing outward his borders. Though, indeed, it was becoming increasingly difficult to raise money for war and political ventures, it was less difficult than in England where Edward too often had to call assemblies of the three estates and grant them concessions in return for grudging consent to taxes. It was common knowledge on the Continent that lack of funds had delayed Edward in launching his campaign from the Low Countries against Philip. Had not his financial exactions from the clergy, his prises of food and matériel, his seizure of wool and hides, his innovation known as the *maletote*, and his insistence upon foreign military service forced his igno-minious surrender of royal power in the confirmation of the Charters?

There is no record of Edward's replies to these observations of Philip, but it is certain that he could not refute them and that he must have agreed that Philip's powers were considerably greater. If this is a reasonable reconstruction of the conversation at Tournai, one seems justified in asking why it has recently become fashionable to regard Philip the Fair as a "constitutional king." If English historians are agreed that Edward was a "sort" of constitutional king, how, given the disparity in power, could Philip have also been a constitu-tional king? It is conceivable that he was constitutional, though less so than Edward, and that the French criteria for a king's being con-stitutional differed from the English, but what one really wants to know is what made a medieval king constitutional.

If in the thoughtful and provocative article of Professor J. R. Strayer, published a few years ago, one follows the shifting opinion of historians on the nature of Philip the Fair's power, he discovers that until twenty-five years ago it was generally agreed that Philip was an illusive, shady character whose intentions and objectives were concealed by the efficient, ambitious councillors and servants who surrounded him and who initiated and implemented royal policy. The prevailing view was that Philip was not an attractive or

Lord Treasurer's Remembrancer, Memoranda Roll 69, membrane 54
Public Record Office. Document E368/69M54
Crown copyright

reliable person, that he was ineffective and quiescent in government, and that the tremendous power achieved by the Capetian monarchy during his reign stemmed mostly from his capable ministers.[2]

Robert Fawtier challenged this interpretation, asserting that Philip dominated his government and was active in its work, that he was responsible for the achievements of his reign.[3] The Fawtier position gained the support of Professor Strayer who investigated the performance of Philip by looking at him through administrative and legal records of the central government rather than through the eyes of contemporary chroniclers. Professor Strayer concluded that Philip "controlled and directed the routine work of the government. He was the one who assigned tasks to his councillors, and he reserved the right to act directly and personally in any matter which interested him. ... At the very least, the king was busier than any member of his Council." Furthermore, Philip not only concerned himself with the "small details" but was involved in the "greater affairs." He was responsible for the struggle against Boniface VIII, the affair of the Templars, and diplomatic and political moves involving an important range of subjects. Philip was no figurehead![4]

In the last part of his study Professor Strayer portrays Philip as a constitutional king. His thesis is that Philip behaved in a constitutional manner because he conformed to the traditions and practices of French government, observed the customs and laws of the realm, obtained consent from those concerned when he went beyond normal practices or the law, worked through established legal procedures and courts, and invariably asked for the advice of his council. Though acknowledging that ultimately Philip controlled all, Professor Strayer contends that because Philip stayed within the letter of the law and took counsel he was a constitutional king.[5]

While Professor Strayer has reinforced Fawtier's position that Philip the Fair was an active and powerful king, in portraying him as a constitutional king he has parted from Fawtier who saw no effective control exercised over his power. Fawtier's last words on the question were that in the kingdom of France there was no control

2 J. R. Strayer, "Philip the Fair: A 'Constitutional' King," *AHR*, LXII (1956), 18–32.
3 Robert Fawtier, *L'Europe occidentale de 1270 à 1380*, in *Histoire générale*, ed. Gustave Glotz (Paris, 1940), VI, i, p. 299. See also Ferdinand Lot and R. Fawtier, *Histoire des institutions françaises au moyen âge: Institutions royales* (Paris, 1958), II, pp. 24, 26–27.
4 Strayer, "Philip the Fair," 24–9.
5 *Ibid.*, 30–2.

over the king and that although kings might consult with their councils they were never bound by the advice received. Even the assemblies of estates convened by Philip wielded no control: "Le roi est le maître de faire ce qu'il croit bon pour le gouvernement du royaume."[6] There are other modern opinions on the problem but, as Professor Strayer has said, "this is not a problem which can be settled by accumulating authorities."[7] The problem can only be clarified, it seems, by comparing what Philip did and was able to do with what Edward I did and was able to do. Essentially the problem reduces itself to the practical consideration of what each king could "get away with." Regardless of theory on limitation of royal power and regardless of the restrictive influence of law and custom, the "constitutionalism" of both kings was largely a matter of practical politics.

There is not enough evidence to support the generalization that a succession of ineffective, untalented, and inactive kings necessarily contributed to the rise of constitutional government, but it is a fact that weak kings were more easily controlled, and controlled by various political configurations, and that such control could lead to constitutional government. Although some French kings, such as Charles VI, were controlled by political factions of nobles and although, as dauphin, the future Charles V was temporarily restricted in the exercise of royal authority by Etienne Marcel and his followers in the estates, such control was transitory and led to no permanent limitation of royal power.[8] In England, however, the undeniably weak reign of Henry III, as well as the reigns of Edward II, Richard II, and Henry VI, encouraged baronial control in the form of councils,

6 Lot and Fawtier, *Institutions françaises*, II, p. 555. At another point Fawtier writes: "Et cependant cette monarchie, née de l'élection, a abouti très rapidement à une monarchie, sinon absolue, du moins complètement libre du contrôle" (p. 547).
7 Strayer, "Philip the Fair," 20.
8 Unfortunately, little work has been done recently on Charles V and his relations with the assemblies and Etienne Marcel. See, however, L. Lazard, *Un bourgeois de Paris: Etienne Marcel* (Paris, 1890); S. Luce, *Histoire de la Jacquerie, d'après des documents inédits* (2nd ed., Paris, 1894); R. Delachenal, *Histoire de Charles V* (Paris, 1909–28), I–IV; E. Lavisse, "Etude sur le pouvoir royal au temps de Charles V," *Revue historique*, XXVI (1884), 233–80; A. Coville, "Les états-généraux de 1332 et 1357," *Le Moyen Age*, VI (1893), 57–63; Coville, in E. Lavisse, *Histoire de France* (Paris, 1911), IV, i, pp. 98–144; E. Faral, "Robert le Coq et les états généraux d'octobre 1356," *Revue historique de droit français et étranger*, XXIV, 4th ser. (1945), 171–214; Lot and Fawtier, *Institutions françaises*, II, pp. 563–70; E. Perroy, *The Hundred Years' War* (London, 1951), pp. 133–4.

control that led ultimately to constitutional government.[9] It seems to follow, therefore, that active and able kings were controlled only with difficulty.

Concurring with Professor Strayer that Philip the Fair was an active king in control of his government, but doubting his "constitutionalism," let us now consider the activity and power of Edward I. That Edward took a keen interest in the routine affairs of government is apparent. Few of England's kings, perhaps not even Henry II or John, had a better record.[10] Whether in council, chancery, or wardrobe one feels the royal omnipresence. If, as Professor Strayer has contended, the test of a king actively concerned with routine government is how frequently and regularly he was personally involved, there is ample evidence of Edward's participation by such phrases in the records as "Teste me ipso," "Teste rege," and "per ipsum Regem."[11] Another indication almost as reliable are the orders and decisions authorized under the privy seal. The keeper of the privy seal, who was either the controller of the wardrobe or his deputy, was always with the king and acted as a private secretary who could

---

9 See especially F. M. Powicke, *King Henry III and the Lord Edward: Community of the Realm in the Thirteenth Century* (Oxford, 1947), I, pp. 290–409; II, pp. 411–502; E. F. Jacob, *Studies in the Period of Baronial Reform and Rebellion, 1258–1267* (Oxford, 1925); R. F. Treharne, *The Baronial Plan of Reform, 1258–1263* (Manchester, 1932); V. H. Galbraith, "Good and Bad Kings in Medieval English History," *History*, xxx (1945), 119–32.

10 Documentation does not permit an intensive check on Henry II, but from the great series of enrolments beginning with John which enable one to observe routine government, one can only conclude that John was amazingly concerned with routine decisions and orders. This has, of course, been the conclusion of J. E. A. Jolliffe, *Angevin Kingship* (2nd ed., London, 1963), pp. 139–65, 301–50.

11 In the *Memoranda de Parliamento* (London, 1893), pp. 328–38, F. W. Maitland has printed excerpts from the Gascon Roll of 1305 dealing with routine government and petitions of Gascony. Edward I witnessed a few more than half of the twenty-four documents issued between 24 and 30 March. A more thorough investigation of the Gascon rolls supports this finding. Of the twenty-six documents issued during November 1274, Edward I witnessed all of them. During 1275–76 the phrase "Teste me ipso" accompanies with monotonous regularity documents concerned with routine affairs. It is the same for the year 1305. See C. Bémont, *Rôles gascons* (Paris, 1900–6), II, pp. 1–24; III, pp. 437 ff. The Close and Patent rolls are filled with orders and directions of Edward, showing his concern with details. Typical is the order of Edward on 16 January 1297 to the sheriff of Lincoln to deliver a ship and its tackle to a certain Adam de Welle (*Calendar of Close Rolls, 1296–1302*, p. 11), and that of 8 December 1306 granting safe-conduct to Philip Bourge, merchant of the society of the Mazi of Florence (*Calendar of Patent Rolls, 1301–1307*, p. 484).

draft or authorize documents.[12] To counter the objection that the keeper of the privy seal could act without the royal command and could assert a power independent and unknown to the king, it should be said that all personnel of the Edwardian household, particularly those of the wardrobe, were invariably loyal and devoted servants ever mindful that Edward was master and that to him they owed their position and advancement. Typical of such officers was John Benstead, controller of the wardrobe for almost ten years, who became chancellor of the exchequer.[13]

Further evidence of royal control over government, though perhaps less reliable, are the documents issued under the great seal by authority of the chancellor.[14] We know that by the reign of Edward the great seal could be used only upon authorization by an order under the privy seal. Such procedure assured tight control of the king over his chancellors, all of whom, despite periodic separation from the king, never usurped authority that was not theirs or mishandled the authority that was theirs. Like the wardrobe personnel, the chancellors were devoted to Edward. Chancellors like Robert Burnell (1274–92) and John Langton (1292–1302) came to their position only after long and faithful service in the wardrobe and chancery. The wardrobe was the school for the typical Edwardian official; it was a school dominated by one master – Edward – who observed the performance and talent of his servants and appointed them to key positions in his government.[15] Almost without exception these officials were interested mainly in their professional tasks; they left politics and intrigue for high stakes to the great magnates. It seems reasonable to conclude, therefore, that whether Edward was per-

12 See, for example, the range of routine business authorized in April 1302 by the privy seal on pp. 26–34 in *Cal.Pat.R., 1301–1307.*
13 T. F. Tout, *Chapters in the Administrative History of Mediaeval England* (Manchester, 1937), II, pp. 18–20, 37–8. In 1302 Benstead was referred to as "the royal clerk who stays continually by the king's side" (*Cal.Cl.R., 1296–1302,* p. 606).
14 On 31 August 1306 there was a memorandum drawn up regarding various letters "sent to the chancellor out of Scotland, sealed in the form of charters by the king's command by writ of the *targe,* and were then sealed with the great seal in the above form, and the said charters under the *targe* were sent to the wardrobe under the chancellor's seal" (*Cal.Pat.R., 1301–1307,* p. 460).
15 Tout, *Chapters,* II, pp. 60–84. On 30 December 1304 John Benstead was appointed *locum tenens cancellarii* and held the great as well as the privy seal until 17 January 1305 (Tout, *Chapters,* II, p. 69). The careers of Robert Burnell and John Langton are described in Tout, *Chapters,* II, pp. 11 ff. See also Powicke, *The Thirteenth Century 1216–1307* (Oxford, 1953), pp. 333–40.

sonally responsible for routine governmental decisions or whether he left them to officials in the wardrobe or chancery, he retained control. To deny that there was intrigue in the wardrobe and chancery would be incorrect, but it was petty intrigue aimed at personal advancement within one of these departments rather than at political power and position that would challenge royal authority. When officers were removed from office or otherwise punished, it was for inefficiency or maladministration rather than for acts committed against the king. It should be emphasized that maladministration by royal officials customarily occurred during the king's absence. After three years spent in Gascony (1286–89) reorganizing the government, Edward had to deal with the most blatant cases of corrupt and inefficient administration in England. Upon his return he immediately appointed commissioners to hear complaints. Trials followed the complaints and among those removed from office, exiled, imprisoned, or fined were well-known justices of the royal courts and lesser administrative officers who had used their official position to enhance their personal wealth and to acquire land.[16] That Edward swiftly and relentlessly punished such offenders buttresses the assertion that he was in full control of his government.

By the late thirteenth century medieval government had reached a level of sophistication and complexity that demanded specialization by the officers of such organs as the chancery, exchequer, wardrobe, and royal courts. Chancellors like Robert Burnell and John Langton, treasurers of the exchequer like Walter Langton, wardrobe officers like John Benstead, Ralph Manton, and Antony Bek, and many justices became experts in finance, in detailed aspects of administration, and in equitable and common law. But none became so specialized in his skill and knowledge, so essential and unassailable, that Edward's mastery was ever challenged.[17] G. O. Sayles has studied in detail the

16 For the inquests and trials see Powicke, *Thirteenth Century*, pp. 361–6. Ralph de Hengham, chief justice of the king's bench, was heavily amerced. Thomas of Wayland, chief justice of the bench of common pleas, was dismissed and forced to abjure the land. The clerk Adam de Stratton was imprisoned in the Tower as a felon and died shortly thereafter.

17 Walter Langton served Edward I as a wardrobe clerk, and as cofferer, controller, and keeper of the wardrobe. He then became treasurer of the exchequer and, finally, bishop of Lichfield. Through most of his career he was close to Edward; he constantly served on confidential and difficult diplomatic missions and was a member of the council. See Tout, *Chapters*, II, pp. 15–16; B. Lyon, "Un compte de l'échiquier relatif aux relations d'Edouard Ier d'Angleterre avec le duc Jean II de Brabant," *Bulletin de la Commission*

careers of clerks who worked up through the royal service to become justices on the king's bench but has found none who "was allowed to concentrate his undivided attention upon the work for which he was nominally paid or even upon judicial business in general."[18] These justices were called upon to assess and collect taxes, to act as commissioners of array and as inspectors of boundaries and rivers, to serve in administrative capacities in Wales and Scotland, and to go on diplomatic missions.[19] Even in the efficient government of Edward there was a "disregard of specialisation."[20] The Wardrobe Books clearly show how adept wardrobe officers had to be in finance, secretarial work, diplomacy, and logistics.[21] These men were typical of the rank and file of royal officials who were expected to carry out the royal will and who were almost always responsive to it.

   In the routine business of the realm Edward took an active interest throughout his long reign. The records indicate no slackening in zeal for the slightest affair even toward the end of his life. He maintained an iron grip over routine, never losing communication with members of his council or with his officers in England, Wales, Scotland, and Gascony. To the end he was in control.[22] Knowing that a king such as John often involved himself in minutiae while ignoring and leaving unsolved essential problems, we cannot assert that kings who mastered routine government *ipso facto* initiated or participated in the formulation of decisions and policies affecting great affairs of the realm. But Edward, like Philip the Fair, excelled in all levels of government. Much more, however, is known about Edward's role in the great events of his reign than about Philip the Fair's. The Gascon,

royale d'histoire de Belgique, cxx (1955), 67–93; G. P. Cuttino, "Bishop Langton's Mission for Edward I, 1296–1297," *Studies Soc. Sci. U. Iowa*, xi (1941), 147–83. In vol. II of his *Chapters* Tout has sketched the careers of most of Edward's principal officials. See especially C. M. Fraser, *A History of Antony Bek, Bishop of Durham 1283–1311* (Oxford, 1957), and G. P. Cuttino, "King's Clerks and the Community of the Realm," *Speculum*, xxix (1954), 395–409.

18 Sayles, *Select Cases in the Court of King's Bench under Edward I* (Selden Society, London, 1936), I, p. lxv. For the careers and work of these justices see pp. xli–lxiii.

19 *Ibid.*, pp. lxiii–lxvii.

20 Powicke, *Thirteenth Century*, p. 341.

21 Highly informative for the year 1297 is Wardrobe Book 25 Edward I, Brit. Mus. Add. ms. 7965.

22 Powicke, *Thirteenth Century*, p. 337: "So far as the general business of the realm was concerned, Edward, to the last days of his life, neither lost grip and interest nor made any change in his ways of co-operation with his counsellors, judges, and ministers."

French, German, and Patent rolls, the miscellaneous records included under the rubric of Diplomatic Documents of the Exchequer, and the treaties, agreements, contracts, and negotiations printed in *Foedera* describe the serious military, political, and administrative problems of Edward on the Continent and underscore his constant efforts to solve them. The policies adopted, whether concerning the stance to be taken toward Philip III and Philip IV of France, the diplomatic relations with princes in Germany, the Low Countries, and France, or the reorganization of Gascon administration, were Edward's.

In the decade between 1275 and 1285, despite family ties with Champagne and Navarre, despite the efforts of Peter of Aragon and Alfonso of Castile to involve Edward against Philip III of France, the records show Edward making decisions which kept England free from military involvement and which committed him to the solving of political problems with his French overlord by formal treaties and legal settlements in the parlement of Paris. He refused to be sucked into war, he served as a mediator between the kings of Aragon and France, and he attempted to serve as a peacemaker. Although his political interests coincided with those of Rudolf of Habsburg and although economic and political interests dictated involvement in the tortuous politics of the Rhine, Rhône, and Savoy, Edward avoided any real commitment against France until the aggressive action of Philip the Fair forced counter diplomatic moves and war in Gascony and Flanders.[23]

As duke of Aquitaine, responsible for a land notoriously unstable, Edward assumed personal responsibility for Gascon affairs immediately upon his return from the Holy Land in 1273. After doing homage at Paris in July 1273 to Philip III of France, he went directly to Gascony, remaining there until the following summer. Realizing that he and his lieutenants were ignorant of his rights and of the obligations of his Gascon vassals, he initiated a series of inquests designed to ascertain not only his feudal rights but his relations with the towns and rural communities. These investigations resulted in

23 Powicke, *Thirteenth Century*, pp. 237–64; Fawtier, in *Histoire générale*, VI, i, pp. 261–325; Ch.-V. Langlois, *Le règne de Philippe le Hardi* (Paris, 1887); F. Kern, *Die Anfänge der französischen Ausdehnungspolitik bis zum Jahre 1308* (Tübingen, 1910). For more information on the relations of Edward with Rudolf of Habsburg and Peter of Aragon see the articles of Kern in *Mitteilungen des Oesterreichischen Instituts für Geschichtsforschung*, XXX–XXXI (1909–10), 412–23, 54–70. See also Cuttino, *English Diplomatic Administration 1259–1339* (Oxford, 1940).

the *recognitiones feodorum,* a compilation of tenures and customs comparable to those which issued from the *Quo Warranto* proceedings about a year later in England.[24] Even more comprehensive were the ordinances issued in May and June of 1289 after Edward had resided in Gascony for three years and had personally investigated every aspect of Gascon government. By these ordinances Edward reorganized the haphazard administrative system and made it serve him as efficiently as did his English government.[25] One feels throughout these ordinances the firm hand of Edward, his sense of order, and his desire for conciseness.

Feudal relations between the English kings and their Gascon vassals, which had never been easy, continued to plague Edward, particularly after Philip the Fair's intrigue began to ferment. With this problem, as with others on the Continent, Edward personally decided upon a policy and then adhered to it. Typical of his approach to the unruly and temperamental Gascon vassals is his treatment of Gaston de Béarn. From 1273 to 1279, although Gaston committed virtually every crime known to feudal law, Edward refused to be needled into committing some outrageous act against him. Never did he attempt to crush Gaston by force. Finally, after a duel of wills lasting almost six years, Edward arranged a settlement so satisfactory that Gaston remained a loyal vassal until his death in 1290.[26] It was in a similar vein that Edward negotiated with Philip III and Philip IV for the return of the Agenais. By the treaties of Amiens and Paris concluded in 1279 and 1286, which were negotiated by Edward in person, he obtained the cession of the Agenais. Edward entered into these delicate negotiations only after he had been thoroughly briefed by advisers on his rights to the Agenais.[27]

After Edward was beguiled by Philip the Fair in 1293 and forced

---

24 C. Bémont, *Recueil d'actes relatifs à l'administration des rois d'Angleterre en Guyenne au XIIIe siècle (Recogniciones feodorum in Aquitania)* (Paris, 1914).

25 J.-P. Trabut-Cussac, *Le livre des hommages d'Aquitaine* (Bordeaux, 1959), "L'administration anglaise en Gascogne sous Henri III et Edouard I de 1252 à 1287," in *Positions des thèses de l'Ecole des Chartes* (Paris, 1949). See also the chapters of Y. Renouard and Ch. Samaran on Aquitaine and Gascony in Lot and Fawtier, *Institutions françaises,* I, pp. 157–207.

26 The details of these relations are in P. Tucoo-Chala, *La vicomté de Béarn et le problème de sa souveraineté des origines à 1620* (Bordeaux, 1961), and *Histoire du Béarn* (Bordeaux, 1962). See also Powicke, *Thirteenth Century,* pp. 285–7.

27 Cuttino, *Diplomatic Administration,* p. 7; Powicke, *Thirteenth Century,* pp. 289–93.

the next year into war in order to regain Gascony, the records portray another facet of his character and ability – his tremendous flair for military organization. The Gascon and Patent rolls abound with his orders for soldiers, supplies, and ships. His commands ring clearly in communications to his lieutenants.[28] His trusted wardrobe and chancery officials were dispatched to the Low Countries and the Rhineland to build up an anti-French coalition.[29] In the Wardrobe Book of 1297 is the story of the brief Flemish campaign of that year. Here, intertwined with the details on the daily operations of war, are the details showing Edward as the core and essence of the operation. What is true for the Flemish campaign is even truer for the Welsh and Scottish wars when, less harassed by domestic political pressures, Edward could give more thought and energy to the preparation and conduct of war.[30] Five days before he died at Burgh-upon-the-Sands Edward, already a sick and dying man, set out at the head of his army to engage the Scots.

As evident as his mastery over military, diplomatic, and political moves outside England is Edward's prominence in domestic affairs. His relations with the church, like those of Philip the Fair, were marred by conflict over the royal right to tax the clergy without papal consent. It is a pity that this issue clouded what could have been a harmonious relationship with Archbishop Winchelsey. Even before Winchelsey assumed his duties as archbishop of Canterbury in January 1295, Edward had clashed with the clergy over his demands made in September 1294 that he be granted one half of the church revenue newly assessed for the tenth of Pope Nicholas. When the

28 See, for example, Bémont, *Rôles gascons*, III, pp. 226–398. There is similar information in the Issue and Liberate rolls (PRO, E 403/105; PRO, C 62/75).
29 Lyon, *From Fief to Indenture* (Cambridge, Mass., 1957), pp. 161–80, 210–3; J. de Sturler, *Les relations politiques et les échanges commerciaux entre le duché de Brabant et l'Angleterre au moyen âge* (Paris, 1936), pp. 141–319; F. Boch, "Englands Beziehungen zum Reich unter Adolf von Nassau," *Mitteilungen des Oesterreichischen Instituts für Geschichtsforschung*, XII (1932), 199–257; H. S. Lucas, "Diplomatic Relations of Edward I and Albert of Austria," *Speculum*, IX (1934), 125–34; F. Funck-Brentano, *Philippe le Bel en Flandre* (Paris, 1897), pp. 97 ff.; F. Trautz, *Die Könige von England und das Reich, 1272–1377* (Heidelberg, 1961), pp. 117–91.
30 Wardrobe Book 25 Edward I, Brit. Mus. Add. ms. 7965. See also E. B. Fryde, *The Book of Prests of the King's Wardrobe for 1294–1295* (Oxford, 1962); *Liber Quotidianus Contrarotulatoris Garderobae, Anno Regni Regis Edwardi Primi Vicesimo Octavo* (Society of Antiquaries, London, 1787); S. Lysons, "Copy of a Roll of the Expenses of King Edward the First at Rhuddlan Castle," *Archaeologia*, XVI (1812), 32–79; J. E. Morris, *The Welsh Wars of Edward I* (Oxford, 1901).

clergy only offered two tenths, Edward terrified those assembled in the refectory of Westminster. It was, however, Pope Boniface VIII's *Clericis Laicos* of February 1296 that blocked any rapport between Edward and Winchelsey, who felt compelled to abide by the bull. Highly intelligent and practical, Winchelsey could see both sides of the dilemma. When Edward demanded a fifth in 1297, Winchelsey left the answer to each cleric's conscience. He could understand those who paid the tax, and yet he believed it wrong to ignore the bull. Winchelsey, driven to repeated compromise to maintain an uneasy peace with Edward, in the spring of 1298 finally had to refuse a request for a tenth and prayers from the clergy for the projected Scottish campaign, saying that there would be prayers but no tenth without papal approval. Edward, however much he respected Winchelsey and admired his ability, could never forgive such defiance; he hounded Winchelsey until he prevailed upon the new pope Clement V in February 1306 to suspend the archbishop. Edward's vendetta with Winchelsey was wholly personal; he alone was responsible for Winchelsey's final disgrace.[31]

Edward's role in the legal and institutional development of medieval England is well known. No king, not even Henry II, had a more intelligent interest in the law. His drive and intelligence lay behind the great statutes enacted between 1274 and 1290. He initiated the famous inquest of 1274, a forerunner for much of the subsequent legislation. Other inquests followed and after them, more statutes.[32] These inquests were conducted by officials close to Edward. Royal justices such as Ralph de Hengham were directed to prepare statutes that would say and do exactly what Edward intended them to do.[33] His statutes were meant to achieve the decency and order so dear to him, and to meet the pressing legal, economic, and social problems uncovered in the inquests. He well knew the legal problems because he assiduously participated in the difficult cases, discussing them

---

31 Rose Graham, "Archbishop Winchelsey: From His Election to His Enthronement," *Church Quarterly R.,* CXLVIII (1949), 161–75, *English Ecclesiastical Studies* (London, 1929), pp. 302–16; Powicke, *Thirteenth Century,* pp. 672–8, 704–5, 717–8; W. E. Lunt, *Financial Relations of the Papacy with England to 1327* (Cambridge, Mass., 1939).

32 See especially T. F. T. Plucknett, *Legislation of Edward I* (Oxford, 1949), *Edward I and Criminal Law* (Cambridge, 1960); H. M. Cam, *Studies in the Hundred Rolls* (Oxford, 1921), *The Hundred and the Hundred Rolls* (London, 1930); D. W. Sutherland, *Quo Warranto Proceedings in the Reign of Edward I, 1278–1294* (Oxford, 1963).

33 Plucknett, *Legislation of Edward I;* Sayles, *Select Cases in King's Bench,* I, pp. xli–cxv, cxxix–cxxxiii; Powicke, *Thirteenth Century,* pp. 352–80.

with his justices and councillors.[34] No statute was enacted without Edward's scrutiny.

The evidence thus far supports the position that Edward was active in the routine and great affairs of the realm, that he was in control of them and of the men who counseled him and who exercised delegated authority. Edward has emerged as a probably more active king than Philip the Fair and one who exercised even more control over his government. In Edward, England had an ambitious, industrious, observant, keen, and practical king. But was such a strong king also constitutional, and are the arguments of Professor Strayer, depicting Philip the Fair as a constitutional king, valid also for Edward?

Philip the Fair, according to Professor Strayer, regarded his grandfather Saint Louis as the model of what a king ought to be. Philip therefore tried to be honest, pious, and dignified. Above all, he had a sense of the mission of French kingship and, as Robert Fawtier has expressed it, assumed the role of high priest of the "religion of monarchy."[35] In some ways Edward resembled Philip. As a young man Edward had known Saint Louis and had admired his lofty concept of kingship. He agreed with Saint Louis that kingship was a high trust for which a king was responsible only to God, that kings could not be shorn of their rightful prerogatives by mortal men. But although he emulated the good qualities of Louis, and despite his high concept of royal power, it would be difficult to prove that Edward regarded himself as the high priest of the "religion of monarchy."[36]

But what does this have to do with constitutionalism? History has shown that even virtuous kings who acknowledged responsibility only to God for their acts were not constitutional; they were, in fact, despotic. Although the medieval successors of Philip the Fair continued to share his admiration for Saint Louis and considered themselves pious Christians, the French monarchy did not emerge from the middle ages as a constitutional monarchy; it emerged as a very absolute one. Few are the historians who would defend the thesis

34 Powicke has written: "Perhaps the most remarkable thing in Edward was his readiness, amid all his distractions, to discuss knotty legal details, as they arose, with his advisers. ... The hearing of a difficult case or petition reserved for talk with the king would suggest a general provision. ..." (*Thirteenth Century*, p. 375). See also F. Pegues, "The Clericus in the Legal Administration of Thirteenth-Century England," *EHR*, LXXI (1956), 529–59.

35 Strayer, "Philip the Fair," 30; Fawtier, *L'Europe occidentale*, pp. 300–1. See also Fawtier, *Les Capétiens et la France* (Paris, 1942), p. 41.

36 See the shrewd remarks of Powicke, *Thirteenth Century*, pp. 229–30.

that Richard II, James I, or Louis XIV were constitutional kings because of their elevated concept of kingship or their admission of
responsibility only to God. It simply does not follow that because
Saint Louis was a good and just king who respected the rights of his
people he was constitutional, or that because Philip the Fair and
other kings admired Saint Louis and gave the impression of following in his footsteps they were constitutional.[37]

Philip the Fair, Professor Strayer contends, followed the guide-
lines of his grandfather by conforming to the traditions of French
monarchy, by governing through the existing system of courts and
administrative officials, and by adhering to established law and
custom. He managed, as Professor Strayer says, "to stay at least
within the letter of the law."[38] But cannot some of these conclusions
be questioned? Did Philip work within the existing framework of
administration, respect the law, and use established courts and judicial procedure? To be sure, he still used *enquêteurs*, but were they
the same kind of official as Saint Louis used and were their instructions still to weed out bad government and corrupt officials and to
remedy the grievances of subjects?[39] Would Saint Louis have proceeded against the Knights Templars in the fashion that Philip did?
In this celebrated struggle did Philip respect law and allow accepted
procedure to be followed in the proper courts?[40] These queries are

37 After noting that Philip the Fair did model his actions after those of Saint
   Louis and did attempt to emulate the Christian faith of his grandfather,
   Fawtier immediately concludes: "Mais ce n'est pas la foi de saint Louis"
   (*Les Capétiens*, p. 41). Fawtier completely disagrees with Strayer when he
   sums up Philip as a king: "Cet homme froid et silencieux a marqué profondé-
   ment de son empreinte l'histoire de la monarchie. C'est sous son règne
   qu'achève de se constituer l'administration royale, insatiable, tatillonne,
   passionnément dévouée à sa tâche, plus attachée à la couronne que le roi
   lui-même et faisant pénétrer son action partout, opposant plus ou moins
   consciemment aux tendances du droit féodal, qui mettait volontiers le roi
   au-dessous de la loi, le droit romain, conservé dans ce Midi récemment an-
   nexé au domaine, avec sa théorie de la volonté du prince comme seule loi"
   (*Ibid.*, p. 42).
38 Strayer, "Philip the Fair," 30.
39 Lot and Fawtier have clearly expressed the transformation of the *enquêteurs*
   under Philip: "Trop souvent, ils substituent arbitrairement leur autorité à
   celle des officiers du roi et des pouvoirs locaux. Pourvoyeurs du Trésor, ils
   transforment la justice en instrument de fiscalité. L'institution dévie, et
   comme l'a dit un historien, 'sous la robe du juge se cache l'agent financier'"
   (*Institutions françaises*, II, p. 157).
40 The account of the affair of the Templars by Langlois in Lavisse, *Histoire de
   France* (Paris, 1901), III, ii, pp. 174–200, remains one of the best. Cf. G. Leg-
   man, *The Guilt of the Templars* (New York, 1966).

perhaps best answered by Professor Strayer's phrase: "He tried to stay at least within the letter of the law."

But what bearing do these questions have for Edward? Having among his predecessors no such model as Saint Louis, Edward yet never turned his back upon the institutional and legal traditions established by Henry I and Henry II. No English king worked harder to make the institutions of government function efficiently for the general good of the realm. Edward's name has come to epitomize justice. He laboured to strengthen the common law, to make it meet the shifting needs of the thirteenth century, and to give his courts a reputation for the best justice in the realm. His was a great age of legal innovation, but innovation accomplished by established legal methods and through the medium of existing institutions and procedures.[41] Edward's record is better than Philip's; it would be unfair ever to suggest that he did what he did within the letter of the law. Yet it would be rash to conclude that Edward's respect for tradition and law, however commendable, made him a constitutional king. The fundamental question remains: why did Edward behave so well?

According to Professor Strayer, Philip the Fair, knowing that a good king never acted arbitrarily, always deliberated with his council before making decisions. This is not to say, however, that Philip had to take counsel or that he acted upon the counsel given. Professor Strayer is careful to emphasize that Philip was never bound by the advice of his council, that he made his own decisions, decisions often contrary to the counsel received. He controlled the council and "in the last analysis he controlled the government."[42]

Though the relations of Edward with his council were much the same, there was a basic difference. Edward was wary of his council; he knew the embarrassment it could cause a king. He remembered that in 1215 the barons had tried to control John by means of a

41 Helen Cam has argued that the preambles to Edward's statutes afford proof of his concern for justice. They also show that fundamental changes in the law were made only with consent of parliament. Typical of Edward's reasons for legislation are: "to make good the oppressions and defects of former statutes" and "having diligently meditated on the defects in the law and the many grievances and oppressions inflicted on the people in time past we wish to provide a remedy and establish the certainty of the law." Miss Cam observes that "without any intention of calling the nation into partnership with him, it is clear that Edward was to some extent permitting his subjects to suggest, if not to dictate, matters for legislation" ("The Legislators of Medieval England," in *Law-Finders and Law-Makers in Medieval England* [London, 1962], pp. 143–4).

42 Strayer, "Philip the Fair," 30, 32.

baron-dominated council. He knew from experience all the trouble councils had caused his father. First, the barons had complained that Henry III's council was composed only of foreign favourites and sycophants. Then, after they forced Henry to accept the Provisions of Oxford, they rigged the council to control him. Although the Mise of Amiens had helped the royal cause, ultimately the barons had to be crushed in order to restore the royal prerogatives. With these lessons before him, Edward generally selected his councillors from Englishmen but tried to secure loyal men, men he could trust and control, men from the wardrobe, chancery, and royal courts. At times he even found it expedient to bypass the council and to govern almost completely through the wardrobe.[43] Edward took advice from his council and used it much as did Philip the Fair. But, despite his control of the council, he distrusted it; it made him nervous. Could he not lose control of it? Could it not control him? Such thoughts never entered Philip's mind. Never had councils controlled his predecessors and never would they control him.

That Philip and Edward took counsel from their councils does not make them constitutional kings; both controlled their councils and both had the ultimate decision. But Edward had less control; he knew that at times his control was precarious and feared that it might be challenged. Though a strong king, Edward must have known that he was less powerful than Philip and that he had to scheme and struggle to retain control over his council and government. He lived under the shadow of a powerful baronage which could not be ignored, and he therefore had less freedom of action than Philip. Encounters of Edward and his predecessors with the baronage afforded dramatic proof that royal power was not absolute, that Edward's desires and objectives must take into account the desires and objectives of the barons. Neither Philip the Fair nor his predecessors had known such a limitation of their authority.

It is true, as Professor Strayer has stated, that when Philip the Fair embarked upon important projects or demanded extraordinary support and pecuniary contributions, he summoned large assemblies to Paris or consulted with local assemblies to obtain counsel, consent,

43 Tout, Chapters, II, pp. 60–84, 146–55. Tout observed that "the king's view was that he might take counsel with whomsoever he liked, and that in the long run the wisest counsel came from the loyal officers of his household, who spent their lives in his service, who had learnt by long practical experience the art of government, and who considered his interests above all other things" (p. 150).

and a wide consensus of support.[44] Edward behaved similarly, but again with some important differences. He seldom dealt with local assemblies; usually, he summoned large assemblies increasingly composed of clergy, baronage, knights of the shires, and burgesses of the boroughs to give him counsel, consent, or support for weighty affairs of the realm. Edward was either unable or seldom tried to negotiate with regional assemblies; almost invariably he dealt with one large assembly-parliament which spoke more and more for the whole realm. Unlike Philip who only used his assemblies to obtain money, to propagandize his policies, or to gain support from his subjects, and who never felt compelled to grant or promise concessions in return for what he wanted and got, Edward had to negotiate with parliament ever more frequently and to make concessions in return for what he obtained. He realized that when he had to summon a parliament he would have to deal with it on a *quid pro quo* basis. On those occasions when he demanded service considered unjustified by custom, when he taxed arbitrarily and heavily, when he forcibly seized the goods of his subjects, or when he introduced unpopular innovations, he was backed into a corner and humbled by the confirmation of the Charters and the *Articuli super cartas*.[45]

For actions and demands far more arbitrary than Edward's, Philip the Fair suffered no such indignity. He was never humbled or forced to admit any definite restriction of his authority. Imagine what his reaction would have been to a restriction that henceforth on no account would he "take from our kingdom such aids, taxes, prises, except by the common assent of the whole kingdom and for the common benefit of the same kingdom, saving the ancient aids and prises due and accustomed"![46] After his death there was revulsion against what was considered an arbitrary reign and his sons were faced with regional leagues of nobles demanding concessions that would limit royal authority and return conditions to those known under Saint Louis. The outcome is well known. Philip's sons were able to delay and to negotiate, to isolate the leagues, and finally to reduce them to impotence. They emerged virtually unscathed and passed on their majestic power to their Valois successors.[47] Not under Philip the

44 Strayer, "Philip the Fair," 30–1.
45 C. Stephenson and F. G. Marcham, *Sources of English Constitutional History* (New York, 1937), pp. 164–5, 175.
46 From the confirmation of the Charters (Stephenson and Marcham, *Sources*, p. 165).
47 Fawtier, *Les Capétiens*, p. 43: "Le mouvement de réaction, un instant vic-

Fair, not under his sons, and not under their successors of the fourteenth and fifteenth centuries was there any force or group of forces
powerful and united enough to compel real and permanent limitation
of royal authority.

What, then, made a medieval king constitutional? To call Philip
the Fair a constitutional king because he gave the appearance of
respecting tradition and law, took counsel from his council, and occasionally consulted with assemblies about extraordinary demands
and problems is unrealistic. Although Philip did these things, he was
not forced to do them; his control over council and assemblies was
supreme. If he used established legal apparatus and administrative
organs, he did so just within the letter of the law. Never did he have
to work out his problems with a strong political bloc that had the
power to make him govern according to defined principles of government. How he behaved was really his own affair, and so it was for
most of his successors.

Edward welcomed limitation of his authority no more than Philip,
but he had to govern his realm knowing that there were effective
limitations.[48] He had always to negotiate with a united and resource-
ful baronage. Increasingly this negotiation had to be in parliament
which, in addition to the baronage, came to include the clergy,
knights, and burgesses. Despite his efforts to ignore these groups and
to govern without their general approval, he could not; he had to
acknowledge that on great affairs of the realm, such as taxation and
fundamental legislation, parliament held the trump cards. Edward

torieux sous le court règne de Louis X, disparaît sans laisser de traces pro-
fondes. Comme l'avaient voulu Philippe Auguste, saint Louis et Phillippe le
Bel, il n'y aura qu'un roi en France. La monarchie s'oriente vers l'absolu-
tisme." After commenting upon the failure of the estates to establish effective controls over the French kings in the fourteenth and fifteenth centuries,
Fawtier thus characterizes royal power at the time of Charles vii and Louis
xi: "Le roi attira peu à peu tout à lui et reprit toute initiative. C'est bien la
monarchie exclusive, absolue, qui va triompher et une monarchie du genre
de celle-là n'admet aucun contrôle" (Lot and Fawtier, *Institutions françaises*,
ii, p. 577). See also Fawtier, "Parlement d'Angleterre et Etats Généraux de
France au moyen âge," *Comptes rendus de l'Académie des Inscriptions et
Belles-Lettres* (1953), 275–84.
48 The following words of Maitland are relevant: "That the king is below the
law is a doctrine which even a royal justice may fearlessly proclaim. The
theory that in every state there must be some man or definite body of men
above the law, some 'sovereign' without duties and without rights, would
have been rejected. Had it been accepted in the thirteenth century, the
English kingship must have become an absolute monarchy. ..." (*History of
English Law* [2nd ed., Cambridge, 1899], i, 181–2).

was forced into being a constitutional king by political realities expressed in that institution known by the late thirteenth century as parliament. Because Philip the Fair never had to live with or make accommodation with these political realities, he never became a constitutional king. It was not theory, not professed belief in tradition and established institutions and law, not admiration of a saintly king, and not counsel from a council, but political pressure become constant and institutionalized that made medieval kings constitutional. To understand medieval constitutionalism otherwise is to misunderstand medieval politics.

Statutes of Edward I: Huntington Library ms. H.M. 25782 V. H. GALBRAITH

The manuscript H.M. 25782 in the Huntington Library, San Marino, California, is catalogued as follows:

Statutes from Magna Carta (1215) to the Statutes of Exeter (1286).
c. 1290 England.
MS. Vel. 87 leaves. Latin and French. 8½ inches × 5½ inches. 32 lines to the page.
Legal hand: initials red and blue: pen ornamentation.
Quires: [1–4]⁸, [5]⁴, [6]⁸, [7]¹⁰, [8–10]⁸, [11]¹⁰; lacks [11]⁹.
Catchwords in 4 quires. Legal notes in a later hand on some blank leaves.

4to brown calf; rebacked.

There is unfortunately no formal indication of its medieval provenance,[1] though we may guess that it passed into the possession of Gilbart Forman of Rodwell, yeoman in the county of Yorkshire, a draft of whose will, dated 21 May 1500, is entered on f.32ᵛ. For the rest, it is a handsome little book, as books of statutes go, written by a single scribe, with fine bold rubrics[2] and pleasant red and blue initials. The only significant medieval annotation is found on f.82ᵛ where a fourteenth-century scribe has added the text of Westminster the Third (*Quia Emptores*, 1290): that is to say the act which followed the Statutes of Exeter (1286) with which the book ends. This addition indicates that our statute book is complete, while the evi-

---

1 A more modern owner is suggested by a small round bookplate inscribed "Lowther" inside the front cover. ? William Lowther, second earl of Lonsdale, 1787–1872.
2 The rubrics, being in colour, were added after the ms. was written. The scribe left a space for the rubric, the text of which he added in tiny writing, high above the top margin. These guides to the rubricator were normally cut off when the ms. was finally trimmed to size: but in this ms. they survive in whole or in part on folios 8, 12, 21, 57, 58, 62, 84, and 85ᵛ.

dence of the script suggests that it was written very soon after that date. Ornamental though it is, the book clearly served a practical purpose before the coming of printing. A fourteenth-century scribe, to facilitate reference, has added in the upper margin of the recto of each folio the title of the statute set out below: and several of the statutes have been collated with and corrected from the statute roll in fifteenth- and sixteenth-century hands. Moreover, at an early date small parchment (? or leather) tabs have been sewn on to the top right-hand corner of a dozen or more leaves, indicating to the searcher where each major statute began in the manuscript.[3] The tabs have all gone, but the sewing marks remain and the space occupied by each tab is still markedly whiter and cleaner than the rest of the vellum. In this connection it is noticeable that there the pagination is not medieval: readers depended on the tabs.

The contents of the volume are as follows:[4]

f.1   *Incipiunt provisiones de Ronnemede scilicet carta Regis Iohannis*

f.6ᵛ   *Expliciunt provisiones de Ronnemede*
       Magna Carta (1215), here (incorrectly) described as "data per manum nostram apud Wyndesor."

f.7   Exposiciones verborum antiquorum anglicorum[5]
       The meanings of more than thirty old English terms (e.g., soken, saka, tol, etc.) given in French.

f.8   De ponderibus et mensuris[6]
       Cf. *S.R.* 1, 204

f.9   *Hic incipit Dictum de Kenilworthe de tempore Regis Henrici*
       S.R. 1, 12

f.12   *Capitula que placitantur coram Justiciariis Itinerantibus*
       S.R. 1, 233

f.14   *Expliciunt Capitula Incipit extenta manerii*
       Expliciunt f.15
       S.R. 1, 242

f.15ᵛ *Assisa Panis*
       S.R. 1, 199

---

3 E.g., f.17 (Magna Carta, 1225); f.25 (Provisions of Merton); f.27 (Provisions of Marlborough); f.37 (Westminster I); f.63 (Westminster II).
4 Headings of documents, when rubricated, are printed in italics. The references are to the *Statutes of the Realm*, 1 (1810), with the abbreviation *S.R.* In this volume the charters of liberties precede the statutes and have a separate pagination.
5 No rubric though a space has been left for it, and the scribe's note in the upper margin still remains.
6 No rubric, but the note for it remains in the upper margin.

f.16   *Assisa Ceruisie*
        S.R. 1, 199
f.16   *Capitula franci plegii*
        Cf. S.R. 1, 246 which is in French and very different.
f.17   *Magna carta domini Henrici Regis filii Regis Iohannis de libertatibus*
        communibus
        Magna Carta (1225): S.R. 1, 22, but with two differences: (1) for
        the address of the 1225 charter it substitutes that of 1217 as
        printed by Holt, *Magna Carta*, p. 350, n.1; (2) it omits the date
        and all the witnesses except Stephen Langton.
f.21   *Carta domini Henrici Regis filii Regis Iohannis de libertatibus foreste*
        Charter of the Forest (1225): S.R. 1, 26, somewhat inaccurate,
        and retaining a clause from the charter of 1217 printed by Holt,
        Magna Carta, p. 362, n.1., and omitting the witnesses, except
        Stephen Langton.
f.23   *Sentencia super infringentes libertates predictarum cartarum*
        S.R. 1, 6
f.23ᵛ   *Capitula foreste*
f.24ᵛ   *Expliciunt capitula foreste*
        "Chapters of the Regard." See G. J. Turner, *Select Pleas of the*
        Forest (Selden Society), p. lxxv, and *Patent Rolls 1225–1232*,
        p. 286.
f.24ᵛ   [   ] i breve primo uenerit in Octabis sancti Michaelis etc.
        20 lines. A list of *Dies communes in Banco* added by the scribe,
        without a rubric after the book was illuminated. A space was left
        for a large coloured S which was not added. S.R. 1, 208
f.25   *Prouisiones de Mertone*
f.26ᵛ   *Expliciunt prouisiones de Mertone*
        S.R. 1, 1
f.27   *Incipiunt prouisiones Marlebergie de tempore Henrici Regis*
f.32   *Expliciunt prouisiones Marlebergie*
        S.R. 1, 19
f.32ᵛ   In the name of God amen etc.
        The will of Gylbart Forman of Rodwelle (Yorks) 21 May 1500.
f.33   *Rubrice de primis statutis Westm'*
f.34   *Expliciunt* [65 capitula]
f.34ᵛ   *Rubrice de statutis Gloucestr'*
        Expliciunt [20 capitula]
f.35   *Rubrice de secundis statutis Westm'*
f.35ᵛ   *Expliciunt* [56 capitula]
f.36   [hec sunt capitula que inqueri debent etc...
        A fifteenth-century scribe has added about one half of the *uisus*
        franci plegii (above f.16) on what was a blank leaf; f.36ᵛ is still
        blank.
f.37   *Ces sunt les establissemenz ke le Roy Edward fiz le Roy Henry fist a*

Wemust' a son primer parlement general apres son coronement lendemeyn de la cluse Paske lan de son regne tierz par conseil e par assentement de Arceuesk', Euesk', Abbees, Priors, Cuntes, Barons, e la communalte de la terre ilokes somunse
The first statute of Westminster: *S.R.* 1, 26.

f.48 *Expliciunt statuta prima Westm'*
        S.R. 1, 39

f.48ᵛ *Ces sunt les estatuz del Eschek' fez a Westmust' a la cluse Paske en le roy Edward fiz le roy Henry tierz*
        S.R. 1, 197, among "Statutes of uncertain date."

f.51ᵛ *Ces sunt les estatuz de la Ieurie ke nostre seignur le roy Edward fiz le roy Henry fist a Wemust' a son parlement a la quinzeyne de seint Michel lan de son regne tierz*
        The title of the statute written at the foot of the page to guide the rubricator describes the parliament as a "parlement general."
        S.R. 1, 221, among "Statutes of uncertain date."

f.53ᵛ *Ces sunt les estatuz de Gloucestr' fez a la feste seint Per ad Uincula en lan del regne le roy Edward fiz le roy Henry sime*

f.56 *Expliciunt statuta Gloucestrie*
        S.R. 1, 45–50

f.56ᵛ *Explanaciones statutorum Gloucestrie*
        S.R. 1, 50

f.57 *Statuta de religiosis facta apud Westm' Anno r.r.E. filii regis Henrici septimo*
        S.R. 1, 51

f.57ᵛ *Expliciunt statuta de Religiosis*

f.58 *Ces sunt les estatuz fez a Actone Burnel al parlement procheyn apres la seint Michel lan del regne le Roy Edward fiz le roy Henry unzime*
        S.R. 1, 53

f.59 *Expliciunt*

f.59ᵛ *Ces sunt les estatuz de marchaunz fez a Acton Burnel declarez e enuoietez al parlement de Wemust'*
        S.R. 1, 98

f.61ᵛ *Expliciunt statuta de mercatoribus apud Westm'*

f.62 Rex concessit quod omnes qui milites esse debent et non sunt ... fines admittant [f.62ᵛ]
        No rubric. Upper margin "De militibus faciendis." An addition of the original scribe, leaving space for a large R[ex]. *S.R.* 1, 229

f.63 *Statuta domini Edwardi Regis filii Regis Henrici facta apud Westm' in parliamento suo post Pascha Anno regni sui Terciodecimo*

f.83 *Ces sunt les estatuz le Roy Edward fiz le Roy Henr' fez a Wyncestre a son parlement apres la feste seint Michel lan de son regne Treszym*

f.85ᵛ *Ces sunt les estatuz le Roy Edward fiz le Roy Henry fez a Excestre a la feste seint Hillarii lan de son regne Quatorzim*
        S.R. 1, 210–212, among "Statutes of uncertain date."

The quires, as so often, reveal the compiler's *modus operandi*. The pre-Edward I documents fill exactly four quires, each of which begins with a major text: Q.1, Magna Carta 1215; Q.2, the Dictum of Kenilworth (1266); Q.3, Magna Carta 1225; Q.4, the Provisions of Merton. In no case does a text run on from one quire to the next. Each quire forms a complete booklet: and it may be that Q.3 has been wrongly bound, and should have been number 2. Each quire having been allotted its main text, the remaining leaves were filled by smaller routine and mostly undated texts, like the assizes of bread and ale, and the *capitula franci plegii* (f.16). In Q.4, the Provisions of Marlborough (1267) immediately follow the Provisions of Merton (1236) and the two together filled it nicely leaving only f.32ᵛ blank.

The second portion of the book, containing the statutes of Edward I to the year 1286 (Statutes of Exeter), is constructed with the same economy of parchment. Here again are two very lengthy documents – Westminster I (1275) and Westminster II – and each begins a new quire; but as each of them requires more than one, the compiler has no difficulty in copying all his statutes in chronological order without leaving many blank pages. When this was done, he seems to have prefaced the whole with a small quire of four leaves (fols. 33–6) setting out the chapter headings of the statutes of Westminster I, Gloucester, and Westminster II – a sort of table of contents.

The book having been thus completed, it was next illuminated and rubricated, and in the upper and lower margins the binder has still left us in tiny writing the headings of the statutes exactly reproduced in red in the text. The book was thus technically complete, but the compiler – whom I assume to have been the scribe – added a few more documents which are an integral and interesting part of the book. These additions were intended, like the others, to begin with an illuminated capital letter and a rubricated heading, though this was never in fact done. They are: on f.7, the little Anglo-Saxon glossary; on f.8, the tract on weights and measures; on f.24ᵛ the list of *dies communes in banco*; and on f.62 a treatise entitled *De militibus faciendis*, described in the *Statutes of the Realm* as "a statute for knighthood." Today the only completely blank page left in the book is on f.36ᵛ. So precious was parchment in the middle ages.

For whom are we to suppose such a fine, costly volume was compiled? At first sight it could well have belonged either to a lawyer or to a landowner; but a variety of reasons suggest the latter rather than the former. A typical British Museum volume, Harley ms.

4975,[7] which seems to be of about the same date contains, like so many of these collections, a sprinkling of purely procedural tracts (e.g., *Fet assaver*) and ends with a register of writs. The Huntington ms. is much smaller, containing only the basic information necessary for a landlord of great estates. Some such provenance too is suggested by the inclusion of the sentence of excommunication and anathema against all who infringed the charters as confirmed in 1253 (f.23). The list of antiquated Anglo-Saxon legal terms (f.7) with their contemporary vernacular (i.e., French) meanings suggests some old established monastery with estates guaranteed by ancient charters. So too the other undated texts dealing with traditional matters long since committed to writing, though of course the greater part of English law was still unwritten custom. Such were the tract on weights and measures (f.8); the Pleas of the Crown (f.12); the procedure for extending, that is, surveying, a manor (f.14); the assizes of bread and ale (fols. 15–16); the view of frank pledge (f.16); and that entitled *De militibus faciendis* (f.62). These texts will be found in nearly all books of this kind, but their prime interest is for the landowner rather than the common lawyer. The same is true of the much less common *Capitula foreste* (f.23ᵛ) which were a set of interrogatories called the Chapters of the Regard. The regard was the triennial inspection of the woods within the metes and bounds of the forest. Twelve knights, called the regarders, were required to find answers to the regard questionnaire. All the above, then, deal with the problems that faced the owner of great estates – his lands, his woods, his villeins. The cumulative evidence of the contents of the volume thus seems to justify the tentative conclusion that the book was made for a landlord, and if so, probably a landlord in the north of England, in view of the presence of the Yorkshire will on f.32ᵛ.

At this point my general conclusion regarding the provenance of the manuscript was unexpectedly confirmed by my friend Mr. Derek Hall, whose eagle eye detected in the text of the second Statute of Westminster (f.66ᵛ) an allusion to the manor of Naseby in Northamptonshire. The reference to this trouble-spot goes near to proving that the manuscript belonged to perhaps the most famous, and certainly the most litigious woman of Edward I's reign: Isabella de Fortibus (Forz) 1237–93, dowager countess of Aumale and countess of Devon, who held vast estates from Holderness in the north to the Isle of Wight in the south. Mr. Hall's conclusions upon the

7 I have to thank Mr. Godfrey Davis for directing me to this manuscript.

legal struggle over Naseby, set out below in the appendix, are of particular interest to lawyers. They are, too, a characteristic example of the value of these statute volumes to the historian.[8]

The special value of the book lies in its relatively early date. It throws light on the attitude of lawyers and landowners, still living in Edward I's time, towards the half-century before his accession: the texts they included and those they left out. Custom had already fastened upon Magna Carta as the starting point of English law-making, and this manuscript, most intelligently, includes both the 1215 and 1225 versions. There followed a period of just fifty years about which lawyers might differ in their selection of texts: but, for our compiler, from Edward I's accession, or more precisely from his first "general" parliament in 1275, all was plain sailing. He ceases to be selective, the statutes follow one another in chronological order, and each one is preceded by a full and accurate rubric. We are left in no doubt that, for him at least, true "statute"-making goes back to Edward's first parliament and no further. For him that was a turning point.

This conclusion follows plainly from the titles he gives to the main documents he selects from the period 1215–72. He refers to Magna Carta (1215) as the "Provisions of Runnymede, that is to say the Charter of King John." The title "Magna Carta de libertatibus com-munibus" is reserved for the final version of 1225, together with the charter "de libertatibus foreste." The distinction he draws between the two is a valid one, and implies some understanding of their history. Much the same thinking lies behind his preference for the title Provisions of Merton (1236) as against the later practice of calling them the Statute of Merton. The title Dictum of Kenilworth, being accurate, he lets pass, but again prefers Provisions of Marl-borough to Statute of Marlborough. These are his five main texts, and it is significant that neither the Provisions of Oxford nor the Provisions of Westminster find a place in the volume. With the year 1275 we arrive at the "statutes" of Edward I, and the precision of their rubrics suggests that their texts may well have been derived from sealed copies.

To the political historian, if not to the lawyer, the most interesting item in the book is the last: the statutes made at Exeter on the feast

---

8 For a full discussion of what follows see "The Early Statutes" by H. G. Richardson and G. O. Sayles, *Law Q. R.* (April and October, 1934); and V. H. Galbraith, "A Draft of Magna Carta (1215)," *Proceedings of the British Academy*, LIII (1967).

Ces sunt les estatuz le Roy Edward fitz le Roy Henry fer
a Everwyk a la feste seint Hillari lan de son regne
quatorzim. Purueu est cu come... les en ...

Primerement manndent al ... del ... ke il face
... a un certein iour. e ... Tou ... manner
Ceo cea pay les auant... enquerrons tuz les
bailifs dedenz les ... ... ffraunchises ke sunt
... ont este bailifs ou bedeus s'il en bie serrunt del tens
ke p . de C. fu corouney nostre seignur le Roy en cel tem
te. Ceo fet a entendre tuz les bailifs ou bedeus ... sunt
... ont este dedenz la ... de la baillie apurtenant
a tel corouney ou dehors ... mester sent.
E ke il facent au bien deuant cus le corouney de ki il
prendrunt lenqueste oue tuz les roules de tut son tens ke
il fust corouney nostre seignur le Roy. e tuz ses clerks ke
en bie sunt. E les enquerrons meintenant de sur lur
scale tuz les roules ... Coroun ... en ...
les ... al coroun ke il les eit prest quel hure
ke les Justices en eyre ... soey en cel ... . ou ke
le Roy ... ... de ... chose. E si le coroun seit
mort: seit fet en meme la manere a son heir del tens son pere.
Issi ke le coroun ne son heir, ne lur clerks ... ...
lur roules ... la venue de Justices, ne ...
ke ... ... les poinz de la coroune en ... del
Roy. e damage del poeple e en ... ... de ... a
... com auant ... ... fet .

E apres facent tuz les auant... Enquerrons tuz les auant
... bailifs ... . e ... frunt ... ke eus
lur charg... de par le Roy. e le conseil le Roy concede
... . E puis tant il auerint fet le serment: seit chef
con bailif de ... ... charge par
... ke il ... deuant les auant... enquerrons a ...

of St. Hilary (13 January) in the fourteenth year of Edward's reign (1286),[9] and therefore associated with no parliament. It is a statute not very often found in these little books and its presence is best explained by the fact that it was made shortly before our manuscript was written. Four months later Edward crossed to France, and he did not return till 1289 when he found the whole administration of the law in scandalous confusion. The statute may thus have quickly become a dead letter, and certainly it has almost wholly escaped the notice of recent historians and lawyers.[10] Yet it is more typical of the bulk of Edward's statutes than the famous and enduring measures dealing with subinfeudation, new manors, entails, and such-like, for it is an administrative act dealing entirely with procedure. Its genesis and meaning have lately been examined by Mr. Hunnisett,[11] and it throws a flood of light on the coroner's office when it was at the zenith of its efficiency. In the later thirteenth century, we are told, the coroner's office was second only to that of the sheriff, both in dignity and in its chronic practice of oppressing and fleecing the king's subjects. Kirkby's *Quest* in 1284–85 had looked into the mis-deeds of local officials, including the coroner; and it was realized that a detailed statement of the procedure by which peccant coroners could be brought to book, was badly needed. This was set out in the Statutes of Exeter, which elaborately detailed the process of summon-ing a jury to hold the grand inquest before the royal inquirers and then "demanded detailed information of all duties performed by coroners and their clerks and inquired of almost every possible op-pression and extortion. No special inquiry was intended immediately. ... The Statute of Exeter seems rather to have been intended as the basis of all future inquiries into Coroners' offences."[12] The statute gives us a picture of local administration at work, that is vivid and depressing, so widespread were its evils. A brighter sidelight is thrown upon the progress of social integration in the clauses of the statute concerned with the choosing of jurors for the grand inquest.

---

9 *Statutes of the Realm,* I, pp. 210–2 (among statutes of uncertain date) bears the date 28 December 1285, and may be right. Edward I had left Exeter on 9 January 1286.

10 I find no mention of it in Stubbs' *Constitutional History* (4th ed., Oxford, 1896) nor in Professor Cam's *The Hundred and the Hundred Rolls* (London, 1930) or in Plucknett's *Legislation of Edward I* (Oxford, 1949). It is misdated in Holdsworth's *History of English Law:* but there is a reference in the second edition of Powicke's, *The Thirteenth Century* (Oxford, 1953), quoting a short notice of mine on the ms. in the *Huntington Lib. Q.,* XXII, 2 (1959).

11 R. F. Hunnisett, *The Medieval Coroner* (Cambridge, 1961).

12 *Ibid.,* p. 119.

They were to be chosen from the "meillurs e plus leawz gens," and each man chosen was to have a seal to be attached to the presentments made by the jurors. But (the statute continues), where there is a shortage of free men, a juror may be chosen from the "plus sages et leals bunds," that is to say, the unfree: but, if so, he too must be a man with a seal. A century earlier Henry II's justices had scoffed at a poor knight (*militulus*), who produced a charter under his father's seal, for aping the manners of the great. By Edward I's reign we meet peasants with seals, and by Edward II's reign we encounter *cartae nativorum*[13] which no doubt were all sealed.

"In the long array of his legislative and administrative reforms," writes Miss Cam,[14] "we see the evidence of a passion for law, order, seemliness and subordination unequalled in any who came before or after him." To read the statutes in their entirety is to acquire a new respect for Edward's heroic, though largely unavailing, struggle against administrative oppression of his subjects, a great part of which arose from the actions of the king's own officials.

The book has also its interest for the constitutional historian, intent upon the development of parliament, and the gradual limitation of *de facto* royal authority in government. Thus, the question "What was a 'statute'?" is now, I think, generally answered by: "the word, in the sense of a specific type of legislation, did not come into common use until towards the end of the thirteenth century"[15] – a conclusion fully supported by the text before us, which denies the title of "statutum" to the whole of lawmaking in England before the reign of Edward I. Professor Sayles and Mr. Richardson, relying upon an intensive scrutiny of the plea rolls, would draw the line between the old conception of legislation and the new, "without much hesitation at 1258, the year of the Parliament at Oxford,"[16] mentioning *inter alia* that the Provisions of Westminster (1259) were being cited in pleading as early as 1260. Yet one cannot but notice that our (early) text of statutes takes no cognizance of the various documents connected with the barons' wars of 1258–65. Nor is this, in my view, the result of either accident or ignorance. The omission is surely deliberate, and suggests that the narrow pur-

13 *Cartae Nativorum* ed. C. N. L. Brooke and M. M. Postan (Northamptonshire Record Society, vol. 22, 1960).
14 Cam, *The Hundred and the Hundred Rolls*, p. 240.
15 H. G. Richardson and George Sayles, "The Early Statutes," *Law Q. R.* (April and October, 1934).
16 *Ibid.*, 1.

suit of English legal procedure is an imperfect guide to the development of the English constitution. Throughout the middle ages kingship worked at two levels, inseparable in practice but notionally quite distinct. For the common lawyer England was a feudal kingship, the legal workings of which have been traced in detail by Professor Holt in his book on Magna Carta. But centuries before we have much record of the kingly power as envisaged by his feudal magnates, England was also what Professor Ullman[17] describes as "a theocratic kingship," an aspect basically at loggerheads with that of the feudal sovereign. The dichotomy is of vital significance to constitutional, if hardly to legal, history and carries with it certain inferences of importance to critical study. First, it is a fact that the conception of the king as full sovereign under God, whose prerogative knows no earthly superior (theocratic kingship) reached its height at precisely the period that the feudal king first ran into revolutionary trouble with his greater subjects. Secondly, it is a fact that the vast influence of the papal monarchy was consistently exerted in support of the theocratic sovereign from the moment that King John made his peace with Innocent III (in 1213) until the death of Henry III in 1272. From that point it began to fail, though Edward I in 1305 found papal release from his legal undertakings towards his barons, and from about the year 1327 England was, if hardly even yet in principle, in practice a monarchy so limited in the exercise of power by the magnates as eventually to give rise to a widely different order of society. From all this it follows that in the thirteenth century at any rate, the historian must hesitate to draw constitutional precedents from the events happening in crises when the kings made promises to their subjects under duress. They were in every case subsequently released by their feudal suzerain the pope from their obligation to adhere to them; and this release was generally approved, when the heat of the moment had passed, by their subjects. So, in the middle ages we are dealing neither with simple legal theory, nor even political theory but with a working Christian principle, which was a compound of both, supported by moral and religious considerations. We shall hardly exaggerate if we say that the papacy so far christianized society as to make it suspicious for centuries to come of all encroachment on royal power imposed by revolution. And when at last, in 1539 or so, the long-waning spiritual

17 Walter Ullman, *Principles of Government and Politics in the Middle Ages* (1961).

power of the papacy was taken into the competent hands of Henry VIII, Magna Carta (1215) lost its appeal – Shakespeare does not even mention it in *King John* – only to be painfully resurrected by the early seventeenth-century antiquaries.

Considerations of this kind must be in our minds as we examine this very early and well-informed little book. They explain why the compiler began with Magna Carta (1215) but was careful to add the real and permanent Magna Carta (1225), exactly describing the first as the Provisions of Runnymede, and the other as the Great Charter. Equally, they suggest why 1258–65 was ignored, though some of its achievements were permanently embodied in law by the Dictum of Kenilworth and the Provisions of Marlborough – both of which were included since both had been approved and largely directed by papal legates. But only with Edward I does he arrive at "Statutes" – enactments made by a sovereign king freely and with the traditional help of his natural advisers. No one, not even a lawyer or a feudal magnate, would have felt quite happy about describing England as simply "in principle a limited monarchy"[18] in the thirteenth century. The concept was more complicated than that, for thinkers had not yet canalized thought into the separate categories of "politics," "law," and/or "administration."

And so one is led to the view that the constitutional advance made by England in the thirteenth century was in great part the achievement of the papal concern and suzerainty over England. Without it, Magna Carta, as well as the whole achievement of 1258–65, might have disappeared from history. Alternatively, to some it may seem likely that without papal interference the advance might have been much greater still. What we can say as a fact is that the actual advance made towards limited monarchy was mainly secured by direct papal action, and that by the same token it is due to the papacy that it was not either more or less. Nor must we forget that these highly educated papal legates – Guala, Pandulf, Otto, Gui, Ottobuono – knew little and probably cared less about the detailed operation of English common law in the courts. Their influence was on the whole exerted in favour of a growing sense of community participation in government, but always subject to the exercise of a full royal prerogative, modified only by the force of good customs established in the past. With the decline of the papacy in the fourteenth century,

18 Richardson and Sayles, "Parliament and Great Councils in England," *Law Q. R.* (April 1961), 223.

the English monarchy had both less to gain from papal support, and less to fear from papal opposition.

These mixed collections of statutes and legal tracts, then, which survive by the score in our greater libraries have much to teach us, and deserve closer attention than they have received from either the compilers of the very unsatisfactory *Statutes of the Realm*[19] or from more recent historians of the law. They were equally essential to working lawyers and to owners of land: and this Huntington ms. seems likely to prove to be among the earliest surviving examples.

𝕬𝖕𝖕𝖊𝖓𝖉𝖎𝖝 G. D. G. HALL

"The common law was reluctant to give judgment by default. ... A tenant [in fee simple] who lost by default was not for ever barred, but could regain his land if he succeeded in a writ 'of a higher nature'; thus, if he had lost by default in an assize he could still recover (if his title was sufficient) in a writ of entry, or if he had lost by default in a writ of entry he could resort to a writ of right. Even in a writ of right a judgment by default will not bar a future writ of right except in certain circumstances."[20] But not all tenants were tenants in fee simple. A tenant in tail, in *maritagium*, for life or in dower, was called a particular tenant. "A particular tenant could not use the writ of right; [and so,] if he lost by default after being duly summoned, he could have no new action."[21]

In 1285 the Statute of Westminster II, c.4, established a new remedy to deal with this problem, the writ *quod ei deforciat*.[22] The statute gives four specimen writs: one of these is a writ for one who claims land as *maritagium*. The formula given in the statute (printed in the *Statutes of the Realm* from the chancery statute roll) is as follows: "Precipe A. quod iuste etc. reddat B. tale manerium de C. cum pertinenciis quod clamat esse ius et maritagium suum et quod A. ei iniuste deforciat." But in the statute book under discussion the

---

19 Cf., Richardson and Sayles, "The Early Statutes," 46–7, who call attention to the need for a new, critical edition of the *Statutes of the Realm*. Volume I, published in 1810, is positively antediluvian, and reminds us, as so often, upon what shaky foundations so much modern research upon medieval English history rests.

20 T. F. T. Plucknett, *Concise History of the Common Law* (5th ed., London, 1956), pp. 385–6.

21 S. F. C. Milsom, *Novae Narrationes* (Selden Society, 80, 1963), p. cxxix.

22 See *ibid.*, pp. cxxviii–cxxxi.

writ reads: "Precipe A. quod iuste etc. reddat B. manerium de Navesby cum pertinenciis quod clamat esse ius et maritagium suum et quod predicta talis ei iniuste deforciat."[23] There are two significant variations here from the form given in the statute: "tale manerium de C." has become "manerium de Navesby," and for the second mention of the tenant "A." we have the feminine "predicta talis." If we take the words at their face value, this writ is a simplified copy of an actual writ of *quod ei deforciat* in which a man or woman claimed the manor of Navesby (Naseby in Northamptonshire) as *maritagium* against a woman who had won it on a default in a previous action between them. What do the printed sources tell us about Naseby?

In January 1238 Richard de Clare, earl of Gloucester, married Maud de Lacy, daughter of the earl of Lincoln, "and by this marriage he became possessed of Navesby lordship" which had been a Lacy fee since the beginning of John's reign.[24] In "33 Henry III" (1248–49) Richard and Maud by final concord conveyed the manor and advowson of Naseby as *maritagium* to the recently married William de Forz, count of Aumale, and Isabella, daughter and sister of successive earls of Devon and niece of Richard; there was to be a reversion to Richard and Maud and the heirs of Maud if Isabella died without heirs of her body.[25] The death of her husband William in 1260 and of her brother Baldwin in 1262 left Isabella as dowager countess of Aumale, countess of Devon and lady of the Isle of Wight; by November 1274 all her children were dead.[26] Richard de Clare died in 1262 leaving Maud as dowager countess of Gloucester. The two widows fought a battle over Naseby. Isabella was in possession of Naseby in 1260–64,[27] and probably in 1274–75.[28] She is said to have lost it to Maud in the bench "in the third year of Edw. 1"[29] and this is

23 At f.66ᵛ. The writ was later collated with the statute roll and corrected accordingly.
24 J. Bridges, *Northamptonshire* (Oxford, 1791), I, p. 576; *Calendar of Patent Rolls, 1232–47*, p. 208; and see below, n.40.
25 Bridges, *Northamptonshire*, I, p. 576, vouching "Ped.fin.anno 33 Hen. III"; *Cal.Inq. Post Mortem*, III, no. 156. For the fine, see below, n.34.
26 Isabella and her dealings with Edward I are discussed by F. M. Powicke, *King Henry III and the Lord Edward* (Oxford, 1947), pp. 707–11, and K. B. McFarlane, "Had Edward I a 'policy' towards the earls?" *History*, L (1965), 152–3.
27 Revenues from Naseby, 1260–64, disputed with her mother Amice: N. Denholm-Young, "The Yorkshire Estates of Isabella de Fortibus," *Yorks. Arch. J.*, XXXI (1934), 393, 412. Presentation to Naseby, 1262: *Rotuli Ricardi Gravesend* (Lincoln Record Soc., 20), p. 101.
28 *Rot.Hundr.*, II, p. 7.
29 Bridges, *Northamptonshire*, I, p. 576, vouching "Placit. de Banco anno 3 Edw. I."

probably the case between them in which judgment was entered on 15 November 1275.[30] Isabella's famous, but abortive, arrangements with Edward in 1276 seem to refer to this loss: "If the countess recover the manor of Navesby, which she claims as her right, then she shall give it to the king" in part-exchange for the manor of Tiverton; "if she does not recover the manor of Navesby and she recover the manor of Craft, which she claims, then she shall give the latter manor to the king for the manor of Tiverton."[31] Perhaps by 1286,[32] certainly before her death in 1293,[33] Isabella had recovered Naseby again.

This evidence suggested two interesting possibilities which might be checked against the plea rolls of the bench. First, that when Isabella lost Naseby to Maud "in the third year of Edw. I" it was on a default. This is so. In May 1275 Maud brought a writ of entry *cui in vita* against Isabella, claiming that Richard had alienated it against her will. Isabella appeared and set up in defence the final concord of "33 Henry III,"[34] but, after a further appearance on 20 October, she defaulted on 24 October. She subsequently appeared *coram rege* with Maud, but was unable to cure the default, and she later defaulted again in the bench. Judgment was given for Maud, almost certainly on 15 November.[35]

The second possibility was that Isabella took advantage of the new remedy given in 1285 by the Statute of Westminster II, c.4, and recovered Naseby by *quod ei deforciat* soon after the passing of the statute; given Edward's interest in Naseby, it was even possible that the statute owed something to Isabella's plight. But this is not so.

---

30 *Calendar of Close Rolls, 1272–79*, p. 256, "concerning the manor of N...etby."
31 *Cal.Cl. R., 1272–79*, p. 348. This is no. 4 of four documents enrolled; No. 2 is irrelevant; Nos. 1 (dated 14 January 1276), 3, and 4 (both undated) are, to judge from the changing arrangements for the manor of Craft, in chronological order.
32 When she presented Master William of Cherrington to Naseby; *Rolls and Register of Bishop Oliver Sutton* (Lincoln Record Soc., 43), II, p. 53: but the advowson is not said by Bridges to have been in issue in the litigation of 3 Edw. I.
33 *Cal.Inq. Post Mortem*, III, no. 156.
34 The full text of the fine as given on the plea roll corresponds exactly with the fine itself which is P.R.O. CP 25(1), 173/36, no. 574. The fine is dated 20 January 1249 and was levied then or shortly afterwards at Worcester before Roger de Thurkelby and his fellow itinerant justices; no plea roll survives.
35 P.R.O. CP 40/9, m.47ʳ, the Bench roll for Easter 1275: pleas for one month and five weeks from Easter, 12/19 May. The later proceedings are entered here as *posteas*. No dates are given after 24 October, but the Close Roll memorandum of judgment on 15 November concerning "N...etby" (above, n.30) fits the chronology.

What actually happened is more remarkable. In 1276, shortly after
the previous action and nine years before the passing of the statute,
Isabella sued Maud by *quod ei deforciat*: "Isabella de Fortibus Comitissa Albermarl' petit versus Matellidem de Clare Comitissam Glouc'
et Hertf' manerium de Navesby cum pertinenciis quod eadem Isabella clamat esse ius et maritagium suum de dono Ricardi de Clare
quondam Comitis Glouc' et Hertf' et predicte Matillidis et quod
eadem Matillis ei iniuste deforciat."[36] It is hardly surprising to find
that Maud's attorney objected that he ought not to answer to the
writ. The argument is interesting enough to be given in full:

Et Matillis per attornatum suum venit et dicit quod non debet ei inde ad
hoc breve respondere. Dicit enim quod breve istud non est conceptum
secundum communem formam Cancellarie, immo quoddam novum breve
est absque consilio regni provisum. Dicit eciam quod ipsa Comitissa Glouc'
alias in curia regis hic recuperavit predictum manerium cum pertinenciis
versus ipsam Comitissam Albermarl' per defaltam ipsius Comitisse Albermarl', unde petit iudicium si ipsa modo posset petere predictum manerium
versus ipsam per aliud breve quam per breve de recto. Et predicta Comitissa Albermarl' dicit quod predicte raciones non debent ei obesse. Dicit
eciam quod ipsa non clamat ius in predicta terra per descensum heredi-
tarium ita quod per breve de recto sibi perquirere posset, eo quod breve de
recto, sive sit patens sive clausum, facit mencionem de iure et hereditate.
Dicit eciam quod licet huiusmodi brevia communiter hucusque non fuerint
impetrata, hoc fuit eo quod consimilis casus prius non accidit, et oportet
quod in quolibet novo casu nova provideantur remedia per brevia de
Cancellaria domini regis.
Et predicta Comitissa Glouc' non potest hoc dedicere. Ideo consideratum
est quod respondeat.

Without the additional evidence which a report in year-book style
might give, we cannot tell how long or furious a debate preceded the
laconic ruling against Maud.[37] Her orthodox argument accords with
the general rules stated at the beginning of this appendix. Isabella's

---

36 P.R.O. CP 40/15, m.10[d] (false start at m.6[r]), the Bench roll for Trinity 1276.
I would never have looked for the case in 1276 but for a reference in a sixteenth-century abbreviation of the 1275 case in P.R.O. Index no. 17114, f.13[d],
which ends, "In T. 4 rot. 3 iterum placitatur inter eos"; this led to CP 40/16,
m.3[d], a second roll for Trinity 1276. CP 40/15, m.10[d], is a slightly better text
and has a *postea* with further proceedings. The case may have begun earlier:
in Easter 1276 Maud appointed attornies against Isabella "de placito terre" in
Northamptonshire; CP 40/14, m.79[d].
37 The case might well have been, but was not, reported in the two collections
of Anglo-Norman reports, c.1274–c.1278, which were printed by W. H. Dun-

reply is one more piece of evidence for the controversy about the power of chancery to issue original writs. On the face of it the case sits well with Professor Wilkinson's observation: "There is a belief, for which I can find no evidence, that the extension of the chancery's powers by the *in consimili casu* clause 24 of Westminster II in 1285 was caused by the conservatism of the office."[38] But it may be that royal interest was decisive for Isabella in chancery and bench. Ordinary people would have had to wait a further nine years for relief.[39]

Forced to answer, Maud went on, unsuccessfully, to demand a view of the land and to challenge, on technical and substantive grounds, the fine of 1249.[40] On 9 February 1277 judgment was given for Isabella.[41] Had Edward a "policy" towards the countesses? If he did in fact exert pressure in 1276–77 to protect the small and contingent interest in Naseby which his arrangements with Isabella had given him, then he may have regretted it by 1290, for Isabella held Naseby until her childless death in 1293 when it reverted, under the terms of the 1249 fine, to Gilbert, earl of Gloucester, as heir of Maud; from Gilbert it passed in 1295 to his infant son Gilbert.[42] Had Maud been successful in 1276–77 Naseby would, as *maritagium*, have passed to earl Gilbert not in 1293 but when Maud died in 1289, and would have been available in 1290 for inclusion in the arrangements which Gilbert made with Edward when he married Joan of Acre.[43] In the end it made little difference to Edward himself.[44]

ham, *Casus Placitorum* (Selden Society, 69), pp. 45–141: collection II, no. 4, is a novel disseisin against Isabella in the same term, Trinity 1276.

38 B. Wilkinson, *Constitutional History of Medieval England, 1216–1399* (London, 1958), III, p. 125, n.52.

39 Coke thought, wrongly, that a tenant in tail or in *maritagium* could use a writ of right in such cases before the statute, and that it was only because c.1 of the statute (*De Donis*) changed their estates from fee simple to estate tail that c.4 had to give them *quod ei deforciat*: 2 *Institutes* 350.

40 As part of her case Maud said that when Naseby was given to Richard and her in 1238 it was as *maritagium*.

41 CP 40/15, m.10^d; a *postea* on the same membrane as the rest of the case.

42 *Cal.Inq. Post Mortem*, III, nos. 156 and 371.

43 *Calendar of Charter Rolls*, II, pp. 350–1. For the non-inclusion of Naseby see *Calendar of Fine Rolls*, I, p. 517.

44 McFarlane, "Had Edward I a policy?" 154.

The Letters of John Mason: A Fourteenth-Century Formulary from St. Augustine's, Canterbury W.A. PANTIN

The subject of this essay is a formulary or collection of letters emanating from St. Augustine's Abbey, Canterbury. These letters were written at various dates between about 1307 and 1350 and survive in three manuscripts:

Merton College (Oxon) ms. 122, fols.104–120^v. Written in a mid-fourteenth-century hand; containing 72 letters; bound up with the chronicle of Martinus Polonus and the letters of Piero della Vigna, Frederick II's chancellor (popular as models of style); given to Merton by John Bohun.[1]

Bodleian Library (Oxon) ms. Rawlinson c 7, fols.1–50^v. Written in a hand of c. 1400; containing 83 letters; incomplete, breaking off in the middle of the last letter (quire missing); bound up with the *Secreta philosophorum* (a treatise on the seven liberal arts); formerly belonged to St. Augustine's, Canterbury (see below), and to Dr. John Dee; inscribed on flyleaf, "Epistole Mason de librario [sic] sancti Augustini."[2]

Worcester Cathedral, Library, ms. F 80, fols.120^v, 97–108^v (misplaced in binding). Written in an early or mid-fifteenth-century hand; containing 65 letters; incomplete, breaking off in the middle of the last letter (quire missing); described as "Epistole Mason"; bound up with nine other treatises, such as the *Gesta Romanorum*, the pseudo-Seneca *De remediis fortuitorum*, the declamations of Seneca, *Metaphora creaturarum* (on the seven vices), the *Parvum bonum* of Bonaventura, Ruysbroek *De nuptiis spiritualibus*, and two sets of *Distinctiones*. At first sight this literary and theological miscellany would seem to have little in common. However, it contains the sort of material that would be useful for a preacher, and

---

1 H. O. Coxe, *Catalogus Codicum MSS qui in Collegiis Aulisque Oxoniensibus hodie asservantur* (Oxford, 1852), Merton mss, 55; F. M. Powicke, *The Medieval Books of Merton College* (Oxford, 1931), 232 (hereinafter M).
2 *Bodleian Quarto Catalogue*, v (Rawlinson), ii, 1; *Summary Catalogue*, 11874 (hereinafter R).

probably Mason's letters, with their moralizing preambles, would also serve this purpose.[3]

Of the three surviving manuscripts, the Merton ms. is the earliest and has the best text. The Rawlinson ms. is the most complete, though even this was originally longer. It is possible that letters 73 through 83, found only in R, are an addition made by someone later than John Mason. The Worcester ms. is the latest and least valuable of the three. The readings of R and W often agree as against M, so perhaps they derive from the same original. In printing some of the letters in the course of this essay I have based the text on M as far as it goes, and thereafter on R. I have provided the numbering of the letters.

The late fifteenth-century library catalogue of St. Augustine's, Canterbury, includes two copies of the *Epistole fratris Iohannis Mason*, numbers 953 and 954.[4] Number 953 is to be identified (by the second folio) with ms. Rawlinson c 7 described above. Number 954 has not been identified. It was bound up with *Epistole Pharaonis*, Alan of Lille's *De planctu nature*, a *tractatus de arte dictandi*, and the *Cosmographia* of Bernard Silvestris. The manuscript was given by John Hawkherst, who was abbot from 1427 to 1430. The letters of John Mason also formed one of the works which John Whetham-stede, the fifteenth-century abbot of St. Albans and himself an amateur of *florida verborum venustas*, had transcribed.[5]

Although the letters were practically all issued, so far as we can tell, in the name of the abbot or the abbot and convent of St. Augustine's, Canterbury, the collection evidently circulated under the title "Epistole fratris Iohannis Mason" or "Epistole Mason." Presumably this means that they were in fact composed by a monk of St. Augustine's called John Mason. Mason appears as one of the committee of seven monks who elected Thomas Poucyn abbot in 1334, being then presumably a man of some seniority.[6] This identification fits in well with the period covered by the letters, which corresponds roughly with the abbacy of Ralph of Bourne, 1310–34. Mason was probably born in the 1270s and entered the monastery in the 1290s. It is likely that he is the "Iohannes dictus Machun," monk of St. Augustine's,

3 J. K. Floyer, *Catalogue of MSS preserved in the Chapter Library of Worcester Cathedral* (Oxford, 1906), 39–41 (hereinafter W).
4 M. R. James, *Ancient Libraries of Canterbury and Dover* (Cambridge, 1903), 298–9, 519; the identification of number 954 with M is incorrect.
5 T. Tanner, *Bibliotheca Britannico-Hibernica* (London, 1748), 518.
6 *Calendar of Papal Letters*, II, 405.

who was ordained priest in 1297.[7] There is no evidence as to whether or not he was at the university. Apparently he left no books to the monastic library and the Rawlinson ms once at St. Augustine's is too late to have belonged to him.

At St. Augustine's the precentor was responsible for the letters sent out under the common seal of the abbot and convent: "scripta in capitulo legenda legere, componenda componere, corrigenda corrigere, atque sigillanda sigillare." He kept one of the keys of the common seal and was also responsible for the library. On the other hand it was the duty of the monk who acted as abbot's chamberlain to compose and write the letters which went out under the abbot's seal: "ipsius est dictare et precipue scribere ea que sub sigillo abbatis sunt mittenda." The chamberlain had to be at hand day and night, and was something of the nature of a confidential secretary.[8] John Mason might have held either office, but that of abbot's chamberlain seems more likely. These letters are not the formal legal documents that would need to be read out in chapter.

These letters were evidently collected together as models of style. Thus the addresses and subscriptions were unfortunately omitted and the names mostly reduced to initials, so that it is sometimes quite difficult to piece together what the letter is about. The compiler was probably mainly interested in those parts that least interest the modern historian, such as the long-winded and flowery "proverbia" or introductions. However, the letters seem almost all to have been real letters, not just imaginary exercises. Many were written to further causes that really mattered, such as the great lawsuit against the archbishop of Canterbury in the Roman curia. No doubt they were written in this flowery style because it was found by experience that this had the desired effect. Style could be more important than one might imagine; a mistake in addressing a letter to the abbot instead of to the abbot and convent could give offence.[9] As is well known, princes in the fifteenth century thought it necessary for reasons of prestige to employ humanist secretaries.

The letters themselves are not arranged in chronological order, nor are they grouped according to subject-matter, although some

7 *Register of Archbishop Robert Winchelsey* (Canterbury and York Society, 1940), 916.
8 *Customary of St. Augustine's, Canterbury, and St. Peter's Westminster*, ed. E. M. Thompson (Henry Bradshaw Society, 1902), I, 96, 53.
9 *Chapters of the English Black Monks*, ed. W. A. Pantin (Camden Series, III, xlv, 1931), I, 30.

letters addressed to the king (numbers 14–19) are grouped together. Unlike some formularies, the letters in John Mason's collection are not classified according to type, as *Supplicatoria, Deprecatoria, Preceptoria, Excusatoria,* etc. In fact there does not seem to be any key to the arrangement of these letters. Presumably Mason kept the original drafts of the letters as he composed them and copied from these.

There are plenty of such formularies, made up of real letters, which survive from the fourteenth century. Notable among them are the *Liber epistolaris* compiled by Richard de Bury and a number of formularies connected with Oxford.[10] These were a necessary adjunct to the *ars dictandi,* the art of letter-writing. What is remarkable about this collection is not so much that a monk of St. Augustine's should have put together a formulary of his choicest compositions, but that this should have gained some currency outside Canterbury, and that quite soon. The Merton manuscript seems almost contemporary, and only one of the three surviving manuscripts comes from St. Augustine's.

A large number of the letters in the formulary, nearly a third of the total, are connected with the struggle between the monks of St. Augustine's and the archbishop of Canterbury, c.1329–33. The major issues were the monastery's claim to exemption from the archbishop's jurisdiction and its rights over its churches.[11] It was part of a prolonged struggle that went on throughout the twelfth, thirteenth, and fourteenth centuries and finally ended with a composition in 1397. With an ancient and powerful monastery on the doorstep of the archbishops, such a struggle was inevitable. In 1257 a compromise had been arranged with St. Edmund, but the struggle broke out again in 1297 with archbishop Winchelsey. Boniface VIII afterwards resolved the matter first in favour of the monks and then in favour of the archbishop. When Simon Mepham became archbishop in 1329 he attempted to include St. Augustine's in his visitation of his diocese. The monks appealed to Pope John XXII who appointed in

10 *Oxford Formularies,* ed. H. E. Salter, W. A. Pantin, H. G. Richardson (Oxford Hist. Soc., N.S., IV–V, 1939–40), *passim.*
11 For this struggle see William Thorne's chronicle of St. Augustine's, Canterbury, ed. R. Twysden, *Historiae Anglicanae Scriptores Decem* (London, 1652), esp. cols. 2039–53; English translation by A. H. Davis (Oxford, 1934); *Dict. Nat. Biography,* s.n. Mepham, Simon; on exemption in general cf. David Knowles, *The Monastic Order in England* (Cambridge, 1940), 575ff; *Religious Orders in England* (Cambridge, 1948), 277ff.

July 1330 a canon of Salisbury and much-used papal agent, Itherius de Concoreto, to act as judge-delegate to decide the case. Early in 1331 the monks' proctor went to the archbishop's manor of Slindon in Sussex to summon him to attend Itherius' court. The monks alleged that the proctor was seized and maltreated by the archbishop's servants. In November 1332 Itherius gave sentence in favour of the monks, and awarded costs against the archbishop in the enormous sum of £700 (perhaps £35,000 in modern values), under threat of excommunication. The archbishop had not paid when he died on 12 October 1333. In 1334 the monks obtained papal ratification of their privileges and exemption.[12] A minor operation accompanying the main struggle was the appropriation of three churches to support four monks as students at Oxford. This had been granted as early as 1327, but was not finally effected until 1349.[13]

Two of the St. Augustine's monks were sent as proctors to the Roman curia at Avignon: John Mankael, D.D. (nos. 2, 10; M fols.104, 106) and Robert of Fekenham (nos. 2, 4, 5, 9, 10; M fols.104, 106). Mankael died at the curia, a severe loss to his colleague and to the monastery, as he was the ablest scholar and the first doctor of theology they had produced – an interesting example of the way contemporaries used graduates for practical purposes. Another agent was a secular, Master Robert of Worcester,[14] for whom the monks requested a benefice (no. 53; M f.116). Many letters are addressed to various people at the curia who might help in the case, from Pope John xxii downwards (nos. 3, 50, 51; M fols.104, 114ᵛ, 115). The men addressed or referred to include, besides Itherius de Concoreto; Matthew Orsini, o.p., cardinal priest of SS. John and Paul, 1327–38 (nos. 8, 53, cf. 6; M fols.105ᵛ, 116); Edmund, bishop of Ardfert, sent as nuncio to England (no. 52; M f.115ᵛ); Hugh of Angoulême (see no. 59 below); and a prelate addressed as "in eterni regis edificio columpna preclara et insignis" whom this description is said to suit "nomine et re simul" – probably Cardinal John de Colonna, 1327–48 (no. 5; M f.105).

This prolonged struggle over St. Augustine's exemption, like others of its kind, will no doubt seem to the modern observer a prodigious waste of time, energy, and money by spiritual men over a

12 *Calendar of Papal Letters*, II, 401.
13 *Ibid.*, II, 278, 315; Thorne, *Historiae Anglicanae*, cols. 2086–7.
14 Robert of Worcester, alias de Humbultone, D.C.L., A. B. Emden, *A Biographical Register of the University of Oxford to A.D. 1500* (Oxford, 1959), III, 2086.

matter of little or no spiritual importance. But it was not just a display of bloody-mindedness. To a conscientious medieval bishop, any claim to exemption seemed a hindrance to religious discipline and the cure of souls. On the other hand, a well-intentioned but misguided bishop might do real harm to a religious order or community. Archbishop Pecham had tried hard to quash the most enlightened parts of the reform policy of the Black Monks' general chapters, namely liturgical retrenchment and the revival of studies.[15] St. Augustine's was only claiming the same freedom from outside interference that most religious orders today enjoy as a matter of course. One cannot blame the monks if they felt about exemption rather as we feel about academic freedom.

One of the great developments in canonical procedure in the late twelfth century had been the way in which the papal *plenitudo potestatis* had been put at everyone's disposal by the appointment of papal judges-delegate, who could give a final decision, with local knowledge, on the spot. But this lawsuit shows that, although a judge-delegate was appointed, prolonged and expensive lobbying at the curia was still necessary to get the case settled and the sentences, even when already given, implemented. Moreover the *plenitudo potestatis* did not produce that finality that one might have expected. It was for this reason that Prior Henry of Eastry advised Archbishop Mepham to settle with the monks in 1330, "because lawsuits in the curia which seem to be dead, commonly come to life again and become immortal."[16] Again and again, over three centuries, the issue was taken to the papacy, and though the pope or his judges-delegate would make a ruling, a few years later the dispute would break out once more. When the dispute was finally settled in 1397,[17] it was not because of any ruling from the papacy, but simply because the two parties were tired of fighting, and the archbishop accepted the monks' claims. This illustrates the importance of compromise in the unceasing litigation of the middle ages, at every stage, high and low, ecclesiastical and secular, from the Roman curia to the chancellor's court at Oxford. It also shows that the government of the medieval church was in practice less authoritarian, and more dependent on consent, than one might suppose.

The prosecution of a great lawsuit needed rhetoricians as well as

15 Pantin, *Chapters*, I, 6off; Knowles, *Religious Orders*, I, 12ff.
16 *Literae Cantuarienses*, ed. J. B. Sheppard (Rolls Series, 1889), I, 334.
17 Thorne, *Historiae Anglicanae*, cols. 2199–2202.

lawyers. These letters are interesting for they illustrate the barrage of persuasive letters (the masterpieces of John Mason's art), addressed to useful people, from pope and king downwards, which would accompany the formal, basic legal documents, the proxies, articles, sentences, and appeals. These latter are not included in the formulary, but they may have been entered into the monastery's registers or letter-books, which have not survived for this period.

It is possible to print here only a small number of the letters dealing with the struggle with the archbishop. The following letter, number 60, shows the monastery summoning all the lawyers sworn to its service to come to a council at Michaelmas (29 September). It was feared that the newly elected archbishop might attempt a visitation on his return from the Roman curia. Simon Mepham was consecrated at Avignon on 25 May 1328, and landed in England on 5 September; so this letter may perhaps be dated in the summer of 1328, thus anticipating the whole struggle. This date would also fit in with the reference to the appropriation of churches. The mandate for the appropriation of Willesborough, Burmarsh, and Stone-in-Oxney to support four monk students at Oxford had been obtained in November 1327. It was renewed in January 1329, although it was not finally carried out until 1349[18] (cf. also nos. 59, 70 below). The bishop of Worcester in 1328 was Adam Orleton, who had had much experience as an envoy to the Roman curia, and had been at one time auditor of causes there. Obviously he would be well qualified to press Master Andrew Sapiti to hand over the mandate. The recipient of the letter was perhaps at the Roman curia.

Number 60. To a lawyer, perhaps at the Roman curia, Summer, 1328
Illata gravamina transacti temporis, ea passis dancia[19] cautele sollerciam de futuris, expertos edocent, ut adversus consimilia oportunis se defensionibus muniant, per quas illis insurgentibus securius se opponant. Solent namque ad archipresulatus Cantuariensis regimen evocati, mox in sue creacionis novitate contra nos et monasterium colore quesito capitose procedere, et exempcionis nostre iura suam visitando diocesim graviter impugnare.[20] Ut itaque in eventum nos vestro ceterorumque peritorum assistencium nobis armatos consilio, patris ipsius iam ad sedem suam episcopalem a Romana curia revertentis, volentisque forsitan, ut timetur, in

18 *Calendar of Papal Letters*, II, 278, 315; Thorne, *Historiae Anglicanae*, cols. 2086–7; in the event Brookland was substituted for Burmarsh.
19 dancia M; habundancia R W
20 graviter M; *omit* R W; impugnare R W; pugnare M

gravando predecessorum suorum vestigiis inherere, previsa[21] iacula minus ledant, necesse habemus omnes iurisperitos iuramento nobis fidelitatis astrictos ab undique locorum hac de causa convocare nostro lateri assistendos. Inter quos de vestra fidelitate, circumspeccione et industria pleniorem in arduis fiduciam optinentes, qualitate negocii nos urgente, ex cordis intimis vos rogamus, quatenus non vos tedeat labor itineris, nec assumpta detineat occupacio in agendis, quin de status vestri circumstanciis taliter per omnia ordinetis quod citra festum sancti Michaelis proximo nunc futurum vestram apud nos exhibeatis presenciam in agendorum nostrorum consilium et succursum. Ceterum ut graciam de appropriandis ecclesiis a sede apostolica impetratam, quam magister Andreas Sapeti penes se hucusque detinuit, in formam debitam redigendam, exhibitis sibi litteris domini Wygorniensis[22] episcopi, quas lator presencium tradet vobis, cum effectu nitamini ab ipsius eripere manibus, ut secura ad nos delacione perveniat, quod hactenus non permisit malicia detinentis. (M, f.117ᵛ; R f.36; W, f.108)

Letter number 7, addressed to a judge at the Roman curia, explains how the case has been committed to Itherius de Concoreto (in July 1330) who was to hear and determine the case in England. It also explains that the archbishop had objected that Itherius was a pensioner of St. Augustine's. Monasteries had a practice of retaining useful clerks, lawyers, and royal officials with a pension in return for an oath of fidelity,[23] rather as the king retained certain cardinals with pensions. Parties in a law suit had the right to object to a judge-delegate, but it looks as though the archbishop's objection was overruled in this instance. To get the right judges was half the battle; the prior of Durham realized this when he wrote to his agent at the curia in 1284–85: "And for the passion of Christ, act so circumspectly that we have at least two of the judges in whom we can have confidence."[24]

Number 7. To a judge at the Roman curia, c. 1330
De facili non labitur fundatum in solidum, nec potest cause negocium maliciosis adversancium conatibus occumbere, quam tanti patris autoritas potenti decreverit dextera sustinere. Nuper itaque causa litis mote inter dominum Cantuariensem archiepiscopum ex parte una, et nos ex altera, per procuratores nostros exhibita coram vobis, vestraque paternitate ami-

---

21 previsa R W; emissa M
22 Wygorn. R W; W. M
23 W. A. Pantin, *The English Church in the Fourteenth Century* (Cambridge, 1955), 33.
24 R. Brentano, *York Metropolitan Jurisdiction and Papal Judges Delegate* (University of California, 1959), 153ff, 217.

cissima procurante, ad audiendum et terminandum[25] in partibus Anglicanis venerabili et discreto viro magistro Itherio de Concoreto, sedis apostolice in partibus eisdem nuncio, a dicta sede commissa tanquam iudici delegato, ipsoque super eadem in forma iuris iudicialiter procedente, pro parte dicti archiepiscopi dedignantis comparere personaliter coram eo clericorum, advocatorum et notariorum comparens nimia multitudo, obiiciendo eidem excepciones frivolas et mendaces, falsoque et maliciose inponendo eidem, quod clericus familiaris ac pensionarius noster erat, verbis minatoriis et probrosis tantum fecerunt clamorem et strepitum coram ipso,[26] quod in sue iurisdiccionis contemptum permissum non est ei in causa commissa facere quod est iuris. Ex quibus apparet quantum dicte sedis autoritatem pro minima habeat, eiusdemque execuciones et iusta iudicia parvipendat, ad hoc quod nititur ut in[27] sue diocesis et provincie confidens incolis, per excepciones vanas dictum possit iudicem recusare. Acta igitur in dicto negocio, que in instrumento quodam publico inde confecto vestreque si placet reverencie exhibendo plenius continentur, apostolice dignemini sanctitati suggerere, ac parti adverse, ne latenter in audiencia seu alibi pendente causa coram dicto iudice in nostri preiudicium aliquid impetretur, circumspeccione provida congruisque temporibus obviare. (M, f.105ᵛ; R, f.5; W, f.98)

The following letter is addressed to Hugh of Angoulême, who had just been made bishop of Carpentras in February 1332. Hugh, an old friend of St. Augustine's, had hitherto been archdeacon of Canterbury, and was thus a valuable ally in the enemy's territory. In fact he shows how useful a well-placed alien provisor could be. By this time the sentence had been given in favour of St. Augustine's, but the problem was to get it confirmed. It was also desired to get the grace for the appropriation of the three churches redrafted, so as to omit any explicit reference to the purpose of maintaining scholars. If one was too explicit it only gave a handle to the malice of one's adversary. One is reminded of the maxim of an experienced academic politician: "Never argue; it only clears your opponent's mind."

Number 59. To Hugh of Angoulême, c. February 1332
Ad ortum nove lucis, quam lucis auctor, in persona vestra virtutibus radiante, ad presulatus Carpentoracensis apicem evocata, clarescere voluit inter sidera splendida[28] orientis nos de virtutis eius influencia, ceteris alcius sencientes, inter anxias huius temporis passiones, spiritu consolacionis

25 terminandum M; determinandum R W
26 coram ipso *omit* R W
27 in M; *omit* R W
28 splendida M; splendencia R W

assumpto consurgimus, et immensa tante beatitudini vestre leticia con-
gaudemus, plenam in hoc solidantes fiduciam, quod in agendis monasterii,
tanto pocioris apud vestram excellenciam aditus nobis patefiet iuvaminis,
quanto ipse qui cornua iusti prophetice memorat exaltanda, honoris vobis
et dignitatis gradum dederit alcioris.[29] Unde inter illa negocia,[30] que
speciali recommendacione vestra paternitas in se suscipere dignabitur et
amplecti, nostra quesumus, quibus vestra sincera deleccio promta semper
affuit et propicia, a vestris non fiant affectibus aliena. Ex nostrorum
namque relatibus ac variis epistolis nostris innotuit satis vobis, quantis
oneribus et pressuris humeros submiserimus, in sustinendo et prosequendo
negocium cause nostre, quam demum suffragante iusticia adeo voluit
altissimus prosperari, quod ipsa iam pro parte nostra per sentenciam
diffinitivam iudicialiter est decisa. Post que, quia ad robur plenum aliud
non requiritur, nisi ut lata sentencia de apostolice sanctitatis gracia con-
firmetur, ad quam consequendam necessaria valde nobis est tanti instancia
promotoris, paternitatem vestram quantis possumus affectibus deprecamur, quatinus ad consecucionem dicte gracie, sanctissimo patri[31] pater
pro filiis bona suggerat dulci[32] interloquio, paternam ad hoc sanctitatem
alliciat, et ad optinendum quod petitur oportunis pro nobis temporibus
intercedat. Absque hoc eciam quod superaddendo preces precibus, vestram
quod absit benevolenciam offendamus, placeat vobis manus ad hoc exten-
dere adiutrices, ut gracia appropriacionis trium ecclesiarum ob vestri
favorem rogaminis impetrata, de speciali domini nostri pape gracia in
melius transmutetur, ita videlicet quod ubi in prima suggeritur monasterium ita extenuatum esse in substancia, quod absque apostolice sedis
presidio non sufficit ad sustentacionem quatuor fratrum scolarium exhi-
bendam, de suggestione huiusmodi, que etsi racionabilis sit[33] et vera, per
diocesani tamen se volentis opponere potest maliciam inpugnari, nulla fiat
mencio in secunda, set quod dominus ipse mero motu et ex certa sciencia
ipsas ecclesias in usus eosdem monasterio uniat, incorporet et annectat de
apostolice plenitudine potestatis. Nosque assignatis vestris constitutis a
vobis ad vestra exequenda negocia in partibus Anglicanis, iuxta beneplaciti
vestri mandatum assistemus pro viribus in consiliis, favoribus et auxiliis
oportunis. (M, f.117; R, f.35; W, f.107ᵛ)

Another letter, number 70, seems to be a further reminder to Hugh
of Angoulême written soon after his return to the Roman curia. Like
number 59 it presses for the confirmation of the sentence in the
monks' favour, and for the redrafting of the grace for the appropriation of the three churches. It concludes by reporting that Peter
of Dene had conceded certain articles and read them out before the

29 alcioris M; alciorem R W
30 negocia *omit* R W
32 dulci M; *omit* R W

31 M *adds* patᵐ
33 sit M; *omit* R W

high altar at St. Augustine's in the presence of the community, four notaries, and a multitude of citizens; and so the monastery was quit of this affair. Apparently the ceremony occurred in February 1333. Peter of Dene was an important ecclesiastical lawyer, a pensionary clerk of St. Augustine's from 1300, and a great benefactor to the monastery. In 1322, as a supporter of Thomas of Lancaster, he took refuge in the monastery and became a monk, but under special conditions. He had his own books and plate, his own house and household within the monastic precincts, and gave public lectures on canon law. In 1330, when things were politically safer, he left the monastery but was brought back. After an appeal to the pope, and a rather stormy investigation by the prior of Christ Church, Peter remained at St. Augustine's. He was one of the committee that elected Abbot Poucyn in 1334.[34]

Several letters illustrate the monastery's relations with the king. In the following two, numbers 14 and 15, the monastery asks the king's help in its struggle against the archbishop. It is the king's duty to protect a monastery which his predecessors have founded and made their burial place – the Westminster Abbey, so to speak, of the Kentish kings. The monastery stresses this all the more as the pope has by his letters appointed the king defender of its rights. The king thus appears as a secular counterpart of those ecclesiastical executors who were appointed to carry out every papal mandate. In number 14 the king is apparently being asked to use writs of prohibition to ward off the archbishop's attacks – a move which would have shocked ecclesiastical purists like Grosseteste or Pecham. The second letter opens with a preamble about government as a remedy for man's fall (in the stoic and patristic tradition) and about the duty of the two swords to help each other. It is clear that the monastery felt no incongruity in calling in the king to implement the papal *plenitudo potestatis*, nor would the king feel any embarrassment in a case in which, unlike some papal provisions, the king's own interests and claims were not involved.

Number 14. To King Edward III, c. 1330
Glorioso principi cedit ad gloriam efficiturque in dominantis obsequia fide ac dileccione devocior plebs subiecta, si sub ipsius temporibus pacis et iusticie unitas observetur, ipseque eterni regis exemplo pia compassione,

34 For Peter of Dene, see Thorne, *Historiae Anglicanae*, cols. 1979, 2037–9, 2055–66; Emden, *Biographical Register*, III, 2168–9; the "articles" he read were probably those printed in: *Literae Cantuarienses*, II, 9.

ut capud nobile membris languentibus condescendens, benignum se prebeat clamoribus oppressorum. Ab olim siquidem notorium fuit mundo,
qualiter prefatum monasterium, quod primum huius regni progenitorum
vestrorum fundavit antiquitas, ad instanciam beatissimi doctoris Anglorum Augustini, latoris fidei Christiane, ab omni cohercione iurisdictionis
ordinarie semper liberum extitit et exemptum. Quibus se irreverenter
opponens, pater iste dominus Cantuariensis archiepiscopus suam diocesim
visitando, etsi sibi non liceat in nos quicquam excercere iurisdiccionis aut
iuris, non obstantibus tamen appellacionibus nostris legitime interpositis
in defensionem et subsidium iuris nostri, per citaciones iniuriosas et
penales sentencias nos in contemptum sedis apostolice, cui immediate subicimus, non desinit molestare; verum iusto iudice oportunum de quolibet
iniusto gravamine remedium providente, ipsius in terra vicarius, princeps
ecclesie militantis, per suas reales literas, coram regia si placet excellencia
recitandas, exempcionis nostre iurium vos in brachio seculari constituit defensorem. Ad cuius execucionem negocii, ob dicte sedis reverenciam, eo si placet benignius se inclinet regia sublimitas, progenitorum
suorum vestigia clara sequens, quo speciale in eodem iuris apostolici interesse vertitur, et ad diffinitivam ipsius sentenciam dictam causam esse
constat iuris ordine devolutam. Placeat igitur providencie regie dicto patri
sue inhibicionis mandata dirigere, ne in offensam regiam, pendentibus
appellacionibus eisdem, quicquam gravaminis innovet vel attemptet, sed
ipsarum iudex parcium, discussis hinc inde iuribus, super lite mota
decernat[35] et iudicet quod est iustum. (M f.107; R, f.8ᵛ; W, f.99)

Number 15. To the king, c. 1330
Ad tutelam proni ad lapsum hominis, in duobus componentibus subsistentis, rex regens omnia duo regimina, sacerdocii videlicet et regni, in
orbe constitit, ut utroque in iudicio et iusticia confirmato, spiritualis
temporali et vice mutua temporalis spirituali gladius subveniret. Sancta
namque et apostolica mater ecclesia in suis actibus provida semper circumspeccione procedens, varios ecclesie gradus, quos privilegiis et libertatibus
sic munire disposuit, ut solum dumtaxat Romanum pontificem ordinarium
in spiritualibus iudicem recognoscant, ne per ordinarios locorum exempcionibus eorundem aut iuribus derogetur, regum et principum terre potencia protegi constituit et defendi. Ab olim siquidem tam in remotis quam
propinquis terre finibus notum fuit, quod exempcionis nostre status adeo
fuit et est in iuribus suis validus et securus, quod observata utrobique
iusticia, ordinarie iurisdictionis impetus non timeret. Verum pater iste
Cantuariensis archiepiscopus frustra nitens in dominio ecclesie transcendere principatum, ipsius iura irreverenter invadit, ius et verum non considerans, sed motus illicitos animi sui sequens. Omnia enim servitutis
honera cervicibus nostris imponere satagit, a quibus indulta nobis gracia

35 decernat M; determinet R W

ipsius examen separat et excludit. Ne igitur existente in remotis eximentis iuvamine, prepotens agentis insecucio subito[36] precipitet defendentes,[37] clare memorie progenitorum vestrorum temporibus solita fuit nobis regalis dignitas potenter assistere, quod apostolico vos invitante rescripto, vestre si placet excellencie exhibendo, vestris temporibus nobis deposcimus annui[38] graciose. Dignetur itaque innata vobis pietas eo benignius devotis intercessoribus vestris in suis pressuris condescendere, quo prefatum monasterium regie fundacionis primum extitit, in quo tot sanctorum regum Anglie et pontificum humata[39] corpora requiescunt. (M, f.107; R, f.9; W, f.99)

The following letters, numbers 16 and 17, show the monastery again appealing to the king, in the first against their tenants, in the second on their behalf. The first begins by pointing out how the primitive equality of man, owing to the fall, needs to be modified by subjection and lordship – the same doctrine as in letter number 15. The monastery then proceeds to ask for the king's help against some of its tenants in Thanet. In 1318 these tenants attacked the manors of Minster and Salmestone (as also described by the chronicler Thorne[40]) in protest against the abbot's claim to exercise the view of frankpledge. They went on to attack the instruments of agriculture, rather like the machine-breakers and rick-burners of the early nineteenth century. Unlike the similar insurrections against monastic landlords at Bury St. Edmunds, St. Albans, and Abingdon in 1327,[41] this Kentish rising seems to have been caused not by contemporary political disturbance and outside agitators, but by the insistence of Kentish peasants on their traditional freedom and rights. They claim that the monastery is "disinheriting" them and they threaten action in the king's courts; they are conservatives rather than revolutionaries. The second letter pleads on behalf of the monastery's tenants of Fordwich, a small town and port on the Stour two miles from Canterbury. These tenants had violently rescued certain of their beasts that had been taken by the king's purveyors and as a result the liberty of Fordwich had been forfeited into the king's hands – a blow to the monastery as well as to its tenants. This was a

---

36 subito M; debito R W
37 defendentes M; insecutos R W
38 annui: animi R; aĩ M W
39 humata W; humana M R
40 *Historiae Anglicanae*, cols. 2034–6.
41 G. Lambrick, "Abingdon and the Riots of 1327," *Oxoniensia*, xxix–xxx (1964–5), 129ff.

period during which some indignation was being expressed against the abuse of royal rights like purveyance and forced labour. These form the subject of the letter written to Edward III by the canonist William of Pagula (c. 1331), and the *Speculum regis* addressed to him, probably by archbishop Mepham (c. 1332).[42]

Number 16. To the king, c. 1318
Etsi humane ingenuitas nature dignitate creacionis sit eadem in singulis individuis speciei, ne tamen in homine contracta fragilitas, iusto destituta regimine, facilius ad devia declinaret, humanis cervicibus iugum est subieccionis impositum, ut domini iuste ac pie vivendo presint subditis, et servi subiecti sint dominis in timore. Nuper itaque inter preclara et ampla beneficia, quibus regia dignitas ecclesiam Dei prospicere non desistit,[43] ipsa sui gracia prefato Augustinensi monasterio, cuius vos et progenitores vestri fundatores extitistis, domini et patroni, libertatem visus hominum et tenencium eiusdem, coram iusticiariis itinerantibus in comitatu Kancie, tanquam ipsius ius antiquum adiudicatam, per cartam suam roborans et confirmans, ut res ipsa stabilis permaneat in futurum, ipsam nobis preclari doni sui contulit[44] novitate. Verum aliqui nostrorum tenencium de Thaneto, concesse nobis libertati ex conspirata se malicia opponentes,[45] et a servitutis huiusmodi iugo colla excutere molientes, in nos et nostros vi et armis hostiliter insurgunt, loca nostra confractis foribus, bonis inventis spoliant, inventos in eisdem gladiis et fustibus letaliter sauciant, ea[46] ut asserunt flammis voracibus incensuri. Nec hiis contenti iniuriis, tanto furore incipiunt insanire, quod excercicia ruralia, per que victus noster adquiritur, illis in locis fieri non permittunt, sed quasi demoniosi[47] ipsa aratra cum iugis inpositis inhumaniter dilacerant et confringunt. Et ut multa sub brevibus concludamus, omnibus nocendi viis quas excogitare possunt in nos et nostra crudeliter insevientes,[48] ut colore quesito suam possint nequiciam palliare, iam in curia regia aliisque locis solempnibus in multitudine copiosa conquesti graviter conclamarunt, quod nos in execucione debita iuris nostri, ad ipsorum exheredacionem ex certo proposito agebamus. Sicque in nostram ex certa sciencia innocenciam mencientes, in nostri lesionem regiam nisi sunt excellenciam provocare. Exurgat igitur quesumus rex noster et dominus in servorum suorum refugium et succursum, et cuius est facere iudicium et iusticiam in terra, dexteram sue magestatis potenter extendat in tantorum excessuum debitam ulcionem. (M, f.107ᵛ; R, f.9ᵛ; W, f.99ᵛ)

---

42 Cf. L. E. Boyle, "The *Oculus Sacerdotis* and Some Other Works of William of Pagula," *TRHS*, ser. v, v (1955), 104, 107.
43 desistit M R; decessit W   44 contulit M; constituit R W
45 opponentes M; exponentes R W   46 ea M; eos R W
47 demoniosi M; demoninati R; demoniaci W
48 insevientes M; sevientes R W

Number 17. To the king, c. 1332?

Rex regum altissimus suos erudiens mites et humiles esse corde, in punien-
dis culpis cadencium semper misericordiam preferendam esse iudicio, et
sermone docuit et opere demonstravit. Per quem regnantes in orbe principes, tam pii magistri inherendo vestigiis, eo clemencius condecet lap-
sorum culpis ignoscere, quo de propria fragilitate conscii, se inter ceteros
prospiciunt miserantis Dei misercordia indigere. Cum itaque communitas
ville de Fordwico,[49] libertatis quinque portuum, que ad nos de dono claris-
simorum progenitorum vestrorum noscitur pertinere, in hoc regiam graviter offenderit[50] magestatem, quod provisa infra libertatem eandem
usibus regiis quedam animalia arestantes, non ex contemptu, sed ex sim-
plicitate et discrecionis ignorancia, a provisorum vestrorum manibus cum
strepitu et violencia abstulerunt, cumque nichil tanto domino in regno suo
licite possit aut debeat denegari, quanto dominantis in quem delinquitur
status eius[51] est alcior, tanto delinquencium necesse est ut gravior sit
offensa. Propter quod edictum regium libertatem eandem tanquam foris-
factam in manus suas capi voluit et mandavit. Nos igitur facti eiusdem in
nullo participes nec conscii teste Deo, ipsorum compassi miserie, nos
invitante solo intuitu caritatis, mesto corde una cum ipsis recognoscimus
nos in hoc facto contra regie dignitatis honorem penaliter deliquisse, nec in
vestris aspectibus favore seu gracia dignos esse, de reverentissimi tamen
domini nostri confisi misericordia, que semper afflictis consuevit et veniam
poscentibus esse pia, humili subieccione gracie et voluntati regie submit-
timus nos et nostra, innatam serenitatis[52] vestre clemenciam deprecantes,
quatinus inflicta reis condigna penitencia pro reatu, regia benignitas
admittere dignetur ad graciam, quos excessiva transgressio gracia spoliavit.
(M, f.107^v; R, f.10^v; W, f.99^v)

The following letter, number 77, is addressed to a bishop who has
recently accompanied the king on a triumphant expedition against
his enemies. The abbot asks for permission to send a proctor to a
forthcoming parliament, instead of attending in person, in order to
economize, on account of his expenses at the Roman curia on his
recent appointment. The abbot concerned may have been either
Thomas Poucyn, elected in 1334, writing perhaps to John Kirkby,
the bishop of Carlisle, who had led a retinue in a campaign against
the Scots in June-September 1335; or else, perhaps more probably,
John Devenish, provided to the abbey in May 1347, writing (with a
view to the parliament of January 1348) to Bishop Thomas Hatfield
of Durham, who had accompanied Edward III and had taken a promi-

---

49 Fordwico M; Fordewico R W   50 offenderit R W; offenderint M
51 eius M; *omit* R W   52 serenitatis R W; serenitati M

nent part in the Crécy campaign.[53] The phrase, *ad defensionem sumpti diadematis*, may refer to the claim to France and therefore favour the later date. 1347 seems a good deal later than most of Mason's letters, but this part of the collection (numbers 73–83) may have been added by a later writer, as already suggested.

Number 77. *To a bishop, 1335 or 1347*

Quam sinceris affectibus amor paternus pro statu zelaverit regni pacifico, in quantumque sacerdocium oportuna prestando iuvamina, sana et salubria communicando consilia subvenerit ipsi regno, strenui et famosi actus vestri, qui abscondi nequiunt, iam produxerunt in puplicum, et magne laudis preconio per orbem lacius est diffusum; voluntariis namque pro rege eodem assumptis laboribus, pater in spiritu adoptivum filium terrenum, in temporalibus dominum, in expedicione sua bellica non deseruit, sed varia cum eodem subeundo pericula, ad defensionem sumpti diadematis viriliter animavit, sicque cooperante sapiencia paterni pectoris assistrice hostilis est devicta malicia, omniaque suaviter et gloriose sunt disposita circa progressum et regressum principis triumphalem. De prospero itaque ipsius atque vestro ad propria regressu nos immensa merito leticia exultantes, beatitudini vestre congratulamur in Domino, utpote qui in subiectum tam venerabile omnia virtutum insignia que pontificalem beatificant dignitatem veraciter credimus convenisse. Inter que signanter illud vobis utinam profuturum merito laudabile recitamus, quod propositis[54] racionabiliter coram vobis benignum semper prebetis auditum, et implendo iuxta sentenciam apostolicam legem Christi manus libenter adiutrices extenditis ad relevandas sarcinas oppressorum. Satis namque novit vestre reverende paternitatis industria, quam onerosum sit et grave vocatis ad regimen in Romana curia sue creacionis negocium prosequi, illi qui in suis hoc senciunt facultatibus, in curie[55] eiusdem extorciones actualiter sunt experti. Nos quoque qui racione vacacionis[56] ultime domus nostre ac subsequenter nostre creacionis eodem in presenti laboramus incommodo, urgente nos negocio, ad forinsecas pro tempore partes concessimus, ut ad relevacionem omnium precedencium aliqualem in moderandis expensis nobis et nostre familie poscemus caucius providere; ubi per breve regium nobis exhibitum ad instans parliamentum sumus personaliter advocati,[57] previdentesque quod per accessum nostrum huiusmodi nos subire debere onera graviora, tam in expensis propriis quam aliis donativis, que in ista status nostri

---

53 R. G. Nicholson, *Edward III and the Scots* (Oxford, 1965), p. 249; *The Anonimalle Chronicle*, ed. V. H. Galbraith (Manchester, 1927), pp. 22, 161. I owe these references to Mr. James Campbell.
54 prepositis R
55 *sic* R; *perhaps* in *should read* et?
56 vocacionis R
57 sumus ... advocati: suum ... advocatum R

novitate non possemus effugere absque honoris[58] nostri nimia lesione, paternitatem vestram amicissimam, que in sui gracia tam in remotis, quam in propinquis partibus nobis semper affuit graciosa, quanta possumus devocione requirimus et rogamus, quatinus per procuratorem ydoneum, plenam ac liberam potestatem habiturum, in dicto parliamento fieri possit in omnibus, quicquid in effectu nostra faceret presencia personalis; hoc nobis dignetur paterna bonitas conferre presidii, ut apud dominum nostrum regem nostra possit hac vice absencia excusari. Aderit enim assensus[59] noster plenus voluntarius et expressus omnibus que in parliamento eodem per vos ceterosque prelatos ibidem convenientes ad honorem Dei et sancte matris ecclesie pro statu regni ac regie dignitatis ipso fuerint inspirante corditer ordinata. (R, f.46ᵛ)

Other letters to the king include a request to be excused from granting a corrody (no. 18; M f.108); a request for help in capturing an apostate monk who is threatening the abbot's life and is said to be in the king's army (no. 19; M f.108); an offer of 100 quarters of wheat and 200 quarters of oats towards the king's expedition to "repress the insolence of the perfidious Scots," perhaps the expedition which led to Halidon Hill in 1333 (no. 36; M f.112). However, when the king asks for an aid towards the expenses of the recent marriage of his sister Eleanor, the abbot pleads impoverishment through the lawsuit with the archbishop and reminds the king of the grant already made towards the Scottish expedition. Rather ingeniously the abbot offered to write off three years of arrears of an annual payment due to the monks from the royal manor of Milton by Sittingbourne, which amounted to a grant of £30 to the king, although as this payment was later challenged by the king,[60] perhaps he did not see it in that light (no. 62; M f.118). Eleanor had been married in May 1332, but the aid may have been demanded as late as March 1333, when the prior of Christ Church declined a similar request.[61]

Some of the most interesting letters in the formulary are those concerning monastic studies and contacts with the university. Between 1277 and 1279 the general chapter of the English Black Monks, in which the then abbot of St. Augustine's, Nicholas Thorne, played a leading part, had introduced a twofold programme for the revival of monastic studies: first, the setting up of a common house of studies (Gloucester College) to which monk students could be sent, and secondly, the establishment of theological lectures at home in

58 honoris: oneris R   59 assensus: assencius R
60 Thorne, *Historiae Anglicanae*, col. 2072.
61 *Literae Cantuarienses*, II, 20.

the various monasteries, to be given either by monks or by theologians brought in from outside.[62] Number 27 (M f.110) is a reply to a request from the university of Oxford for help in meeting the expenses of lawsuits in defence of their rights. This must refer to the university's struggle either with the mendicants, c. 1312–20, or more probably with Cardinal Gaillard de la Motte, archdeacon of Oxford, who challenged the university's jurisdictional rights, c. 1325–45.[63] The university (as distinct from the colleges) had practically no endowments, and so needed to send out appeals of this kind. The abbot sends £5 (approximately £250 in modern values), thanking the university for the benefits and honours it has conferred upon Dom J. Mankael,[64] probably referring to his inception as doctor of divinity, c. 1325–29 (cf. no. 29 below). Mankael, as we have seen, died at the Roman curia, c. 1329–31. He must have been the star theologian among the St. Augustine's monks, and left an extremely interesting collection of thirty-nine volumes to the monastery library.[65] They range over philosophy, theology, and canon law, and include some quite recent works by the Mertonian philosophers Walter Burley and Richard Campsale, roughly Mankael's contemporaries. The monk students very quickly took up the latest intellectual trends at Oxford.

The following letter, number 29, probably refers to Mankael's inception feast. Evidently this was the first time that a monk student from St. Augustine's had got so far as incepting as a doctor of divinity, although some may have already been at Oxford without getting as far as that degree. The reference to the *examinacio consueta* is interesting; this of course was not a written examination in the modern sense (which did not exist before 1800), but meant taking part in disputations, giving lectures, and the *sermo examinatorius*. The provision of food and cash is formidable; £60 would be something like £3,000 in modern values; it would include the distribution of robes to the regent masters.[66] All this was in fact a lump payment, in kind, of university fees covering a man's whole career. A great

---

62 Pantin, *Chapters*, I, 60ff; Knowles, *Religious Orders*, I, 21ff.
63 Oxford Historical Society, *Collectanea*, II (1890), 193ff; *Collectanea*, I (1885), 16ff.
64 Emden, *Biographical Register*, II, 1214–5.
65 M. R. James, *Ancient Libraries*, index of donors, s.n. Mankael.
66 Cf. other inception expenses at Canterbury College in 1395 (feast, £46 7s 11d) and in *c*. 1410 (feast, robes, travelling, etc. £118 3s 5½d), *Canterbury College Oxford*, ed. W. A. Pantin (Oxford Hist. Soc., N.S., VIII, 1950), III, 54ff, 63ff.

house like St. Augustine's would be expected to do such things on a grand scale, and this was just before the expensive trouble with the archbishop started again.

Number 29. Probably to John Mankael, c. 1325–29

In agro vitis dominice palmes nostre plantacionis proficiens, post expansum florem odoris suavia diffundentem, sic ad fructuum maturitatem completam dicitur pervenisse, ut ex ipsis cordibus siciencium delectabile vinum fluat. Cuius rei novitatem felicitati magne merito ascribentes, eo ampliori leticia totis nos condecet precordiis exultare, quo hoc ad honorem et laudem ordinis nostris videmus temporibus fieri, quod nulli predecessorum nostrorum hucusque permissum est oculis intueri. Cum itaque nuper nobis leto nuncio suggerente, universitatis Oxoniensis examinacio consueta vos ad docendum in sacra theologia dignum honore decreverit magistrali, futurum nos allicit commodum quod videmus, ut congruis honoribus tam fructuosi operis preveniamus inicium, et quod invitata vicine plebis presencia illud celebre faciat et festivum. Ne igitur incepcioni vestre, quam nos quatenus ad hoc sufficimus honorificam[67] esse volumus, paterne provisionis subvencio grata desit, ecce quod preter ea que vobis mittimus de providenciis domus nostre, videlicet cignos octodecim, quatuor scuta aprina, et sex corpora carnium ferinarum, pro robis et ceteris vestris necessariis, quantumcumque nobis sit modernis temporibus onerosum, sexaginta libras, quas tedio fecimus magno recolligi, vobis de fratrum consilio duximus assignandas. Quarum administracionem committi volumus providis et dicretis viris, qui in talibus sunt experti, et qui ab utroque extremorum, superfluo videlicet et minimo, declinantes, virtute medii dirigant actus suos. Ipsa assignacio satis vobis sufficiet ad honorem, si[68] in faciendis providenciis et dispensandis eisdem sufficiens non desit industria provisorum. (M, f.110^v; R, f.17; W, f.102)

In letter number 28 (M f.100), not here printed, the abbot grants an increase of £4 per annum to a monk student who has found his original grant insufficient. This is a reward for the good reports of his progress, and for his now increased needs. The monk may be John Mankael at an earlier stage in his career, perhaps when he had just been made a bachelor of divinity and would be requiring more books (we have seen what a large collection he formed). He is told to follow the early Christians' example by sharing all things in common, which probably implies that he had one or more monk students from St. Augustine's living with him in the *camera* at Gloucester College.

67 honorificam M; honorificatam R W
68 si M; etsi R W

The two following letters are both addressed to Gloucester College.[69] In the first, number 33, the abbot apologizes for having recalled his monk students without sending replacements. He has done this for two reasons: first, because he needs his graduates to teach at home – probably a reference to John Mankael, who had just incepted (cf. no. 32 below); secondly, because he needs their help and support under the attacks of the archbishop of Canterbury. This letter probably dates from early in the dispute with the archbishop, perhaps c. 1329–30. Each monastery had its own set of chambers in Gloucester College (some of which can still be seen today on the south side of Worcester College), and the abbot asks that the St. Augustine's chambers be kept free for their future use.

In the second letter, number 78, the abbot agrees that the monk students from Christ Church, Canterbury may occupy these chambers until such time as a fresh lot of students from St. Augustine's are sent. The monk who has just been recalled, T. de N., may be Thomas de Natyndon, one of the proctors afterwards sent to the archbishop's manor of Slindon and there maltreated (see above, p. 196). He had presumably not taken a degree, hence the *dolenda precisio*. The reference to something like a college-meeting at Gloucester College – *tota vestra comitiva* – is interesting. It was perhaps the return of the monks of St. Augustine's to reclaim their chambers in Gloucester College that led the monks of Christ Church to hire a hall near St. Peter's-in-the-East in 1331.[70] One sees here how litigation and studies were interconnected: litigation necessitated the temporary withdrawal of students, but one of the subsidiary aims in the litigation (as we have seen) was the appropriation of churches to support students.

Number 33. To Gloucester College, Oxford, c. 1329–30
Dudum altissimo disponente [preamble omitted]. Processu namque temporis quosdam de nostris a studio ad matris gremium revocavimus, ut post assumptum magistratus honorem, documentis suis fructus nobis communicent adquisitos; quibus alios nondum subrogavimus, iuxta quod esse perpendimus placitum votis vestris, pro eo quod super iniuriosis processibus quibus dominus Cantuariensis archiepiscopus nos in exempcionis nostre lesionem non desinit nolestare, omnino[71] necessarium esse conspicimus, ut oppresse matri filiorum omnium assistat consilium,[72] ut quod

---

69 For Gloucester College cf. *Oxoniensia*, XI–XII (1946–7), 65ff.
70 *Literae Cantuarienses*, I, 392.
71 omnino M; *omit* R W   72 consilium M; presencia R W

omnes tangit, ab omnibus approbetur. Et quia proficiendi in studio iam anni presentis multum temporis est elapsum, pro anno venturo[73] citra principium eiusdem, de mittendis illuc fratribus ad Dei laudem et honorem ordinis, quatenus ad hoc sufficimus, vires et animos apponemus. Quibus si placet in eorum adventibus non preiudicet consuetudo edita loci vestri, quin cameras illas, quas pro nostris fecimus studentibus construi, pacifice possint ingredi et tenere, set in hiis et aliis apud vos inveniant favorem et graciam consuetam. (M, f.111; R, f.19; W, f.102ᵛ)

Number 78. To Gloucester College, Oxford, c. 1329–30
Cum ab assumpte religionis ingressu nostre[74] intime voluntatis extiterit, ea semper appetere per que[75] ordinis ipsius accrescat honoribus, eaque semper pro viribus procurare, que fratrum ordinis eiusdem in actibus studialibus proficere satagencium commoditatem respiciant et quietem. Relacione fidedigna ad nostram noticiam iam deducto, cameram illam infra mansum vestrum predictum constitutam, quam monasterii nostri sumptibus constructam, nos et confratres nostri[76] nobis quondam associati inhabitantes iteratis fecimus sumptibus innovari, iam vacantem esse per venerabilis[77] viri fratris T. de N. revocacionem a studio, in qua palmitis fructiferi dolendam nimis precisionem a vite totum ordinem anxie ferre decet; quia cari nostri nobis fratres et commonachi ecclesie Christi Cantuarie studentes Oxonie, quamdiu ex permissione nostra processerit, desiderant et procurant dictam cameram occupare; nos specialis amoris intuitu, quo ad fratres eosdem afficimur, tanquam nostros benevolentes et vicinos, votis ipsorum duximus in hac parte amicabiliter annuendum, dummodo ipsi confratribus nostris et commonachis ad dictum studium proximo dirigendis in ipsorum adventum cameram eandem sine[78] molestia et contradiccione resignent, consideracioneque gracie sibi prestite amicabiliter cedant eis. Quocirca fraternitatem vestram nobis semper gratissimam ex intimis deprecamur, quatinus si coram vobis et tota vestra comitiva ad hoc specialiter convocanda dicti fratres ecclesie Christi Cantuarie nostris fratribus ad studium accessuris, quo ad occupacionem camere eiusdem, bona fide promiserunt se[79] cessuros, nobisque suas literas idipsum[80] continentes in testimonium fecerint premissorum, tunc ipsos dictam cameram interim inhabitare et libere ingredi permittatis. (R, f.47ᵛ)

Two other letters, numbers 55 and 56 (M f.116ᵛ), are replies to further appeals from the university for help, which St. Augustine's has to decline because of the struggle with the archbishop. The second of these is written in the first person singular, and implies

---

73 venturo M; futuro R W   74 nostre: nostro R
75 que *omit* R   76 nostri: nostros R
77 venerabilis: venerabilem R   78 sine *omit* R
79 promiserunt se: commiserunt et R   80 idipsum: ad ipsum R

that the writer was once an Oxford student: "ego quem quondam tenera matris pietas uterinum filium in deliciis enutrivit" (happiest days of my life). There is no evidence that the abbot, Ralph of Bourne, had been at the university, so perhaps this is John Mankael replying to a personal appeal sent to him, as a distinguished alumnus, as well as to the monastery. The letter is addressed to the university's congregation, since it speaks of "reverentissimi cetus vestri."

The other part of the monastic-studies programme, the finding of a lecturer to teach theology to the monks at St. Augustine's, was probably more difficult than the sending of monks to study at Oxford. At Christ Church, Canterbury, the monks had had to start the process, from 1275 to 1314, by getting in Franciscan lecturers.[81] At St. Augustine's the monks apparently had no one of their own qualified until John Mankael incepted c. 1325–29, and he was untimely cut off. But before this they were for a time able to get the services of a distinguished monk theologian from Worcester, John of St. Germans.[82] He had been at Oxford from 1298 to 1302, when he was elected bishop of Worcester by his brethren, but without success; the days of monk bishops and even of schoolman bishops were nearly over. He went as theological lecturer to St. Augustine's from 1308 to 1310, where he won golden opinions. With the encouragement of St. Augustine's, Worcester sent him from 1310 to 1315, to the university of Paris, where he graduated with a doctorate in divinity. At some period after his return from Paris, c. 1315–20, St. Augustine's asked Worcester to let him come again to lecture to their monks. There are several letters from St. Augustine's about him in the Worcester letter books; here are two from our formulary, probably asking for him to come for the second time, number 30 being addressed to the prior of Worcester, number 31 to John of St. Germans himself.

Number 30. To the Prior of Worcester, c. 1315–20
Peregre profectus servorum dominus ideo ipsorum sollicitudini supposuit bona sua, ut vigili ipsorum operacione in adquisito lucro multis proficerent, que torpencium ignavia abscondita nil prodessent. Ecce enim quod venerabilis vir confrater et commonachus vester, magister Iohannes de Sancto Germano, in multiplicando lucro dominico circa talenta tradita sic

81 C. Cotton, *The Grey Friars of Canterbury* (British Soc. Franciscan Studies, extra series, II, 1924), 34ff.
82 Emden, *Biographical Register*, III, 1626; J. M. Wilson, *The Worcester Liber Albus* (London, 1920), 76ff, 106ff, 132ff.

studuit et profecit, ut ipsius sollicitis adquisita laboribus, et ordini hono-
rifica, et ecclesie sunt fidelium luminosa. Cuius ut documenta salutaria
ceteris proficiant ad commodum, per quod de administratis fideliter racio-
cinium premiabile Domino faciat redeunti, lucernam que in ipso ad tempus
latuit, in altum decet erigi, ut in obiecta disposita diffundat lacius lumen
suum. Nos igitur ad devota et assidua confratrum nostrorum rogamina,
qui ipsum sinceris amplectuntur affectibus, fama celebri commendante, ad
hoc totis insistentes viribus, ut ex eius doctrina, cooperante Domino qui
dat parvulis intellectum, per studii exercicium fructum proferant aliqualem, fraternitati vestre amicissime sedula instancia supplicamus, quatinus de benivolencia unanimi et consensu eidem fratri vestro, quem futuri
ipsius discipuli tam instanter, quam devote, sibi in lectorem postulant et
magistrum, ut sibi liceat pro lectura sacre pagine, iuxta quod honeste per-
mittit religionis idemptitas, inter nos personaliter conversari, liberam
dignemini concedere facultatem, ut ex novi fructus germine proveniat
honor Deo, et firmius inposterum robur accipiat mutue inter nos vinculum
caritatis. (M, f.110^v; R. f. 17^v; W, f.102)

Number 31. To John of St. Germans, c. 1315–20
Terra Germanica, optima et fecunda, ex infuso doctrine semine fructum
centuplum germinavit, quo veri solis beneficio ad complete maturitatis
temperiem iam deducto, mentes famelice refici concupiscunt. Cum itaque
profecti peregre abscondi non debeant talenta tradita, nec[83] accensa lu-
cerna sit modio supponenda, confratrum nostrorum precibus excitati, qui
afficiuntur ad vos in sinceris amplexibus caritatis, quique in lectura divine
pagine vos in doctorem desiderant et magistrum, amiciciam vestram caris-
simam instanter[84] duximus exorandam, quatinus ad ipsorum informa-
cionem placitum vobis sit labores subire voluntarios, et pro lectura apud
nos ad tempus continuanda, optenta pro qua scribimus dominorum prioris
ac fratrum[85] vestrorum licencia, quanto potestis celerius ad nos dirigere
gressus vestros. Quod si deliberacione previa[86] super circumctanciis oneris
et honoris, votis instancium ac nostris precibus senseritis annuendum, tunc
nos curetis per vestras literas harumque baiulum efficere cerciores, citra
quem terminum potestis ad plenum de rebus vestris disponere, et versus
partes nostras duce Domino arripere iter vestrum, ut equi et familia pro
vestro ac rerum vestrarum vehiculo providende, parate veniant ad diem et
locum, quos in vestris duxeritis literis nominandos. (M, f.111; R, f.18; W,
f.102)

The following letter, number 64, is addressed to someone who has
been staying at Canterbury, and to whom a horse has been lent for
use, first abroad, and then to take him to the west of England. It may
be that it was John of St. Germans who borrowed the horse for his

---

83 nec W R; in M
85 fratrum R W; vestrum M

84 instanter R W; *omit* M
86 previa R W; prima M

trip to Paris. If this is the case, it seems sad that his cordial relations
with St. Augustine's should have ended in misunderstanding, with
some offence taken and the return of the horse demanded. Just about
this time, in 1318, Worcester lent another monk-lecturer, Ranulph
de Calthrop, to Ramsey Abbey and then demanded him back which
led to a heated correspondence. Lending, however well-meant, can be
dangerous.[87]

Number 64. Perhaps to John of St. Germans, c. 1315–20
Merito nos excitant ea que in vestris literis confratri et commonacho nostro
A. de B. post recessum vestrum a partibus Cantuarie transmissis, nobisque
per eundem exhibitis iuxta quod regularis exigit institucio, sub querula[88]
demonstracione vidimus contineri, ut quo ad palfridum nostrum, qui vobis
ad votum deserviuit, ut dicitur, in partibus transmarinis, et quem vobis
ulterius comodari usque ad occidentales partes Anglie postulastis, excusa-
cionem nostram tunc factam vobis non fictam fuisse, sed veram et legiti-
mam reverencie vestre tenore presencium nunciemus, nec aliquid in eadem
tepide caritatis fuisse compositum, quod paternitatem vestram debuerat
offendisse. Nam equum eundem, si recolitis, usque ad regressum vestrum
a dictis partibus occidentis gratanter et benivole vobis optulimus servi-
turum; taleque[89] super hoc per vos responsum accepimus, quod vobis provisum fuerat aliunde; super quo, quia vobis ut intelleximus non accidit ut
optastis, ipsum quem habemus unicum vobis mittimus, vestris serviciis,
que nostris preferimus, utinam oportunum. (M, f.118ᵛ; R, f.38; W, f.108ᵛ)

In time, St. Augustine's was able to provide its own lecturer. The
following letter, number 32, evidently commands a monk student of
the house to leave Oxford in order to arrive at Canterbury on August
1 (St. Peter ad Vincula). After a summer holiday in his native countryside, he was to begin lecturing to the monks on the Sentences at
Michaelmas (29 September). This may well have been addressed to
John Mankael, who had just obtained his doctorate (cf. nos. 27, 29,
33 above). The claustral lectures evidently followed the university
terms, beginning at Michaelmas. Mounts have to be provided not
only for the monk student himself but also for his servant or servants (*familia*); a house like St. Augustine's had to do things in
proper style (cf. no. 31).

Number 32. Perhaps to John Mankael, c. 1325–9
Inest precipue nostris affectibus, avidisque ad hoc desideriis aspiramus,
ut in[90] commisso nobis orto dominico novelle plantule exculte proficiant,

---

87 Pantin, *Chapters*, I, 181ff.   88 querula R W; querela M
89 taleque R W; tale quod M   90 in R W; *omit* M

infusoque desuper incremento, congruis temporibus proferant fructus suos, ex quorum ornatu ipse decorem accipiant, eorumque fomento suavi corda famelica sacientur. Cum itaque personam vestram ad fructificandum virtuose dispositam, ut magis proficeret, ad solum fecundius duximus transponendam, speremusque firmiter sic eam celestis agricole graciam fecundasse, quod studialis laboris excercicio fructus placidi in ipsa creverint iam maturi, incumbit nobis cura pensare solicita,[91] qualiter ceteris proficere cupientibus fructuosum cedat ad commodum, quod est ex Dei dono vestris laboribus adquisitum. Nostris siquidem fratribus unanimiter et devote poscentibus, de lectura sibi in sacra pagina[92] provideri, cum magis deceat ut de lectore ex proprio provideatur gremio, quam nostra insufficiencia supplemento indigeat alieno,[93] circa vestrum ad nos hac de causa regressum de fratrum consilio taliter duximus ordinandum, quod huc[94] ad festum beati Petri ad vincula proximum futurum de adventu vestro, cum rebus illis que pro negocio huiusmodi fuerint necessaria, sic in omnibus disponatis, ut instanti tempore autumpnali nativi soli dulcedine recreati, in laboris subsidium, qui vobis postmodum restat grandis, post sequens festum sancti Michaelis ad lecturam sentenciarum apud nos continuandam efficaciter vos paretis. De mittendis igitur pro adventu vestro eveccionibus et familia, quo ad diem et numerum, per vestras nos expedit literas premuniri. (M, f.111; R, f.18ᵛ)

The last of the letters printed here, number 65, illustrates the lighter side of monastic reading. The abbot asks a friend to lend him a book about Godfrey de Bouillon and the conquest of the Holy Land, probably one of the medieval French *chansons de geste* on the subject, such as the *Chanson d'Antioche* and the *Chanson de Jérusalem*. The library of St. Augustine's contained a number of French books, some of them religious, some romances.[95] The suggestion that the book might be sent wrapped up in livery cloth seems to imply that the recipient of the letter (whether religious or secular) may have had property or tenants in Kent.

Number 65. To a friend, for the loan of a book
In auribus audientis illius supplicantis vox emissa de facili non offendit, cuius prerogativa speciali persona diligitur, forisque clamans, intus in cordis amplexibus continetur. Ne tamen pulsantis ad ostium sepius iterata peticio animi vestri mitissimi dulcedinem inquietet, intencionis mee non existit[96] aliter precum mearum onus imponere, nisi quatenus ipsas per-

91 incumbit ... cura ... solicite M; incumbunt ... cure ... sollicite R W
92 pagina R W; *omit* M
93 alieno M; aliorum R W
94 huc R W; hinc M
95 M. R. James, *Ancient Libraries*, nos. 1504–35, pp. 371–4.
96 existit R W; existat M

pendero placitas vobis esse. Confidens itaque et infra claustra pectoris carum gerens, vos illud velle gratanter annuere, unde michi consolacionis aliqualis grata possit iocunditas provenire, habeatque vestra dileccio libros aliquos, ex quorum lectura interponi solent solacia curis vestris, pro uno ipsorum michi pro tempore commodando, illo videlicet qui temporibus Godefridi de Bolon'[97] aliorumque nobilium conquestum continet terre sancte, pro quo eciam me vobis pluries memini supplicasse, preces iterum precibus superaddere, solidata in vobis ab antiquo fiducia, meis in hac parte motibus ausum prebet. In quibus si excessus aliquis seu presumpcio appareat indiscreta, hoc totum[98] absorbeat illa grandis affeccio, quam vos ad indignam personam meam hactenus habuistis. Si igitur dignum duxerit vestra reverencia condescendere in hoc quod petitur votis meis, nisi per aliquem de vestris ad partes Kancie accessurum michi afferri possit commode liber ille, inter robas liberacionis vestre ad partes easdem dirigendas secure satis et absque tedio duci potest. Quem ego vester cum suppplici graciarum accione receptum salvo custodiam, sub omnium que possideo ac fidei caucione. (M, f.118ᵛ; R, f.38ᵛ; W, f.108ᵛ)

There are some letters of condolence. One of these, number 38 (M f.112), seems to be on the death of Edward I in 1307, since it refers to his service as a crusader "adversus inimicos crucis Christi." Another letter, number 37 (M f.112), appears to be addressed to a king or queen on the death of their eldest son. This was a situation that did not arise until the death of the Black Prince in 1376, long after the date of this collection, and this must have been an imaginary composition. Another letter, number 39 (M f.112ᵛ), is on the death of the bishop of Winchester, described among other things as "ecclesiastice libertatis columpnam solidam." Presumably this refers either to Rigaud of Assier (d.1323) or Adam Orleton (d.1343). Several letters concern an abbatial succession, presumably at St. Augustine's: the abbot's death and an invitation to his funeral (no. 41; M f.113); a request to the king for a *congé d'élire* (no. 42; M f.113); a request to tenants for an aid towards expenses *in sua creacione* (no. 44; M f.113ᵛ); an invitation to be present *in missa et mensa* at the writer's installation as abbot on June 12 (no. 43; M f.113). This last letter gives the name of the deceased abbot as Thomas. This can hardly be Thomas Fyndon (d.1310), as his successor's installation feast (described in detail by the chronicler Thorne[99]) was on 16 November; so it was presumably Thomas Poucyn (d.1343). Possibly these letters do not all refer to the same abbatial succession.

97 Bolon' R W; B. M
98 totum R W; tamen M
99 Thorne, *Historiae Anglicanae*, col. 2010.

There are other letters recommending postulants for the religious life to various monasteries (nos. 24–26; M f.109ᵛ; nos. 82–83; R f.49ᵛ). Two letters concern a monk (called Thomas de W.) sent away to live for a year in another monastery, apparently for penance and reform, who returned at the end of the year with a good testimonial (nos. 48, 68; M fols. 114, 119).[100] Another is a letter of confraternity granted to a benefactor or official (no. 46; M f.114). One letter is an abbatial confirmation of a licence granted by the diocesan (the arch-bishop of Canterbury) for an oratory within the manor of Ores in the parish of Chislet, on account of the distance from the parish church and the bad roads in rainy, wintry weather (no. 47; M f.114). St. Augustine's, as both patron and appropriator of the parish and lord of the manor, was careful to assert its rights. In another letter (no. 49; M f.114ᵛ) the abbot apologizes for his delay (on account of illness) in granting permission to hunt "in our park of C." – probably the park which the abbey had at Chislet, so perhaps the same man (no doubt the abbey's tenant) had both his spiritual and temporal needs catered for. Another letter (no. 22; M f.109) apologizes to a friend of the monastery who, coming on the king's business when the abbot was absent, was refused hospitality. A prelate who is coming to make peace after the "lethal discords" between the kings of Eng-land and France, is invited to come and rest "in your domicile of St. Augustine's" after his channel crossing (no. 21; M f.108ᵛ). The abbot writes to reprove the monastery of Battle for showing ingrati-tude towards their former abbot, John de Northbourne, who had resigned in 1318. After treating the ex-abbot well at first, the mon-astery is now proposing to treat him less generously and to relegate him from the monastery to somewhere outside. Perhaps St. Augus-tine's was particularly interested in John de Northbourne because he can be assumed to be a native of Northbourne in Kent which manor belonged to St. Augustine's (no. 23; M f.109). The abbot writes to another monastery on behalf of a *domicellus*, William de L., asking for the restoration of an annual livery (no. 66; M f.119). In another letter the abbot asks a prelate to remove from his councils an excom-municated priest who has maligned St. Augustine's (no. 75; R f.44ᵛ). Some monks are sent for ordination at Rochester, in spite of a law-suit between Rochester and St. Augustine's over the church of P., probably Plumstead (nos. 79, 80; R fols. 48, 48ᵛ). The abbot refers to

100 Cf. a similar case from Worcester, Pantin, *Chapters*, I, 178ff; Wilson, *Worcester Liber Albus*, 65ff.

the marriage of his brother to the sister of his correspondent (no. 61; M f.118). He welcomes proposals for a reconciliation with a neighbouring monastery (clearly Christ Church) on account of its "antiqua familiaritas, religionis idemptitas, locorum vicinitas et sanctorum inibi conquiescencium venerabilis sanctitudo" (no. 67; M f.119).[101]

Although John Mason's letters were copied and circulated as models of style, every individual letter had originally been written for a particular, practical purpose. Thus the collection as a whole provides a most interesting cross-section of the various problems, large and small, top-level and local, ecclesiastical and secular, that faced a fourteenth-century abbot.

101 Perhaps relations with Christ Church had been strained by the prior's intervention in the affair of Peter of Dene (see *supra*, p. 202).

Isabella and the Bishop of Exeter

F. D. BLACKLEY

The refusal of Isabella of France, queen of Edward II of England, to return from a diplomatic mission she undertook in 1325 to arrange for a treaty between England and France has been presented as one of the final stages of her opposition to her husband and the Despensers, dating back to the royalist triumph of 1322. Professor May McKisack writes that "almost certainly, it was the position accorded to the Despensers after the royalist victory [of Borough-bridge] which finally alienated Isabella from Edward II; and it may have been not long afterwards that she began to attach to herself the little group of bishops and lay magnates who were to be her principal supporters for the rest of the reign." The leaders of this group were the bishops of Hereford and Lincoln, Adam Orleton and Henry Burghersh, the former the protégé of Roger Mortimer of Wigmore, with whom, in 1321, he "had thrown in his lot." Presumably for this association, the queen suffered penalties in 1324 and was glad of the opportunity in 1325 to escape to France where she "came out at last into the open."[1] The purpose of this essay is to examine the grounds for assuming that the queen was indeed a member of any opposition group before November, or December, of 1325. It adds to the existing evidence an original letter from the queen to Walter Stapledon, bishop of Exeter, dated 8 December 1325.

It should be noted that it is not until 18 March 1326, when Isabella had been gone for more than a year, that Edward II, in his letters about and to his queen on her failure to return home, mentions that she is associating with his exiled enemies. At that time he specifically mentions Roger Mortimer of Wigmore as one of these. Many his-

---

1 M. McKisack, *The Fourteenth Century, 1307–1399* (Oxford, 1959), pp. 80–82.

torians assert that the queen began her liaison with that marcher lord long before, in England.

Professor Denholm-Young in the introduction to his edition of the *Vita Edwardi Secundi* (a chronicle whose reliability he asserts and which contains not the slightest hint of an Isabella-Mortimer relationship) informs us with apparent certainty that, "The liaison between Isabella and Roger Mortimer of Wigmore probably dates from the autumn of 1321" after the birth of the queen's last child, on 5 July of that year.[2] Professor J. Conway Davies holds that the queen's interest in Mortimer "was not of sudden growth."[3] The author of the only lengthy study of Isabella, Miss Agnes Strickland, thinks that the storms of 1321 "brought Isabella and Roger Mortimer into personal acquaintance." She conjectures about meetings in the Tower while the marcher lord was a prisoner in that palace-fortress.[4] The popular biographer, Thomas Costain, states that, "It is not recorded when or where he [Mortimer] first saw Queen Isabella, but it is agreed that it must have been while he was in the Tower."[5]

The earliest English writers to suggest that the queen had had a close relationship with Mortimer before she left England in 1325 are the English dramatists Christopher Marlowe and Michael Drayton, the former in his play *Edward II* (1593) and the latter in three of his works: "Mortimeriados" in 1596, revised as "The Barons Warres" in 1619, and "England's Heroicall Epistles" in 1619. Drayton makes the queen, with Bishop Orleton of Hereford, responsible for the escape of Mortimer from the Tower. But the English chronicles had given these dramatists no grounds for their romantic fictions.

As Bishop Stubbs pointed out long ago, "On the relations of the queen and Mortimer the chronicles of the time are very reticent."[6] One must admit, however, that the French *Chronographia Regum Francorum* does say that Mortimer was imprisoned in the Tower because of suspicions of the queen implanted in the mind of her

2 *Vita Edwardi Secundi Monachi Cuiusdam Malmesberiensis,* ed. and trans. N. Denholm-Young (London, 1957), p. xiii, n.1. The translations from the *Vita Edwardi Secundi* used in this essay are those of Professor Denholm-Young.
3 J. Conway Davies, *The Baronial Opposition to Edward II* (Cambridge, 1918), p. 107.
4 A. Strickland, *Lives of the Queens of England* (London, 1864), I, pp. 338, 341.
5 T. B. Costain, *The Three Edwards* (New York, 1958), p. 198.
6 W. Stubbs, *The Constitutional History of England* (4th ed., Oxford, 1896), II, p. 374, n.3.

husband by Hugh Despenser the younger. When the marcher lord escaped, the chronicle asserts, Despenser advised the king to seize the queen.[7] However, Mortimer was not arrested for the reasons given nor does any English chronicle suggest a part for the queen in his escape.[8]

Mortimer's escape from the Tower was fully investigated by royal officials and not the slightest suspicion of the queen appears to have emerged.[9] Had doubts about her loyalty been entertained, it is hard to explain why she was trusted to go to France, where Mortimer had fled. Indeed, when the trip of the queen there was being considered, Thomas de Asteleye was instructed by the king to ensure, if possible, "qe le Mortimer et les autres treiturs et enemis du roi voident le roialme de France avant le venir de ma dame pur perils et deshonurs qe a lui ou as soens purroient avenir sur chimyn, qe Dieu defende."[10]

It is possible, as Miss Strickland suggests, that the queen saw Roger Mortimer when he was a prisoner in the Tower from 1322 to 1323. However, we can dismiss any romantic notion of a first meeting there, for Mortimer must have been well known to the queen at that time. Along with three others, Mortimer had carried the royal robes at the coronation of the queen and king in 1308.[11] He was an important member of the not very large English baronage and so, despite his extensive absences in Ireland and his normal residence in the Welsh march, it would be most surprising if the two had not met from time to time. He could not have escaped the queen's notice in the part he played in the Treaty of Leake and its aftermath.

The assertion of Professor Denholm-Young that the queen began her liaison with Mortimer in the fall of 1321 after the birth of her last child (5 July) is hard to accept. An examination of the events of that period shows little time for any romantic interlude. Mortimer, as a contrariant, attended the troubled parliament of July 1321, at

---

7 *Chronographia Regum Francorum*, par H. Moranvillé (Paris, 1891), I, pp. 267–8.

8 Henrici de Blaneforde, *Chronica monasterii S. Albani (Johannis de Troke-lowe et Henrici de Blaneforde)* (Rolls Series, 1866), pp. 145–6, gives the fullest account of the escape.

9 See E. L. G. Stones, "The Date of Roger Mortimer's Escape from the Tower of London", in *EHR*, LXVI (1951), 97–8; G. A. Williams, *Medieval London* (London, 1963), pp. 293–4; *Registrum Ade de Orleton, Episcopi Herefordensis*, ed. A. T. Bannister (Canterbury and York Society, vol. 5, 1908), pp. xxvi–xxix.

10 *The War of Saint-Sardos (1323–1325)*, ed. P. Chaplais (Camden Society, 3rd. series, LXXXVII, 1954), p. 196.

11 *Complete Peerage*, VIII, p. 434.

which the majority of the barons demanded the exile of the Despensers. The king, who wished to save his favourites, only agreed to meet the contrariants on the intervention of the moderate earls, Pembroke and Richmond. Isabella reinforced their arguments by falling on her knees before her husband.[12] On the evidence we possess, the action of the queen, who had a reputation as a peacemaker,[13] cannot be construed as support for the contrariants, especially Mortimer. Richmond, it might be noted, along with the earl of Arundel, was to be sent by the king to plead for the recall of the Despensers before a council of prelates in December of the same year.[14]

Mortimer, although he and other contrariants obtained a royal pardon for the action they had taken against the Despensers,[15] was hardly a person who would be welcome at the royal court after the break-up of parliament on 22 August 1321. His opportunities for seeing the queen would have been very limited, if they existed at all. Unfortunately we know nothing of the whereabouts of either Mortimer or the queen until 13 October 1321, when Isabella had her celebrated brush with Lady Badlesmere at Leeds castle. The forces of Edward II were besieging that castle by 23 October, the castle falling by 31 October. The marchers, including Mortimer, had assembled at Kingston-on-Trent during the siege but, having accomplished little, returned to their homes after a fortnight. By the end of the year Mortimer, with his uncle Mortimer of Chirk, was again in the field, both surrendering to the king at Shrewsbury, 22 January 1322.

On the surrender of Mortimer his estates were sequestered, but the king granted his wife, Joan, an allowance for her necessities. On the subject of this allowance Isabella wrote, 17 February 1322, to the acting treasurer, Walter of Norwich, urging him to be as liberal as he could to "our dear cousin," Lady Mortimer. It is this letter which seems to suggest to Conway Davies that a long liaison existed between the queen and Roger Mortimer of Wigmore.[16] The request,

12 *Annales Paulini* (Rolls Series, 1882), pp. 294–300.
13 *Croniques de London*, ed. G. J. Aungier (Camden Society, old series, XXVIII, 1844), p. 49.
14 *Calendar of Close Rolls, 1318–23*, p. 410.
15 *Calendar of Patent Rolls, 1321–24*, p. 15. The pardons were dated 20 August 1321.
16 Davies, *The Baronial Opposition*, p. 107. The letter (P.R.O., S.C. 1/37, no. 45) reads as follows: "Isabel par la grace dieu Roine Dengleterre Dame Dirlaunde et Duchesse Daquitaine / a nostre cher et feal monsire Wautier de

however, could be explained as a simple act of kindness on the part of the queen. Lady Mortimer was of immediate French ancestry[17] and the queen was a French princess. Isabella had a kindly streak in her character, illustrated by her concern for the little Scottish war orphan, Thomelino.[18] Had she wished to help the wife of a lover, she could have done so in a far more discreet fashion.

Froissart, who is utterly unreliable for this period, says that trouble arose between the queen and Hugh Despenser the younger when the latter learned that she blamed him for the execution of her uncle, the earl of Lancaster.[19] As a result, he "fomented such discord between the King and Queen that the King would not see the Queen nor come into any place that she was." The queen at least had some reasons for annoyance with her husband. When she followed him north on his abortive Scottish expedition of 1322 he took with him Adam, his bastard son,[20] and, when he was forced to retreat, left her behind at Tynemouth Priory from which she was forced to escape to safety in a small coastal vessel. There was a long period, apparently, when the king did not see the queen: on 23 December 1322, Edward informed his sheriffs "and other bailiffs" that the queen was depart-

Norwyz Lieutenant le Tresorier nostre trescher le Roi / saluz et bon amour. Pour nostre cher et bien aimee Cousyne La Dame de Mortemier vous prions tant affectueusement come nous poons qe de ce qe nostre trescher seigneur le Roi Li agrante pur sa sustenance Li vueilliez faire paier en si gracieuse manere come vous pourrez par lamour de nous / Issint qe elle se puisse apercevoir en effeit de ces nos prieres / et qe nous vous en puissons tresbon gre savoir. Nostre seigneur vous guart. Donnez at la Tour de Londres le .xvii. iour de fevrier." Walter of Norwich's tenure of the Treasury dates the document as 1322. Davies says that the queen sent this letter "before she had left England." This is true, but she sent it more than three years before leaving England. All translations and transcriptions of crown copyright records in this article appear by permission of the Controller of H.M. Stationery Office.

17 *Complete Peerage*, VIII, p. 441. Lady Mortimer was the daughter of Piers de Geneville and Joan, daughter of Hugue XII, count of La Marche and Angoulême.

18 Strickland, *Lives of the Queens*, I, p. 333, refers to Thomelino. The orphan is mentioned in Isabella's wardrobe book for the fifth regnal year of Edward II (Brit. Mus. ms. Cotton Nero C VIII, fols. 135, 137^r).

19 *Chroniques de Jean Froissart*, par S. Luce (Paris, 1869), I, pars. II, p. 14. The *Lanercost Chronicle* (p. 244) blames the execution of the Earl of Lancaster "ad suggestionem aemulorum comitis et maxime Domini Hugonis Dispensatoris, junioris." The *Vita Edwardi Secundi* (p. 135) says "Small wonder if she [the queen] does not like Hugh, through whom her uncle perished."

20 For Adam see my note, "Adam, the bastard son of Edward II," *Bull. Inst. Hist. Research*, XXXVII (1964), 76–7.

ing on a long pilgrimage to various places within the kingdom until
the following Michaelmas (29 September 1323).[21]

Restrictions, however, were in store for the queen. On 18 September 1324, her lands were seized on the excuse of the threat of a
French invasion, Cornwall being held as particularly vulnerable to
enemy attack.[22] In return for the revenue of these lands she was
allowed 8 marks a day and an additional allowance of 1,000 marks a
year. "To spend only a little over £37 a week on housekeeping meant
considerable economy according to the standards of the time," writes
Miss Hilda Johnstone, "but the allowance was at any rate far more
substantial than the £7 a week of which the chroniclers talked."[23]

The Close rolls show that the 1,000 marks a year was to pay for all
the expenses of the queen beyond the food and drink of her inner
household, charged against the daily allowance of 8 marks.[24] For the
fifth regnal year (1310–11) the queen spent, in addition to payments
for the food and drink of her inner household, the sum of
£1,592 2s. ½d.,[25] considerably more than the 1,000 marks now to be
allowed to her.

On 28 September 1324, by an ordinance of the king's council, the
arrest was ordered of all those in England "of the dominion and
power" of the king of France.[26] The order, which appears to have
been rigorously applied, was to affect both the king's household and
that "of our dearest consort." The arrest of the French members of
the queen's household seems to have struck the people of the time.
Her brother, Charles IV of France, expressed his surprise at the move,
to the embarrassment of the English envoys in France.[27] The earl of
Richmond was able to mainprize twenty-six members of his household
who were of French allegiance; the widowed countess of Pembroke was able to obtain royal protection for two of her ladies; and
the heir to the throne received royal permission to retain his
treasurer, William de Cusancia.[28] No such exceptions are recorded

21 *Cal. Pat. R.*, 1321–24, p. 227.
22 *Foedera*, II, p. 569.
23 T. F. Tout, *Chapters in the Administrative History of Mediaeval England*
    (Manchester, 1930), V, pp. 274–5.
24 *Cal. Close R.*, 1323–27, p. 260.
25 Brit. Mus. ms. Cotton Nero C VIII, f.150ᵛ.
26 Gascon roll 36, m.22 (Porchester, 28 September 1324) quoted in Chaplais,
    The War of Saint-Sardos, p. 128, n.1.
27 Chaplais, *The War of Saint-Sardos*, pp. 128, 130–1.
28 *Cal. Pat. R.*, 1324–27, pp. 30, 57–8.

for members of the queen's household. When Prior Eastry of Canterbury wrote to his archbishop, 8 February 1325, he suggested that before the queen went to France she should be restored to her former state.[29]

The *Lanercost Chronicle*, which attributes the seizure of the queen's estates and the arrest of the members of her household to Hugh Despenser, says that at this time Despenser was attempting to secure a divorce between the king and Isabella, employing for that purpose, at the *curia*, Robert Baldock and "a certain irreligious man of religion," Friar Thomas Dunheved. The chronicle also asserts that "the wife of the said Hugh was assigned to the Queen as a chaperone, and carried her seal, nor could she write a letter to anyone without the espionage of Lady Despenser; whereupon the Lady Queen was greatly enraged, and for securing revenge and satisfaction wished to visit her brother, the King of France."[30]

Dunheved, a Dominican friar, certainly did go to the papal *curia* on secret business, but when he wrote to the king on his mission, 7 October 1325, he said nothing about a divorce.[31] The chronicler Murimuth was at the *curia* in 1324[32] but he said nothing in his chronicle about negotiations for a divorce. To engage in such proceedings, at a time when relations between France and England were very strained, would have been a most unwise procedure. Moreover, as will appear below, by the end of 1324 Edward II already was considering sending Isabella as an ambassador to France to obtain a treaty, a peculiar idea for that monarch to have if he was seeking to end his marriage with her.

During this period it is generally accepted, as we have seen, that the queen was associating with bishops Orleton of Hereford and

---

29 *Literae Cantuariensis* (Rolls Series, 1887), I, p. 137.
30 *Lanercost Chronicle*, p. 254. Lady Despenser was the queen's principal lady-in-waiting in 1310–11 (Brit. Mus. ms. Cotton Nero C VIII. f.141ʳ). With the Despensers in power it would be surprising if Lady Despenser did not have her former position in the queen's household. The *Annales Paulini* (p. 337) reports the rumour of the divorce proceedings.
31 For Dunheved see F. J. T. Tanquerey, "The Conspiracy of Thomas Dunheved," in *EHR*, XXXI (1916), 119–24; R. Clarke, "Some Secular Activities of the English Dominicans, 1272–1377," unpublished University of London M.A. thesis (1930), pp. 190–201. Some of Dunheved's secret business was connected with Alexander Bicknor, the archbishop of Dublin.
32 Murimuth went abroad to Naples about 28 August 1323. Later in that year he was at Avignon, where he was still staying on 22 May 1324 (*Cal. Pat. R., 1321–24*, pp. 331, 414; Murimuth, *Continuatio Chronicarum* (Rolls Series, 1889), p. xi).

Burghersh of Lincoln, the *alumpni Iezebele* of the chronicler Baker.
Dr. Kathleen Edwards, the authority on the political activities of the
bishops for the reign of Edward II, thinks that "At this time Adam's
[Orleton] chief connexion with Isabella was probably through
Mortimer."[33] Baker says that Orleton inflamed the queen over her
treatment and, with the assistance of Burghersh of Lincoln, was
responsible for the suggestion that the queen visit France, with the
secret purpose of imploring the help of the queen's brother against
the Despensers. Through pressure upon the royal council, the two
bishops were successful in obtaining the adoption of the plan to send
the queen to France as her husband's deputy.[34]

However, Orleton, by March of 1324, was in such disgrace[35] that
he scarcely can have had the easy access to people of importance that
Baker assumes for his story to have been true. It is hard to see how
the bishop can have been in touch with Queen Isabella and mere conjecture supports the idea that the queen was in touch with Mortimer.
The king said that he sent Isabella to France on the counsel and
request of his ambassadors in France, the bishops of Norwich and
Winchester and the earl of Richmond.[36]

The idea of sending the queen to France arose naturally from her
relationship to the king of France. Perhaps, as Professor McKisack
suggests, the original suggestion came from the pope.[37] As early as
April 1324, a draft was prepared in England of an appeal the queen
might write to Charles IV on the subject of the dispute.[38] The pope,
2 July 1324, sought her intervention.[39] When the ambassadors mentioned above were sent to France at the end of 1324, they were
charged with advancing the suggestion that the heir to the throne,
invested with the English possessions in France, might give homage
to the king of France. The bishop of Winchester, reporting back in

33 K. Edwards, "The Political Importance of the English Bishops During the
   Reign of Edward II," in *EHR*, LIX (1944), 331–47, esp. p. 343.
34 *Chronicon*, pp. 17–8.
35 *The Register of Thomas de Cobham, bishop of Worcester, 1317–1327*, ed. by
   E. H. Pearce (Worcestershire Historical Society, XL, 1930), p. 169, contains a
   letter, dated March 1324, written by Bishop Cobham in which he informs the
   cardinal archbishop of Albano that, while Burghersh has been taken back
   into royal favour, "Dominus Herefordensis episcopus apud Regem graviter
   est turbatus."
36 Chaplais, *The War of Saint-Sardos*, p. 198.
37 McKisack, *The Fourteenth Century*, p. 110.
38 Chaplais, *The War of Saint-Sardos*, pp. 42–3.
39 *Lettres secrètes et curiales du pape Jean XXII (1316–1334) relatives à la
   France*, Auguste Coulon and S. Clémencet (Paris, 1965), no. 2131.

January 1325, said that the French royal council favoured the sending of both the prince and the queen. A great council, meeting on
7 February 1325, opposed the sending of the Lord Edward, but sent
Thomas de Asteleye to the English ambassadors in France to see if
the queen, coming alone, might be able "purchacer pees honurable
et sanz desheriteson."[40]

The pope, if he did not initiate this development, was well informed on developments. When, on 5 March 1325, the king wrote to
his ambassadors that the queen was coming,[41] the pope was writing
to congratulate Isabella on her new responsibility.[42] Edward did not
inform the pope officially of the decision until three days later.[43]
However, outside of court circles in England it was known as early
as 8 February that the queen was to go abroad.[44] Letters of protection
were issued on 20 February to some of the people who were to
accompany her.[45] She departed for France on 9 March 1325, with
considerable state. Her treasurer was given £1,000 for expenses, with
authority to draw for more upon the Bardi in Paris.[46]

One can follow the queen from day to day by the entries in her
expense roll. At Poissy she met, 22 March, the three principal English ambassadors whom she entertained on that and on the following
day. They seem to have accompanied her to Paris, where she arrived
on 3 April to spend considerable time visiting relatives, friends, and
shrines. It is difficult to imagine that Isabella was plotting against
anyone: she appears as a French princess, home for a visit, renewing
acquaintances and indulging her fondness for sacred relics. She went
off on a short trip but returned to Paris for a meeting with the French
council, 30 May 1325, to arrange for a peace by the terms of which
her husband was to come to France to do homage to her brother for
his continental possessions.

Edward made some rather convincing preparations for this trip to
France,[47] but using the excuse of illness sent his eldest son in his

40 Chaplais, *The War of Saint-Sardos*, pp. 192–6.
41 *Ibid.*, p. 198.
42 Coulon and Clémencet, *Lettres secrètes et curiales*, no. 2409.
43 *Foedera*, II, p. 595.
44 *Literae Cantuariensis*, I, p. 137.
45 *Cal. Pat. R., 1324–27*, pp. 91–2.
46 For the queen's journey to France and her stay there see J. Hunter, "Journal
   of the Mission of Queen Isabella to the Court of France, and of her long
   residence in that country," *Archaeologia*, XXXVI (1855), 242–57. The queen's
   itinerary (9 March–14 November 1325) is given in Chaplais, *The War of
   Saint-Sardos*, pp. 267–70. The expense rolls of the queen are P.R.O., Exchequer K.R., Accounts Various, 380/9, 380/10.
47 *Cal. Pat. R., 1324–27*, pp. 162, 166–8.

place, after investing him with his French possessions. It is possible that the Despensers did convince the king of this course of action, fearing to go to France with him, or to remain in England without him.[48] It is interesting to note, however, that the prince's mission had been a possibility as early as the end of 1324.

Since the prince was a minor, he was assigned as governors the bishops of Exeter and Winchester and the Lord Henry Beaumont.[49] Of these three, the man of interest for this study is Walter Stapledon, bishop of Exeter. Scholars are far from unanimous on an assessment of this cleric. To Dr. Kathleen Edwards, "though he often gave valuable support to the king, [he] was a man of independence and courage who refused to be bound to any political party." She admits, however, that the bishop had a great "unexplained personal unpopularity."[50] T. F. Tout, however, sees Stapledon as "a worldly, greedy, and corrupt public minister" whom even Edward II thought it wise to remove as treasurer in June 1325.[51] Miss M. V. Clarke describes the bishop as a man who "understood the value of constitutional forms." He perhaps prudently did not attend either the parliament of 1321, which condemned the Despensers, or the somewhat amorphous clerical assembly at the end of the same year which declared their exile to be illegal. When pressed by the king for his opinion of the latter declaration, Stapledon said that what had been done by parliament ought to be undone by that same body.[52] While these actions might be construed as opposition to the Despensers, the rolls of Parliament, when certain of his measures were repealed after his murder, declared that the bishop had been a supporter of the Despensers.[53] The queen's expense roll shows that she did not entertain the bishop of Exeter when he arrived in France. The people of London certainly thought that Stapledon was her enemy. After his murder in 1326 they sent to her his severed head.[54]

In France, the bishop was present at the formal render of homage by the Lord Edward to Charles IV. He had some responsibility for

---

48 For the decision see N. Denholm-Young, "Edward of Windsor and Bermondsey Priory," in *EHR*, XLVIII (1933), 431–43.

49 *Cal. Pat. R.*, 1324–27, p. 174.

50 Edwards, "The Political Importance," 328, 347.

51 T. F. Tout, *The Political History of England, 1216–1377* (London, 1905), p. 292. In discussing Stapledon's removal from the Treasury the *Vita Edwardi Secundi* (p. 139) says that the bishop was "unreasonably avaricious."

52 M. V. Clarke, *Medieval Representation and Consent* (London, 1936), pp. 133–6, 138 n.2, 168–70. Cf. Edwards, "The Political Importance," 338–9.

53 *Rot. Parl.*, II, p. 5.

54 *Annales Paulini*, p. 316; *Flores Historiarum* (Rolls Series, 1890), III, p. 234.

articles concerning the restitution of the duchy of Aquitaine, and he made some payments to English proctors at the French court.[55] Then he left abruptly.

The chroniclers speculate on his sudden departure. The *Vita Edwardi Secundi* asserts that Stapledon was treated by the officials at the French court as "if he were guilty of some crime." He avoided any danger to himself, if danger there was, by fleeing. To confuse his enemies, he left his household behind "to pretend that he was there," escaping to England disguised "as a merchant or pilgrim."[56] Baker says that the bishop, although ordered not to leave, fled secretly when he found his rightful place in the queen's confidence was taken by Roger Mortimer and other English exiles.[57]

Stapledon's expense account reveals that he departed from France with all his household. He had gone to France in three ships with a retinue of forty-nine men and thirty-three horses; he returned in three ships with all of the men and thirty-two of the horses.[58] One cannot think that he left one horse behind to confuse his enemies.

The queen's expense account shows that she left Paris on 22 October, was joined by her son at Le Bourget the next day, and with him went to Rheims. Stapledon remained in Paris until his departure for England, on or about 31 October. He was gone when the queen returned on 12 November. At some point she received a letter, or letters, from him, concerning his departure. In reply, she sent him an irate letter.[59]

Par la roine Dengleterre

Nous avoms bien entenduz ce qe vous nous avez mandez par voz letres / et coment qe vous vous excusez devers nous de ce qe vous partistes de Paris en la manere qe vous feistes Sachez qe puis qe nostre trescher seigneur le roi Dengleterre / vous avoit envoiez avecques Edward nostre filz es parties de France / et nous vous avions promis certeinement / qe nous vous gar-

<hr />

55 Chaplais, *The War of Saint-Sardos*, pp. 243, 245 n.1. He was supposed to bring back Charles IV's official remission of rancour against Edward II, but this remained in the custody of the prince's treasurer, William de Cusancia (*Cal. Pat. R., 1324–27*, p. 175).

56 *Vita Edwardi Secundi*, p. 142.

57 *Chronicon*, p. 20.

58 The bishop's expense account (P.R.O., E. 101/309/31) shows that he drew personal wages, at 40s. a day, from 12 September to 31 October. It lists the various expenses of his crossing, re-crossing, etc. He was given little money but had authority to draw upon the Bardi in Paris.

59 P.R.O., S.C.1/49, no. 188. The document is missing its lower right-hand corner.

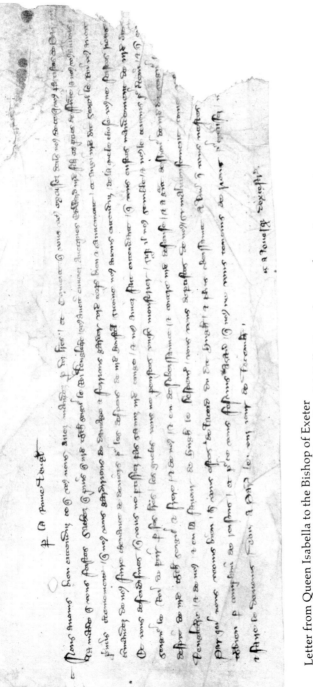

Letter from Queen Isabella to the Bishop of Exeter
Public Record Office Ancient Correspondence, Special Collection 1/49, number 118
Crown copyright

dirions de damage et ferrions garder vostre corps bien et sauvement / et auxi nostre dit seigneur le roi vous avoit commandez de nous faire chevance de deniers pour les despens de nostre houstel / sicome nous avoms entenduz / de la quele chose vous ne feistes riens / Et vous defendismes / qe vous ne partissiez pas saunz nostre conge / et vous aviez fait entendant / qe vous eustes mandement de nostre dit seigneur le roi de partir par ses letres / les queles vous ne peustes unques monstrier / sique il nous semble / et nous le tenoms pour certein / et qe en despit de nostre trescher seigneur et frere / et de nous / et en desobeissaunce / et contre nostre defense / et a grant deshoneur de nostre dit seigneur... [lacuna of about 5 letters, presumably "le roi"] Dengleterre / et de nous et en la favour de Hugh le Despenser / vous vous departistes de nous / si maliciousement comme... [lacuna of about 11 letters, perhaps "vous feistes"]. Par qoi nous veoms bien / qe vous estes de lacord du dit Hugh / et plus obeissaunt a lui qe vous nestes... [lacuna of about 20 letters] tresbien par complein de reisons / et pour ce vous fesoms a savoir / qe nous ne vous tenoms de riens pour excusez / n... [lacuna of about 20 letters] et faire le devoms / Don' a Paris le viij iour de Decembre.

a levesque dexcestre

From this letter it is apparent that the queen and the bishop had quarreled before her departure to Rheims. He wished to return to England, claiming a royal mandate to do so that he was unable or unwilling to show. That he had fears for his safety is shown by the queen's promise to protect him. The queen had been informed that the bishop was to provide her with money for her household but this he did not do. He left France against her express orders "to the great dishonour of our said lord [the king] of England and of us and in favour of Hugh le Despenser." She holds him to be in league with that magnate.

The roll of the queen's expenses ceases on 14 November, immediately after her return to Paris from Rheims. On 31 December she was forced to borrow 1,000 Paris *livres* from her brother, King Charles.[60] The departure of the bishop of Exeter without paying the queen any money apparently was a great financial blow.

The queen claimed that the bishop acted to the great dishonour of her husband. She doubted that he did receive a royal letter of recall. Her dismay may have been great when she received a letter from Edward II, dated 1 December 1325, supporting the bishop of Exeter. On the same day her husband wrote also to the king of France. Both

---

60 *Les Grandes Chroniques de France*, Jules Viard (Paris, 1937), IX, p. 43 n.3, citing *Journaux du trésor de Charles IV le Bel*, no. 9419.

letters are concerned with the departure of the bishop from the French court and Isabella's failure to return to England.[61]

To Isabella the king says that he had ordered her to come home "both before and after the homage," a statement that is supported by the chroniclers.[62] At first she excused herself on the grounds of the "advancement of the affairs." Now, the king understands from the bishop of Winchester, who has lately returned to England with letters from the French king, "that she will not return now for danger and doubt of Hugh le Despenser." Since Exeter does not seem to have had this information, Winchester may have seen the queen after her return to Paris on 12 November; he was abroad on 20 October, when he was instructed to prorogue the truce with the duke of Brittany.[63]

Edward expresses himself as amazed that his wife should fear Hugh Despenser, who has never done her any harm and always held her in high honour. When she departed for France she took an affectionate farewell of Hugh and from abroad she has sent him "loving letters." She whom he sent to France to arrange a peace should not be the cause of trouble, "especially for feigned and untrue reasons." He can think of no reason why Isabella should feel that she has been treated badly, except that on some occasions he "addressed to her in secret words of reproof."

The queen is informed by Edward that the bishop of Exeter departed because "some of the king's banished enemies lay in wait for the bishop to have done him harm of his body if they had seen a fitting time." He himself ordered Stapledon to come home "to eschew such perils and by reason of the great affairs of the king's that the bishop had to do." The king of France is asked to excuse the hasty departure of the bishop, and he and Isabella are assured that Stapledon left the French court for the reasons he gives, and no others.

While Edward does not state that he has cut off the household money of the queen, he knows that she is short of cash, and seems to imply that she has complained to him of this fact. "As to her expenses," he says, "the king will, when she has returned to him as a wife ought to do to her husband, ordain so that she shall have no lack of things appertaining to her, whereby neither the king nor she may

---

61 *Foedera*, II, p. 615; *Cal. Close R.*, 1323–27, pp. 580–1.
62 Baker, *Chronicon*, p. 20; Murimuth, *Continuatio Chronicarum*, p. 45; *Vita Edwardi Secundi*, pp. 142–3.
63 *Foedera*, II, p. 614.

be dishonoured in any wise."[64] By her letters of credence, taken to her by the bishop of Winchester, she is free to return home at any time, a fact confirmed by her brother, the king of France.

The *Vita Edwardi Secundi* recounts an odd interview said to have been held between English messengers and the queen, in the presence of the king of France. At this, Isabella is reported to have said:

> I feel that marriage is a joining together of man and woman, maintaining the undivided habit of life, and that someone has come between my husband and myself trying to break this bond; I protest that I will not return until this intruder is removed, but, discarding my marriage garment, shall assume the robes of widowhood and mourning until I am avenged of this Pharisee.[65]

The French Chronicle of London states that the queen in France began to use "simple raiment as a lady in mourning who had lost her husband."[66] There were soon many other stories circulating in England about the queen's failure to return home.[67]

According to the *Vita Edwardi Secundi*, the king raised the refusal of the queen to return home at a parliament held in November of 1325. At this he suggested that someone evil was putting ideas into the head of the queen, ideas that she could not have fabricated herself. The bishops present were ordered to write a common letter exonerating Hugh Despenser from charges of malice towards the queen, whom they were to urge to come home.

In this common letter, given by the chronicler, references are made to earlier communications received from the queen. In these she has stated what she and her brother, with the help of French supporters, plan to do, which "will turn out not to the prejudice of the lord King or anyone else, but to the destruction of Hugh alone." The bishops urge that a French invasion of England will be disastrous.[68]

Prior Eastry, in a letter written on Christmas Day 1325, makes guarded comments to the archbishop of Canterbury on letters recently received from Isabella. No one, he says, is liked by everyone and some, through no malice or evil on their own part, are disliked,

---

64 *Les Grandes Chroniques de France*, IX, p. 43, states that, instead of going to England, the queen sent home most of her household. *Cf.* Walsingham, *Historia Anglicana*, I, p. 177.
65 *Vita Edwardi Secundi*, pp. 142–3.
66 *Chroniques de London*, p. 49.
67 Baker, *Chronicon*, p. 20; Walsingham, *Historia Anglicana*, I, p. 177; Murimuth, *Continuatio Chronicarum*, pp. 45–6.
68 *Vita Edwardi Secundi*, pp. 143–5.

obviously a reference to the queen's hatred of Hugh Despenser. The prior continues that "no real or personal calumnious charge should be instituted against our lord the King of England, or any people subject to him, as the letters recently sent to us by the Lady Queen of England most amply set at issue."[69]

A letter of Isabella, dated 5 February 1326, is contained in Twysden's *Decem Scriptores*. In this she says that no one must think that she left the king "without very great and justifiable cause." This cause was Hugh Despenser who "wished to dishonour us by all means in his power." She admits that for long she held secret her dislike of that magnate, but only to escape from danger. "We desire," she says, "above everything else, after God and the salvation of our soul, to be in the company of our said Lord and to die with him."[70] The *Vita Edwardi Secundi* gives some support for this long hatred; when she went abroad it advances the opinion that the queen "will not (so many think) return until Hugh Despenser is wholly removed from the king's side."[71]

It was in December of 1325 that Isabella seems to have recruited her first important English supporter. This was not the exiled Roger Mortimer but the earl of Richmond, John of Brittany, who, as we have seen, had been sent to France as one of the principal ambassadors in the Saint-Sardos affair. The chronicler Walsingham says that he was one "qui cum Regina familiaris fuit."[72] Isabella's household expenses show that he was much in her company before and after the homage ceremonies. Like the queen he was to ignore the king's orders to return home. On 14 March 1326, the king was to order his arrest on the grounds that he had refused to come to England to give an account of his mission, offering only frivolous excuses for his failure to do so.[73] The king was to justify his seizure of the earl's lands – for the earl remained in France and could not be arrested – in a letter to the pope, dated 18 June 1326, in which Edward says that John of Brittany has been consorting with, and aiding, his enemies.[74]

Walsingham has a strange story concerning the earl, relating that he was ordered by the king to murder both the queen and her son

69 *Literae Cantuariensis*, I, pp. 162–3.
70 R. Twysden, *Historiae Anglicanae Scriptores Decem* (London 1652), col. 2766.
71 *Vita Edwardi Secundi*, p. 135.
72 *Historia Anglicana*, I, p. 179.
73 *Foedera*, II, p. 622; *Cal. Close R.*, 1323–27, p. 552.
74 *Foedera*, II, p. 630.

"sed Deo prohibente, illa machinatio fuit penitus impedita."[75] This rumour may have arisen to explain the seizure of the earl's lands by the king.

However, the seizure may have been the result of an agreement made by the earl, for himself and his heirs, with the Lord Edward, handing over to the latter his English possessions in return for an annual grant of 10,000 Tournay *livres petites* based upon the revenues of the duchy of Aquitaine. While this agreement was subject to confirmation by the king of England, it states that the prince, on Christmas 1325, had already received the earl into his "faith and homage." The document waives all benefits of the prince's minority and ends with a request for the approval of the king of France. Miss I. I. Lyubimenko, the biographer of the earl, thinks that this convention is an alliance between the queen and John of Brittany since the Lord Edward was too young at this time really to be acting for himself.[76]

It is hoped that this study shows that Isabella, before her departure to France, had reason for dissatisfaction with her treatment in England, but that there is little to suggest, beyond the stories of the chronicler Baker, that she was in league with the enemies of the Despensers, in particular with Roger Mortimer. In France the crucial episode seems to have been the visit of the bishop of Exeter who, in some way, made the queen assert that she would not return while Hugh Despenser remained in power in England. Receiving no support from her husband, Isabella moved towards active revolt, perhaps with the encouragement of John of Brittany but not yet, as far as we know, with the support of Roger Mortimer.

75 *Historia Anglicana*, I, p. 179.
76 I. I. Lyubimenko, *Jean de Bretagne, Comte de Richmond* (1908), pp. 113–5.

The Summons of the English Feudal Levy, 5 April 1327   N. B. LEWIS

he English expedition against the Scots in 1327 is of special interest to the military historian in a number of ways: it was the first campaign in the historic military career of Edward III and prompted the last in that of Robert Bruce; it illustrated with unusual clarity some of the permanent characteristics of Anglo-Scottish warfare in the middle ages and, at the same time, was the occasion for the first appearance of some features which were to be peculiar to its final phase.[1] Of no less interest is the fact that this was the last occasion but one when a general summons was issued to the feudal levy of the English kingdom, so that it marks the penultimate stage in the long decline of the feudal military organization which ended with the summons of 13 June 1385. On that occasion it seems that, although the summons was full and formal and although an unusually large army mustered for the campaign, no properly feudal service was done. The king explicitly renounced any claim he might have to levy scutage; there is no available evidence of the payment of fines or the proffer of corporal service; all the troops of whose presence we have evidence were paid the normal contemporary rate of wages; and when an over-zealous sheriff molested the abbot of Cerne for alleged failure to do his service, he was told peremptorily to desist since the

1 Some of these features of the expedition are described by Jean le Bel, *Chronique*, ed. J. Viard and E. Déprez (Société de l'Histoire de France, Paris, 1904–5), pp. 37–77, and by John Barbour, *The Bruce*, ed. W. Skeat (Scottish Text Society, no. 32, Edinburgh, 1894), II, pp. 148–69; others are brought out by A. E. Prince, "The Importance of the Campaign of 1327," *EHR*, L (1935), pp. 299–302, and R. Nicholson, "The Last Campaign of Robert Bruce," *EHR*, LXXVII (1962), pp. 233–46. The most recent and detailed account of the campaign is in R. Nicholson, *Edward III and the Scots* (Oxford, 1965), chapters 2 and 3.

abbot had "caused the service which he owed to the king ... to be performed" by men we know, in fact, to have drawn the king's wages.[2] Apparently, therefore, the only practical purpose of the summons was not to secure the performance of the very limited amount of gratuitous feudal service due from the tenants-in-chief but, by reminding them of their legal obligation, to stimulate them to raise more substantial forces in return for pay.

And if this was the main purpose and the achievement of the writs of 1385, it seems worth enquiring just what share those of 1327 had in raising the army which won even less distinction for itself at Stanhope Park than its successor did on its march to the Forth and back. The writs themselves, dated 5 April and summoning the host to assemble at Newcastle-on-Tyne on 18 May (Monday before the Ascension), give little indication of whether they were intended to be a genuine or only a token summons to a feudal muster; for though, on the one hand, this seems to be the only known occasion on which all nineteen bishops and both archbishops were summoned, on the other hand the number of lay tenants to whom the individual summons was sent was unusually small; and though the writs were otherwise conventional in form, they omitted, rather surprisingly, the clause frequently included in the late thirteenth and fourteenth centuries, requesting the lay tenants to bring as large a force as possible in addition to their strict obligation.[3]

That the government, nevertheless, intended to rely heavily on the service of paid volunteers is evident from the fact that they not only engaged a force of foreign troops (variously estimated as totalling from 500 to 780 men)[4] under the command of the count of Hainault but advanced substantial sums to some English leaders and incurred debts to others for the wages of troops under their command.[5]

---

2 N. B. Lewis, "The Last Medieval Summons of the English Feudal Levy, 13 June 1385," *EHR*, LXXIII (1958), 1–26.

3 *Reports from the Lords Committees Touching the Dignity of a Peer of the Realm* (5 vols., 1829), IV, p. 373, and H. M. Chew, *The English Ecclesiastical Tenants-in-Chief and Knight Service* (Oxford, 1932), p. 76. Six earls and 80 other lay tenants-in-chief were summoned in 1327 as against a normal range of 100 to 150: the smallest number summoned (apart from 1385 when only 56 were summoned) seems to have been 81 in 1323, *Peerage Report*, III, pp. 334 and *passim*.

4 Nicholson, *Edward III and the Scots*, p. 20.

5 Public Record Office, Exchequer Accounts, Various, 383/8, fols. 11, 17. Only four payments of advances on f.11ʳ are clearly assigned to the date of the Stanhope campaign: those on f.17ʳ are assigned merely to the first and second years of the reign, but since the Stanhope campaign was the main

The records of these payments do not constitute a complete pay-roll of the army so that it is impossible to form from them any esti-mate of the total strength of the paid forces raised by these com-manders. It is, however, noteworthy that they include some of the leading figures in public life. The king's eldest uncle, Edmund of Woodstock, earl of Kent, received an advance of £1,000 on the wages of himself and his men; another uncle, Thomas de Brotherton, earl of Norfolk and earl marshal, together with his colleague, the heredi-tary constable, earl of Hereford (whose joint duty it was to receive proffers of feudal service and to array the feudal host) received smaller advances:[6] and although there is no known record of pay-ment being made to another "royal" earl – Henry, earl of Lancaster – the issue of numerous letters of protection to men serving under his command seems to leave no doubt that he also brought a paid contingent.[7]

No less conspicuous among those to whom the king owed wages for service during his first and second years was Roger Mortimer of Wigmore (soon to be, but in 1327 not yet, earl of March) the virtual ruler of the country, to whom the king's debt was even greater than the advance received by the earl of Kent. Four other major tenants-in-chief who received an individual summons to the host are also found receiving advances or being owed wages by the king:[8] and to these lay tenants must be added two bishops, one of whom – John Hotham, bishop of Ely – certainly brought a substantial paid contin-gent and the other of whom – Henry Burghersh, bishop of Lincoln – probably brought a smaller one.[9] It is, moreover, noteworthy that

military undertaking of these two years it is probable that the bulk of the expenditure was for that army.

6 P.R.O., Exch. Accts, 383/8, f.11ʳ. The constable and marshal received £200 each.

7 P.R.O., Scotch roll, 1 Edward III, m.6. Fifty-eight men going in his company to Scotland on the king's service received letters of protection on 4 and 5 June to be valid till Michaelmas.

8 Hugh Audley (200 marks), John Crumbwell (£85), Henry Percy (£330), Wil-liam Roos of Helmsley (£533). The total sum due to Roger Mortimer was just under £1,400. P.R.O., Exch. Accts, 383/8, fols. 11ʳ, 17ʳ.

9 The bishop of Ely brought a contingent of two bannerets, 35 knights, and 138 squires most of whom served from 28 May to 17 August, and whose wages totalled £864/19/0. (P.R.O., Pipe roll, 175, m.46). No payments to the bishop of Lincoln are recorded but fifteen men had letters of protection to go in his company to serve in Scotland (P.R.O., Scotch roll, 1 Edward III, m.5), and as the bishops of Lincoln recognized a service of only five knights (Chew, Knight Service, p. 32), it seems that a retinue of at least fifteen must have been a paid one.

Hotham was chancellor and Burghersh, treasurer at the time of the expedition;[10] and the fact that the two principal officers in the national administration as well as so many of the lay magnates most closely associated with the king and with the control of national affairs probably, if not certainly, brought paid contingents, seems to make it plain that the government was willing to accept – and probably preferred to have – large paid contingents from tenants-in-chief rather than small, though gratuitous, feudal ones.

But, though these paid forces must have been substantial,[11] the government, unlike its successor in 1385, also claimed, and took practical steps to secure, the fulfilment of all three forms of feudal military obligation – scutage, fine, and corporal service. Scutage, it is true, was not put in hand till October 1337, ten years after the expedition was over, and the demand then met with such universal resistance that the collectors were unable to secure any payment; four months later, in the parliament of February 1338, the king agreed, in response to a petition, to recall the writs of collection and supersede the levy.[12] The delay in demanding scutage and the king's

10 T. F. Tout, *Chapters in the Administrative History of Mediaeval England* (Manchester, 1933), VI, pp. 11, 21. The probability that Burghersh brought a paid retinue in 1327 is strengthened by the fact that he did so on the expedition to Flanders in 1339 (A. E. Prince, "The Strength of English Armies in the Reign of Edward III," *EHR*, XLVI (1931), 361); and the likelihood that it was their official position which prompted both bishops to bring paid contingents is also strengthened by the fact that bishops very rarely raised paid forces. John Kirkby, bishop of Carlisle did so in 1337 (N. B. Lewis, "The Recruitment and Organization of a Contract Army, May to November 1337," *Bull. Inst. Hist. Res.*, XXXVII (1964), 17), but his action, like that of Burghersh, was very exceptional. It is interesting, in connection with the service of government officers, to note that in 1327 John de Roos, steward of the king's household, also brought a contingent, three of whose members took out letters of protection (P.R.O., Scotch roll, 1 Edward III, m.5). Whether he was discharging feudal service or not is uncertain. A "John de Ros" received a feudal summons (*Peerage Report*, IV, p. 374) and a "John le Rous" proffered a fine for the service of a quarter of a knight's fee (P.R.O., Lord Treasurer's Remembrancer, Miscellaneous roll, 1/13, m.15ᵈ): so that it seems likely that these two men were identical and that the steward, like the chancellor, brought a paid (though comparatively small) contingent.

11 If all the tenants-in-chief whose wages are recorded served for the same length of time and made up their contingents in the same proportion of knights and squires as the bishop of Ely, their forces would have totalled about 800 men.

12 H. M. Chew, "Scutage in the Fourteenth Century," *EHR*, XXXVIII (1923), 39–40. The returns of the collectors in nine counties survive: they report unanimously that they had been unable to collect anything. Writs *de scutagio habendo* were issued to the king's son and to the abbots of Glastonbury and Ramsay (P.R.O., Scutage roll 13, m.2) but, in view of the king's supersession of the levy, it is doubtful if they were able to collect anything.

readiness to abandon it in the face of resistance do not, however, constitute evidence of any disposition on the part of the government to renounce the royal claim to feudal service in general or, on the part of the tenants, to repudiate it, since Edward I had changed the character of scutage by levying it in addition to, instead of as a substitute for, corporal service or fine. This attempted change, and the continued efforts of Edward I and Edward II to exact payment on the new basis, had provoked such vigorous and tenacious opposition and caused so much friction between king and baronage,[13] that Edward III had good reason not to press for the payment of an impost which had proved itself so "sterile of revenue and fertile of discontents."

In its demand for the payment of fines in lieu of corporal service, moreover, the government showed much more resolution, though with only partial success. Permission to make fine was limited by a writ dated 26 April, to "those who do not hold a whole knight's fee and to abbots, priors, abbesses, prioresses and others of the clergy and widows and other women"; in response fines totalling £778, to be paid before the Ascension (21 May), were proffered by seven abbots, one abbess, three other women, fourteen men holding fractional fees and one man acknowledging the service of a mounted crossbowman.[14] Payment was not made at the time of the proffer but the exchequer was very active in pressing for it. On 13 and 14 July,

13 Chew, "Scutage in the Fourteenth Century," and "Scutage under Edward I," *EHR*, XXXVII (1922), 321–36.

14 P.R.O., Lord Treasurer's Remembrancer, Miscellaneous roll, 1/13, m.15 and *Rotuli Scotiae* (Record Commission, 1814), I, p. 208. The wording of the writ is vague in dealing with clergy other than monastic ("alii de clero") and the exchequer officials themselves seem to have been uncertain how to interpret it since they first entered a fine proffered by the bishop of Bath and then cancelled the entry with a marginal note saying that the barons of the exchequer had no warrant to accept fines from bishops in this army. Those who proffered fines were: the abbots of Abingdon (£60), Ramsay (£80), Peterborough (£100), St. Albans (£120), Sherborne (£40), Bury St. Edmund's (£120), and Glastonbury (£60); the abbess of Wilton (£20), Joan Botetourt, sister and heir of John de Somery (£20), Margaret Handlo (£10), Margaret, widow of Bartholomew Badlesmere (£40), Ralph de Camoys (£2), John de Segrave (50/–), Geoffrey de Besile (£5), Nicholas de Beauchamp of Fyfyde (£10), Lapinus Roger (£6 13s. 4d.), John le Rous (£5), Richard de la Ryvere (£10), John de Blyton of Lincoln (13s. 4d.), John Sturmy (£5), Reginald Fitz Herbert (£3 6s. 8d.), Ralph Whitewell (6s. 8d.), Edward Charles (£1), John de Enefield (£1 6s. 8d.), and John de Metham (£10). The abbots of Bury and Glastonbury were given respite for a week by letters dated respectively 13 and 12 May (P.R.O., King's Remembrancer, Memoranda roll 103, mm.88 and 83[d]). These writs state explicitly, if mistakenly, that the barons were ordered to take fines from bishops as well as from abbots and others of the clergy.

not quite eight weeks after payment had been due, the treasurer sent, either directly or through the sheriffs, to all but one of those who had made proffers, ordering them, since the king was in urgent need of money for the Scottish war, to pay their fines by 2 September on pain of the king's severe displeasure and in peril of their baronies.[15] The only positive result of this second demand was the payment on 24 July of an instalment of £40 by the abbot of St. Albans out of his due total of £120,[16] and on 26 July writs were sent to a number of sheriffs ordering them to summon fourteen of the major tenants to come to the exchequer on 30 September to hear the decision of the court.[17] The only payments recorded on the Memoranda roll on this occasion are those of £20 due from the abbess of Wilton and £10 due from Richard de la Ryvere; but five of the others are not included in any later list of summonses so that we may, perhaps, conclude that their fines – totalling £340 – were paid before the next demand was made.[18] This was done on 12 November when sheriffs were ordered to summon nine of the defaulters to come to the exchequer at York on 14 January to hear the decision of the court: the sheriffs were also ordered to be there with all relevant writs and the names of their messengers.[19] This summons apparently succeeded in securing an instalment of £5 from Margaret Badlesmere, and on 1 January Joan Botetourt was given leave by the king to discharge her fine of £25 by half-yearly instalments of 5 marks at Easter and Michaelmas:[20] but on 14 January new writs were issued to the sheriffs ordering them to

15 P.R.O., Lord Treasurer's Remembrancer, Memoranda roll 99, m.113. The exception was Ralph Whitewell whose fine was 6s. 8d. Three days previously a writ had been drafted ordering the sheriff of Essex to collect fines from the abbot of St. Albans and John de Enefield on 2 August, but this was vacated, *ibid.*, m.112^d.

16 *Ibid.*, m.113. Neither John le Rous nor any of the six holders of fractional fees whose fine was less than £3 (Blyton, Camoys, Charles, de Enefield, Segrave, and Whitewell – totalling £8 3s. 4d.) received any further demand after 14 July: either because they had paid or, perhaps, because collection was not worth further effort.

17 All those who owed £10 or more, *ibid.*, m.114.

18 The abbots of Abingdon, Glastonbury, Peterborough, Ramsay, and Sherborne. Payment by the abbots of Glastonbury and Ramsay is confirmed by the issue to them, on the ground that they had made fine, of writs *de scutagio habendo* when scutage was put in hand ten years later, *supra* n.12.

19 P.R.O., Lord Treasurer's Remembrancer, Memoranda roll 100, m.77. Margaret Badlesmere, Nicholas Beauchamp, Geoffrey de Besile, Joan Botetourt, the abbot of Bury, Margaret Handlo, John de Metham, Lapinus Roger and John Sturmy.

20 P.R.O., King's Remembrancer, Memoranda roll 104, m.31^d, and *Calendar of Patent Rolls, 1327–1330*, p. 198.

levy fines on the lands of the other eight defaulters who had been summoned in November and on those of two who had been omitted on that occasion.[21] Further search through the exchequer records might produce evidence of additional payments, but the history of the first nine months of the levy is perhaps enough to show the extent of passive resistance on the part of the recalcitrants and the degree of pressure from the exchequer which had been necessary to secure, in that time, payment of a little more than half the sum due.

The extent of corporal service is more difficult to assess. The clearest and most unequivocal case is that of William Melton, archbishop of York, who on 5 May concluded, at Bishopthorpe, an indentured agreement with Sir Robert Constable of Flamborough, by which the latter undertook to discharge the feudal service which the archbishop had then been summoned to do by the king's writ. This contract – recorded in the archbishop's register[22] and printed in J. Raine's *Historical Papers and Letters from Northern Registers*[23] – is a very rare and perhaps uniquely surviving example of this type of agreement and is exceptionally valuable not only in showing that the written contract, which had for so long been used to embody undertakings for non-feudal service,[24] had also been adopted to engage troops to fulfil the feudal obligation before the system was finally abandoned,[25] but in giving us some interesting side-lights on the details of its working in the final stage of its existence.

The terms of the contract accord, in the main, with what we know

21 P.R.O., Lord Treasurer's Remembrancer, Memoranda roll 100, m.54[d]. The two additional defaulters were Reginald Fitz Herbert and the abbot of St. Albans. Richard de la Ryvere was also summoned though he was recorded to have paid his fine on 30 September, *supra*, p. 241.
22 Borthwick Institute, York, Archbishop Melton's Register, f.21[d].
23 Rolls Series no. 61 (London, 1873), pp. 342–4. A revised text is printed in an appendix at the end of this article for convenience of reference.
24 The earliest surviving contract for paid military service at present known seems to be that of 1270 printed in H. G. Richardson and G. O. Sayles, *The Governance of Mediaeval England* (Edinburgh, 1963), p. 464.
25 In 1306 (34 Edward I) Ralph de Gorges covenanted with the abbot of Abbotsbury to do the military service due from his fee, but the phrase "fist covenant" used in the abbot's petition on the subject, P.R.O., Ancient Petitions 330, no.E995, leaves it uncertain whether the agreement was written or verbal and gives no clue as to its detailed terms. The bargain proved a bad one for the abbot because Ralph arrived late at the muster and failed to get the marshal's certificate of service, so that the abbot was prosecuted for failure to serve and it was not till four years later that he got a certificate from the constable and was freed from distraint. See, Chew, *Knight Service*, p. 87, which cites the Ancient Petition referred to above, and P.R.O., Lord Treasurer's Remembrancer, Memoranda rolls 77, m.18[d], and 80, m.6[d] (rectius 62[d]).

in general of the organization of feudal service in the fourteenth century and with that of the archbishops of York in particular. Progressive sub-infeudation and the unpopularity of compulsory corporal service having made it increasingly difficult for overlords to exact personal service from their tenants, it had become a common practice for ecclesiastical overlords either to fine with the king for their service or to raise a hired troop.[26] This had been the case with the archbishops of York since the last quarter of the thirteenth century and in 1282 there is direct evidence of the payment of a mercenary troop.[27] There seems to be no indication that overlords normally found leaders for these troops among their own tenants and this appears not to have been so in the case of archbishop Melton and Sir Robert Constable who, though a personal associate of the archbishop, holding land in the county in which his see was situated, does not seem to have been his tenant.[28] The amount of service specified – that of ten men-at-arms with barded horses – is also in accordance with the service of five knights recognized by the archbishops in the thirteenth and fourteenth centuries,[29] two men-at-arms, so mounted, being normally equated with one knight.[30]

26 Chew, *Knight Service*, chap. IV, iii.
27 *Ibid.*, p. 156, n.2. Sir John Eyvile was paid £100 "ad expensas suas pro servitio nostro faciendo in Wallia."
28 In his article, "Archbishop Melton, his Neighbours and his Kinsmen," in *J. Ecclesiastical History*, II (1951), 54–68, Professor L. H. Butler describes Sir Robert as a "lay tenant" of the archbishop (p. 60, nn. 5, 6). He cites f.27 of the archbishop's register where there is an entry, dated January 1329, in which the archbishop asks the cellarer of Bridlington Priory to go to Flamborough to collect the farm of £20 due to the archbishop last Martinmas from Sir Robert's tenants there. This entry, however, hardly proves that Sir Robert was the archbishop's tenant – the farm might well have been assigned to him by Sir Robert in repayment of the loans which, Professor Butler tells us, he had been receiving from the archbishop for some years previously; and it is noticeable that Sir Robert's name is not included in the list of homages and fealties recorded on folios 593–5 of the register. In Kirby's Quest (1284–85), moreover, it is recorded that William le Constable holds ten carucates in Flamborough of the honour of Chester; a later inquest of 1302–3 records that the honour of Chester has 16 carucates in Flamborough; and in 1346 Sir Marmaduke Constable and others contributed to the aid for knighting the king's eldest son in respect of 19 carucates of land in Flamborough and elsewhere, held of the honour of Chester, *Feudal Aids* (London, 1920), VI, pp. 29, 142, 211. But although, therefore, the Constables were apparently mesne tenants of modest holdings, they were a well-established family and their arms appear, with those of other county families, in the windows of York minster. See F. Harrison, *The Painted Glass of York*, pp. 26, 204.
29 Chew, *Knight Service*, p. 32.
30 J. E. Morris, *The Welsh Wars of Edward I* (Oxford, 1901), pp. 54–5. It is not clear, however, whether Sir Robert himself is to be counted as being equiva-

The remaining terms of the contract, which are stated with great particularity, define Sir Robert's duties in detail and the rewards he is to receive in varying circumstances. He is to proffer and discharge the archbishop's service if the king goes forward ("aille avant") in his war in Scotland or in England and if other great men of the land do their service; and Sir Robert pledges himself, his heirs and assigns, his lands and tenements, his goods, moveable and immoveable, to discharge the service loyally and to secure the archbishop from any damage on its account. He shall also bring the archbishop a letter of acquittance in due form, sealed by the constable and marshal, certifying that he has discharged the service so that the archbishop will suffer no loss and will be able to collect scutage when it is current.

Sir Robert, in return, is to have £20 for his trouble in equipping the troop if he takes it to the muster ready for service, even if by reason of peace or truce or for any other cause, he is not called on to make the proffer; if he makes his proffer and it is accepted he is to have a further £30 and if he and the troop serve for twenty days he is to take £100 all told. In addition, if Sir Robert has to wait eight days at the place of muster, through no fault of his own, before being able to make his proffer, the archbishop will pay his expenses from then until the proffer is accepted.

Some of these terms are in accordance with traditional feudal practice. The proviso that Sir Robert shall do service if the king carries on the war may well be an implied assertion of the long-standing baronial claim, accepted with so much reluctance by Edward I, that feudal service was due only under the king's personal command;[31] and the strict stipulation requiring Sir Robert to bring an official letter of acquittance safeguarding the archbishop from any charge of neglect and securing his right to collect scutage recognizes one of the essential formalities of the feudal muster.[32] It also calls attention, indirectly, to one of the anomalies of the tenurial situation, and may help to explain why the archbishop was willing to pay £100 to have his feudal obligation discharged when he could, presumably,

---

lent to two of the ten men-at-arms. In fourteenth-century contracts it is usual for the leader to be included in the total of those "with" whom he is to serve, but Dr. Morris maintains that in feudal retinues each knight must be presumed to have at least two troopers in attendance, in which case the troop would consist of ten men-at-arms in addition to Sir Robert himself.

31 Chew, *Knight Service*, pp. 100–1.
32 The experience of the abbot of Abbotsbury (*supra* n.25) shows what inconvenience might result from neglect to secure the official certificate of service.

like the bishop of Ely, have raised a troop without expense to himself, to serve at the king's wages. For although the archbishop recognized a service of only five knights, his predecessors had created 43½ knight's fees on their lands,[33] so that if he had been able to collect a full scutage at the rate of 40/– on the knight's fee authorized in the writs *de scutagio habendo*,[34] he would nearly have recouped the outlay on his troopers' pay.

The proviso that Sir Robert is to do the service "if other great men of the land" do the same suggests, at the outset, however, some doubt in the archbishop's mind as to whether feudal service would generally be discharged or not; and a number of the other terms show more affinity with the conditions of voluntary contract service than with feudal practice. The definition of the area within which service is due is a normal feature of fourteenth-century military contracts,[35] and the allocation of a specified sum to Sir Robert for his initial work of raising and equipping the troop corresponds to the "regard" normally paid to the leader of a contract troop for this part of his service.[36] The undertaking also that if Sir Robert is kept waiting more than eight days at the place of muster to make his proffer, the archbishop will maintain the troop till it is accepted, bears some resemblance to the promise, which appears in some voluntary contracts, that wages shall begin from the time when the retainer leaves home to attend the muster:[37] it also concedes, in part, the demand unsuccessfully made on two occasions in the thirteenth century by the tenants of St. Albans abbey that the abbot should pay their expenses during their journey to the place of muster and till their service actually began.[38]

Just how much service Sir Robert and his troop rendered we cannot say, as the entry in the archbishop's register, dated the kalends of June 1327, simply orders his receiver of York to pay Sir Robert £30 "in perpacationem et plenam solutionem C librarum quas sibi solvere conventum fuit pro servitio nostro quod pro nobis faciet domino nostro Regi in partibus Scotie";[39] but since payment in full

33 Chew, *Knight Service*, p. 19.
34 P.R.O., Scutage roll 13, m.2.
35 A. E. Prince, "The Indenture System under Edward III," *Historical Essays in Honour of James Tait*, ed. J. G. Edwards, V. H. Galbraith, and E. F. Jacob (Manchester, 1933), p. 291.
36 *Ibid.*, p. 293.
37 *Ibid.*, p. 292.
38 Chew, *Knight Service*, pp. 152–3.
39 Borthwick Institute, York, Archbishop Melton's Register, f.21ᵈ.

was ordered and not, apparently, cancelled, we must conclude that Sir Robert discharged at least the minimum service of twenty days stipulated in his contract.[40]

Archbishop Melton is the only tenant-in-chief of whose discharge of corporal service we can be certain but there are indications that he was not alone in doing so. In 1337, for example, when scutage was put in hand, the collectors in Wiltshire demanded payment from certain manors of the earl of Surrey on the ground that they had been in the king's hand in 1327 and had not rendered corporal service: the earl maintaining, on the contrary, that the manors had been in his own hands at the time and that he had done service for them.[41] An enquiry was accordingly ordered to ascertain the facts, and although the findings do not seem to be on record, some confirmation of the earl's claim may be found in the fact that only six retainers took out letters of protection to go with him to Scotland[42] – a number quite compatible with the *servitium* of eleven knights recognized by his grandfather in 1277 and 1282.[43] The enrolled letters of protection also indicate that some other lay tenants-in-chief may have fulfilled their feudal obligation since seven of those who received an individual summons to the army each had one or two followers to whom such letters were granted.[44] The letters themselves, of course, give no indication of the nature of the service being discharged, but the smallness of the number of protections issued to the followers of each leader is much more suggestive of feudal than of paid contingents.

And there is positive evidence that some other tenants-in-chief,

40 On what basis the fee of £100 was arrived at is not clear. If Sir Robert served, like the bishop of Ely, for 82 days (*supra* p. 238, and n.9), his fee of £20 for raising and equipping the troop would have been at about the normal rate of "regard" paid in Edward's reign (*supra* p. 245, and n.36); but wages for himself and the men-at-arms for the same period at the current rates paid to the bishop of Ely, would have amounted to just under £50, so that even if he served for double the conventional 40 days of the feudal obligation he would still have made a clear profit. Perhaps the archbishop simply adopted the fee paid by his predecessor to Sir John Eyvile in 1282 (*supra* p. 243, and n.27).

41 *Calendar of Close Rolls, 1337–1339*, p. 285. The wording is, "servitium suum per manerios et feodis predictis nobis in exercitu predicto fecit," P.R.O., Close roll, 2 Edward III, pt. ii, m.6ᵈ.

42 P.R.O., Scotch roll, 1 Edward III, m.6.

43 *Parliamentary Writs* (Record Commission, 1827–34), I, pp. 199, 228.

44 Fulk Fitzwarin, John de Grey of Rotherfeld, Richard de Grey (of Codenor), William de Latymer, John Marmyon, John de Mowbray, and Thomas de Veer, P.R.O., Scotch roll, 1 Edward III, mm.5 and 6.

even if they didn't serve, nevertheless did not disregard their obligation. On 5 June, for example, the barons of the exchequer were ordered to receive from the king's cousin, John of Brittany, earl of Richmond, reasonable fine for his service, since he lived overseas ("es parties de dela") and was not provided with men-at-arms in England ("par decea") to discharge the service;[45] and in the following month the bishop of Winchester was given quittance of his service for a fine of 100 marks, and was granted the right to take scutage from his fees when the king did the same, "since he was abroad on the king's service when the summons was issued and was thereby prevented from proffering his service."[46] On 29 June the bishop of Norwich was given complete remission of service in Scotland as he was staying on the king's service in Gascony; and on 3 July a writ was issued exempting Thomas de Berkeley from service in Scotland "because the king has imposed certain special services on him for this occasion".[47]

How many tenants-in-chief, other than those for whom we have direct evidence, discharged their feudal service, we can only conjecture:[48] but if the action of the seven earls who owed service[49] is characteristic of the king's feudatories in general, the feudal contribution to the strength of the army must have been a very small proportion of the whole. For the earls are so small and so prominent a group that our information about them is almost complete – the one exception being the earl of Oxford, of whom we have no record. And

---

45 P.R.O., King's Remembrancer, Memoranda roll 103, m.91ᵈ.
46 The date was 29 July, *Calendar of Fine Rolls, 1327–1337*, p. 60.
47 *Cal. Pat. R., 1327–1330*, p. 131, and P.R.O., Lord Treasurer's Remembrancer, Miscellaneous roll, 1/13, m.15ᵈ.
48 The lists of those to whom the individual summons was sent give an exaggerated impression of the amount of service due and, consequently, of the possible extent of default. Of the twenty-one members of the episcopate summoned, for example, six had never owed military service; and that of the archbishopric of Canterbury had, apparently, been allowed to lapse for over a century (Chew, *Knight Service*, pp. 10–13); thus there are only eight bishops – those of Chichester, Coventry, Durham, Exeter, Hereford, London, and Salisbury – who should have served but of whose action we have no record. The case of the regular clergy is less straightforward. Of the twenty-four heads of religious houses who were summoned, only fifteen owed service, and of these six proffered fines; but there were also nine houses which had owed service in the past (*ibid.*, pp. 5–16) which were not summoned, and of these only two – Sherborne and Witney – proffered fines.
49 Those of Hereford, Kent, Lancaster, Norfolk, Oxford, Richmond, and Surrey. Thomas de Beauchamp, earl of Warwick, was only thirteen years old and was not summoned, G.E.C., *Complete Peerage*, XII, pt. ii, p. 372.

of those whose course of action we do know, one had permission to make fine, another claimed to have provided corporal service (which, at the most, can hardly have reached a total of more than some twenty to thirty men-at-arms); three others certainly, and a fourth probably, brought paid contingents which – judging from the advances made to them and the numbers of protections issued to their followers – may well have reached ten times that strength.[50]

How far, if at all, the issue of the feudal summons may have contributed to the strength of the army as, apparently, it did in 1385, by prompting feudal tenants who would not otherwise have done so, to bring paid contingents is, once again, a matter of conjecture. It would appear, however, that King Edward found it less than satisfactory for this purpose since he never again issued a general summons to the feudal levy but resorted to other methods of raising troops[51] when he took personal charge of affairs. But whether it was effective for this purpose or not, the formal exemptions from service granted while the army was being assembled, no less than the corporal service rendered and the financial service which the exchequer was at such pains to exact, show unmistakably that the summons of 1327 was a genuine one and not just a token, issued merely to stimulate the recruitment of paid contingents. In 1385 feudal military service was a relic of a bygone past; few men then of military age could have had personal experience or recollection of it: in 1327 it was still a reality, if only an expiring one and soon to be extinct.

Appendix

Contract for feudal military service between William Melton, archbishop of York and Sir Robert Constable of Flamborough.[52]

Fait a remembrer qe acovenu est entre sire William par la grace de dieu Ercevesque Deverwyk, Primat dengleterre, et monsire Robert le Conestable, seignur de Flaynburgh, dautre; cest assaver qe le dit monsire Robert ad enpris et enprent de faire a nostre seignur le Roi le service qe lavantdit Ercevesque lui est tenu a faire a ore, par somounce de son brief, ove dis

50 *Supra* pp. 237, 245–7.
51 A. E. Prince, "The Army and Navy," in *The English Government at Work,* *1327–1336,* ed. J. F. Willard and W. A. Morris, I, p. 350–1.
52 Archbishop Melton's register, f.21ᵛ, Borthwick Institute, York; reproduced by courtesy of the archivist of the Borthwick Institute. In transcribing the document contractions have been extended and punctuation and the use of the letters *u, v, i,* and *j* have been modernized.

hommes darmes as chevaux coverts, daler ove meisme le service au lieu assigne, et de faire le proffre et parfaire entierment le dit service, si [nostre] seignur le Roi aille avant en sa guerre descoce ou en Engleterre, et autres grantz de la terre facent leur services. Et si par cas le dit monsire Robert neit mester defaire le dit proffre, par cause de triewe, ou de pees, ou par autre cause quele qele soit, et viegne au dit lieu assigne prest defaire duement le dit service, mes qil ne le face poynt; le dit Ercevesque grante au dit monsire Robert vynt livres desterlinges pur son travaille, et pur son apparaille. Et le dit monsire Robert enprent le dit service faire, et oblige lui et ses heirs et ses assignetz, et totes ses terres et tenementz, et ses autres biens, moebles et nounmoebles, de leaument faire le dit service, et de sauver le dit Ercevesque saunz damage en chescun poynt, en quant qe attient a meisme le service. Et si le dit monsire Robert proffre le dit service, et il soit resceu, adonqes eit meisme le jour de proffre trente livres estre les vynt livres avantdites. Et si le dit monsire Robert face le dit service par vynt jours apres ceo qe le proffre soit resceu, adonqes lui soit paie le remenaunt de cent livres avantdites, cest assaver, cinkaunte livres. Et si le dit monsire Robert apres le jour assigne gise a lieu assigne outre oyt jours saunz sa defaute, avant ceo qe son proffre soit receu, demoerge apres les oyt jours avantditz a les coustages le dit Ercevesque, tanqe il soit resceu afaire le dit service. Et le dit monsire Robert soit tenu deporter lettre de acquitaunce au dit Ercevesque en due fourme, seale des seals le conestable et mareschal del oust le Roi, qe le dit monsire Robert ad fait le service pur le dit Ercevesque issint qe le dit Ercevesque par tant soit sauve de damage, et puis avera escuage quant y court. Et a ceaux covenantz leaument tenir, dune parte et dautre, les avantditz Ercevesque et monsire Robert se sount obligez par ceste endenture. En tesmoigniaunce de quele chose, les ditz Ercevesque et monsire Robert a cestes presentes endentures entre-chaungeablement ount mis leur seals. Done a Thorp pres deverwyk, le v^te jour de Maii, lan de grace M^l ccc et vintseptisme.

Parliament and the French War, 1336-40

E. B. FRYDE

I n the absence of the rolls of parliament from 1334 to the autumn of 1339, the parliamentary history of those years is regrettably obscure.[1] Yet important proceedings did take place in parliaments and great councils during this period. Representative assemblies were repeatedly consulted about Edward III's dealings with Scotland and France. It will be one of my objectives to show that parliamentary support was carefully secured by Edward for his war with France. The need, after 1336, for continuous and unusually heavy taxation inevitably increased the importance of the commons. When the existing series of parliament rolls does restart in October 1339, the commons appear as leaders in the resistance to a speedy concession of further money grants. A tax-grant offered by the magnates had to be postponed because the members of the commons present on this occasion declared themselves insufficiently qualified to give their assent. They requested the king to summon another parliament. As far as is known, the knights and burgesses had never done this kind of thing before and their action effectively delayed a tax-grant for another six months. Their resentment at the unusually heavy burdens imposed upon the kingdom was coupled with a demand for the redress of a multitude of serious grievances.[2] It was not a sudden and

1 There is one exception to this. A common petition of an uncertain date, with a royal reply to it, is edited by H. G. Richardson and G. Sayles, in *Rotuli Parliamentorum Anglie Hactenus Inediti, MCCLXXIX–MCCCLXIII* (Camden 3rd ser. LI, 1935), pp. 268–72. They probably form part of the records of the parliament of March 1337 (see *infra* for a fuller discussion) and would, in this case, have been presumably enrolled on the parliament roll for that assembly. All references to unpublished sources are to documents in the Public Record Office in London, unless otherwise stated. I owe thanks to my wife for much help.
2 *Rotuli Parliamentorum*, II, pp. 104–5.

unexpected storm but the culmination of complaints and protests voiced in a number of earlier assemblies, echoes of which have survived in various classes of records. I shall try to reassemble here this scattered evidence. The piecing together of a fuller record of the parliamentary proceedings during this initial phase of the Hundred Years' War may contribute to a better understanding of the internal crisis in England in 1340–41 on which the writings of Professor Bertie Wilkinson have thrown so much valuable light.[3]

On the eve of the war with France in 1336–37, Edward III and his advisers were well aware of the internal disturbances provoked in England by the earlier Anglo-French conflicts. Among a large collection of memoranda on Anglo-French relations dating from the first decade of his reign, there are several documents drawing attention to such dangers.[4] Not all of this is good history,[5] but they convey clearly the government's anxiety to avoid the errors of the past. The longest of those documents recalls the complaints made to the council of Edward I by his subjects about the burdens imposed upon them and consequent injury done to their ancient franchises and customs. In the opinion of the author of the memorandum, if Edward I had not provided suitable remedies, a civil war might have resulted, such as had occurred in the reign of his father, King Henry.[6]

As England drifted gradually into war with France in 1336–38, there were repeated consultations with parliamentary assemblies at each stage of the slowly developing conflict; the king was trying in this way to anticipate and diminish the internal troubles that had hampered his ancestors in wartime. Edward's capacity to secure adequate financial support for his French venture was bound to depend, to some extent, on the amount of consent he could secure beforehand for that war from both the lords and the commons.

Several reliable texts explicitly record that the actual decision to start the war had been taken by an assembly including both lords and

---

3 Cf. "The Protest of the Earls of Arundel and Surrey in the Crisis of 1341," *EHR*, XLVI (1931), 181–93; *Studies in the Constitutional History of the Thirteenth and Fourteenth Centuries* (Manchester, 1937), especially section III (pp. 55ff.); *Constitutional History of Medieval England 1216–1399 (1307–1399)*; II, chap. 5, pp. 176ff., "The Crisis of 1341."
4 Chanc. misc., C.47/28/5, nos. 17, 18, 36, 41, 44, 50; C.47/28/9, no. 2; C.47/30/7, no. 9.
5 One memorandum (C.47/28/5, no. 17) links the arbitration of Louis IX in 1264 with the stirring of rebellion that followed in England, which singularly misrepresents that king's motives.
6 C.47/28/5, no. 36.

commons. One very clear statement to this effect occurs in the roll of the parliament of 1343.[7] On 1 May 1343 Bartholomew Burghersh requested on the king's behalf that the lords and the commons debate in their separate assemblies whether negotiations for peace should be started. He explained that it was the king's wish to seek their consent to measures that might end the hostilities as "this war had been undertaken by the common assent of the prelates, magnates and commons."[8] It is not, however, certain which particular assemblies were consulted about the really vital decisions and a patient survey of all the relevant meetings is, therefore, desirable.

Two great councils in the summer and autumn of 1336 were apparently concerned with Anglo-French relations. The first, held at Northampton in June and consisting only of magnates and prelates, sanctioned the sending of a solemn embassy to Philip VI. We learn about this decision from the writs summoning another assembly to Nottingham for 23 September.[9] On this occasion knights and burgesses were also present and the failure of the negotiations with France was presumably one of the main subjects discussed, as the meeting was held some weeks after the return of the royal envoys.[10]

More decisive consultations took place in the parliament of March 1337. Originally summoned for 13 January to York, it was twice prorogued before assembling on 3 March at Westminster, in order, so the royal writs said, to sit nearer the source of the perils that were threatening the kingdom.[11] In the course of its session the king bestowed a dukedom on his eldest son, created six new earldoms, and lavished grants of lands and franchises on numerous magnates. It was the most spectacular of a series of measures taken by Edward III in 1337–38 to enlist the support of the magnates for his policies. About a month after the conclusion of this parliament, the vitally important embassy of Henry Burghersh, bishop of Lincoln, and the earls of Huntingdon and Salisbury left for the Netherlands to procure allies on the continent.[12] It is worth noting that in a subsequent

---

7 *Rot. Parl.*, II, p. 136.
8 For other evidence see below.
9 *Reports from the Lords Committees touching the Dignity of a Peer of the Realm* (1829), IV, pp. 460–1.
10 The embassy, headed by the bishops of Durham and Winchester, was away from late July to the beginning of September: cf. L. Mirot and E. Déprez, *Les ambassades anglaises pendant la Guerre de Cent Ans* (Paris, 1900), p. 14.
11 *Peerage Report*, IV, p. 470.
12 E. Déprez, *Les préliminaires de la Guerre de Cent Ans* (Paris, 1902), pp. 152ff.

letter of privy seal, sent from Antwerp in July 1338, the king asserted that he had been advised by the lords and the commons to seek these alliances.[13] He was clearly referring, in part at least, to the deliberations of this very parliament of March 1337. The treaties concluded by the embassy of bishop Burghersh in the late spring of 1337 were to determine the pattern of the English strategy on the continent until 1340. The envoys also carried with them instructions for further negotiations with the king of France "according to a form agreed upon in parliament,"[14] obviously in March 1337.

When a great council of prelates and magnates met on 30 May at Stamford it was commanded by the king to continue its deliberations until news should arrive from the envoys who were abroad.[15] The preliminary agreement for setting up an English wool company, which promised to finance the continental war, was concluded in the course of this session at Stamford.[16] A second great council was summoned for 21 July at Westminster to hear a full report of the achievements of the bishop of Lincoln and his fellow envoys. On this occasion the previous agreement with the wool merchants was confirmed by a larger and more representative assembly of English business men.[17] Yet another great council, attended this time also by the commons, was ordered to assemble at Westminster at the end of September to sanction arrangements for the defence and good government of the realm during the king's projected absence abroad.[18] It made the unusually generous grant of three fifteenths and tenths spread over 1337–40,[19] which provided one of the best securities for the contraction of loans during those years. On 7 October 1337, a few days after the departure of the commons, Edward III formally asserted his title to the crown of France.[20]

In December the further progress of the war was suspended by the arrival in England of two cardinals entrusted by the pope with the mission of securing a truce. They arrived probably at the beginning of that month.[21] The king consulted prelates and magnates.

13 *Ibid.*, p. 418.
14 Gascon roll, C.61/49, m. 22ᵛ: "aut pacis tractatus ... iuxta formam concordie in parliamento nostro nuper inde facte" (letter of 24 June 1337).
15 Ancient Correspondence, S.C.1/45, no. 229 (1 June 1337).
16 E. B. Fryde, *The Wool Accounts of William de la Pole* (York, 1964), p. 5, n.16.
17 *Peerage Report*, IV, p. 475; Fryde in *History*, n.s., XXXVII (1952), 11–14.
18 *Peerage Report*, IV, p. 479.
19 See *infra*, p. 257.　　　　　　　20 Déprez, *Préliminaires*, pp. 171–2.
21 On 2 December according to a document in Brit. Mus. ms. Royal 12 D XI, f.18. This is a formulary compiled by someone with ready access to the register of Archbishop John Stratford and to the records of the chancery.

The cardinals were told, in Edward's presence, that his subjects had previously offered in full parliament to defend his kingdom and seek his rights. Therefore, he and his councillors did not dare to decide upon a truce of any length without consulting with the magnates and the commons of the land. A fresh parliament would have to be summoned for this purpose.[22] In a formal letter to the cardinals, of 24 December, the king informed them of the decision to summon parliament for 3 February 1338 and explained that the need to refer matters of such importance to parliament was a laudable custom of his kingdom. At the same time the cardinals were notified that a temporary truce was to be in operation from 22 December 1337 to 1 March 1338.[23]

Perhaps Edward, in this instance, made such great play with the need to submit the issue of war or peace to parliament because he wanted to gain time for consulting the royal envoys abroad about the wisdom of concluding a prolonged truce. They assured the king that this would destroy the continental grand alliance against France that had been so laboriously created in the course of 1337.[24] Their advice was accepted. We have the king's own version of the proceedings at the February parliament in a letter he addressed to the council on 24 July 1338.[25] We are told that the continuation of the war was upheld and the continental alliances were confirmed by the assent of all the magnates and others present in parliament. The king was urged to hasten his expedition overseas and all those present, unanimously and of their own free will, provided the required financial aid, pledging themselves to give in future other support necessary for the success of the king's venture. This rosy picture of generous financial aid is somewhat at variance with the facts,[26] but the policy of war was undoubtedly upheld by this parliament.

There is thus evidence of consultation about the French war in most of the assemblies held after May 1336. But the real quality of

22 Chanc. misc., C.47/32/18 (a confidential message to the royal envoys in the Netherlands).
23 Rymer, Foedera (Record Commission ed., 1821), II, ii, p. 1007. The truce was notified to the seneschal of Gascony on 22 December (Ancient Correspondence, S.C.1/45, no. 232) and the warrant to the chancellor to summon parliament, but without specifying its business, is dated on the same day (Chanc. warrants, C.81/240, no. 10.493).
24 The king's messages to Bishop Burghersh and the other envoys and their replies are copied in Chanc. misc., C.47/32/18.
25 Déprez, Préliminaires, p. 418.
26 See infra, pp. 260–1.

all these discussions nowhere emerges very clearly. Were the magnates and commons ever allowed to debate seriously the issues of peace and war or did Edward III merely seek from them a purely formal consent for policies already settled beforehand in the narrow circle of the king's closest advisers? It is a pertinent question because all these consultations did not ensure enduring support for the war. By the autumn of 1339, when things were obviously going badly both in the Netherlands and in Scotland, while burdens were mounting at home, it proved impossible to secure quickly fresh supplies from parliament.

To understand better the crisis of October 1339 we must review in some detail the complaints voiced in the earlier assemblies about the financial requirements of the crown and about other burdens imposed upon the country. One basic feature of the financial situation was the fixed yield of the taxes on movables. Since 1334 a fifteenth and tenth assessed on movable property amounted to around £38,000; largely for political reasons it could not be made to produce a bigger sum.[27] The origins of this arrangement only in part went back to 1334, for it was a subject of further debate in 1336 and, perhaps, in 1337 as well. The fifteenth and tenth granted by parliament in 1334 had been assessed in a peculiar way, designed to avoid the flagrant abuses connected with the earlier taxes. An exceptionally reliable group of collectors was appointed and they were instructed to negotiate with particular localities about the amount each village was prepared to pay. The resulting tax charges were thus, for the first time, assessed on localities, not on persons, and apparently each village was then left to collect its quota by methods of its own choice. It could be assumed that a particularly fair assessment had been achieved in 1334.[28]

When a direct tax was next demanded in the parliament of March 1336, the king, in response allegedly to the requests of the magnates, knights, and burgesses, agreed that the new grant should be identical with what had been levied in 1334. If we accept this official version, derived from the preamble to the commissions of the chief taxers,[29] the initiative for perpetuating this change came from parliament.

27 J. F. Willard, "The Taxes upon Movables of the Reign of Edward III," *EHR*, xxx (1915), 69–74. The amounts assessed on each county from 1334 onwards are tabulated on p. 73.
28 *Ibid.* and Willard, *Parliamentary Taxes on Personal Property, 1290 to 1334* (Cambridge, Mass., 1934), pp. 5–6.
29 King's Remembrancer Memoranda roll E.159/112, recorda, Easter, m. 40.

When a fresh grant was secured in September 1336, it was again ordered to be levied on the assessment of 1334.[30]

One feature of the new arrangements was that the old rules about the exemption of the poorer persons disappeared. In 1332 no one possessing less than 10s. worth of taxable goods was to contribute to a fifteenth, while the taxable minimum for the urban taxpayers, paying a tenth, was 6s.[31] From 1334 onwards it was left to the men of each locality to decide who should contribute to the fixed quota for which their village was liable. There was henceforth a possibility that the burden might be spread more widely over most of the inhabitants, including many poorer men who had enjoyed exemption in the past. This certainly happened in Kent in the case of the first wartime taxes of 1338–39.[32] The greater oppressiveness of the new arrangements may help to account for the exceptional difficulties experienced by the collectors of the fifteenths and tenths in 1339–40.[33]

While the idea of a fixed assessment was apparently accepted by parliaments after 1336, on one subsequent occasion, possibly in March 1337, the commons petitioned that the over-all total of the tax should be lowered, so that the sum exacted by the king should correspond to the somewhat lighter tax of 1332.[34] Edward III's reply

30 K.R. Mem. R., E.159/113, m.146 (commissions of the chief taxers of 16 December 1336).
31 Willard, *Parliamentary Taxes*, p. 88.
32 C. W. Chalklin and H. A. Hanley, "The Kent Lay Subsidy of 1334–5," *Kent Archaeological Society, Records Branch*, xviii (1964), p. 58 (while 11,016 persons contributed in 1334, some 17,000 were taxed in 1338); K.R. Exch. subsidies, E.179/123/14 (extension of the levy in 1339 to taxpayers too poor to pay more than 5d. or 6d., compared with the minimum of 8d. in 1332).
33 See *infra*, p. 264.
34 Richardson and Sayles, *Rot. Parl. Hactenus Inediti*, pp. 269–70. Both a date in March 1337, suggested by me, and a date in February 1339, preferred by Richardson and Sayles, raise some chronological difficulties. The statements that the petition of the commons was presented on the eighth day of the parliament (p. 268) and that it was answered on Thursday in the first week of Lent (p. 270) cannot be reconciled with what is otherwise known of the chronology of either of the two assemblies. The resultant conflicts of evidence are somewhat greater if the hypothesis of Richardson and Sayles is accepted (I owe thanks to Sir Goronwy Edwards for advice on this point). The case for 1337 must rest entirely on the contents of the commons' petition. There is no obvious reference in it to any events after March 1337, while all its statements are compatible with what is known of the happenings up to this date. It is most improbable that a petition presented after 1337 could have treated the hostilities against Scotland as the main war waged by the king (pp. 268–9). The lack of all references to the king's absence from the country and to the council governing in his place also points to 1337 rather than 1339.

was completely evasive.[35] If our dating of this incident is correct, there may be some connection between this request and the negotiations pursued by the government in September 1337 with the individual county courts for separate grants from each shire.[36] It is impossible to offer any other adequate explanation for the adoption of such an exceptional procedure. Some counties are known to have offered sums of money, differing slightly from the amounts that they normally contributed to the fifteenths and tenths and somewhat smaller in most cases.[37] These local grants were superseded soon afterwards by the concession of three fifteenths and tenths by the parliament which met on 26 September 1337. The assessment of 1334 was again adhered to. The levy was intended to be spread over the period from October 1337 to February 1340.[38] Its collection occasioned serious difficulties in several counties in the course of 1339–40.[39]

It was natural for an English king in the first half of the fourteenth century to base his hopes for the financing of a continental coalition on the exploitation of the wool trade. One way of doing it was to increase the duties on exported wool. A heavy subsidy, over and above the traditional "ancient custom" of 6s. 8d. per sack, was bound to be unpopular with the wool producers. They justifiably feared that the merchants might use it as an excuse for purchasing wool in England at lower prices. But the increased duty on wool formed an indispensable part of Edward's plans for financing the war in 1337: it was meant to provide the security for the loans that he wished to contract in the Netherlands from the English Wool Company which he was specially creating for this purpose. It was as a preparatory measure for the wool scheme that a merchant assembly, sitting at Nottingham in September 1336, agreed to an additional subsidy of 20s. per sack.[40] Their meeting coincided with the session of a great

---

35 *Ibid.*, pp. 271–2.
36 J. F. Willard, "Edward III's Negotiations for a Grant," *EHR*, XXI (1906), 727–31. The difficulties inherent in trying to make local grants by individual county courts binding on everybody are discussed by J. G. Edwards, "Taxation and Consent in the Court of Common Pleas, 1338," *EHR*, LVII (1942), 473–82.
37 For a few figures cf. Willard, "Edward III's Negotiations," 729; L.T.R. enrolled acc. (subsidies), E.359/14, m.27ᵛ (£1,051 received in Northamptonshire).
38 Commissions of the chief taxers dated 6 October 1337 (K.R. Mem. R., E.159/114, m.173).
39 See *infra*, p. 264.
40 As an embargo on wool export had been in operation since 12 August 1336 (*Calendar of Close Rolls, 1333–37*, p. 700), the new rates of duty began to be applied only in the autumn of 1337. They were notified to the collectors of

council at Nottingham, but the granting of the new subsidy was always attributed in the official records to the merchant assembly and to no one else.[41] There is nothing to show that the magnates and commons present at the great council were consulted. Here lay the seeds of a future conflict between the king and the parliament of October 1339.[42]

One of the most immediate and effective concessions won by the parliament of October 1339 concerned purveyance.[43] This royal right to buy supplies on credit for the king's household became in wartime a source of ruinous exactions. Its application was then extended to providing continuously for the needs of a chain of garrisons in Scotland and it was also employed on several occasions to feed and equip entire armies and fleets. While ordinary taxation was always based on some kind of assessment related to the means of each tax-payer, the seizures of supplies by purveyors tended to be quite arbitrary. They often spared the more influential persons and took instead an excessive proportion of the goods belonging to unimportant and poorer people. In theory everything was supposed to be paid for but these promises were often carried out very slowly and, in some cases, no payment was ever made. Thus purveyance was inherently oppressive by its very nature, but matters were made far worse by the abuses to which it gave rise. In the period here studied, it proved quite impossible to devise some effective means of control over the royal purveyors or to audit their accounts properly. Between 1336 and 1339 purveyance became apparently the most execrated of all the burdens thrust upon the population: it could and did seriously impoverish individuals and might even cause complete ruin of particular persons.[44]

customs by writs of 26 July 1337 (*Cal. Close R., 1337–39*, p. 97). By a subsequent agreement between the king and the English wool merchants, concluded on 4 May 1338 (K.R. Mem. R., E.159/117, recorda, Easter t., m.12), the subsidy payable by Englishmen was raised to 33s. 4d. per sack. The total duty, including both the Ancient Custom and the new subsidy, was thus increased to 40s. per sack. The government also decided that the corresponding aggregate rate for aliens was to be 63s. 4d. per sack. These new rates of duty came into operation at various harbours "by the order of the council" in the course of June–July 1338 (L.T.R. enrolled acc., customs, E.356/5, m.4.).

41 E.g. *Cal. Close R., 1337–39*, p. 97 (26 July 1337): the grant of the subsidy "made by the merchants of the realm at Nottingham."

42 *Rot. Parl.*, II, p. 104.

43 See *infra*, p. 266.

44 This summary of the effects of purveyance is based on a considerable body of evidence which I intend to discuss in more detail in a future publication.

The undated commons' petition, which I incline to attribute to March 1337, was much concerned with purveyance. In article one, after requesting the confirmation of the Great Charter and of the other charters and statutes, the petitioners go on to specify in particular the statutes enacted about purveyors.[45] In a subsequent article they affirm that nobody was obliged by law to contribute supplies except of his own free will and demand the cancellation of the current commissions to purveyors "because no free man ought to be assessed or taxed without the common consent of parliament."[46] If our dating of this petition is correct, the commons were especially invoking the observance of a statute of 1331, re-enacted in 1336, under which purveyors guilty of improper conduct were liable to be hanged as thieves.[47] The king's answer was completely evasive. If our petition was indeed presented in March 1337, Edward continued to ignore its main request that purveyance should cease to be used for supplying armies and fleets. On 24 March, a few days after the conclusion of the parliament, his government issued fresh commissions for the purveyance of supplies for the forces destined for Gascony.[48] The government would have to be in a much greater fear of the parliamentary opposition, before it would accept the alternative policy of raising all the needed supplies through purchase by merchants. This happened ultimately only in October 1339.

The same petition also contained requests that the government should bear the cost of equipping the men-at-arms summoned for military service under commissions of array and that it should pay the wages of the arrayed soldiers before they set out to join the king's forces.[49] These were intractable problems and no satisfactory com-

The main sources used are: (1) Accounts of the purveyors in L.T.R. miscellaneous acc., E.358/1 and E.358/2 and the particulars for the same among K.R. exchequer acc. various (E.101), especially the accounts of the two chief receivers William Dunstable and William Wallingford, whose arrest had to be ordered in 1339 (E.101/20/7, E.101/20/13, E.101/21/4, E.101/21/40). (2) Records of inquiries held in 1339–40, especially E.101/21/38, E.101/21/39, E.101/22/1, E.101/22/4 and E.101/35/4. (3) Records of inquiries held in 1341 on assize rolls (Just. Itin. 1), especially the roll for Lincolnshire (no. 521). (4) Numerous records of proceedings before the exchequer on the Memoranda rolls for 1338–41.

45 Richardson and Sayles, *Rot. Parl. Hactenus Inediti*, p. 268.
46 *Ibid.*, p. 269.
47 T. F. T. Plucknett, "Parliament," in *The English Government at Work, 1327–36* (Cambridge, Mass., 1940), I, pp. 117–9.
48 L. T. R. miscellaneous acc., E.358/2, mm. 5, 33v. (appointment of Stephen le Blount on 24 March 1337 and subsidiary commissions to sheriffs).
49 Richardson and Sayles, *Rot. Parl. Hactenus Inediti*, p. 269.

promise solution was found for several more years.[50] The parliament
of March 1337 was perhaps acting in response to this petition when
it tried to settle temporarily one of the issues raised in it: an agreement was reached that the cost of the men-at-arms should be borne
by landowners having property worth annually 40s. or more.[51]

The long-term prospects for financing the war were greatly im-
proved by the grant for three years of fifteenths and tenths by the
great council or parliament[52] that sat from 26 September to 4 October
1337. At that time the English Wool Company also seemed to be
successfully launched. The government may have thought it unlikely
that fresh parliaments would be needed for quite a while. The time
may have seemed ripe for a survey of the prerogative financial rights
of the crown, which was sure to be unpopular with the groups
usually represented in parliament. A few days after the dismissal of
the commons, orders were sent to hold inquiries into the revenue due
from the chattels of felons and fugitives which had been neglected
for several years.[53] The king also bethought himself of his right to
levy a scutage for the Scottish campaign of 1327, as the feudal levy
had been called out on this occasion.[54] All these projects were put in
jeopardy by fresh developments in the course of December. The
papal requests for a truce compelled Edward to convoke a parliament
for 3 February 1338. Worse still, the royal envoys abroad had quar-
relled with the leaders of the English Wool Company and the king
found himself in the position of having to seek a fresh parliamentary
grant to compensate him for the collapse of the wool scheme.[55] He
secured the permission to levy a forced loan in wool,[56] but had to
agree to the suspension of inquiries into the chattels of criminals and

50 The most recent discussion is to be found in M. Powicke, *Military Obligation
   in Medieval England* (Oxford, 1962), chap. 10, pp. 182ff., and in H. J. Hewitt,
   The Organisation of War under Edward III, 1338–62 (Manchester, 1966),
   chap. 2, especially pp. 40–2.
51 K.R. Mem. R., E.159/113, m.13.
52 Both terms were used in the official records; cf. *Handbook of British Chronology* (2nd. ed., 1961), p. 520.
53 Writ of 6 October 1337, discussed by G. O. Sayles in *Select Cases in the
   Court of King's Bench* (Selden Soc., vol. 74, 1957), IV, p. lxvi; E. 137/216/2.
54 Commissions to levy scutage of 10–12 October 1337; *Calendar of Fine Rolls,
   1337–47*, pp. 52–5.
55 E. B. Fryde, "Edward III's Wool Monopoly of 1337," *History*, n.s., XXXVII
   (1952), 24.
56 This loan is discussed in chapter 3 of my D.Phil. thesis, "Edward III's War
   Finance, 1337–41" (Oxford, 1947, in the Bodleian Library).

to the abandonment of the scutage, before that tax had begun to yield any revenue.[57] The relevant royal mandates, dated on 15 and 16 February, explicitly refer to parliamentary petitions on these matters. The king proclaimed his readiness to renounce these prerogative revenues in view of the grant made to him by parliament.[58] There had obviously been some tough bargaining.

The forced loan in wool, known as the levy of the moiety of wool, soon proved a lamentable failure. It was left to a great council summoned to Northampton for 26 July 1338, ten days after Edward's departure from England, to devise a fresh wool grant. Both magnates and commons were present and they accepted a properly assessed tax in wool, which turned out to be a success.[59] But other financial proposals aroused hostile comments from the magnates. Shortly before his departure overseas Edward III had promulgated at Walton an ordinance regulating the government of the kingdom during his absence.[60] Among other things it inaugurated a policy of financial stringency that challenged many of the established usages. At Northampton the magnates absolutely refused to give their consent to a royal injunction that debts due to the king should henceforth be collected integrally and that all payments of debts by instalments should cease while the current financial difficulties lasted. According to a report sent subsequently to the king by his councillors in England, the magnates had declared that payments by instalments had been allowed since time immemorial and were a part of the custom of the kingdom. Such things could not and should not be changed

57 Pipe Roll, E.372/183, m.15 (enrolled accounts for the scutage).
58 K.R. Mem. R., E.159/114, m.68ᵛ. (chattels of criminals); H. M. Chew, "Scutage in the Fourteenth Century," *EHR*, xxxviii, (1923), 39–40 and the sources there quoted; K.R. Mem. R., E.159/114, mm.49, 130ᵛ (instructions to the exchequer about the scutage and the resultant measures).
59 A writ of 1 August, notifying the exchequer, expressly attributes the grant to the prelates, magnates, and community of the kingdom present in the council at Northampton (K.R. Mem. R., E.159/115, m.18ᵛ). This tax is discussed in chapter 4 of my thesis, *supra*, n.56. Some concessions were secured in return for the grant. The taking of tin by royal agents in Devon and Cornwall was stopped and an order was issued for the restitution of the tin seized since May 1338 (treaty roll, C.76/12, m.17; *Cal. Close R., 1337–39*, p. 449).
60 The best edition of the "Walton ordinances" is in T. F. Tout, *Chapters in the Administrative History of Mediaeval England* (Manchester, 1928), iii, pp. 143–50. His discussion of them (pp. 69–80) needs revision and does not supersede the more detailed account in D. Hughes, *A Study of Social and Constitutional Tendencies in the Early Years of Edward III* (London, 1915), chap. 4.

without the assent of the magnates and that had to be given in parliament.[61] The council at home had no desire to take any action in this matter, but was compelled to do so a year later by a royal order issued from Antwerp on 6 May 1339.[62] All existing payments by instalments were cancelled and the king expected to receive abroad the additional funds accruing from the prompt collection of the entire debts due to him. Officials in England were also forbidden to sanction new payments by instalments notwithstanding any custom to the contrary. The royal order was, indeed, unrealistic as his councillors in England pointed out. It was not in practice likely to yield any more revenue since the main beneficiaries of the existing arrangements were magnates whom it was impossible to distrain for debts.[63] On 5 September 1339 Edward at long last gave way and recalled his former orders. He abandoned at the same time several other injunctions contained in the ordinances of Walton and the order of 6 May 1339.[64] He was presumably already aware that another parliament had been summoned by writs dated 25 August and it was becoming impolitic to enforce measures that were arousing so much resistance among influential people.

A parliament held during the first half of February 1339 appears to have been convoked mainly to make provision for the defence of the coastal areas against the French raids or a possible full-scale invasion.[65] It is most improbable that any fresh grant of taxes was requested by the government on this occasion and certainly none was granted. But it gave men a chance to voice their grievances. On 12 February, while parliament was still in session, the exchequer appointed a commission to enquire into the misdoings of William

61 Parl. and council proc., C.49/file 7/7 (a royal message and the council's reply, probably in May, 1339). There is a brief reference to this in Tout, *Chapters*, III, p. 92 and it is discussed by Hughes, *Social and Constitutional Tendencies*, pp. 68–9.

62 Rymer, *Foedera*, pp. 1080–1; K.R. Mem. R., E.159/115, m.267 with a marginal heading "De assignacionibus, respectibus, debitis et atterminacionibus revocatis."

63 There is an useful recent discussion of the prolonged debate between the king abroad and the council at home about fiscal policies in G. L. Harriss, "The Commons' Petitions of 1340," *EHR*, LXXVIII (1963), 631–5.

64 K.R. Mem. R., E.159/116, m.12 (noted by Harriss, "The Commons' Petitions," 635). The message was brought back to England by John Thorp, who was sent to the Netherlands by the council in August 1339 (he was abroad on 1 September, E.404/493/146). The exchequer received these new instructions on 1 October.

65 J. R. Lumby, ed. *Chronicon Henrici Knighton* (Rolls Ser., 1895), II, p. 3; Hewitt, *The Organisation of War*, chap. 1; treaty roll, C.76/14, mm.16–14.

Dunstable "on clamorous information of diverse men of York-shire."[66] It may be significant that one of the commissioners, William Scargill, was sitting as knight of the shire for Yorkshire in that very parliament of February 1339.[67] William Dunstable had been in trouble before. His activities as the chief receiver of victuals north of the Thames since October 1336 were ended on 10 August 1338.[68] The council in England ordered his arrest by a letter dated at North-ampton on 28 July and a more general mandate was sent by the king from Antwerp, dated 3 August, ordering the seizure of William, his brother Thomas, and their deputies, and appointing commissioners who were to receive complaints against them.[69] By February 1339 William and his associates were also facing charges of having con-cealed and sold for their own benefit goods destined for the king, and William was trying to shift all the blame on to his former agents.[70] But other purveyors, guilty of similar malpractices, continued to act until October 1339.

The period of Edward's absence abroad (July 1338 to February 1340) was a time of increasing economic depression in this country. Chroniclers mention several signs of distress and throw light on some of the causes. An anonymous poem, which most probably dates from 1338–39, contains particularly illuminating comments because the author expresses the grievances and bewilderment of the common people.[71] Private estate accounts and various classes of

66 K.R. Mem. R., E.159/115, m.8: "ex informacione clamosa diversorum de predicto comitatu Ebor."
67 A. Gooder, "The Parliamentary Representation of the County of York, 1258–1832," (*Yorkshire Archaeological Soc.*, Record Ser. xci, 1935) I, pp. 79–81. Scargill had held every kind of office in his native county, though he was never a sheriff.
68 K.R. exch. acc. various, E.101/21/4. For other accounts of Dunstable see references *supra* n.44.
69 *Calendar of Patent Rolls, 1338–40*, p. 145 and chanc. warrants, C.81/248, no. 11274.
70 C.81/251, no. 11516.
71 The best edition is in I. S. T. Aspin, "Anglo-Norman Political Songs," *Anglo-Norman Text Society* (1953), XI, 105–15. She suggested a time between 1337 and 1340, but was unable to date the poem more precisely. It was written during the absence of a *young* king and his army overseas. This rules out the date of 1297–98, formerly suggested by T. Wright (*ibid.*, 105). The references to taxes make it clear that it could have been written only during Edward's first continental expedition: there is mention of the fifteenths year after year and of concurrent wool levies. A poet writing at the time of Edward's second expedition (June–November 1340) would presumably have referred to the very peculiar ninth of 1340. Only a wool levy was being col-lected in 1342–43 (the Breton expedition) and the mention of the collection

exchequer records provide corroborative information about prices of food. Lastly there is the evidence of the tax records suggesting that there were excessive delays in payments,[72] which would be readily intelligible in a time of economic stagnation and mounting popular anxiety about the worsening situation.

The harvests of 1336, 1337, and 1338 had all been good, the last two quite outstanding.[73] In normal times this would have been highly welcome, but in 1338–39 the resultant low prices of food-stuffs[74] were being depressed still further by heavy taxation and other royal exactions. The decline in the purchasing power of the population was so considerable that economic activity was becoming seriously discouraged. One chronicler speaks of "such plenty of goods and scarcity of money that a quarter of wheat was fetching at London [only] two shillings, and a fat ox half a mark.[75] The well-informed contemporary Adam Murimuth attributed the low prices not to the special abundance of corn, but to the lack of money.[76] The poem describes graphically a deflationary situation. "There is a desperate shortage of cash among the people. At market the buyers are so few that in fact a man can do no business, although he may have cloth or corn, pigs or sheep to sell because so many are destitute." The passage occurs in the middle of impassioned complaints against excessive taxation. The author claimed that because "now the fifteenth runs in England year after year" men were driven into much hardship to raise the necessary money "and common people must sell their cows, their utensils and even clothing."[77] There had

of the fifteenths year after year fits the 1336–40 period better than the time of Edward's next expedition in 1346–47. There were no further wool levies after 1347. Nothing in the poem is incompatible with a date of 1338–39. I owe thanks to Professor E. Miller for first drawing my attention to this poem.

72 K.R. and L.T.R. Mem. R., 13–15 Edward III, views and audits of accounts (the sections of "visus et status compotorum"), passim; Chanc.misc. C.47/87/4/-30 and Cal. Close R., 1339–41, pp. 175–6 (July 1339).

73 J. Titov, "Evidence of weather in the account rolls of the bishopric of Winchester," Econ. Hist. R., 2nd. ser., xii (1960), 363, 394–6.

74 J. E. Thorold Rogers, A History of Agriculture and Prices in England, ii, pp. 106–9; M. M. Postan and J. Titov, "Heriots and Prices on Winchester Manors," Econ. Hist. R., 2nd. ser., xi (1959), table facing p. 410; K.R. Exch. extents and inquisitions, E.143/11/1, nos. 21ff. (inquisitions post mortem on Thomas, earl of Norfolk in the autumn of 1338). For purveyors' accounts which contain abundant evidence about prices see supra n.44.

75 J. R. Lumby, ed., Polychronicon Ranulphi Higden (Rolls Series, 1883), viii, p. 334 (under 1339).

76 E. M. Thompson, ed., Adae Murimuth Continuatio Chronicarum (Rolls Series, 1889), p. 89.

77 Aspin, "Anglo-Norman Political Songs," 109, 111, 112–3 [stanzas 3 and 14].

been very heavy rains in the autumn of 1338 followed by intense and prolonged cold so that the ground remained covered with ice for about twelve weeks. By the spring of 1339 it became abundantly clear that the crops sown in the previous autumn had suffered great damage.[78] This was bound to increase the anxiety of the population about the future and presumably increased men's reluctance to spend money. Murimuth implies this when he notes that the bad winter was not followed by a rise in prices.[79] A rise occurred only in the autumn of 1339 when men found themselves short of seed for sowing.[80] The parliament of October 1339 assembled at a time when men were full of bitterness about the current conditions and were filled with even gloomier forebodings about the future.

In preparation for the new meeting of parliament summoned for 13 October, Edward III authorized his representatives in England to offer valuable concessions to his people in return for an expected grant of taxes.[81] Various prerogative rights of the crown could be bargained away in exchange for fines of money. On the proffered list of possible concessions there figured a number of royal claims that had aroused opposition during the preceding years, including the scutage and the revenue from the chattels of felons and fugitives. But nothing was said about the more fundamental grievances of both lords and commons and the inadequacy of royal offers became plain very rapidly.

The magnates demanded the abolition of the higher duties on exported wool and a binding pledge that they would not be levied again. The commons concurred in the demand for a return to the normal pre-war ancient custom of 6s. 8d. per sack and pointed out that the rate of duty had been raised without the assent of either the magnates or of "la Commune."[82] The unsatisfactory state of the wool trade in 1339 may have aggravated the sense of grievance against the high duties. Exemptions from the payment of the customs in favour of the royal creditors were so common in 1338–39 that only those who had them could hope to make appreciable profits. The non-privileged exporters were at a grave disadvantage.[83]

---

78 Murimuth, *Continuatio Chronicarum*, pp. 88–9. The severe winter also mentioned by Higden, *Polychronicon*, p. 334.
79 Murimuth, *Continuatio Chronicarum*, p. 89.
80 *Ibid.*, p. 89, n.3 (an addition found in two of the surviving manuscripts).
81 Rymer, *Foedera*, p. 1091 (26 and 27 September).
82 *Rot. Parl.*, II, pp. 104 (no. 5) and 105 (no. 13).
83 Fryde, *Some Business Transactions of York Merchants 1336–49* (York, 1966), pp. 7–8.

Their plight was made worse by the steady decline in the price of wool abroad, because of the vast stocks thrown on the foreign market by Edward III and the magnates serving with him in the Netherlands. Sales at a loss did not vitally matter to the king and his followers as long as they received enough to maintain themselves abroad, but the prospects of the ordinary exporters were greatly depressed thereby.[84]

The outcry against purveyance came to a head in the October parliament where the commons demanded that unless the purveyors paid for what they took, they should be arrested and treated as breakers of the king's peace. It was subsequently agreed in parliament that the commission of William Wallingford and all the other commissions to purvey victuals should be cancelled forthwith.[85] Wallingford ceased to act on 15 October,[86] two days after the opening of parliament. He was a clerk of the king's household[87] and had been acting since July 1338 as the chief receiver of the supplies for the royal army abroad. He had gone to Brabant, probably in charge of victuals, and on 1 February 1339 he was given a fresh commission at Antwerp. He returned to England immediately afterwards.[88] In the October parliament it was resolved that Wallingford and his deputies as well as other notoriously evil purveyors should be arrested and kept under detention until enquiries into their misdeeds could be completed.[89] Wallingford was arrested on 23 October for alleged failure to account at the exchequer and was lodged in the Fleet prison.[90] Commissions of enquiry were appointed in many counties in late October and November[91] and by early February 1340 Wallingford was being searchingly examined about their findings.[92] Purveyances did not completely cease,[93] but judging by the absence

84 Fryde, The Wool Accounts of William de la Pole (York, 1964), p. 12.
85 Rot. Parl., II, pp. 105–6 (nos. 13 and 19).
86 He accounted subsequently for the period up to 15 October (K.R. Exch. acc. various, E.101/21/40).
87 Chanc. warrants, C.81/248, nos. 11262–63 (a list of household clerks deserving ecclesiastical preferment, dated 25 July 1338).
88 Wallingford's enrolled accounts, E.358/2, mm.12 and 27.
89 Rot. Parl., II, pp. 105–6 (no. 19).
90 K.R. Mem. R., E.159/116, m.167.
91 Ibid., m.5ʳ and 5ᵛ.
92 K.R. Exch. acc. various, E.101/21/38 is a record of complaints against Wallingford and of his answers to them. He was being interrogated on 9 February 1340.
93 Stephen le Blount was continuing the purveyances for Gascony until 20 November 1339 (E.358/2, m.7); on 23 December 1339 the king commissioned from abroad Richard Potenhale to purvey fish "a nostre oeps pur noz deniers paiantz" (Chanc. warrants, privy seal no. 12495).

of complaints about Wallingford's successor, there was some improvement in administrative arrangements. On 21 December Thomas Baddeby, another household clerk, was appointed to survey all the purveyances made in the kingdom.[94]

At the opening of the October parliament the assembly was told of the king's immense financial difficulties. Archbishop Stratford and the other royal envoys, who had just returned from the king's camp,[95] declared that he had incurred obligations amounting to £300,000 or more[96] and there was no exaggeration in this.[97] The magnates were willing to give an aid forthwith. The tax grant recommended by them was a levy in kind modelled on the ecclesiastical tithe. It was to apply to the commodities that were the main components of the tithe, comprising all kinds of corn, wool, and lambs. The magnates justified this particular choice of a tax in kind on the ground that there was "a great shortage of money in the land."[98] They were clearly being influenced by the belief that some abnormal economic conditions prevailed in England. The magnates also discussed the possible remedies for this alleged monetary crisis, but no decision could be reached.[99] The commons excused themselves from making a grant by pleading that an exceptionally large sum was required and that there was therefore a need for a more prolonged consultation in the counties. Hence their request for the summoning of another parliament.[100] It may be worth recollecting that in the subsequent common petition presented in the parliament of March 1340 it was claimed that "the community of the land was so impoverished" by previous taxes "that they could survive only with great difficulty."[101]

The second parliament met on 20 January 1340. For a long time the government confidently expected that it would be able to secure a fresh grant of taxes. As late as 11 February Thomas Rokeby, the keeper of the castles of Edinburgh and Stirling, was promised payment "out of the first issues of the new aid that will be granted to

94 Chanc. warrants, privy seal no. 12494.
95 They returned to England on 10 October (K.R. Exch. acc. various, E.101/311, nos. 35 and 36).
96 *Rot. Parl.*, II, p. 101 (no. 4).
97 Cf. my thesis, *supra* n.56, chap. 6 and *Revue Belge de Philologie et d'Histoire*, XL (1962), 1186, n.5; and XLV (1967), 1180–1.
98 *Rot. Parl.*, II, pp. 103–4 (no. 4).
99 *Ibid.*, p. 105 (no. 14).
100 *Ibid.*, p. 104 (no. 8).
101 A. W. Goodman, ed., *Chartulary of Winchester Cathedral* (Winchester, 1927), p. 131.

the king in this parliament."[102] The magnates were willing to repeat
their previous proposal and granted a tithe of the produce of their
demesne lands for themselves and their peers.[103] The commons departed from their usual procedure and, instead of granting a tax,
they merely made a conditional offer of one on 19 February.[104] We
have not got the text of the indenture containing their conditions, but
the council dared not pronounce on them and referred the whole
matter to the king. In view of the scholarly speculations about the
significance of this incident[105] one hitherto overlooked feature may
be worth noting. The grant offered by the commons may have been
thoroughly distasteful to Edward III. The commons were recommending on this occasion a levy of 30,000 sacks of wool. But by the end
of 1339 the king appears to have conceived an aversion to wool levies
in general. When subsequently a tax of wool was granted by a later
parliament, in July 1340, the council informed the king of this decision in terms that were clearly designed to allay his dislike of such
a levy.[106] On a still later occasion, in 1347, he referred scathingly to
his previous experiences with the wool taxes and he was then presumably recollecting the disappointments suffered in 1337–39.[107]
When a fresh parliament met on 29 March 1340, after Edward's return from abroad, the proposal for a tax in wool was discarded in
favour of a "tithe" advocated by the magnates.

No *communes petitiones* are mentioned in the roll of the first
parliament of 1340 and we can therefore learn nothing about the
grievances that may have been aired on this occasion. But the arrangements made in that parliament for the supplying of the English

102 K.R. exch. acc. various, E.101/23/1.
103 *Rot. Parl.*, II, pp. 107–8 (nos. 7–9).
104 J. G. Edwards, *The Commons in Medieval English Parliaments* (London,
    1958), p. 24, n.1.
105 The most recent discussion is in Harriss, "The Commons' Petition of 1340";
    his account of this parliament is unfortunately marred (652–3), by his
    failure to note that the entries in the *Cal. Pat. R., 1338–40*, pp. 377–8 (called
    membrane 29) and pp. 408–9 (called membrane 1) are misplaced in the
    calendar, though not in the original roll (C.66/201) as repaired today. Hence
    the mandates of January–February on pp. 408–9 really belong to 1339 and
    not 1340. These mistakes, which had led Mr. Harriss into error, are corrected
    in the Public Record Office copy (Literary Search Room) of *Cal. Pat. R.,
    1338–40*.
106 *Rot. Parl.*, II, p. 122 (no. 29): "l'entente ... est qe cest aide ne soit pas mys en
    mayns de tielx come vos autres leines ont este mys avant ces houres, ou
    vous n'avez este serviz de riens."
107 Chanc. warrants, C.81/318, no. 18251, quoted in Fryde, "The last trials of
    Sir William de la Pole," *Econ. Hist. R.*, 2nd. ser., XV (1962), 19 and n.2.

garrisons in Scotland represented the working of a new policy. Purveyance was being avoided in favour of the making of contracts with important merchants who would not hold any special royal commissions.[108] This anticipated the procedure prescribed by the statute enacted in the next parliament which met on 29 March 1340.[109]

Its assembly must mark the end of the present study. I have tried, in Professor Wilkinson's phrase, "to put parliament back at the center of ... the political life and struggles,"[110] in the obscure period before March 1340 and thus to render more intelligible the concessions that the king was forced to make in April and May of that year. The story told here tries to bring out the importance of the parliamentary sessions for providing opportunities to air the complaints about "the hurts done to *commune poeple*."[111] Government officials must have felt somewhat more insecure whenever a parliament was sitting. An incident in July 1340 provides one unusual illustration of this.[112] Adam de la Mare, the attorney of the sheriff of Somerset and Dorset, had been put in the custody of the marshal of the exchequer because of debts totalling £75. 19s. 2d. which his master had failed to collect. This happened on 20 July and two days later, because the exchequer had been closed for the summer vacation, Adam was consigned to prison. But parliament happened to be in session. The imprisonment of the sheriff's attorney contravened the statute enacted in the previous parliament absolving sheriffs and other local officials from the liability for debts that they had never collected.[113] On 26 July, at the request of the chancellor and other magnates present in parliament, it was agreed by the treasurer, with the assent of the judges and others of the king's council, that Adam should be released on mainprise. One of his two sureties was John de Hungerford, knight of the shire for Somerset in that very same parliament.[114]

108 *Rot. Parl.*, II, p. 109 (nos. 25–27). The account of two of these merchants is in K.R. Exch. acc. various, E.101/22/36 and is enrolled on E.358/2, m.12.
109 *Statutes of the Realm* (Record Commission ed.), I, p. 288.
110 Quoted by G. P. Cuttino, "Mediaeval Parliament Reinterpreted," *Speculum*, XLI (1966), 686.
111 Parliament roll of 1352 quoted by D. Rayner, "The forms and machinery of the 'Commune Petition' in the fourteenth century," *EHR*, LVI (1941), 209.
112 L.T.R. Mem. R., E.368/112, m.202.
113 *Statutes of the Realm*, I, p. 291.
114 *Return of the Name of every Member of the Lower House of Parliament, 1213–1874* (House of Commons Parliamentary Papers of 1878), I, p. 133.

Some Notes on Walter Burley's Commentary on the Politics L. J. DALY

he *Politics* of Aristotle was one of the last of the master's works to be rediscovered in the movement which has come to be known as the "Renaissance of the Twelfth Century," and it does not seem to have become accessible to western scholars until about 1260. There were apparently two translations: the so-called *vetus versio* is anonymous, and the few manuscript copies which contain it have only the first two books, although the commentary of St. Albert the Great is adduced as evidence that the *vetus versio* originally contained a translation of the whole of the *Politics*. The more usual translation is that of William Moerbeke.[1]

There seem to be only four commentaries on the *Politics* by scholars of the thirteenth and fourteenth centuries: those of Albert the Great, of Thomas Aquinas, of Peter Auvergne, and of Walter Burley. All of them have been printed except that of Walter Burley. The commentary of Thomas Aquinas goes only as far as chapter six of book three of the *Politics* and is then continued by Peter of Auvergne.[2] Burley's work is virtually unknown to modern political theorists – a strange fate for his commentary, for he himself seems to have been one of the more widely known and popular writers of his day.

Historians today are accustomed to a lack of detailed knowledge even about the more popular medieval authors, and Walter Burley is no exception to this situation. As an editor of one of his writings remarked, "Magister Walter Burleigh, born in 1275, probably in

1 Georgius Lacombe, *Aristoteles Latinus* (Rome 1939), pp. 74–5; 163–5.
2 Alfred O'Rahilly, "Notes on Saint Thomas II: The Commentary on the *Politics*," *Irish Ecclesiastical Record*, xxx (1927), 614–22.

England, is a personality of whom little is known."[3] Fortunately an essay by C. Martin has now assembled the available materials and presented us with a biographical sketch, as complete as can be expected from the limited data, and on this the following historical summary is largely based.[4]

HIS LIFE AND WORK

Walter Burley was born about 1274 or 1275; his surname, de Burley, would indicate a northern English origin, perhaps a town in Yorkshire, either Burley-in-Wharfdale or Burley near Leeds.[5] Holinshed believed that Walter was a relative of Sir Simon Burley who was a companion-in-arms of the Black Prince, and he refers to Stow's account of Burley, but modern scholars have discounted the story on chronological grounds.[6] We do know that Burley was an Oxford student during the 1290s and that by 1301 he was a master and fellow of Merton College for there is extant a manuscript entitled, "*Questiones* given by Master Walter de Burley on the Book of the Perihemeneias in A.D. 1301."[7] Burley is not mentioned in the Merton bursars' roll for Easter to August of 1307 which is the next surviving one after the rolls of 1305, one of which names him as a fellow of the college. There is a note in a Lambeth Palace manuscript which says that Burley had an unusually long regency at Oxford and then went on to the theological faculty at Paris.[8] It would seem then that Burley had begun his Parisian studies in theology at least by 1308.

While at Paris Burley became the pupil of Thomas de Wilton, himself a former Mertonian (1288 to 1301), who had taken his doctorate in 1314.[9] The date of Burley's own doctorate is not certain

---

3 P. Boehner, *Walter Burleigh: De Puritate Artis Logicae* (Franciscan Institute Publications: Text Series no. 9, 1955), p. vii.

4 C. Martin, "Walter Burley," in *Oxford Studies Presented to Daniel Callus* (Oxford Historical Society, Oxford, 1964), pp. 194–230.

5 *Ibid.*, p. 200.

6 *Ibid.*, p. 200, n.4; T. F. Tout, *Chapters in the Administrative History of Mediaeval England* (Manchester, 1928), III, p. 331, n.2; A. B. Emden, *Biographical Register of the University of Oxford to A.D. 1500* (Oxford, 1957–1959), I, p. 313. This last is most helpful.

7 Martin, "Walter Burley," p. 201. The manuscript is Gonville and Caius College (Cantab.), ms. 668.

8 Cf. S. H. Thomson, "Unnoticed *Questiones* of Walter Burley on the Physics," *Mitteilungen des Instituts für österreichische Geschichtsforschung*, LXII (1954), 392 quoting from Lambeth Palace ms. 70 f.109vb as cited in Martin, "Walter Burley," p. 202 n.2.

9 Emden, *Biographical Register*, III, p. 2054.

although one of his many writings (the *Tractatus de quattuor con-
clusionibus*) would seem to imply that he had graduated as early as
1322, for that tractate seems to have been written after Burley took
his doctorate since he speaks of himself as having held a *disputatio
de quolibet,* which he could only do as a doctor. He was a fellow of
the college of the Sorbonne in 1324 according to the *explicit* of a
Paris manuscript copy of his *Tractatus de puritate artis logice.*[10]

Continuing his writing programme, Walter completed the fourth
book of his commentary on the *Physics* of Aristotle in March 1326,
and within another year had finished the sixth book.[11] Then, sometime in 1327, he left Paris on a mission for his sovereign, King
Edward III. In a letter to Pope John XXII, dated 28 February 1327, the
king asked that the preliminary inquiries for the canonization process
be begun in regard to Thomas, earl of Lancaster, and one of the
delegation to expedite the matter was "Master Walter de Burley,
sacrae paginae professor."[12] Burley was back at Avignon again in
1330 on the same mission but at neither time was he successful.

From 1331 to 1341 Burley remained in England. It was perhaps at
this time, as a canon of Wells, that he met Richard de Bury who was
to be one of his chief patrons. Bury was also a canon of Wells, becoming dean on 20 March 1333; in December 1333 he was consecrated bishop of Durham. Bury gathered around him a remarkable
group of scholars, three of whom were Mertonians (Burley, Thomas
Bradwardine, and Nichols Maudit), and in addition there were
Richard Fitzralph, Richard de Kilvington, Robert Holcot, a Dominican, and Richard Bentworth, a civil servant. During these years
Burley did considerable writing, apparently finishing a commentary
on the first six books of the *Ethics*, the seventh and eighth books of
his revised work on the *Physics,* and a revision of his work on the
Ars Vetus. It must have been a pleasant scholarly atmosphere in
which to work, and we are told how Bishop Bury used to have his
scholars dispute before him after dinner.[13] During this same period
Burley was in casual service as a royal clerk, once at least (in September 1338) "going beyond the seas on the king's service." It must

10 Martin, "Walter Burley," p. 209, n.1, quoting Dr. Weisheipl's information on
   Bibl. Nat., ms. lat. 16130, f.110ᵛ: "Explicit tractatus de puritate artis logice
   Magistri Gualteri Burley socii domus de sorbona parisius."
11 *Ibid.,* p. 213.
12 T. Rymer, *Foedera* (London, 1816–30), II, pp. ii, 695.
13 W. A. Pantin, *The English Church in the Fourteenth Century* (Cambridge,
   1955), p. 139.

have been a short stay, for Burley was apparently back in England by the Easter of 1339.[14]

In 1338 and 1339 he continued his writing on the *Ethics* and began his commentary on the *Politics*. Although Bentworth had originally encouraged Burley, he had died on 8 December 1339, and so both works were ultimately dedicated to Bury. Probably both men aided him with money as well as encouragement. It is interesting to note that Burley, like so many other medieval scholars, had to depend for his subsistence upon the system of provisions either from king or pope. His pluralism developed in parallel with his distinction as a scholar, but generally he never held more than one rectory in addition to one canonry with prebend.[15]

In 1341 Burley returned to Italy where we have record of his disputation in the faculty of arts at Bologna. In November 1343, if not earlier, he was at Avignon where he presented a copy of his commentary on the *Politics* to Pope Clement VI whom, during his student days at Paris, he had known and admired as Peter Roger, a French Benedictine. In the dedicatory letter he refers to Peter as having been a most distinguished doctor of theology "lecturing on the Bible and carrying out the other academic exercises."[16] Burley did not rely in vain on Clement's liberality, for in January 1344, he received papal favours for a relative, two servants, and his clerk.[17]

It would appear from the manuscript tradition of his popular *De vita et moribus philosophorum* that this work was written while he was abroad since of the more than one hundred extant manuscripts, not one seems to be in an English hand.[18] There is a note in the register of Robert Wyvil, bishop of Salisbury, that Burley received a living at Great Chart in Kent on 19 June 1344,[19] but whether he came back to England for his last days the documentation so far discovered does not tell us.

14 *Calendar of Patent Rolls, 1338–1340*, p. 123, quoted in Martin, "Walter Burley," p. 225. Burley was given protection until the Easter of 1339.

15 Cf. the discussion in Martin, "Walter Burley," pp. 223–4, and the more general one in Pantin, *The English Church*, pp. 47–75.

16 "... temporibus quibus ibi lecturam sacrae scripturae ceterosque actus scholasticos exercebatis tamquam doctor in theologia excellentissimus et veritatis perscrutator subtilissimus ..." Vatican codex Borgh.129.

17 Martin, "Walter Burley," p. 229.

18 J. O. Stigall, "The Manuscript Tradition of the *De vita et moribus philosophorum* of Walter Burley," *Medievalia et Humanistica*, XI (1957), 44–5.

19 *Wyvil's Register*, II, fols. 139ᵛ–140ʳ as quoted in Martin, "Walter Burley," p. 230.

THE COMMENTARY

The medieval commentary could take various forms. For instance there was a commentary *ad litteram* which was really only a simple explanation of the key words and phrases of the text. There was also the commentary *ad sensum* which was generally a more elaborate paraphrase of the text, clarifying the meaning, and one in which the author could insert some personal reflections by the way he emphasized this or that point. Lastly there was the commentary *ad sententiam* in which the commentator explained the text much more fully and often, in his *ad intelligendum* or *notandum*, gave his own comments.[20] Burley's work is somewhat of a mixture of the three types but in general he is a laconic writer, though giving one the impression of a careful and methodical teacher who is anxious to make clear to his readers the basic structure and chief ideas of Aristotle's work. He planned his commentary thus: each of the eight books of Aristotle's *Politics* is subdivided into a number of *tractatus*, which in turn are subdivided into *capitula*, these into *partes principales*, and these last into *particulae*. Burley further planned to have a list of principal questions treated in each book at the beginning of that book and at the end a series of conclusions reached. From the following excerpt from his introduction to the third book the reader can see how Walter directed his attack on the citadel of the *Politics*.[21]

20 M. D. Chenu, *L'étude de Saint Thomas d'Aquin* (Paris, 1950), pp. 70–1, 175–83.
21 S. Harrison Thomson, "Walter Burley's Commentary of the *Politics* of Aristotle," *Mélanges Auguste Pelzer* (Louvain, 1947), p. 564 gives a list of various manuscript copies of Burley's commentary to which some additions were made by Anneliese Maier, "Zu Walter Burley's Politik-Kommentar," *Recherches de théologie ancienne et médiévale*, XIV (1947), 332–6. The citations in the present article are from the Vatican codex Borgh. 129 which is a beautifully written fourteenth-century copy with a dedicatory letter (possibly in Walter's own hand) to Pope Clement VI. The corrections too may possibly be Burley's. On this codex see the description by A. Maier, *Codices Burghesiani Bibliothecae Vaticanae*, Studi e Testi 170 (Città del Vaticano, 1952), p. 172. The italicized phrases are those from the medieval translation of Aristotle's *Politics* on which Burley was commenting and are almost always underlined in Borgh. 129. The numbers which I have inserted refer to the paragraph numbers of the medieval Latin translation of the *Politics* as printed in R. M. Spiazzi, *S. Thomas Aquinatis in libros Politicorum Aristotelis Expositio* (Rome, 1951). Generally speaking, except for a stray "enim" or "autem," I have found that the phrases cited in Borgh. 129 correspond word for word with those in the printed text of Spiazzi, at least for the sections of the third book under consideration here. The present quotation of Burley's commentary is at the beginning of the third book, Borgh. 129, f. 33ʳ, col. 1.

Incipit liber tertius. *Ei qui de policia* [223]. Iste liber tertius qui specialiter et principaliter est de regno et rege continet tres tracatus. In primo determinatur de civitate et cive. In secundo ibi *Quoniam autem haec determinata sunt* [244] determinatur de politiis et principatibus in generali. In tertio ibi *Forte autem bene habet* [334] determinatur specialiter de rege et regno.

Tractatus primus continet dua capitula in quorum primo ostenditur quid est civis et quid civitas et a quo habet civitas unitatem; in secundo capitula ibi *Hiis autem que dicta sunt habitus est* [233] movetur et solvitur quaedam questio circa virtutem civis: an sit eadem virtus boni viri et civis studiosi.

Capitulum primum continet quinque partes. In prima ostendit hic esse determinandum de civitate et cive et ordine determinandi de hiis. In secunda ibi *Eos quidem* [225] ostendit de quo cive hic intendit. In tertia parte ibi *Civis autem simpliciter* [226] ponitur diffinitio civis simpliciter et etiam civitatis. In quarta parte ibi *Determinant autem* [229] removetur unam falsam opinionem circa quiditatem civis. In quinta parte ibi *Dubitant enim quidem* [230; ms. lacks *enim* but supplies it when this paragraph is more fully treated on f.34] movetur et solvitur quaedam dubitatio circa unitatem civitatis.

Prima pars continet duas particulas. In prima narrat quod volenti considerare de politia primo oportet scire et considerare quid est civitas. In secunda particula ibi *Quoniam autem civitas* [224] ostendit ordinem considerandi de civitate et cive qui est quod prius est determinandum de cive quam de civitate, in prima ostendit Philosophus inquirendum esse quid est civitas et quid est civis et continet duas particulas. In prima narrat quod volenti considerare de politia primo est ostendendum quid est civitae. In secunda particula ibi *quoniam autem civitas* ostendit quod prius est determinandum de cive quam de civitate.

In prima igitur particula dicit narrando quod volenti considerare de politia prius est ostendendum quid est civis et quid est civitas et est ratio duplex. Prima est quia hoc est dubium: an civitas sit principes vel non, nam cum principes civitatis aliquid faciunt dicitur quod civitas facit illud et e converso; et ideo secundum aliquos civitas est idem quod princeps vel principes; et secundum alios non sunt idem civitas et principes. Secunda ratio ad idem est quia omnes legislatores et politici tendunt circa ordinationem civitatis quia politia nihil aliud est quam ordinatio habitantium civitatis.

Quoniam autem civitas [224] haec est secunda particula etc.

Burley's method of commentary is well described by Martin who is discussing the commentaries on the *Politics* as a whole.

... Their method indicates that they purpose to explain the meaning of the text. They take each book of the *Politics* and divide and sub-divide each, again and again, until they reach its smallest logical components; they then proceed to paraphrase or clarify the meaning of each component. At the head of any division which contains subdivisions, a plan is given of these subdivisions. In this way they combine minute penetrating analysis with an astonishing breadth of accurate synthesis.[22]

TEACHING TECHNIQUES IN THE COMMENTARY

The third book of Burley's commentary provides a good example of the various aids which he designed for the student and reader in order that they would more easily grasp the thought of Aristotle. At the beginning of the third book he has placed a series of questions together with Aristotle's answer in abbreviated form and the reference to the text where it occurs. There are eighteen of them and the following examples will show his technique.

Quid est civis? Movetur et solvitur, tractatu primo, capitulo primo, quod civis simpliciter est qui habet potestate[m] communicandi principatu consiliativo vel iudicativo in civitate.

Quid est civitas? Movetur et solvitur, tractatu primo, capitulo primo, quod civitas est multitudo civium habentium potestatem communicandi in principatu consiliativo vel iudicativo, habens per se sufficientiam ad vitam.

A quo civitas est una? Movetur et solvitur, tractatu primo, capitulo primo, quod civitas est una ab unitate policiae.

Utrum sit eadem virtus boni viri et civis studiosi? Movetur et solvitur, tractatu primo, capitulo secundo, quod non cuiuslibet civis studiosi est eadem virtus cum virtute boni viri; sed civis sic studiosi, ut possit bene et iuste principari, est eadem virtus in specie cum virtute boni viri.

Quae politiae sunt rectae et quae non rectae? Movetur et solvitur, tractatu secundo, capitulo primo, quod politiae quae principaliter intendunt bonum subditorum vel totius multitudinis sunt rectae, quae autem intendunt principaliter bonum principantium sunt iniustae et transgressae.

Quae sunt per se differentiae politicae democraticae et oligarche: utrum multitudo et paucitas vel divitae et paupertas? Movetur et solvitur, tractatu secundo, capitulo secundo, quod per se differentiae harum politiarum sunt paupertas et divitiae.

Quid debet rationaliter esse dominans in civitate? Utrum multitudo vel unus, et hoc vel unus homo vel lex? Movetur et solvitur, tractatu secundo, capitulo tertio, quod multitudo non vilis sed multitudo comprehendens in se consiliarios, iudices, concionatores et aliquos prudentes.

Utrum melius sit regi ab optimo rege vel ab optimis legibus? Movetur et solvitur, tractatu tertio, capitulo secundo, quod melius est regi ab optimis

22 C. Martin, "Some Medieval Commentaries on Aristotle's *Politics*," *History*, XXXVI (1951), 33.

legibus, intendo per leges legem universalem et legem particularem quae est intellectus sine admixtione appetitus sensitivi, cuiusmodi est intellectus epikeis.

Utrum melius sit habere regem secundum succesionem hereditariam vel secundum electionem? Movetur et solvitur, tractatus tertio, capitulo secundo, quod quibusdam melius est habere regem uno modo et quibusdam alio modo.[23]

At the end of the third book we find a series of propositions which Burley has more or less made up directly from key sentences of the section of Aristotle which is under consideration. There are some sixty-five statements here which certainly gave the medieval student a fairly detailed outline of the whole book. It is reminiscent of the modern habit of underlining key sentences in the textbook, and it must have proved helpful to the average medieval student who had to work through the *Politics* using a very literal translation with the consequent difficulty of understanding some of the thought. Here are a few examples of these propositions:

Politia est ordo quidam habitantium civitatem [223].

Civitas est civium multitudo [224].

Neque per habitare neque per iustorum participare est quis civis; hiis participant adventitii et qui contractibus participant [225].

Civis simpliciter nullo aliorum determinatur magis, quam per participare iudicio et principatu [226].

Principatuum quidam determinatus et divisus per tempora ut et quibusdam omnino non liceat eumdem bis principari vel per aliqua determinata tempora alius indeterminatus ut praetor et concionator; hiis non est commune, scilicet praetori et concionatori; sit igitur determinationis gratia, indeterminatus principatus [226].

Oportet regem habere potentiam majorem unius cuiusque potentia et minorem potentiam totius multitudinis [366].

De rege qui secundam suam voluntatem omnia agit sermo instat nunc; principatus regis secundum legem non est species regni; ordo enim lex [367, 369].

Qui intellectum iubet principari, videtur iubere principari deum et leges; qui autem hominem iubet, apponit et bestiam [372].

Sine appetitu intellectus lex est [372].

Exemplum autem artium videtur esse falsum, quod secundum litteras medicari sit pravum [373].

Oratio Agamemnonis: tales mihi sodales; ut non iam principari iustum [377].

---

23 *Borgh. 129*, f. 32[r]–33[r].

Quoniam autem quaedam est comprehendi legibus, quaedam autem impossibilia a lege comprehendi. Haec sunt quae faciunt dubitare et quaerere, utrum optimam legem principari elegibilius (ms. ? elegibilibus) quantum optimum unum [378].
Oculos multos monarchiae faciunt sibi et aures et manus et pedes [379].
Eos qui principatui et sui sunt amici, faciunt comprincipes [379].[24]

Then, at the very end of the third book, Burley writes out a list of twenty-two conclusions. These had already been underlined in the text in the course of his commentary, and they had also been duly noted in the margin as "conclusion 1" etc. The reader could hardly miss them, but to be sure that he would not, they were written out separately at the end of the book. Since they represent what at least one important commentator thought were the significant conclusions to be derived from this third book (probably the most important book for the average reader), they are worth consideration:

1. Primus est determinandum de cive quam de civitate.
2. Non est aliquis civis simpliciter propter participationem iustitiae in civitate.
3. Non solum ille est civis qui descendit a parentibus civibus.
4. Civitas non est una propter unitatem murorum.
5. Civitas habet unitatem ab unitate politiae.
6. Oportet principem bonum habere disciplinam bonae subiectionis.
7. Principantis et subiecti sunt diversae virtutes secundum speciem tam intellectuales quam morales.
8. Magnam utilitatem consequitur homo ex hoc quod est pars civitatis vel societatis.
9. Principatus politici iuste commutantur ab uno cive in alium.
10. Politiae quae intendunt principaliter bonum subditorum seu bonum commune sunt rectae, aliae autem non rectae.
11. Civitas est communicatio propter vitam perfectam et sufficientem habendam, quod est feliciter vivere.
12. Illi qui perfectius et felicius vivunt in civitate magis et essentialius sunt cives.
13. Magis conveniens est quod multitudo comprehendens in se consiliarios, iudices, concionatores et alios prudentes principentur quam unus vel pauci virtuosi.
14. Non secundum cuiuslibet boni excessum debent distribui principatus.
15. Divites, nobiles liberi et virtuosi requiruntur ad civitatem.
16. Leges rectae sunt ferendae ad conferens toti civitati.

24 *Borgh. 129*, f. 48ᵛ–50ʳ.

17. Sine comparatione excedens omnes alios de civitate non est pars civitatis, intellectus huius patet in quarto notabili.

18. Dominatio secundum legem non est regnum nec politia aut species eius, quid intelligitur secundum legem tantum.

19. Lex debet principaliter principari.

20. Rex et lex compaciuntur se in principando.

21. Eadem est virtus regis optimi et aristocratici et politici.

22. Eadem est disciplina regis optimi et aristocratici et politici.[25]

BURLEY'S USE OF THE AQUINAS-AUVERGNE COMMENTARY

There is no doubt but that Walter Burley used the commentary on the *Politics* begun by St. Thomas and finished by Peter of Auvergne. Here is an example taken from the third book which shows the close dependence, at times almost word for word. The commentators are considering Aristotle's advice (Bekker 1288a 17) on what should be done when there is a whole family or a single individual whose virtue far exceeds that of others. Peter of Auvergne writes thus.

[525] Deinde cum dicit *cum igitur*. Declarat quis est ille modus, secundum quem expedit unum principari pluribus, et qualiter. Et primo facit hoc. Secundo recapitulat, ibi, *De regno quidem* etc.

In prima dicit, quod si contingat unum totum genus vel unum inter alios sic differre in genere ab aliis secundum virtutem, ut virtus eius excedat virtutem omnium aliorum, iustum est hoc genus esse regale, vel illum si sit unus, et regnum et dominium esse unum omnium: hoc enim est secundum naturam, quod ille qui excedit secundum virtutem sit dominus aliorum. Ergo si virtus alicuius excedat virtutem aliorum, naturale est quod iste sit rex et dominus.

Nec solum propter hoc iustum est illum esse regem, quia excedit absolute, sicut est prius dictum quod omnes illi qui instituerunt politias dixerunt quod iustum est principari illum qui excedit, sicut et qui optimatum et qui paucorum potentium et qui popularem statum instituerunt. Omnes enim considerantes ad excessum dixerunt illum qui excedit debere principari: quamvis non eumdem excessum ponerent: sed quidam secundum virtutem, quidam secundum divitias, alii secundum libertatem; sed expedit istum principari qui excedit alios secundum virtutem; nec expedit interimere, vel relegare, vel fugare; hoc enim esset tollere regulam vivendi a civitate vel regione.

Iterum non expedit istum principari secundum partem, sed omnibus; nec secundum aliquod tempus sed semper; quia pars non est nata excedere suum totum; sed iste in virtute excedit omnes alios; ergo alii sunt pars respectu istius; ergo non sunt nati excedere ipsum, sed semper excedens magis secundum virtutem debet principari. Quare relinquitur istum debere principari omnibus et semper, et dominum esse et omnes illi tali obedire quasi ex inclinatione naturali.

Sed est intelligendum quod quamvis multi conveniant in virtute et disciplina, oportet tamen quandoque unum principari principatu regali. Est enim aliqua multitudo virtuosorum et haec dignitatem habet, et dicitur multitudo politica. Alia est quae deficit a ratione multorum, et haec dicitur dominativa.

Utramque expedit regi principatu regali; primam, inquantum est unus qui excedit omnes alios in virtute; aliam autem expedit regi uno, inquantum est aliquis qui excedit omnes alios in virtute.

Sed differt: quia in prima principatus politicus multum distat a dominativo principatu; in secundo autem multum appropinquat quia multitudo ista a ratione deficit, prima autem non. Item differt quia secundum regnum diuturnius est quam primum, quia ad secundum minus de virtute sufficit quam ad primum; et ideo facilius potest inveniri unus qui excedat alios, in primo non. In prima enim multitudine, quia omnes attingunt ad rationem, contingit esse aliquos qui possunt invenire diversas vias et modos ad expellendum principem. Non sic est in secunda, quia in secunda deficiunt a ratione; et ideo non possunt invenire vias et cautelas contra principantem; et ideo secundus principatus plus durat quam primus.[26]

Here is the corresponding section in Burley's commentary.

Cum igitur haec est secunda pars huius capituli, in qua ostendit quis est ille modus secundum quem expedit unum principari pluribus et qualiter, dicens quod si contingat unum totum genus vel unum inter alios ita differre ab aliis secundum virtutem et virtus eius multum excedat virtutem omnium aliorum, iustum est hoc genus esse regale, vel illum qui omnes alios multum excedit in virtute et regnum et dominium esse unum omnium. Hoc enim est secundum naturam quod iste qui excedit sic omnes alios in virtute sit rex et dominus, et non solum est hoc iustum quia excedit, nam sicut dictum est prius omnes illi qui in omnes instituerunt politias, posuerunt principari debere esse secundum aliquem excessum, licet non secundum eundem; illi enim qui instituerunt politias dixerunt quod iustum est illum principari qui excedit. Omnes enim illi ut democratici et oligarchici considerabant ad excessum dicentes illum qui excedit debere principari licet non eundum excessum ponerent; sed quidam secundum virtutem, quidam secundum divitias, alii secundum libertatem. Expedit autem illum principari qui excedit alios secundum virtutem, nec expedit illum interimere vel relegare vel fugare; hoc enim esset tollere regulam vivendi a

26 Spiazzi, *S. Thomas Aquinatis*, p. 185, #525.

civitate vel regione; sed expedit talem principari non solum secundum partem vel secundum tempus sed omnibus et semper.

Intelligendum quod est aliqua multitudo quae dicitur multitudo politica et alia est multitudo quae multum deficit a ratione et haec dicitur multitudo dispotica; et utrumque expedit regi principatu regali, primam in quantum unus est qui excedit omnes alios in virtute, aliam in quantum illa multitudo deficit a ratione et virtute. Primus principatus multum distat a principatu dispotico; secundus multum appropinquat quia multitudo ista multum deficit a ratione, sed prima non; differunt etiam in hoc quod secundus principatus seu regnum diuturnius est quam primum quia ad secundum minus de virtute sufficit quam ad primum, et ideo facilius est invenire unum qui excedit alios. In prima etiam multitudine quia omnes attingunt ad rationem contingit invenire aliquos qui possunt invenire diversas vias et modos ad expellendum principem; sed non est sic in secunda, quia secunda multitudo deficit a ratione, et ideo non potest invenire vias et cautelas contra principem. Ideo secundus principatus plus durat.[27]

Unfortunately, in this commentary at any rate, Burley is often a laconic writer and his presentation gives one the impression of a methodical teacher anxious most of all to make clear to his readers the basic structure and important conclusions of Aristotle. He generally passes over the historical examples given in Aristotle's text; and, sad to say, does not add any of his own. Often too his text is but a paraphrase of the Aristotelian paragraph on which he is commenting, nor does he cover all the ideas within a given section. Yet his commentary was evidently a popular one, for the number of manuscript copies of it exceeds that of Marsiglio of Padua's *Defensor Pacis* and this gives us some idea of its popularity among students.[28] Furthermore, the series of questions, conclusions, and notable propositions which Burley added to his commentary gives us a good insight into what the medieval professor thought was important for the student of Aristotle's *Politics* to know and understand; and this in turn aids us in gaining a better understanding of the medieval political mind in general.

27 Borgh. 129, f. 48ʳ, col. 2.
28 S. H. Thomson, "Walter Burley's Commentary," p. 563, n.26.

The Structure of Commutation in a Fourteenth-Century Village J. A. RAFTIS

hile fires raged and blood flowed in the south-east during the great English peasant revolt of 1381, social conditions in the midlands – the very heartland of villeinage – remained comparatively quiet.[1] But rebellions were not foreign to the areas of champion husbandry,[2] and accumulated economic pressures were to bring commutation of villein services along with farming of manorial demesnes as rapidly in the midlands as in the east.[3] What precisely is meant by this term "commutation," the central concept[4] in descriptions of the resolution of rural social tensions in the medieval manor? The historiography of commutation grew up in the context of such evolutionary expressions as natural economy, barter, and subsistence that have become increasingly less acceptable as descriptions of actual economic decisions in pre-industrial societies.[5] More intimate ac-

1 Edgar Powell, *The Rising in East Anglia in 1381* (Cambridge, 1896), p. 57; A. Reville and Ch. Petit-Dutaillis, *Le Soulèvement des travailleurs d'Angleterre en 1381* (Paris, 1898), p. cx.
2 R. H. Hilton, "Peasant Movements in England before 1381," *Econ. Hist. R.,* 2nd ser., II (1949), 117–36.
3 E. F. Jacob, *The Fifteenth Century, 1399–1485* (Oxford, 1961), pp. 370ff.
4 E. Lipson, *The Economic History of England* (London, 1949), I, chap. 3.
5 "The process [commutation] was not uniform and the older view that commutation was a necessary result of the growth of 'money economy' in other spheres, has had to be abandoned in the light of more recent research." May McKisack, *The Fourteenth Century, 1307–1399* (Oxford, 1959), p. 324. But Professor McKisack was as yet unable to supply a coherent replacement for the "older view." Cf. Mildred Campbell, *The English Yeoman under Elizabeth and the Early Stuarts* (2nd. ed., 1960), for a good example of the difficulties historians of later periods experience with the current historiography of the peasant in the fourteenth century.

It should be recognized that archaeologists and social anthropologists have been instrumental in forcing revisions of some of these concepts by economic historians. E.g. Grahame Clark and Stuart Piggott, *Prehistoric Societies* (London, 1965), p. 165, where it is argued that neolithic man may

quaintance with the personal economic decisions of individual peasants is now required of the economic historian. In the following study some of the possibilities for further scientific investigation of commutation are probed through a sample of only one village over a brief period of time.

Shortly before the year of the peasant revolt, Ramsey Abbey's account rolls for the village of Broughton in Huntingdonshire began to append a list of names of tenants together with the amounts of property each held and the conditions of the tenure. Complete lists are extant for the years 1378–79, 1380–81, 1383–84, 1392–93.[6] Properties in these lists were either virgates (thirty-two acres),[7] one-half or one-quarter virgates, or cotlands (probably of two or three acres). The conditions of tenure were ordinary villein services (*ad opus*), "official" village duties (the *officiales* are noted as reeve, beadle, ploughmen), partial commutation (*ad censum*), or more complete commutation (*ad arentatum*). The material from these four years has been combined in tables I and II.

TABLE I

Total Disposition of Villeinage*

	1378–89	1380–81	1383–84	1392–93
Ad opus	20¾ *v.*	22½ *v.*	22 *v.*	19½ *v.*
Ad censum	7 *v.*	5½ *v.*	6½ *v.*	9 *v.*
Ad arentatum	½ *v.*	½ *v.*	½ *v.*	½ *v.*
Ad officium	3¼ *v.*	3¼ *v.*	3 *v.*	3 *v.*
Ad opus	3 *cot.*	3 *cot.*	3 *cot.*	3 *cot.*
TOTAL	31½ *v.*, 3 *cot.*	31¾ *v.*, 3 *cot.*	32 *v.*, 3 *cot.*	32 *v.*, 3 *cot.*

*In tables I and II the following short forms are used: *v.* = virgate; *cot.* = cotland; *ad op.* = ad opus; *ad c.* = ad censum; *ad A.* = ad arentatum; *ak.* = akerman (ploughman); *bed.* = beadle.

be more properly understood by economic models in terms of progressing beyond subsistence economics. On the same point, see also, K. W. Butzer, *Environment and Archaeology* (London, 1964), chap. 23, "Early Subsistence and Settlement Patterns." Raymond Firth, *Elements of Social Organization* (3rd ed., London, 1961), chap. 4, "The Social Framework of Economic Organization," is a useful expression of the anthropologists' discovery of how negative a by-product of western classical economics the concept of non-monetary economies has become.

6 Brit. Mus. Additional Rolls 39535, 39536, 39537, 39539. For the Broughton account roll for 1386–87 (39538) the rent roll is missing.

7 *Cartularium Monasterii de Rameseia*, ed. W. H. Hart and P. A. Lyons (Rolls Series, 79, 1884–93), I, p. 333.

TABLE II

Villein Tenure at Broughton

	1378–9	1380–1	1383–4	1392–3
Asplon, Simon	1 v. ad op., ¼ v. ad c.	1 v. ad op., ½ v. ad c.	1 v. ad op., ½ v. ad c.	
Asplon,[8] William			1 v. ad op., ¼ v. ad c.	1 v. ad op., ¼ v. ad c.
Balde,[9] Robert	½ v. ad op.	½ v. ad op.	½ v. as ak.	¾ v. ad op.
Balde, Richard	1 v. ad op.	1 v. ad op.	1 v. ad op.	1 v. ad op.
Bernewell, John	¼ v. ad op., 1 cot. ad op.	¼ v. ad op., 1 cot. ad op.	¼ v. ad op., 1 cot. ad op.	1 v. ad op., ¼ v. ad c.
Bigge,[10] William	½ v. ad c., ½ v. as ak.	1 v. ad op.	1 v. ad op.	
Bigge,[11] John	¼ land	¼ land		½ v. ad c.
Boon, John	½ v. ad op.	½ v. ad op.		
Boon John jr.	¼ v. ad op.	¼ v. ad op.	¾ v. ad op.	1 v. ad op.
Boteler, Thomas	1 v. ad op.	½ v. ad c., ½ v. as ak.	1 v. ad op.	1 v. ad op., ¼ v. ad c.
Boteler, William	1 v. ad op., ¼ v. ad c.	1 v. ad op., ½ v. as ak.[12]	1 v. as reeve, ¼ v. ad c.	1 v. ad c., ¼ v. ad c.
Bouk, Richard	¼ v. ad op.	¼ v. ad op.	¼ v. ad op.	1 v. ad op.
Brington, John	½ v. ad op.	½ v. ad op.	½ v. ad op.	¼ v. ad op.
Broughton, William	¼ v. ad op.	¼ v. ad op.	¾ v. ad op.	1 v. ad op.
Cabe, John	1 v. ad op. ¼ v. ad c.	1 v. ad op., ¼ v. ad c.	1 v. ad op., ¼ v. ad c.	1 v. ad op., ¼ v. ad c.
Catoun,[13] John	1 v. ad op., ¼ v. ad A.	1 v. ad op., ¼ v. ad A.	1 v. ad op., ¼ v. ad A.	½ v. ad op., ¼ v. ad A.

Holder					
Catoun, John jr.					½ v. ad op., ½ v. ad c.
Clerk,[14] John	1 cot. ad op.	1 cot. ad op.	1 cot. ad op.	1 cot. ad op.	1 cot. ad op., ½ v. ad op., ½ v. ad c., 1 v. ad op.
Clerk, John jr.					
Couper, Thomas	1¼ v. ad c., ½ v. as ak.	1 v. ad op., ¾ v. ad c.	1 v. ad op., ¼ v. ad c., ½ v. ad op.		
Couper, John					½ v. ad op., ½ v. as ak., ½ v. ad c., ¼ v. ad c.
Couper, William	1 v. ad op., ¼ v. ad c.	1 v. ad op., ¼ v. ad c.	1 v. ad op., ¼ v. ad c.		
Couper, Adam					½ v. as ak., ¾ v. ad c.

8 A John Asplon, said to hold one-quarter "terra" in the revenue sections of the account rolls, is not included in this table since such land is not listed in the rent roll and probably is freehold. There is also some evidence (1392–93) that this John is of the Shepherd family rather than the main Asplon group.

9 A Robert the son of Richard Balde, said to hold one-half virgate *ad censum* in 1378–79, has not been entered here; nor has the ? John Balde holding one-half virgate as a ploughman in 1380–81 been entered.

10 The account roll of 1386–87 notes that William Bigge died during that year.

11 The one-quarter land held by John Bigge for these first years appears to be freehold, since it is not entered in the villeinage rent roll.

12 William Boteler shared this holding with another villager for plough services.

13 A Beatrice Cateline, noted only in 1378–79 as holding one-quarter virgate *ad censum*, has not been entered here.

14 A William Clerk pays rent in the account rolls of 1378–79, 1380–81 and 1386–87 for a virgate that is probably freehold, and so is not listed here.

TABLE II (*continued*)

	1378–9	1380–1	1383–4	1392–3
Crane, John		¾ v. ad op.	¾ v. ad op.	
Crane, Agnes				½ v. ad op.
Cros, Ivo atte	1 v. ad op.,	½ v. as ak.,	½ v. as ak.,	1 v. ad op.,
	¼ v. ad c.	¾ v. ad c.	¾ v. ad c.	¼ v. ad c.
Elyner, William	¼ v. ad op.	¼ v. ad op.		
wife of William Elyner			¼ v. ad op.	
Everard, William	½ v. ad op.	½ v. ad op.	½ v. ad op.	1 v. ad op.
Fisher,[15] Simon	1 v. ad op.,	1¼ v.	1 v. ad op.,	1 v. ad op.,
	¼ v. ad A.	as reeve & bed.	¼ v. ad A.	½ v.,
				¼ v. ad A.
Gernoun,[16] Richard	¾ v. ad c.,	1 v. ad op.,	¼ v. ad c.	¼ v. ad c.
	½ v. as ak.	¼ v. ad c.		
Gore,[17] Thomas	½ v. ad op.	½ v. ad op.		
Grymesby, Robert			½ v. ad c.	½ v. ad op.
Hale, Emma de				¼ v. ad op.
Justice, Edward	1 v. ad op.,	1 v. ad op.,	1¼ v.	¾ v. ad c.,
	¼ v. ad c.	¼ v. ad c.	ad op.	½ v. as ak.
Leighton, William	1¼ v.			
	as reeve & bed.			
Leighton, Margaret		1 v. ad op.,		
		¼ v. ad c.		
Lomb, William	1 v. ad op.,	1 v. ad op.,	¾ v. ad c.,	
	1 v. ad c.	¼ v. ad c.	½ v. as ak.	
Mohaut, Simon				½ v. ad c.
Neel, John	1 v. ad op.	1 v. ad op.	½ v. ad c.,	1 v. ad op.,
			½ v. as ak.	¼ v. ad c.

Othehill,[18] Stephen	1 v. ad op., ¼ v. ad c.	1 v. ad op., ¼ v. ad c.	1 v. ad op., ¼ v. ad c.	
Othewold, John	1 v. ad c., ½ v. as ak.			
Othewold, Thomas		½ v. ad c.	1 v. ad op., ½ v. ad c.	1 v. ad c., ½ v. as ak.
Prat, John	½ v. ad op.	½ v. ad op.	½ v. ad op.	
Pye, Benedict	½ v. ad op.	½ v. ad op.	½ v. ad op.	½ v. ad op., ½ v. ad c.
Randolf, John	½ v. ad op.	½ v. ad op.		
Shepherd, William	1 cot. ad op.	¼ v. ad op., 1 cot. ad op.	¼ v. ad op., 1 cot. ad op.	1 cot. ad op.
Shepherd, Nicholas	¼ v. ad op., ½ v. ad c.	¼ v. ad op., ½ v. ad c.	¼ v. ad op., ½ v. ad c.	
Shepherd,[19] John	½ v. ad op.	½ v. ad op., ½ v. ad c.	?	½ v. ad op., ½ v. ad c., ½ v. ?
Shepherd, John jr.				1 v. as reeve, ¼ v. as ak?
Stivecle, Thomas	¼ v. ad op.	½ v. ad op.	1 v. ad op.	1 v. ad op.
Wrighte, John	½ v. ad c.	½ v. ad c.	½ v. ad c.	½ v. ad c.

15 A William Fisher pays rent in the account rolls of 1378–79, 1380–81 and 1386–87 for a virgate that is probably freehold.

16 In 1383–84 a Thomas Gernoun is noted as holding one virgate *ad opus*, but this may be a scribal error since there is no further reference to Thomas, and so his name is not entered here.

17 The account rolls of 1378–79, 1380–81 and 1386–87 note that Thomas Gore also holds one virgate of freehold.

18 A William Othehill pays rent in the account rolls of 1378–79, 1380–81 and 1386–87 for a virgate that is apparently freehold.

19 There are several difficulties not yet resolved in identifying the properties of the John Shepherds.

From table I it can be seen that there were only slight variations in the over-all figures for tenurial categories during this period. The *arentatum* lease, introduced to Ramsey Abbey manors after the Black Death, was only employed for a one-half virgate. Three cotlands remained *ad opus*. Properties allowed to officials for their services only varied slightly from three and one-quarter to three virgates. More flexibility was introduced between the virgates *ad opus* and *ad censum*, but in proportion to the number of virgates involved, even these variations were not very considerable.

Figures for the individual tenants in table II present a strikingly different picture of change from the relatively stable over-all aggregate. Over these years nearly every tenant in the list had changes in tenurial conditions or in the total amount of property held. Of the sixteen villagers increasing their holdings over this period, five (Simon Asplon, John Boon jr., William Broughton, John Shepherd sr., Thomas Stivecle) did so in the early 1380's, and eleven by 1392. For only two villagers is there clear evidence for a decline in the amount of property held, and these were not important villagers at Broughton: John Brington decreased his holdings from one-half to one-quarter virgate by 1392; Agnes Crane was only able to hold one-half virgate after the death of her husband John. Additional properties were made available to the above villagers by the death and disappearance of their neighbours. For table II it has been calculated that the total number of these tenants gradually declined from forty-one to thirty-five over the period of our study (1378–79: 41; 1380–81: 39; 1383–84: 37; 1392–93: 35).

How were villagers able to extend their holdings over these years? In nearly all instances the increased holding seems to be associated with an ability to provide services, that is to have lands *ad opus*.[20] With some (Robert Balde, John Bernewell, John Boon jr., Richard Bouk, William Broughton, John Clerk, William Everard, Thomas Stivecle) there was quite simply an increase in the size of the holding *ad opus*. For others (Simon Asplon, Thomas Boteler, Simon Fisher, John Neel, John Shepherd, Benedict Pye) lands *ad censum* were able to be added to considerable holdings *ad opus*. Perhaps the nearest one can come to the decisions involved in this process of increased

20 Alternatively, an inability of women to work lands is illustrated by the very short periods of their tenure in the late fourteenth century. Beatrice Cateline, the widow of William Elyner, Margaret Leighton, widow of William, and Emma de Hale are such examples at Broughton. Prior to the Black Death widows and other women often held many villein lands for long periods.

holdings is through the arrangements for special services as officials. "Official" services were paid the price of a regular unit of land free of regular services, as well as the premium of commutation of services for the remaining land of the villager. In 1378–79 William Bigge received one-half virgate for ploughman services, and his own one-half virgate was freed for money rent (*censum*). Thomas Couper received one-half virgate as ploughman, and one and one-quarter virgates *ad censum*; Richard Gernoun received one-half virgate as ploughman and three-quarters of a virgate *ad censum*; John Othewold received one-half virgate as ploughman and one virgate *ad censum*. Similar arrangements were made for Thomas Boteler, Ivo atte Cros, ? John Balde and William Boteler in 1380–81; for Robert Balde, Ivo atte Cros, William Lomb, and John Neel in 1383–84; for John Couper, Adam Couper, Edward Justice, and Thomas Othewold in 1392–93. Parallel arrangements were made for reeve and beadle duties, so that under this title William Leighton held one and one-quarter virgates free of other services in 1378–79, Simon Fraser one and one-quarter virgates free in 1380–81, William Boteler one virgate as reeve and one-quarter virgate *ad censum* in 1383–84, John Shepherd one virgate as reeve (and one-quarter ? *ad censum*) in 1392–93.

The economics of villeinage at this time seems, therefore, fairly clear. First of all, there is a labour and service market whereby fewer villagers are able to obtain increasingly larger holdings for their services as reeve, beadle, ploughman, or simply as regular villein. For some of these villagers this was indeed an "increase of serfdom" over certain years in the 1380s. But that it was not an increase of impoverishment is perhaps best borne out by the ability of such main tenants to rent bits of demesne as these became available. Richard Bouk had by 1392 a one-acre piece, and another holding of three furrows from the demesne; John Cabe (and associates) had five sellions; John Clerk sr. had two pieces of one acre each; Ivo atte Cros had one-half acre; William Everard had one acre; John Neel leased a capital messuage; and Thomas Othewold had ten furrows and a three-acre piece. There was a turnover in these small holdings that is difficult to trace since they are not listed in the appended rent roll, but it is clear that other portions of demesne were held before 1392 by important villagers: Thomas Couper, one-half acre; John Clerk sr., one acre, one acre, three furrows; Nicholas Shepherd, three acres, four acres; John Prat, five furrows; Benedict Pye, one messuage, six acres.

same rate; from the badly decayed account roll for the year 1312–13[26] it can be determined that at least 728 works were sold at the same rate. These early fourteenth-century account rolls also show that the category *ad censum* was being applied to annual commutation of services in addition to the above seasonal arrangements. Four virgates were *ad censum* in 1307–8, and four virgates were also at this money rent in 1311–12 and 1312–13.

Appended to the account roll for the year 1314–15 (Michaelmas to Michaelmas) is a detailed listing of the *opera* owing to the lord, and the disposition of these services.[27] The calculations are based upon two periods, the first from Michaelmas of 1314 to early August 1315, and this in turn was divided into a period to the feast of the birth of St. John the Baptist (29 September to 24 June) and from 24 June to early August; the second or "autumn work" period embraced a five-week period from the "Gules" of August to the feast of the nativity of the Blessed Virgin Mary (8 September). For the first period it was estimated that thirty-one and one-half virgates owed three works[28] a week for thirty-eight weeks (3,591 works), four cotmen owed one work a week for thirty-eight weeks (152 works); the same virgates owed three works a week for the remaining five weeks and two days (535.5), and cotmen owed at one work or 24 works for this period. This total of 4,302.5 works was accounted for in the following fashion: 838.5 works (or 19.19 per cent) were allowed for the lands of the reeve, beadle, woodward, four ploughmen, and three virgates *ad censum*; 712 works (or 16.19 per cent) were allowed the twenty-five remaining virgates and four cotlands for twenty-eight feast days; 48 works (or 1.1 per cent) were allowed for illness; 69 works were expended upon cutting and collecting thatch; 623 works were expended for ploughing and related work; 147 works were expended on threshing, 63 works on building, 24 works on watching (at the fair of St. Ives), 40 works on gathering manure, 271 on gates and hedges, 94 on carpentry, 168 on cutting wood and thorns, 220

26 P.R.O., SC 6, Port. 875, no. 9.
27 This text is added as an appendix below.
28 The precise requirements of the various work units owed by villeins are described in detail in the thirteenth-century extent, *Cartularium Monasterii de Rameseia*, I, pp. 335–8. Some work units are defined by the "piece," e.g. cutting 40 bundles of reeds in the marsh, ditching a length of 16½ feet, 3 feet at the top, and 2 "spadgraffs" in depth. In other work the unit is time, as repairing buildings or spreading manure when the work must be from morning to evening.

on cutting fen, 97 on weeding, and 60 on marling; the remaining 868 works (20.08 per cent) were sold.

For the second period or autumn work of this year (1315) the thirty-one and one-half virgates owed five works a week for five weeks (and three work days in the next week) for 882 works; one work was demanded for the day after the boon, and four works per virgate were collected for (? boon) work (127.5 works); cotmen or cotlanders paid 20 works for the same period; for the three weeks from the feast of the nativity of the Blessed Virgin Mary to the vigil of Michaelmas the virgates owed five works per week (472.5) and the cotmen one work (12); special units of land contributed another 11 works. This total of 1525 works was accounted for in the following fashion: 246 (or 16.13 per cent) were allowed for lands of the officials and *ad censum* as in the earlier part of the year; 178.5 (or 11.70 per cent) were allowed for seven feast days; illness accounted for only 8 works (.5 per cent); 597 works were expended on cutting and collecting corn; ditching accounted for 22 works, stacking for 40 works, cutting thorns for 15 works, and five "Bethsolewes" for 127.5 works. The remaining 291 works (19.08 per cent) were sold.

No doubt the fact that this detailed account of *opera* was often appended to the main account roll by a small piece of parchment that could easily be torn away explains why it could frequently fail to survive. Of the dozen account rolls extant for Broughton before the Black Death, the detailed *opera* account is found only for this year and for the year 1342–43. But several *opera* accounts survive after 1378, and these have been gathered into the summary table (table III).

The total works possible from villeinage during the annual session and the special autumn season varied somewhat from year to year. Slight variations in the total amount of land in villeinage account for some of these differences.[29] Other variations appeared from a few extra works in the annual and autumn seasons. The reason for these extra works is not clear, and certainly they are not sufficiently significant to suggest a policy of extra works. The greater variable was simply the incidence of work days owing to use of a religious liturgical calendar. A better understanding of these variations may emerge by breaking down the *opera* owed per virgate. Beyond the

29 E.g., works are listed separately for Beatrice Beneyt in the autumns of 1314–15 and 1342–43. And from 1378 John Clerk and William Shepherd did a few works for "furrows" that may have been taken out of demesne.

TABLE III

The Structure of Villein Work Payments

	1314–15	1342–43	1378–79	1380–81	1386–87	1392–93
Annual Works Due*	4,323	3,555	2,868	3,114	3,181	2,766
		(4,281)	(4,221)	(4,362)	(4,276)	(4,386)
Annual Works† Allocated:						
Services and Censa	839	(726)	(1,353)	(1,188)	(1,095)	(1,620)
percentage	19	17	32	27	26	36
Feast Days	712	676	332	267	296	293
percentage	16	16	8	6	7	7
Illness	48	9	0	0	5	34
Work Done	1,865	2,251	2,260	1,798	2,251	2,027
percentage	43	53	54	42	53	46
Work Sold	868	636	521	1,049	630	412
percentage	20	15	12	24	15	9
Autumn Works Due	1,525	1,131	961	999	1,020	861
		(1,362)	(1,412)	(1,386)	(1,385)	(1,365)
Autumn Works Allocated:						
Services and Censa	246	(231)	(451)	(387)	(365)	(504)
percentage	16	17	32	28	26	37
Feast Days	179	104	104	22	23	39
percentage	12	8	7	2	2	3
Illness	8	4	4	0	27	8
Work Done	802	810	770	802	805	682
percentage	53	58	55	58	59	50
Work Sold	291	212	84	175	166	133
percentage	19	16	6	13	12	10

*The bracketed figures in this line include the works owed from services and *ad censum* lands, that is, the addition of the bracketed data of the next line, which data were not calculated in the summations at the end of the rolls for these years. All figures and percentages in this table have been rounded.

†Except for the year 1314–15, the total works accounted for every year tally almost exactly with the totals owed, so the totals of allocated works are not entered in this table.

thirty-eight, five and three week units and before the terminal feast-day of each period, were a few days that might or might not be week-days on which work was owed; such added work days are indicated by the plus figure in table IV.

Work allowed for the special official services did not vary much over the whole period under consideration here. Over 1314–15 the

TABLE IV

Opera owed per Virgate

	1314	1342	1378	1380	1386	1392
38 weeks @ 3 opera	114	114+1	114+1	114	114	114+1
5 weeks @ 3 opera	15+2	15+2	15	15+3	15+3	15+3
extra	0	0	2	2	2	2
Annual total	131	132	132	134	134	135
5 weeks @ 5 opera	25+3	25+1	25+3	25+2	25+2	25+1
3 weeks @ 5 opera*	15	12	12	12	12	12
extra	5	4	4	4	4	4
Autumn total	48	42	44	43	43	42
Work Year Total	179	174	176	177	177	177

*From 1342 this second autumn work session was three weeks at four opera.

reeve, beadle, woodward, and four ploughmen were allowed work on three virgates. In 1342–43 the reeve and four ploughmen were allowed work on two and one-half virgates, and the bailiff on one virgate. As noted above, work was allowed on three or three and one-quarter virgates over the 1380s. It was the *ad censum* figure that brought a long-run increase in percentage of work allowed in this category, though the amount of land *ad censum* could fall after 1314–15, and again after 1378–79.

Perhaps some of the most interesting evidence in these documents is that for feast days. These medieval "holidays" could bring more than fifteen per cent work allowance in the early fourteenth century at Broughton. Unfortunately, the pre-Black Death accounts do not give any details about what feast days were actually allowed. By the later period, however, specific detail may be found. During the three-work weeks work was only required on Monday, Tuesday, and Wednesday for the annual work session. In 1378–79 work was not demanded for the feast of All Saints (Monday), Saint Andrew (Tuesday), Conception of the Virgin Mary (Wednesday), Saint Thomas the Apostle (Tuesday), for the three days in Christmas week, for the feast of the Purification (Wednesday), for the three days of Easter week, for the three days of the week of Pentecost, for Saints Peter and Paul (Wednesday), and Saint James (Monday). During the autumn session work was not demanded for the feast days of Saint

Lawrence (Wednesday), the Assumption (Monday), Saint Bartholomew (Wednesday), the nativity of the Virgin Mary (Thursday),
Saint Mathew the Apostle (Wednesday). The reason for the long-
run decline in work allowed for such feast days, which can be seen
in table III does not emerge from the Broughton records. Indeed this
very important question of labour and religious feasts deserves an
attention that cannot be given in this brief study.[30]

The mid–thirteenth-century extent of Broughton shows how sickness was to be allowed in the villein service structure:

Ad omnes etiam precarias autumni veniet ipse, vel uxor eius, cum tot
operariis quot habet; et si minus quam tres operarios habeat, alter eorum
operabitur; et si plures, deferet virgam ultra suos operarios et non uxor;
et si ipse infirmetur, uxor eius domi remanebit ad ipsum custodiendum;
et nihilominus omnes operarios mittet ad precariam.

Et quotiens infirmetur, erit quietus ab omni opere praeter aruram.

Et si ejus aegritudo per annum duret et diem, toto illo tempore ob [ab!]
omni opere erit quietus, praeterquam de arura.

Post annum vero et diem, a nullo opere per aliquam infirmitatem excusa-
bitur.[31]

Opera allowed for sickness were not a significant percentage in
the total structure: there was over one per cent of annual work
allowed for illness in 1314–15, as high as two per cent of autumn
works in 1386, but for the other years much less than one per cent.
So far it does not seem possible to employ these data on illness for a
wider study of patterns of sickness.[32] But in any case "sickness benefits" are a very personal matter, and although there were no personal
details in the 1314–15 account, later rolls are more informative. Over
the annual session of 1342–43 a semivirgater, Simon ad Portam, was
allowed two works for one week's illness, Richard the son of Hugh,
semivirgater, was allowed three works excluding feast days for a
fortnightly illness; John Crane, holding a quarter virgate, was allowed one and one-half works for a fortnightly illness; William of
Broughton, holding a three-quarter virgate, was allowed two works
for an illness of (? one)[33] week. During the autumn work period a

30 A wider study of this question is being undertaken by Mr. Edwin DeWindt.
31 *Cartularium Monasterii de Rameseia*, I, pp. 336–7.
32 It is not certain, for example, how often the *operarii* of the above text
replaced their villein master when he was ill. I am making a wider survey of
this evidence in order to attempt to correlate this specific village evidence
with studies of wider patterns of plague and sickness.
33 The court roll is badly stained at this point.

semivirgater, Thomas Balde, was allowed four works for a fortnightly illness. Over 1378–79 only John Crane was allowed four
works for illness of a non-specified period. No sickness allowances
are noted for 1380–81. Over 1386–87 the semivirgater Benedict Pye
was allowed four and one-half works for a three-week illness; William Couper (tenant of two virgates) was allowed ten works for
being sick one week, and an additional seventeen works (probably
from the property at his death). Over 1392–93 John Catoun, semivirgater, was allowed nine works for an illness of six weeks; John
Neel, virgater, was allowed twelve works for a four-week illness (he
died later that year, at which time a further thirteen works were
allowed from his property); John Shepherd sr., semivirgater, was
allowed seven and one-half works for a three-week illness.

The sale of works is, perhaps surprisingly, one of the more difficult parts of the *opera* structure to interpret. Undoubtedly the sale
of works was to some degree simply a by-product of the whole
system. With a relatively fixed system of labour obligations for
tenure, but with changing labour needs resulting from the open-
field system, climate, repair, size of harvest, and a multitude of such
variables, arrangements for the sale or commutation of works was
an elementary wisdom. Furthermore, any sensible lord would keep
a safe margin of labour at his disposal.[34] But surely a margin that
varied from more than twenty-four to ten per cent for annual work
was more than a safe margin required! For the autumn works, varying so much with harvest requirements and more stringent time
schedules, there might be expected a wider safety margin. But in
the later fourteenth century when labour was in such short supply,
one finds an average of ten per cent of the *opera* sold.

An alternative explanation for the sale of *opera* has been that of
profit motive on the part of the lord. But as a long run interpretation
of the economics of manorial administration this interpretation is
somewhat less than compelling. Above all, the price of the *opera*
does not seem to have changed from the mid-thirteenth century,
despite the competition for labour in the later fourteenth century.

Actual work done would seem to be the objective of the administration of villeinage. And yet the work done in table III above is a
quite stable percentage over the years: varying from about forty-
three to fifty-three per cent both before and after the Black Death.
A somewhat higher percentage of work was able to be extracted for

34 Lipson, *The Economic History of England*, I, pp. 96f.

TABLE V*

Sale of *Opera*[35]

1314–15: 860 @ ob.	1380–81: 925 @ ob.
291 @ 2 d.	159 @ 1 d.
	137 @ 2 d.
1342–43: 638 @ ob.	1386–87: 466 @ ob.
221 @ 1 d.	170 @ 1 d.
45 @ 2 d.	152 @ 2 d.
1378–79: 486 @ ob.	1392–93: 286 @ ob.
36 @ 1 d.	210 @ 1 d.
83 @ 2 d.	49 @ 2 d.

*In this table *opera* figures have been rounded for convenience. The price of *opera* indicated on the mid-thirteenth-century extent are given in the text, quoted *supra* p. 290.

autumn work requirements, but the range – from fifty to fifty-eight per cent – was still quite stable in view of the many changes in the labour market and the policies of labour administration over the century. It would appear that the inflexibilities of the manorial structure were such that the lord was able to tap only some fifty per cent of the pool of labour represented by villeinage services.

It is now possible to return to the consideration of the reasons for the capacity of the villeins to accumulate land over the period from 1378–93. For such an investigation the inability of the lord to extract more than fifty per cent of *opera* owing from villein tenants may be translated into the labour supply condition of the individual villein tenant. The virgater who owed 179 works in 1314–15 could expect some 25 works to be cancelled by feast days. Since there is no evidence that the sale of *opera* was restricted by regular policy to one villager more than to another, this virgater could expect to purchase for his own use a further 36 works. This left 118 works (one can usefully designate these as work days) for the lord. It should be recalled that many villagers held three-quarter or one-half virgates, and so would owe proportionately fewer works.

By 1378, the virgater would have only one-half as many work

35 This sale of *opera* is part of a wide context of fixed rents that structured the lord's profit policy. The main money rents paid by villeins along with their *opera* (heusire, tallage, and assized rents) remained the same from the mid-thirteenth century until the end of the fourteenth century. Virgates were put *ad censum* at a standard 14s. 8d. at least from 1307 to the end of the century.

units freed by feast days; over 1378–79 he would sell fewer works also, though in 1380–81 he could sell more works than in 1314–15. But by 1378, as against the earlier part of the fourteenth century, the virgater would have nearly twice as many opportunities of having services commuted (*ad censum*) for additional lands he might wish to hold, and from the later 1380s this opportunity would greatly increase. The actual disposition of his labour in relation to land tenure became a very individual matter of the villein, as was seen above in table II. Further evidence of the individual nature of villagers' decisions can be seen in the patterns of avoidance of works for which villagers were fined through the local court. Over the period from 1378 to 1393, 29 of the main tenants of table II were fined for avoidance of work, and 20 were not charged at all for avoiding work.[36] Those refusing to work might be smaller landholders like Robert Balde (7 offences) or important landholders like Thomas Boteler (3 offences); alternatively, a lesser landholder like Thomas Stivecle as well as a more important landholder like Ivo atte Cros, might have performed all their services.

This study has merely attempted to describe the structure of villein labour supplied in the village of Broughton in order to isolate the many elements that may underline a casual concept such as commutation. Once it becomes possible to establish the limits of the lord's direct control over the labour supply in the village,[37] the investigation of villagers' economic activity can be undertaken. There are some indications that a study of this activity can be as fruitful for the pre-Black Death as for the later period. Specialized services, such as that of the reeve, were creating a wealthy village group in the early fourteenth century.[38] Tax assessments of the early fourteenth century also indicate a noticeable variety in the taxable wealth of villeins.[39] Further studies into the individual patterns of villein ownership and wealth should be encouraged.

36 P.R.O., SC 2, Port. 179, no. 41 (1377–78); no. 42 (1386–88); no. 43 (1391–92). Brit. Mus., Add. Rolls 34306 (1382–83); 34901 (1384–85); 39474 (1387–88); 34815 (1390–91); 39475 (1391).
37 Because of the nature of administrative documents, studies of manorial administration have usually been unable to describe this detailed structure of villein labour supply. Cf. such useful studies of commutation as H. P. R. Finberg, *Tavistock Abbey* (Cambridge, 1951), pp. 83, 245f.; Edward Miller, *The Abbey and Bishopric of Ely* (Cambridge, 1951), pp. 102f.; Marjorie Morgan, *The English Lands of the Abbey of Bec* (Oxford, 1946), pp. 101f.
38 J. A. Raftis, "The Concentration of Responsibility in Five Villages," *Mediaeval Studies*, XXVIII (1966).
39 53 Broughton villagers are listed in the subsidy roll for 1 Edward III, and 41 villagers for the roll of 6 Edward III.

Appendix

The *Opera* Account for 1314–15[40]

Compotus operum

Idem respondet de .M^{D}M^D.ix^C.v^{xx}.xi. operibus de .xxxi. virgatariis et dimidio a festo Sancti Michaelis usque festum Nativitatis Sancti Johannis Baptiste pro .xxxviii. septimis et duos dies non operabiles quorum quilibet facit .iii. opera per septimam. Et de .cxxxii. operibus de quatuor cotmannis ibidem per idem tempus quorum quilibet facit .i. opus per septimam. Et de .cccclv. operibus et dimidio de eisdem virgatariis a festo Sancti Johannis predicto usque ad gulam Augusti per quinque septimas et duos dies operabiles quorum quilibet facit .iii. opera per septimam ut supra. Et de .xxiiii. operibus de predictis quatuor cotmannis per idem tempus quorum quilibet facit .i. opus per septimam ut supra per diem lune.

Summa .iii.M^D.V^{xx}.ii. opera et di.

De quibus allocantur preposito bedello wodewardo .iiii. akermaniis et .iii. virgatis terre ad censum per supradictum tempus .DC.v^{xx}.xviii. et di. Iterim xxv virgate terre in opere pro .xxviii. diebus festivis .D.V^{xx}. Interim .iiii. cotmanni pro ebdomada Natale, Pascale et Pentecoste .xii. Infirmis .xlviii. In stipula falcanda et colligenda .lxix. In caruce fuganda frumento et semine quadragesimali hercianda et waterforewyng .D.iii. In blada trituranda .vii^{xx}. vii. In domibus cooperiendis .lxiii. In vigilandum ad feriam Sancti Ivonis .xxiiii. In fymis colligendis .xl. In foreis et haiis facienda circa curiam .ccxxxi. In carpentria in curia .iiii^{xx}. xiiii. In spino prostrando et meremio .viii^{xx}. viii. In falcatione et levatione feni .cxx. Iterim apud hydek .lx. In serculatione .iiii^{xx}. xvii. In fymis marlandis .lx. In venditione .Dcc.xxviii. inter festa sanctorum Michaelis et J. Baptiste, pretium operis obulus.

Et eque

Opera autumpna

Idem respondet de .Dccxlii. operibus de supradictis .xxxi. virgatis et dimidia a gula augusti usque Nativitatem beate Marie per .v. septimas et .iii. dies operabiles quorum quilibet facit .v. opera per septi-

---

40 P.R.O., SC 6, Port. 875, no. 10. Except where multiples of twenty are explicitly employed, the long hundred was used in the above accounting. While the autumn works are exactly accounted for, twenty more works were allocated during the year than can be traced in this first paragraph above.

mam. Et de .xxv. operibus et dimidio de eisdem in crastino prime
precarie que dur' bouzeld quilibet facit .i. opus qui est in opere. Et de
.v^{xx}. ii. operibus de eisdem per predictum tempus quorum quilibet
virgatarius in opere facit .iiii^{or}. opera in autumpno preter opera
predicta. Et de .xx. operibus de predictis quatuor cotmannis per idem
tempus videlicet de quolibet .i. opus per septimam. Et de .v. operibus
de Simone ate Dam per idem tempus videlicet quolibet die lune .i.
opus. Et de .iii. operibus de Beatrice Beneit per idem tempus. Et de
.cccv^{xx}. xii. operibus et dimidio de supradictis virgatariis et dimidio
a festo Nativitatis beate Marie usque festum Sancti Michaelis per tres
septimas quorum quilibet facit .v. opera per septimam ut supra in
autumpno. Et de .xii. operibus de quatuor cotmannis per idem tempus de quolibet .i. opus per septimam. Et de .iii. operibus de Simone
atedam per idem tempus videlicet quolibet die lune .i. opus.

Summa operum .M^D. cciiii^{xx}. v. opera
De quibus allocantur preposito bedello .iiii. akermannis et .iii.
virgatis terre ad censum per supradictum tempus .ccvi. Iterim .xxv.
virgate et dimidia terre in opere pro .vii. diebus festivis .clviii. et di.
Infirmis .viii. In blada metenda et colligenda .iiii^c. v^{xx}. xvii. In sicera
facienda .xxii. In meya facienda .xl. In spinis prostrandis .xv. Iterim
pro .v. Bethsolewes .c.vii. et di. In venditione .ccli. in autummno, pretium operis .ii .d. an' nat'.

Et eque

The Wealth of Richard Lyons   A . R . MYERS

ll students of fourteenth-century England are familiar with the impeachment of Richard Lyons in the Good Parliament of 1376 and know that in the next year he was pardoned. They probably have the impression that he was an unscrupulous London merchant; but much further than this they usually do not need to go. Yet there are some other aspects of his career that merit attention.

In the first place it is of interest that in an age that prized birth and family connections so much, a man of illegitimate birth and obscure ancestry should have been able to rise so high in the greatest city of the land. That he was a bastard is reiterated in various legal proceedings after his death relating to his estate.[1] Yet in April 1374 he became an alderman of the city of London and in October of the same year he was elected one of the sheriffs of the city.[2] How he had achieved this exalted position we do not know. A decade earlier he was already prominent as a vintner, for in 1365 he received a ten-year lease, for the considerable annual rent of £200, of the three taverns in London assigned for the sale of sweet wines.[3] At this stage his rise cannot have been wholly or even largely because of royal favour, for in the previous year he had been mainprised to keep the

---

1 *Calendar of Plea and Memoranda Rolls of the City of London. 1381–1412*, p. 104; *Calendar of Patent Rolls, 1381–5*, pp. 52, 164; P.R.O., C66/311.
2 *Calendar of Letter-Books of the City of London, Letter-Book G (c. 1352–1374)*, pp. 322, 327, 332. He had been made lieutenant to the admiral of the fleet by December 1371: *Calendar of Patent Rolls, 1370–4*, p. 180.
3 *Letter-Book G*, p. 199. He had been buying several houses and shops as early as 1359 (Hustings rolls 87 (33 Edward III), no. 85). The first extant record of him may be in 1353 when a Richard Lyouns of Winchelsea was accused of conspiring to rob John de Bures of a bond for £3,043 4s. 0d. due to John from another conspirator (*Rotuli Parlimentorum*, II, 263ª); but it is not certain that this is the same Richard Lyons.

peace with Alice Perrers and not to interfere with her going where she wished on the king's business and on her own.[4] A man who dared to clash with a royal favourite was hardly likely to be in receipt of royal bounty. Yet he was already in a position to acquire rural property, doubtless, as many other rising London merchants did, to advance in status. The manor of Overhall-in-Liston which he gained in 1364[5] was of especial value for this purpose, for it carried the right for its lord to make wafers for the king for his coronation feast and to serve them to him on that very symbolic occasion. After the disaster of 1376 Lyons recovered this manor and was able to exercise his right at the coronation of Richard II in 1377.[6]

By the early 1370s Lyons had soared high in the government's estimation. In December 1372 he received the farm of the petty custom and subsidy of nearly all the ports of England, a valuable grant which was renewed in December 1373 and November 1375.[7] The government did this in order to obtain loans on the security of the customs, as Edward III had done in the 1340s.[8] As had happened then, the farmer of the customs was allowed to redeem old royal debts at a discount, or on commission;[9] but there is reason to think that some at least of the accusations of great and extortionate gain, made against Lyons in the Good Parliament, were exaggerated.[10]

---

4 Cal. Plea and Mem. R., 1364–81, p. 11. In spite of this early hostility, Alice Perrers is said to have been the person chiefly responsible for the restoration of Richard Lyons to all his property in March, 1377 (Cal. Pat. R., 1374–77, pp. 439–40; Rot. Parl., III, 13).

5 Cal. Pat. R., 1361–64, p. 476. This manor was in Essex, the shire which he represented in parliament in 1380.

6 Calendar of Close Rolls, 1377–81, p. 5.

7 Calendar of Fine Rolls, 1368–77, pp. 197, 227, 316. The grant for London was lost in April 1375: (Cal. Close R., 1374–77, pp. 135–6); but by this time he was wealthy enough to be acquiring properties in London rapidly (Hustings roll 101 no. 141; roll 102, nos. 140, 196; roll 105, nos. 34, 49, 59).

8 Cf. E. B. Fryde, "The English Farmers of the Customs, 1343–51," T.R.H.S., 5th ser., IX (1959).

9 E.g., Cal. Pat. R., 1370–74, p. 411, Cal. Close R., 1374–77, p. 379. The financial repute of the government was so low that creditors preferred to take hard cash, at the cost of a heavy discount, rather than face the very doubtful possibility of repayment by the crown at some unspecified future date. For the large loans of Richard Lyons to the crown, amounting to as much as £20,000 in 1374, see Cal. Pat. R., 1370–74, pp. 319, 383, 411; Cal. Pat. R., 1374–77, pp. 5, 36, 254.

10 Cf. P.R.O., Ancient Petitions 662, 10378, 10377, and Rot. Parl., II, 374[b], for representations of Richard Lyons and his deputy William Elys in 1377 that they had been falsely accused by John Botild, William Coupere, and others of their "gang" in 1376, whereas these men had in fact been attempting to evade payment of customs and had been properly resisted by Lyons and

Nevertheless his accumulations of wealth put him in the first rank of London merchants, as the inventories of his confiscated possessions clearly show.[11] The account of the sheriffs of London, made up after March 1377, naturally relates only to his assets within the city; yet these were reckoned to amount to over £2,443, comprising over £1,925 worth of goods and chattels, £68 of debts still due to him, and revenues from lands and tenements, such as houses, shops, and taverns, totalling nearly £450.[12] He had a ship, the *Grace Dieu*, valued at £200, which was good enough to be given to Edmund, earl of Cambridge.[13] This prince did not disdain to take over quite a number of the fallen merchant's household furnishings, just as his brother, Thomas of Woodstock, was glad to have various lots of timber, freestone and ragstone, laths, and bricks, amounting to £69 in value, from Lyons' stock.[14] At the time of his arrest he had in his possession valuables such as the jewels of the duke of Brittany.[15] As a vintner he not only held stocks of wine but had debts due to him for the supply of wine amounting to £228. Like many other London merchants, he traded in more than one commodity; he held stocks of cloth worth nearly £198, iron valued at just over £649, and lead priced at nearly £103.[16] Other London merchants of the time prob-

Elys. Such representations might be discounted as a mere unjustified counterattack were it not that in each case Lyons and Elys declared themselves ready to stand by the findings of a judicial enquiry or of the king's council. As for the charge of lending at a high rate of interest to the king, the low financial credit of the crown made this almost inevitable, even if the payment of interest was still illegal and condemned by the church. Ambitious Lyons certainly was, and unscrupulous he may have been; but the evidence does not seem to justify the description of him as an "arch-thief": G. M. Trevelyan, *England in the Age of Wycliffe* (New edn., 1909), p. 11.

11 P.R.O. Sheriffs Accounts, Middlesex, E199/25/70. For some reason this inventory did not cover even all his possessions within the jurisdiction of the city, Cf. *Cal. Pat. R.*, 1374–77, pp. 298, 343. The return of the escheator of Essex for the sale of his possessions in that shire shows that his manors of Gosfield and Liston were well stocked with cattle, sheep, pigs, poultry, crops, tools, and furniture (E199/10/42).

12 E199/25/71.

13 E199/25/70; E199/25/72, document 8.

14 E199/25/70; E199/25/72, documents 11, 17, 22. He is said to have tried to save his wealth by attempting to bribe the Black Prince, and then the king, with £1,000: T. Walsingham, *Chronicon Anglie*, ed. E. M. Thompson (Rolls Series, 1870), pp. 78–79.

15 *Cal. Pat. R.*, 1374–77, pp. 296–7.

16 E199/25/70. Cf. E101/508/25 & 26, rolls of Adam de Hertyngdon and Robert de Sybthorp of the controlment of the goods of Richard Lyons, sold in London. In 1374 Lyons had been given permission to ship 200 quarters of oats from Rye to Bordeaux (*Cal. Close R.*, 1374–77, p. 10) and to bring wine back from Bordeaux.

ably had more wealth than Lyons.[17] Nevertheless his accumulation of possessions, stock, and influence was quite enough to excite an envy that may well have been sharpened by the reflection that he had begun life as a bastard of obscure parentage.

Secondly, it is remarkable how quickly Lyons recovered in wealth, and in social position, after the onslaught of the commons in 1376. It is true that the hostility of the leading merchants of London prevented him from securing reinstatement as an alderman.[18] John of Gaunt might wish to undo the work of the Good Parliament; but some circumspection was needed, especially in view of the opposition of the Londoners, and there could be no question of restoring Lyons to his former role as a favoured farmer of customs and a principal lender to the crown.[19] Yet by 1379, when a war loan was raised and paid to William Walworth and John Philpot, the special war treasurers, Lyons contributed £40, which was more than most of the lenders did.[20] He served as knight of the shire for Essex in the parliament that met in January 1380;[21] but he may have found that service of this kind interfered too much with business, for before the parliament ended he had obtained an exemption for life from being put on assizes, juries, etc., and from being made sheriff, escheator, coroner, justice of the peace, or collector of taxes, against his will.[22] However this may be, it is certain that by the time he was murdered by the rebels in Cheapside, London, on 14 June 1381,[23] he had built up a complex of property, both in the capital and in the countryside, much greater than he had enjoyed in 1376.[24] It is true that the inquisitions taken after his death were able to produce very little as having been held by him as tenant-in-chief. The sheriff and escheator of Essex

17 Cf. S. Thrupp, The Merchant Class of Medieval London (Chicago, 1948), chap. 3, pp. 103 ff.
18 He was deprived of the dignity on 1 August 1376: Letter-Book H, c. 1375–1399, p. 38.
19 In spite of his restitution at law to his goods and lands: Rot. Parl., II, 374.
20 Cal. Pat. R., 1377–81, p. 636.
21 Cal. Close R., 1377–81, p. 356.
22 Cal. Pat. R., 1377–81, p. 446.
23 Memorials of London and London Life, 1276–1419, ed. H. T. Riley (London, 1868), pp. 449–51, from Letter-Book H, f. cxxxiii; Cf. Letter-Book F, p. 289.
24 We catch glimpses of his accumulation of rural property in the references to robbery from his groom near Chelmsford in Essex of two horses with their harness and from his manor of Great Delse in Kent of 26 sheep (Cal. Pat. R., 1377–81, 499, 483). We see something of his acquisitions of property in London from entries on the Hustings Rolls between his pardon in 1377 and his death in 1381 (Hustings roll 105, nos. 59, 60, 61; roll 106, no. 27; roll 108, nos. 115, 125).

and Hertford could report only the manor and advowson of Over-hall-in-Liston, where the rebels under John Wrawe had recently wrecked the house;[25] and William Walworth, mayor and escheator of London, knew of only one messuage and wharf in London.[26] But, as we have seen, to be tenant of Overhall was a specially honourable position; and the messuage in Dovegate ward had been kept in the tenancy of Lyons for some special reason that is not clear. Almost all his other property had been conveyed to feoffees to uses, as William Walworth explained. Some of the London properties had been so conveyed as early as 21 May 1377. This had evidently been done without permission from the crown and Richard's executors paid 2,000 marks for a royal confirmation of the transaction. From this pardon and confirmation it appears that at the time of his death Lyons had held thirty messuages, a toft, sixty shops, twelve cellars, and six gardens in London and its suburbs on the north bank of the Thames; two shops and seven gardens in Southwark; the manor of Great Delse in Kent; the manors of Gosfield and Netherhall-in-Liston in Essex; and other parcels of arable land, meadow, pasture, and woodland in Kent and Essex.[27] Richard is said to have died without heirs,[28] and it therefore seems likely that at least part of his property would have been devoted to charitable purposes, including a chantry foundation for his soul. Of this we have no record, though Stow tells us that in Elizabeth's reign there was still in the church of St. James, Garlickhithe, London, a fine tomb of Richard Lyons, with an impressive effigy of the merchant.[29] It is also clear that with such a considerable estate available, the lady who considered herself to be his widow was determined to have her share. The executors held that Richard had obtained a divorce from her as long ago as 1363. They produced what might have appeared to be a trump card in the shape of a certificate from the bishop of London to the effect that the marriage between Richard Lyons and Isabella Pledour had been quashed and annulled. But Isabella held that the marriage had continued until Richard's death, and that he had left goods and chattels

25 P.R.O., C136/19/33, documents 2 and 5; E. Powell, *The Rising in East Anglia* (Cambridge, 1896), pp. 9, 10.
26 P.R.O., C136/19/33, document 10. This messuage and the manor of Over-hall escheated to the crown because Lyons died without heirs. *Cal. Pat. R.*, 1381–85, pp. 68, 164.
27 *Cal. Pat. R.*, 1381–85, p. 52.
28 C136/19/33, documents 2, 3, 5, 7, 10.
29 *The Survey of London*, by John Stow, ed. C. L. Kingsford (Oxford, 1908), I, 249.

in the parish of St. James, Garlickhithe of the value of 3,000 marks, to half of which she was entitled by the custom of the city. When the case was renewed in the Guildhall two and a half years later, in June 1391, her claim had risen to 5,000 marks, a considerable fortune for the time and more than the total assets for which the sheriffs of London had accounted in 1376–77. She now pleaded that she had appealed against the divorce and that the bishop's commissary had confirmed the marriage. The executors would not accept this and took their stand on the bishop's recent certificate. At last, in 1394, Isabella lost hope and renounced all claims to Lyons's property; but the case confirms the impression that Lyons left a large estate, well worth a prolonged law suit.[30]

Finally, the inventory of the goods of Richard Lyons, drawn up by the sheriffs of London at the time of the seizure of his property in the summer of 1376, is of unusual interest. This is not because it is the only inventory of the period. There are a number of extant inventories of fourteenth-century London merchants, and some are more detailed than this.[31] But this appears to be the first inventory of a London merchant's house which lists the contents room by room in such detail.[32] It is doubtful whether the house of Richard Lyons gives "the earliest indication of any concern for privacy."[33] We have a brief description from 1349 of the house of the vintner Henry Vanner, who was later to be one of the executors of Richard Lyons. His house in Royal Street in the parish of St. Michael Paternoster, in the Vintry ward, had a hall built above a stone wall, with three chambers, a kitchen, and a store room, with a stone chamber below the hall, a shop to the south of it, and a cellar adjacent to (probably behind) the shop.[34] Even earlier, in 1327, another vintner left his wife two adjacent houses, one of which had a parlour and chamber as well as the hall, and the other had a parlour, bedchamber, and a kitchen with a chamber next to it, in addition to the hall.[35] But none of these earlier references describes the contents of the rooms. The inventory of the possessions of Richard Lyons not only does this

30 *Cal. Plea and Mem. R.*, *1381–1412*, pp. 151, 184; Hustings roll 122, no. 97.
31 The inventory of the possessions of Sir John Pulteney, taken between 1349 and 1351, is much bulkier and records not only the goods and chattels in his London houses but provides a detailed valuation of the stock on his nineteen manors: P.R.O., E101/508/12.
32 E199/25/70. His house eventually passed to the abbey of St. Albans in 1456: Stow, *Survey of London*, I, p. 234.
33 Thrupp, *The Merchant Class*, p. 134.
34 London Guildhall Record Office; Hustings roll 77, item 66.
35 Hustings roll 56, item 55.

but lists the contents of his drapery shop and the furnishings of the three taverns which he controlled – a very rare kind of record. A transcript of the inventory is therefore printed below.

This inventory is one of a series of documents resulting from the confiscations. First the chamberlains of the receipt of the exchequer had an inventory made of Lyons's household possessions and stock-in-trade, by the oversight of fifteen London merchants – six drapers, three pelterers, two mercers, four upholsterers, two armourers, and two joiners (P.R.O., Exchequer K.R., various accounts, E101/509/26). Then this inventory was reshuffled into a more coherent order and a few details of where some of the goods had been found were omitted (E101/509/25). The third inventory, printed here, follows closely the arrangement of the second inventory, but adds some information, such as a list of the contents of the "counter" of Richard Lyons, and provides notes on the disposal of the possessions, whether by sale, by gift, or by return to him. The sheriffs of London, who drew up this third inventory, also produced an account for the £2,443 5s. 8¾d., which they reported as the total value of Lyons's goods and chattels (E199/25/71). They also returned to the Exchequer a sheaf of twenty-seven documents which included writs from the king for the sale of the property, receipts for payments and deliveries of property and, finally, the king's pardon and order of restitution of Richard's remaining goods, an order dated 20 March 1377 (E199/25/72).

The Inventory of the Goods of Richard Lyons, 50 Edward III (1376)
(P.R.O., Sheriff's Account, Middlesex. E199/25/70)

Fait a remembre qe ceux sont les parcelles des biens qe furont a Richard Lyouns trouez en la Citee de Loundres queux John Hadle et William Neuport, nadgairs Viscountz de la dite Citee de Loundres aresteront et furont venduz par comandement de brief par le surviu et countrerollement de le Tresourer et Chaumberleyns de leschequer.

LA SALE

Vendita
In primis 1 doser, 2 costers, 3 banquers[36] oue 6 cossyns
staynt dun suyte usez, pris 20s.

36 doser = seat-back cover; coster = wall-hanging; banquer = bench-cover.

Liberata Comiti Cantebrigg'
Item 2 tables, 2 peir tristels oue 1 fourme, 1 launcet[37]
vsez, pris 13s. 4d.
Vendita
Item, 1 tabeler oue le meisne pur iuer[38] vsez, pris 6d.
Liberata Comiti Cantebrigg'
Item 1 chaundeleur pendant oue 5 chaundeleurs petitz[39]
et 1 coppeborde[40] 21s. 4d.
Item 1 lauour de plumb',[41] pris 10s.
Summa, vendita 20s. 6d.
Summa liberata Comiti Cantebrigg' 44s. 8d.
Summa £3. 5s. 2d.

PARLOUR

Vendita
Item 2 banquers oue 6 cossyns vsez, pris 2s.
Liberata Comiti Cantebrigg'
Item 1 table, 2 pair tristels, 3 formes, et
1 coppeborde, pris 8s. 8d.
Summa, vendita patet
Summa liberate predicto Comiti patet
Summa 10s. 8d.

LA CHAMBRE PRINCIPALE

Vendita
Item 1 lit pale de rouge say[42] et blank, cestassavoir
1 coverlit, 1 tester, 1 celour, 3 redelles,[43] 5 costers,
oue 2 bankers et 12 cussines dun suyte vsez et feblez,
pris 33s. 4d.
Item 1 federbed de Flaundre oue 1 bolster vsez,
pris 20s.

---

37 launcet = settle, called "cheier longe" in E101/509/26; the earl of Cambridge to whom this was given was Edward III's fifth son, later duke of
   York.
38 probably a small table for playing dice.
39 E101/509/25 here records "1 screne," and E101/509/26 lists separately
   "1 spere" (screen).
40 sideboard.   41 leaden wash-bowl.
42 thin woollen stuff or serge.   43 curtains.

Item 1 coffre auncien, pris 6s. 8d.
Liberata Comiti Cantebrigg'
Item 1 coppeborde, 1 launcet, 1 table, 1 fourme,
1 quek,[44] 2 aundernes,[45] pris 13s. 4d.
Item, diuerses mappes[46] de Flaundre ordeignez pur
4 chaumbres vsez, pris en grosse 40s.
Summa, vendita 60s.
Summa, liberata Comiti Cantebrigg' 53s. 4d.
Summa 113s. 4d.

LA SECONDE CHAUMBRE

Vendita
Item 1 lit pale rouge de say et bleu, cestassauoir
1 coverlit, 1 tester, 2 curteyns, 2 costers, 1 celure,
oue 12 cussins de mesme la suyte, vsez et feblez,
pris 26s. 8d.
Item 1 quilt blank pur le dit lit, 1 quilt de
silk feble rouge, pris 10s.
Item 3 lintheux[47] aunciens et 2 pilous, pris 6s. 8d.
Item 1 federbed oue 1 bolster de Flaundre vsez,
pris 15s.
Item 1 couuerte pur 1 lit de pealx de lipard
vsez, pris 20s.
Item 3 cussins de sengle camaca[48] bleu auncien et
feble, pris 10s.
Summa £4 8s. 4d.

LA TIERCE CHAMBRE[49]

Vendita
Item 1 lit rouge de say feble, cestassauoir
1 coverlit, 1 tester, oue 1 redell de bolter,[50]
1 banquer de soy, dun suyte vsez, pris 13s. 4d.

---

44 counting-frame. E101/509/26 has "j cheker pur le queke" and lists also
"1 schrene."
45 fire-dogs.   46 cloths.
47 linen sheets.   48 sengle camaca: unlined silk.
49 E101/509/26 describes this room as "la chambre iuxst la gardyn, poudre de
Lyons" and "la seconde chambre" as "la chambre iuxt la chapelle."
50 coarse reddish-brown cloth.

Item 1 materas de bleu carde[51] vsez, pris 6s. 8d.
Item 1 blank materas auncien feble, pris 3s. 4d.
Item 1 peir de lyntheux feble, pris 1s. od.
Liberata Comiti Cantebrigg'
Item 2 bord, 1 peir de tristels, 1 stole,
1 launcet, pris 13s. 4d.
Vendita, non in contrarotulo
Item 1 cheste auncien et feble, oue 1 firpreik,[52]
pris 4s.
Summa, vendita 24s. 4d.
Summa, liberata predicto Comiti, patet
Summa 41s. 8d.

LA CHAPEL

Vendita
Item 4 ridelles, 1 doser de vert taffata ray,
1 drap' pend' de mesme, et 3 autreclothes, oue
1 vestment de bustian[53] auncien et feble, pris de
tout 20s.
Item 1 table nouel peynte dor de Flandre, pris 20s.
Item 1 portos[54] auncien et feble, pris 20s.
Summa 60s.

LA GARDEROBE

*Liberata predicto Ricardo Lyons per litteram de privato sigillo
datam vj^{to} die Augusti anno L° vnde summa £49 7s. 10d.*
En primes 1 slop'[55] de drap' vert partie de ray furr'
de fuyns vsez,[56] pris 16s.
Item 1 slop' rosset furr' de fuyns vsez, pris 20s.
Item 1 slop' de rouge drap' furr de fuyns vsez, pris 13s. 4d.
Item 1 slop' de scarlet, 20s.
Item 1 slop' partie de ray et de rouge furr des agnell'
blank, pris 8s.

51 an inferior silk.
52 poker. E101/509/25 has "firepike."
53 coarse cloth.
54 portable breviary.
55 E101/509/26 usually has "gown" where this inventory has "slop."
56 striped fur of used marten.

Item 1 slop' partie de vert medle ray furr' de agnell'
blank, pris 6s. 8d.
Item 1 slop' partie de rouge et medle furr' dagnell'
blank vsez, pris 2s.
Item 3 doublettes de rouge poniez vsez, pris 9s.
Item 1 doublet de stayne[57] bleu feble, pris 2s. 6d.
Item 1 doublet partie vsez, pris 2s.
Item, 1 partie cote punye vsez, pris 4s.
Item 32 chaperons pris de chescun 12d., amounte 32s.
Item 7 peir de chauces rouges vsez et 1 peir de
vert pris 8s.
Item 2 gounes de russet lyne de blank drap, pris 11s.
Item 1 autre partie oue blue vsez, pris 5s.
Item 2 singles sloppes parties vsez, pris 8s.
Item 1 slop' de russet faldyng furr de beure,[58] pris 26s. 8d.
Item 1 slop' de camaca furr de gray gris,[59] pris 36s. 8d.
Item 1 slop' furr de boge[60] vsez, pris 4s.
Item 1 clothe partie de vert ray furr de gray, pris 5 marks
Item 1 clothe partie de rouge et ray furr de gray 6 marks
Item 1 autre clothe partie de rouge et ray vert
furr oue gray, pris 5 marks
Item 1 clothe partie de bleu et ray furr oue
crispegray, pris 40s.
Item 1 clothe partie de tauny et ray furr de
calabr',[61] pris 40s.
Item 2 sloppes de baudekyn[62] de silk furr de calabr',
pris 40s.
Item 1 clothe de tauny lyne oue vert, pris 13s. 4d.
Item 1 clothe partie de vert et de rouge lyne de
taffata, pris 10s.
Item 1 clothe sengle partie de plonket,[63] pris 6s. 8d.
Item 1 clothe de velvet noir vsez, pris 20s.
Item 1 sengle cloche de bleu vsez, pris 6s. 8d.
Item 1 mantel rouge vsez, pris 3s. 4d.
Item 7 sloppes lynes de taffata, cestassauoir
2 rouges, 3 vertz, et 2 partie vsez, pris 46s. 8d.

57 E101/26 has "satyn bleu."
58 beaver.
59 miniver.
60 high-grade lamb-skin.
61 a kind of foreign squirrel.
62 brocade.
63 a kind of cloth and also a shade of blue-grey.

Item 1 slop' partie rouge et ray furr de gray
vsez, pris 20s.
Item 1 slop' partie de blank et ray single
vsez, pris 4s.
Item 1 clothe sangwyn lyne oue rouge pris 13s. 4d.
Item 1 slop' de camaka oue 20 belles dargent
pris 20s.
Item 1 slop' partie de medle et ray furr de
calabr', pris 13s. 4d.
Item 1 slop' partie de bleu furr de calabr'
vsez, pris 10s.
Item 1 goune court de scarlet, pris 5s.
Item 2 sloppes 1 clothe de vert single, pris 13s. 4d.
Item 1 goune de bokesyn[64] blank oue 1 roket et
1 peir de chauz[65] blank pris 6s. 8d.
Item 1 slop' de camelet rouge vsez, pris 4s.
Item 4 jakk' de guerre cestassauoir 3 de silk
et camaca, 1 autre de fustayn, pris £6 13s. 4d.
Item 1 lit de vert tartarin[66] ray de 2 pieces, pris 26s. 8d.
Item 1 capel de beure, pris 3s. 4d.

Vendita

Item 15 pilous, 5 de blu camaca 4 de vert
camaca et 6 blanc, pris 15s.
Item 1 furr blank dagnell' pris 1s.
Item 8 cotes de bokeram et westenale
ordeignez pur releu',[67] pris 3s. 4d.
Item certeins remenantz de bokeram et carde,
pris 10s.
Item 13 cotes de bokeram de westenale ordeignez
pur releu', pris 8s.
Item 1 doser 1 banquer de drap'daras, pris 5 marks
Item 1 coverlit 1 tester 3 costers 3 banquers
7 cussins de drap daras, pris 5 marks
Item 1 lit rouge enbroude couerlit et tester, pris 13s. 4d.
Item 1 sarpell pur 1 chapel, pris 3s. 4d.
Item 1 auncien quilt, pris 1s.

64 bocasine (a thin fabric).
65 stockings.
66 rich silk fabric.
67 Both E101/509/25 and 26 have "reveler" "for the watch," here and below.
which seems to make more sense.

Item 1 clotheseke et 2 males[68] oue 2 bosages,[69] pris 3s. 4d.

Summa, vendita £9 11s. 8d.

Summa £58 19s. 6d.

NAPARIE[70]

Vendita

Item 8 pieces de towells de Denant[71] cont' 82 knottes
nouelles, pris 26s. 8d.

Item 3 pec' de drap' lyne cont' 7 douzaine et
9 aunez,[72] pris le alne 9d.   69s. 9d.

Item de nap' de Paris cont' 48 aunez, pris le aln' 5d.   20s.

Item 1 autre nap' de Paris feble, pris 2s.

Item 7 peces de towells vsez cont' 18 aunez et
demi 2 aunez, acompte pur 1, pris lalne 6d.   9s. 3d.

Item 3 peces de towells de denant nouelles cont'
12 aunez doubles, pris lalne 8d.   8s.

Item 3 peces de sanap'[73] vsez cont' 7 aunez doubles
et demi, pris le alne 4d.   2s. 6d.

Item 13 peir de lintheux, pris le peir 4s.   52s.

Item 1 pece de drap' pur le sanenap' pris 8d.

Item 1 pauilon pur 1 bathfatte,[74] pris 4s.

Item 1 cotarmur, pris 3s. 4d.

Item 60 peces feblez de diuerse naparie, pris 20s.

Item 2 chestes, 1 almory oue presse,[75] pris 10s.

Summa £11 8s. 2d.

LA PETIT GARDEROBE[76]

Item 6 bacenettes saunz aventailles vsez, pris 20s.

Item 3 pair de legharnoys vsez 30s.

Item 2 pair de legharnoys plufeblez, pris 6s. 8d.

---

68 trunks.
69 bags.
70 E101/509/26 here notes: "En un cofre iuxst la capelle en la ale."
71 towels of fine material.
72 ells.
73 surnape, strip of cloth to protect table-cloth.
74 tent for a bath-tub.
75 E101/509/26 has: "l'almarye, 2 chestes, ove 1 presse en 1 faus chambre devers la cosine pres la gardyn."
76 E101/509/26 describes these goods as kept "En la chambre en la ale."

Item 1 peir de vaimbras et 1 peir de splentes
feble, pris 1s.
Item 6 arblastes vsez, pris 26s. 8d.
Item 1 basenet oue aventaille et healme vsez,
pris 22s.
Item 1 hache vsez, pris 3s. 4d.
Item 1 espee les gayn[77] et ceynture garnise
dargent endorre pris 4 marks
Item 1 peir de plates couerez de rouge velvet,
pris 20s.
Item 1 pauad garnise dargent vsez, pris 13s. 4d.
Item 10 cestes pur claues[78] de guerre vsez, pris 1s. 10d.
Item 1 coppegorge auncien, pris 3s. 4d.
Item 1 bedewe garnise dargent 3s. 4d.
Item 1 dagger garnise dargent, pris 2s.
Item 2 peir de gauntes de plate, 2 peir vaimbras,
2 peir rerebras, 2 pair de sabatons,
1 bristplate vsez, pris 13s. 4d.
Item 1 haubergeon vsez, pris 10s.
Item 1 peir de paunces, 2 peir brace, et
2 aventailles febles, pris 12s.
Item 10 hastes de launces pris 8s. 4d.
Item 1 clothsak et 1 quek vsez pris 1s. 8d.
Item 2 peir prasses pris 3s. 4d.
Item 2 blankettes vsez pris 8d.
Item 1 reuers[79] or oue demi aune de baudekyn de
say, pris 20s.
Item 30 aunces de drap' de reyns[80] en un pece,
pris le alne 2s.   60s.
Item 30 auncez de drap' de reynes, pris lalne 10d.   25s.
Item 1 petit barell de file cont' 32 lb., pris le lb. 7d.   18s. 8d.
Item demi C azure de liys, pris 3s. 4d.
Item 2 colers pur vn chene, pris 4d.
Item 1 peir de balaunce, pris 6d.
Item 1 drap' dor, pris 60s.
Item 6 auncez de drap' de lyne raw de Flaundres,
pris 3s.
Item 1 bere pur 1 bolster, pris 3s. 4d.

---

77 sheath.   78 horseshoes.   79 collar.
80 Rennes, noted for fine linen cloth.

Item 2 graundes beres pur 1 lit, pris 20s.
Item 1 pauncher de silk, pris 3s. 4d.
Item 1 cappe furr de gray, pris 1s. 8d.
Item 3 coffres aunciens, pris 13s. 4d.
Item 6 coffyns de Flaundre 1s. 6d.
Item 6 mazers, pris 13s. 4d.
Item 1 grepeshey et 2 cokyls,[81] pris 7s.
Item 6 lb. de gingibrede, pris 6s.
Item 4 lb. de maces, pris 18s.
Item 4 lb. de grayn de Paris,[82] pris 8s. 8d.
Item quibibis,[83] pris 10s.
Item reyn de canell,[84] pris 6s.
Item 48 lb. de peper, pris 48s.
Item figges de raycyns,[85] pris 6s. 8d.
Item 10 poyntes, pris 1s. 8d.
Item 1 riban et 1 burse, pris 1s. 8d.
Item 2 boteners dargent, pris 10d.
Item garnettes pur 1 frountel, pris 1s. od.
Item 1 peir de gauntes furr, pris 2s. 6d.
Item 5 telles[86] de worsted de diuerses colours, pris le pice 4s.   20s.
Summa £32 11s. 4d.
Gerard Clokmaker
Item 1 clok, pris[87] 20s.
Item 1 graunt merure, pris 2s. 6d.
Vendita
Item 3 arblastez, pris 20s.
Item 1 coffyn oue viritons,[88] 1 bauderik, et
1 poleyne,[89] pris 3s. 4d.
Summa 45s. 10d.
Remenants de drap esteant en la Garderobe
Item 1 pece de motteley cont' 12 verges,[90] pris £6 os. od.
Item 4 peces de scarlet cont' 10 verges et 1 quart,
pris la verge 8s.   £4 2s. od.

81 spoons.
82 grain of paradise (spice).
83 pepper.
84 fine cinnamon.
85 E101/508/25 has "fyges et raycyns."
86 lengths, rolls.
87 This and the following three items are described in E101/509/26 as "En la chambre sur la porche."
88 arrows (presumably for the three crossbows of the previous item).
89 steel knee-cap. Described as "colt" in E101/509/25.
90 yards.

Item 6 verges et demi de rouge eyreyne,[91] pris la
verge 5s.   32s. 6d.
Item 12 verges de blanket, pris 22s. od.
Item 12 verges de blanket, pris 20s. od.
Item 2 courtz draps de bleu, pris de chescun 24s.   48s. od.
Item 3 draps cont' 24 alnes de drap' medle, pris de
chescun drap 32s.   £4 16s. od.
Item 21 alnes de mesme le drap' en 9 peces, pris de
chescun verge 15d.   26s. 3d.
Item 1 pece de medle cont' 13 verges et demi, pris
la verges et demi, pris la verges 16d.   18s.
Item 1 pece de bleu medle cont' 11 verges et demi,
pris la verge 18d.   17s. 3d.
Item 2 peces de marbryn[92] medle cont' 4 verges, pris
la verge 16d.   5s. 4d.
Item 1 remenant de blu cont' 1 verge et demi, pris
la verge 20d.   2s. 6d.
Item 2 verges 1 quart drap', pris la verge 12d.   2s. 3d.
Item 1 remenant de blu cont' 1 verge, pris 2s. 6d.
Item 1 demi verge de bleu, pris 15d.
Item 2 verges de poire medle, pris la verge 16d.   2s. 8d.
Item 1 verge et 3 quarts de marbryn medle, pris la
verge 15d.   2s. 2¼d.
Item 3 quarts de medle vert, pris 2s.
Item 1 quart et demi de russet blank, pris 8d.
Item 1 verge de bleu, pris 3s. 4d.
Item 1 petit remenant de plonket, pris 4d.
Item 1 drap' de ray, dount le chaump' russet cont'
23 verges, pris la verge 10d.   19s. 2d.
Item 2 verges et demi de ray, dount le chaump' murre,
pris la verge 2s.   5s.
Item 1 pece de ray murre cont' 8 verges et demi,
pris la verge 16d.   11s. 4d.
Item 2 peces de ray murre cont' 5 verges, pris la
verge 18d.   7s. 6d.
Item 1 verge 3 quarts de ray sangwyn, pris la verge 2s.   3s. 6d.
Item 1 verge et 3 quarts de ray, dount le chaump'

91 copper-red.
92 cloth of parti-coloured worsted, resembling veins of marble, whence the
name.

bukhorn,[93] pris la verge 2s.   3s. 6d.
Item 1 remenant de ray cont' 1 quarter et demi, pris 12d.
Item 1 remenant de medle vert et de ray, pris 8d.
Item 1 verge et 3 quarters de ray, dount le chaump'
bleu, pris la verge 2s.   3s. 6d.
Item 1 remenant de russet cont' 1 verge, pris 1s. 8d.
Summa £28 3s. 10¼d.

CHAPMAN CHAUMBRE

Vendita
Item 1 testour, 1 coverlit, 2 costers darras, pris 4 marks
Item 1 lyt, 1 coverlit, 1 testour rouge broude avec
lyouns, pris 6s. 8d.
Item 1 lit, 1 testour de rouge broude de wodewoses,
pris 5s.
Item 2 federbeddes, 2 bolsters, 1 pilou, 1 pair de
lintheux, prix 20s.
Item 1 coverlit de blank worsted poudr' de ermyn, pris 5s.
Quia supra[94]
Item beddes de bord pur 12 litz, pris [*sic*] 6s.
Summa £4 16 0d.

1 AUTRE CHAUMBRE PUR AUTRES[95]

Vendita
Item 1 coverlit, 1 testour de worsted blu enbroude de
lyouns, pris 3s. 4d.
Item 1 de double worsted, pris 3s.
Item 1 federbed, 1 bolster oue 1 pilou, pris 6s. 8d.
Summa 13s.

PANETRIE ET BOTELLERIE

Vendita
Item 3 masers petitz oue bendes dargent garniz dor, pris 10s.
Item 14 chaundelers de laton, pris chescun 6d.   7s.
Item 4 torches, 5 tortises, 5 priketes, 9 stompes de

93 buckram.
94 In spite of this note this item was not entered earlier, and in E101/509/26
it appears in the next section.
95 E101/509/26 describes this as "la middel chambre."

torch, et 8 chaundelers et autre cire auncien bruse[96]
poisant 1 centene 1 quarter oue 14 lb., pris. lb. 4d.   51s. 4d.
Item 1 galounpotte, 1 potel, 2 quarts, 5 salers de
peautre, pris 3s.
Item 2 cultelles oue 1 gayne pur la table, pris 8d.
Liberata Comiti Cantebrigg'
Item 1 garn' pur payn, pris 6s. 8d.
Vendita
Item 40 lb. de auncien peautre, pris lb. 2d.   6s. 8d.
Summa, vendita 78s. 4d.
Summa, liberata Comiti Cantebrigg' 6s. 8d.
Summa, £4 5s. 4d.

LA CUSYNE

Liberata Comiti Cantebrigg'
Item 8 spites, 3 tryuettes, 1 gerdern,[97] 2 aundernes,
2 fryyngpannes, 2 rackes, 2 greespannes, 2 dressyngknyfs,
1 autre cultel, 3 petitz copardes,[98] 1 fleshoke de fer,[99]
2 pestels de fer poisantz 4 centaines et demi,
et 24 lb. pris le centaine, 8s.   38s.
Item 8 pottes darrein, 1 chaufour, 1 possenet saunz,[100]
poisantz 2 centaines, 34 lbs., pris lb. 1½d.   32s. 3d.
Item 6 payles darrein, poysantz demi centaine et 24 lb., pris la
lb. 1½d.   10s.
Vendita
Item 3 morters darrein poysantz 3½ centenes 4 lb.,
pris lb. 1½d.   49s. 6d.
Summa liberata Comiti Cantebrigg' £4 0s. 3d.
Summa £6 9s. 9d.

LARDER

Vendita
Item 1 barell de meel.[101] pris 16s.

96 E101/509/25 and 26 both have "brise."
97 E101/509/25 has "gryderne": gridiron.
98 The words "2 standardes de fer pur 1 fenestre" are here crossed out: they
remain uncancelled in E101/509/25 and 26.
99 The words "1 chymeney de fer" are here crossed out; they remain uncancelled in E101/509/25 and 26.
100 "1 sound small basin"; then comes the cancelled phrase "et 1 potte
rompuz." "Darrein" means "of brass."
101 honey.

Item par estimacion 3 quarters de seel, pris 10s.
Item 1 pipa de vynegre oue 2 remenantz de vynegre et
de verguis, pris 20s.
Item 1 bale dalmoundes de gardeyn, poisantz 2½ centimes,
pris C 20s.   50s.
Item 99 lb. de chaundell' de parys, pris la lb. 1½d.   12s. 4½d.
Liberata Comiti Cantebrigg'
Item 1 remenant de blak sope, poisant 80 lb., ¾d. (un lb.)   5s.
Item 8 tobbes, pris 4s.
Vendita
Item 1 peir de balaunce 1s.
Summa, vendita 114s. 4½d.
Summa, liberata Comiti Cantebrigg' 4s.
Summa 118s. 4½d.
Liberata Ricardo Lyons
Item divers cotes et sloppes liveres a dit Richard, pris £6 13s. 4d.
Item 3 quarters de furment[102] par estimacion, pris 20s.
Vendita
Item del encres de choses vendues a John Colshull £40
Item 13 panys rouges, pris 13s. 4d.
Summa liberata Ricardo Lyons patet
Summa vendita £41 13s. 4d.

DEBITA[103]

Liberata Ricardo Lyons
Item Thomas Cornealeys 2 tones faut de gauge 2 cesters,
pris le ton £7. Summa clara £12 15s. 4d.
Item Henry Vanner 2 tones faut 4 cesters. Summa clera £13 10s. 8d.
Item Galfridus Newenton 2 tones faut 9 cesters demi.
Summa clera £12 17s. 10d.
Item William More 2 tones faut 4 cesters. Summa clera £13 10s. 8d.
Item Richard Blake 2 tones faut 5 cesters demi. Summa £13 7s. 2d.
Item John Edrop' 2 tones faut 5 cesters. Summa clera £13 8s. 4d.
Item Richard Longe 2 tones faut 2 cesters demi.
Summa clera £13 13s. 2d.
Item John Willyngham 2 tones faut 5 cesters. Summa £13 8s. 4d.

102 Both E101/509/25 and 26 note that the 3 quarters of wheat and 13 red
cloths (below) were in "La Garner."
103 E101/509/28 records "Item en un celer en la Vintery trouez, 34 tonnes de
vin vendue as diverses marchantez par attornez Richard Lyons. £228-9-
10d."

Item Thomas Heyward 2 tones faut 4 cesters demi. Summa £13 9s. 6d.
Item Thomas Kyrton 2 tones faut 2 cesters demi. Summa £13 14s. 2d.
Item John Andreu 2 tones faut 9 cesters demi. Summa £12 17s. 10d.
Item Richard Paris 2 tones faut 7 cesters. Summa £13 3s. 8d.
Item Richard Heydok 2 tones faut 5 cesters. Summa £13 8s. 4d.
Item Walterus Lynet 2 tones faut 7 cesters. Summa £13 3s. 8d.
Item Geffrey Chauntflour 2 tones faut cester demi. Summa
£13 14s. 2d.
Item Roger Wilford 1 ton 1 pipe faut del ton 1 cester £10 7s. 8d.
Item Dame Agnets Fraunceis et le Recordour 1 ton 1 pipe
faut 4 cesters £10 0s. 8d.
Item le tresourer 1 pipe pleyn gauge, pris 70s.
Item William Sharpyng 1 pipe faut 1 cester. Summa 77s. 8d.
Summa £228 9s. 10d.

LA STABLE

Vendita
Item 5 selles dount 2 sommers, 2 malesadels, et 1 sele
pur 1 hakenay, pris 8s. 4d.
Liberata Comiti Cantebrigg'
Item 1 bynne pur provendre, pris 3s. 4d.
Item 1 porcion de fuell,[104] pris 20s.
Summa vendita 28s. 4d.
Summa liberata Comiti Cantebrigg' 3s. 4d.
Summa 31s. 4d.

DRAPERIE[105]

Item 1 pice de drap' ray oue le chaump' bleu cont'
22 verges de ray, pris la verge 2s. 8d.   58s. 8d.
Item 1 drap' de chaump mene blu ray, pris 66s. 8d.
Item 1 drap' ray chaump' murre, pris 66s. 8d.
Item 1 drap' ray chaump' blu, pris 66s. 8d.
Item 1 pice de drap' ray le chaump' murre cont' 21
verges, pris la verge 2s. 4d.   49s.
Item 20 verges de ray en 2 peces, dount le chaump' plonket,
pris la verge 16d.   26s. 8d.

104 In E101/509/26 this item is given as "1 porcion de talwode" and is said to
be in the "wodehous."
105 In E101/509/26 this section is described in the left margin as "En la schope
en Taimstrete."

Item 3 verges de ray dount le chaump' est vert, pris la
verge 3s. 4d. 10s.

Item 6 verges de ray dount le chaump' bleu, pris la verge 2s. 6d. 15s.

Item 1 drap' noir cont' 30 verges, pris la verge 4s. 6d £6 15s.

Item 1 pice de drap' rouge cont' 22 verges demi, pris la
verge 3s. 4d. 75s.

Item 1 pice de murre medle cont' 19 verges, pris la verge 3s. 4d. 75s.

Item 1 pice de taune medle cont' 19 verges, pris la verge 3s. 6d.
66s. 6d.

Item 1 pice de sangwyn demi greyn cont' 11 verges demi,
pris la verge 5s. 6d. £3 3s. 3d.

Item 1 pice de drap' noir cont' 28 verges, pris la verge 3s. 4d.
£4 13s. 4d.

Item 1 pice de rouge cont' 3 verges et demi pris la verge 4s. 14s.

Item 1 pice de rouge cont 1 verge 3 quarters pris la verge 7s. 12s. 3d.

Item 1 pice de sandryn medle cont 1 verge, pris 2s. 6d. 2s. 6d.

Item 1 pice de tauny medle cont' 28 verges, pris la verge 3s. 6d
£4 18s.

Item 1 pice de russet noir cont' 7 verges demi, pris la verge 2s. 8d.
20s.

Item 1 pice de grene bukhorn cont' 12 verges, pris la verge 3s. 4d.
40s.

Item 1 pice de drap' de noir cont' 20 verges, pris la verge 2s. 8d.
53s. 4d.

Item 1 pice de rouge cont' 10 verges, pris la verge 2s. 8d. 26s. 8d.

Item 1 pice de noir drap' cont' 7 verges, pris la verge 4s. 8d. 32s. 8d.

Item 1 pice de bleu cont' 10 verges et demi, pris la verge 3s. 4d. 35s.

Item 4 verges de noir, pris la verge 4s. 16s.

Item 1 pice de vert cont' 6 verges 3 quarters, pris la verge 3s. 4d.
22s. 6d.

Item 1 autre pice de vert cont' 9 verges et 1 quarter, pris la
verge 3s. 4d. 30s. 10d.

Item 1 pice de blanket cont' 2 verges 3 quarters, pris la verge 2s. 4d.
6s. 5d.

Item 1 pice de plonket cont' 16 verges, pris la verge 3s. 8d. 58s. 8d.

Item 1 pice de broune tawny cont' 25 verges, pris la verge 3s. 4d.
£4 3s. 4d.

Item 1 pice de russet cont' 12 verges, pris 2s. 2d. 26s.

Item 1 douzaine de blue medle, pris 16s.

Item 2 pices de drap' violet cont' 12 verges, pris la verge 6s. 72s.

Item 3 verges de rouge drap', pris la verge 4s. 12s.

Item 3 verges de plonket, pris la verge 3s. 8d.   11s.
Item 8 verges et demi de plonket, pris la verge 15d.   10s. 7½d.
Item 1 verge de noir drap', pris 2s. 6d.
Item 1 drap' long de brounetaune cont' 28 verges 70s.
Item 1 drap' long de plonket, pris 70s.
Item 1 drap' medle vert cont' 22 verges demi, pris la verge 3s. 4d.
75s.
Item 9 verges de blanket, pris la verge 3s. 4d.   30s.
Item 1 pice de russet cont' 24 verges, pris la pice 46s. 8d.
Item 1 pice de rouge cont' 28 verges, pris la verge 3s. 4d.   £4 13 4d.
Item 1 drap' court de brounetaune cont' 24 verges, pris la verge 3s.
72s.
Item 10 verges et demi de rouge, pris la verge 2s. 4d.   24s. 6d.
Item 1 drap' de noir cont' 26 verges, pris la verge 2s. 8d.   69s. 4d.
Item 1 drap' de blu cont' 28 verges, pris la verge 4s. 6d.   £6 6s.
Item 1 pice de russet cont' 14 verges, pris la verge 4s.   56s.
Item 1 drap' de blu cont' 29 verges, pris la verge 3s. 8d.   106s. 4d.
Item 1 drap' de plonket long' chaufed, pris 40s.
Item 1 pice de blu pers[106] cont' 20 verges et demi, pris la verge 6s.
£6 3s.
Item 1 pice de scarlet rouge cont' 6 verges, pris la verge 8s.   48s.
Item 13 verges de drap' vert, pris la verge 4s.   52s.
Item 25 douzaines de drap' de diverses colours, pris de chescun
douzaine, 16s.   £20
Item 19 douzaines de drap' de diverses colours, pris de chescun
douzaine 13s. 4d.   £12 13s. 4d.
Item 6 verges de drap' en 2 peces de acole mellez, pris de les 2 peces
16s.
Item 70 douzaines de drap' de diverses colours, pris de chescun
douzaine 8s.   £28 0 0d.
Item 36 peir de chaux de diverses colours, pris de chescun peir 18d.
54s.
Summa £197 15s. 2½d.

VINS ET OYLE

Vendita
Item 9 tonnes, 14 sestres doyle, pris le ton £7   £64 12s. 8d.
Item 2 tonnes doseye, 2 pipes de vin de Fraunce,

106 dark blue.

1 rondell de vin cokete et 2 doles et 4 vesseaux voidez pris[107]
£10 13s. 4d.
Summa £75 6s. 0d.

FERR' ET PLUMB'

Vendita
Item 252 milles demi centaine 2 lb de ferr, pris de mille lb. 51s. 6d.
£649 0s. 8d.
Item 14 fothers 8 weys 8 cloves de plumb, pris le fother
10 marcz et demi £102 16s. 11d.
Summa £751 17s 7d.

NAVIS LIBERATA COMITI CANTEBRIGG'

Item quedam navis vocata la Grace Dieu arestata etc et postmodum
deliberata fuit per breve de privato sigillo Edwardo Comiti
Cantebrigiensi cum eius attilio et[108] apparatu, appreciata ad £200
Summa – patet

BORDES

Liberata Roberti Sybthorp pro operibus regis de Shene
Item 4 centaines bordes appelles righolt[109] a 50s.   £10
Vendita W. de Sleford ut patet per 1 talliam de £25 1s. 8d.
Item 990 bordes appellez rigolbordes,[110] pris le centaine 50s.
£24 11s. 8d.
Item 50 bordes de waynscotte 10s.
Summa £35 1s. 8d.

MERESME[111] ET PERES

Liberata Thome de Wodstok
Item en la paroche seint Benet de Fynk meresme novel framee et
nient framee, peres franks et ragg',[112] preisez par maszons et
carpenters £50

---

107 This wine is said in E101/509/26 to have been found "En la seler de son
hostell demesne."
108 gear.
109 Riga wood, deal timber from the Baltic.
110 Riga boards.
111 timber.   112 dressed stone and rubble.

Item une porcion de meresme en la paroche de seinte Etheldrede
deyns Bisshopegate[113] £4
Item une porcion de meresme en la paroche de la Trinite la petite,
pris £4
Item une porcion des peres ragges en la paroche de seint Martyn
Otteswich, pris 53s. 4d.
Item illoeqes veil meresme et lathes, pris 20s.
Item illoeqes 1 porcion de tygles de Flaundres, pris 66s. 8d.
Item 1 porcion de peres franks en la Veil Iuerie,[114] pris £4
Summa £69

VIN FLORE[115]

Vendita
Item delyuere a boteller 2 tones de vin flore, pris £13 6s. 8d.
Summa – patet

DETTOURS PUR VINS ET POVERE[116]

Liberata Ricardo Lyons vnde summa £411 0 0d.
Item Thomas Heyward, £11 2s. 4d.
Item Thomas Cornwaleys et John Clyvelee, £19 1s. 9d.
Item Walterus Doget et Thomas Neel, £18 13s. 4d.
Item Thomas Medelane et Willelmys Sharpyng, £18 16s. 6d.
Item Ricardus Blake et Ricardus Sprot, £18 11s. 2d.
Item Willelmus Stokesby et Thomas Kirketon, £18 18s. 10d.
Item Nicholas Rote et Geffrey Chaumflour, £18 13s. 4d.
Item Willelmus Stokesby et John Croydon, £18 16s. 3d.
Item de Willelmo Coke pro pipere sibi vendita per attornatum
Ricardi Lyons, £268 7s. 3d.
Item John' Hothom pro minutis rebus sibi venditis, 6s. 8d.
Vendita
Item Bartholomeo Taverner al Galeye en Lombardestrete pro
minutis rebus sibi venditis, 53s. 3d.
Item un chaundeller pro 2 tonnis de raspeys[117] venditis per
Sire Rauf' de Kesteven, £8

113 A mistake for St. Ethelburga within Bishopsgate; St. Etheldreda's is in
Ely Place, Holborn. The other parishes are St. Benet Fink and St. Martin
Oteswich in Bread St. ward, and Trinity the Less in Queenhithe ward.
114 Old Jewry.   115 scented wine.   116 small items.
117 wine freshened after it had gone stale.

Item Willelmo Bys stokfisshmonger pro ferris, £96 3s. 5d.
Summa vendita £107 3s. 4d.
Summa £518 4s. 1d.

LA TAVERNE APPELLE LA GALEYE DE LOMBARDESTRETE

La mountaunce de 2 tonnes de vin vermaille de Gascoigne en
4 tonnes, pris 8 marks
Vendita
Item 1 boute pleyn de vin de ryn et 3 remenants de vin vernage
romeneye et malviasyn[118] que furont 1 autre boute par esme,[119]
pris 20s.
Item 2 remenants de vin de la Rone, 1 remenant de vin coit,[120]
pris 6s. 8d.
Item 6 tonnes et pipes voidez, pris. 3s.
Item 1 lavoir de plumb', pris 6s. 8d.
Item 7 tables ou les seges, pris 5s.
Item 1 table, 2 tristells, 1 fourme long', pris 1s. 4d.
Item 6 quartepottes, 4 potelpottes, et 1 demi-pynt de peautre, pris 4s.
Item 1 stole, pris 6d.
Item 7 canevas pur les seges, pris 1s. 9d.
Summa £7 15s. 7d. *et lencres* 25s. 10d.
Summa totalis £9 1s. 5d.

LA TAVERNE APPELLE CHICHESTRE SELER[121]

Vendita
Item 1 demi boute de vernage, pris 40s.
Item 1 ton de vin vermaille 12 pouz meyns. Item 1 demi ton de vin
vermaille, pris 40s.
Item 1 demi ton de vin Oseye,[122] pris 6s. 8d.
Item 1 demi boute de romeneye, pris 46s. 8d.
Item 3 quarters dun boute de vin malviasie, pris 5s.
Item 1 remenant de vin renissh, pris 3s. 4d.
7 pipes voides, 4 rondelles voidez, pris 4s. 2d.

118 Rhine wine, Vernaccian wine, Greek wine, and Malmsey wine.
119 estimation.
120 short for "cocket."
121 According to E101/509/26, this tavern also stood in Lombard Street and
was valued, like the tavern called "la Galeye," on 30 July 1376.
122 sweet wine, perhaps from Alsace.

Item 1 galoun potte, 2 potelpottes, 2 pyntpottes, pris[123] 4s.
Summa £7 10s. 8d. *Et lencres*
Non in contrarotulo
Item en le graunt celer 4 pipes et demi de vin vermaille vendus a
William More a 4 marcs le pipe dount faut de gauge 7 cestres[124]
12s. 6d.   £11 7s. 5d.
Vendita
Item vendu au dit William More le vyn douce et roman en le dit
celer, pris 20 marks
Item vendus 2 bales de almandes qe peysent 461 lb.; pris le centaine
25s.   115s.
Item 3 tonnes de vin rouge, pris le ton 40d.   10s.
Summa £30 19s. 1d.

LES BIEN ESTEAUNTZ DEINS LE COMPTOUR RICARD LYOUNS PREISEZ
PAR THOMAS BERCH RICHARD CHIRTON ET JOHN PONCHON

Le Comptour
Item 1 gipser[125] de riban dor de luke oue annel dargent endorrez oue
1 scurrey de soy dargent endorrez, pris 16s. 8d.
Item 1 autre gipser vsez oue annels dargent endorrez en manere
come lautre, pris 8s.
Item 1 braunch de corall, pris 1s. 6d.
Item 1 muge [126] garnise dor, pris 20s.
Item 1 agnus dei garniz dargent enamaylez pris 1s.
Item 1 bolle de cupre florez de figure de sarsenye pardehors,
pris 1s. 10d.
Item 7 bursez petit dount les deux de rouge velvet pris 8d. 3 autres,
pris 8d., 1 bourse garniz de botons dargent endorrez, pris 20d.,
1 petit bourse de noir velvet garniz des perles, pris 2s.   5s.
Item 1 peir de cisours dargent, pris 6s. 8d.
Item 2 piles de la tour,[127] pris 6s. 8d.
Item 1 peir de petit balauncz oue les poys deyns un cas, pris 1s.
Item 1 peir de balauncz de 6 lb., pris 2s.
Item 1 peir de balaunce de 2 lb., pris 1s.

---

123 After this item E101/509/26 has: "Item 1 grant fonel de fust(wood), 1 petit
funel de peautre, 1 pote de wykers, pris – 10d." This was omitted from
E101/509/25 and E199/25/70, perhaps because it was too insignificant.
124 sesters.   125 girdle.
126 nutmeg shell made into a cup.   127 sets of weights.

Item 1 petit balaunce, pris 4d.
Item 1 merour, pris. 1s.
Item 1 chaundeler de laton, pris 6d.
Item poys de plumb, pris 1s.
Item en or et argent del signe de coigne de la tour 23s. 8d.
Item 1 peir appelle baleys, pris 40s.
Item 43 perles oue 2 petitz pieces dor debrusez, pris 20s.
Item 2 franks, 1 noble leger debrusez, pris 12s.
Item 1 annel dor pris 4d.
Item 1 livre appelle manual oue diuerses trehotez,[128] pris 6s. 8d.
Item 1 livre de la chauncellerie appelle regestre, pris 2s.
Item 1 livre appelle Breton' escript en frauncais, pris 1s
Item 1 livre appelle legende sanctorum en engleis, pris 10s.
Item 1 countour, 1 fourme, 1 doser, 5 shelves oue autres meyns,
pris 3s. 4d.
Summa £9 13s. od.
Liberata Ricardo Lyons
Item al crane 22 peres de moleyns
Item 1 porcion de woldesborde
Item 1 porcion des cables
Item 1 porcion de piche
Item 1 porcion de remes[129]
precio in toto, £71 4s. od.
Les queux choses demureront nient venduz et sont delyuerez a
Richard Lyouns come ils furont arestuz par vertue dun brief.
Summa £71 4s.
Summa totalis onerationis £2443 7s. 10d.

CEUZ SONT LES PARCELLES DE LA DESCHARGE DEL SOMME AUAUNT
ESCRIPT[130]

Item paiee pur frett des vins a Thomas Baker, mestre du nef Sire
William Wyndesore, par brief £9 12s. od.

128 treatises.
129 wood.
130 E199/25/72 is a file of 27 documents, amongst which are receipts from
Thomas Baker, Henry Selby, Margaret Picard, John Desterny, for the payments made to them, and acknowledgements from Robert Sybthorp,
Thomas of Woodstock, Edmund earl of Cambridge, and Richard Lyons
of the goods delivered to them.

Item paiee pur fret des vins a Henry Selby par brief £7 5s. 4d.
Item paiee a dame Margarete Pykard par brief du grant seal[131]
£11 15s.
Item paiee a Janyn Desterne par brief 26s. 8d.
Item paiee pur peiser fer et plumb et as wyndrawers et al couper[132]
71s
Item lyvere al countee de Cauntebrigg par lettre du prive seal la
nef appelle *la Grace Dieu* qe fuist preise ouesqe toute lappareille £200
Item lyuere a Sire William Sleford al oeps du Roy 990 bordis
appellez Righolde a 50s. le centaine Summa £24 11s. 8d.
Item[133] lyuere au dit Sire William al oeps du Roy 50 bordes
appellez waynscotte. Summa 10s.
Item liuere a Sire Robert de Sybthorp al oeps nostre seigneur le roy
pur sus ouereinys[134] en pris de 400 bordes appellez ryngholt £10
Item lyuere a monsieur Thomas Wodestok meresme framee et nient
framee peres raggs et franks par comandement dune lettre de
monsieur Robert de Asshton adonqez tresourer come piert par
endenture ent fete qamountent a £69
Item[135] ils demandont allowance en ceste acompt de surplusage de
lacompt de lour office de viscounte de £13 4s. 3d.
Item[136] lyuere a Richard Lyouns les biens esteauntz deyns
son compte par comandement le tresourer qamountent a £9 13s.
Item[137] lyuere a monsieur de Cantebrigg [et au dit Richard par les
mayns John Colshull] en diuerses parcelles touchantz [sa garderobe
et des] autres choses du maison par [comandement dune lettre] 1
lettre de priue seal qamount come piert par bille escript del mayn
Sire Rauf Kesteuen a £10 14s. 3d.
Summa[138] £1765 14s. 1d.
Summa allocationum – £369 16s. 11d.

131 E199/25/72 makes it clear that the payment to Margaret Pickard was for
rents for a crane situated on the banks of the Thames, 10 cellars, and
another tenement in the vintry, all let on yearly rent by her to Richard
Lyons. The rents had already been paid into the exchequer.
132 This item is entirely crossed out.
133 This item and the preceding one are entirely crossed out and in the margin
are the words: "disallocantur quia habent postea tallias de £25 1s. 8d."
134 works.
135 This item is entirely crossed out and above it are the words: "quia pro
sequitur in pede compoti."
136 This item is entirely crossed out.
137 The sections in brackets are crossed out. The original sum named was
£70 17s. 11d.
138 This item is crossed out.

Item lyuere au dit Richard Lyouns par comandement dun brief
diuerses parcelles come piert par endenture fete parentre eux et le
dit Richard qamountent al somme de £766 15s. 9d.[139]
Summa – patet.
Summa totalis solucionum – £29 19s. od.
Et debent £1356 18s. 1od.
*Summa totalis solucionum talliis et liberacione
denariorum* £1386 17s. 1od.[140]

De aliquibus exitibus siue proficuis terrarum seu tenementorum que
fuerunt predicti Ricardi Lyons predicto 17° die Junii anno 50 seu
postea non receperunt per breve Regis datum 20° die Marcij anno
51° per quod rex precepit dictis vicecomitibus quod omnia terrae et
tenementa ac redditus predicti Ricardi per ipsos vicecomites similiter
in manu Regis capta una cum exitibus inde a tempore capcionis in
manu Regis precepto prefato Ricardo restituant.

139 Amended from £552 11s. o¾d.
140 The addition of these sums plainly does not come to £2443 7s. 1od., stated
above to be the total sum for which the sheriffs were responsible. In the
consolidated account of the sheriffs (E199/25/71) the figures are corrected
to: Summa oneris et recepte: £2443 5s. 8¾d.; Summa solucionum £1086 6s.
1o¾d. Et debent £1356 18s. 1od.

The Holy Oil of St. Thomas of Canterbury

T. A. SANDQUIST

Historians have generally eschewed prophecy when discussing intellectual history. The reasons for their reluctance are not far to seek: there is no satisfactory way to discover the impact of prophecy on the minds of contemporaries; whatever connections exist between belief and action in such ethereal matters cannot be readily discerned.[1] Prophecy confronts the historian with difficult questions for which few historians would be so foolhardy as to propose easy answers. Surely most would admit that in its total scope prophecy is beyond the grasp of current methodology and evidence. Yet the widespread occurrence of prophecies during the middle ages means that a medieval historian cannot easily avoid contact with this phenomenon.

Prophecy, for the political and constitutional historian of the medieval period, is seen usually not as a philosophical and psychological problem of the first order, but rather in the guise of political prophecy and in connection with a specific incident. Thus it becomes something that must either be woven into the composite analysis or simply ignored. For many the latter course is preferable and surely it is the safer. The author rejects the prophecy as being of no consequence, or at least of so little consequence that it need not be considered a factor in the total analysis. The temptations to adopt this attitude toward prophecies are great. If the historian attempts to deal with prophecy at all he is immediately brought face to face with the problems referred to above – problems which are not satis-

---

1 To limit these considerations to the category of prophecy will doubtless seem absurd to the more philosophically inclined historian. However, I think it is generally the case that prophecy raises doubts in the minds of historians who do not suffer from such misgivings when dealing with other materials.

factorily met by making the particular prophecy a kind of *et cetera*, the last of several "reasons for" or "causes of" the outcome of a battle, usurpation, or deposition. And on occasion the prophecy is yet more loosely associated with the incident in question.

This discussion does not attempt to answer those fundamental problems posed by the mere existence of prophecy. Even to offer tentative suggestions in this area is beyond the present frame of reference and obviously the present format is not the place for such a study. Yet despite the existence of these larger problems the utility of studies of particular prophecies is undeniable. Indeed the historian is unable even to approach intelligently the more general questions until he possesses a sound knowledge of particular prophecies.[2] This brief study attempts to bring together the evidence relating to a particular political prophecy of the fourteenth and fifteenth centuries.

The prophecy in question is tolerably well known.[3] According to the common version[4] the Virgin Mary appeared to St. Thomas of

2 A vivid illustration of the danger in writing without adequate knowledge and consideration of the history of particular prophecies is found in R. Taylor, *The Political Prophecy in England* (New York, 1911).

3 It has been printed many times, although no edition based on a substantial number of the manuscript texts has ever been published. A few of the more accessible are: *Patres Ecclesiae Anglicanae: Vita S. Thomae Cantuariensis Archiepiscopi et Martyris*, ed. J. A. Giles (Oxford, 1845), II, 246–7, reprinted with minor alterations in *Patrologiae latina*, ed. Migne, cxc, 393–94, the source of this text is Lambeth Palace ms. 577, pp. 9–10; *English Coronation Records*, ed. L. G. Wickham Legg (Westminster, 1901), pp. 169–70, Legg printed his text from Oxford Bodleian Ashmolean ms. 1393, fols. 52–54, and where necessary Ashmolean ms. 57, f.77; *Chronica Monasterii S. Albani, Johannis de Trokelowe et Anonymorum Chronica et Annales*, ed. H. T. Riley (Rolls Series), pp. 297–8, this copy is found in the *Annales Ricardi Secundi et Henrici Quarti* by Thomas Walsingham and the manuscript source is a collation of Corpus Christi College (Cantab) ms. VII, and Brit. Mus. ms. Cottonian Faustina B IX.

4 This essay is based upon a fairly extensive examination of the English manuscript texts of the prophecy. Throughout the essay the term "common version" is used to refer to the remarkable uniformity among these manuscripts. I had originally intended to make a scholarly edition of the prophecy but in the end decided that for my present purposes such an edition was neither useful nor justifiable. It was hoped that a study of the manuscripts would reveal some interesting variations in the text of the prophecy and add to our knowledge of how the Lancastrian dynasty used the prophecy for political purposes. Neither hope was in fact realized. In addition to the printed texts of the prophecy the following manuscript texts were examined: Brit. Mus. mss.: Additional 7096, f.167; Additional 10374, f.16; Arundel 219, f.386; Cottonian Cleopatra B I, f.182; Cottonian Cleopatra C IV, f.114 (fragment); Cottonian Claudius E VIII, fols. 1–2; Cottonian Titus D VII, fols.

Canterbury in a vision while the latter was praying in the church of
St. Colombe in Sens.[5] The Virgin presented Thomas with a golden
eagle which contained a stone flask filled with oil. She informed
Thomas that the oil was to be used for the anointing of future, but
unspecified, kings of England. These kings would recover peacefully
certain lands lost by their predecessors. The king first anointed with
the oil would recover Normandy and Aquitaine without the use of
force and would be "greatest among kings."[6] This same king would
build many churches in the Holy Land and drive the pagans from
Babylon, building many churches there also. As often as the king
carried the eagle in his bosom he would have victory over his
enemies and his kingdom would prosper. The remainder of the
prophecy relates to the immediate disposal of the eagle and the oil.[7]

The text of the prophecy makes clear that the Virgin was the
source of the prophetic material. In large part the account purports
to be a faithful transcription of the Virgin's own words. St. Thomas
served as the human agency for the transmission of the prophecies
and the disposal of the eagle and its vessel of oil. Anyone at all
familiar with the posthumous fame of the archbishop will not be
surprised by this association. St. Thomas was frequently connected
with vaticination. Even the earliest of his biographers attributed to
him prophecies relating to his own career and the lives of his contemporaries. And, as the reputation of the saint increased, Thomas
was associated with visions foretelling more distant events.[8]

28–29; Cottonian Vespasian E vii, fols. 115–16; Harleian 495, f.10; Lans-
downe 762, fols. 6–7; Royal 12 C xii, f.16ᵛ (incomplete); Royal 13 E ix, f.27ᵛ;
Oxford Bodleian mss.: Ashmolean 59, f.77; Digby 196, f.22; Rawlinson A
389, f.73; Lambeth Palace mss.: 12, f.254; 577, pp. 9–10; College of Arms
ms.: Arundel 1, f.234ᵛ.

5 At the time the archbishop was in exile having fled England because of the
dispute with Henry ii. One of the printed texts of the prophecy gives the date
1167 for the delivery of the treasure by St. Thomas to the monk William
(see *infra* n.7). *Eulogium Historiarum*, ed. F. S. Haydon (Rolls Series), i,
pp. 406–7.

6 *maximus inter reges*.

7 The archbishop was instructed by the Virgin to deliver the treasure to a
monk of St. Cyprian of Poitiers by the name of William. William would
transport the eagle to Poitiers and conceal it in the church of St. Gregory.
The leader of the pagans would be responsible for the discovery of the eagle.
The prophecy concludes by stating that Thomas delivered everything,
enclosed in a leaden vase, to William the monk.

8 The legends associated with the life and martyrdom of St. Thomas of Canterbury have been studied by P. A. Brown, *The Development of the Legend
of Thomas Becket* (Philadelphia, 1930). For the material referred to see
especially chapters four and ten.

This prophecy can then be seen as part of the well-established prophetic tradition of St. Thomas of Canterbury. It sheds valuable light upon the saint's posthumous reputation and also reveals something about the intellectual milieu of later medieval England. The number of manuscripts which contain the prophecy, their date and geographical distribution, the uniformity and/or disparity of the text, are some of the important factors in establishing the context within which such a discussion can profitably take place. Viewed as an episode in the development of the cult of St. Thomas, the prophecy has yet to be systematically studied.[9] However, for English historians this particular prophecy has achieved the status of something rather more than an episode, however interesting, in hagiography. This is entirely due to the association of the prophecy with the accession of the Lancastrian dynasty in 1399.

These Lancastrian connections of the prophecy place it in a somewhat different context of which the focal point is the fulfilment of the prophecy by Henry IV; the extent to which the prophecy was a factor in Henry's immediate success; and the long-term consequences, if any, for the Lancastrian dynasty. Some areas of interest are common, as for example, the popularity of the prophecy during the fifteenth century. But even here careful distinctions must be maintained. The prophecy, *qua* prophecy, was of no use whatever to the Lancastrians; it had to be made clear that Henry IV and his successors fulfilled its terms. Thus the mere fact that the majority of the manuscript texts of the prophecy now extant date from the fifteenth century in no sense demonstrates that the prophecy was used by the Lancastrian kings during that century to bolster their claim to the English throne.

It is necessary to clarify certain problems of dating in connection with this prophecy before proceeding further. The author and the circumstances of the origin of the prophecy are not known. In so far as is known it is not one of the earliest prophecies associated with St. Thomas. It is not mentioned by Becket's earliest biographers. From internal evidence – the mention of the recovery of Aquitaine and Normandy – it would seem impossible for the prophecy to be earlier than 1204.[10] The oldest manuscript copy discovered thus far

9 In addition to the work cited *supra* n.8 see Taylor, *The Political Prophecy in England*, pp. 99–100. Neither is in any sense a systematic study of this particular prophecy.
10 It is unwise to put too much stress on this type of argument when dealing with prophecies. Cf. however, Brown, *The Development of the Legend of Thomas Becket*, p. 229.

dates from the first half of the fourteenth century.[11] Still more con-
cretely, there is unmistakable reference to the prophecy in a papal
letter of 1318.[12] This letter relates the prophecy in considerable
detail and gives an account of the circumstances surrounding the
discovery of the oil. With respect to the prophecy proper the papal
letter contains a number of variants on the common version found
in the later manuscripts.[13] This papal letter and the earliest manuscript copy of the prophecy reveal one fact of central importance in
so far as the Lancastrian association is concerned: the Lancastrians,
whatever else they might have done, certainly did not invent the
prophecy.[14] The prophecy of St. Thomas and the holy oil exists *in*

11 Brit. Mus. ms. Royal 12 C xii. According to Ward, *Catalogue of Romances in
   the British Museum*, I, pp. 316–7, the date of this manuscript is "about A.D.
   1340"; cf. J. P. Gilson, *Catalogue ... Royal and King's Collections*, ii, 29,
   where the manuscript is dated *c.* 1320–40. John Morris, a nineteenth-century
   biographer of Becket, used a manuscript in which the scribe stated that the
   prophecy was "accidently found by my lord the King of England, on the
   vigil of St. Gregory, in the year of our Lord 1337, in an old chest." J. Morris,
   The Life and Martyrdom of St. Thomas Becket (2nd ed., London, 1885), ii,
   p. 496. None of the manuscripts I have examined fits Morris' description,
   either of the manuscript he used or of the exemplar therein referred to.

12 The letter is a papal reply to inquiries made on behalf of Edward ii asking
   if the king should be anointed with the oil of St. Thomas and if such unction
   would be beneficial. John xxii replied that although there would be neither
   superstition nor sin in receiving the unction, he was not willing to give advice
   as to whether or not Edward should actually receive unction with the oil.
   The pope declared that, should the king decide to undergo the re-anointing,
   it should be kept secret and private. This letter is printed in Legg, *English
   Coronation Records*, pp. 69–72.

13 The oil is intended for the unction of the fifth king from that "now reigning," thus making it clear that the Virgin intended Edward ii to be the first
   king anointed with the oil. This king was to be a good man, a champion of
   the church, and would recover the Holy Land. There is no mention of any
   golden eagle, building of churches, or recovery of lands lost by predecessors.
   The papal letter does not contain a text or even extracts from a text of the
   prophecy. It reports the oral presentation of Nicholas de Stratton who, according to the letter, had in his possession a copy of the prophecy and details
   of the immediate disposition of the treasure in a writing that only Nicholas
   could read. Marc Bloch identified the "fratris N., ordinis predicatorum" of
   the papal letter with Nicholas de Stratton, *Les Rois thaumaturges* (Paris,
   1924), p. 238, n.1.

14 Bishop Stubbs, for example, consigns the prophecy to the rank of the Lancastrian claim of legitimate descent from Edmund Crouchback, and hints
   that the same party may be responsible for both fabrications. W. Stubbs,
   The Constitutional History of England (Oxford, 1891), iii, p. 11. Cf. also,
   G. Lapsley, "The Parliamentary Title of Henry iv," *EHR*, xlix (1934), 598–9.
   Both Stubbs and Lapsley, and a host of earlier authors, thought that the
   prophecy as well as the account of the fate of the golden eagle during the
   fourteenth century was manufactured in 1399. Most recent authors have

toto at least as early as *c.* 1340.[15] Inquiries made by Edward II (*c.* 1318) indicate that the prophecy was known then, though no extant text appears to be that early.

This prophecy cannot at present be firmly associated with any particular incident in the thirteenth or early fourteenth centuries. It has been suggested that the troubles of Edward II's reign provide the proper sort of background for the devising of the prophecy.[16] The papal letter certainly indicates that Edward II took seriously the suggestions that his difficulties were caused by omission of the unction and that his fortunes would improve if he were anointed with the oil.[17] It is not beyond belief that the king or some one of his friends concocted the prophecy in the hope that it would benefit the royal cause. The pope's refusal to sanction the unction and his insistence that if it were to be performed this was to be secret and private doubtless disappointed the king and his adherents. It seems quite likely that the whole point of the appeal to the pope in this matter was to obtain papal sanction for the widespread publication of the event. As a result of the pope's attitude it is not known whether or not Edward II was anointed with the oil of St. Thomas. If he was so anointed his miserable fate must have given second thoughts to those who knew the prophecy.

In view of the hypothetical character of the connections between Edward II's troubles and the origin of the prophecy it should be kept in mind that the problem can be seen in more general terms. The

recognized that the prophecy itself has pre-Lancastrian origins. Marc Bloch, although he firmly believed that Henry IV was culpable in certain respects, wrote, "on [Henry IV] répandit à cette occasion dans le public une version légèrement retouchée de la première légende," *Les Rois thaumaturges*, p. 241. Cf. also, H. G. Wright, "The Protestation of Richard II in the Tower in September, 1399," *Bull. John Rylands Library*, XXIII (1939), 9–12. One may add to the later group John Webb. Webb, though writing nearly a century and a half ago and drawing his conclusions from quite unacceptable information he found in Bouchet's *Annales d'Aquitaine*, believed it probable that the "story about the ampulla" was earlier than 1399: John Webb, "Translation of a French Metrical History ..." *Archaeologia*, xx (1824), 1–423, here 99, 264–67; J. Bouchet, *Les Annales d'Aquitaine* (Poictiers, 1644), pp. 146–7.

15 Collation of the earliest extant manuscript, Brit. Mus. ms., Royal 12 C XII, f.16ᵛ, reveals that it differs little and only in non-essentials from the many later copies.

16 Cf. *Liber Regie Capelle*, ed. W. Ullman (Henry Bradshaw Society, XCII), p. 34; Taylor, *The Political Prophecy in England*, especially chapter four, "Relation of the Prophecies to Political Events," pp. 83–107.

17 The letter is carefully phrased and indicates that Edward II was not the author of these suggestions.

prophecy may be nothing more than the English counterpart of the French legend of the Sainte Ampoule. Thus its origin may not be found in any specific event or series of events but rather in the desire of the English to have an oil for the unction of their kings with as miraculous an origin as the oil of Clovis.[18] Marc Bloch, who incidentally knew the papal letter well, best characterized this point of view when he suggested that the prophecy was, "une médiocre imitation de la Sainte Ampoule, née, plus de quatre siècles après Hincmar, des inquiétudes de princes impopulaires ou illégitimes."[19]

For the better part of a century the prophecy appears to have been moribund in so far as political history is concerned, although manuscript evidence indicates that it circulated in connection with the cult of St. Thomas. In 1399 the prophecy appears once again in a political context, this time linked with the accession of Henry IV. There is little doubt that the prophecy of St. Thomas and the holy oil is best known to historians in the context of the Lancastrian usurpation. Moreover, in so far as this prophecy has provoked their interest, it has done so in connection with Henry IV and not Edward II. Therefore the circumstances of the reappearance must be examined with some care.

The most valuable source of information for 1399 is the work of the contemporary St. Alban's chronicler, Thomas Walsingham. Among this writer's many works, the *Annales Ricardi Secundi et Henrici Quarti* contains the longest and most detailed account.[20] The *Annales* gives the complete text of the prophecy[21] together with a

18 Viewed in this light the prophecy cannot be said to have had much success. The oil of St. Thomas never assumed for the English anything like the important role played by the oil of Clovis in French history. For a recent study of the French legend see Sir Francis Oppenheimer, *The Legend of the Sainte Ampoule* (London, 1953).

19 *Les Rois thaumaturges*, p. 243.

20 *Annales Ricardi Secundi et Henrici Quarti*, printed in *Chronica Monasterii S. Albani, Johannis de Trokelowe et Anonymorum Chronica et Annales*, ed. H. T. Riley (Rolls Series), pp. 297–300, hereafter cited as *Annales*. Abbreviated versions with a few significant differences which have been noted are found in *Historia Anglicana*, ed. H. T. Riley (Rolls Series), II, pp. 239–40; *Ypodigma Neustriae*, ed. H. T. Riley (Rolls Series), p. 388. All these St. Albans chronicles of the late fourteenth and early fifteenth centuries are the work of Thomas Walsingham. Cf. V. H. Galbraith, "Thomas Walsingham and the Saint Albans Chronicle, 1272–1422," *EHR*, XLVII (1932), 12–30, and *The St. Albans Chronicle, 1406–1422*, ed. V. H. Galbraith (Oxford, 1937), pp. ix–lxxv.

21 The text of the prophecy differs only in minor respects from what I have referred to as the "common version." Most noteworthy of the differences is

graphic report of the subsequent fate of the golden eagle and holy oil. According to Walsingham the golden eagle lay hidden for a long time in the church of St. Gregory. At length the secret was revealed to a certain unnamed holy man. This discovery took place during the reign of Edward III when Henry, first duke of Lancaster, was fighting "in those parts," presumably near Poitiers. The holy man gave the treasure to the duke of Lancaster who in turn presented it to Edward, eldest son of King Edward III. It was intended that the oil would be used at the unction of the Black Prince. Walsingham notes that at the time of the discovery it was hoped that the Black Prince would be the king designated in the prophecy but that this hope proved false for the prince died before his father. When the Black Prince received the eagle he placed it in the Tower of London in a locked chest.[22] A search was made for the eagle before the coronation in 1377 but it could not be found. Thus Richard II was not anointed with the oil of St. Thomas.

In 1399[23] Richard II, whom Walsingham claims was something of an antiquary,[24] came across several chests in the tower and inspected them. One was found to be so securely locked that the king was not able to open it. Richard ordered it broken open so that he could discover what it contained. In this chest the king found the eagle containing the ampulla of holy oil together with the "writing" of the blessed martyr Thomas. When Richard learned the powers of the holy oil he asked the archbishop of Canterbury, Thomas Arundel, to anoint him with it.[25] The archbishop refused, saying that once the

the statement near the conclusion of the prophecy: "et erit unctio Regum Anglorum qui erunt capita paganorum," probably a conflation; *Annales*, p. 298.

22 This detail is found only in the *Historia Anglicana*, II, p. 239.

23 The date 1399 for Richard II's discovery of the eagle is given in the *Historia Anglicana*, II, p. 239. In the *Ypodigma Neustriae*, p. 388, the discovery is said to have taken place in the twenty-first year of Richard's reign (22 June 1397–21 June 1398). In the *Annales*, p. 299, Richard is said to have discovered the treasure "post multos annos transactos regni."

24 "Curiosus perscrutator rerum progenitoribus relictarum," *Annales*, 299, cf. *Historia Anglicana*, II, p. 239.

25 There is something of a problem here. Archbishop Arundel was relieved of the temporalities of the archdiocese of Canterbury in September 1397. Shortly afterward he was translated to St. Andrews and replaced at Canterbury by Roger Walden. Walsingham is one of the prime sources for the events in the stormy parliament of 1397 and his works give a full account of the fate of Archbishop Arundel: *Annales*, pp. 209–25, *Historia Anglicana*, II, p. 224, *Ypodigma Neustriae*, p. 376. Walsingham's dating of Richard's discovery of the eagle is referred to *supra* n.23. The *Eulogium Historiarum*

sacrament had been administered by the metropolitan it should not be repeated. When the king discovered that he would not be able to obtain the archbishop's willing consent he desisted in his attempts to have the unction repeated. However, Richard carried the treasure about with him, hoping thereby to turn away all dangers.[26]

Richard II returned from Ireland late in the summer of 1399 and the eagle and holy oil were taken from him at Chester Castle by archbishop Arundel[27] who informed the king that it was quite clear that the divine will had decreed it was not he who should be anointed with the oil of St. Thomas. Archbishop Arundel kept the oil until the time of the coronation of Henry IV who was thus the first king to be anointed with it. "Because of this," concludes Walsingham, "it is believed by many that this is that king, elected by God, who will be preserved by such a miraculous unction, and to whom so great grace will be promised, greater than any who were kings before him."[28]

gives 1399 as the date for the finding of the eagle, though it does not mention any request by the king for unction with the oil of St. Thomas, *Eulogium Historiarum*, ed. F. S. Haydon (Rolls Series), III, pp. 379–80. Obviously if the date 1399 for Richard II's discovery of the eagle is correct, and the evidence seems to indicate that this is the case, then Walsingham has made an error in designating Arundel as archbishop. It seems likely that Walsingham had forgotten that Arundel, who again became archbishop with the accession of Henry IV, was not archbishop of Canterbury during the last two years of Richard's reign. Historians have accepted that it was Arundel who refused to anoint Richard with the oil of St. Thomas. For a recent example see *Liber Regie Capelle*, ed. W. Ullmann, p. 35. A. P. Stanley, though he cites Walsingham where the reference is to Arundel, says quite inexplicably that it was Archbishop Courteney (1381–96) who refused to anoint the king, *Historical Memorials of Westminster Abbey* (4th ed., London, 1876), 67.

26 Cf. the words of the prophecy: "Quocienscumque Rex portabit aquilam in pectore, victoriam habebit de inimicis suis et regum eius semper augmentabitur."

27 Richard II's movements during the weeks following his return from Ireland are a subject of considerable importance. The sequence Conway, Flint, Chester (c. 14 August to c. 19 August) established in 1930 by M. V. Clarke and V. H. Galbraith has been accepted by recent authors, "The deposition of Richard II," *Fourteenth Century Studies*, ed. L. S. Sutherland and M. McKisack (Oxford, 1937), pp. 66–76. More importantly, the betrayal of Richard by Henry of Bolingbroke and his co-conspirators seems now accepted by scholars. See, in addition to article cited above, A. Steel, *Richard II* (Cambridge, 1941), p. 268; M. McKisack, *The Fourteenth Century* (Oxford History of England, Oxford, 1959), p. 493; R. H. Jones, *The Royal Policy of Richard II* (Oxford, 1968), pp. 102–105. Archbishop Arundel may have been a member of the delegation to Conway, he certainly was present at Flint and again at Chester where Richard confronted Henry of Bolingbroke for the first time. Either Flint or Chester would appear an appropriate site for Arundel's seizure of the ampulla.

28 *Annales*, p. 300.

A second contemporary or near-contemporary source, the continuation of the *Eulogium Historiarum* tells a much simpler story.[29] Richard II, returning to London from a visit to Canterbury in the spring of 1399, went to the Tower of London and found there the golden eagle which contained the stone ampulla. The king also found a certain writing, "quadam scriptura," which related how the eagle was delivered by the Virgin Mary to St. Thomas while the archbishop was in exile. The continuator of the the *Eulogium Historiarum* then quotes a part of the "writing."[30] This is followed by the statement that Richard always carried the eagle hanging about his neck thereafter, presumably a reference to the king's expedition to Ireland. A few pages later the chronicle refers again to the oil of St. Thomas. It states that Henry IV was anointed by Thomas Arundel with the oil from the eagle and notes that Henry was the first king to be anointed with this oil.[31] This source entirely omits any explanation of the fate of the treasure from the time it was delivered to St. Thomas until Richard II came across it in the Tower of London.

These two accounts constitute the sum total of contemporary or near-contemporary reference to the oil of St. Thomas in connection with the accession and coronation of Henry IV. This, in itself, seems a quite remarkable fact. That garrulous and credulous fifteenth century chronicler, Adam of Usk, knows nothing of the oil of St. Thomas. Adam was actually present at the coronation of Henry IV,[32] and he does not seem the sort of writer that would pass up a good story, whatever its probable credibility. Moreover, if this situation is compared to the efforts of Henry IV in making public the charges against Richard II, the so-called *Record and Process*, the point becomes still clearer.[33] The Lancastrians were certainly capable of

29 *Eulogium Historiarum*, III, pp. 379–80, 384.
30 The passage quoted concerns the prophecy of the Virgin respecting the deeds of the king first anointed with the oil and the future discovery of the eagle, approximately one-fifth of the whole of the prophecy.
31 In addition to these notices in the continuation of the *Eulogium Historiarum*, the *Eulogium Historiarum* itself contains a text of the prophecy among a group of miraculous narratives at the conclusion of book III, *Eulogium Historiarum*, I pp. 406–7. It is obvious from a comparison of the passage quoted in the continuation of the *Eulogium Historiarum* and the text of the prophecy found at the conclusion of book III that the author of the continuation did not use the text found at the conclusion of book III.
32 *Chronicon Adae de Usk*, ed. and trans. E. M. Thompson (London, 1904), pp. 187, 298. The *Chronicon* was not composed until after 1415.
33 M. V. Clarke and V. H. Galbraith, "The Deposition of Richard II," *Bull. John Rylands Library*, XIV (1930), pp. 129–55.

mounting a propaganda offensive if they desired to do so. Yet the evidence which links the new dynasty with the oil of St. Thomas will not support the notion that in 1399 the Lancastrians sought to bolster their claim to the English throne by emphasizing the special character of Henry IV's unction.

In addition to the lack of contemporary comment in 1399 there is one further consideration that should be noted. The whole story of Richard II's discovery of the eagle in the Tower, his transporting the eagle to Ireland, and the subsequent recovery of the eagle by Archbishop Arundel seems unduly complicated. If the account is no more than pure fiction dreamt up by some unknown Lancastrian public relations man why did it need to be so elaborate? One can easily imagine many far simpler, more edifying, and less vulnerable fictions that would account for the appearance of the eagle and Henry IV's possession of it in 1399.

The finding of the golden eagle in the Tower of London is mentioned in both contemporary sources. As is widely known, one of the charges made against Richard II at the time of his deposition was that of transporting the royal jewels to Ireland.[34] Moreover a bit of evidence that may throw some added light on the story of Richard's discovery in the tower is found in an account of the coronation expenses of Edward I. In the Pipe Roll for 8 Edward I there occurs the following entry: "Et pro una aquila auri cum rubettis et aliis lapidibus preciosis, XLVIII £ xvs."[35] Is there not some chance that it was this eagle, long mislaid among the royal treasures in the tower, that Richard discovered late in his reign and carried off to Ireland? Ob-

34 "Item, [Richard] leaving the kingdom for Ireland took away treasures, crowns, and relics, and other jewels, that is to say goods of the realm that had from ancient times been set apart in the archives of the realm for the honour of the king and the preserving of his kingdom." Walsingham, *Annales*, p. 270. This is from the text of the so-called *Record and Process*. In addition there is a summary of the charge found in the chronicle proper, *Annales*, p. 239.

35 "For one eagle of gold with rubies and other precious stones, £ 48 15 s.," P.R.O., E372/124, m.26ᵈ. The physical appearance of the eagle used for the unction during the middle ages is a problem. There are no detailed descriptions. In the later fifteenth century the eagle is described as, "an Eagle of gold garnysshed with perles and precious stones," Westminster Abbey Muniments 9482. The full text is printed in, J. W. McKenna, "The Coronation Oil of the Yorkist Kings", *EHR*, LXXXII (1967), 103. In 1649, just before the destruction of the regalia, the eagle is noted as, "a dove of gould sett with stones and pearle," Legg, *English Coronation Records*, p. 274.

viously this is mere conjecture; the evidence does not warrant any firm conclusions in this, as in many other matters. However, this evidence does open the way for a possible explanation of the appearance of the prophecy in 1399 which does not necessitate seeing its appearance as a clever piece of Lancastrian propaganda.[36]

If one looks forward in time from 1399 one of the strangest aspects of this whole curious story is the all but complete lack of any reference to it in the fifteenth century. The later authors, almost without exception, fail to mention the oil of St. Thomas when they write about the coronation of Henry IV.[37] The only important exception is John Capgrave and all of his information could have been taken straight from Walsingham.[38] In fact, references to the oil of St. Thomas in connection with the coronations of the Lancastrian kings are so scarce that some writers have believed that the story must have been quite forgotten.[39] In 1959 Professor Walter Ullman printed an English manuscript now in Portugal which contains a reference to the oil of St. Thomas.[40] This, together with a writ from Henry VI ordering delivery of the "Aquilam auream cum ampulla qua Reges consecravi solebant" for Henry's coronation in 1429,[41] has been

36 I am well aware that a fabricator often attempts to give verisimilitude to his creations by the admixture of truth and also that the evidence now available does not link the eagle purchased by Edward I with either the unction or the prophecy.

37 Cf., for example, *The Great Chronicle of London*, ed. A. H. Thomas and I. D. Thornley (London, 1938), pp. 72–4; *Ingulph's Chronicle of the Abbey of Croyland*, ed. and trans. H. T. Riley (London, 1854), p. 354; *The Historical Collections of a Citizen of London*, ed. J. Gairdner (Camden Society, 1876), p. 102; *Three Fifteenth Century Chronicles*, ed. J. Gairdner (Camden Society, 1880), pp. 28, 51; Richard Grafton, *The Chronicle of John Hardyng with the Continuation by Richard Grafton*, ed. H. Ellis (London, 1812), pp. 350–2; Robert Fabyan, *The New Chronicles of England and France*, ed. H. Ellis (London, 1811), pp. 564–5; Edward Hall, *Chronicle*, ed. H. Ellis (London, 1809), I, pp. 13–14; Richard Grafton, *Chronicle: or History of England*, ed. H. Ellis (London, 1809), I, p. 478.

38 John Capgrave, *Chronicle of England*, ed. F. C. Hingeston (Rolls Series), pp. 273–4. The prophecy is not mentioned in Capgrave's *Liber de Illustribus Henricis*, ed. F. C. Hingeston (Rolls Series).

39 P. E. Schramm, *A History of the English Coronation*, trans. L. G. Wickham Legg (Oxford, 1937), p. 138.

40 *Liber Regie Capelle*, ed. W. Ullmann (Henry Bradshaw Society, XCII), pp. 35–8, 90, n.3.

41 P.R.O., E404/46/136. Printed in, *Proceedings and Ordinances of the Privy Council*, ed. H. Nicolas (London, Record Commission, 1836), IV, p. 7; T. Rymer, *Foedera* (Holmes ed.), X, p. 437; A. Taylor, *The Glory of Regality* (London, 1820), p. 382.

taken by Professor Ullmann to be clear proof of the use of the miraculous oil during the fifteenth century.[42] This may indeed be true, but in addition to the usefulness of the reference as evidence of the continued use of the oil, the discovery serves to emphasize the extraordinary lack of contemporary comment.[43] The mere fact that historians are forced to rely upon such evidence is, from one point of view, most revealing.

Here also the situation ought to be compared with the efforts of the Lancastrians in other directions. Recently J. W. McKenna has examined in detail some propaganda efforts on behalf of Henry vi.[44] He demonstrates a substantial and sophisticated effort on the part of the new dynasty. The talents of genealogists, poets, engravers,

42 It should be pointed out that Professor Ullmann attributes certain changes in the coronation service, namely the abandoning of anointing with two kinds of oil, to the introduction of the oil of St. Thomas. This strengthens the case he makes for the continued unction with Becket's miraculous oil during the later middle ages. Professor Ullmann's remarks on the eagle itself, *Liber Regie Capelle*, pp. 36–8, should be compared with *supra* n.35. Cf. also, W. Ullmann, "Thomas Becket's Miraculous Oil," *J. Theological Studies*, n.s., viii (1957), 129–33.

43 After this article was written J. W. McKenna published a note in *EHR* drawing attention to and printing Westminster Abbey Muniment 9482; see *supra* n.35. He also noted the fact that the Pseudo-Elmham states that the oil of St. Thomas was used at Henry v's coronation: *Thomae de Elmham, Vita & Gesta Henrici Quinti Anglorum Regis*, ed. T. Hearne (Oxford, 1727), p. 21. The *Vita & Gesta* contains the only even moderately detailed account of the coronation in 1413. It was written about 1446 and the eighteenth-century editor, Thomas Hearne, wrongly attributed the work to Thomas Elmham. For speculation about the authorship see: C. L. Kingsford, "The Early Biographies of Henry v," *EHR*, xxv (1910), 71; Kingsford, *English Historical Literature in the Fifteenth Century* (Oxford, 1913), pp. 58–9. The *Vita & Gesta* is an expanded version of Tito Livio de Foro-Juliensis' *Vita Henrici Quinti*, with one of the more notable additions being the description of Henry v's coronation. The source of this particular addition is not known. If Kingsford is correct in his suggestion that Vincent Clement was the author of the *Vita & Gesta* it can hardly be an eyewitness account of the coronation in 1413; moreover the date 1446 makes it somewhat doubtful that the author, whoever he may have been, was present at the ceremony. None of the earlier biographies of Henry v – Thomas Elmham's *Gesta Henrici Quinti* and *Liber Metricus* or the *Vita Henrici Quinti* – mention the oil of St. Thomas in connection with the coronation of 1413. Therefore the *Vita & Gesta* hardly seems conclusive evidence for the use of the holy oil of St. Thomas at the coronation of Henry v. The work does indicate, however, that in some quarters in the 1440s it was believed that this oil was used in 1413. How widely this belief was held cannot be determined. The proximity in date of the *Vita & Gesta* to the *Liber Regie Capelle* should be noted, *supra* n.40.

44 J. W. McKenna, "Henry vi of England and the Dual Monarchy: Aspects of Royal Political Propaganda, 1422–1432," *J. Warburg and Courtauld Insts.*, xxviii (1965), 145–62.

and manuscript illuminators were utilized by the house of Lancaster in a sustained effort "to improve its image."

Perhaps, it might well be urged, the well-known decline and degeneration of the sources in the later middle ages should be held responsible for the lamentable lack of contemporary comment. Every medieval historian recognizes that arguments from silence are rarely convincing. In this instance the possibility that this is the case seems much reduced by an examination of the Lancastrian-Yorkist debate of the later fifteenth century. If the oil of St. Thomas played any part in shoring up the Lancastrian claim to the English throne one would naturally expect to see it defended and/or attacked when these claims were the subject of detailed and acrimonious debate, in parliament and elsewhere. Even the duke of York felt obliged to counter the Crouchback legend before the lords,[45] while chief justice Fortescue assiduously sought arguments to re-inforce his defence of the Lancastrian claim.[46] Nowhere in these debates is there any reference to the oil of St. Thomas.

Thus may we end our account of the miraculous oil of St. Thomas of Canterbury. It must appear to many as a strange story of unfulfilled promise and missed opportunity. The prophecy is one that had certain attractions for contemporaries, a fact amply illustrated by its continued popularity in the fifteenth century as a part of the cult of St. Thomas. That it had similar attractions as a piece of political propaganda or that any effort to exploit it for these purposes was made has yet to be demonstrated. It is clear that historians can no longer hold, as did Maskell and other earlier authors, that, "it is obvious that this legend was *invented* in order to supply a hereditary defect, and give additional sacredness to the character of King Henry the fourth."[47] The evidence does not even support the notion that

45 *Rotuli Parliamentorum*, v, pp. 375–9.
46 This is a tangled problem because of the diverse nature and sometimes fragmentary survival of Fortescue's writings. The standard edition is, *The Works of Sir John Fortescue*, ed. Thomas Lord Clermont (2 vols., London, 1869). Cf. also, J. Fortescue, *The Governance of England*, ed. C. Plummer (Oxford, 1885), pp. 74–9, 353–6; J. Fortescue, *De Laudibus Legum Anglie*, ed. S. B. Chrimes (Cambridge, 1942), p. 151; L. H. and C. Nelson, "A Lost Fragment of the *Defensio Juris Domus Lancastriae*," *Speculum*, XL (1965), 290–3; S. B. Chrimes, *English Constitutional Ideas in the Fifteenth Century* (Cambridge, 1936), pp. 9–13, 64–5.
47 W. Maskell, *Monumenta Ritualia Ecclesiae Anglicanae* (2nd. ed. Oxford, 1882), II, p. xix n.26 (italics mine). Cf. the comment of Froissart's editor, "une fable grossière fut inventée," *Œuvres de Froissart*, ed. Lettenhove (Brussels, 1872), XVI, p. 359.

the prophecy was, in the words of Marc Bloch, "carefully retouched" by the Lancastrians to cover their illegitimacy.[48] It would appear certain that neither Henry IV nor his successors made any effort to utilize the oil of St. Thomas as a support for their dynasty. On close examination, even the status of a minor factor in the Lancastrian success seems much too exalted a role for Becket's miraculous oil.

Quite unwittingly Adam of Usk may have written the final word on the Lancastrian connection with the oil of St. Thomas. In citing the omens which foreshadowed the miserable death of the first of the Lancastrian kings Adam wrote:

That same rotting did the anointing at his coronation protend; for there ensued such a growth of lice, especially on his head, that he neither grew hair, nor could he have his head uncovered for many months.[49]

48 Bloch, Les Rois thaumaturges, p. 241.
49 Chronicon, ed. Thompson, p. 298.

The Canterbury Convocation of 1406

E. F. JACOB

he year 1404 is a difficult one for the historian of convocation. There were two meetings that year. In the table of parliamentary and convocation grants for the reign of Henry IV which I drew up several years ago,[1] no mention was made of any meeting of convocation before that of 24 to 28 November. In point of fact the convocation of Canterbury met on 21 April,[2] to be asked for a subsidy as well as for a tenth. On 17 May writs went out to the dioceses for (besides a tenth) the collection of a subsidy of 2s. in the pound:

From all ecclesiastical benefices and offices to which spiritualities are annexed, but which are not assessed nor accustomed to pay a tenth, but which exceed the sum of 100s according to a true estimation of the yearly values of the same to be made by the bishops of the places in which the said benefices and offices are situated; a subsidy of 2s in every 20s to be paid at Midsummer next and to be at the king's disposal and for his use.[3]

The clergy had conceded both subsidy and tenth. It is very difficult to find out whether the subsidy was in fact paid. I believe not. There is no mention of it in the writs making anticipatory drafts upon the ecclesiastical collectors in the dioceses, and the normal reference to the grant then made is to "the tenth granted to the king in the last Convocation of the Province of Canterbury."[4] The Receipt rolls do not record the collection of any such 2s. subsidy. The reason may lie in the attitude of the clergy during the second meeting of convocation in the late autumn.

1 *The Fifteenth Century, 1399–1485* (Oxford, 1961), pp. 118f.
2 Lambeth Palace Library, Register Arundel, I, f.57; Wilkins, *Concilia*, III, p. 279.
3 *Calendar of Fine Rolls, 1399–1405*, p. 246.
4 E.g. *Calendar of Close Rolls, Henry IV*, II, pp. 349, 395, 413, 414.

This was a definite refusal to concede the demand that a subsidy should be levied upon the great mass of clergy that did not contribute towards the ecclesiastical tenth. The majority of these were of the hired or stipendiary group, whether chantry priests, parochial chaplains, schoolmasters, or hospital chaplains. Convocation met at St. Paul's from 24 to 28 November. In December Archbishop Arundel had to report to the king that despite the pleading of the bishop of Winchester and one of the earls (nameless), the clergy were adamant. Three times they had been asked, but to no avail. They were quite prepared to make a grant of 1½ tenths, but the other type of grant would (it is implied) involve great numbers not represented in convocation. It would also involve a formidable amount of administration for lists of non-payers would have to be drawn up by the dioceses and forwarded to the exchequer and a flat rate for the non-payers decided.

The purpose, as we said, was to tax the numerous seculars, beneficed or unbeneficed, who ministered and were subject to no assessment of any kind. To bring them in, was, in 1404, an obvious step. It had been tried, as an exceptional measure under both Winchelsey and Islep.[5] For all the exemptions attached to every convocation grant, ecclesiastical taxation was more flexible and capable of extension than was secular: three times the assessments had been revised upwards, whereas the level of civil taxation collected had stayed still. Mr. H. C. Johnson has calculated that in the county of Surrey between 1334 and 1422 the amount collected showed very little variation, falling a little by the middle of the fifteenth century (this was before the larger deduction granted for the whole country).[6] It may be wondered whether the tax bore any relation to the wealth of the country during the fifteenth century. It was the policy of the commons to force this, if possible, upon the convocations: strictly speaking, it was not their business, but they had a weapon to hand, unsheathed in the parliament of 1404. It must have been the resistance of the clergy which provoked the scene recorded by Thomas Walsingham between Sir John Cheyne and the archbishop.

Cheyne[7] was an old opponent of Arundel. In 1399 the archbishop

5 Jacob, The Fifteenth Century, pp. 420–1.
6 Surrey Taxation Returns, Fifteenths and Tenths, ed. H. C. Johnson (Surrey Record Society, XXXIII, 1932), III, pp. lvi–lvii. On the difficulties of collecting an ecclesiastical tax cf. Jacob, The Fifteenth Century, pp. 421–2.
7 See the biography of him in J. S. Roskell, The Commons and Their Speakers in English Parliaments, 1376–1523 (Manchester, 1965), pp. 353–4.

had got him removed from the speakership of the commons for his Lollard sympathies. He was not elected to the parliament of 1404, so what was he doing at Westminster? It seems likely that, besides lobbying, he was presenting in person the petition of a group of knights "for the annexation by the Crown of clerical temporalities"; and the acerbity of the archbishop's reply was heightened by the knowledge that this Gloucestershire knight had done very well out of alien priories – was in fact drawing £230 a year from that source. Cheyne's demand was for a year's annexation of the temporalities – not enough to make a very great fuss about, but it was the principle that mattered.

Walsingham represents the altercation that took place between Cheyne and Arundel, who was replying to the charge that the clergy were not taking their full share in public burdens, in this manner: "The chosen knights of parliament could not find any remedy for the relief of the King other than that of confiscating the patrimony of Christ throughout all the realm: namely that the Church should be generally deprived of all its temporal goods." From this there arose a great dispute between the clergy and the laity. The royal knights declared that they had often set forth on behalf of the king, and with the king, against rebels and enemies. They had not only spent their goods very profusely but had also exposed their bodies to many dangers and labours whilst the clerics had sat idly by at home, offering no manner of support to the king.[8]

To such clap-trap (if it were ever uttered) Arundel would have had no difficulty in replying; but seeing that his defence made little impression where it should, he appealed to the king to maintain the promise made in the coronation oath to "honour and sustain the Church," and to the knights to consider how small gain had accrued to the crown when the alien priories were confiscated. Their petition was based, he observed, on sheer cupidity; and his argument eventually carried weight with the king. However, according to Walsingham Arundel, not trusting the knights' intentions, set about forming a party among the lords to defend the temporalities of the church and so defeat the plans formed in the lower house for their confiscation. So strong was the primate's reply that those knights who had stubbornly persisted in this error begged the lord of Canterbury to

8 *Historia Anglicana*, ed. H. T. Riley (Rolls Series), II, pp. 264f. The passage is translated in B. Wilkinson, *Constitutional History of England in the Fifteenth Century* (London, 1964), 306–8.

forgive them: "they acknowledged their malice and guilt and offered thanks that the Church had abated its anger for this time." It may be that Arundel had threatened a general sentence of excommunication.

In 1406 therefore, when the situation caused by the expenses incurred in 1405 was even more pressing, the commons were insistent upon a greater effort from the clergy. They were determined, as before, to touch all those who were not assessed for the tenth, which meant the great body of chaplains and stipendiaries throughout the province of Canterbury. These stipendiaries had already provoked the criticism of the beneficed clergy in the provincial constitution which was to be renewed by Chichele.[9] In this statute the conduct of the stipendiaries in churches governed by the beneficed clergy is regulated in terms which suggest that their position since the early fourteenth century may well have been growing stronger financially, a result of the large number of pious bequests for masses and services found in later medieval wills and elsewhere. Why should these men make no contribution? What may have been in the thirteenth century a comparatively poor class had outgrown its depression and its progress cannot have been lost upon the jealous knights in parliament.

In composition the 1406 convocation follows the normal pattern; its summons was less usual. The writs were transmitted by the bishop of Lincoln, London being vacant and the bishop of Winchester, next in order, being abroad. This is carefully explained in the minutes, which Wilkins abbreviated so severely as to make the gathering one of scant importance procedurally.[10] They were in fact drawn up with the utmost care, and by their detail emphasize the vital connection between convocation and its president, the archbishop. In his absence the convocation was allowed to discuss reform in the church; it was not allowed to decide upon taxation, from which arose the numerous adjournments that kept the reluctant clergy at Westminster until agreement was reached. The grant demanded the personal attendance of the president.

The minutes of the 1406 convocation emphasize its close connection with parliament, and the "Long Parliament" proved one of the

---

9 *Presbiteri stipendiarii*, text in F. M. Powicke and C. R. Cheney, *Statutes, Synods and other Documents* (Oxford, 1964), II, p. 1136. The editors consider the attribution to Archbishop Winchelsey doubtful.
10 *Wilkins, Concilia*, III, p. 284.

most contentious in later medieval history.[11] The Canterbury province began to sit on Friday 14 May in the chapter house of St. Paul's,[12] when the certificates and proxies were examined by Nicholas Risshton, the archbishop's auditor, and William Milton, his registrar. This done, convocation stood adjourned until Monday 17 May. On that day the archbishop appeared, but not for long; because of various items of parliamentary business the two houses were adjourned until the 21st, the intervening time to be occupied in discussing and framing articles on reform.[13] On Friday the 21st the archbishop and bishops were occupied elsewhere in parliament "on the business of the king and kingdom," and at the archbishop's command John Chaundeler, dean of Salisbury, adjourned convocation to the following Monday (the 24th). At the reassembly, parliamentary business again supervened and Chaundeler was told to adjourn until Thursday 27 May at 8 AM. But on the 27th also parliamentary business kept the archbishop from convocation till 3 PM, and for the morning the members were sent away. In the afternoon meeting, after various public matters had been discussed, convocation was visited by "certain nobles sent by the king" who, led by Edward, duke of York, thanked the clergy for their generosity in the past and made a strong plea for assistance: "Considering the reign of misfortunes to which the Kingdom is calamitously subject from the insults of rebels and adversaries and the expenses in repelling them necessitated by the King's laborious march around the country."[14] After discussion, the archbishop adjourned convocation till the next day, Friday 28 May, when, however, he was *aliunde occupatus* and had to adjourn till Saturday. On the Saturday Arundel had to go for Whitsuntide celebrations to Maidstone until Wednesday in the full week (2 June). The bishop of Exeter, named as his commissary for summons or adjournment, indicated Tuesday, 1 June as the date for meeting, but two more adjournments were to come: on Thursday,

---

11 The debates till 24 May were concerned with the nomination and duties of a new king's council, the names of which were publicly declared. Among them, significantly for Arundel, was that of Sir John Cheyne.

12 Lambeth Palace Library, Register Arundel, I, f.66.

13 We do not know what these were, but some may have found their way into Richard Ullerston's *Petitiones quoad reformationem ecclesie militantis,* written in the summer of 1408. For Ullerston, see A. B. Emden, *A Biographical Register of the University of Oxford to 1500 A.D.* (Oxford, 1957–59), III, pp. 1925–9.

14 Lambeth Library, Register Arundel, I, f.66.

3 June, and, because more parliamentary business intervened, 7 June at 8 AM.

On the 7th, unfortunately, the archbishop could not attend "on account of difficult matters to be discussed with the king and his council," and Risshton, the auditor, again adjourned till the morning of Tuesday the 8th. The archbishop was then free to join his colleagues, and on Tuesday a novel delegation arrived in the chapter house. Though Arundel's registrar takes it all in his stride, what he wrote was this:

Et post varia inter eosdem communicata intraverunt certi milites et armigeri, milites comitatuum in parliamento nuncupati, missi ex parte communitatis et aliorum militum communitatuum tunc absentium et exposuerunt pro parte communitatis et militum huiusmodi absentium prefatis reverendissimo patri archiepiscopo et suis suffraganeis pericula et necessitates regis et regni ac insufficienciam ac paupertatem et inopia [sic] quibus communitas Anglicana circumducitur. ...

The writer may have mixed up the declensions of comitatus (fourth) and communitas (third), inventing a new and most expressive word communitatus, but of the meaning there is no doubt: milites comitatus are the knights of the shire; comunitas is the community of the realm represented by the commons, and aliorum militum communitatuum [sic] "other knights of the commons" away at Westminster. The people who entered St. Paul's on that Tuesday morning were the parliamentary knights, the colleagues of Cheyne and Arnold Savage speaking on behalf of the communitas Anglicana.

While the knightly delegates were pleading, the prelates and proctors of the clergy "stood around them" and listened. On the Wednesday the parliamentary knights appeared again to continue the discussion, after which the clergy withdrew to the undercroft. On Thursday, returning upstairs, they granted the lord king "a subsidy for resisting the perils and the besetting necessities that surrounded the kingdom, one tenth and a certain subsidy under a special form stated in the schedule named."[15] The special form concerned the 6s.8d. payable the following June (but collected well before that):

from every chaplain, secular or religious, even of the order of mendicant, stipendiary or hired, or taking a salary or stipend, and from every chaplain or warden of chantries, and from every other person beneficed or any other

15 *Ibid.* fols. 66, 66ᵛ. The collection of the subsidy is in ɪ, f.67, *Deputacio collectorum ad nobilia.*

benefices, parsonages or offices whatsoever, who have been unaccustomed to pay to the tenth or tenths hitherto granted to the king and also from all vicars or others beneficed in cathedral and collegiate churches, and from all rectors and vicars of churches whatsoever likewise unaccustomed to pay such tenth. ...[16]

Lists of non-contributing clergy had to be drawn up for the Exchequer, and the diocese, archdeaconry by archdeaconry, had to classify them as best it could. The king was in a hurry. On 5 August the prior of St. Mary Overy, collector in the archdeaconry of Surrey was advised under pain of £100 "for urgent causes which nearly concern the king and the defence of the realm, to leave all else and ceasing every excuse to be in person before the king and council before the Assumption next, bringing with him all sums of money due and pertaining to the king within his collection."[17] The prior brought no more than £4.[18] That was better than the prior of Wenlock (in a notoriously Lollard area) who could only muster £2.0.0.

To collect the subsidy was a formidable task for the dioceses. The returns are by no means complete but one group can at any rate be checked: the returns of the archdeaconry of Worcester. Besides the eight deaneries the Worcester list includes the exempt jurisdiction of the Vale of Evesham belonging to the abbot of Evesham. In each deanery are enumerated first the non-paying beneficed clergy, rectors, and vicars, then the chantry priests and chaplains; stipendiaries and other hired priests (*conductitii*) as well as the wardens of hospitals, and cathedral and collegiate chaplains are also listed. Against each the tax is carefully written: vjs. viiid. At the end of the document a note on procedure tells us that the archdeacon's official drew up the list at the bishop's instructions, then handed it to the collectors.

Quorum quidem capellanorum stipendiariorum et aliorum quorumcumque huius subsidii soluencium nomina et cognomina cum locis, beneficiis et officiis in quibus moram trahunt et beneficiati existunt singillatim annotantur in quadam indentura sigillo officialis domini archidiaconi Wyg' consignato [sic] prefatis collectoribus per dominum officialem ex mandato Ricardi Wygorniensis episcopi facta, tradita et super huius complementum liberata.
Summa totalis Recepte ... cxx li.[19]

This is a correct figure. For the various deaneries the following

16 *Cal. Fine R., 1405–1413*, 35.   17 *Cal. Close R., Henry IV*, III, 57.
18 P.R.O., E401/640.   19 P.R.O., E179/58/35.

number of clerks were leviable: Worcester, 56; Kineton, 54; Warwick, 56; Pershore, 67; Powick, 14; Droitwich, 24; Kidderminster,
33; Blockley, 30; Vale of Evesham,[20] 27. There were 361 leviable
clerks in all. In Pershore, the largest, non-paying rectors and vicars
were 20; non-paying cantarists 5; stipendiaries 42; 67 in all. Did
everyone pay, and is the full figure of £120 a real one or purely
notional?

The abbot of Evesham accounted on 10 December for £18 13s. 4d.
Clearly he must have collected more than this, if his target was £120,
but there appears to be no later entry in the Receipt roll. The list
drawn up in each archdeaconry by the official of the archdeacon,
probably with the help of the bishop's register, may have been a
correct statement, but it is not likely to have satisfied the Receipt,
which was used to larger sums from the dioceses. In the see of Winchester, for example, one-third of a tenth produced £148 17s. 9½d.
The sums paid in are neither striking nor abundant. The largest, as
one might expect, were for the great archdeaconry of Richmond and
for the archdeaconry of Wiltshire and Berkshire, where two instalments were received.

Between 7 October 1406 and 11 February 1407 (inclusive), seventeen archdeaconries sent in their subsidies with a total of £359 6s.
6d:[21] that means that 1,078 stipendiaries were laid under the flat rate
of contribution (6s. 8d.); but it is evident that we have only a portion
of a much bigger list which may have amounted to well over £1,500.
The details are set out in Table 1.

The Receipt roll for the months from April through July 1407 has
the following additions (we give the dates of receipt):[22]

1 June	The Prior of Hereford, collector for the dioceses of Hereford	£40.0.0.
8 July	The Prior of Durham, collector for the diocese of Durham	£40.0.0.
8 July	The Prior of Wenlock, collector in the diocese of Hereford [sic]	£9.5.6.
8 July	The Abbot of Abingdon, collector for the arch-deaconry of Berks. and Wilts.	£9.6.8.[23]
15 July	The Cellarer of the Abbot of St. Albans, collector for the abbot's exempt jurisdiction	7.8.[24]
15 July	The Abbot of St. Mary of Graces near the Tower	19.6.
		£99.19.4.

20 The abbot of Evesham.   21 P.R.O., E401/640.   22 P.R.O., E401/641.
23 Second instalment.   24 A mistake for 6s. 8d.?

TABLE I

archdeaconry	collector	sum
Barnstaple	Abbot of Hartland	£ 4. 6. 8.
Bedford	Prior of Newnham	19. 6. 8.
Buckingham	Abbot of Notley	1. 11. 10.
Chester	Abbot of Chester	39. 6. 8.
Cornwall	Prior of St. German's	13. 6. 8.
		1. 0. 4.
Derby	Prior of Gresley	13. 19. 2.
Lancaster (county of)	Prior of Burscogh	25. 13. 4.
Norwich	Prior of Castelacre	3. 18. 4.
Nottingham	Prior of Newland in Shirwood	50. 0. 0.
		3. 0. 0.
Richmond	Abbot of Fountains	63. 6. 8.
Salop	Prior of Wenlock	2. 0. 0.
Stafford	Abbot of Burton	10. 0. 0.
Sudbury	Prior of Thetford	2. 7. 8.
Suffolk	Prior of Butley	15. 0. 0.
Surrey	Prior of St. Mary Overy	4. 0. 0.
Wilts. and Berks.	Abbot of Abingdon	60. 0. 0.
Winchester	Abbot of Hyde	8. 7. 4.
Worcester	Abbot of Evesham	18. 13. 4.

Some of these figures look suspicious, especially Wenlock and St. Mary of Graces: perhaps the collector paid in all he could get. At any rate, as far as the recorded figures go, the total for these units gathered between October 1406 and July 1407 is no more than £420. But the king wanted every penny, and the commons, through their pressure, had asserted a principle.

Hermeneutics and History:
The Problem of Haec Sancta   B. TIERNEY

he decree, *Haec sancta*, enacted by the Council of Constance in 1415, declared that a general council could claim the obedience of all men "of whatsoever rank, state, or dignity, even if it be the papal." A few years ago a historian could discuss this proposition with much the same happy detachment that he might bring to a consideration of the decline of feudalism or the causes of the Hundred Years' War. Quite recently, however, a lively theological controversy has grown up concerning *Haec sancta* and the historian can hardly ignore the literature it has produced without retreating into a sort of professional provincialism even though he may at first feel that the theologians' problems are no concern of his.[1]

Nowadays a historian is likely to be interested in *Haec sancta* most of all as a document of major importance in the transition from medieval to modern constitutionalism. The theologians, on the other hand, are asking whether the decree embodies a permanent truth about the nature of the Christian church. The difference is fundamental and typical. A historian's purpose is primarily to understand the past for its own sake; a theologian's is to expound a structure of religious revelation that he considers valid for the present. But although these purposes are different they are not necessarily antithetical nor mutually exclusive. The documents of religious revelation themselves – whatever else they may be – are historical

---

1 The question of *Haec Sancta*'s validity was a matter of perennial theological debate from the fifteenth century to the nineteenth. After 1870 the discussion died away for a time. Protestants were not interested in the question and, for Catholics, it seemed settled by the pronouncements of Vatican Council 1 on papal sovereignty and infallibility. The issue is still not one of denominational controversy. The scholars whose views are discussed below all write from a Catholic standpoint.

documents. The possibility of fruitful dialogue between theologians and historians exists because they have common interests as well as divergent ones.

Both disciplines are concerned in different ways with the interplay between past and present. A historian can approach objectivity only by making himself understand how the circumstances of the present tend to influence his interpretations of the past. The theologian's objectivity consists in understanding how the circumstances of the past have shaped the doctrinal structure of the present which he expounds. This implies that, while a theologian will normally appeal to modern doctrine in judging the theological pronouncements of the past, he must also be prepared to acknowledge that existing doctrinal formulations may sometimes need reconsideration in the light of a deepening understanding of historical reality.

The hermeneutical considerations involved in a theological interpretation of *Haec sancta* have been set out with admirable clarity in a recent study by Helmut Riedlinger.[2] A valid decree of a general council, he points out, does not necessarily express a permanent, irreformable truth of Christian faith. It may refer to some changing point of church discipline. Moreover, even those decrees that are intended as solemn dogmatic definitions will always be expressed in language and buttressed by arguments that are conditioned by the cultural climate of a particular age. This means that, even when a conciliar decree contains a permanent truth, that truth may be faultily articulated or even expressed in language that is downright misleading for a modern reader. The theologian's task is to separate the grain from the chaff, to distinguish permanent truth from time-conditioned modes of expression and argumentation.

A historian may well object that this principle opens the way to the most fanciful exegesis of historical documents. The theologian seems to be saying that he can take them to mean anything he wants them to mean. But, precisely in order to avoid mere irresponsible subjectivism, Riedlinger insists that, if theology is not to "wither away in blind isolation," theological conclusions must be supported

---

2 Helmut Riedlinger, "Hermeneutische Ueberlegungen zu den Konstanzer Dekreten," *Das Konzil von Konstanz*, ed. A. Franzen and W. Müller (Freiburg/Basel/Wien, 1964), pp. 214–38. An equally lucid and excellent presentation of the historical problems that arise in the exegesis of *Haec sancta* has been provided by K. A. Fink, "Zur Beurteilung des grossen abendländischen Schismas," *Zeitschrift für Kirchengeschichte*, LXXIII (1962), 335–43.

by convincing historical analysis. "Theology ... cannot rest content," he writes, "until it has succeeded in making its position intelligible on historical grounds." Thus it is not enough for a Catholic theologian merely to assert that the decree *Haec sancta* is invalid because it conflicts with the decree *Pastor aeternus* of Vatican Council I. If he wants to carry conviction he has to wrestle with the realities of the fifteenth century (as well as with those of the nineteeth). He has to be at least open to the possibility that there may be a good historical case for the validity of *Haec sancta* and that *Pastor aeternus* may need some re-interpretation in the light of the earlier decree. Again, if a theologian wants to argue that some particular document is to be interpreted in a sense which it only obscurely expresses, he has to show how the meaning he discerns would naturally have come to be expressed in the actual words used by an analysis of the historical context in which his document took shape.

If historical credibility is to be a criterion of sound theology, then evidently the historian has a role to play – especially as critic – in the discussions of the theologians. I propose to criticize two recent, extremely opposed, interpretations of *Haec sancta* which both use historical argumentation to reach theological conclusions, and, in so doing, to present a different interpretation of my own.

Let us begin with the text of the decree:

> This holy synod of Constance, constituting a general council and lawfully assembled to root out the present schism and bring about the reform of the church in head and members ... declares that ... representing the Catholic church militant, it holds power immediately from Christ and that anyone of whatsoever state or dignity, even if it be the papal, is bound to obey it in matters which pertain to the faith, the rooting out of the said schism and the general reform of the church in head and members. Further it declares that any person of whatsoever rank, state, or dignity, even if it be the papal, who contumaciously refuses to obey the mandates, statutes, ordinances, or instructions made or to be made by this holy synod or by any other general council lawfully assembled concerning the aforesaid matters or matters pertaining to them shall, unless he repents, be subjected to fitting penance and duly punished, recourse being had, if necessary to other sanctions of the law.[3]

3 J. D. Mansi, *Sacrorum conciliorum nova et amplissima collectio* (Venice, 1784), XXVII, p. 585, "Haec sancta synodus Constantiensis, generale concilium faciens, pro extirpatione praesentis schismatis et unione ac reformatione ecclesiae Dei in capite et membris ... legitime congregata ... declarat quod ...

Haec sancta was enacted in an atmosphere of crisis: John XXIII had fled from Constance and the assembled prelates feared that he might try to dissolve the council. It is by no means a simple and straightforward decree. As Bertie Wilkinson wrote of another important constitutional document of the middle ages, "there is no plain meaning of these particular words."

The text was drafted in haste, even in panic. Moreover, although it was sponsored by the more radical members of the assembly, it had to be formulated in language that would be acceptable to the council as a whole, and the council included prelates of various shades of opinion. Not surprisingly, therefore, the decree is full of ambiguities. Probably for this reason Cardinal Zabarella opposed it. He argued for a shorter draft which claimed supremacy only for the particular council assembled at Constance and only in matters "pertaining to the faith and the ending of the present schism."[4] There seems nothing in the actual substance of *Haec sancta* that was opposed to Zabarella's own views as expressed in his *Commentaria* on the decretals – and in the end he did indeed acquiesce in the promulgation of the decree – but he probably saw that the language in which it was formulated would give rise to difficulties of interpretation in the future.

These difficulties continue to the present day. The most extreme variations of opinion have been expressed in recent work on *Haec sancta*. Joseph Gill, for instance, has restated the traditional Catholic view that the decree was a radical and invalid attempt to subvert the divinely ordained constitution of the church. Hans Küng, on the other hand, has argued that *Haec sancta* was an irreformable decree of a licit general council and as such binding on the church forever.[5]

Professor Gill, the distinguished historian of the Council of

ecclesiam catholicam repraesantans, potestatem a Christo immediate habet, cui quilibet cujuscumque status vel dignitatis, etiamsi papalis existat, obedire tenetur in his quae pertinent ad fidem et extirpationem dicti schismatis et reformationem dictae ecclesiae in capite et in membris. Item declaret quod quicumque cujuscumque conditionis, status, dignitatis, etiam si papalis, qui mandatis, statutis seu ordinationibus aut praeceptis hujus sacrae synodi et seu cujuscumque alterius concilii generalis legitime congregati, super praemissis seu ad ea pertinentibus, factis vel faciendis, obedire contumaciter contempserit, nisi resipuerit, condignae paenitentiae subjiciatur et debite puniatur, etiam ad alia juris subsidia, si opus fuerit, recurrendo."

4 Mansi, *Sacrorum conciliorum*, p. 584.
5 Hans Küng, *Strukturen der Kirche* (Freiburg/Basel/Wien, 1962). Subsequent references are given to the English translation by S. Attanasio, *Structures of the Church* (New York, 1965).

Florence, presented his views in an article published in 1964.[6] He deplored the fact that, "The principle of the superiority of council over pope, forgotten and denied in the intervening centuries (since Constance) is being revived." The issue at stake, he noted, was a theological one; but he claimed that, even without appealing to the principles of dogmatic theology, it was possible to establish the invalidity of *Haec sancta* on purely historical grounds.

His argument runs like this. The Council of Constance represented the church to the same extent that the Council of Pisa had done. Moreover, it was summoned by a "pope" whose authority was derived from Pisa. Thus, by attendance and convocation the Council of Constance had the same authority as the Council of Pisa. But Pisa is not recognized as a general council. Therefore Constance was not one either, at least in its opening stages. It became a legitimate general council when the true pope, Gregory XII of the Roman line, convoked it as such on 4 July 1415. But the decree *Haec sancta* was enacted before this, on 6 April. Therefore *Haec sancta* was not a valid decree.

Most of Gill's article is devoted to proving that, besides having been illicitly enacted in the first place, *Haec sancta* never received the papal confirmation necessary for any valid decree of a general council. The facts here are not in dispute though, as usual, the interpretation of them is. Martin V, the pope elected at Constance, declared in an unpremeditated speech toward the end of the council that he would "inviolably observe ... everything enacted *conciliariter* in matters of faith by the present Council." More importantly, in the carefully considered bull *Inter cunctas*, he required suspects accused of the Hussite heresy to affirm "that what the sacred Council of Constance, representing the universal church, has approved and approves in favor of faith and salvation of souls must be accepted and be held by all the Christian faithful." But this same Pope Martin also forbade an appeal from the pope to a future general council. The next pope, Eugenius IV, declared on one occasion, "We accept, embrace and highly respect the Council of Constance," but his attempt to dissolve the Council of Basle before it had undertaken any significant work of reform indicates a lack of any real sympathy with

---

6 Joseph Gill, "The Fifth Session of the Council of Constance," *Heythrop J.*, v (1964), 131–43. See also Gill's *The Council of Florence* (Cambridge, 1959), *Eugenius IV* (London, 1961), *Constance et Bâle-Florence* (Paris, 1965).

conciliarist doctrines; and Eugenius bitterly opposed an attempt by the dissident fathers of Basle to define the principle of conciliar supremacy as a doctrine of faith. Much ingenious theological argumentation has been deployed in attempts to prove that the papal confirmations of the Constance decrees were deliberately so worded as to exclude *Haec sancta*.[7] Gill does not rely heavily on such arguments which are indeed highly unconvincing. He is content to emphasize that no pope ever confirmed *Haec sancta* in a bull that explicitly mentioned the decree by name.

All this amounts to a moderate and reasonable argument for a widely held point of view. But it is hard to agree with Gill when he insists that his argument is a purely historical one. On the contrary, it seems to rely at every point on theological premises that would be disputed by the scholars who reach a different conclusion concerning *Haec sancta*. For example, the question whether Pisa was a valid general council seems to be essentially a theological one. There is no coherent, irrefutable historical tradition that would settle the matter beyond doubt. Lists of general councils in Catholic sources have usually omitted Pisa but lists of popes have very commonly included Alexander v, the pope elected at Pisa; and the next pope who took the name Alexander called himself Alexander vi (though of course the next John was another John xxiii).

In general Gill seems to have tacitly assumed throughout his argument that the regulations of modern canon law which lay down requirements for a legitimate general council are expressions of universal truth, valid for all time; and he never seems to realize that this is a theological presupposition, not a historically demonstrable fact. (In fact, judged by these modern criteria, the canons of the Council of Nicea are more certainly invalid than those of the Council of Constance.) One might argue that the requirements of papal convocation and papal confirmation had been clearly formulated before the fifteenth century so that it is entirely proper and not anachronistic to condemn Pisa and Constance for failing to conform to these requirements. But this is not altogether true. The canonists of the twelfth century who formulated the medieval conception of a "papal

7 For a typical statement of these arguments see A. Baudrillart's article, "Constance (Concile de)" in *Dictionnaire de théologie catholique* and, for a recent criticism of them, Paul De Vooght, "Le conciliarisme à Constance et à Bâle," *Le Concile et les conciles* (Paris, 1960), pp. 143–81.

general council" had clearly recognized that in time of schism a legitimate council could be assembled without formal papal convocation and that, in certain grievous emergencies (as when a pope was suspected of heresy), a council without the pope could enact valid decrees.[8] One can make a very good case for the legitimacy of Pisa and Constance in terms of medieval canon law. Cardinal Zabarella did so, of course.

In determining whether a given assembly (like Constance) was a true general council it is legitimate to enquire whether it was accepted as such by the whole church, including the pope. But it is anachronistic to make the validity of the particular decree, *Haec sancta*, depend on explicit papal ratification. From the terms of the decree itself it is self-evident that if *Haec sancta* were valid at all it was valid from the moment of its enactment, "this holy synod ... holds power immediately from Christ." This was obvious to contemporaries. The idea that *Haec sancta* should be presented to the pope for his *ex post facto* approval never presented itself to Martin V or to the fathers of the council or to anyone else.[9] The assumption that papal ratification is a necessary condition for the validity of all conciliar decrees involves the assumption that *Haec sancta* was invalid (precisely because its terms exclude the necessity for such ratification); but the initial assumption is derived from theology and not from history.

8 See my *Foundations of the Conciliar Theory* (Cambridge, 1955), pp. 57–67, 76–7 and "Pope and Council: Some New Decretist Texts," *Mediaeval Studies*, xix (1957), 197–218.

9 This was pointed out long ago by B. Hübler, *Die Constanzer Reformation* (Leipzig, 1867), but the point was usually forgotten until Fink insisted on it again, "Zur Beurteilung," 339. Gill was justified in devoting so much attention to the question of papal approbation since he was replying directly to De Vooght who also treated the matter at length. De Vooght's own position is ambiguous. In the article cited above (n.7), he maintained that (1) it is doubtful whether the Council of Constance represented the universal church adequately in the opening sessions because it consisted of only one obedience (p. 150), but that (2) none the less Pope Martin and Pope Eugene lent the weight of their authority to *Haec sancta* (pp. 160, 171) although (3) these papal approbations were not infallible decrees (p. 180). In a subsequent article, "Le conciliarisme aux conciles de Constance et de Bâle (compliments et précisions)," *Irenikon*, xxxvi (1963), 61–75, De Vooght maintained that (1) the ecumenicity of the fifth session of Constance was recognized by the other two obediences (p. 61) and that (2) in a strict sense no papal ratification took place because contemporaries did not regard it as necessary (pp. 64–5). He also warmly approved Küng's view that (3) the definitions of Constance were "définitions sans appel, qui engageaient l'avenir de l'église" (p. 73).

Gill's view that the legitimate papacy remained always with the Roman line is important to his argument for, if this is accepted, one can maintain that Gregory xii's resignation made possible the ending of the schism without any need for conciliar action against a true pope. But once again, while the persistence of the papacy in the Roman line is an interesting theological theory, it is quite impossible to demonstrate its truth as a matter of historical fact. The one thing that a historian can affirm with reasonable assurance is that it was impossible in 1415 to know with certainty who was the true pope. The possibilities are endless. The election of Urban vi in 1378 may have been invalid because the cardinals acted under coercion. The election may have been valid in form but the candidate mad.[10] (He certainly acted like a madman.) In either case, however, it does not follow that the cardinals could legitimately proceed to a second election without any judicial process against the man whom they had solemnly crowned as Roman pontiff and who was recognized as pope by the whole of Christendom. It may well be that the elections of Urban vi and of Clement vii were both carried out illicitly. It may also be the case that the sentences of deposition pronounced at Pisa against the popes of the Roman and Avignonese lines were canonically valid. Again, the canonists and theologians of the middle ages commonly taught that a pope could divest himself of his office if he cut himself off from the church by persistence in heresy or schism. The argument that all the "popes" of 1415 had so degraded themselves by willfully prolonging the schism has to be taken seriously and it applies with special force to John xxiii after his flight from Constance. Perhaps there was no true pope at the time when *Haec sancta* was enacted. If there was one it was quite impossible for contemporaries – as it is for us – to know whether he was John or Gregory or Benedict.

The historical event which broke the deadlock of the Great Schism and made possible the restoration of a legitimate papacy was the enactment of *Haec sancta*. Moreover, the historian can reasonably

10 On the dubious nature of the election see M. Seidlmayer, *Die Anfänge des grossen abendländischen Schismas* (Münster, 1940), O. Přerovsky, *L'elezione di Urbano VI e l'insorgere dello scisma d'occidente* (Rome, 1960), and K. A. Fink, "Zur Beurteilung." Walter Ullmann, *Origins of the Great Schism* (London, 1949), argued in favour of the claims of Urban vi, but his analysis of the juridical literature of the fourteenth century shows how impossible it was for men of that time to resolve the issue without appealing to a general council.

assert that the schism could not have been ended in any other way than by the enactment of a decree asserting authority over the legitimate pope, whoever he might be. The question whether Gregory XII was pope in the eyes of God is not really relevant to the issue. The point is that, short of a miracle – which was not vouchsafed – he could never have been established as such in the eyes of man. For a judgment in favour of any one of the competing "popes" to have been accepted by the adherents of the other two was plainly out of the question. The ideal solution of a simultaneous resignation by the rival pontiffs had proved unattainable in twenty years of tortuous negotiations before Pisa when there were only two "popes" to deal with. It passed out of the realm of practical possibility after Pisa when there were three. The only possible way out of the impasse was for some qualified body to assert jurisdiction over all three claimants.

Theologians teach that the church is indefectible, that it will endure through all the ages, and for Catholic theologians this implies the continuity of a visible church in communion with the pope. To deny the validity of *Haec sancta* is to deny the validity of the only means by which, in a real historical situation, such continuity could be preserved. The greatest flaw in Gill's argument is that this fact does not seem to interest him in the least.

Hans Küng, in presenting the opposing argument in favour of *Haec sancta*, appeals like Gill to "the most recent research in church history." He naturally emphasizes the importance of the decree as a decisive step towards the ending of the schism and, following Fink, he correctly points out that Martin V never explicitly granted or withheld approbation of *Haec sancta* because his approval was never asked for. For Küng the universal acceptance of Constance's work of re-unification and the acceptance of its decrees in general terms by Martin V and Eugenius IV are sufficient to establish that those decrees "had the authority of the whole church and of the pope behind them" and that, accordingly, "to drop the definitions of the Council of Constance ... is not allowable to a Catholic."[11]

Küng's major contribution was to set *Haec sancta* in the context of a far-ranging theological discussion on the intrinsic nature of general councils. His argument in favour of the validity of the decree seems to me very persuasive. As De Vooght observed, Küng is the first Catholic theologian in modern times who has been prepared to con-

11 *Structures of the Church*, pp. 253, 257.

sider seriously all the historical circumstances surrounding the enactment of *Haec sancta,* and his views provide a valuable and refreshing
corrective to many old-fashioned opinions. But Küng overlooked
one possibility (later suggested by Riedlinger) – the possibility that
Haec sancta might well be a licit enactment of positive constitutional
law without being in the technical sense "irreformable." There have
been many such canons in the history of the church – canons relating
to episcopal and papal elections for instance. Such laws have profoundly changed the constitutional structure of the church. They
are not without theological significance. They were intended by their
framers to be permanently valid and some of them have been in
force for centuries. But they are not technically "irreformable." If
we regard *Haec sancta* as such a decree we can preserve the substance of Küng's argument while avoiding certain objections that
have been made to it, above all the objection that, in order to reach
his conclusions, Küng had to rely on a strained interpretation of the
text of *Haec sancta.*

Arguments about which particular ecclesiastical enactments (if
any) are infallible and so irreformable usually lead into swampy
terrain. A historian can contentedly leave its exploration to the dogmatic theologians (provided that the dogmatists get their history
right). But all theologians would agree that the quality of irreformability, if it exists at all, inheres only in dogmatic definitions on faith
and morals. And the main difficulty in Küng's argument is that
Haec sancta is not cast in the form of a solemn dogmatic definition.[12]
It does not demand belief, like a dogmatic definition; it exacts
obedience, like a decree of positive law. In its preamble, *Haec sancta*
does not purport to define an article of faith. It does not appeal to
scripture or tradition. It does not pronounce anathemas against
unbelievers. We cannot be sure that it was intended as an immutable
dogmatic decree, and in such cases it would surely be wise to adopt
a variation of Ockham's razor and abide by the principle that "Infal-
libilities are not to be multiplied without necessity."

One can well understand why Küng did consider it a necessity to
classify *Haec sancta* as irreformable. He discerned a principle of

12 On this point see A. Franzen, "Das Konzil der Einheit," in *Das Konzil von
Konstanz,* pp. 69–112, here 103. Hubert Jedin, in his finely balanced study,
Bischöfliches Konzil oder Kirchenparlament (Basel/Stuttgart, 1963), notes
that, when the Council of Basle tried to define the principle of conciliar
supremacy as an article of faith, it was raising a new issue and that contemporaries were well aware of the fact.

permanent value in the decree and wanted to reply in advance to the argument that it had been implicitly repealed by subsequent legislation which emphasized the doctrine of papal primacy in a one-sided fashion. But we can defend the view that *Haec sancta* has a permanent theological relevance without insisting – against the evidence of the text – that it was deliberately promulgated as an irreformable dogmatic decree. It is impossible, for instance, to accept *Haec sancta* as any kind of valid decree and also to accept the extreme doctrine of papal power that was fashionable in the Roman curia for half a century before the Great Schism and that, unfortunately, was revived soon after the Schism had ended. This doctrine is crystallized in a phrase of Augustinus Triumphus, "The pope who can be called the church. ..." As developed by Augustinus himself and by other theologians of the fourteenth century it maintained that Christ originally conferred on Peter alone a divine right to rule the church. Peter in turn conferred authority on the other apostles. Similarly, in later ages, no licit jurisdiction existed in the church except jurisdiction derived directly or indirectly from the pope.[13] The fathers of Constance, at the time of the enactment of *Haec sancta*, obviously did not act by virtue of a jurisdiction derived from the pope. Therefore, on the curialist theory they had no authority to act at all. To accept *Haec sancta* as licit is to reject the fourteenth-century curialist doctrine of the church.

An alternative theology of the church existed in the fourteenth century. It had been developed mainly by the canonistic commentators on Gratian's *Decretum* and by the theologians who defended the episcopalist position in the medieval conflicts between mendicants and seculars.[14] According to this second doctrine Christ conferred jurisdiction on all the apostles and not on Peter alone. Subsequent bishops, created by election and consecration, also received

---

13 M. J. Wilks describes these "high papalist" theories and provides a good guide to the modern literature on them in his *The Problem of Sovereignty in the Later Middle Ages* (Cambridge, 1963). Hervaeus Natalis explained that bishops did not hold a status in the church similar to that of feudal lords in a secular kingdom. Rather they stood to the pope like stewards and bailiffs to a king, *De iurisdictione*, ed. L. Hödl (Munich, 1959), pp. 28, 29, 34. Johannes de Torquemada went further and held that the pope stood in relation to the bishops as God did to his creatures, *Oratio Synodalis de Primatu* ed. E. Candal (Rome, 1954), p. 85.

14 See Y. Congar, "Aspects ecclésiologiques de la querelle entre mendiants et séculiers," *Archives d'histoire doctrinale et littéraire du moyen âge*, xxxvi (1961), 35–151.

their authority directly from Christ. Episcopal authority was normally exercised under the presidency of the pope but, if the papal headship temporarily failed, the episcopal office was still qualified by its intrinsic nature to represent both God and the Christian people. This second theory would evidently justify legislation by a council in time of emergency when the papacy was prevented from functioning. The first theory seems tenable only on the assumption that such an emergency never has arisen and never can arise.

To sum up then: If *Haec sancta* had not been enacted, the Great Schism could not have been ended; *Haec sancta* could not have been licitly enacted if the more extreme medieval theories of papal power were valid. These facts never ceased to be true. It became convenient for a later school of theologians to forget them.

There remains one final question to consider. What was the actual nature of the claim for the general council embodied in *Haec sancta*? Here again Gill and Küng are far apart. Gill, regarding the decree as in any case invalid, asserts that it proclaimed the doctrine of conciliarism in a most extreme and radical form.[15] Küng, committed to accepting not only the validity but also the irreformability of the decree, has to advance a decidedly minimalist interpretation of its content.[16] In his view, *Haec sancta* did not claim for the general council a regular role in the government of the church but only a "control authority" in time of emergency. That is to say, the fathers of Constance foresaw that a crisis like the Great Schism might arise again at some time in the future and they wished to make provision for such a contingency. But, as Küng's critics have pointed out,[17] this is not an easily defensible interpretation of the actual text of *Haec sancta*. The decree did not merely assert a right to "control" dubious claimants to the papacy in time of schism. It also claimed a permanent superiority for future councils in all matters "which pertain to the faith ... and the general reform of the church."

It is easy to understand how these provisions came to be written into *Haec sancta*. The claim to obedience in matters of faith had to be made, not only because of the possibility that a charge of heresy might be framed against John xxiii, but above all because of the

15 *Constance et Bâle-Florence*, p. 51, "C'était le conciliarisme sous sa forme la plus extrême."
16 *Structures of the Church*, p. 255, "Conciliar parliamentarism (along the lines of a radical conciliarism) was *not* defined."
17 E.g. H. Hürten, "Zur Ekklesiologie der Konzilien von Konstanz und Basel," *Theologische Revue*, LIX (1963), 362–71.

impending trial of John Hus. (*Haec sancta* was enacted at the fifth
session of the council on 6 April; the commission to investigate Hus
was set up at the sixth session on 17 April.) A claim for the authority
of future general councils, and not merely for the particular synod
assembled at Constance, had to be put forward – so the majority
decided – because at the time when *Haec sancta* was drafted it
seemed altogether possible that the Council of Constance would
dissolve before the schism had been brought to an end.[18] And once
it had been agreed that this general claim for future councils had to
be included because of the very nature of the immediate crisis it was
hardly possible to exclude some reference to the reform of the church.
To have ignored the reform issue would have tacitly conceded in
advance to the papacy a right which the fathers of Constance were
determined to claim in some form for the council. In the two weeks
of intrigue and emotional debate that preceded the enactment of
Haec sancta it naturally proved impossible to frame a lucid and
detailed statute on such a difficult point of church law. Perhaps if the
fathers of the council had had ample time for cool deliberation they
would have worded their decree differently. But it is with the actual
text which they adopted that we have to deal.

In interpreting this text it seems possible once again to find a middle ground between the two extremely opposed views that we have
mentioned. Küng observed that the framers of *Haec sancta* never
meant to reduce the pope "to a subordinate executive organ of the
conciliar Parliament." This is true enough. Even if *Haec sancta* had
always been held in honour and *Frequens* fulfilled to the letter, the
pope, controlling all the central machinery of church government,
could hardly have become a mere executive agent of a council that
met only once every ten years. Probably no one at Constance had any
such intention. But it was entirely possible, without any such intention, to claim for the general council a regular role, in association with
the pope, in the great task of reforming the church that lay ahead.
This was one of the purposes of *Haec sancta*.

The all-important point to grasp in interpreting *Haec sancta* – a

---

18 *Haec sancta* did not make any reference to possible future schisms. It mentioned only "the present schism" and required future popes to obey future
councils in all matters pertaining to "the rooting out of the said schism." No
doubt the fathers of Constance would have upheld the right of a general
council to settle any other schism that might arise, but the wording of the
decree makes it plain that the immediate crisis was uppermost in their minds
when they framed the clause relating to future councils.

point that has been overlooked in modern interpretations – is that the decree used the word "council" in an ambiguous fashion and that the ambiguity was probably deliberate. *Haec sancta* certainly did not state, and its framers probably never intended to state, that the members of a council, acting in opposition to a certainly legitimate pope, could licitly enforce their will on such a pope in any circumstances. As regards the immediate situation, the prelates at Constance claimed authority for themselves at a time when there were three "popes," all of doubtful legitimacy.[19] As regards the future, *Haec sancta* laid down that all popes were to be subject to the decrees of lawfully assembled general councils in certain defined spheres. But in normal circumstances, once the schism was ended, a lawfully assembled council would not consist of the members alone – bishops and other representatives – but of pope and members together. The decrees of future councils, which were to be binding on the pope, would, in normal times, be decrees of pope-and-council acting jointly, not decrees of the members acting against the head. There was nothing revolutionary in claiming supremacy for such an assembly. For two hundred years before *Haec sancta* every young canon-law student, plodding through his elementary course on the *Decretum* and its *Glossa ordinaria*, had been taught that, "Where matters of faith are concerned a council is greater than a pope."[20] All the major conciliar theorists who were present at Constance affirmed that, when a legitimate pope existed, supreme authority in the church inhered in a general council that included the pope – not simply in the pope alone and not simply in the members of a council separated from the pope. And they intended that this supreme authority of pope-and-council should carry through the programme of reform envisaged in *Frequens*. The claim of the members to over-ride a legitimate head was of course put forward at Basle, but it is a radically different claim from that of *Haec sancta*.[21]

19 Some members believed that they were claiming authority for the council at a time when no true pope existed. See H. Zimmerman, "Die Absetzung der Päpste auf dem Konstanzer Konzil; Theorie und Praxis," in *Das Konzil von Konstanz*, pp. 113–37, here 120–2. This position was provided for in the rather roundabout wording of *Haec sancta* with its reference to any rank, state, or dignity, "even if it be the papal."
20 *Glossa ordinaria ad Dist.*, 19, c.19, "Videtur ergo quod papa tenetur requirere concilium episcoporum, quod verum est ubi de fide agitur, et tunc synodus maior est papa. ..."
21 The distinction we are emphasizing was brought out with great clarity by Pierre d'Ailly, *Tractatus de materia*, ed. F. Oakley: *The Political Thought of*

The distinction that we have drawn between the term "council," understood as pope-and-members together, and "council," as the members alone separated from the pope, is not an over-ingenious refinement of modern scholarship. On the contrary this distinction had been employed in debates about conciliar supremacy ever since the twelfth century. Among the canonists there was a universally held opinion that a general council, understood in the first sense of the term, possessed supreme authority in matters concerning the faith and the universal state of the church. But the canonists differed sharply among themselves concerning the authority of a council understood in the second sense of the term. At the end of the twelfth century, for instance, the French author of the *Summa, Et est sciendum* suggested that, if the members of a council disagreed with a pope, the decision of the members should be accepted. Huguccio, on the other hand, taught that, even if all the bishops of the church stood in oppostion to the pope, the judgment of the pope should prevail. Alanus held that the opinion of the members of a council in opposition to the pope was to be accepted in matters of faith but not in any other matter. Johannes Teutonicus, in his *Glossa ordinaria,* presented the various opinions and favoured the ultimate authority of the pope. A century later John of Paris hedged on the issue. There existed in the church, he wrote, an authority "equal to or greater than" the pope's. At the time of the Great Schism itself Zabarella held that the judgment of the members should prevail against that of the pope in matters of faith and he was inclined to extend their authority also to matters touching the general state of the church.[22]

This is not the place for a history of the whole problem. The point is that the leaders of the Council of Constance, men who had devoted years of study and debate to these questions, could not have been unaware of its existence. By simply decreeing that, in certain circum-

Pierre d'Ailly (New Haven, 1964), p. 304, "Secunda ad praedictam objectionem dicitur quod minor rationis non est vera, scilicet quod Papa est major et superior concilio, *licet sit major et superior in concilio cum sit caput omnium membrorum.* Et ad hanc probandum videtur esse ratio evidens, quia omne totum sua parte majus est. Sed Papa est pars concilii, sicut caput pars corporis. Ergo totum concilium majus est Papa, et per consequens auctoritas totius concilii major auctoritate Papae." The argument presents both a vindication of *Haec sancta* and a denial in advance of the claims of Basle.

22 On these various opinions see Tierney, *Foundations of the Conciliar Theory,* pp. 55, 67, 171, 232, 250–4 and "Pope and Council." All the authors used the word *concilium* sometimes to mean pope-and-members together and sometimes (especially in discussions on the trial of a heretical pope) to mean the members alone.

stances, popes were to be bound by the decisions of general councils without defining exactly what was meant by the term "council" they were deliberately leaving the issue unresolved.[23] Perhaps some of the prelates at Constance believed in the doctrine later asserted at Basle. But they did not define it. Moreover it is most improbable that a majority could have been found at Constance for any such definition. Two years after *Haec sancta* it was proposed that a decree be prepared affirming the right of the members of a council to depose a pope for crimes other than heresy, but the suggestion attracted only minority support and the decree was never enacted.

A historian might sum up the position of the fathers of Constance by suggesting that they had reached the same stage of constitutional thought as the leaders of the English parliament in 1641, at the point where they were vigorously asserting the sovereignty of king-in-parliament but had not yet advanced a claim for the supremacy of the members of parliament separated from the king. A Catholic theologian, accepting the criteria of Riedlinger set out above, might well maintain that *Haec sancta* was an attempt – a premature, imperfect attempt, perhaps – to formulate a constitutional law for the church that would be in keeping with the ancient and never-forgotten doctrine of "collegiality," the doctrine that eventually found a formal definition at Vatican Council II. He could explain the "imperfection" of the formula which was actually adopted by pointing out that, for reasons which are historically intelligible, *Haec sancta* had to combine in one long tangled sentence both an assertion of the council's authority at moments of crisis and a proposal for future co-operation between pope and council in more normal times.

These considerations can help us to understand the aftermath of the Council of Constance. For a generation after the enactment of *Haec sancta* everyone, including the popes, understood very clearly that an overt attack on the decree would re-open all the wounds of the Great Schism. For practical purposes the decree *had* to be valid. But Pope Martin, and still more Pope Eugenius, lacked any sympathetic understanding of the theology of the church underlying *Haec sancta*, and they were obdurately opposed to the line of moderate

23 Most of Hürten's criticism of Küng and De Vooght is invalidated by his failure to grasp this point. Hürten argues in various ways that the lack of universal approval for the principle of conciliar supremacy enunciated at Basle proves that there was never a consensus in favour of *Haec sancta*. But it was entirely possible to reject Basle and accept Constance.

constitutional development suggested by that theology. The inconsistencies in their attitudes led to a new period of tension and frustration. The conciliarists were driven to assert the extreme claims of Basle. Their opponents came to favour, in opposition to those claims, a variety of extreme but highly unstable papalism which was not supported by a consensus of Catholic opinion, which was dependent for its continued existence on the goodwill of secular monarchs, and which was singularly ill-adapted to carry through the necessary reform of the church. The explosion that came in the next century was as inevitable as anything in history can be.

𝕷ancastrian 𝕮aptains M. R. POWICKE

𝕿he armies of the fifteenth century[1] were composed of companies of irregular numbers serving under captains who first recruited and then commanded them. These retinues were made up of men-at-arms and archers and, at least for a large part of the century, were in a ratio of one of the former to three of the latter. Occasionally a captain undertook to include a specific number of knights amongst his men-at-arms, the rest being esquires. The whole force was usually mounted, though on occasion, especially for garrison forces, foot archers were prescribed.

The names of the captains, the size of the companies they undertook to raise, and in most cases the conditions of service, can be derived from two principal sources. These are the original indentures, of which large numbers have survived,[2] and the warrants for issue of the first payment, which are even more extensive.[3] It is not with the developments in the terms of the contracts that this paper is concerned. The intention is rather to make a preliminary enquiry into the involvement of these captains in the national and local life of the community of England. It is the belief of the writer that the extent and depth of this involvement will provide some clues as to the commitment of the nation to the war. For if the ruling parties in the nation and the county were taking part in the campaigns in France,

---

1 A. H. Burne, *The Agincourt War* (London, 1956); C. Oman, *A History of the Art of War in the Middle Ages* (2nd ed., London, 1924), II; F. Lot, *L'Art militaire et les armées* (Paris, 1949), II; H. Delbrück, *Geschichte der Kriegskunst* (Berlin, 1900–20); R. A. Newhall, *The English Conquest of Normandy* (Yale, 1924); Newhall, *Muster and Review* (Harvard, 1940); J. H. Ramsay, *Lancaster and York* (Oxford, 1892).

2 Public Record Office, Exchequer K.R., Various Accounts: E 101/69–71.

3 P.R.O., Exchequer of Receipt, Warrants for Issues: E 404/31–69. The P.R.O. has now published a list of captains.

they would be that much the more likely to vote taxes for the war and support war measures in those parliamentary discussions which are a feature of the fifteenth century.[4] Against this kind of inference is to be set the consideration that the more professional and, therefore, the less aristrocratic the captains were, the more skilful and efficient they were likely to be. On balance, it seems probable however, that involvement rather than detachment was the most likely pre-requisite for a successful war.

The evidence for participation in national and local political life is plentiful and obvious. The summons of peers to parliament,[5] the returns of knights of the shire,[6] the lists of sheriffs,[7] and the appointments of justices of the peace[8] are the principal material which has been used. Further, there are many relevant references in the chancery rolls to appointments to commissions of "oyer et terminer," "de walliis et fossatis," and to a wide miscellany of other local responsibilities. All these have been drawn upon to build up our picture of community involvement.

A further observation may be made about the great lords. It is a commonplace that the peerage of the fifteenth century played a role of increased importance in the life of the nation. Without their support in council and parliament the war with France could not go on for a moment. Yet their obvious leadership in the army had been put in question by the cessation of the feudal summons after 1327. Before that year, the same lords, broadly speaking, were summoned alike to parliament and army.[9] Nevertheless, many peers continued to serve in the army by making military contracts with the king. It will be part of our task in the following pages to discover how many parliamentary lords continued to serve in the army, and whether that number grew or declined.

While an attempt will be made to say something of the military participation of the non-parliamentary barons, the main discussion

4 Ramsay, *Lancaster and York*; W. Stubbs, *Constitutional History of England* (3rd ed., Oxford, 1884); A. B. Steel, *The Receipt of the Exchequer 1377–1485* (Cambridge, 1954); A. R. Myers, "A parliamentary debate of the mid-fifteenth century," *Bull. John Rylands Library*, xxii (1938).
5 *Reports from the Lords' Committees touching the Dignity of a Peer of the Realm*, iv.
6 *Members of Parliament (Members)* (House of Commons, 1878), i.
7 P.R.O. Lists and Indexes, no. ix (H.M. Stationery Office, 1898).
8 *Calendar of Patent Rolls, passim.*
9 M. R. Powicke, *Military Obligation in Medieval England* (Oxford, 1962), pp. 162–3.

will concern the knights and esquires of the shire communities. The influence of these local groupings of landlords on politics and war alike was prodigious. We shall be concerned to see whether their participation remained steady, waxed, or waned.

The Agincourt campaign involved Henry v in prolonged and extensive preparations.[10] The magnates were strong supporters of the English king's claims, and their enthusiasm was kindled in parliament and council. The participation of the peerage in the war was reflected in the sharp drop in the numbers summoned to the parliament of November 1415, by writs of 12 August.[11] Correspondingly, there was a large contingent of peers among the contractors for forces for the campaign. Pre-eminent among these were the dukes and earls. Thomas, duke of Clarence contracted for the largest single company, of 240 men-at-arms and 720 archers (240/720). Close behind was Humphrey, duke of Gloucester with 200/600. Thomas, earl of Arundel was to lead 100/300, the earl of Cambridge 60/160, the earl of Dorset 100/300, Edward, duke of York 100/300, the earl marshal 50/150, the earl of March 60/160, the earl of Oxford 40/100, the earl of Salisbury 40/80, and the earl of Suffolk 40/120.[12] Thus the dukes and earls comprised well over a third of the total of 2,262/6,275.

The other peers contracted for fittingly smaller retinues, though all were substantial. Lords Camoys, FitzHugh, Scrope, Talbot, Willoughby, and Clifford each undertook to find thirty men-at-arms; lords Botreaux, Zouche, and Clinton contracted for twenty men-at-arms each; while Lord Ferrers was least of the peers with 12/36.[13] The total undertaking of these remaining peers was for 252 men-at-arms and 636 archers. This brought the contribution of the peerage to just over half the total force.

It is proposed to classify the retinues of twenty or more men-at-arms as "great" companies. In 1415 the peers contributed a marked majority of such great companies. Besides the twenty peers, however,

10 E. F. Jacob, *The Fifteenth Century* (Oxford, 1961), chap. 4; N. H. Nicolas, *History of the Battle of Agincourt* (London, 1853); for other authorities, see references cited *supra* n.1.
11 *Peerage Report*, IV, 828.
12 P.R.O., E 101 69/4/389; P.R.O., E 404/31/263, 250, 149, 276, 278, 170, 169, 254, 174, 178. See also "The Agincourt Roll" in Nicolas, *Agincourt*, pp. 333f.
13 PRO., E 404/31/357, 279, 384 and 400, 179, 183, 358, 151, 351, 346, 249.

were sixteen others who had twenty or more men-at-arms. Not that
these were mostly professional soldiers. There were two lords –
Bourchier and Matrevers. Three were scions of noble houses – Sir
Edward Courtenay, Michael Pole, and Gilbert Umfrevill. Seven of
the commoners among them served at one time or another as shire
representatives in parliament.[14] Of these seven, some were figures of
national importance – such as Sir Thomas Erpyngham and Sir
Walter, later lord, Hungerford.

All the commanders of great companies in 1415 were at least
knights; there was not a solitary esquire among them. Many were
parliamentary knights, and Sir Roger Leche may be taken as typical
of this group. He represented Derbyshire in the commons in 1406
and 1413.[15] He received various valuable favours from the crown,
including the custody of church lands, for example, the Cistercian
abbey of Combermere and the priory of Holy Trinity, Repyndon.[16]
He served the crown in various capacities: as commissioner of array
in 1415,[17] on an enquiry into the concealment of royal rights and the
misbehaviour of royal officials in Derbyshire and other midland
counties in 1413,[18] in the searching out and arrest of Lollard rebels
in Nottinghamshire and Derbyshire,[19] and as justice of the peace
in both Derbyshire and Staffordshire in 1413 and 1415.[20]

The title "king's knight," into which further research is required,
was bestowed by chancery clerks on several of these great captains.
Such were Sir William Bourchier, Sir Thomas Erpyngham, Sir John
Philipp, Sir Gilbert Umfrevill, and Sir John Cornwall.[21] In all probability this was an honorific title without fixed duties or emoluments;
but it possibly implied a special availability for the king's service
which perhaps marks off its recipients from their fellow captains.

The majority of the contractors for military service were not great
captains. For purposes of analysis these leaders may be divided into
lesser captains who contracted for anything between three and nineteen men-at-arms, and individual soldiers who served simply with a
quota of archers and perhaps with one fellow warrior. There were
fifty-two lesser captains in 1415, promising a total of 139 men-at-
arms in addition to themselves, normally with three archers for each

---

14 Sir John Blount, Sir William Bourchier, Sir Walter Hungerford, Sir John
   Philipp, Sir Thomas West, Sir Gerard Ufflete, Sir Roger Leche.
15 *Members*, pp. 268, 278.   16 *Cal. Pat. R. 1413–16*, pp. 73, 393–4.
17 *Ibid.*, p. 408.   18 *Ibid.*, p. 113.
19 *Ibid.*, pp. 177–8.   20 *Ibid.*, pp. 418, 423.
21 *Cal. Pat. R. 1416–22*, 320, 29, 150, 130; *Cal. Pat. R. 1413–16*, 270, 380.

man-at-arms. The majority were still knights, only sixteen being esquires or lesser men. Seven were "king's knights," five "king's esquires," and one a "queen's esquire."[22] The proportion of parliamentary knights drops from the half of the "great captains" to one third; there were eighteen M.P.'s; of these eighteen many also served as sheriffs of their counties. Seven of the M.P.'s, all of whom served as sheriffs, were justices of the peace, as were six other lesser captains.[23] It is difficult to single out any one knight or esquire as "typical" of their group; but as an example we may note Sir Richard Hastings of Yorkshire, who also figured on the Agincourt roll.[24] He served as knight of the shire for Yorkshire in the parliaments of 1425 and 1429;[25] he was sheriff in 1426;[26] in 1413 he was commissioned to arrest certain malefactors.[27]

The individual soldiers who may have served either alone or with one companion or follower were almost all esquires. Of these there were 176. But there were also five knights in this category. A remarkable number of these men were of the county ruling class although the proportion was not as great as was that of the great and lesser captains. There were about thirty members of parliament among them: men such as John Butiller, representative for Huntingdonshire in 1414,[28] John Belle, who represented Lincolnshire in 1413,[29] and William Brokesby, who served as both sheriff and parliamentary representative of Leicestershire.[30] I think in these cases one must picture the essentially non-military county esquire setting off to do his duty in the wars.

Perhaps the first observation that naturally arises in turning to the armies levied for the conquest of Normandy (1417–21) concerns

---

22 The king's knights were Sir Richard Arundel, Sir Hertank van Clux, Sir Thomas Dutton, Sir Simon Felbrigg, Sir John Grey, Sir William Haryngton, and Sir Roland Lenthall (*Cal. Pat. R., passim.*); the king's esquires were John Peryent, William Porter, John Steward, Walter Beauchamp, and Janico Dartas (*ibid.*); the queen's esquire was Nicholas Alderwych (*Cal. Pat. R., 1413–16, 272*).

23 The following were M.P.'s, J.P.'s, and sheriffs: John Burgh, Sir Thomas Chaworth, John Cheney, Sir John Greyndor, Sir Ralph Shyrley, Sir William Talbot, and Thomas Chaucer. The other J.P.s were Walter Beauchamp, Thomas, baron of Carrew, Sir Simon Felbrigg, Sir Roland Lenthall, William Porter, and Sir Richard Tempest.

24 Nicolas, *Agincourt*, p. 353. 25 *Members*, pp. 309, 317.

26 *List of Sheriffs*, p. 162. 27 *Cal. Pat. R. 1408–13*, p. 478.

28 *Members*, p. 281. 29 *Ibid.*, p. 279.

30 *Ibid.*, p. 265; *List of Sheriffs*, p. 145.

the continuity of leadership. Did the Agincourt captains lead the ensuing conquest? The answer is no. A nucleus of only thirty-one of the 177 captains indenting in these years were veterans of Agincourt. Moreover, only twenty-five of them went on to serve in the armies of Henry VI. This absence of a sizeable corps of regular captains at the height of English achievement in France suggests a fundamental weakness in the English armies of the period.

We turn, first, to the peerage. The great dukes and earls remained in the forefront during the years 1417–21. Thus John, duke of Bedford served with 120 men-at-arms and 360 archers in 1420;[31] Thomas, duke of Clarence with 60 men-at-arms and 180 archers in 1418;[32] Thomas, duke of Exeter, with 260 men-at-arms and 780 archers in 1418;[33] John, earl marshal with 100 men-at-arms and 300 archers in 1417;[34] and Edmund, earl of March with 30 men-at-arms and 90 archers in 1421.[35] Large retinues were also contributed by two earls who did not receive summons to parliament: William de la Pole, earl of Suffolk, contracted for 30 men-at-arms and 90 archers in 1417,[36] and Humphrey, earl of Stafford, for ten men-at-arms and thirty archers in 1421.[37] Yet the proportion of men contributed by dukes and earls dropped considerably from 1415; they contracted for 610 men-at-arms and 1,830 archers out of a total force of 1,771 men-at-arms and 5,031 archers. Other baronial peers contributed nothing to these forces. Hence the contribution of the peerage dropped from just over half to just over a third of the total.

The other great captains of 1417–21 were twenty-four in number, contributing a total of 721 men-at-arms and 2,163 archers. Six of these were non-parliamentary barons. Lord Henry FitzHugh, one of this group, contracted for the largest retinue outside the peerage: 80 men-at-arms and 240 archers.[38] The other lords were Lord James of Audeley (with 21/63 in 1420), Edward, lord Ferrers of Charteley (with 20/60 in 1417), John, lord Furnivall (with 30/90 in 1421), John, lord of Matrevers (with 40/120 in 1417), and Lord Scales (with 20/60 in 1421).[39] Another group were those of noble family or who were later ennobled. These included Sir Edward Courtenay (with 30/90 in 1417), Sir John Grey of Ruthyn (with 30/90 in 1417), Sir Edward Holland (with 40/120 in 1418), Sir John Tiptoft (with 30/90

---

31 P.R.O., E 404/35/273.   32 P.R.O., E 404/33/219.
33 P.R.O., E 404/33/216.   34 P.R.O., E 101/70/576.
35 P.R.O., E 101/70/704.   36 P.R.O., E 101/70/575.
37 P.R.O., E 101/70/724.   38 P.R.O., E 404/33/217 (1417).
39 P.R.O., E 101/70/638, 580, 706, 604, 699.

in 1417), and Sir Gilbert Umfrevill (with 60/180 in 1418).⁴⁰ Six of
the great captains served as representatives of their shire in parliament; these were Sir John Tiptoft, Sir John Cornwall (with 30/90 in
1421; M.P. for Shropshire in 1407),⁴¹ Sir William Porter (with 20/60
in 1421, M.P. for Cambridgeshire in 1413),⁴² Sir John Radcliff (with
20/60 in 1417; M.P. for Norfolk in 1420 and 1427),⁴³ Sir Gerald Urs-
flete (with 20/60 in 1417; M.P. for Yorkshire in 1400–01),⁴⁴ and Sir
Hugh Lutterell (with 20/60 in 1417; M.P. for Somerset in 1414).⁴⁵
One captain served as sheriff: Sir Richard Arundel in Herefordshire
in 1412.⁴⁶ Some served as J.P.'s: for example Sir Ralph Rochefort in
Kesteven, Lincolnshire.⁴⁷ Most of the "M.P. captains" also served on
various commissions in their counties. Thus Sir Hugh Lutterell was
J.P. in both Devon and Somerset in 1422; he was on a special commission to bring three wanted men before chancery in 1417; he was commissioned in 1421 and 1422 to negotiate a loan in the counties of
Devon and Cornwall; and in 1422 he was on a commission of "oyer
et terminer" in the southwestern counties.⁴⁸ The knightly class continued to monopolize the position of great captains, and seven of
these eighteen knights were referred to in chancery documents as
"king's knights."⁴⁹

The lesser captains of 1417–21 (those with 3–19 men-at-arms)
formed a larger proportion of the captains as a whole, and brought
substantially larger companies, than in 1415. They were fifty-nine in
number, contracting for a total of 396 men-at-arms and 1,202
archers. Although leading large retinues, they were less likely to be
knights than in the Agincourt campaign: only twenty-seven had that
status. Once again, about a third served also as parliamentary
knights; 21 and a possible 3 others, were in this category. Eleven of
the "M.P. lesser captains" served as sheriffs and another eleven as
justices of the peace. (An additional four of these leaders, neither
M.P.'s nor sheriffs, served as J.P.'s.) Sir Roger Fyenes, for example,

---

40 P.R.O., E 101/70/582, 590, 621; and E 404/33/218, 220.
41 P.R.O., E 101/70/708; *Members*, p. 272.
42 P.R.O., E 101/70/694; *Members*, p. 278.
43 P.R.O., E 101/70/600; *Members*, pp. 295, 313.
44 P.R.O., E 101/70/587; *Members*, p. 261.
45 P.R.O., E 101/70/263; *Members*, pp. 282, 284.
46 *Lists of Sheriffs*, p. 60.
47 *Cal. Pat. R. 1416–22*, p. 455.
48 *Ibid.*, pp. 452, 459; 385, 417; 141, 445.
49 Sir Richard Arundel, Sir Ralph Boteler, Sir John Cornwall, Sir Ralph Rochefort, Sir John Radcliff, Sir John Tiptoft, and Sir Gilbert Umfrevill.

who also served in 1415 and in some of Henry vi's campaigns, was
M.P. for Sussex in 1429,[50] sheriff for Surrey and Sussex in 1423,[51]
and J.P. in Sussex in 1416 and 1417.[52] He was a "king's knight," as
were four others. Five of the lesser captains were called "king's
esquires."[53]

Of the eighty-eight men-at-arms serving either alone or with one
companion in 1417–21, a surprisingly large number – fourteen all
told – were knights, but I have only been able to find five who served
as representatives in parliament,[54] and two who were sometime
sheriffs.[55]

Certain generalizations may be attempted as a result of this survey
of the contracts of Henry v's reign. The army was dominated by the
peerage, though less so in the latter wars. About a third of the captains of middle-sized retinues served as members of parliament.
There was a decline in the number of individual M.P.-soldiers setting
off for the wars. In brief, there was a decline, not cataclysmic but
noteworthy, in the involvement of the political leading class after
the high point of the Agincourt campaign.

Only one expedition of Henry vi's reign was comparable to the
great muster of 1415. This was the coronation march of 1430–31,
deliberately planned in council to counter the effects of Joan of Arc
and of Charles vii's coronation at Rheims.[56] The expedition was
under the king himself, though Henry was but nine years old, and
every effort was made to ensure that it represented the might of
England. The military successes were slight, though some important
places were taken. The expedition was the swan-song of Lancastrian
military glory.

In 1430, once again the peers accounted for over half the total of
1,352 men-at-arms and 5,593 archers for whom contracts or war-

50 *Members,* p. 317.   51 *List of Sheriffs,* p. 136.
52 *Cal. Pat. R. 1416–22,* pp. 460, 54.
53 Nicholas Merbury, Nicholas Pecche, John Stiward, Roger Salveyn, and
   Christopher Standissh.
54 Sir Hugh Cokesey, M.P. for Worcestershire in 1442; Sir John Grisley, Staffordshire in 1422 and 1427; Sir John Gra'de Ingelby, Lincolnshire, 1422; Sir
   William Meryng, Nottinghamshire, 1425; John Pygot Esq., Lincolnshire,
   1432; *Members,* pp. 334, 303, 314, 303, 308, 321; J. C. Wedgwood, *History
   of Parliament 1479–1509* (London, 1936–38), I, p. 202.
55 Thomas Clarell, sheriff of Lincolnshire in 1413 and 1422, *List of Sheriffs,* 19,
   39; Sir John Kyderowe, sheriff of Cornwall in 1413.
56 Ramsay, *Lancaster and York,* I, pp. 409f; Steel, *Receipt,* pp. 172–6; *Proceedings and Ordinances of the Privy Council,* III, pp. 322f; IV, pp. 10f.

rants for issue exist. There were sixteen peers, of whom seven were of ducal or comital rank. The latter were the earl of Warwick (80/240), the earl of Arundel (60/180), the earl of Devon (7/21), the earl of Huntingdon (80/240), the earl marshal (120/360), the earl of Ormond (40/120), and the earl of Stafford (80/240). The other parliamentary peers were John, lord Beaumont (20/60), Sir Ralph Boteler (20/60), Lord Bourgchier (35/105), Lord Lovett (30/90), Lord Morley (25/64), Lord Roos (40/120), Lord Tiptoft (35/105), Lord de la Ware (30/90), and Lord de Welles (24/72).[57]

The non-peers among the great captains were outnumbered by the peers. Of the former there were thirteen. Three of these were of the nobility: the Bastard of Clarence (50/700), the Lord of Duras (20/40), and Lord Grey (40/120). The development of retinues in which the archers greatly exceeded the traditional ratio of 3:1 is a typical feature of Henry vi's reign. It probably represents a drying up of the source of men-at-arms rather than a deliberate military policy and, as such, reflects the growing disenchantment of the English middle-class with the war in France. Besides that of the Bastard of Clarence, two other retinues of great captains reflected this tendency: those of Thomas Burgh and Henry Fenwick esquires (joint commanders, 80/600), and of Sir John de Kyghley (30/500).[58] The other great captains of 1430 were Henry Bourgchier esquire (35/105), Sir John Cobham (20/60), Sir Philip Courtenay (20/60), Sir William Philip (20/60), Sir William Porter (20/60), Sir John Robessart (20/60), and Sir Ralph Rocheford (20/60).[59] For the first time some of the great captains were not knights, though the knightly class continued to predominate. Only two of them served in parliament – Sir Philip Courtenay for Devonshire in 1427 and 1455,[60] and Henry Fenwick esquire for Northumberland in 1430.[61] Courtenay was active on many commissions in Devon, Somerset, and Cornwall. More than once he was ordered to enquire into piracy and smuggling; he also served as commissioner of array in coastal defence, as commissioner of "oyer et terminer," and as negotiator for a local loan to the king. He was J.P. for Cornwall and a "king's knight."[62] Fenwick

57 P.R.O., E 404/46/188f.; E 101/70/672.
58 P.R.O., E 404/46/45, 149
59 P.R.O., E 404/46/190, 230, 231, 255, 256, 209, 259.
60 *Members*, pp. 313, 350, 360; Wedgwood, *Parliament*, pp. 229–30.
61 *Ibid.*, p. 319.
62 *Cal. Pat. R.*, *1429–36*, pp. 299, 197, 280, 301, 358, 469, 473, 519, 198, 273, 358, 361, 354, 615.

was less active, but had a term as sheriff of Northumberland and was once a commissioner of array.[63] Others were also active in local and national affairs. Thomas Burgh esquire was given the custody of the castles of Scarborough and Newcastle in 1423, and was to have robes from the great wardrobe; in 1431 he was commissioner "de kidellis" in Norfolk.[64] Sir John de Kyghley was a "king's knight"; he had valuable appointments as keeper of the temporalities of the bishopric of Bangor and as collector of Irish customs; in 1432 and 1433 he served as J.P. for Surrey.[65] Sir William Philip had an even more active and prolonged career as J.P. – in his case for Norfolk and Suffolk, in which counties he was also frequently commissioned to raise loans. Although not a "king's knight," Philip had once been a "king's esquire."[66] Another active J.P. and commissioner of loans was Sir Ralph Rocheford, "king's knight."[67] Probably Sir John Robessart was of a different type – perhaps a professional soldier. He doesn't appear as an active M.P., J.P., sheriff, or commissioner; but he received considerable money fees and was awarded letters of denization in recognition of his good services to the king.[68] Our list does not exhaust the active political administrators among the great captains of 1430, and is perhaps enough to show how fully the nation was involved in this expedition.

There were twenty lesser captains in 1430, contracting for 145 men-at-arms and 658 archers. Fifteen of the twenty were knights, and one, Thomas, lord of Echyngham (12/36), was a noble. As with the larger companies, there were several cases where the companies were primarily bodies of archers with a small nucleus of men-at-arms. Such were the followings of William Heyward esquire (6/120), Maykeyn Longworth esquire (10/100), and Nicholas Cok esquire (3/60).[69] Perhaps the most astounding fact about the lesser captains of 1430, however, was that fourteen of the fifteen knights and one of the four esquires served as parliamentary knights. Three examples will suffice. Sir William Montfort served as M.P. for Warwickshire

63 List of Sheriffs, p. 98 (1427); Cal. Pat. R., 1422–29, p. 405.
64 Cal. Pat. R., 1422–29, p. 116; Cal. Pat. R., 1429–36, p. 625.
65 Cal. Pat. R., 1422–29, pp. 213, 287, 353; Cal. Pat. R., 1429–36, p. 625.
66 Cal. Pat R., 1422–29, pp. 570, 39, 355, 481; Cal. Pat. R., 1429–36, pp. 621, 625; 50, 354.
67 Cal. Pat. R., 1422–29, pp. 63, 354, 481, 565; Cal. Pat. R., 1429–36, p. 50. He was also commissioner of array and "de walliis et fossatis," ibid., pp. 128, 469, 521–2.
68 Cal. Pat. R., 1422–29, pp. 13, 229.
69 P.R.O., E 404/46/148, 150, 147.

in 1422, 1423, and 1437;[70] he was sheriff in 1432 and J.P. in 1433–34.[71] He negotiated loans in the county on several occasions in the 1420s and 1430s, and assessed the parliamentary grant of 1431.[72] Sir John Popham was active in Hampshire as M.P., J.P., commissioner of array, and negotiator of a loan.[73] Our third example, Sir Robert Roos, served Lincolnshire as M.P., J.P., commissioner of "walliis et fossatis" and commissioner of array.[74] The thorough involvement of the political community in the coronation expedition is thus more than confirmed.

There were eighty-eight individual contractors in 1430, all but one esquires or clerks. About a dozen were clerks of the household, and another twenty-five esquires of the household. This number also included a chaplain and almoner. A far smaller percentage of these individual contractors served in the house of commons; I have been able to discover only eighteen of the eighty-eight serving in this capacity. However, this was still a rise compared with the figures for 1417–21, and about the same as the ratio in 1415. The thesis of a high political involvement in the coronation expedition is sustained.

It would be tedious, even if it were possible, to enquire in this way into all the expeditions of Henry VI's reign. In the relatively small expeditions of 1434 and 1436 the peers were still dominant, though there was a decline in the knightly class and a very poor representation of past and future parliamentary members. Lord John Talbot's company comprised almost half of the 1434 force,[75] and a group of peers led by Richard, duke of York accounted for most of the army of 1436.[76] Four M.P.'s are to be found among the captains of 1434 – Sir William Chamberlin, Sir Henry Norbury, Thomas Hoo esquire, Foulkes Vernon esquire[77] – but none appears among those of 1436. The persistent interest of the court aristocracy in the war was all that kept the English effort alive.

Even this aristocratic interest disappeared, or all but disappeared, in the closing campaigns of the war. Sir Thomas Kyriell, in 1450,

70 *Members*, pp. 304, 307, 331.
71 *Cal. Pat. R.*, 1422–29, p. 1571; *Cal. Pat. R.*, 1429–36, pp. 188, 626.
72 *Cal. Pat. R.*, 1422–29, pp. 354, 481; *Cal. Pat. R.*, 1429–36, pp. 50, 126, 137, 529.
73 *Members*, p. 342 (1449); Wedgwood, *Members*, I, 692; *Cal. Pat. R.*, 1422–29, p. 563; *Cal. Pat. R.*, 1429–36, pp. 51, 473, 522.
74 *Members*, p. 303 (1422); *Cal. Pat. R.*, 1422–29, pp. 172, 500, 565, *Cal. Pat R.*, 1429–36, pp. 273, 348, 469, 521, 619.
75 P.R.O. E 404/50/159.
76 P.R.O. E 404/52/196, 208, 211, 226; E 101/71/3/894, 895.
77 Wedgwood, *Members*, I, pp. 172, 466, 635, 907.

was accompanied by only one other knight;[78] one of the esquires, John Clyfton, who led ten men-at-arms and one hundred archers, may have represented the city of Lincoln in parliament in 1429.[79] The ratio of archers to men-at-arms was at times as high as 14:1, though 10:1 was more normal. The short supply of men-at-arms may have contributed to the defeat at Formigny;[80] at any rate, this force was notable for its unruliness and insubordination.[81]

The army of 1453, like that of 1450, also met defeat on the battle-field. This time the commander was a peer, Lord John Talbot, and three of his captains were non-parliamentary lords.[82] Almost half of the remaining captains were of knightly status, and two of these were active in county government, though not as M.P.'s.[83] One of the esquire-captains was also modestly employed in local affairs.[84] The ratio of ten archers to one man-at-arms, emergent in 1450, was standardized in 1453.

This analysis supports the conclusion that the English lost the Hundred Years' War because, at the very time when the French nation was being roused, the solid core of the English nation was losing interest and withdrawing its support. We only claim to have told one part of the story. Equally important, and probably causally related, was the decline of parliamentary taxation and therefore of the loans which that taxation underwrote. The one great national effort of Henry VI's reign which can compare with the almost crusading fervour of 1415 was the coronation expedition of 1430–31 which culminated in the French coronation of the boy king. But apart from that militarily sterile enterprise, the story is one of disillusionment, loss of faith, and withdrawal.[85]

78 Sir Thomas Dring (30/100), P.R.O. E 404/66/28.
79 *Members*, p. 316.
80 A. Burne, *The Agincourt War*, p. 317.
81 Ramsay, *Lancaster and York*, II, p. 104.
82 William, bastard of Exeter, Lord Robert Moleyns, and Lord William Say.
83 Sir Richard Frogenhale and Sir John Lisle.
84 John Baker esquire.
85 The writer leaves open the question whether there were clearly defined reasons for these new attitudes. Preoccupation with internal problems seems dominant in the parliamentary debate of 1449 (Myers, "A parliamentary debate"); this seems confirmed indirectly by R. L. Storey, *The End of the House of Lancaster* (London, 1966).

The Huntingdonshire Parliamentary Election of 1450 J. G. EDWARDS

I
n spite of the large mass of archival evidence about English parliamentary elections in the fourteenth and fifteenth centuries, there are several important aspects of the subject that remain surprisingly obscure. The two documents printed below (pp. 392–95) help to illuminate a few of these obscurities. These documents relate to the election of two knights of the shire to represent the county of Huntingdon in the parliament of November 1450. We must premise that such an election would present a variety of possibilities. It might be contested (if more than two candidates were nominated for the two seats that had to be filled) or uncontested. It might also be disputed (if some irregularity was alleged to have occurred in the course of the electoral proceedings) or undisputed. Such irregularities were particularly apt to occur, of course, if an election were contested hotly, and for that reason contested elections were often also, but not necessarily, disputed elections.

Document I below, in Latin, is the indenture by which the sheriff of Huntingdonshire in 1450 returned to chancery the names of the two persons who had been elected; Robert Stonham and John Styuecle, both of them esquires. Instruments of this sort normally confined themselves to stating the names of the persons elected and the names of the persons whose seals were appended to the document as a guarantee of its authenticity. Rather exceptionally, this particular indenture contains in addition a statement to the effect that there is "stitched" to it what it calls a *certificatio* containing some further particulars of the election. From this *certificatio* it becomes evident that the Huntingdonshire election of 1450 was both contested and disputed: contested in that three candidates had been nominated for the two seats; disputed in that the electoral proceedings were alleged to have been interrupted and brought to a stand by threats of force on the part of the supporters of Henry Gymber, one of the three candidates. The *certificatio* itself states that it was put forward by 124 named supporters of the other two candidates, Stonham and Styuecle, and that it bore their seals, though these by now have all disappeared.[1] This *certificatio* is printed below as document II; it is an interesting specimen of mid-fifteenth-century English, and although it is no longer actually "stitched" to the indenture, the two documents are preserved together in the Public Record Office.

Both documents were printed by Prynne as long ago as 1662, and the *certificatio* was again printed by Wedgwood in 1938, so they are very familiar to historians.[2] Neither of these printed versions is free from incidental errors, and even more regrettably, neither Prynne nor Wedgwood printed the *certificatio* in full. They omitted nearly all the names of the 124 persons who are stated to have "severally" put their seals to the document. They seem to have thought that a sentence in the concluding part of the *certificatio* – "we the saide ffreholders to the nombre of cxxiiij have putte to oure seales severally" – would adequately summarize the string of names. By taking this short cut, however, they unwittingly did a double disservice to the historical study of the document. If they had printed the names in full, the mere existence of the list in print might possibly have suggested, and would certainly have facilitated, the necessary identification of the people and the establishment of some estimate of their social and economic position in the Huntingdonshire of 1450. (That necessary but lengthy operation still remains to be performed, and naturally it could not even be attempted in the limited compass of the present paper.) Again, if the list had been printed in full, one significant point would at once have become obvious: it is more than a mere list of names. It is in fact a list of 124 persons arranged in a way that provides a preliminary but significant clue to their social and economic position as expressed in fifteenth-century terms. Reference to

1 In its original state, complete with seals, it must have been quite an impressive document. In its present state the parchment measures some 52.4 centimetres across, 20 centimetres down its left edge and 19 centimetres down its right edge. On its left edge is the usual torn "root," which is all that remains of what was presumably a considerable number of "tongues" of parchment that would have been requisite to accommodate the 124 seals which purport to have been appended.

2 William Prynne, *Brevia Parliamentaria Rediviva* (1662), pp. 156–9; Josiah Wedgwood, *History of Parliament, 1439–1509, Register* (London, 1938), pp. ciii–civ.

the full text of the *certificatio* printed below shows two things: (1) that all the 124 persons who are stated to have appended their seals are comprehensively described as "ffreholders and duellyng withinne the same shire of Huntyngdon havyng frehold to valewe clerely overe all charges yerely xls."; but also (2) that one of them is further described as "knyght," that eight others are further described as "esquyers," and that ten others are further described as "gentilmen." In other words, the unabbreviated *certificatio* provides among other things a contemporary, categorized list of 124 of the Huntingdon county electors of 1450 divided into four classes – "knyght," "esquyers," "gentilmen," and undifferentiated forty-shilling freeholders. This feature could not emerge from the abbreviated version printed by Prynne and Wedgwood. Now that it does emerge, it immediately suggests two reflections. First, that such a categorized list of county electors at a date as early as 1450 is a rarity. Second, that such a list with as many as 124 names is perhaps sizeable enough to be of some service as a provisional but concrete "sample" of the vanished Huntingdonshire electorate of the mid-fifteenth century.

There are of course various reservations that must be duly kept in mind. The *certificatio* is avowedly a statement made by one of two groups of contending electors. An *ex parte* statement of any kind is apt to manipulate numbers upwards or downwards to suit its own purpose. In the present case, however, what is actually said seems to be worded with some care. The only precise figure mentioned is that of the 124 who promoted the *certificatio* and who are alleged to have all been forty-shilling freeholders: the interruption of the electoral proceedings meant that the forty-shilling status of the 124 was never verified, but at any rate the number is supported by actual names. The 300 others who are said to have supported Stonham and Styuecle, and the 70 who are said to have supported Gymber, are actually expressed as "a ccc" and "a lxx," and in English usage from the fourteenth to the sixteenth century the indefinite article "a" followed by a numeral normally "expresses an approximate estimate."[2] It is also noticeable that whereas the 70 are called "ffreholders

3 *Oxford English Dictionary*, s.n. "a." Stubbs, *Constitutional History* (5th ed.), III, p. 423, does not remark that the "300" and the "70" are not intended as exact numbers. He also says that the 70 "had voted for" Gymber: in fact 48 of them were "examined" on oath by the undersheriff, with what result is not stated, but any of them who failed to survive the "examination" would not be polled.

comuners," the 300 are called "*goode* comuners," which may mean that the certificators were cautiously taking refuge in the indefinite-ness of "goode" as well as in the indefiniteness of "a ccc." In any case, as the *certificatio* was submitted through the sheriff, it was going to someone who was not totally unacquainted with the facts, so that even if the certificators were indifferent to literal accuracy, they presumably had some regard for "artistic verisimilitude."

Another reservation concerns the meaning of two of the four categories into which the 124 certificators are divided. "Knights" were a clearly defined class, and "forty-shilling freeholders" were at any rate clearly definable. The terms "esquires" and "gentlemen," however, were not clearly differentiated in the fifteenth century.[4] Nevertheless, each local community seems to have had some sort of consensus about who were called "esquires" and who were called "gentlemen." Moreover the existence of the terms was reflected in the statute book. A statute of 1413 (1 Henry v, c. 1) described the county electors as consisting of "les chivalers, les esquiers et autres." A statute of 1430 (8 Henry vi, c. 7) referred to "chivalers" and "esquiers" and "gentiles" as participating in county elections. At the time of our Huntingdonshire election in 1450, a very recent statute (1445, 23 Henry vi, c. 14) had provided that the persons elected to represent the shires should be "notablez chivalers des mesmez les counteez ... ou autrement tielx notablez esquiers gentils hommez del nativite des mesmez les counteez come soient ablez destre chivalers," and that none should be so elected "qi estoise en la degree de vadlet et desouth." The certificators of 1450 were clearly very conscious of this statute of 1445: they themselves recall that it had been "re-hearsed" in the writs summoning the parliament of November 1450,[5] and they assert that the candidate Henry Gymber was not of gentle birth as the statute required. So, although "esquire" and "gentle-man" cannot be clearly differentiated by us, we may surmise that in the *certificatio* they probably had some intelligible relation to the facts, in the minds both of the certificators who employed them and of the sheriff who vouched the *certificatio* to warrant his returning Stonham and Styuecle as the successful candidates.

For what it may be worth, then, our "sample" of 124 Huntingdon

4 See the remarks of Professor H. L. Gray, "Incomes from land in England in 1436," *EHR*, xlix (1934), 625–6.
5 The enrolled writ of summons is printed in *Report from the Lords Commit-tees touching the Dignity of a Peer of the Realm*, iii, pp. 928–9.

county electors in 1450 was actually made up as follows: knight, 1; esquires, 8; gentlemen, 10; plain 40/-freeholders, 105. An obvious query is whether this proportion of 1 knight to 8 esquires is likely to have been a typical sample. This question happens to have been touched upon by Professor H. L. Gray who, basing his study upon some lengthy lists of names recorded by some commissions in 1434, concluded that between knights and esquires "an intelligible ratio emerged. Although this varied considerably, the average for fifteen counties was 1 knight to 5 esquires." For Huntingdonshire he found that the ratio in 1434 was 1 knight to 6 esquires. When he tried an alternative count based mainly on the tax-lists of 1436, it gave him a ratio for Huntingdonshire of 1 knight to 7 esquires.[6] Now of course such ratios are notional, but at least they are not essentially divergent from the ratio of 1 knight to 8 esquires in our Huntingdonshire "sample" of 1450; thus they tend to strengthen rather than weaken one's inclination to regard the "sample" as a reasonably serviceable one – at any rate for Huntingdonshire. In that case, one would estimate that the county electorate of Huntingdon in 1450 would be made up somewhat as follows: knights, about 1%; esquires, about 6%; gentlemen, about 8%; plain 40/-freeholders, about 85%.

In respect of parliamentary "experience," too, our Huntingdonshire list of 1450 seems reasonably typical. Shire representatives were, in practice (a practice prescribed by statute since 1445), chosen from among the knights, esquires, and gentlemen of the shire, of whom nineteen are specified in our list. The two who were elected for the parliament of November 1450 – Robert Stonham and John Styuecle, both esquires – had previously been elected for Huntingdonshire: Stonham eight times and Styuecle twice. The single knight on the list, Nicholas Styuecle, who may have been the father and was almost certainly a relative of John Styuecle, had been seven times knight of the shire for Huntingdon between 1420 and 1435. On the other hand the three who had thus served repeatedly are adequately balanced by the equally typical sixteen who had not been called upon (and perhaps did not particularly aspire) to represent their shire in parliament.[7]

Stubbs has rightly described the documents of the Huntingdonshire

6 Gray, "Incomes from land," 626, 634–5.
7 Two of the "gentilmen" seem to have each served twice as representatives of the borough of Huntingdon: Thomas Charwalton in 1431 and 1433, John Chyksond in 1431 and 1435.

election of 1450 as "an important illustration of a contested election." That is indeed their direct interest, but indirectly they illuminate other aspects of medieval parliamentary elections besides contests. One such aspect has already been discussed above. Another concerns the problem of interpreting the evidence of election indentures. After the statute of 1406 which prescribed that the names of persons elected as parliamentary representatives should be returned by indentures drawn up between the sheriff and those who made the election, the indentures naturally become of capital importance for parliamentary history; they have survived in very considerable numbers, though not as consecutively in the second half of the fifteenth century as historians would wish. But, as often happens when archival evidence is used for historical purposes, these indentures present the historian with a sort of façade which challenges scrutiny. They usually state that the shire court was held at such a place on such a date, that so and so were then elected, and that the indenture is "data die et loco supradictis." Consequently, it usually seems to have been tacitly assumed that these indentures were drawn up on the spot in the shire court which made the election. Reference to document I will show that the Huntingdonshire indenture of 1450 conforms almost precisely to the usual pattern: it states that in the shire court at Huntingdon on Saturday next before the feast of St. Luke the Evangelist (17 October 1450), Robert Stonham and John Styuecle, esquires, were elected to be representatives of the shire in parliament, and that "Hec indentura ibidem facta in pleno comitatu" is "data die et loco supradictis." Nothing could be more categorical. In the middle of the text of this particular indenture, however, there comes the sentence to the effect that there is "stitched" to it what is called a *certificatio* giving further details about the election. Clearly, therefore, this particular indenture was drawn up after the certification which was stitched to it. Reference to document II below will show that the *certificatio* also mentions the same place and date of the election as the indenture, but mentions it in a way that is in one respect significantly different. The *certificatio* states that the election occurred "at Huntyngdon the Saterday next before Seynt Luke day the Evangelist nowe last passid"; thus it is obvious that the *certificatio* was being drawn up after the election day. Since the indenture was in turn drawn up after the certification, it follows that the indenture, in spite of its categorical talk of "data die et loco supradictis" was in fact drawn up on some date, unknown but later than that of the election day. And that significant fact is indicated in another way as well. In the *certificatio* the certificators say that "what the shireve will returne in this behalf we can have no notyse." Yet the five persons who are named as sealing the indenture containing the sheriff's return, are none other than five of the certificators – one knight, two esquires, and two gentlemen.[8] Presumably, therefore, when they said in their *certificatio* that they could "have no notyse" what the sheriff would return, they said so because they had not then sealed the indenture, for five then did have "notyse" of what names the sheriff was returning. This then adds proof that this particular indenture was drawn up after the *certificatio*. As the election day was already "passid" when the *certificatio* was drawn up, then *a fortiori* it was "passid" when the indenture was made. Yet the indenture itself purports to have been "made" and "dated" on the actual election-day. It is therefore clear that whatever the wording of these indentures may purport, they were not necessarily drawn up in the shire court at the time when the election was made. This conclusion is reinforced by another consideration which is also indicated by the Huntingdon documents of 1450.

The fact that the sheriff was always a party to the election indentures does not necessarily imply that he was always present at the actual election. The Huntingdonshire documents prove that the sheriff was not present at the election on that occasion, and that his place was taken by the undersheriff. Why this happened then is not indicated, but sheriffs were subject to normal human accidents like ill-health, and they had many things to attend to, particularly if their bailiwick happened to consist not of one shire but of two. In the fifteenth century there were no less than nine such pairs of sheriff-doms, one of which, incidentally, happened to consist of the two shires of Huntingdon and Cambridge. Quite possibly the sheriff of paired shires tended to make more use of his deputies. It seems clear, however, that when a parliamentary election took place, the responsibility for making the return rested absolutely upon the sheriff himself, whether or not he was actually present at the election. Thus on 15 June 1461 the shire court of Norfolk made an election under the presidency of the undersheriff as the sheriff's deputy. (The sheriffdom of Norfolk, incidentally, was paired with that of Suffolk). One candidate whose name had been proposed was John Paston, and

---

8 I assume that the "William Walker" of the indenture was probably the same person as the "William Waller" of the *certificatio*.

on 18 June the undersheriff wrote to Paston telling him briefly what had happened in the shire court three days earlier. He concludes thus:[9] "I purpose me, as I woll answer God, to return the dieu [due] eleccion, that is after the sufficiente [that is in accordance with the votes of the qualified electors], yow and Mastir Grey. Never the latyr I have a master." The last remark is significant. The undersheriff says that he "purposed" to "return" (i.e., to the sheriff) that the voting had gone in favour of Paston and Grey. But he "had a master." In other words he was merely undersheriff, the sheriff was his "master," and it was the "master" who would make the final return to chancery. Clearly the sheriff's final return to chancery might not necessarily be in accord with what the undersheriff "purposed" to "return" to him.

It is thus evident that on occasions when the sheriff was not actually present at the election, some interval, shorter or longer, would almost necessarily occur between the actual election and the time when the sheriff finally gave the word for drawing up the indentured return that went to chancery. In the Huntingdonshire election of 1450 the length of such an interval cannot be estimated. In the Norfolk election of 1461 it probably ran to several days because three days after the election the undersheriff was still only at the stage of "purposing" to inform the sheriff what had happened at the election.[10] The Huntingdonshire indenture of 1450, though it was not made in the shire court, seems nevertheless to have been accepted without question by the chancery. So there was presumably no legal necessity that the indenture be drawn up in the shire court. Indeed one can gather as much from the statute of 1406 which inaugurated the indentured returns. All that the statute says is that "after they [the representatives] have been elected ... their names shall be written on an indenture under the seals of all those who elected them": it does not prescribe that the writing and sealing must be done in the shire court.

These considerations have an interest beyond that of mere "parlia-

---

9 J. Gairdner, ed., *Paston Letters* (1904), III, 36. For the dates see K. B. McFarlane in *T.R.H.S.*, 4th ser., XXVI, 59.

10 Unluckily the returns for the 1461 parliament are not extant. It may be that no return was made by the sheriff of Norfolk, for the election was greatly disputed and led to litigation. The statements of the undersheriff to Paston and those of the sheriff in the course of the litigation are not easy to reconcile. See Professor C. H. Williams, *EHR*, XL (1925), 79–86, and K. B. McFarlane, *supra* n.9.

mentary antiquities." The question whether the election indentures were sealed in the shire court has a bearing upon one of the most important practical problems of medieval parliamentary elections in England – the problem of the "false return." A "false return" was an indenture in which the sheriff named certain persons as having been duly elected when the outcome of the election had in fact been different. That this was a serious problem is very evident from the Statute Book. The statute of 1406 providing for returns by indentures was avowedly designed to remedy this very abuse. A supplementary statute of 1410 prescribed penalties for breaches of this statute of 1406: sheriffs were to incur a penalty of £100 payable to the king, and any representatives who had been "unduly" returned were to lose their "wages" for going to the parliament which they had attended. A statute of 1430 increased the sheriff's penalties by adding a year's imprisonment to the penalty. A statute of 1445 brought the elections of city and borough representatives, as well as those of shire representatives, within the scope of the legislation, and greatly increased the penalties all round. The growing severity of these statutes doubtless indicates that they were not effective, but it also proves that the problem of "false returns" was persistent. It was indeed a problem that was never solved in the medieval period.

To say that some indentures were demonstrably not drawn up in the shire court, and that the sheriff was under no legal obligation to make the indentures in the shire court, is not to imply that he never made them there. The reasonable probability seems to be that he would be guided by circumstances and his own convenience. There is no need to suppose that every sheriff on every occasion was out to make a false return. It would seem that, from the sheriff's point of view, one convenience of making the indenture in the shire court might be that in the shire court he would have a number of electors readily at hand to append their seals to the indenture. So on any occasion when he was not meditating a false return, he might well find it convenient to draw up the indenture in the shire court. If, however, he was intending to make a false return, one would be inclined to surmise that he might achieve his purpose more unobtrusively and therefore more safely if the indenture were drawn up and sealed at some time and place other than the shire court. At this point, however, we find ourselves baffled by the common form of the indentures, which all purport to have been made in the shire court. One value of the Huntingdonshire *certificatio* of 1450 is that it

some errors, and with an illustration which is described as "reduced by one-third."[13] The manuscript was already difficult to read in parts when seen by Prynne, and a number of words are now doubtful because of gall stains. Fortunately, however, a transcript of the document was made for the Record Commission, probably in the eighteen-thirties, and that transcript is still preserved in the Public Record Office (Parliamentary Writs, Record Commission Transcripts, 29–31 Henry vi, pp. 12–16). Possibly the gall stains date from the making of that transcript. In any case, the maker of the transcript was rather more careful than Prynne, and perhaps the document was then more legible in parts than it is now. In the version below, words printed in italics are the readings of the Record Commission transcript.

To the Kyng oure gracious erthly sovereyngne lord

Please it youre highnes for many dyversez urgentz causez be the assentz of your lords spirituell and temporell have assigned youre parlement to be holden at Westmynster in the fest of Seynt Leonard nowe next coming that is to wite in the yere of youre most gracious reigne the xxix [6 November 1450] and theruppon to send youre writtes for elections of knyghtes citeseynes and burgeis to all the shirefs of this youre noble lond and among other to your shiref of youre shires of Cantebrig and Huntyngdon. And atte Huntyngdon the Saterday next before Seynt Luke day the Evangelist nowe last passid [Saturday 17 October 1450] the undershyreve of youre saide shyre of Huntyngdon there in the pleyn shire dide youre saide writte of election to be proclamyd to chese ii knyghtes for the saide shire like as in your saide writt is more pleynely conteynyd for youre sayde parlement, and in the same writt is rehersid dyuerses estatuz and ordynaunces and among other that the ii knyghtes that shuld be chosen shuld be notable knyghtes or esquyers or of gentell berth to be chosen be the ffreholders in youre saide shire. And we Nicholas Styuecle, Knyght; Robert Stonham, John Styuecle, John Knyvet, Richard Bevyle, William Waller, William Druell, Thomas Clyrevayx, John Aysshfeld, esquyers; John Collan, Richard Spray, William Morys, John Cheker, John Chyksond, Edmund Wareyn, Baudwyn Wedyngfeld, John Purdy, Thomas Charwalton, John Lord, gentilmen; William Ffaunt, Thomas Barbour, William Botiller, John Ancy,

---

13 The scale is correctly stated, but it is necessary to add that the illustration covers less than half of the text of the original document.

Thomas *Clift*, John Draper, Waulter West, John Sewale, John Kyng, William Kyng, John Redman, John Sykard, John Clyflok, John Hosyer, John West, John Couper, John Crysp, John Horwode, Richard Baker, John atte Water, John Redman the yonger, William Blenche, Thomas Burton, Richard Boys, John Judde, John Mody, Laurens Merton, John Pulter, John Pagraue, Henry Gylour, John Smyth, John Bayle, Richard Judde, William atte Tounesend, John Rauen, Thomas Sebern, Richard atte Tounesend, John Motte, Thomas Aungevyn, John Nicholas, William Nicholas, William Porthos, John Porthos, Richard Smyth, Thomas Joynour, Thomas Parker, Henry Corbet, John Roper, John Bonour, John Annfles, John Bolyon, Thomas Wattisson, Thomas Kyng, Edward Ffyssher, Richard Baker, William Gelam, Thomas Garlek, Robert Walton, Robert Beteswell, John Charwalton, Edmund Ulff, Rauf Ramsey, Robert Dernewell, John Bruys, John Smyth, William Mayster, Robert Spervyle, John Hendisson, Henry Ffitzion, John Mayster, John Belle, Robert Dalton, William Moyne, John Roper, William Peet, William Moyses, John Gosselyn, Richard *Herry*, Richard *Porpworth*, John Mathewe, John Ffyssher, Richard Clerk, John Clerk, William Wardale, Thomas *Reece*, Edmond Cotsale, John Broun, John Galewey, John Kelston, Thomas Ibot, John atte Brigge, John Roode, John Leuynge, John Allumby, John Reppesle, Thomas David, John Rychard, Richard Somer, Laurens Juet, John Bayle, Richard *Motte* (?), John Boton, John Aysshelyn, Richard *Deke* and Symond *Trewe*, ffreholders and duellyng withinne the same shire of Huntyngdon havyng frehold to valewe clerely overe all charges yerely xls., with a ccc moe goode comuners of the saide shire, youre trewe humble sugettz obeyng and wilfully endendyng the [14] of your said writt; Consideryng the grete nedefull ayde that is behofull for youre most royall estat and conseruing the save gard of youre most gracious persone, endendyng the judiciall pease of yowe oure erthely souereyngne lord and of this youre noble realme, consideryng these premyssez that youre men of youre honorable houshold namyd in youre chekir rolle shuld be most like the expedycion and to execute and assente to the saide aydes for yowe our souereynge lord youre realme and us youre trewe sugettz and ligemen; and by the saide consideracions we namyd and chosen for knyghtes [15] Robert Ston-

14 One word illegible: Prynne's suggestion *tenor* seems unlikely.
15 Prynne's reading is *at this time*: the Record Commission transcript leaves a blank at this point.

ham and John Styuecle, esquyers of your sayde honorable houshold. Notwithstonding these premysses there apperid be labour of dyvers gentilmen of other shires and of your saide shire of Huntyngdon [16] number of a lxx ffreholders comuners namyd Henry Gymber to be i of the saide knyghtes, whiche is not of gentell berth according to your saide wryt. And there uppon the saide undershireve went to examynacion according to the estatutz rehersid in your saide Writt, and hadde xlviii [17] examyned of fforyners and receantz withoute interrupcion of us, and ffewe of theym contrybutors to the knyghtes expenses. And whanne we the ffreholders before namyd shuld be examyned in like wyse, tho on the saide Henry Gymber parte wold not suffre us of our parte to be examyned and to geve voys thow he myght clerely yerely expende xx marc, with oute that we shuld have offendid the pease of yowe oure most doutyd sovereyngne lord, and so we depardid for drede of the *many* inconvenientz that was likly to be don of manslaughter. And what that the shireve will returne in this behalf we can have no notyse, for which causes we youre trewe humble sugettz and legemen in oure most lowely wyse besechyng yowe our most doutyd souereyngne lord and king these premysses may be considered for your most ayde and our ffredom, that the saide shireve may be by your grete highnes strytely chargyd to returne the saide Robert Stonham and John Styvecle as for knyghtes atte this tyme for your said parlement as oure election was, as oure endeles lord God knowith. And that this was and is oure wille and dede we the saide ffreholders to the nombre of cxxiiij have putte to oure seales severally as it aperit and as youre lawe will to do and abyde thereby to oure lyves ende.

16 Prynne's reading is *the*; the reading might be *to the*.
17 Prynne's reading is *xlvii*.

Bibliography of the Published Works of Bertie Wilkinson M. TYSON

1924

"The authorisation of Chancery Writs under Edward III," *Bulletin of the John Rylands Library*, VIII, 107–39. Also reprint.

1925

"A letter to Louis de Male, Count of Flanders," *Bulletin of the John Rylands Library*, IX, 177–87. Also reprint.

1927

"A Letter of Edward III to his Chancellor and Treasurer," *English Historical Review*, XLII, 248–51.

"The Seals of the Two Benches under Edward III," *Ibid.*, XLII, 397–401.

"The Household Ordinance of 1279," *History*, XII (new series), 46–7.

Review: Sir H. C. Maxwell-Lyte, *Historical Notes on the use of the Great Seal of England*. In *ibid.*, XII (new series), 158–9.

1929

The Chancery under Edward III. Manchester University Press, Historical Series, no. LI.

1931

The Mediaeval Council of Exeter. Manchester University Press, The University College of the South-West of England, History of Exeter Research Group, Monograph no. 4.

"The protest of the Earls of Arundel and Surrey in the Crisis of 1341," *English Historical Review*, XLVI, 177–93.

1933

"The Coronation Oath of Edward II," in *Essays in Honour of James*

Tait, edited by J. G. Edwards, V. H. Galbraith, and E. F. Jacob, Manchester University Press, pp. 405–16.

1937

Studies in the Constitutional History of the Thirteenth and Fourteenth Centuries. Manchester University Press, Historical Series, no. LXXIII.

1938

"Freeman and the Crisis of 1051," *Bulletin of the John Rylands Library,* XXII, 368–87. Also reprint.
Review: J. E. A. Jolliffe, *The Constitutional History of Medieval England.* In *Law Quarterly Review,* LIV, 431–4.

1939

"The Deposition of Richard II and the Accession of Henry IV," *English Historical Review,* LIV, 215–39.
"Northumbrian Separatism in 1065 and 1066," *Bulletin of the John Rylands Library,* XXIII, 504–26. Also reprint.

1940

"The Chancery," in *The English Government at Work, 1327–36,* edited by James F. Willard and William A. Morris, The Mediaeval Academy of America, I, pp. 162–205.
"The Peasants' Revolt of 1381," *Speculum,* XV, 12–35.
"Canada's Place in an English-speaking Union," *Saturday Night,* November 30, 1940.

1941

Review: Adolf Hitler, *My New Order.* In *University of Toronto Quarterly,* October 1941, 123–6.

1943

"The Council and the Crisis of 1233–4," *Bulletin of the John Rylands Library,* XXVII, 384–93. Also reprint.
Review: G. C. Homans, *English Villagers of the Thirteenth Century.* In *The Journal of Political Economy,* LI, 85–6.

1944

"The Coronation Oath of Edward II and the Statute of York," *Speculum,* XIX, 445–69.
"The Government of England during the absence of Richard I on the Third Crusade," *Bulletin of the John Rylands Library,* XXVIII, 485–509. Also reprint.

1944-5
"Stories from Canadian History," Nos. 1 – xxxix. Imperial Optical
Co., Toronto.

1945
"Canada in the Modern World," *Talks : Series No. 2*, from broad-
casts sponsored by the Imperial Optical Co., Toronto.

1946
"Tendencies in Fourteenth-Century Constitutional Development,"
Report of the Canadian Historical Association, 1946, 18–29.

1947
"An Aspect of the Decline of Citizenship in the Later Roman
Empire," *The Phoenix : Journal of the Ontario Classical Association*,
I (supplement), 19–29.
Review: *Readings in European Economic History*, edited by K. F.
Helleiner. In *Canadian Historical Review*, xxviii, 445.
Obituary Notice: "Tribute to G. G. Coulton," Toronto *Globe and
Mail*, Thursday, March 13.

1948
*The Constitutional History of England, 1216–1399, with Select
Documents*, 1: *Politics and the Constitution, 1216–1307*. Reprinted
in 1959 as *Constitutional History of Medieval England, 1216–1399*,
I, Longmans, Green and Co.
"The negotiations preceding the 'Treaty' of Leake, August 1318,"
In *Studies in Medieval History presented to Frederick Maurice
Powicke*, edited by R. W. Hunt, W. A. Pantin, and R. W. Southern,
pp. 333–53
"The Sherburn Indenture and the Attack on the Despensers, 1321,"
English Historical Review, LXIII, 1–28.
Review: Hilda Johnstone, *Edward of Carnarvon, 1284–1307*. In
History, xxxiii, 263–4.

1949
"The 'Political Revolution' of the Thirteenth and Fourteenth Cen-
turies in England," *Speculum*, xxiv, 502–9.
Review: S. B. Chrimes, *English Constitutional History*. In *The
Annals of the American Academy of Political and Social Science*,
CCLXII, 211–12.

1950

Reviews: (with D. J. McDougall and F. H. Underhill). Keith Feiling, *A History of England.* In *Canadian Historical Review*, XXXI, 406–8.

W. Ullmann, *Medieval Papalism: The Political Theories of the Medieval Canonists.* In *University of Toronto Law Journal*, VIII, 438–9,

J. E. Neale, *The Elizabethan House of Commons.* In *The Annals*, July 1950, 186–7.

1951

Reviews: S. Painter, *The Reign of King John.* In *The Annals*, CCLXXIII, 274–5.

J. F. Willard *et al. The English Government at Work*, III. In *ibid.*, CCLXXIV.

S. K. Mitchell, *Taxation in Medieval England.* In *Political Science Quarterly*, LXVI, 472–3;

M. P. Charlesworth, *The Roman Empire.* In *Canadian Historical Review*, XXXII, 389.

1952

Constitutional History of Medieval England, 1216–1399, II: *Politics and the Constitution, 1307–1399.* Longmans, Green and Co.

Studies in the Constitutional History of the Thirteenth and Fourteenth Centuries. Manchester University Press, Historical Series, no. LXXIII. Second Edition.

Reviews: *The Heritage of Western Culture,* edited by Randolph Carleton Chalmers. In *Canadian Historical Review*, XXXIII, 182,

A. L. Rowse, *The England of Elizabeth.* In *The Annals*, CCLXXX, 222–3.

1953

The Coronation in History. Historical Association pamphlet, G. 23. (general series), London, G. Philip and Son.

Reviews: B. H. Putnam, *The Place in Legal History of Sir William Shareshull, Chief Justice of the King's Bench, 1350–61.* In *History*, XXXVIII, 68–9.

The Shorter Cambridge Medieval History, edited by C. W. Previté-Orton. In *Canadian Historical Review*, XXXIV, 183–4.

1954

Reviews: Sir Maurice Powicke, *The Thirteenth Century, 1216–1307* (Oxford History of England). In *Canadian Historical Review*, XXXV, 256–8.

A. R. Myers, *England in the Late Middle Ages*. In *History*, XXXIX, 109–10.

1955

"English Politics and Politicians of the Thirteenth and Fourteenth Centuries," *Speculum*, xxx, 37–48.

"Notes on the Coronation Records of the Fourteenth Century," *English Historical Review*, LXX, 581–600.

1956

"In Appreciation: Charles Rupert Sanderson, 1887–1956," *Ontario Library Review*, XL, 165–6.

Reviews: V. H. H. Green, *The Later Plantagenets*. In *Canadian Historical Review*, XXXVII, 91–2.

Sir Winston Churchill, *A History of the English-Speaking Peoples*, I: *The Birth of Britain*. In *ibid.*, XXXVII, 371–3.

1958

Constitutional History of Medieval England, 1216–1399. III: *The Development of the Constitution, 1216–1399*. Longmans, Green and Co.

"The Duke of Gloucester and the Council, 1422–8," *Bulletin of the Institute of Historical Research*, XXXI, 19–20.

1959

Review: William C. Bark, *Origins of the Medieval World*. In *Canadian Historical Review*, XL, 62.

1961

Review: May McKisack, *The Fourteenth Century, 1307–1399* (Oxford History of England). In *Canadian Historical Review*, XLII, 65–7.

1962

"The Teaching and Writing of the History of Mediaeval Europe," *History Newsletter*, 4–5.

Review: Bryce Lyon, *A Constitutional and Legal History of Medieval England*. In *Canadian Historical Review*, XLIII, 159–60.

1963

The Foundations of the West. With D. Fishwick and J. C. Cairns, Toronto, Clarke Irwin, The Background of our Times, series 2, book I.

Review: George Holmes, *The Later Middle Ages, 1272–1485*. In *Canadian Historical Review*, XLIV, 350–1.

1964

The Constitutional History of England in the Fifteenth Century, 1399–1485. Longmans, Green and Co.

Reviews: Mary C. Hill, *The King's Messengers, 1199–1377*. In *Canadian Historical Review*, XLV, 157.

Robert L. Baker, *The English Customs Service, 1307–1343*. In *Ibid.*, XLV, 333–4.

H. G. Richardson and G. O. Sayles, *The Governance of England from the Conquest to Magna Carta*. In *American Historical Review*, LXIX, 427–9.

Book of Prests of the King's Wardrobe for 1294–5, edited by E. B. Fryde. In *ibid.*, LXX, 702–3.

1965

Review: David C. Douglas, *William the Conqueror: The Norman Impact upon England*. In *American Historical Review*, LXX, 752–3.

1966

Reviews: J. C. Holt, *Magna Carta*; I. Jennings *Magna Carta and Its Influence in the World Today*. In *American Historical Review*, LXX, 930–31.

J. R. Lander, *The Wars of the Roses*. In *ibid.*, LXXI, 1316–17.

J. T. Appleby, *England without Richard, 1189–1199*. In *ibid.*, LXXII, 154–5.

The Letters of Frederick William Maitland, edited by C. H. S. Fifoot. In *University of Toronto Law Journal*, XVI, 468–9.

1967

"Fact and Fancy in Fifteenth-Century English History," *Speculum* XLII, 673–92.

Reviews: C. Warren Hollister, *The Military Organization of Norman England*. In *Canadian Journal of History*, II, 86–7.

F. J. West, *The Justiciarship in England 1066–1232*. In *Speculum*, XLII, 209–11.

1968

The Late Middle Ages in England, 1216–1485, Longmans, Green and Co., History of England, vol. 4 (general editor W. N. Medlicott). In the press.

"English Historians and the Later Middle Ages in England," in *The Medieval World*, edited by G. S. Couse. In the press.

LIST OF SUBSCRIBERS

Mrs J. G. Althouse
Margaret Archer
C. A. J. Armstrong

Professor Frank Barlow
Professor C. C. Bayley
J. M. Beattie
J. M. Beauroy
The Library, Bedford College
Thomas N. Bisson
Mr and Mrs W. R. Bland
Harry Bober
Leonard E. Boyle, o.p.
Christopher N. L. Brooke
Dr Alfred L. Brown
Mr and Mrs P. A. Brown
Robert Craig Brown
J. Brückmann
Mrs Neil Bryson
Dr Curt F. Bühler
Professor L. H. Butler

John C. Cairns
J. Campbell
Harry Caplan
J. M. S. Careless
Professor E. M. Carus-Wilson
Professor and Mrs Fred A. Cazel, jr.
Mrs Marjorie Chibnall
Professor S. B. Chrimes
The Library, Christ Church College,
   Oxford
Mrs H. J. Cody
R. V. Colman
J. B. Conacher
Mrs J. K. Conway
The Librarian, Corpus Christi
   College, Oxford
G. M. Craig
Professor D. G. Creighton

James Crompton
Eleanor Cruickshank
Professor G. P. Cuttino

Mr and Mrs Roland Daly
William and Madelyn Dick
Miss Barbara Dodwell
Mr and Mrs Peter Draimin
William Huse Dunham, jr.

Kathleen Edwards
A. Jean Elder
Professor G. R. Elton
Dr A. K. B. Evans
The Library, Exeter College, Oxford

Wallace K. Ferguson
The Most Reverend G. B. Flahiff,
   c.s.b.
Dr Constance M. Fraser
Leslie B. From

Astrik L. Gabriel
F. L. Ganshof, Professor Emeritus
Felix Gilbert
Walter Goffart
Antonia Grandsden
Edgar B. Graves
J. W. Gray
Professor Joan G. Greatrex
Dr V. H. H. Green
Philip Grierson
Ralph A. Griffiths

G. D. G. Hall
G. L. Harriss
Cynthia L. Hawker
Professor Denys Hay
Karl F. Helleiner
Richard J. Helmstadter

Sydney Hermant
Mrs Florence M. G. Higham
Rosalind M. T. Hill
Professor J. N. Hillgarth
The Library, the History Faculty,
  Oxford
Christopher Holdsworth
Albert E. J. Hollaender
C. Warren Hollister
Urban T. Holmes
Professor J. C. Holt
Professor Robert S. Hoyt
R. W. Hunt
Joan Hussey

The Library, Institute for Advanced
  Study, Princeton
Milton Israel

R. I. Jack
Robin Jeffs
Eric John
Professor Richard H. Jones

Howard Kaminsky
Keble College, Oxford
The Library, University of Keele
The Rev. Canon Eric Waldram
  Kemp
N. R. Ker
Pearl Kibre
Ruth King
J. L. Kirby
Dr C. H. Knowles
Milton Krieger
Professor Stephan Kuttner

Margaret Wade Labarge
Gerhart B. Ladner
J. R. Lander
Gavin I. Langmuir
Professor M. Dominica Legge
Professor John Le Patourel
P. S. Lewis
John Leyerle
The Library, Lincoln College,
  Oxford

Robert W. Linker
F. Donald Logan
Bryce Lyon

Catherine McCauliff
James Kelsey McConica, c.s.b.
Professor May McKisack
James C. McRuer
Professor Domenico Maffei
Magdalen College, Oxford
Professor Kathleen Major
Kemp Malone
Dr G. H. Martin
Merton College, Oxford
Edward Miller
A. Taylor Milne
W. L. Morton

Hilda Neatby
Harold Nelson
W. H. Nelson
The University Library, Newcastle
  upon Tyne
Philip H. Niles

Charles E. Odegaard
Professor H. S. Offler
Elisabeth M. Orsten
Professor A. J. Otway-Ruthven

W. Pantin
The Reverend Dr T. M. Parker
E. Franklin Perry
Gaines Post
Ruth Green Price and Vincent Price
George and Linda Provost
The Library, the Public Record
  Office, London
Professor Ralph B. Pugh

The Library, Reading University
Dr C. F. Richmond
William Roach
Ann Wilkinson Robson
John M. Robson
Elliot Rose
Peggy and Don Rose
Joel T. Rosenthal

Professor J. S. Roskell
The John Rylands Library,
  Manchester

The Librarian, University Library,
  St. Andrews
The Library, St. John's College,
  Oxford
John J. Saunders
Professor G. O. Sayles
Herbert and May Sharp
Margaret Sharp
J. W. Sherborne
Grant G. Simpson
R. C. Smail
Miss B. Smalley
R. W. Southern
Dr William B. Spaulding
Robert Spencer
Dr Peter Spufford
Professor C. P. Stacey
Geoffrey Stagg
Mrs Margaret Douglas Stamp
  (neé Higgins)
Colin Steele
Eric Stone
Professor and Mrs E. L. G. Stones
Joseph R. Strayer
Roberta M. Styran
Department of History,
  University College, Swansea

E. A. Synan

Arnold J. Taylor
John Taylor
Dr Geoffrey Templeman
Mrs Mary M. Thompson
Professor S. E. Thorne
The Library, Trinity College,
  Hartford
John H. Trueman
Joseph M. Tyrrell

Professor W. Ullmann
Francis Lee Utley

Keith Wallis
John O. Ward
Andrew M. Watson
Sister Christina Maria Weber
The Library, Westminster Abbey
Frank Wilkinson
Harry Wilkinson
Isobel and John Wilkinson
J. W. Wilkinson
Michael Wilks
Dr B. P. Wolfe

Yale Mediaeval Studies
Phyllis and Douglas Young

Norman P. Zacour